MW00773422

Bodies of Song

Bodies of Song

Kabir Oral Traditions and Performative Worlds in North India

LINDA HESS

OXFORD
UNIVERSITY PRESS

OXFORD
UNIVERSITY PRESS

Oxford University Press is a department of the University of Oxford. It furthers the University's objective of excellence in research, scholarship, and education by publishing worldwide.

Oxford New York
Auckland Cape Town Dar es Salaam Hong Kong Karachi
Kuala Lumpur Madrid Melbourne Mexico City Nairobi
New Delhi Shanghai Taipei Toronto

With offices in
Argentina Austria Brazil Chile Czech Republic France Greece
Guatemala Hungary Italy Japan Poland Portugal Singapore
South Korea Switzerland Thailand Turkey Ukraine Vietnam

Oxford is a registered trademark of Oxford University Press in the UK and certain other countries.

Published in the United States of America by
Oxford University Press
198 Madison Avenue, New York, NY 10016

© Oxford University Press 2015

All rights reserved. No part of this publication may be reproduced, stored in a retrieval system, or transmitted, in any form or by any means, without the prior permission in writing of Oxford University Press, or as expressly permitted by law, by license, or under terms agreed with the appropriate reproduction rights organization. Inquiries concerning reproduction outside the scope of the above should be sent to the Rights Department, Oxford University Press, at the address above.

You must not circulate this work in any other form and you must impose this same condition on any acquirer.

Library of Congress Cataloging-in-Publication Data

Hess, Linda, author.
Bodies of song : Kabir oral traditions and performative worlds in North India / Linda Hess.
pages cm
Includes bibliographical references and index.
ISBN 978-0-19-937417-5 (paperback) — ISBN 978-0-19-937416-8 (hardback) 1. Kabir, active 15th century—Criticism and interpretation. 2. Oral tradition—India—Malwa (Madhya Pradesh and Rajasthan) 3. Malwa (Madhya Pradesh and Rajasthan, India)—Religion. I. Title.
PK2095.K3Z696 2015
891.4'312—dc23
2014036589

1 3 5 7 9 8 6 4 2
Printed in the United States of America
on acid-free paper

Contents

List of Figures vii

Acknowledgments ix

Transliteration xiii

Introduction 1

1. "You Must Meet Prahladji!" 19

2. Oral Tradition in the Twenty-First Century: Observing Texts 73

3. True Words of Kabir: Adventures in Authenticity 112

4. In the Jeweler's Bazaar: Malwa's Kabir 149

5. Oral Tradition in the Twenty-First Century: Exploring Theory 203

6. A Scorching Fire, a Cool Pool 249

7. Fighting over Kabir's Dead Body 315

8. Political / Spiritual Kabir 345

Notes 399

References 439

Index 449

List of Figures

I.1. Prahladji and group performing on stage in Bangalore, with Shabnam Virmani. Photo by Jackson Poretta. 12

1.1. Prahladji sings with his younger brother Ashok. Photo by Kedar Desai. 21

1.2. Rural audience late at night, showing women's and men's sections. Photo by Smriti Chanchani. 52

2.1. Prahladji's hand on an old handwritten bhajan notebook. Photo by Smriti Chanchani. 83

2.2. Shabnam and Prahladji singing together. Photo by Smriti Chanchani. 100

2.3. Audio and video CD covers. Photo by Linda Hess. 105

4.1. Shantiji, Prahladji's wife, makes chapatis during conversation in kitchen. Photo by Shabnam Virmani. 176

6.1. R. N. Syag, during our car conversation presented in chapters 6 and 8. Photo by Shabnam Virmani. 256

6.2. Dinesh Sharma, who organized and documented the Kabir *manch* with the NGO Eklavya, holds a picture of the great Dalit anticaste leader B. R. Ambedkar. Photo by Shabnam Virmani. 259

6.3. Hiralal Sisodiya. Photo by Shabnam Virmani. 284

6.4. Narayanji breaks into dance at a village performance. Photo by Hari Adivarekar. 289

6.5. Kaluram Bamaniya singing. Photo by Smriti Chanchani. 298

6.6. Dinesh Sharma with singer Dayaram Sarolia. Photo by Shabnam Virmani. 314

7.1. Prahladji performs *chaukā āratī* ritual during his period as a *mahant* of the Kabir Panth. Photo by Smriti Chanchani. 334

Acknowledgments

DOING ACKNOWLEDGMENTS ALWAYS reminds me of Thich Nhat Hanh's table. In one of his early books the Vietnamese Buddhist teacher asks, "What is the table and how did it get here?" He starts with wood and carpenter, and eventually, having acknowledged items like merchants, tools, truck drivers, forests, sky, and rain, he demonstrates that we must include the whole world in appreciating what this table is and who made it possible.

That doesn't actually help me write the acknowledgments. True, everything is connected and my debt is incalculable. But even as the Mahayana Buddhists say that form is emptiness (emphasizing the oneness and boundlessness of everything), they also say that emptiness is form, bringing us back to particularities.

First, I bow to the Kabir singers and musicians of Malwa. Among them my greatest gratitude belongs to Prahlad Singh Tipanya, whose fame has grown ever larger since we met at the end of 1999. Prahladji's high spirits, glorious music, astonishing energy, profound knowledge, generosity, and lively sense of humor have changed my life. Since the Rakhi celebration of August 2002, he has been my official brother. He has taught me immeasurably—by singing, discussing, explaining, laughing, hanging out, taking many trips together.

Other performers in Malwa with whom I've become particularly close are Narayan Singh Delmia, Kaluram Bamaniya, Ajay and Vijay Tipanya, and Devnarayan Sarolia—all amazing and wonderful musicians and human beings. I'm delighted and fortunate to know and work with them.

When Prahladji became my brother, his whole family became my sisters, brothers, nieces, nephews, and grandchildren (our English kinship terms are poor compared to the Hindi). I embrace Prahladji's wife Shantiji—a welcoming, good-humored, capable, and caring female head of family and manager of the performing artist's home world. His brothers Ambaram and Ashok, their wives Kamla and Sumitra; Shantiji and Prahladji's sons and daughters-in-law Ajay and Sangeeta, Vijay and Seema; their daughter Sona; all the nieces and nephews and babies; the very old patriarch, Prahladji's father, who was called "Da-ji" and who passed away from this earth at a very old age in 2014—they have become part of my life.

Shabnam Virmani of Bangalore and beyond—filmmaker, singer, media artist, friend, collaborator, soulmate—most recently helped me figure out how to end chapter 8 and how to break through my confusion in booking a flight to India. She taught me not to say "thank you" and "sorry" too much to a real friend.

Smriti Chanchani of the Kabir Project in Bangalore, a beautiful friend, has lent her amazing artistic talents and technical skills on many occasions. Many of the pictures in the book, including the cover, were taken by her.

Anu Gupta and Arvind Sardana of Eklavya in Dewas, unstintingly generous, kind, delightful, living their values at home and in the world, have been my hosts, companions, and advisers over more than a decade of coming and going.

R. N. Syag, the original director of Eklavya's *Kabir bhajan evam vichār manch*, is a wise and kind man with clarity in his commitments, skill in dialogue, and a great smile that lights up the space even when he's respectfully disagreeing with me.

The Soni family of Dewas—Kailash and Garima, Ambuj, Rati, Utkarsha, and Oj—have been my hosts and helpers in countless ways. Ambuj is my go-to person for all sorts of needs. I love the warm, bright, friendly feeling of their home.

I extend warm appreciation to Indore friends in the organization Kabir Jan Vikas Samuh, especially Suresh Patel, who remains dedicated to connecting Kabir's inspiring poetry and song to social justice and equality.

Purushottam Agrawal is a brilliant and passionate Kabir scholar, creative writer, and social-political commentator with Kabirian streaks of irony and satire, underlain by a warm love of humanity. To him and to his wife, the poet Suman Keshari, I offer gratitude for hospitality and many wonderful conversations.

Ashok Vajpeyi—extraordinary poet, prose-writer, cultural leader, a person of effervescent spirits and reliable humanitarian values—has helped me in fundamental ways on two book projects in the last decade. He was the first to direct me to Malwa and Prahlad Singh Tipanya. He was my invaluable liaison to the family of Kumar Gandharva. Here's to the IIC Annexe Lounge, where many of his creative activities flourish!

Ramachandra Guha has been a generous friend, consultant, and inspiration as a writer and historian. Among other gifts, he introduced me to Rukun Advani, whose wonderful Permanent Black I had dreamed might become the publisher of my book in India. The dream came true, thanks to the kindness of Rukun and Ram.

The Berkeley Zen Center has been my warmhearted spiritual home for quite a long time. How improbable and lucky! Lots of emptiness, lots of form. Symbolically, I'll mention Sojun Mel, Hozan Alan, Laurie, Mary, Christy, Colleen, Marie, Susan, Anne, Karen. There could be many more. They all helped me finish the book.

Gay Searcy gets a paragraph of her own. Though quite an everyday thing, I find it mysterious.

Who would have guessed that Stanford University—after a somewhat tormented undergraduate life there in the 1960s, then three decades moving about—would in the 1990s become a nourishing professional home that would give me everything I needed (and thought I'd lost) to imagine and carry out a project like this? Special thanks to the people of the Department of Religious Studies, as well as others, whose generosity, support, and collaboration have opened many doors for me.

Bulbul Tiwari did a very helpful round of editorial work on an earlier draft of the book. Francesca Orsini responded with warmth and learned detail to a penultimate version. Jack Hawley has always been amazingly ready and quick to inform, comment, and advise at my request, and I have requested often. (When he answers an email within a few hours, he apologizes for the delay.) My friend and fellow Kabir scholar David Lorenzen has shared vast knowledge, generous support, and kind suggestions since we met in Varanasi nearly forty years ago. Encouragement and support from Laurie Patton, Kirin Narayan, Ann Gold, Philip Lutgendorf, and Wendy Doniger have been crucial along the way. Carolyn Karcher commented generously on an early draft; my long and precious friendship with her and Martin Karcher has been like the priceless jewel in a Kabir poem.

My good friend Matthew Rahaim, hanging out with me in a café at Stanford, suggested that the sleepy picture I had chosen for the cover was not the best choice, and that the one we have used, bursting with energy, would be a great. He was so right.

The American Institute of Indian Studies (AIIS) has supported my life and study in India on multiple occasions, from the initial summer language program in 1973 to a senior fellowship in 2002 for the first year of fieldwork on this book. All the India-based work I have ever done is interwoven with gratitude to AIIS. A Guggenheim fellowship in 2011 allowed me to complete the first draft of the book. I thank all the people who made such generous support possible.

The editorial team at Oxford University Press has been extremely helpful, careful, and in all ways admirable. My thanks to Cynthia Read, Glenn Ramirez, David Joseph, Kay Kodner, and Sudha Ramprasath.

I am unspeakably grateful to have a close family: my husband Kaz Tanahashi, daughter Karuna Izumi Hess Tanahashi, and son Ko Hanshan Hess Tanahashi. Both kids got middle names of great Asian poets (Izumi a passionate/romantic/contemplative woman poet of eleventh-century Japan, Hanshan a laughing Zen hermit of ninth-century China who wrote poems on the rocks and trees of Cold Mountain). Kaz, whose art, writings, and activism have inspired many, also has translated poetry of great Japanese Zen writers like Ryokan, Hakuin, and Dogen. I join the family circle with my fifteenth-century Indian iconoclastic mystic oral poet.

Transliteration

THIS BOOK USES a modified scholarly transliteration, in which certain letters are shown as they are pronounced, rather than in the standard scholarly way, which would likely lead to mispronunciation. The exceptions to standard transliteration are the following:

> ś = śh; ṣ = ṣh; c = ch; ch = chh; ṛ = ṛi; jñ = gy.

For mid-word nasal sounds, "n" or "m" is used, whichever mostly closely approximates the right pronunciation; for end-word nasal, "ṇ." The Hindi letter representing the palatal "d," and the same letter with a dot underneath in Hindi, are both transliterated as *ḍ* (creating a slight ambiguity). For capitalized names of people and places, diacritical marks are not used, and English spellings normally used in India are preferred to "correct" transliteration (thus "Tiwari" instead of "Tivari").

Two Hindi words are used so often that they are not italicized after the first use: "bhakti" and "bhajan."

Bodies of Song

Introduction

THIS BOOK IS about Kabir; about oral tradition and the oral-performative lives of texts; about poetry and music; and about communities that coalesce around Kabir, his poetry, and music. Widening the lens, we could also say that it is about religion, literature, society, and expressive culture in North and Central India—particularly in the Malwa region of Madhya Pradesh—in the early twenty-first century, as revealed by the study of Kabir oral traditions.[1]

One of the great features of oral tradition is that it is embodied, with givers and receivers physically present in the same place and time. So if you want to meet it, you have to do so through people. Reading this book, you are going to meet a lot of people; I hope you will feel that you have come to know some of them fairly well, and that you are getting to know Kabir through them. Poets of India's vernacular devotional and mystical traditions (commonly referred to as *bhakti*) generally use a signature line, or *chhāp,* that identifies them near the end of the poem. Kabir's *chhāp* is unique in that it nearly always begins with a version of *kahe kabīr suno*: "Kabir says, listen!" It is not, as Ashok Vajpeyi quipped at a literary gathering in Delhi, *kahe kabīr paḍho*: "Kabir says, read!" "Listening" implies live engagement of the body, a wholehearted presence that is contrasted with the insubstantiality of mere words and ideas. Here is one of the Kabir verses that became a joking commentary about me and my scholarly pursuits:

Maiṇ kahatā ānkhoṇ kī dekhī
tū kahatā kāgaz kī lekhī
terā merā manavā ek kaise hoi re

I talk of what I've seen with my own eyes,
you talk of what's written on paper.
How can your mind and mine
ever get together?

A pervasive irony of this book is that it is a book. It enthuses about embodied experience through the medium of words on paper. I tell myself different stories about how this endeavor could make sense. If you are reading the book, you may be thinking about it too. I won't try to explain or justify it. Reflecting on the continuing presence of books in our lives, as well as the rapid transformation of their function and importance, is part of the fun for both readers and writer.

Listen

Kabir's signature line is so famous that millions of Hindi speakers will readily produce it when asked: *kahe kabīr suno*. No other Indian poet of popular bhakti tradition is associated with this phrase the way Kabir is.[2] How seriously should we take it? To understand Kabir, is it important to heed his exhortation and listen—to the words, the song, the sound? Whether or not literal listening is necessary, we can say uncontroversially that with this constantly recurring *chhāp*, Kabir calls attention to his own orality. His style is also uniquely associated with the vocative—frequent direct addresses, questions, and challenges to the listener-reader—again emphasizing the oral character of his communication.[3] Another intriguing fact is that, as a truth-seeker who emphasizes the God without form or quality (*nirguṇ*), he repeatedly tells us that the ultimate experience of reality is in a sound, one that is profoundly different from those we ordinarily hear, yet still sound—the *anahad nād*, often translated as "unstruck sound," but more closely rendered as "boundless sound."[4]

In 2002, after studying well-known written collections of Kabir for some years, I plunged into the living oral/musical tradition. The first metaphors to arise from that experience were aquatic. I lost my moorings in that ocean. Or was it a river? Solid lines of print turned into multiple streams, swirling currents. Surging with the exhilaration of music, I was thrilled one day to hear my experience echoed in the words of a Kabir song: *Laharī anahad uṭhe ghaṭ bhītar*—"Boundless waves are rising in my body." The word for waves, *laharī*, meant the ones we find in water, but the word for boundless, *anahad*, also suggested waves of sound.

Kabir traditions have been alive and transforming since he composed orally nearly six centuries ago. Most scholars of Kabir think it likely that he never wrote.[5] His words lived in his own lifetime and afterward largely through the voices of people who sang and said them, made meaning out of them and changed them. This realization, which was literally fleshed out during my first few months on the road with Kabir singers, gave rise to an axiom in my mind: to know Kabir, you should know people. The axiom soon expanded to include the places and circumstances in which people meet. I carried on imaginary conversations with you, my reader. You should try immersing yourself in the experience of a place and its worlds of meaning, discovering the relationships of texts, foods, social organization, music, weather. I want to give you an inkling of how much you are missing if you don't hear the music; if you don't take (or at least imagine taking) a series of conveyances, packed in closely with local people, over roads, rails, and trails, through heat, cold, and rain, to arrive in places where you sit on the ground or in chairs, where you listen, watch, discuss, take part in rituals, eat and drink; and where all this is what it means to know Kabir. I want you to consider that you may get your best insights into the meaning of a poem while you are humming it.

Entering oral tradition changes the textual scholar. First, everything changes with the simple fact that each poem is a song. As purely textual scholars, we dealt only with words; now words and music are inseparable. Music affects us physically and emotionally. Emotions shake up the patternings of thought. Mind and body interact. Singing is interpretation. The meanings of the text change when we hear it sung. These are the barest hints of how music affects text.

Further, in oral tradition, there is no such thing as text without context. It is easy enough to ignore context when we are sitting in an office or library, or in any sort of private chair—situations that we are conditioned to believe are the "natural" places to read books.[6] Actually these contexts do influence how we make meaning, but we screen out that fact. In performative situations, context rushes into awareness. It will not be ignored.

A village house. A stage in the midst of a country fair where bullocks are bought and sold. Rain dripping. Electricity failing. Moods changing, emotions rising and falling as the bhajans roll along. Different groups vying for their chance to sing. Glasses of tea, platters of *dāl-bāṭī* (*bāṭī* being ball-shaped breads, baked amid glowing dried-cowdung-cake coals and ashes till they come out hard on the outside and soft on the inside, to be cracked open, doused with *ghee* and dipped in *dāl*). Speeches, sermons, discussions, controversies. Men and women enacting their gendered roles. Children pointing, giggling, crying. Calves staring, mosquitoes biting. Cultural programs on riverbanks in small cities. Concert stages in Bhopal and Mumbai. A village singer performing at a government officer's house in the capital. A classical singer in an art gallery at Delhi's Habitat Centre with the American ambassador in attendance.

In the academic study of religion and literature, working with written texts is our expertise, our dharma. It is the skill in which we have been schooled by our gurus, and which we hone and pass on to our academic offspring. This book argues that if we want to know Kabir, we should also engage seriously with oral traditions. As oral traditions are embodied, we should engage with learning in the body—not just with the part of the body that's in the skull, but with quite a few other parts—ears, skin, organs, feet, and so on.

Written texts have a quasi-sacred status in the humanities partly because they are convenient. Texts hold their shape. We can xerox them. Performances are dizzyingly varied, changing through different times and locations. We have to go out of our way to experience them. But in truth, Kabir is much more an oral-performative tradition than a written one. We may ignore that for our convenience. What happens if we don't?

When I talk like this, some colleagues think: "Linda wants to be an anthropologist. It's fine if she feels compelled to change fields late in life, but why does she have to lecture me about giving up the study of texts?" A European scholar, hearing of my work at an early stage, looked at me with earnest concern and asked, "Why have you abandoned texts?"[7] In fact, I am neither abandoning texts nor encouraging anyone else to do so. In this book we refer continually to written texts, trying to make sense of their existence along with oral performance and other media. I am trying to develop a method in which fieldwork and textwork inform and change each other. Perhaps we can imagine together a larger world of "text," where one mode of inquiry does not need to eclipse the other.[8]

Who Is Kabir?

Kabir has been introduced in English before, by me among others.[9] But it must be done repeatedly, as our knowledge and our ideas about how it is possible to imagine Kabir keep changing.

It is easy to summarize the points on which nearly everyone agrees. Regarded as one of the great poets of Hindi literature, Kabir lived in fifteenth-century Varanasi, North India.[10] He is a revered figure in religious history, an iconoclastic mystic who bore marks of both Hindu and Muslim traditions but refused to be identified with either. Stories about his life come to us as legends, most of them unverifiable. He grew up in a family of Muslim weavers and practiced the weaving craft himself.[11] He is widely believed to have had a Hindu guru, and poetry that bears his name is full of Hindu terminology and references to Hindu beliefs and practice. Muslim singers in India and Pakistan still sing Kabir's verses in Sufi musical styles, their texts showing a greater frequency of Perso-Arabic vocabulary. In the late sixteenth century he was adopted as one of the exemplary devotees whose poetry was inscribed in the sacred book of the nascent Sikh religion.[12] Meanwhile some of his admirers turned him into a divine avatar and took to worshiping him in a sect called the Kabir Panth.[13] His own poetry subverts and criticizes religious identities and institutions, but such subversion has never stopped religions from co-opting their critics. Kabir also has a life beyond established religions, his couplets taught to schoolchildren all over India, his poems and songs appreciated by people of all classes and regions. Such people may think of themselves as religious, spiritual, secular, or atheist, but they all have their reasons for liking Kabir.

Compositions associated with Kabir have a uniquely powerful style, expressing his own spiritual awakening, urging others to wake up, observing delusion in individuals and society. Kabir's voice is direct and anti-authoritarian. He was of a low social status, and most of his sectarian followers belong to communities now called Dalit (the former "untouchables"). His poetry has a vivid streak of social criticism, making trenchant observations on caste prejudice, religious sectarianism, hypocrisy, arrogance, and violence. At the same time it is profoundly inward-looking. It examines the nature of mind and body, points out the tangle of delusions in which we live, and urges us to wake up and cultivate consciousness. The imminence of death and the transiency of all things are frequently invoked. The journey within is permeated with the imagery of yoga—its map of a subtle body made of energy, lotus-centers, coursing breath-streams, sound and light. A keyword associated with Kabir's spiritual stance is *nirguṇ*—"no quality"—indicating an ultimate reality that can't be visualized in form or described in language. While invoked negatively, it conveys simultaneously emptiness and fullness.

Scholars in Hindi, French, English, and other languages have gradually expanded our knowledge of Kabir texts and developed ever-more sophisticated modes of literary and historical analysis. The most disconcerting fruit of our diligent efforts to date has been the revelation that Kabir, like his "not-one-not-two" ultimate reality, is ungraspable. He almost isn't there. Never mind that we can't pin down the details of his biography. We can get along pretty well without the poet's life-story, as long as we feel safe in the consensus that he actually did exist around the fifteenth century. But text! A scholar could howl in distress at the absence of a stable text.

In the past, scholars have used the terms "oral" and "written" in tandem, as if they existed side by side. Now we know that oral Kabir is an ocean whose boundaries remain unmapped after nearly six hundred years of continuous rolling, its coastlines curling unpredictably, its depths and currents shifting. It rolls on today. Written texts have from time to time crystallized out of it, then have been sucked back in, altered, and spewed out again. The oral continually transforms the written, and the written equally transforms the oral.[14] The textual situation is further complicated by newer modes of transmission such as cassettes, CDs, film, mobile phones, and computers.

Authentic Texts?

The words of Kabir circulate in conversation and in music, among urban and rural people at all levels of education and status. Kabir is common property. Someone said to me: "Do the scholars who search for authenticity want to take away my favorite Kabir poetry? I'd recommend throwing away the scholars rather than the poetry."

Vinay Dharwadker (2003) has said that "Kabir" is a community of poets who have been pooling their creativity for centuries. That is certainly true. So should we just relax and enjoy "Kabir," whatever happens to come our way? Often that is exactly what we should do. I have been doing that for the last several years, and the quality of my life has improved dramatically.

Yet I would not like to remove the tension of wanting to know who Kabir is more particularly and more rigorously, in different social and geographical spaces, performative situations, moments in time. The methods of investigating this question are ethnographic, textual, and historical. We can move around South Asia today and discover what is happening in different places and among different people. To some extent observations in the present may shed light on how oral traditions functioned in the past, though we must be modest in our claims. The tools of historical and sociological research can uncover contexts: how caste, class, gender, sect, region, language, rural-urban divides, and religious-secular differences, along with economic and political factors, play their roles in defining Kabir. To delve into the question of who Kabir was in the more distant past, we must make use of dated manuscripts. But even the oldest manuscripts provide precarious grounds on which to make claims of authenticity.

Can we even gesture toward the *real* Kabir? Can we make any limiting statements about what he is likely to have said? Can the earliest dated manuscripts provide clues to Kabir's original utterances? The intellectual atmosphere in which I presently write is charged with skepticism about the project of searching for the phantom author.

I have the same skepticism, but also an undeniable attraction. I occasionally try to dance with this phantom, inspired by the way in which the poems of the Kabir tradition dance with the *śhabda*, the true Word that can never be circumscribed by ordinary words but that is nonetheless real and not to be ignored. This book is largely devoted to the relatively fluid oral Kabir, discovered among living performers and listeners. In the future it would be good (for me or someone else) to revisit stable bodies of text preserved in old manuscripts, making use of fine-grained new research that wasn't available when I undertook such a study over twenty-five years ago.[15] Between extensive, intimately detailed fieldwork that follows the flowing streams of Kabir tradition on the surface today, and vertically probing text study that delves like a tube-well toward some imagined groundwater below (passing through subterranean pools and channels at different levels along the way), perhaps it will be possible to come up with a more satisfying answer to the question, "Who is Kabir?"

If representations of Kabir across time, space, social locations, textual records, and performative moments are (for practical purposes) endless, then pursuit of the truth about Kabir may look like a replay of *Rashomon*, the classic twentieth-century artistic statement about unstoppable multivocality. At the end of Kurosawa's stunning film, one might conclude that truth is inaccessible and irrelevant, and that (as one character says) the only important question is who can tell the best story. Or one might feel that in the maze of narratives, truth is somehow hovering, and we are still responsible for discovering it.

Oral Tradition

Kabir is usually studied through collections of poetry attributed to him. But he most likely did not write or read. His words, or words believed to be his, live on in oral-performative as well as in written forms. From the beginning his poems have been sung, spreading across the northern half of the kite-shaped subcontinent, taking on the colors and styles of local folk traditions, as well as entering the repertoires of classical singers. We can't know with any certainty what the original Kabir actually composed. But he has a distinct profile, a flavor, a voice, which shape his identity and importance in religious and social history.

How would our understanding of text, author, and reception change if we took cognizance of the nature and history of oral transmission, its interactions with written and recorded forms, and the paramount importance of context in creating the words and meanings of texts? How far can we go in treating texts as embodied?

Letting the words rise up off the written page creates a cascade of consequences for us as scholars. First we attend to the dynamics of oral traditions, the forms of recorded text with which they interact (manuscript, print, audio, video, internet), and the conditions of performance. We discover how meanings change when music is wedded to words. All this transforms our way of understanding text, which is a big thing. But it is not the only thing. The words—their forms and meanings—also live in communities. They are enmeshed in people's aspirations and choices, organizations and rituals, ways of striving for power. Thus we study "Kabir" through singers, listeners, music, performative circumstances, the fluidity and stability of texts, communities, and the interpretations produced in particular religious, social, and political contexts.

Studying oral tradition has proved to be much more complicated than I suspected at the outset of the project. I have learned to separate inquiries that are mostly concerned with text, both oral and written, from inquiries into the experience and cognition of listeners and readers. If we have a particular interest in the dynamics of text under oral-performative circumstances, we can immerse ourselves in those circumstances and learn many new things about text. Such ethnographic work related to text and performance is central to chapters 1, 2, 4, and 6. Still focusing on text, if we want to juxtapose oral and written, we can instigate a conversation between our ethnographic material and the history of written (and otherwise fixed) texts, as in chapter 3. When it comes to theories of orality, the task is much more daunting as it involves the receiver's experience and cognition. I venture into that strange land in chapter 5. The phenomena to which the term "oral tradition" refers are far from clear. As Bruce Rosenberg asks, "[D]o we mean orally composed, orally transmitted, or orally performed?" (Rosenberg 1987, 75). To demarcate a domain in which the discussion in this book will take place, I define "oral-performative" as referring to live performance where physical bodies are interacting, and where sound is produced by singers and heard by listeners who are present in the same place at the same time. But that does not mean that I propose to wall off what is "oral" from what is transmitted through other media.

Since text and context become inseparable in oral performance, our study of oral tradition inevitably takes us to study of reception and meaning-making. Chapters 6, 7, and 8 emphasize the presence of text and performance in communities, turning toward the social and political, while continuing to listen to poetry and music and to examine the connections between inner and outer worlds. A persistent theme in the book is the relation between the religious-spiritual and the social-political. There is a mystic Kabir who speaks of inner sound and light, who urges meditation, devotion, and nonattachment, who reminds us relentlessly of death and the transitory nature of all relationships. There is a social critic and satirist Kabir who speaks of the injustice of caste, the omnipresence of greed, the stupidity of puffed-up authority and hypocritical religiosity. We study how different constituencies appropriate, negotiate, and argue about these Kabirs.

The Genesis of This Project

My work in North India over several decades has turned gradually from the purely text-based toward reception, performance, and cultural embeddedness. When I first engaged with Kabir, in the late 1970s, I was interested in poetry as language, form, meaning, craft. My task was to translate and interpret. I also studied the history of manuscript traditions in order to position myself on the question of authenticity, which was compulsory for a scholar. But even then, I was drawn to investigate the experience of the audience, imagining the voice of the poet actively doing things to the reader-listener. Stanley Fish's early theory and practice of reader-response criticism inspired me.[16] Living in Varanasi while writing a dissertation on Kabir, I also began to study the Ramlila of Ramnagar, a month-long annual performance based on Tulsidas's sixteenth-century poetic rendering in Hindi of the *Rāmāyaṇa* epic. This took me into a complex performative space where I was able to explore how texts live in people, beyond the covers of books.[17]

The *Rāmāyaṇa* is a long narrative. My true literary home was in short poems, like those associated with bhakti in Indian vernaculars. Bhakti poetry, as anyone knows who has ventured out of a classroom, is song. It is as much music and performance as it is literature. Both fascinated and intimidated by the prospect of plunging into music, I mulled over it for years. Eventually this project took shape: to study Kabir oral traditions, inevitably in musical forms. The initial plan was to survey a vast swath of North India. Kabir oral traditions thrive throughout the Hindi heartland (Uttar Pradesh, Bihar, Rajasthan, Madhya Pradesh) and beyond—from Gujarat to Bengal, Punjab to Chattisgarh. I also considered going to Pakistan, to see whether and how Kabir existed there.

Once in the field, I abandoned the plan to "cover" the northern half of the subcontinent. Little visits to different regions, short encounters with singers, interviews with gurus and scholars by appointment—this would not satisfy. For one thing, each area had a different language. Dialect, one may say—but each dialect was very different from standard Hindi and from the other regional tongues. It took time to begin to understand the local language. Then the musical styles were different, and the people and situations were different. How could I connect, fluttering around like a butterfly, checking regions off my list? A well-known Kabir couplet says that doing one thing thoroughly is better than trying to do everything.

ek sādhe sab sādhe, sab sādhe ek jāī
mālī sīnche mūl ko, phūle phale aghāī

Do one thing fully, all is done.
Try to do all, you lose the one.
For plentiful flowers and fruit,
a gardener waters the root.

Having fallen in love on the first encounter with the songs of Malwa, and having been welcomed by a remarkable folksinger of Malwa, I decided to settle there.

Malwa is a region with no formal borders, defined principally by language (the Malwi dialect of Hindi), then more haphazardly by certain geographical associations, preferences in dress, or favorite foods. Most of Malwa is in western Madhya Pradesh (M.P.), but it also extends into southeastern Rajasthan and Gujarat. From the colorful turbans that men wear, to the *dāl-bāṭī* that people eat, to the forms of their local languages and the osmosis of song texts and melodies, this part of M.P has much in common with Rajasthan. Various political entities have been associated with the region and with the name Malwa over many centuries—a sixth-century kingdom, a fifteenth-century sultanate, eighteenth-century Maratha-ruled centers of power, a set of princely states under the British collectively known as the Malwa Agency.

Two major cities of Malwa are Indore and Ujjain. Forming a triangle with them, about an hour's drive from each, is a third city, which is smaller but looms larger in the study of Kabir: Dewas. It was here that the great classical singer, Kumar Gandharva, lived from 1948 until his death in 1992. Kumarji was extraordinary in many ways; one was the way he sang Kabir bhajans. He brought bhajans and bhakti poetry into the classical repertoire in an entirely new way, and he was especially famous for his renderings of Kabir and other *nirguṇ* poets. He was also drawn to and influenced by folksingers (see Hess 2009a).[18]

Another Dewas connection was Eklavya, the educational NGO active in Madhya Pradesh since 1982. I had met Dr. Namvar Singh, a very prominent scholar of Hindi literature, at a 1998 conference in Heidelberg celebrating the 600th anniversary of Kabir's birth. He had urged me to meet the people of Eklavya and to learn about the extraordinary work they had been doing with Kabir singing groups, which had left a lasting mark on the Kabir culture of Malwa. Eklavya's Kabir project, carried on through most of the 1990s, is the subject of chapter 6.

Lunyakhedi was the village of Prahlad Singh Tipanya, the singer who opened his home, his knowledge, and the treasury of Malwa's Kabir music to me. It took about an hour, by bus or shared jeep-taxi, to get from Dewas to Maksi, the nearest point to the village on a paved road. From Dewas and Lunyakhedi, my connections gradually spread to other villages as well as to the big city of Indore. And so I had a home in Malwa.

My longest continuous period of fieldwork was in 2002, when I spent a total of nine months in India. Since then I have been in India once or twice

FIGURE I.1. Prahladji and group performing on stage in Bangalore, with Shabnam Virmani. Photo by Jackson Poretta.

a year, staying about two months each year, sometimes longer. I hosted Prahlad Singh Tipanya and his *mandalī* on performance tours in the United States and Canada in 2003 and 2009. Each tour lasted two months (See Figure 1.1).

Since 2003 I have been associated with the Bangalore-based Kabir Project, headed by filmmaker Shabnam Virmani. Shabnam's journeys and mine, along with those of the Kabir Project team and their extended circles of artists and friends, have intertwined in countless ways, as the following pages will show. Sometimes audiences of Shabnam's work and mine aren't sure who has done what. (Sometimes we ourselves aren't sure.) People may see me in a film and think that I am a filmmaker, or they may see connections between a film by Shabnam and an article by me, and based on the dates of publication infer that one is derived from the other. Here is what happened. Shabnam and I bonded from our first meeting in December 2002. We recognized that we were on the same trail, excited by the same questions, meeting the same people. She was a film and media person; I was a writer and scholar. We became friends, mutual consultants, sometimes collaborators, often joyous traveling companions. Working full-time on her project, Shabnam completed four feature-length films along with a rich collection of audio, video, and print products, bringing them into public view in 2009 (see www.kabirproject.org). During that period I was teaching full-time, with more limited time to work on the book. Besides, I'm just slower. So the book is coming out several years later than the films. But they were all researched and largely put together in the same period.

More than any other project in my professional life, this has been a journey of friendship and connection. I entered deeply into the worlds I was studying and became part of them (which included sometimes recognizing when I was separate from them). In December 2013, I came to Malwa after finishing my book and sending it to the publisher. In gratitude to the Kabir singing groups of Malwa, I planned an all-day function in the city of Dewas. Many groups would sing, and I would offer gifts, food, and appreciation. When I arrived in Lunyakhedi village, Prahlad Tipanya's wife Shantiji said to me, "Your work is finished, so now you won't be coming here any more." I replied, "Of course I'll be coming here. This is not a work relationship. This is a heart relationship." She smiled broadly and said, "This is a heart relationship."

Summary of Chapters

Chapter 1. "You Must Meet Prahladji!"

The book's main themes are introduced through the story of a village singer, Prahlad Singh Tipanya, and the story of how I entered into relationship with him, his family, neighbors, friends, and the worlds of Kabir song. Emerging from a poor Dalit family with no musical tradition, Prahladji became an honored and beloved singer/interpreter of Kabir, constantly performing in rural and urban spaces. I join the family (by ritually becoming Prahladji's sister), travel with him and his group, learn songs, observe who invites him, how he relates to audiences and other singers, and the issues that arise in his life and representation of Kabir.

Chapter 2. Oral Tradition in the Twenty-First Century: Observing Texts

We learn how texts are brought into being again and again in the matrix of interactions between performers, audiences, media, and circumstances. We discover how all forms of text interact dynamically across media as well as across history and geography. These processes are vividly enacted in present-day Kabir oral traditions among singers, speakers, listeners, and readers.

Chapter 3. True Words of Kabir: Adventures in Authenticity

Once we have seen the fluidity, immensity, and complexity of oral tradition, does the old question of authenticity have any meaning? Though deconstruction and reception theory have undermined old-fashioned notions of author and authenticity, more subtle and multilayered notions are still interesting. Either "Kabir" is a vast undifferentiated mishmash of everything ever associated with his name in the last 600 years, or some process of clarification is possible. This chapter reflects on ways of imagining such a process. We notice various discourses of authenticity and see where they lead.

Chapter 4. In the Jeweler's Bazaar: Malwa's Kabir

A collection of songs from Malwa repertoires, organized under thematic categories that can be seen separately but that also interpenetrate each other. Many songs are translated, discussed, and shown in performative contexts.

Chapter 5. Oral Tradition in the Twenty-First Century: Exploring Theory

"Orality" has been central to many studies of literature, performance, and communication since 1960, starting with landmark works such as Albert Lord's *The Singer of Tales* and Marshall McLuhan's *The Gutenberg Galaxy*. Some thinkers distinguished sharply between "oral" and "literate" and then, to support "essential" differences between orality and literacy, posited "essential" differences between the ear and the eye—views that are no longer tenable. When we recognize the dynamic interactions of media over time and space, can the category of oral-performative stand? When we understand that the senses do not operate separately, can we say anything about the differences between hearing and reading? In the light of current neuroscience and communication studies, does "orality" exist?

Chapter 6. A Scorching Fire, a Cool Pool

Is Kabir a blazing social revolutionary or a promoter of detached spiritual quietism? Is he both? Or neither? In the 1990s Eklavya, an educational NGO, created a platform for Kabir singers in Malwa, foregrounding the social-political, rational, and secularist impulses in his works. They called it a stage for singing and discussing (*Kabīr bhajan evam vichār manch*). The all-night sessions that they hosted every month for eight years left a strong mark on the Kabir culture of the area. They brought village performers into dialogue with each other and with city-educated activists. The religious/spiritual/social/political aspects of Kabir were examined and debated. NGO workers didn't just push their agenda on the traditional singers but listened to and learned from them. Through all the meetings and serious conversations, the spirit of music and the joy of singing kept the energy flowing.

Chapter 7. Fighting over Kabir's Dead Body

We enter one major lineage of the sectarian Kabir Panth, where Kabir is claimed as an avatar of the Supreme Being, and sect gurus are claimed as avatars of Kabir. Their institutional structures, traditions of guru worship, social attitudes, and uses of Kabir-attributed texts are observed. We follow a dramatic story in which Prahlad Tipanya, introduced in the first chapter, radicalized in his thinking in the Eklavya forum (as seen in the sixth chapter), decides to become an authority figure in the Panth, taking on the role of a *mahant* and guru, presiding over a controversial ritual that he helped to criticize in the days of the forum. Through the local and personal lens of this story, we examine processes in the history of religion: institutionalization and iconization of a radical and charismatic figure; battles over ownership of the "founder's" story; uses of ritual; and tensions between authoritarian and anti-authoritarian tendencies, between organized religion and the quest for mystical insight. We see the debates that rage over Prahladji's decision among his family and peers, his own grappling with the situation, and the surprising outcome.[19]

Chapter 8. Political/Spiritual Kabir

In this concluding essay on the theme of political and spiritual, which has threaded through the whole book, we review the tendency to split

Kabir along political/spiritual lines and the convictions that lead different people to valorize one side and reject the other, or to try embracing both. The scope widens to include urban intellectuals, activists, and artists. We cite debates in ancient India about social responsibility as opposed to world renunciation. The story of Lenin's conversation with Gorky about Beethoven's *Appassionata*, and a reply in the form of the 2006 German movie, *The Lives of Others*, sharpens and contemporizes the discussion. Can too much music, too much beauty and bliss, wreck your revolutionary spirit? Does turning inward make you forget the harsh realities of our world? If you use Kabir's social messages for your own purposes and push the spiritual ones away with distaste, are you enacting a crude and misguided political appropriation? What do music, spiritual practice, and self-knowledge have to do with politics? What is at stake in asking and answering these questions?

Arguments

A major argument that emerges from these chapters is for more embodied study—in research and in the classroom—of literature that lives in performance. I have read articles about North Indian poetry that had "performance" or "oral tradition" in the title but turned out to consist of close readings of texts in which the authors merely looked for verbal markers of orality. This book argues that to know Kabir, you should know people, places, and times. You should use your ears, voice, nose, and skin as well as more cerebral capacities. You should appreciate the local in performance, starting with the first location: your own body.

Even while arguing for the richness and particularity of place, I see the substance of "the local" growing thinner. Cassettes and CDs take Malwi folk tunes to other parts of India and beyond. The grandly tolerant oral tradition welcomes film tunes, *qawwālī* or ghazal styles. A producer in Bhopal convinces a singer to make a video CD and illustrates the songs onscreen in low-grade Hindi film style: garishly flashing "divine" lights, waterfalls, and women dancing. My friend Shabnam Virmani, documenting in video and audio the content and styles of different regions, brings artists of Malwa, Kutch, Rajasthan, and Pakistan into contact with each other. They start to sing and even to record each other's material. I play a role in the globalizing process—not only by engaging with Kabir singers, devotees, and admirers in Malwa but also by taking the leading folksinger of the region and his group on U.S. tours.

Particular chapters have their own arguments. Chapter 2 proposes that distinct versions of Kabir can be identified by locating textual and cultural ecoregions. Along with familiar variables like the presence of manuscript traditions and the marks of regional languages, we can inquire into matters that reveal themselves through performance. For example, what religious and sectarian traditions tend to rub shoulders in a particular area? How do Kabir texts therefore become inflected with the language of the Nath Yogis or the Sufis, and how does Kabir the poet sometimes become interchangeable with the poets of those traditions? Chapter 5 argues that despite the complexity of multiple mediations, it is still possible to speak meaningfully of oral-performative texts and experiences. Chapter 6 demonstrates that oral interpretation by singers can take an honored place along with published exegeses by scholars and religious pandits. Chapter 7 reveals the contentious encounters of sectarian and nonsectarian claims to ownership of Kabir.

Embrace

mil lyo mil lyo re, bhāī mhārā mil lyo
lambī bāṇh pasār, ab ke bichhuryā re sadho kad milāngā jī

Embrace, embrace, my brother,
stretch out your arms and embrace.
Once we're parted, seeker,
when will we meet again?

A. K. Ramanujan and I got together three weeks before his utterly unexpected and greatly lamented death in 1993. The poet-scholar-translator-folklorist-classicist of Kannada, Tamil, and English had come to Berkeley for some lectures. He called me on arrival, and I asked if he'd like to drive to some scenic place, or go to a performance. No, he replied, he didn't care to see a play or a regional park. More and more, he had come to realize, what he wanted to do was simply to spend time with friends. That statement has lingered with me in the years that followed. Though he was only thirteen years older, I always considered him vastly my senior, my greatest model and inspiration for undertaking to translate Indian bhakti poetry. Now well past the age he was at that last meeting, I feel his statement about friends is also mine. To me, this doesn't mean that we would rather be with our friends than do our work. It means that the people we work with can be our friends. Our movements between professional and personal, America and India, text and field, work and leisure, art and intellect, can trace a network of warm human feeling that becomes, increasingly, the constant in all our activities.

This brings me to a final thesis that I am trying to prove only to myself. It is that scholarship can be an act of love, that the war between head and heart can finally be undeclared in the territory of my own body. Actually, I believe that this thesis is relevant to understanding Kabir, that Kabir would like us to understand it and will shed light on it. "Head and heart" here correlate with certain other pairs, such as outside and inside, social and individual, objective and subjective, two and one. Let us proceed.

I

"You Must Meet Prahladji!"

"YOU MUST MEET Prahladji." This is what people kept saying when I announced my interest in doing a project on Kabir oral traditions. So in January 2000 my friend Jeanne Fleming and I took off on a scouting expedition to Prahladji's village in the Malwa region of western Madhya Pradesh. Ashok Vajpeyi in Delhi had mentioned Prahladji and referred us to the Adivasi Lok Kala Parishad (Tribal and Folk Art Institute) in Bhopal.[1] Kapil Tiwari, the director of the institute, graciously received us and offered help. Many fruitless phone calls on a Saturday morning culminated in a successful contact, and we were finally off in our rented white Ambassador taxi. It was a long day's adventure. Four hours' travel from Bhopal brought us to the little market town of Maksi, where Prahladji and various members of his family met us. He had a flashing smile, wavy gray hair, an immediate warmth. Though time was short he insisted that we take a walk through the weekly market, which was in full swing. We threaded our way through lanes crowded with merchants and customers. Jeanne bought a pair of pointed leather shoes. Then we followed his jeep (our immaculate elderly taxi driver visibly tense) over fields and rutted lanes to Lunyakhedi village, ten minutes away.

For us the village on that occasion was just his low-roofed house, whitewashed and bluewashed; his two brothers' nearby houses; two cows with calves; some buffaloes; and an assortment of men, women, and children who seemed to be mostly of his family. It was already 5 p.m. They spread mats along the blue wall. Everybody in sight sat down to listen. The men who were going to make music donned red and yellow turbans—garb that I associated with the neighboring state of Rajasthan. They arranged themselves, Prahladji in the middle with his *tambūrā*, a long-necked, five-stringed instrument, held and strummed with one hand. Slipped over the fingers of the other hand were *kartāl*, two flat-edged wood and metal objects struck together to make a tambourine-like sound. Next to him sat his brother Ashok, who would sing in unison with him. Then one man on *dholak* (a two-headed drum perched on his lap), one on harmonium, one on violin, others with small cymbals or bells. Under the open sky, they started singing. I loved it.

Prahladji explained the sequence in Hindi and responded to my questions. There was homage to the guru, then a joyful *mangalgīt* (auspicious song) of welcome, songs about inner yogic experience, admonitions about death, and songs in Kabir's paradoxical style called *ulaṭbāṃsī* ("upside-down language"). The imagery was from villagers' lives: a bullock cart with painted wheels, a bird flying from forest to forest, a deer eating up the crops, a woman crying for her dead husband. It was also from the *nirguṇ* spiritual tradition: a subtle voice ringing within the body, a burst of light, a wound from the arrow of the guru's Word. This was without a doubt the Kabir I had encountered in written traditions that had developed in the northeastern Hindi region, around Varanasi. But it also had a distinct taste that came from the western soil and air of Malwa.

The melodies were lovely, captivating, upbeat, with patterns in verse and refrain that were repetitious but for me never monotonous. The male voices were full-throated and clear. Both brothers closed their eyes and seemed to sing to their instruments, to each other, to themselves. The percussion—drums, cymbals, bells—penetrated the body and made it dance even when it seemed to be sitting still. Music had that power, as I (the hitherto impoverished scholar of the printed page) was just beginning to discover: it lit up the nodes and highways of the body, made inside and outside one, began to erase the boundaries between bodies. Opaque flesh became subtle. Our personal outlines were no longer heavy but vibrated together with the strum of the strings, the drumming and ringing, and the human voice, sometimes running and playing, sometimes held on a long, clear note. (See Figure 1.1)

As they sang, the broad blue sky turned inky; a crescent moon rose over the roof and hung directly above the singing group. The audience expanded as shadowy figures slipped in. Someone lit a fire. After about an hour, it stopped. Prahladji suddenly rose with a smile, introduced some "parties" of singers who had come from nearby villages, and went off to see about dinner. We listened to samples from other singing groups until called inside. In the first room we saw many photos of Prahladji in performance

FIGURE I.1. Prahladji sings with his younger brother Ashok. Photo by Kedar Desai.

and in the company of distinguished people. There were two posters of Dr. B. R. Ambedkar, the great twentieth-century leader of the movement of "untouchables" for liberation from caste oppression. Couplets of Kabir were painted on the walls. Seated on the floor of the next room, we were served a vegetarian meal. Then we went back to the room with the photos, now crowded with family and neighbors. Prahladji presented me with a bunch of his commercially recorded cassettes. I presented him with a copy of my book on Kabir and an American flashlight. The feeling was warm, the energy high. There was the illusion of knowing each other well. He said, "You have come into our lives today, we have done all this. When you leave, will you ever come back? Will we ever meet again? Nobody knows!"

We boarded our taxi and drove off into the night.

It took two years for us to meet again. After that the connection was for life. At least that's the way it feels.

In this and subsequent chapters, I will introduce Prahladji as I gradually came to know him: his life story, his family, his beginning as a singer and his growing performative activities, his involvement with religious sects, his interpretations of Kabir's words, and his movement toward being a guru as well as a singer. We will see his orbit grow from village to region and then become national; eventually we will witness the beginning of his globalization. We will also be introduced to what he sings and how this singing is part of the social, religious, economic, and political networks of Malwa. Other singers will enter the story. We will see how Kabir is produced among them.

Telling the stories of Prahladji and others is important because it is also a way of telling the story of Kabir. Kabir lives in singers and listeners, social contexts, and personal histories. Innumerable stories of Kabir could thus be told, mediated through people living in India and Pakistan today. I will tell only a few. Throughout these accounts, we will keep remembering the songs of Kabir that they continue to sing. Unfortunately we can't hear their music in the pages of a book. We'll have to make do with words of Kabir, and not even the Hindi words they sing, just English translations. If you are inspired, find a way to listen!

On the Road

Oh bird, my brother, why do you wander
from forest to forest?
Oh bird, my brother, why do you stray
from forest to forest?
In the city of your body is the holy name.
In your own green garden is the sacred sound.[2]

In January 2002 I returned to India, ready to plunge into the oral tradition. Worried about having been out of touch with Prahladji for two years, I went once more to the Adivasi Lok Kala Parishad in the state capital of Bhopal to ask director Kapil Tiwari to help me in contacting him and finding my way to his village. "You are lucky," he said. "Tipanyaji is singing tonight in Bhopal."[3] That evening at the prestigious Bharat Bhavan auditorium, where he and two other folk artists were performing, I saw him for the first time as a public figure. He was shining. White *dhotī*, white *kurtā*, white swathe of hair streaked with grey, white teeth that I couldn't help noticing because of the bright and frequent smile. After the program, when he came out and chatted with the audience, someone asked what I was doing there. "I've come to learn from him," I said immediately. He smiled slightly and gazed downward. The facial expression spoke modesty, but the body remained large. He was used to this, to his own magnetism. He didn't shrink from it.

Prahladji was born in 1954 in a poor rural family, their caste numbered among the former "untouchables." The family had nothing to do with Kabir or with music. These things he stumbled on in his mid-twenties. The sound of the *tambūrā* attracted him, so he started learning to play it in 1978. Then he took up bhajan singing because that's what people did when they played the *tambūrā*. The people who were teaching him happened to sing Kabir. Some of them belonged to the Kabir Panth, the sect devoted to Kabir, which has many members among the lower castes in Malwa.[4] Kabir intrigued and attracted Prahladji. Though he sometimes sang bhajans of Mirabai and Singaji (a popular bhakti poet of Madhya Pradesh), or bhajans praising the deified hero Ramdev, he became increasingly devoted to Kabir.

When a group says, "We sing Kabir," they might equally say, "We sing *nirguṇ*." *Nirguṇ* is a theological term that refers to a notion of God beyond form and attributes, contrasted with *saguṇ*, which refers to God as represented in concrete forms, having incarnations, icons, and stories. The famous bhakti poets of North India from the fourteenth through seventeenth centuries tended to be associated with either *nirguṇ* or *saguṇ* approaches to the divine, though the two weren't sharply separated. *Nirguṇ* carries its own styles and themes. Kabir is the preeminent *nirguṇ* poet of the North. Prahladji often says, "I sing only Kabir." But in fact the signature lines of a number of other *nirguṇ* poets appear in the bhajans that his *mandalī* and others in Malwa sing. It is understood that they are the planets to Kabir's sun.[5]

Bhajan *mandalīs*, or groups that get together to sing devotional songs, are present in nearly every village. They may sing *nirguṇ* or *saguṇ* or a combination of both. They may consist of men or women (one rarely sees a mixed group). The Kabir *mandalīs* of Malwa are almost exclusively male.[6] Groups that stay together for a while usually collect a few instruments: a *tambūrā*, the five-stringed instrument that migrated to this part of Malwa from Rajasthan; a *dholak*, or two-headed drum; small cymbals and bells; eventually perhaps a harmonium, the box-shaped, hand-pumped keyboard that combines attributes of a piano and an accordion. Recently the violin has become fairly common, along with the *timkī*, a pair of small drums hit with sticks and sometimes called *bāngo* (from the English word for the originally Afro-Cuban bongo drums).

Bhajan *mandalīs* are popular as much for the joy and release of singing as for the religious content of the songs. They are one of the ways in which cultural knowledge—poetry, philosophy, morality, devotional feeling and practice, observations about work, society, and business, and insights into the nature of self and purpose of life—sinks in, seemingly without effort, but with cumulative depth and elaboration. Most *mandalīs* go no farther than the houses or neighborhood hangouts where they get together. Some are asked to sing at local functions, family events, holidays, or religious rituals. After sitting with such *mandalīs* for a while, Prahladji became the leader of one. His group started getting invitations to little events. Through the 1980s, his popularity as a singer grew among the local villages. In 1992 he was discovered by Kapil Tiwari, an influential cultural leader in Bhopal who is devoted to encouraging folk artists and making their voices heard. (We will hear from him in depth in chapter 3.) Tiwari was impressed with his voice and spirit. Now there were invitations to bigger places, including the state capital.

In the early 1990s another development brought the Kabir bhajan *mandalīs* of Malwa together in an unusual way. Eklavya, an NGO that does educational work in Madhya Pradesh and beyond, organized a series of monthly Kabir singing sessions, along with other activities, which went on for eight years. The *Kabir bhajan evam vichār manch*—a "platform for singing and discussing Kabir"—generated a great deal of activity and reflection and left a strong mark on the Kabir culture of the area.[7] (We will refer to this program as the *manch* in ongoing discussions.) Prahladji was very active in the *manch*, as were Narayanji, Kaluramji, and others who will come forth more fully in chapter 6. At the beginning they were all just *sāthīs*, companions in singing and playing, who shared similar backgrounds, family experiences, and work lives. But as the decade went on, Prahladji was becoming more of a stage performer. As an artist, he was offered money for singing. His cassettes, which entered the market in 1993, took off. He became very busy, combining singing engagements with his job as a teacher in a government school. He bought a car.

By the time I reached Malwa in 2002, he was in constant demand. His village had no telephone lines, but he had installed a small solar tower that hooked up to a phone that worked—sometimes. When the cells weren't dead, it rang a lot. Despite his growing reputation among city people, most of the calls were for programs in villages and small rural towns. They wanted him for their annual market-fair, for Shivaratri celebrations, for the inauguration of a college, for a Kabir Panth function. Or they were organizing a program especially for him. He seemed to always say yes. I started traveling with the group. Between February and August of that year, I went on more than twenty trips with them, often staying overnight on the road and in the family's village home between trips. That was my real initiation into oral Kabir. In the rest of this chapter, I will write about Prahladji and our adventures together—sometimes through straight biographical narrative, sometimes through his own words, and sometimes through excerpts from journals I kept on the road.

"We're finally off at 3," I wrote one day when we were supposed to leave by 1 p.m. to make it on time to an 8:30 concert. Inset passages in this section are from my notebooks.

> Prahladji keeps passing in and out of the house, saying, "Don't make us late," but he's the one who isn't ready. At last the instruments and bags are jammed into the Mahindra (a big jeep-like vehicle), as are the seven of us. Some boys push us down a mild slope: the starter rarely works. Prahladji exclaims *Satguru! Satyanām!*, a customary benediction, as we set out. We bump along the dirt road that leads to Maksi, then turn onto the paved but potholed narrow highway. As we pick up speed, the mood lightens. Prahladji is humming. Someone slips one of their own cassettes into the player.
>
> *If you come from the dome of the sky,*
> *if you've given up your head,*
> *then what have you to fear?*
> *Stay alert, the guru is always before you!*
> *If your mind is clear,*
> *what have you to fear?*
>
> Ashok's arm rests lightly on Gokul's shoulder. There's an air of warm camaraderie, easy laughter—at least till we all get deadened by our cramped positions and the cratered road. It's a man's world, but I have a special pass. Here we go.

My journals from February through July 2002 swarm with accounts of trips with "the band." (Yes, I am thinking of myself as a groupie traveling with my favorite band, something I didn't manage to do during my youth in the 1960s.) There were trips to huge Kabir Panth convocations, to tiny villages, to pilgrimage centers, and to events I could never have dreamed of, like the *bailoṇ kā melā*, the Bullock Fair, where they say 100,000 bullocks (along with random camels and horses) are for sale, each attended by a gaggle of humans.

March 9, 2002
The Anjali Literary Society of Nemavar, on the holy Narmada River, presents its annual program associated with the *Pānch Koshī Yātrā*—the pilgrimage of five kosh—about a ten-mile walking trip. Introductory speeches start at 9 and go on nearly 2.5 hours. They all keep referring to Tipanyaji's wonderful singing, but he doesn't get to sing till after 11:30 p.m. The women are leaving in droves because it's too late for them. Lots of men have also left, but thousands remain.

P. [Prahladji] is always bringing his audience back to themselves. "It's great, you're here for the Pānch Koshī journey, but first do the journey within yourself. A pilgrimage is good, but make yourself ready for it, worthy of it. Otherwise it's useless. The swan and the heron look the same, but they are very different."[8]

March 24, 2002
Two ways of reacting to the foreign lady who is writing on Kabir.

1. The Literary Society of Nemavar puts me on the stage, garlands me, and proclaims the international importance of the event.
2. Mangal Das, *mahant* of the Kabir Panth ashram in Dewas, says: "Writing a book doesn't mean you understand Kabir. A criminal can write a book too." So true!

April 18, 2002
The wind comes through the windows like a hot bath. We're on the road again! The starter worked. Great. And the horn is under control, doesn't go off randomly as it did on the last trip. But there's a new problem: the car is overheating. An hour into the trip they've poured all the extra water into the steaming hole, but to no avail. A duct connected to the radiator is broken. We're stuck three hours away from the program, which is supposed to begin in three hours.

We sit in a tiny town where they have relatives. P. has gone back to Maksi try to get another car. Finally we arrive at the concert site hours late. It's a big fair for the Navaratri festival. The audience quickly regroups. 99% are men, a sea of white *kurtās* with pink, orange, yellow, and red turbans bobbing on top. After a ceremonious half-hour of bestowing garlands, lighting a lamp, and praising the artist, the singing starts. There's a terrible din coming from nearby loudspeakers that have nothing to do with our show. I hate it, but Prahladji seems unperturbed.

He always says that when we recognize *paramātmā* (the supreme being) as the same in everyone, then we see no one as Hindu or Muslim, high or low caste, Indian or foreign. Today this serves as introduction to a series of *sākhīs* that feature Muslim vocabulary, followed by a delightful song asserting that everything, even improbable and funny things, are nothing but God. It's a fast rollicking song which I identify by its most frequently repeated phrase, *tū kā tū*, "You, only you."

Hey wise wanderer, what's the secret?
Just live your life well.
In this world flowers, branches—
wherever I look,
you, only you.

An elephant is you in elephant form,
an ant is just a little you. As elephant driver
you sit on top. The one who holds the goad
is you, only you.

With thieves you become a thief,
you're among the outlaws too.
You rob someone and run away.
The cop who nabs the thief is you,
only you.

With givers you become a giver,
you're among the paupers too.
As a beggar you go begging.
The donor is you,
only you.

In man and woman you shine the same,
Who in this world would call them two?
A baby arrives and starts to cry.
The babysitter is you,
only you.

In earth, ocean,
every creature, you alone
shine forth. Wherever I look,
only you.

Kabir says, listen seekers,
You've found the guru
right here, right now!

Now well into the program, the original audience has shrunk, but the attention is better. A guy in the front row sucks on a country pipe and gets a chilling look of disapproval from Prahladji. Still the pipe is being passed.

April 19, 2002, 6 a.m.
We change cars again after a rough night. We were stuck at a truck stop for hours, getting something fixed, and took turns sleeping in a small space in the luggage compartment. Prahladji gives me a glance, then there's a little burst of laughter. It's funny. The big red ball of sun is climbing up over the horizon, as it was climbing down on the outward journey. Ashok puts on the *Dhanya Kabīr* tape, loud. This is the life.

March 10, 2002
I travel with these guys like a Deadhead, to fairs and holy places, resting on the floor with pilgrims, going by car, train, or bus, sharing space and facilities with everyone, washing clothes on the spot, sleeping amidst the blare of loudspeakers, listening to them perform at all hours. After a few days or a week of that, I check into a good hotel, send my clothes to be washed and ironed, pay for hot running water, space and silence, a private flush toilet. Collecting my thoughts, writing, sending and receiving emails.

In Dewas's most luxurious accommodation, the Srishti Club. Was dropped off here at 6:30 a.m. by the car in which we'd been driving for hours. A startling contrast from the life of village and pilgrimage. They all walked in and inspected everything—wide lawns, swimming pool, my light-filled room, which could house a village family. I felt embarrassed.

Becoming a Kabir Singer

Prahladji was born in that same Lunyakhedi village where I first met him, and where he lives now. But he didn't stay there long. At the age of about three he was sent to live with his Nana and Nani (maternal grandparents) in the village of Manpur, about fifty kilometers away. Why did they let their firstborn son go so far away? He just says, "My Nana had no sons, and my mother was his only daughter." A girl born before him had died. A boy born after him, and eventually two more girls, also died. His younger brothers Ambaram and Ashok and his sister Gita survived. They struggled economically. Like most rural people of their caste, they worked on others' land, and income was unreliable. Both parents were illiterate. His father was virtually a bonded laborer, working other people's land in return for food, housing, and a tiny monthly stipend that was paid only once a year. He worked thirty years like that. Why did so many kids die? They had no medical resources. As we discuss this, Prahladji and Ambaram pull up their shirts and show me burn scars. That used to be the cure for illness. They burned them around the stomach with hot clay or iron. "It worked!" he says. I don't believe it. "You have to believe it," he says with a grin. "I'm alive."

Their caste is Balai—a scheduled or Dalit caste, meaning one of those formerly deemed untouchable (also referred to locally as Harijan and Mālvī). Prahladji doesn't like to associate himself with any caste label. Once we went to the inauguration of a new house in the nearby city of Dewas. The house owner, a friend, had asked him to sing a few songs at the function. When we all sat down on the ground in rows to be served a meal (a sensitive moment for people who are queasy about intercaste dining), someone asked him outright: "What's your *jātī*?" *Jātī* means caste, but also race or species. He answered without missing a beat: *mānav jātī*—the human race.

> *When Ram plays inside you,*
> *that's wisdom.*
>
> Parrots can repeat a mantra,
> mynahs can recite the Veda.
> Without a guru
> you'll stay confused. . . .
> The Brahmin is clay, the Vaishya clay,
> the whole creation clay.
> In this clay, everyone mingles.
> That's Kabir's message.[9]

Balais are an important Dalit caste in Malwa. Ranked relatively high among the low, they have tended to be upwardly mobile in recent decades.[10] But to many upper-caste Hindus, they are still very low. Practices and attitudes tied to untouchability are not uncommon (though they are illegal). Lunyakhedi is a two-caste village of about 500 residents, all either Brahmin or "Harijan" (the term used when the village layout was first described to me). It has two distinct sections, each filled with members of one of these groups. In between is an open space that takes a few minutes to walk across. I have crossed that space only about three times in ten years.

Prahladji's move to his grandparents' house had huge consequences for his future. They placed a high value on education, and he went much farther in his studies than the children who stayed in his home village. Manpur also provided a more socially progressive environment. Untouchability was little in evidence, whereas in Lunyakhedi Dalits were not allowed to enter the temple, and Brahmins objected if a Dalit added "Singh" to his name as "Singh" is associated with high-status *kśhatriyā* castes. Prahladji's formal name is Prahlad Singh Tipanya. He changed his little brother's name from Kashiram to Ashok when the younger boy started school, explaining that Kashiram was "not a good name"—no doubt because it was recognizable as a Dalit name. Ambaram studied up to fifth standard. Ashok, the youngest, completed twelfth. Gita, their sister, stopped after fifth. But Prahladji was encouraged to study. "My grandmother," he recalls with emotion in his voice, "used to sit with me while I studied at night. She kept me company until I went to sleep." After twelfth he began his B.Sc., a postsecondary diploma in science. But that was interrupted by a job opportunity. Eventually, through correspondence courses, he completed a Bachelor of Arts degree and a Master's degree in history—unprecedented in his family. He got a job as a teacher in a government school—a coveted position because of its security. His first job was located far off the paved road. He walked thirteen kilometers from the road to the village, holding his sandals in his hand during the monsoon because the mud was so thick. It took two-and-a-half hours each way.

His grandparents were religious in conventional Hindu ways, doing rituals and fasts in which Prahladji participated. Nani was devoted to Ramdevji, a deified saint of Rajasthan popular with both Hindus and Muslims, and having a large following from lower castes. They all ate meat. Nana took alcoholic drinks, and so did Prahladji as a young man. Kabir meant nothing to them. Like most children in North Indian public schools, Prahladji had to memorize *sākhīs* (couplets) of Kabir in school: "Five *sākhīs*, ten marks," he recalls. In the early 1970s he became a vegetarian and stopped drinking alcohol; a few years later he gave up tea.

Prahlad was thirteen and Shanti was eleven when they got married. They didn't live together for a long time after that. Between 1972 and 1974, during college vacations, he came home and worked as a laborer. He said he had helped to dig nearly 200 wells. After finishing the first year of his postsecondary science course in Mhow, he was hired as a teacher and spent a year in training. In 1975 he began his first full-fledged teaching assignment in the village of Kathbaroda, where he lived separately for twelve years with his little brother Ashok. Ashok had his first eight years of school there. Prahladji likes to remind me that he did all the cooking during that period, since I'm fond of pointing out how the men and boys in the house now sit around playing carom and watching TV, not lifting a finger while the women cook, serve, wash, and clean.

> [PT][11] In one of the villages where I stayed, they used to sing bhajans all night. I'd complain to my mother—what is this nonsense? Do they have a stomach ache that keeps them up all night? They don't sleep, and they don't let me sleep. I can't even study. Now people probably complain that way about me! (He laughs.)
>
> One day there was a *purnimā* (full moon) program for Ramdevji in Gorkhedi village. I went along with some other teachers. There were a lot of programs like that. That was when I heard the *tambūrā* for the first time. It was around 1978. The sound of the strings hit me really hard. That vibration, that *brrrrrrr,* went inside my body. I thought, wow, I should learn this. I had heard *dholak* and harmonium and never felt like learning them. But with the *tambūrā* I felt an ache, a pang. People don't all get wounded by the same arrow. Some are struck by a bhajan's words. I was wounded by the *tambūrā*'s strings.[12]
>
> I left my posting in Kathbaroda, got transferred to Gorkhedi so I could learn to play the *tambūrā*. A man called Kakur-da taught me every day. I learned quickly because of my concentration [*lagan*]. I played morning and night and learned from him every day.

Prahladji's wife Shantiji later told us that he made a *tambūrā* himself—cut down a tree and carved it out, wounding his thigh with an ax in the process.

> [PT] People used to get together at night to sing bhajans. They told me I'd learn faster if I sang and played at the same time. I said okay, write out a bhajan for me and I'll sing.

Prahladji recalls the first Kabir bhajan he learned. He just wrote down the words to help him improve his *tambūrā* playing, but later he paid more attention and was deeply affected. He says this song turned his life around. Its imagery came from farming and the common plants and animals of the countryside.

> [PT] "Oh mind, plow your fields in such a way / that you don't cause pain to the bullocks." People always beat their bullocks, so there was that feeling in the bhajan. Then it talked about the *semal* tree. Its flower looks very attractive, but there's nothing inside.[13]

I remembered encountering the *semal* while translating Kabir some twenty-five years earlier—about the same time that Prahladji was learning this bhajan. *Semal* is translated as "silk-cotton" tree. Birds are attracted to its big red blooms, but when they peck into the flower they are disappointed by the dry, inedible cottony strands that fall out of it.

> [PT] The bhajan also said, *ausar khet meṇ bīj mat boye,* don't plant seeds in a barren field. And there was another verse about *haṃsa* and *bagulā,* swan and crane. They look the same but the *haṃsa* eats pearls; the *bagulā* keeps a sharp eye out, and when it gets the chance grabs a fish.[14] So don't be attracted by outer form. See the way a person behaves. At first I just sang the song, but later I started to think about what it meant. I thought I should look behind the outer form of the song, see what deep things Kabir is saying. I went through different levels of understanding. After hearing the lines about *semal,* I went to see the *semal* flower and saw that it was true, the flower is useless.

Here Prahladji inserts a Kabir *sākhī* to emphasize his point. Conversations about Kabir are often punctuated by *sākhīs* (see Schomer 1987).

> [PT] *baḍā huā to kyā huā, jaise per kazūr, / panthī kī chhāyā nahīṇ, phal lāge ati dūr.*
>
> You're big? So what?
> The date palm's big, yet it gives
> no shade to the traveler, and its fruits
> are out of reach.
>
> Don't be attracted to something just because of looks. On the physical level, you might get entranced by some woman's beauty, but you shouldn't leave your own home, pulled by desire and sensuality. On the spiritual level, there are so many fruitless, barren tendencies in yourself. Change them, make them fruitful!
>
> I heard this *sākhī*:
>
> *gāyā bin pāyā nahi, anagāvan se dūr / jin gāyā vishvās se, sāheb hāl hazūr*
>
> You won't reach it without singing / if you don't sing, it's far.
> But when you sing with deep feeling, / Saheb is right where you are!

Hey, who is this *sāheb*? I didn't even know who *sāheb* was! Someone said *sāheb* is *paramātmā*, the supreme being. I got the idea that if you want to meet *paramātmā*, you should learn how to sing with sincere feeling. Before this I thought *paramātmā* was out there somewhere, separate. I'd have to go out and get him (laughs). Now I know that he's in me and everyone. There's no separate God, it's just a matter of connecting.

To change my inner tendencies, to convert them from barren to fruitful, I decided to immerse myself in singing and playing. I learned quickly. Soon I was singing on All India Radio and Doordarshan television. And we were traveling all over.

Prahladji took initation (*dikśhā*), almost casually it seems, in several *nirguṇ* sects: first the Nath Panth in Gorkhedi village, where he learned the *tambūrā*; then the Radhasoami Satsang in the big city of Indore; then the Parakhi Kabir Panth, led by Abhilash Das in Allahabad; then the Damakheda-based lineage of the Kabir Panth (see chapter 7). Taking *dikśhā* means receiving a mantra from a guru or a local *mahant* who has authority from the central sect, and assenting to some principles about God and proper conduct. At the top of the list of proper behaviors is swearing off meat, eggs, alcohol, and cigarettes. Reverence for and service to the guru are also enjoined. The mantra consists of one or more divine names. In *nirguṇ* devotion, these names are understood to refer to a supreme being beyond form. Even if Vaishnav names (like Ram, Govind, Hari) are used, they are not supposed to suggest the concrete forms of Ram and Krishna and their many popular stories. As mantras, they are charged, potent sounds that can evoke an inner experience. All such names are encompassed in more general terms like *nām* (name) and *śhabda* (word) that refer to a sound that is both internal and cosmic. The devotee should practice *sumiran* (also spelled *smaran, simran*), remembering or retaining awareness. This may be understood as continuous awareness of the name or as formal practice of repeating the name. The formal practice, called *jap*, is often done with a *mālā* or string of beads, counting one repetition to each bead.

Why did Prahladji keep trying new sects? I thought there must be an important reason, but he didn't find the question very interesting. The Nath Panth guru just asked, "Do you drink liquor? Do you eat meat?" The answer was no. "Fine, then you can join." So he joined. Later somebody said the top guru of Radhasoami was coming to Indore for the sect's grand annual function (see Juergensmeyer 1991; Bhattacharya 1996). In Radhasoami the head of the sect gives mass *dikśhā* at such gatherings. Prahladji and his friends said, *chalo*, let's go and take the name. Then there was a Kabir Panthi *sant*, Purushottamdas, who wanted to initiate him. "I already took the name in Radhasoami," said Prahladji. "Never mind," said the *sant*, "it's all the same." So he took it again. All these sects had in common the worship of a *nirguṇ* God, reverence for the guru, insistence on "pure" food and drink, and constant reference to the name or the word as opening the door to a liberating experience. Prahladji told me that the Kabir Panth was the last stop: he didn't plan to join any more sects. But later I found out that he had taken *dikśhā* from at least three different Kabir Panth gurus. Eventually our conversations revealed much more about his deepening understanding of "guru" over the years.[15]

Prahladji went on explaining how he explored the meaning of bhajans in those early years of learning to sing. He took a practical approach to mysterious utterances:

> [PT] If you get the secret, you can see my country.
> Veda and Quran can't reach its border,
> beyond speaking and hearing.

What was that secret? I kept thinking about it.

> A guru, a wise one, listens—
> a voice vibrates in the sky,
> subtle, very subtle.

I thought maybe it was about the sound of rain in the sky. But then, Kabir-sahib always talks about looking within—

> *man mathurā dil dvāraka, kāyā kāśhi jān*
> *das dvāre kā pinjarā, yā meṇ jot pahachān*
> Know mind as Mathura, heart as Dwarka, body as Kashi.
> This cage of ten doors: recognize the light here.

Mathura, Dwarka, Kashi—people keep running to these pilgrimage places. But the cage of ten doors is the body. So he must be talking about a voice in your body. I decided to find out if the voice is there or not. So I started to meditate. In the evenings I made my food, said the Kabir Panthi evening prayers, did some reading, and then meditated. After sitting down, I didn't know how long I stayed there. One hour, two hours, four. At first my legs hurt, I got pins and needles in my feet, but that gradually got better. I was sitting, but my mind still wandered—school, home, games, all kinds of things. Then I realized why people do *sumiran*—to stop the mind from wandering. You have to get some control over that mental activity. It takes time for the sound to come. I realized you shouldn't eat too much. What you eat affects your body. So for three years I didn't eat any dinner, just had one meal a day, so I could meditate. Even then it's not enough. You can sit still, close your eyes, reduce your eating, give up other things. But behind closed eyes, you're seeing things. Your mind keeps going. That's the subtle part.

moṭī māyā sab taje, jhīnī tajī na jāī
pīr paigambar auliyā, jhīnī sab ko khāī
jhīnī māyā jin tajī, moṭī gae bilāy
aise jan ke nikaṭ se, sab dukh gae hirāy

Everyone gives up gross illusion, no one gives up the subtle.
Masters, prophets, and priests—the subtle ate them all.
If you give up subtle illusion, the gross goes by itself.
That's the way folks get far from sorrow.

After some time I realized that what I'd heard about the voice was true, it's really there. That voice, that melody, is in everyone, initiated or not, Hindu or Muslim or whatever. Some say it's the sound of blood flowing through our veins. Some say breath. But only that sound can get your mind really centered. Nothing else—not pilgrimage, fasting, temples, rituals, recitation. If your mind is there, it can't be here. They're all outside. This is inside.

khel is brahmānḍ kā pinḍ meṇ dekhiyā
See the play of the whole universe in your body.

With sound, there's light. Both arise from the same place. Lightning and thunder go together. After experiencing this, I had more faith in Kabir's bhajans.

Prahladji remembers those three years—alone except for his young, school-going brother, living simply, doing his own cooking and cleaning, exploring the meaning of Kabir's bhajans within himself—as the happiest time of his life.

[PT] Nowadays I've become a sort of lazy fellow. But the experience I had then—enough! It was lasting [*sthāī*]. Every human being should have an experience like that. Once you've had it, it's with you forever. A laborer by the roadside, if he has had this experience, is happier than anyone.

I asked how he learned to meditate. Did he have a guru? He said he learned some things from Purushottamdas, the Kabir Panth guru from Kharchha village for whom he had great respect. He also learned from reading. Whatever methods he read about, he'd try out.

Inside and Outside: A Singer Makes the Connections

We scholars need to name major themes in the expansive body of Kabir poetry, to give ourselves pegs on which to hang our discussions. But the more I stay among singers, the more I find the themes intertwined. Two broad categories that are almost inevitable in discussing Kabir might be called "inner" and "outer." There are the "spiritual" poems that speak of a profound inner experience, a dissolution of ego, a boundless joy that seems to be matched by boundless freedom from attachments; and there are poems of social criticism and satire directed at caste, religious hypocrisy, hierarchy, violence, and delusion (see chapters 6 and 8 for extensive discussion of these distinctions). Other frequently noted categories include homage to the guru; songs of the (yogic) body; and songs of death, transiency, the urgent call to wake up.[16]

In Prahladji's singing and running commentaries, however, these threads and patterns are inextricably woven together in a larger fabric. After listening to him, I turn to the texts in books and find them less and less amenable to categorization. In this section, temporarily suspending the biographical narrative, I will show how Prahladji's way of singing and interpreting Kabir opened out questions that I have long mulled over in the texts, and also enabled me to understand how the texts are rooted in his life and social world.

Inner to Outer

Prahladji's meditation experience in the early 1980s, with its eventual revelation of the continuous inner sound, the subtle voice so frequently evoked in Kabir, is clearly crucial to his understanding of and convictions about Kabir.

The sound is represented through terms like *nām*/name; *śhabda*/word; bhajan/devotional song; *dhūn*/melody; *tāl*/rhythm; *bājā*/instrument; and particular instruments, such as flutes, drums, and sitars. Sometimes it is linked to the breath—*shvās*, breath, or *oham soham*, yogic terms for inbreath and outbreath.

koī suntā hai guru gyānī, gagan meṇ āvāz hove jhīnā jhīnā
oham soham bājā re bāje, trikuṭī shabad nishānī...
sab ghat puran bolī rahā hai, alakh purush nirbānī

The guru, the wise one, listens:
in the sky a voice, subtle, so subtle.
Inbreath, outbreath, the instrument plays,
the word, a sign at the point
where three streams meet.
He speaks completely in every body,
the unseen, unspoken person.[17]

***

sunn mahal meṇ bājā bāje, kingarī ben sitārā
jo chaḍh dekhe gagan gufā meṇ, darsegā agam apārā

In the palace of emptiness an instrument plays—
lute, flute, sitar.
One who climbs
to the cave in the sky
will see
what's deathless, boundless.[18]

***

śhunya śhikhar par anahad bāje
rāg chhattīs sunāūngā

On the peak of emptiness
the boundless sound resounds
there I'll sing
all thirty-six ragas.[19]

***

laharī anahad uṭhe ghaṭ bhītar, phailī rahā chaho pherī,
re divāne lāgī shabad dhun gaharī, re divāne lāgī bhajan dhun gaharī ...

ulṭā baṇ gagan jaī lāgā, vāṇ bich hai ek dairī
uni dairī mere mālik virājai, vahāṇ par lāgī lau merī
uni dairī meṇ aisā bājā bāje, bājī rahā āṭho paharī
mardang tāl pakhāvaj bāje murlī bāje ghaṇī gaharī

Boundless waves arise in my body, spreading in all directions.
Oh mad one, you've been hit by the word, the deep melody,
oh mad one, you've been hit by the song, the deep melody.

An arrow turns backwards to strike the sky,
in the middle is a space
a space where my master splendidly shines
where all my love gathers
in that space instruments play,
they play night and day, the drums keep rhythm,
the flute plays, it is so deep,
boundless waves arise in my body.[20]

The last two passages above use the key word *anahad*. It literally means "boundless" and in this context implies the term *anahad nād*—a very old concept in Indian cosmology, yoga, and music. *Nād* (*nāda* in Sanskrit transliteration) means "sound." Not just any sound, but primordial sound, the very first evolute in the process of creation, a sound that, although it is the source of all sounds perceived by our sense organs, is yet utterly unlike them. This uncanny difference is expressed by the anti-commonsense term "unstruck sound"—the usual translation of *anahad nād*.[21]

Now, starting with Prahladji's reported experience of an inner sound, which he discovered as a young man investigating whether the words of Kabir's bhajans were true, then lingering with examples of how the bhajans describe or hint at such a sound, we might find it reasonable to propose that this represents the *interior* Kabir, the mystic, the *sādhak* or spiritual practitioner. If there are any grounds for separating his spiritual from his social-political poetry, there will be no question about which side of the divide these verses belong on.

But Prahladji leaps directly from the *anahad nād* to social equality, the folly of claiming superiority on the basis of caste, class, religion, sect, nation, and so on. In a heartbeat, he links up those deeply interior, extremely subtle, notoriously difficult-to-attain states of spiritual exaltation to songs satirizing Hindu and Muslim bigots and phonies, arrogant

Brahmins, foolish Mullahs, clueless pilgrims, and myopic yogis. How does he make that leap?

He is able to do it because that unbroken, always immediately available sound, that ungraspable, luminous, formless form of divinity, resides exactly *in the body*, and *in every body*. Countless Kabir poems carry as a central metaphor the *ghat*, the clay pot, ubiquitous in rural Indian life, and standing for the human body.

kaī dhūṇḍhtī phiro mhārī helī, mat bhāgti phiro mhārī helī
ghaṭ ghaṭ meṇ rāmjī bole rī, par ghaṭ meṇ piyājī bole rī,
kaī hertī phiro mhārī helī

My dear friend, what are you seeking? Why are you wandering?
In every body, Ramji speaks! In every body, the beloved speaks!
My dear, what are you seeking? Where are you running?

I would hazard the claim that, if one could examine the widely varying representations of Kabir across history, geography, and social formations, this theme would be central to all. The fundamental reality you are looking for is within you, right in your own body. You're a fool when you exhaust yourself looking for it outside. And all those others are fools and possibly scoundrels when they tell you to look for the truth in temples and mosques, rituals and scriptures, sacred rivers and mountains, beads and costumes, statues, and their own high and mighty expertise.

kahāṇ se āyā, kahāṇ jāoge, khabar karo apne tan kī
koī satguru mile to bhed batāvai, khul jāve antar khiḍkī

hindū muslim donoṇ bhulāne, khaṭpaṭ māhi riyā *aṭakī*
jogī jangam śhekh sevarā, lālach māhi riyā *bhaṭakī* ...

Where did you come from? Where are you going?
Get the news from your own body!
A true teacher can show you the secret.
The window within will open.

Hindus, Muslims, both deluded, always fighting.
Yogis, sheikhs, wandering Jains,
all of them lost in greed.

The song is satirical, laying on Kabir's characteristic equal-opportunity critique of religious hypocrites and idiots. But in the repeated refrain, we are reminded of the inner world, the source of knowledge that gives us the conviction to excoriate their deluded attitudes: to find out who you really are, where you came from and where you're going, don't turn to the idiot-experts. Rather, get the news from your own body. Open the window within. A true teacher can help you see this, but not a phony one. And beware: the phonies are all around.[22]

Prahladji never ceases to remind his listeners that our true home (*nij ghar*) is in our bodies. In this clay pot, everything is revealed. Most intimately, our home is in the uninterrupted subtle sound (also associated with light) that is present in everyone equally. We don't have to search for it; we just have to open to it, to let the stream of our awareness join with it. No song expresses this more beautifully than "*Yā ghaṭ bhītar*":

Who can know this? The one who knows!
Without a teacher, the world is blind.

In this body forests and hamlets, right here mountains and trees
In this body gardens and groves, right here the one who waters them

In this body gold and silver, right here the market spread out
In this body diamonds and pearls, right here the one who tests them

In this body seven oceans, right here rivers and streams
In this body moon and sun, right here a million stars

In this body lightning flashing, right here brilliance bursting
In this body the unstruck sound roaring, streams of nectar pouring

In this body the three worlds, right here the one who made them
Kabir says, listen seekers: right here my own teacher.

Who can know this? The one who knows!
Without a teacher, the world is blind.[23]

Light in the Body: *Nirguṇ* and Caste

Kabir says,
what have you lost?
What do you seek?
The blind don't see.
Brilliance gleams
in your body.[24]

David Lorenzen (1996) has argued that the *nirguṇ* sects that took shape in early modern North India, in contrast with *saguṇ* Vaishnav traditions, tend to be associated with radical social thought; in particular, they criticize the caste system, attack ideas of purity and pollution, and preach absolute equality. A number of *nirguṇ* sects were founded or inspired by low-caste "saints" and have continued to attract followers largely from low-status groups.[25] Although Vaishnav traditions also assert that all are equal before the Lord and that true devotion obliterates all other considerations including caste, the Vaishnav *sampradāys* have been more ambivalent on this point with a greater tendency to maintain caste ideology and practices.[26]

I agree with Lorenzen that *nirguṇ* bhakti has a special appeal to stigmatized and oppressed groups, and that it is linked to rejection of caste. Lorenzen points out that the *nirguṇ* God is omnipresent—an inherently egalitarian notion. But I am doubtful about his comparison of Kabir's *nirguṇ* bhakti to Shankara's Advaita Vedanta philosophy: "If everything is grounded in Brahman, and the physical world is in some basic sense illusory, then the differences between human bodies, between Brahmin and Shudra, are also finally illusory" (1996, 29). I would not resort to the illusory nature of the material world to explain the egalitarianism and the powerful sense of human dignity associated with Kabir's *nirguṇ* bhakti. Such an interpretation would undercut the real-world potency of Kabir's social critique (a critique that is conspicuously absent in philosophers like Shankara). The explanation is more down-to-earth. In Kabir, the human body does not evaporate into Advaitin illusion. Its clay is continually invoked, held up as the precious container of the most precious reality, the place where we experience freedom, joy, the end of fear. The divine as sound reverberates through that clay pot with its subtle channels and lotuses; the divine as light illuminates the space within and beyond that vessel. At the same time, the clay is mere dust when the life goes out of it. Always the same in every pot, this clay makes us equal in birth, life, and death. In some verses we find the poet explicitly diverging from the path of renunciation—the ideal of *sannyās*, abandoning familial and social ties, that reigns supreme in Shankara's Advaitin sects. Here the garden refers to the everyday (worldly) world, that of the nonrenouncer.

sadhū aisā chāhiye, dukhe dukhāve nāhi
pan phūl chheḍe nahīṇ, par rahe bāg ke māhi.

The kind of holy man we need
doesn't suffer or cause others pain
doesn't disturb leaves or flowers
but stays in the garden.

A more practical factor that creates a strong attraction between *nirguṇ* and the oppressed castes is this: *saguṇ* bhakti requires physical images of divine beings. Those images are consecrated and housed in temples, and the guardians of those temples are Brahmin priests. The priests and images are claimed by the regime of caste purity. Only the priest can touch the statue, only the priest can pronounce the sacred Sanskrit syllables, conduct the rituals, hand back the blessed *prasād* to the worshiper. The sacred image must never be desecrated by an impure touch. Thus we can safely guess that in 99 percent of Hindu temples there is no such thing as a woman priest (who would be subject to monthly impurity), no such thing as a non-Brahmin priest.[27] This regime of purity is responsible for "untouchables" being excluded from Hindu temples over a history that goes back thousands of years. Not only have they not been allowed in the door, but they have often not been allowed to walk on the street in front of the temple.

Postindependence India has seen major changes around the practice of untouchability, beginning with the declaration of its illegality in the constitution. Many temples have ceased to discriminate against worshipers on the basis of caste. But if you ask Dalits whether untouchability has disappeared in the villages, they will laugh at you. In recounting his history, Prahladji pointed out that his childhood move from Lunyakhedi to Manpur presaged a better life for him, because in the former Dalits were still excluded from temple entry, but not in the latter. When he sings a song that criticizes faith in statues, we detect an extra bite in the words. First, there is the basic delusion that God is to be sought outside oneself. Second, there is the bitter collective memory of being treated as tainted, unfit to approach that exalted statue. In a song that emphasizes the constant presence and immediate availability of the divine in the body, one stanza describes, by contrast, the lifeless statue in the temple that is zealously guarded by a priest:

My dear friend, what are you seeking? Why are you wandering?
In every body, Ramji speaks! In every body, the beloved speaks!
My dear friend, what are you seeking? Where are you running?

A sculpted statue stands in the temple.
Its mouth never speaks.
The priest stands at the door.
Who can enter without his order?

Another song more aggressively asserts the superiority of the "unformed god," *anagaḍhiyā deva,* which means the god who is not fashioned by anyone's hand.

God without form, who will serve you?

Everyone runs to the solid form.
Nonstop they jump to serve it.
That full being, that indivisible lord,
no one knows its mystery.

Brahma, Vishnu, Shiva,
have scum on their heads.[28]
Don't put your faith in them,
they haven't found liberation.[29]

Niranjan and the avatars,
they're not really ours,
all stuck with the fruits of karma.
The maker is somebody else.

Yogis, ascetics, renouncers,
they all fight with each other.
Kabir says, listen seekers,
cross over with the Word.

God without form, who will serve you?

Focusing attention on caste suddenly sheds light on other lines that I haven't considered in terms of caste before. The phrase *nirmal hot sharīr* wafts through my mind: "the body becomes pure." The whole *sākhī* (couplet) goes like this:

The guru lives in Banaras, the disciple at the ocean's shore.
When the guru's quality comes forth, the body becomes pure.

I think of a series of examples in which the Word (*śhabda,* always a sign of the *nirguṇ* reality), or the light in the body, or the breath, or the song, conveys instant purity. Sometimes it is the *satguru* whose arrival purifies—the true guru who, Prahladji often says, is not any individual but is that very presence which radiates and resonates in every body.

satguru āngan āyā, gangā gomatī nahāyā
merī nirmal ho gayī kāyā, maiṇ vārī jāūṇ re

When the true guru enters my courtyard,
I've bathed in Ganga and Gomati,
my body has become pure.
I offer myself completely.

Prahladji is sensitive to the feelings and beliefs of others. I have heard him temper the fierce tenor of songs like *Anagaḍhiyā deva* by saying that Kabir was not attacking temples or mosques but was criticizing the common ways of misunderstanding them. Temples can be good, he would say; they are a place to focus your attention, to become calm, to let go of your pride and confusion. Similarly rituals can be good, a way to bring people together in a good atmosphere, for a good purpose. But, he would always conclude, they are for the beginning stages of our journey. Kabir's profound teaching takes us far beyond the need for temples or external forms.[30]

Sometimes when I describe myself as a *nirguṇ* devotee, people respond by saying that *nirguṇ* is for intellectuals; it is abstract, devoid of emotion. They ask rhetorically: How can you love a God beyond form, beyond words, beyond everything? I disagree with this characterization of *nirguṇ*. A God who is not anywhere becomes a God who is everywhere. If you withdraw the special divine energy from the temple image, it immediately suffuses the human form and the whole world. As Prahladji sings in a bhajan often heard at the beginning of a concert: *ek akhandit nāth charāchar dhāve*—one indivisible lord courses through all animate and inanimate beings.

Some *saguṇ* devotees also understand God this way. But the insistence on sanctified forms, spaces, and stories tends to pull in another direction. At least to Dalits who have been excluded from holy places and barred from approaching holy objects, there is a manifest link between *saguṇ* institutions and their own oppression. The liberating potential of *nirguṇ* is undeniable.[31]

[From my notebook] August 2, 2002
When I reached the village at 7 p.m., something unusual was going on. Lots of men were standing in two clumps—one group in front of P's house, the other on a field nearby. It turned out that Brahmins

from the other part of the village were trying to set up a cremation ground practically in front of Prahladji's house, near the low-caste part of the village and far from their own houses. The people here were opposing it. I questioned Prahladji and his elder son Ajay.

LINDA HESS (LH): Are there other more distant spots where they could have their cremation ground, where the smoke of burning bodies wouldn't blow into people's houses?

AJAY: There are plenty of spaces available.

LH: Then why do they want to do it right here?

AJAY: Just to push us down. It's caste exploitation.

LH TO PRAHLADJI (PT): Is it entirely about caste, or is it against you personally?

PT: It's about caste, but they also don't like the fact that so many people come to see me. You come, and many other people come, all the time. They think, "Why do people respect him so much? We're Brahmins, people should respect us." They are jealous. They want to put us in our places.

The Collector was called to settle the dispute. After listening to both sides, he decided that the burning ground should be located at a distance, not in front of any houses.

December 23, 2002
Yesterday Ashok donated blood for a Brahmin girl who is pregnant and who has developed a blood problem. He says her blood has "become like water." She accepted the blood. But her family still practices untouchability. They would not want to take food or water from Ashok, or to touch him, or to have his family's water vessels in the well they use.

Outer to Inner

Just as Prahladji transitions seamlessly from spiritual to political in commenting on a single bhajan, the movement from social commentary into the heart of inner experience is less like switching gears and more like subtly shifting between foreground and background. I will illustrate that move with a conversation in one of Shabnam Virmani's films.

As explained in the introduction, Shabnam is a Bangalore-based filmmaker who arrived in Malwa in December 2002 to start research for a film series on the same subject matter I had been immersed in throughout that year—Kabir's presence and meanings in contemporary South Asia, especially approached through music. We met and had a great time moving through the countryside and meeting singers for a few days. In the years to come, we would become close friends and collaborators.

In the film *Chalo hamārā des/Come to My Country*, Prahladji has a brilliant riff on form and no-form, moving from comments on religious hypocrisy to examination of the very structures of our minds. He spins it out from the idea of a *ghāt*, the built-up space on a riverbank with a stairway and leveled area, which allows people to approach the water, to bathe and do rituals, as well as to perform everyday activities like washing clothes. It is a place where people draw water—an activity that can bring forth caste prejudice, as the "upper" castes have historically tried to keep the "lower" away from their water supply. This discussion takes place on a train headed for Varanasi (or Banaras), Kabir's hometown, famous for its *ghāṭs* along the holy river Ganga. Shabnam is shooting with the camera while two sari merchants of Varanasi strike up a conversation with Prahladji.

MERCHANT: In Banaras, there are always ritual recitations of holy texts going on. All the major spiritual leaders have come there. ... Huge crowds gather.

PRAHLADJI (PT): And nothing changes. I've noticed that in India we have the most temples, the most holy places, the maximum sermonizers, the largest number of devotees, and also the most scoundrels, doing every kind of shady activity. ... Yesterday I sang the song "Why search in temples?" Some may feel this is an attack on temples, but it's not. Temples are merely places [that can support] the first stage to stilling your mind. It's just a medium. Once that's done, you can go to a temple or sit at home, or sit in a jungle, or even sit here. Right now, we could think we're in our temple. But we think we're sitting in a train.

SHABNAM VIRMANI (SV): There's a *sākhī* you sing—

> All draw water from the riverbank.
> No one draws where there's no bank.
> Kabir's bank is no-bank.
> One who draws there becomes pure.

What is this *aughāṭ ghāṭ*, "no-bank bank"?

PT: *Ghāṭs* are steps on the riverside. They're separated. Hindu *ghāṭ*, Muslim *ghāṭ*, a *ghāṭ* for upper castes, one for lower castes. We use *ghāṭs* to draw water, but also to get knowledge, to attain something. These frameworks are also *ghāṭs*. A *ghāṭ* on a river is to bathe. But he has a sari shop. That too is a *ghāṭ*. It's the place where we'll get what it can offer.

MERCHANT (SMILING): Yes, like Scindia Ghat, Raj Ghat [naming well known *ghāṭs* of Banaras].

PT: Those are only for bathing. *Ghāṭs* are also for attaining something. *Ghāṭ* means a place that's defined. . . . Different people have their own *ghāṭs*. So Kabir says, "All draw water from the riverbank,/No one draws where there' s no bank." Very few draw from a place where there's no *ghāṭ*. "Kabir's bank is no-bank. One who draws there becomes pure." A *ghāṭ* will trap you within a boundary. If someone sells Banarasi saris, that's all you'll get there. Other saris you won't get. So you'll get defined by that framework.

MERCHANT: At my shop if you ask for a South Indian sari, I won't have it!

PT: So you remain identified within boundaries. Boundaries are not only of caste, religion, and sect. Boundaries are also of knowledge, art, sensory desires, gender. All these create bounded frameworks. If I think I'm a great singer, I get trapped in that identity. Someone says, "I am an expert." He's bound by that. But for a state of spontaneous simplicity [*sahajtā*—one of Kabir's words for being fully awake and aware] all these bounded identities have to dissolve. We alone can release ourselves from these limits. For instance [to Shabnam], you're holding on to the camera. The camera is not holding on to you. The camera did not say, "Hold me." You chose to hold it. So you're tied to it. Whatever our attachments may be, we've shackled ourselves to them.

Saṃsārā

When I reached the village house in January 2002, I was confused. It wasn't the house I remembered from the first visit, two years before. Where was that modest dwelling, white on one side and blue on the other, with bright handprints on the wall beside the door? Our car drove up in the dark and stopped at a much more imposing structure, something with a tall roof, a fenced yard, and steps leading up to a wide verandah. "Hey, this isn't it," I murmured. But it was. Prahladji had built a new house. It had two big rooms on the ground, with more construction in progress on an upper floor. The old house, a few steps away, was little used.

Go now, you who lived
without a guru, oh yes.
Now you praise the body?
Now you sing its glory?
You built a palace, swan,
but couldn't stay there, oh yes.
You cut the grass,

you wove the roof, oh yes.
Where did he go, the king
of this town? Oh yes.

You built a balcony
on walls of sand, oh yes.
You loved what's worthless, then a knife
took your life, oh yes.

You scattered beds and pillows
in that brilliant palace, oh yes.
Your body has to burn one day
on a pile of wood, oh yes.

Kabir says, do you want to live
for ages, oh yes?
Then burn all your attachments,
drink the ashes, oh yes.[32]

Prahladji faces the daunting challenge of living up to the teachings of Kabir, with whom he is deeply identified and whose words he expounds from the stage, while remaining a worldly man. I use "worldly" in the Indian sense—*saṃsārik*, married, earning, looking after a large extended family, dealing with money and property, sometimes entering the corridors of power, constantly traveling and performing to audiences that number in the thousands, and maintaining his job as a schoolteacher. In Kabir culture, one often hears the juxtaposition *karanī-kathanī*: deeds and words. Like the contemporary American expression "walking the talk," it refers to a standard of consistency between professed values and actions, and it implies criticism of inconsistency. While Prahladji sings of the illusory nature of bright-colored palaces, his own house grows. He creates an institution with a long name, the *Kabīr Smārak Sevā aur Shodh Sansthān*: Kabir Memorial Institute for Service and Research. The institute also requires buildings.

In 1998 the state of Madhya Pradesh gave him one hectare of land, later augmented by 1.5 hectares more, to build an institute dedicated to Kabir. The person largely responsible for this was then Chief Minister Digvijay Singh, who, along with others in Bhopal, had been moved by Prahladji's singing. Digvijay also personally admired Kabir and was building a political identity in which concern for Dalit issues figured prominently. Some of the Brahmins in the village resented this lavish state gift. "They were burning," Prahladji told me. "Even now they think: Why is he getting all this? Why does he think he's so great?"

On my first visit in early 2000, there was nothing on the land but a vertical monument whose shapes symbolized aspects of Kabir's teaching. Since then structures have been added every year: a lovely little white temple with open walls and Kabir *sākhīs* painted around the roof-rim, a couple of concrete platforms on either side of the temple, a hall with one big room, an open area with pillars and a roof, a row of toilets for big events, cisterns for storing water. By 2011, there was a new wing with four upstairs guest rooms, and a spacious schoolroom downstairs for the school he had always dreamed of opening.

Prahladji hosts an annual public function that features bhajan programs, discourses by visiting Kabir Panth gurus, and a chief guest, often from the political world. The first year, the chief guest was Digvijay Singh, chief minister of Madhya Pradesh. He landed in the field in a helicopter. An estimated 50,000 people attended on that occasion, and a like number showed up again a year later when the chief guest was Acharya Prakashmuni Nam Sahab the head of the Chhattisgarh-based Kabir Panth, who has hundreds of thousands of followers.

Every time I returned to Malwa, there were new structures. The main house kept growing, its amenities ever improving. A garage housed a tractor and the car. The Mahindra, afflicted by premature old age because of heavy use, was replaced by a sparkling new Bolero in 2005, followed by a Tata Sumo SUV in 2010.

One day I asked Sumitra, Ashok's wife, how their situation had changed since Prahladji became so successful. She said it had changed a lot. Previously they were very poor. She and the others worked as field laborers to earn a little money. The joint family had only one house (in contrast to their present assets—three older houses and a new one, a few motorcycles, a car, a fridge, a TV for each family, and so on). A few days before this conversation I had gone with Prahladji and his wife Shantiji in the car to Tarana market, fifteen kilometers away. Many greeted him as a prominent man. I was introduced as the American professor here to study Kabir. A man outside the car window said to Prahladji, "Now you are more famous than Kabir was in his time."

Prahladji recalls the days when they had virtually nothing. He remembers working as a laborer, digging wells. His father used to work in bad conditions, almost as a bonded laborer. "He got five rupees a month, but they paid only once a year." He remembers riding a bicycle in the early 1980s, carrying his wife and three children. Once it started to rain. Then it poured. They had to stop and look for shelter. An old lady in a small hut took them in. The moment left a deep impression on him—the old woman's kindness, the raw exposure of the family.[33]

In the mid-1980s, the *mandalī* used to go on foot to the places where they had been invited to sing. Once six of them set out at night, but the power was off, so they couldn't make out the locations of villages. In the pitch darkness they got lost and didn't get to the program till 1 a.m. Some people were still waiting to hear them. Nowadays we travel much farther, and by car, but some things are still the same—like getting lost and delayed.

> [From my notebook] April 29, 2002
> We drive four hours into increasingly remote places, over increasingly bad roads. VERY bad roads. In the darkness, how do they know where to turn? But as usual, they reach the destination—a village called Pachlana—and as usual, they are late. After dinner in a village house, we set out for the stage. Prahladji has class! Walking through the lanes, he gleams, he is in his body, he is gracious to all. To a man in renunciant-orange he says, "*Jay gurudev*, I have come for your *darśhan*." ("Homage to you, revered guru, I have come here to be blessed by the sight of you.") As we approach the stage, we hear his recorded voice booming over the speakers. About 2,000 people suddenly appear in the space that was empty a few minutes before. People crowd around to touch his feet, and the ritual of welcoming him with speeches and *mālās* (garlands) of orange marigolds begins. There are multiple *mālās*; bestowing one on the honored guest is an index of local prestige. As an elderly man reaches up to garland him, he suddenly takes the garland and puts it around the old man's neck. He tells the audience that he is the lucky one, to be able to get their *darśhan*. He asks that the electric fans, set up on stage for the performers' comfort, be turned off, explaining that it's

better for all to sit together in the heat than for a few to be cool. He begins to sing, as always praising the guru in the first piece, then moving to a slow haunting tune about the difficulty of holding fast to what one believes in, followed by a rousing wake-up song:

> Wake up, man, wake up!
> The birds have eaten your field,
> you who didn't have a guru.
> Wake up now in your mind,
> wake up now in your heart.

He puts his whole self into the performance, whether for important people in Bhopal, or for me in his house, or for these villagers. He has a mission. He wants to inspire the audience, to inculcate values. He expounds on Kabir's meanings between songs, or between verses within a song, while his accompanists maintain a low-volume background of melody and rhythm with violin, harmonium, cymbals.

On some of his cassettes too, he introduces each bhajan with a short gloss on the meaning. Some have criticized him for too much preaching. A literary man I met in Bhopal said Prahladji's quality had gone down since the first cassette, in which he just sang. Now he wasn't content with being a singer, he had to be a guru! The Bhopal writer wasn't impressed. I too sometimes feel the ratio between singing and expounding gets skewed, and the commentary disrupts the music. But Mr. Nirguṇe of the Adivasi Lok Kala Parishad described Prahladji's ability to sing and interpret as astounding. Prahladji himself seems to need both—his presentation flows in an unbroken stream.

Two-and-a-half hours into the Pachlana concert, he takes a break, inviting some local singers on stage. Returning, he says he's about to sing his last song. Instead he sings eight more. As the hour gets later he gets funnier, drops standard Hindi and talks purely in Malwi. Audience members crack up at his stories and one-liners, now completely in their own idiom. When he concludes at 2:30 a.m., an old guy in the front row shouts, "Since you've come all the way here, you could at least sing a little more." This after five hours! (See Figure 1.2)

Nowadays the three brothers—Prahlad, Ambaram, Ashok—with their wives, children, grandchildren, and elderly father, appear to be a loosely

FIGURE I.2. Rural audience late at night, showing women's and men's sections. Photo by Smriti Chanchani.

constituted joint family. The brothers, with their wives Shanti, Kamla, and Sumitra, have separate houses, all within a few steps of each other.[34] Though I never inquired into their economic arrangements, the three brothers appear to be autonomous. Ashok worked on and off in a clinic for some years, having had some training as a medical assistant. Later he took to keeping buffaloes and cows and selling the offspring. Ambaram works in a factory. Each family has some cattle and some land to cultivate. Prahladji controls his own money but also shares. Children are in and out of all the houses. When there is extraordinary expense (like illness or a wedding) Prahladji steps in to help.

Once I made fun of Ajay, the older son, for calling his girl cousin when his son peed in his pants, instead of cleaning the mess himself. A man is not supposed to do anything like that, he informed me, or even be too affectionate with his child, in front of his father. When I insensitively used the word "stupid," he came back at me strongly. "It's not stupid, it's our culture. A boy is taught not to say anything to his father for years." I backed off and took another tack. "Sangita [his wife] works so hard, serving everybody."

He replied, "You should know how hard the women in our family used to work. Till about five years ago, the women would get up at 4/4:30, sweep and clean, collect the cowdung, cook food for everyone, then go to labor all day in fields belonging to others."

"Did it change from the cassettes?"

"Yes, and from the performances."

I've ridden on the back of Prahladji's motorcycle through Maksi, stopping to pay the electric bill and the phone bill, to do business at the bank, to see if he had received a fax at Shakti STD. He has shown me his budget for the annual Kabir function that he offers to the public—with carefully noted sources of funds and expenditures for food, tents, lighting, workers, and so on. I have attended the double marriage of his son Vijay, and Ashok's son, Mithun, observing the comings and goings between the grooms' and brides' households for many months before the event. I witnessed the breakup of Vijay's earlier engagement, as the men in the family angrily discussed how the prospective bride's relatives had failed to keep their promise of giving up meat and alcohol. At a sudden medical crisis of his daughter Sona, or Ashok's wife Sumitra, Prahladji has jumped into the car with other family members to drive to the hospital in Ujjain. We have all gone to an Indore hospital on a happier occasion, the birth of Sangita's second child. I have been present amid countless different family moods and encounters—from Prahladji's imperious issuing of orders and scolding of everyone in sight, to Shantiji's fearless scolding back, to the whole family's ganging up and relentlessly teasing him for his foibles. In short, he is fully ensconced in networks of domestic and economic obligations, along with attending to responsibilities as a schoolteacher, meeting with people of high and low stations who continually come to see him, reading the newspapers, and discussing politics with his cronies.

Once Prahladji was nearly co-opted by the then ruling Congress Party of Madhya Pradesh to become a politician. In the 1990s they were on the verge of offering him a ticket as candidate for the state legislature, and he was on the verge of accepting it. Ultimately the plan dissolved, to the relief of his family and many well-wishers. But he continues to have the reputation of one who is connected with the powerful: former Chief Minister of Madhya Pradesh Digvijay Singh (later general secretary of the All India Congress Committee) and Delhi Chief Minister Sheila Dikshit (who held this office 1998–2013), among others. In fact, one day he unselfconsciously linked me and Sheila Dikshit in what I suppose would be a category of older women who are charmed by him. "Sheilaji loves me," he said innocently, "just like you."

There was a moment when Prahladji made an overt attempt to get free of his worldly entanglements. He refers to it as an "amazing event" (*adbhūt ghaṭnā*) in his life. It was in 1986, long before he became so famous and prosperous. Prahladji and his *mandalī* went to sing at a Kabir Panth ashram in Kudarmal, now in the state of Chhattisgarh but then still part of Madhya Pradesh. It was a modest, quiet old ashram. He recalls the troupe being in high spirits along the way. Waiting for a connection at Bilaspur, they sat down at an intersection near the train station and started singing and playing. Such a crowd collected that traffic got snarled, and the police chased them away. The ashram itself was very tranquil, and Prahladji liked the guru. Though the ashram owned quite a spread of land, this *sant* lived simply and had no pretensions. On their second day, Prahladji didn't go to the evening meal. He sat by himself and started singing a bhajan. And for some reason, which he still doesn't understand, he started weeping.

> [PT] I decided, "I won't go home." Right there, I made up my mind. I had never had such a thought before. I told my *mandalī*, "You go home without me, I'm staying here. Tell everyone I'm not coming back." I don't know why it happened, singing a bhajan there. Sometime such things occur in life, such realities hit you. A place can inspire a feeling of detachment. You feel you want to do something for humanity. So I told them all, "You go back. I'm staying here." Well, they were pretty upset! (He smiles, finding it funny now.) "If you stay here, what will happen to your family?" They argued with me a lot. I was determined to stay. It was quite a scene. Finally the guru of the ashram told me I should go home.[35]

"Rural Rock Star"

This is the phrase Shabnam comes up with when introducing Prahladji in the film *Chalo hamārā des/Come to My Country*. Her words, via subtitles, accompany footage of his arrival at a big rural concert. "I've been on the road with Prahladji for a few years now," she says. "We're arriving in Kithor village in Malwa, central India. Prahladji is a schoolteacher, but also a very popular folksinger of Kabir...and in fact (to my urban eyes) almost a rural rock star!" The audio switches to a voice booming from the loudspeakers. "The King of Bhajans—respected Tipanyaji—has arrived here with his full team. His melodious voice and Kabir songs we have heard on TV and audio-video tapes. But this is an auspicious day. He is here in person. We will listen to him and share the joy of *sant* Kabir's songs." On the screen Prahladji, making his way toward the stage, is rushed by admirers who touch his feet, wave a flaming *āratī* tray in front of him, and jostle to put garlands around his neck.

Prahladji's rise from ordinary participation in village *mandalī* culture to megapopularity and success was steady and unstoppable, from the late 1980s onward. When Dinesh Sharma was doing research in 1990 for Eklavya's Kabir project (see chapter 6), collecting information on *mandalīs* in the area, he noted in his work journal: "Wherever I go, one name is on everyone's lips: Prahlad Singh Tipanya." The first cassette in 1993 launched Prahladji's success as a recording artist, which has continued unabated through changes in media—cassette tape, audio CD, video CD. Recognition from the metros soon followed.

Kabir devotion and singing were long established in Malwa. But participants were used to being dismissed as inferior by the upper-caste population. The five-string *tambūrā* was a symbol of their status. Dayaram Sarolia and an unidentified friend discuss this with Shabnam in *Chalo hamārā des*:

DAYARAM: In the past, if we went out carrying our *tambūrā* people would recoil and say, sprinkle water here! The path has been polluted! They'd keep away from us and not touch us.

FRIEND: I bought a *tambūrā* once from Dwarka [Gujarat]. When I stopped at a resthouse, they refused to let me in (laughing). They said, shoo away these beggars!

SV: So the *tambūrā* has this stigma?

DAYARAM: Not any more!

FRIEND: Earlier, the youth were not into singing Kabir. Dust settled on so many *tambūrās*. Thanks to Tipanyaji it got wiped away. (Virmani 2008a)

There was widespread agreement that Prahladji's success had significantly influenced the Kabir culture of Malwa. A number of younger men now aspired to follow in his footsteps. They made cassettes, started giving little commentaries on the poetry in the midst of their performances, and were eager to meet the visitors from larger worlds who came to explore Malwi Kabir music. One example from several who come to mind is Bhairu Singh Chauhan, who in 2002 spoke of Prahladji as a guru. I asked him how it all happened.

> My father used to sing bhajans but I wasn't interested. Our family believed in Baba Ramdev. Then I went to the *melā* [fair—in this case

> the annual festival of Baba Ramdev] in Jaiselmer and started singing. Gradually singing bhajans got deeper into me. Then through the Lord's grace I met Sir [i.e., Prahladji, addressed respectfully as a schoolteacher]. It's all his blessing. We were both singing in a program. I was like a pebble in the trash and he was the *pārakh* [the expert tester of jewels who can recognize genuine value—a metaphor common in Kabir poetry]. He saw something there. He picked me up and started to polish me. We developed a guru–disciple relationship. I started making cassettes with the company that produces his cassettes, then switched to another company in Indore. I've recorded cassettes of Baba Ramdev, Kabir, and Gorakhnath bhajans. He was singing on All India Radio, then I got a chance. He was rated B-grade, then he went to B-high. Now I'm also B-high.

Prahladji became the object of tremendous admiration; occasionally, as his successes multiplied, there was also some criticism and resentment. Mostly what I heard was warm, sometimes over-the-top appreciation. Shabnam caught the flavor of this in her films. At the annual Lunyakhedi Kabir program in 2004, she talked to a small group of men.

1ST SPEAKE.R: Kabir Sahab's getting a lot of publicity nowadays. His value has gone up.

SV: Emotional value or market value?

GROUP (LAUGHING): No, no! Emotional value!

1ST SPEAKER: Many have sung Kabir but no one expressed it in their own words. Our Tipanyaji did just that, and managed to connect people to Kabir. People have been singing Kabir for eons, but it hadn't come to the public square.

An elderly man with a big voice and good-humored energy, who elsewhere in the film is seen singing as he plays his *sārangī*, enthused:

> The first one was [Kabir's] blessed disciple Dharamdas, who looted and devoured Kabir's words. Second to him is only our Tipanyaji, who appeared here in Lunyakhedi village. A third such great one, I can't see on this earth!

Dayaram Sarolia shared with Shabnam a song that someone had composed in honor of Prahladji on the occasion of the release of his cassette "*Pī le amīras*—Drink This Nectar." The verses are first given in transliterated Hindi to show the poetic structure. In one line Prahladji is referred to as "Sir," the common honorific for a schoolteacher. Each stanza is sung with repetitions.

are dhan dhan hai lunyākheḍī, dhan yahāṇ nar nārī
janme haiṇ prahlād tipānyā, kabīr bhajan gāyakārī

are bajā tambūrā satya nām kā, lagā shabda sohaṃkārī
are baje kaiseṭ yahāṇ amīras, galī galī meṇ dhūn bhārī

are amīras kaiset nikalī hai na, sar kī us ke upar batāyā hai
are baje kaiset yahāṇ amīras, galī galī meṇ dhūn bhārī

Oh blessed, blessed is Lunyakhedi, blessed all the men and women here.
This is where Prahlad Tipanya was born, the singer of Kabir bhajans.

Oh he plays the tambura of the true name, true word, true breath.
Oh the Nectar cassette is playing, the profound melody resounds in every lane.

Oh the Nectar cassette has come out, Sir has explained things there.
Oh the Nectar cassette is playing, the profound melody resounds in every lane.[36]

Guru

[From my notebook] April 18, 2002
In today's mail comes a densely written letter from a 25-year-old man in Shahjapur District who heard Prahladji singing in a program. Addressing him as Gurudev or Revered Guru, the man writes at length, imploring P. to give him initiation. After many homages, he says:

"Gurudev Tipanya, Kabir's low servant is at your feet." He explains that though he is Kabir's servant, he lacks *dikśhā (initiation). How can he practice devotion to the name without dikśhā? "I have fallen into darkness. Gurudev, will you lift up this fallen one? Will you help?* . . . Like a mother, Kabir says to me, 'Have faith, my child. Will I let you drown in the well? Will I let Death seize you? No, my child, I will send you to a *sant* who will give you a chance to surrender yourself.'" He begs P. to be his guru. He is ready to give up his family and possessions, as he understands that "to get something you have to give up something." He announces that he doesn't eat meat, drink liquor, or smoke, but admits that he sometimes lies. He begs Gurudev again and again to accept him and vows that he won't take *dikśhā* from anyone else. "As quickly as possible, please answer my letter."

LINDA (L): Will you answer?
PRAHLADJI (P): Yes.
L: What will you say?
P: When I start to write, I'll say whatever comes up.
L: You don't know now what you'll say?
P: No.
L: Have you received other letters like this?
P: Yes, often. Once a man told me he had 30,000 people in a group of villages who would all become my disciples.
L: What did you tell him?
P: I told him that that same *śhabda*, that voice, that tune, is constantly playing in all of us. They should listen to it and lead good lives.

He told this story with added details in a filmed interview with Shabnam:

> Once I had a program in Dhar, got there at 9, had a meal, started singing at 10, went on till 3 or 4 in the night, then left. The people there were very moved by the bhajans. I got a letter with many people's names on it. Your bhajan program was so powerful, from today we regard you as our guru and we want to take *dikśhā* from you. I replied that I don't have that authority. If you feel I'm your guru, fine. Actually the guru is in you yourself. Kabir-*sahib* says:
>
> The seeker's form is the guru, the guru's form is you.
> Kabir says, make it real in your thoughts, words and deeds
>
> Take *dikśhā* from anyone, and keep listening to bhajans. They said no, we are people from twelve villages, and we have all had a meeting and decided that we will only take *dikśhā* from you. I said, brother, I don't give the name. I'm not a *mahant* [ritually empowered authority in the sect]. In the Kabir Panth, the *mahant*s give the name. I don't have that authority. So take *dikśhā* from anyone, and listen to bhajans.
>
> This is the kind of faith that arises from bhajans. People come together because of bhajans. I don't know all these people sitting before me, but because of bhajans, they are mine, and because of bhajans, I am theirs. Sahib is right here. Where else is Sahib? Sahib is in everyone. *Paramātmā* is in everyone. This feeling of *ātmiyatā* [a Hindi word for intimacy, made from the word *ātmā*, one's spiritual essence]—this exactly is the connection, the meeting, the *dikśhā*. This is what binds us together.

I liked Prahladji's response to these people: his saying he wasn't a guru, his reminder that the guru is in each of them, and his recognition that in the singing, the song, the sharing, resided their intimate meeting.

So I was surprised to hear, in the train coming home from a big Kabir Panth *melā* at Bandhavgarh in April, that he had become a *mahant*. Actually, this had happened at a previous *melā* in February, but he only told me in April. "Surprised" is too mild a word. I was shocked. I was dismayed. The first thing I blurted out was, "You're not going to wear one of those pointed hats!" He laughed. Of course he had received a pointed hat, along with other items including a document setting forth his rights and responsibilities as a *mahant*.[37] For one thing, he would be officially authorized as a guru—a function that many people had begged him to perform for them. Prahladji and I began a series of discussions and debates that quickly extended to his family, fellow singers, Kabir Panthis, and friends. His decision to become a *mahant* proved to be quite controversial. The nature and import of the controversy, from 2002 to a resolution in 2005, will be examined in detail in chapter 7.

Time to Go

Don't be proud
of your power, don't admire
your body. The golden color
will fly, the rosy color
will fly.

This world
is a bundle of paper.
A few drops fall, it melts away.
The golden color
will fly, the rosy color
will fly.

This world
is shrubs and sticks.
A touch of fire, it burns up.
The golden color
will fly, the rosy color
will fly.

This world
is a patch of brambles
where you get tangled and die.
The golden color

will fly, the rosy color
will fly.

This world
is a market fair
where a fool wastes his savings.
The golden color
will fly, the rosy color
will fly.

This world
is a glass bangle.
A little blow, it shatters.
The golden color
will fly, the rosy color
will fly.

Kabir says, listen seekers—
No one but you reaps the fruits
of your actions.
The golden color
will fly, the rosy color
will fly.

August is flying. In early September 2002, I have to fly too, back to America and my regular life—family, job, responsibility. Perhaps like Prahladji at Kudarmal, I feel I have been surprised by happiness here. My body has become lighter, my mind clearer. Joy appears simpler. Relationships need no explaining. I don't want to go.

Two Kabir bhajans come to mind with images of flying; they are both about transiency and death. In the first, it is the golden and rosy colors that fly. In the second, a bird flies: the *haṃsa*, a swan or wild goose, the symbol of the free human spirit, that flies off alone at the time of death. This song is uniquely associated with Kumar Gandharva, the great classical singer who lived in Dewas, less than an hour's drive from Prahladji's village. I have never seen it in any printed collection. Kumarji discovered it embossed on a mirror at a Nath Panth ashram in Dewas, and it inspired him to compose a very beautiful melody. The mirror is still there to be viewed by visitors to the Shilnath Dhuni Sansthan, which is devoted to the memory of the great yogi Shilnath, who died in 1921 (Hess 2009a, 21; Virmani 2008c).

It will fly away alone, the swan.
What a sight: the carnival
of this world.

Like a leaf that falls from a tree—
it's very hard for them to meet again.
Who knows where it will land
once caught by a gust of wind?

I don't really know what to do with all the feeling that is in me. Luckily, India provides a host of rituals and festivals to contain unruly feelings. In August comes Raksha Bandhan, the festival celebrating the bonds between brothers and sisters. Married sisters return, if they can, to their natal villages to be with their brothers. If they can't make it, they try to send a *rākhī*, a colored bracelet to be tied around the brother's wrist. Gifts are given. It is a big celebration of family ties. Brother–sister relationships are not only born, they are also made. It is common for people who aren't related by blood to declare such a relationship by tying a *rākhī*. People do it for all sorts of reasons, not necessarily sentimental. In nearly forty years of coming to India, I have never done it. Though some people do it quite casually, it always seemed like more than I wanted to get into.

Among the great majority of Indians, relationships are supposed to be clearly defined, especially between men and women. As the title of a popular Hindi film puts it, *Ham āpke haiṇ kaun?*/Who am I to you? Prahladji could only be my brother, and I his *dīdī*, elder sister. For the first time, I chose to tie a *rākhī*. What I had fantasized as a ceremony something like a wedding, fraught with solemn implications, turned out to be an uproarious party with twenty or thirty people, young and old, simultaneously tying threads, applying red powder and rice on foreheads, placing rupee notes on coconuts, laughing, stuffing sweets into each other's mouths. It was a wedding all right. I married the whole family, all three brothers, their wives Shanti, Sumitra, and Kamla, all the children, the old patriarch, a couple of neighbors—*rākhī*s, *rākhī*s everywhere. And I was surprised that the ritual proved to be (as anthropologists sometimes say) efficacious. My status changed. I was inside in a different way. Everybody, including me, knew where I fit, and we were all freer than before. Intimacy came easier. Even love could be expressed.

It will fly away alone, the swan.
What a sight: the carnival
of this world.

When your time is up,
the order comes down from above.
Here come Death's strong messengers.
You have to tangle
with Death.

Kabir sings the qualities of God
whose boundaries can't be found.
The guru's actions
mark his path.
The disciple's actions
mark his path.

Kumar Gandharva's voice soars and dips with unspeakable beauty as he describes the flight of the swan. The voice loops like a leaf in the wind. How can a song about death be so joyful? Though it is often said that Kabir and other saint-poets teach us to welcome death as a consummation, the moment when, free from the flesh, we will be united with God, I have never embraced that interpretation. What I hear in Kumarji's voice is the joy of fearlessness. He flies, receiving an aerial vision of the world as a teeming carnival, knowing himself as a leaf in the wind. God is markless, we also are without boundaries. But our actions (regardless of status or titles) leave traces that point to where we're going.

With my friends at Eklavya, the educational NGO that became closely involved with Malwa's Kabir *bhajan maṇḍalīs* in the 1990s, I organize a big farewell event for August 31. We invite all the *maṇḍalīs* in the surrounding countryside, distributing announcements and setting word of mouth in motion. In the end we have thirty-five groups, to whom we provide dinner, tea, and bus fare. Hand-painted banners at the higher secondary school in Maksi announce the cohosts in Hindi script: Eklavya Sansthan and Professor Linda Hess, California, America. That the singing will go on all night is taken for granted.

I'm nervous as the crowd assembles and opening statements begin. I fret about whether there's enough space in the narrow hall, then run out to check on the dinner. Syag-*bhāī* says I'm like a mother in charge of a wedding.[38] The rain starts early and pours prodigiously through the night, with lanes all around us getting flooded, a truck ending up marooned in an expanse of water nearby. Someone says the power of our bhajans brought the rain.

I totally fail as a documenter: I don't want to take picture or notes and am relieved when my tape recorder refuses to work. Prahladji reminds me that I should be snapping photos and writing things down. He says it's rare to have such a lot of singing groups, old and young together, from villages all around. He's right but I'm just not motivated.

My memory of the night is blurred—one group after another, endless Kabir, endless faces and voices. As day breaks, I ask them to sing a goodbye song for me: "*Eklā mat chhoḍ jo*," the one where a woman says to someone she loves, "Don't leave me." I am leaving them, but it's the same feeling—don't leave me alone, I don't want to be separated from you. In the song we hear the voices of two characters. The woman begins by addressing a *banjārā*—a romantic character, a nomadic merchant who travels from place to place:

Don't leave me alone, oh traveling merchant, oh traveler!
It's about going to another country—a complicated business, my dear one.
It's about a faraway country—a treacherous business, my dear one.

Though it isn't clear to me which lines belong to which voice, there is talk of a fine house with a garden and a well, which has been built by the "master"—*sāhib*. Maybe the woman is pleading with the *banjārā* to stay with her in that wonderful place. Maybe he is describing it to her. But someone's voice at the end of each stanza suggests that in the very house where she lives, she can find what she desires so much.

My master has built a beautiful house
oh traveling merchant, oh traveler.
There's a latticed window on top,
see the view from there, my dear one.

My master has planted a garden
oh traveling merchant, oh traveler.
The basket is piled with flowers,
string a garland there, my dear one.

My master has dug a well
oh traveling merchant, oh traveler.
It's full, the water is deep,
bathe there, my dear one.

Don't leave me alone, oh traveling merchant, oh traveler!
It's about going to another country—a complicated business, my dear one.
It's about a faraway country—a treacherous business, my dear one.

The song has a lovely, lilting melody. The men surround me and sing, dozens of them, coming up with verses that I've never heard, repeating, swaying with me while I cry. It goes on and on. Then we stop and take a lot of pictures. It's fully daylight. People disperse. I say to Prahladji, let me take a bus to Dewas and get some sleep. He keeps laughing and saying no way, you stay with us. Attempting to drive from Maksi to the village, we discover the road is impassable. The downpour has breached embankments and causeways, forming new lakes and closing roads. We'll have to get out and walk.

"I told you I should have taken a bus to Dewas!" I say petulantly, lying down on the car seat like a child. "I need to sleep and get some work done."

"Stand up like a soldier and march," he says. I do.

Next day in the car, as I talk of the possibility of returning in December for a conference in Delhi and a few weeks in Malwa, Prahladji suddenly says, "*āp ke ūpar satguru kī baḍī dayā hai* … the Satguru has blessed you very much."

I know what he means.

World-Renowned Artist

This chapter has been based almost entirely on experiences that happened in 2002, my first year of fieldwork. The rest of the book incorporates travels and research that continued for a decade more. To conclude the first chapter, I offer a glimpse of what was to come.

By the end of 2002 I was a somewhat transformed person, as attested by family and friends who had never seen me in such a sustained state of lightness and happiness. (This was especially a shock, albeit a pleasant one, to my husband of over twenty years.) Immersing myself in this world of joyful music, profound meaning, and friendship in new places seemed to have done what some of the bhajans claimed was possible: opened the lock of my heart. In a *nirguṇ* variant of the great bhakti theme of *viraha*, longing for the absent beloved, I deeply missed the people, the music, the conversations, the laughter, and I plotted to get them all back.

Without my love I can't breathe, like a fish without water.
Who can unite me with my beloved, oh friend?
I cry, I sob, my friend, the arrow of the song has pierced me!
Come to my country!

This frequently sung Malwa Kabir bhajan, with its repeated refrain, "Come to my country," became my theme song.[39] Though I had never organized a performance tour in my life, it all came together very quickly: an elaborate two-month program starting in September 2003, with performances at about thirty venues in the United States, international airfare for five musicians provided by the Indian Council for Cultural Relations, and domestic expenses covered by universities and others who invited them. I arranged a hiatus in my teaching duties and stayed with them all the way, fulfilling multiple functions—carrying tickets, managing tourist excursions, providing pocket money, organizing food, and at the end of the day putting on a colorful Indian outfit and appearing onstage as introducer and translator.

I flew to India in July 2003 to work on preparations for the tour. Imagine my surprise when Prahladji told me they were taking a quick trip to London in August, to perform in an Indian music festival. Despite my fantasies, I alone was not responsible for their emerging international profile. The moment had come. It was inevitable. We were all at home in the village on the day they were to depart for their first trip abroad.

[From my notebook, July 2003]
So far it was an ordinary day. A few people had come to see Prahladji off. Suddenly about fifty were there, and they had all crowded into one room. The atmosphere changed palpably. There was no electricity. The only light in the room was from the wicks on the *pūjā* tray. Shantiji was circling it in front of him as he sat on the bed. They had washed his feet, there were petals sprinkled on the water. A series of *bandagīs* started. First his wife, then elder son and daughter-in-law, then younger son, then disciples. Bowing to the ground, looking down and up three times into his eyes.[40] When it was over they all went outside on the verandah. The water from the ceremonial foot-washing was being distributed. A grand photo-snapping session ensued. There was a row of chairs, with the old father in the middle, Prahladji on one side of him, me on the other, then three more who were going abroad. Endless flower-garlands materialized.

> They were put on everyone who sat in the chairs of honor, but above all on the old man, who usually spends much of the day stretched out on his cot on the verandah. So much attention, so much excitement, six garlands piled around his neck—suddenly the old man burst out crying, and all the latent emotion in the crowd was channeled through him. Layers of love, untold networks of connection and dreams, were now almost visible in the air as the groups to be photographed expanded and contracted. "One more, one more!" The bonds of family, community, and the land, the vistas of green grass and muddy water, swelled up in our chests. That old man had been a bonded laborer. Now his sons and grandson were going to London.

Bhairu Singh Chauhan was beaming: "This *tambūrā* is going to London!" he declared to me. "This *tambūrā* will be on a stage in London!"

The American tour followed. Shabnam, who by that time had received Ford Foundation support for her documentary film project, joined us for three weeks to shoot scenes of Malwi folk Kabir's arrival in the United States. Eventually she produced a two-part DVD, "*Ajab shahar*/Wondrous City," that presented twelve full bhajans performed on American stages, with charming interludes in which the Indian folk musicians and their wildly improvising American manager (me) entered into various wondrous situations.[41] There is a crackling encounter with a college *a cappella* singing group; a visit to a black gospel church; the proverbial moment of walking through midtown Manhattan, heads craning upward; Devnarayan, our violin player, trying out a pair of ice skates at Rockefeller Center.

> [From my notebook, various dates during the first American tour, October–December 2003]
> At home in Berkeley, when they first arrived, I offered the use of the washing machine. They said no, we wash our own clothes. One week later, in Los Angeles, I said, "Do you want to wash your own clothes or use the machine?"
>
> "Machine!" they all said in chorus.
>
> ***
>
> Prahladji weaves in the local situation. Performing at the home of Colorado College president Dick Celeste, he introduces a stanza

about a dog that barks itself crazy in front of a mirror: "There was a dog—just like this little dog," he says suddenly, pointing to the curious Scottie just trotting past him. Explaining *Chādar jhīnī*, at the verse where the washerman beats the cloth on the stone of the Word, he says with a flashing smile: "Here everyone washes their clothes in a machine, but there we have washermen who beat the clothes on a stone in the river!"

***

At the North Carolina State University radio station, they appear as guests on the weekly Indian music program *Gīt Bāzār*. Afroz Taj and his broadcast partner John patter magnificently as our musicians crowd into the tiny studio where they sing standing up, propping instruments against counters. After they sing "*Zarā halke gāḍī hānko*/Move your cart along gently," a woman calls up and says in Hindi, "*Meṇ abhī tak kāmp rahī hūṇ*"—"I'm still trembling."

Later Prahladji reports that an Indian in Raleigh told him that while they were singing she felt like she was filled with light. And a Sikh in Colorado said he cried throughout the concert.

Time rolls on. Each year I go back to India.

[From my notebook] July 29, 2007
Everything keeps changing. If I didn't keep coming back here, I could be content with my two- or three-year snapshot. Prahladji's moustache has changed shape this year. It's gotten droopier and longer at the ends. Every time I see it, something feels disturbed. All the rooms in the house have changed inhabitants again. The room where Shabnam and I used to sleep upstairs is occupied by various women. We are downstairs sharing a room with Sangita and Ajay. The boys who have reached their mid-teens are so tall it's hard for me to recognize them. Sona has a new baby. Prahladji has carried out his years-long promise that he would move to the Smarak [the Kabir Institute set-up about five minutes walk away, through the fields]. Now he doesn't sleep in the house any more. He still keeps things in his old room. But at night he goes out to the big rough room by the little temple.

The slightly lower moustache ends remind me of the artifice of my book: how it pretends to represent the lives of these people but actually crafts a story based on a little slice of time and on the questions and answers I hammered out then. Yet things keep changing.

In 2008, Shabnam's four feature-length documentary films were nearing completion. I planned another North American tour for spring 2009, this time bringing her along with the musicians, organizing programs that would include film screenings and discussions as well as concerts. Once again the Indian Council for Cultural Relations agreed to support international travel for the musicians. Once again we had a two-month tour, starting with three cities in Canada before moving through the United States.

From 2009, Shabnam's films have been widely shown in India. NDTV, a major cable channel, broadcast two of them and got a very enthusiastic response. Considerable drama was generated when the Karnataka state censor board refused to certify two films. A legal case made its way to the High Court in Delhi, and eventually all the films were approved without changes. In 2011 one of the films that the state censor board had tried to suppress won a Special Jury Award in the annual honors doled out by the national Ministry of Information and Broadcasting. Meanwhile enthusiasm was burgeoning among urban fans of Kabir, of Prahladji, and of other singers featured in the films. Multiday Kabir festivals were organized in Delhi, Bangalore, Mumbai, Pune, Baroda, and beyond. Artists from Madhya Pradesh, Rajasthan, Gujarat, and Pakistan were appearing on the same stage, getting familiar with each other's song texts and musical styles. The ten audio CDs produced by the Kabir Project, together with bilingual books containing lyrics and commentaries, were circulating. Groups in Bangalore and Mumbai called Prahladji for workshops in which they learned bhajans and discussed meanings. Shabnam's excellent singing resulted in her being invited for concerts of her own. Several urban women, inspired by Shabnam, Prahladji, and Kabir, traveled to a small town in Rajasthan to buy their own *tambūrās*.

"Where is your book?" People have been asking me now for years. "I'm a slow writer," I reply. In 2011 a fellowship gives me nine months free of teaching. I spend most of that time in India, writing the book.

[From my notebook] January 26, 2011, 9 a.m.
Yesterday I arrived at the village after eighteen months to discover another huge leap in "development." The life energy has shifted, at least for now, to the Smarak. The grand house that I was so

surprised to encounter in 2002, and that has expanded year by year, for the moment is in little use. Perhaps that's because a new wing is under construction, including a fine new bedroom and hall with tiled floors, a bathroom area divided between bathing room and toilet, a new stairway leading to an extended upper floor verandah.

Construction has been dramatic since my last visit. The school project, long a sketchy fantasy that he occasionally dabbled in, is now moving along, encouraged by a partnership with a group of Kabir devotees in Los Angeles. There is a beautiful classroom with bright paintings all over the walls on the ground floor, and an upper floor featuring four guest rooms, each with a private bathroom. This is incredible. I slept in one of those rooms last night. In ten years, this is the first time I could attend to natural functions in my own space, without going outside to a shared toilet, and without needing to search for a bucket of water. Buckets we still use, but the one in my room now is not available to be picked up by anyone passing by in search of a container. The building is painted bright chartreuse with magenta trim.

Some things don't change. On winter mornings they pile up bricks outside with a wood fire to heat a big pot of water for bathing. They cluster around the fire chatting, their voices occasionally raised in whatever is the controversy of the moment. Later they make *chapātīs* on the same fire. The fields are bursting with fresh growth—wheat, garlic, garden vegetables. Out here, away from the main settlement, I heard strange voices at night, like babies crying, only nonhuman. "What's that?" I ask. Foxes.

January 27, 2011

Yesterday was a very special day. The previous evening, the news had come: Prahladji got the Padma Shri, a huge national award given annually to artists, writers, scholars, scientists. Eighty recipients in a nation of one billion. Hundreds of congratulatory phone calls were coming in, and people were arriving by car and motorcycle to pay their respects.

At night after the visitors left, we gathered in the big lower room. All three families were together—Ambaram and Ashok with their wives, kids, grandkids, as well as the immediate family of PT (growing ever bigger). After a meal, mats were laid out for singing. But instead of PT, only the young guys sang and played. He called it jokingly the *naklī* (fake or copycat) *mandalī*. But the *naklī mandalī* was great! For fun, they started with a film song that everybody enjoyed. Then after a few Malwi Kabir bhajans, sung with full energy and showmanship, they did a song I didn't recognize. It had its own spirit and histrionics. It turned out to be Muralala's song from Kutch, Gujarat. After that came something I couldn't have imagined in 2002—"*Allah Hu*," which they had learned from Mukhtiyar Ali of Rajasthan. Vijay, of the sweet and strong voice, had mastered Mukhtiyar's tune, his dramatic buildups and gestures. Ajay was right there with him on *dholak* and vocals, as was Dharmendra on harmonium. At either end were Ambaram on *timkī* and Ashok with *manjīrā*. Everybody was having fun, including the women and girls clustered close. The beat was intense. The younger generation was singing a 100% Sufi Muslim *qawwālī* song in Lunyakhedi village. They followed with more Kabir in Rajasthani and Kutchi folk-style. Finally Ajay said, "Should we do Farid Ayaz?" This is the Pakistani singer featured in Shabnam's film "*Had-anhad/Bounded-Boundless*," a tremendous musician and showman. They took off with "*Maulā maulā lākh pukāre*," leading us all in the great rhythms, melodies, dramatic rises and falls, pauses and gestures characteristic of Farid Ayaz's flamboyant performance. We ended on a high note. All this mingling of region and religion was influenced by the Kabir Project.

A little later, from the balcony above, I see PT in white passing fresh-picked peas around to everyone in sight, while juggling two cell phones.

In April 2011 I attended the second Kabir Malwa Yātrā (Journey of Kabir in Malwa)—a breathtakingly strenuous, action-packed series of events that took place over eight days in six villages and two cities in the height of summer, when the temperature was nearly always above 100° F. I had missed the first one in 2010. Artists from multiple regions performed and traveled together. A notable phenomenon was the interface of urban and rural worlds. Two buses carried a core group that included artists, organizers, about fifty fans from the metros, and a few stray foreigners. Everywhere we went, we were far outnumbered by the local audiences. But the continuous presence of those busloads of urban participants made the mix of urban and rural cultures—of those who commonly communicated in English and those who didn't—particularly noticeable.

Here is one story from the grand opening day of the *yātrā* in Lunyakhedi village—a story that show how Prahladji's profile kept growing and taking him to new worlds. Ten months earlier Prahladji had received an invitation to perform at a birthday party for Kailash Kher—a megastar singer on stage and in the film world. Sometimes billed as a "Sufi singer," Kailash is not Muslim but favors love songs that have a certain spiritual flavor, including some from the Sufi tradition. He has a magnificent voice and a very impressive way of capturing an audience—whether thousands in an open-air San Francisco amphitheater, or a dozen at a Mumbai dinner party (I have observed both). In 2010 someone gave Kailash the Malwa Kabir audio CDs produced by the Kabir Project—one CD by Prahladji and one by Kaluram Bamaniya. He reported that for three months, he listened to those two CDs nonstop in his car. He became a great fan. His wife Sheetal decided to surprise him by inviting the troupe to their farmhouse in Lonavala (near Mumbai) on his birthday. They met a few more times in the following months.

Prahladji asked Kailash to come to Lunyakhedi for the opening of the *yātrā*, and he did, along with Sheetal and their two-year-old son, named Kabir. They arrived a day early and stayed under conditions that were physically difficult. Kailash joined the opening procession in nearby Maksi, where a chariot-like vehicle equipped with loudspeakers blasted live music produced by musicians who walked behind with microphones. Men, women, and children crowded along, singing and dancing. In the boiling heat, Kailash energetically sang two of his blockbuster hits to the tremendous excitement of the crowds in the street. That night, Kailash and his family sat on the ground in front of the brightly lit stage, along with other guests. Called to the stage, he wore the typical red-and-yellow turban of Malwa. He sang two of his own beautiful numbers, then joined Prahladji in singing two Malwa Kabir bhajans. Here are some of his remarks:

> Through the power of his singing, he has captured the hearts of many. I myself am so captivated that I can hardly believe I have known him in a physical sense for only ten months. I also can hardly believe that we two are alive in the same age. Sometimes I have to pinch myself and ask—is this really true? Friends, some of you appreciate my music and are sending loving smiles my way. Let me tell you: What he is sharing is pure nectar. Nectar in huge quantities. I have never seen nectar pouring in such quantities. When we got here yesterday, I realized that there are some difficulties: shortage of water, and lack of electricity so they have to use generators. But I'll tell you something. There is no richer place on this earth than where we are right now.

We end this chapter with a glimpse of death, which, as usual with Kabir, is also a glimpse of life:

> [From my notebook] January 29, 2011
> Prahladji and group were asked to sing in Indore at a function following the death of a respected 100-year-old lady. There were many guests in a large rented hall. The chief mourner, son of the deceased, appeared to be in his 70s, head shaved, dressed in white. He freely embraced the guests who were introduced to him and wept in their arms—including me. He grooved to the Kabir songs, appropriately chosen on themes of death and transiency, alternately shedding tears, clapping in rhythm, and raising his arm in enthusiastic endorsement. About Prahladji, he said to me, "He is Kabir." I showed some hesitation about this view, having seen so much inflated praise particularly in these few days since the Padma Shri award was announced. Then our host clarified: "You are also Kabir. I am also Kabir. Whoever is expressing and receiving Kabir, at that moment that person is Kabir."

We proceed now to investigate how the words of this joyful and weeping mourner come true: how Kabir's varied identities and manifestations take shape in the mouths and ears and minds of people in Malwa.

2

Oral Tradition in the Twenty-First Century

OBSERVING TEXTS

"I WOULD HAVE liked to do some work on Kabir," said my friend Aditya, a professor at the University of Pennsylvania, "but it's too hard."

"What do you mean, too hard?" I was alarmed at the implications for me, as Aditya's fluency in several Indian vernaculars plus Persian far exceeded mine in the one Indian language I knew, Hindi. His answer was simple:

"There's no text."[1]

We academics, especially in the humanities, want to have a text that sits still. We want it to begin and end, to be contained between the covers of a book. We don't want the letters to squirm and change every time we open the book.

We know that many vernacular texts in South Asia are not actually stable, because they function in the oral realm. But as scholars we have to draw the line, like parents setting boundaries on an unruly child: "OK, enough is enough! You are going to sit still. Things are hard enough in this household without you wildly jumping around all the time." So we settle on a critical edition or popular printed version.

It is understandable that scholars prefer to work on fixed written texts, perhaps venturing so far as to compare recensions. In this book I want to lure them, and a wider readership, into a different field of textual awareness. What happens when texts are understood as oral, performative, musical, contextual—brought into being again and again in the matrix of interactions between performers, audiences, and circumstances? Is it possible to hold in our minds both these dynamically produced texts and the more well-behaved editions and collections with which we are familiar? Can we bear to imagine the texts we study as both bounded and unbounded, somewhat stable and unnervingly out of control, created and recreated by individuals, groups, locations, conditions?

This chapter focuses on the production and reception of Kabir in oral settings, with a particular interest in texts. We will briefly scan the histories of Kabir texts, noting their forms and modes of transmission over centuries. Then we will track oral Kabir on the ground today, observing conditions of performance, with special attention to how texts change. Conclusions will include the following:

(1) Even in the promiscuously mixed media of our time, Kabir-attributed texts show characteristics of oral poetry described by Albert Lord in 1960, and oral performance today reveals much about how textual fluidity operates.
(2) The complex movements of texts—over history, across regions, among religious milieus and (claimed) authors—confound our attempts to draw boundaries around Kabir or anyone else. But we can imagine ecoregions in which the body of Kabir songs emerges with subtly differing colors and forms.

Human Body, Pen and Paper, Print, Magnetic Tape, Film, Digital Disc, Mobile Phone, Cyberspace

Certain kinds of Indian poetry have subsisted in oral tradition for centuries. In the case of Kabir, oral transmission started in the 1400s with the first poetic utterance from his mouth. A far-reaching oral tradition has flourished ever since, but it did not long remain simply oral. As the scribe's pen and the printing press irrevocably changed the functioning of oral traditions in past centuries, in recent decades cassettes, CDs, video, and the internet have joined the mix. When a folksinger becomes a recording artist, oral texts get fixed in a small portable object, travel to new places, and are recycled back into performed repertoires. All the technologies interact with each other as well as with less mediated oral transmission. These processes should be studied with respect to the particularities of time and place; but the nature of media is such that they cause texts and styles to break through the lines of localities. Not all media are equal in given times and places. Some are more dominant. They are always shifting. We can observe closely but should generalize tactfully.[2]

The heading for this section lists in more or less chronological order the main media in which Kabir has circulated from the fifteenth century to the present. These developments were, of course, not linear. As soon as there were two types of media, the feedback between them started. Then three, four, and so on. Mostly, the older media stay and readjust to new situations. In the larger history of information and performance, we should note that the first three items on the list developed over a long period of time, while the rest have spread through the world at blinding speed. The vast power of the internet, at this writing, has developed in less than twenty years.

Kabir (whether he was literate or not) certainly shared his works orally.[3] Others listened, sang, and spread the poetry. It naturally changed as they spread it. Dialects and musical styles transitioned. Slips of the tongue (and ear) and gaps of memory did their work. Deliberate alterations occurred when someone preferred a different order to the stanzas, inserted a favorite name of God, disliked and jettisoned a certain verse, or thought up a great improvement in a line. It wasn't long until Kabir's name was tacked on to whole poems he never composed—whether the source was a song floating around in local tradition or something the performer made up, feeling that the content was suitable to Kabir or that the attribution honored Kabir.[4]

Soon, no doubt while he was still alive, somebody wrote down something heard from or attributed to Kabir. We have no manuscripts from his lifetime, but writing was certainly present. The early manuscripts that have come down to us were mainly the ones sponsored and saved by sects: most importantly, the Dadu Panth in Rajasthan, the Sikhs in Punjab, and the Kabir Panth in more northern and eastern directions (today's Uttar Pradesh [U.P.] and Bihar). These collections, largely post-1600 but with some material traceable as far back as the 1570s, became the core of the most important written collections that exist.[5] They were copied and recopied, combined, altered, and enlarged. In the western collections of Rajasthan and Punjab, Kabir mingled with other poets—the Gurus and Bhagats of Sikh scripture, the five *sants* found in the *Panchvāṇī* of the Dadu Panth, and the thematically arranged multi-poet Rajasthani *Sarvāngī* collections. For the Kabir Panthis who compiled their various versions of the *Bījak* in more easterly regions, Kabir stood alone.[6]

The sects that were writing down these texts were also singing them. Within and outside of sectarian settings, people sing.[7] In each place and time, Kabir found himself in a particular textual, religious, musical, social, political, and economic environment. Each of these aspects of life affected the others. Through continuous singing, sharing, writing, working, joining, separating, buying, selling, making, and ritualizing, ecosystems were formed in which texts grew in their own ways. Different Kabirian ecoregions were both connected and distinct. Given the way in which scholarship on oral and written cultures has tended to dichotomize and imply evolutionary stages, it is important to emphasize this: Once we transitioned from the period of primarily oral transmission to the period in which handwritten collections were being preserved, we had not advanced from the oral to the written stage. We had oral and handwritten traditions, giving and receiving each other's feedback. When printing arrived with its new economies and distribution systems, we had not moved on to the stage of print, leaving behind oral performance and handwriting. We had indeed entered a different era. Writing and print drastically altered the environment. Oral performance continued, still an important but a significantly altered mode of transmitting text.

No one has better captured the scope and intimacy of Indian intertextualities than A. K. Ramanujan,, a master of both literature and folklore. In my explorations of the oral, written, performative, fixed, and fluid in Indian textual worlds, he has been a continuous fountain of inspiration and insight. It is worth pausing with a long quotation from his essay "Who Needs Folklore?" (Ramanujan 1999):

> In a largely non-literate culture, everyone—poor, rich, high caste, low caste, professor, pandit or ignoramus—has inside him or her a large non-literate subcontinent. (533)
>
> Written and hallowed texts are not the only kinds of texts in a culture like the Indian. Oral traditions of every kind produce texts. ... Every cultural performance not only creates and carries texts, it is a text.
>
> ... [W]e can ... see all these performances as a transitive series, a 'scale of forms' ... responding to one another, engaged in continuous and dynamic dialogic relations. Past and present, what's 'pan-Indian' and what's local, what's shared and what's unique in regions, communities, and individuals, the written and the oral—all are engaged in a dialogic reworking and redefining of the

> relevant others. ... In our studies now we are beginning to recognize and place folk-texts in this ever-present network of intertextuality. (535–36)
>
> In all cultures, and especially in the Indian, the oral and the written are deeply intermeshed. ... A work may be composed orally but transmitted in writing. ... Or it may be composed in writing ... but the text kept alive by ... reciters who know it by heart and chant it aloud. ... Thus, over a long history, a story may go through many phases. An oral story gets written up or written down. ... Then (as W. Norman Brown tried to show in a famous paper) the written text may reach other audiences who pick up the story and retell it orally, maybe in other languages, and then it gets written down somewhere else, perhaps starting another cycle of transmissions. ... Many of the differences in our classical texts, like the *Mahābhārata* recensions, may be due to the way the texts do not simply go from one written form to another but get reworked through oral cycles that surround the written word. ... Methods of Western textual criticism aim at making tree-diagrams, relating one written version to another, demonstrating that one came directly from another reaching back to a single Ur-text. Texts like the *Mahābhārata* may not have a reconstructable Ur-text at all, enmeshed as they were in oral traditions at various stages of their composition and transmission. (541)
>
> As Philip Lutgendorf ... has shown ... Tulsidas's *Rāmcaritmānas* is the focus of cults, festivals, formal and informal recitations, tableaus and oral forays into interpretations of the most wide-ranging and ingenious kinds. ... Oral traditions thus enlarge the range and they complicate and balance the texts we know. Yet we ignore the oral. (542–43)

In the early twenty-first century, many of the Kabir singers I met in Malwa were writing down texts in their own little copybooks, loosely stapled-together paper notebooks. Prahladji had thousands of songs written down in copybooks going back to 1977. At his father's house in Devali village, Dinesh Sharma showed me an old collection of handwritten bhajans in dated layers, some of which went back a hundred years.[8] These were not written in copybooks, but on large sheets eventually bound together. A few of the singers I met were not literate, so we might be tempted to say they were operating in a primarily oral realm. But this was not at all the same as in the fifteenth century! Though they didn't read and write down

Kabir texts for their own use, they listened to cassettes, watched videos, and heard performances by singers who did write and read. So the material they were getting was heavily influenced by the whole history of media that we are reviewing here.

Print became a force in Kabir textual dissemination in the nineteenth century, starting with an 1868 lithograph of the *Bījak*. In his book *Kabir: The Weaver's Songs*, Vinay Dharwadker combines the data available from previous textual scholars, providing a chart of major manuscript and print editions, including information on contents, compilers, geographical sources, and sectarian or courtly patrons, from 1570 to 2000. It is interesting to see how manuscripts proliferate in the seventeenth through nineteenth centuries and begin to dovetail with print editions, comprising what we are used to calling the "written tradition."

Now, understanding that oral and written are not a tidy dyad, we think about multidirectional transmission via bodies, objects, devices; texts walking, flying, embracing, and repelling each other, getting written and printed, magnetized and digitized, and turning again into live performances. Amid this media cacophony, how do we understand "oral tradition"? The meaning is far more complicated than I expected when I began this project. Here I will reiterate my definition of oral tradition for the purposes of this book. In this chapter and in chapter 5, the complications will unfold.

I use the term "oral" (interchangeable with "oral-performative") only for live, embodied performance. In this study, the first requirement for "oral Kabir" is that the text must be heard physically, with the ears. It will of course be a multisensory experience, but it can't exclude the ears, as silent reading does. The second requirement is that it be live, body to body. We can study oral tradition through audio, video, and electronic media. But we can experience oral tradition only in live transmission. Even amid the complexity of media and the layering of history, we can "prick up our ears," tuning in to the oral-performative aspects of Kabir traditions, cultivating awareness of how elements of text and performance relate to each other in oral environments. We can accomplish this by observing, listening, thinking, and practicing.

What do I mean by "practicing"? The most direct practice is to go to places where Kabir is sung, heard, and used, and to experience what all that means. That is what this book attempts to represent. Short of that kind of travel and immersion, we can begin to learn about oral tradition by studying our texts in somewhat unconventional ways. For example: Listen to recordings of sung bhajans and *dohās*. Try to sing and memorize the words. This practice will at once strike you with the difference between oral and written modes, even if you depend on written versions to sing and memorize. Notice the differences between bhajan (song) and *dohā* (couplet), both of which are performed by Kabir singers. Observe your own experience (physical, cognitive, emotional) in listening and singing compared to your experience in reading. Experiment with different conditions: live performances (in varying locations and social situations, with or without instruments, amplification, etc.); recordings; singing or reciting in Hindi; improvising a musical composition of a poem in translation.

Making It Up as You Go Along: The Fluidity of Texts

Rajula Shah has made a documentary on Malwa Kabir singers, quite different from the films of Shabnam Virmani in that Shah did not work with singers who were especially musically gifted or who had made a mark as performers. Shah's film, *Śhabad nirantar/ Word Within the Word* (2008), focuses solely on ordinary people who we might imagine as the common core of those who have kept the Kabir singing tradition alive. Unknown beyond their localities, they get together to sing and discuss for no other reason than that they enjoy and feel edified by it.

Shah often shows scenes in real life that reflect the imagery in songs. A grizzled old man plows a small field with two bullocks while we hear a song about symbolic bullocks in a symbolic field. As the old man plows, wields a hoe, and cuts plants, we hear his interview. He has been singing bhajans for many years and has taught his son, Shankarlal. The son, he says, "is literate, keeps scribbling, modifies hymns and makes new ones." The elderly father knows countless songs. "We don't sing in loops, we sing new ones, we have a vast repertoire of hymns. I'm illiterate, but once I begin there's no stopping me. I can go on for eight nights without repeating a hymn. I don't remember how many I remember! Once I start, they just roll out."

We see a close-up of the plow's blade pushing through rocky soil as the sounds of *tambūrā*, cymbals, and men's voices come up. The visuals switch to a man spinning cotton thread and weaving a rope, then to close-ups of handwritten words of Kabir. The singing fades as we see a grey-bearded but younger man—Shankarlal—looking at a notebook, with a group of young and old men nearby. His testimony, delivered with gestures and laughter, is a quintessence of how singers have played with texts for centuries.

Pointing to his copybook, he refers to a particular refrain: "Ink fades to a pale white," he reads out. "Now folks here won't understand that, so we have to explain what ink means. Ink means youth, and white is old age." He breaks into song: "Youth fades, palsy shakes, how will you deal with it, brother?" Explaining again: "Folks need these words, they won't know the meaning of 'ink fades.'" A big laugh. "I tackle it my own way." He sings again: "Youth fades, palsy shakes, how will you deal with it, brother? Sickness torments your frail body. Who will you turn to, brother? Hold fast to God's name!" He is really enjoying this, giggling as he says, "No matter how hard they try, they can't find my line here. We have to rephrase it to make the song work. But of course I don't tamper with Kabir's name. In the end, it's 'Kabir says,' so he's responsible!"

Kabir texts become relatively fluid when sung in live spaces, in contrast to their fixity in written or recorded form. In this section we will look at the ways in which singers and reproducers, consciously and unconsciously, change texts. We will note how written, printed, and recorded forms interact with oral sung texts, and how the very fact that a text is written, printed, or recorded gives authority to that particular version. Eventually we will reflect on the entry of electronic media into the textual field. In chapter 5 we will venture into theories of orality, with respect to the experiences and processes of singers and listeners. After traveling these maze-like pathways, we will consider again the distinctness of oral tradition.

Fluidity in Words, Lines, Passages, Sequences

During my first year of research, I collected hundreds of song-texts, greedy to possess the words but unable to simply hold them in my body the way the people around me did. Often I thought of Ramanujan's vivid evocations of the bodily location of texts, even for literate people, in a largely oral culture:

> [U]ntil recently to read meant to read aloud. I've heard of a grand-uncle who would say he couldn't read a novel because he had a sore throat. ... Pundits and Vedic experts had what Narayana Rao calls "oral literacy": they used an almost entirely oral medium, but were learned in grammar, syntax, logic, and poetics. Their literacy was, as it were, imbued in their bodies. We speak of a learned

> man having all his texts in his throat, *kanṭhastha*; when one is ignorant, one is called "a fellow who has no letters in his belly" or a *nirakṣarakukṣī*. (Ramanujan 1999, 538–39)

I still have those piles of rumpled sheets, sometimes in my handwriting, sometimes penned by Prahladji or a fellow musician in the *mandalī*. The sheets of paper are associated with memories of different places and conditions—sitting on the floor of the village home, on a layer of straw at a Kabir Panth gathering, in a train chugging rhythmically along while curious onlookers watch the process of transcription. One day, at my request, Prahladji wrote down *Bhāv nagarī*, "the city of love." First comes the *ṭek* (refrain), with repetitions that he has written out in full. Then the stanzas, which he has marked by number: 1, 2, 3, 4. My notes jotted over his lines show a further layer in the process of transforming an oral performance into a written artifact—notes by which the literary person seeks to make the text comprehensible to herself: Malwi *thāne* (I wrote) equals Hindi *āpko*. *Eb* means *avaguṇ* or *doṣ*. *Kachanār* is a small tree with beautiful flowers, *bauhinia variegata*, the buds used for vegetables, the leaves for medicine. In the following weeks I translated that song, which to me was a beautiful poem. Each stanza had a ruling image. They built on each other, unfolding a lyrical story of life.

In December 2002, in Malwa, I met Shabnam Virmani—the Bangalore filmmaker beginning to explore Kabir music, poetry, and social settings. Like me, she had heard about Malwa's Kabir singers and Eklavya's Kabir project, and she would work closely with Prahladji and others in the coming years as she created a series of films, audio CDs, and other works. Shabnam and I became close friends, sharing our projects in innumerable ways. Once when I returned to India after nine months at home, I found that she had recorded Prahladji singing *Bhāv nagarī*, and she had transcribed and translated the song. I felt upset to see that she had written the stanzas in a different order than I had. I was attached to my translation. It had an inner logic; it needed to go in that order. Anybody could see that her order was a mistake. I was afraid that hers would take over, overrun mine, and people would think that was the real order.

All of this is utter *māyā* (illusion), of course. Her order and mine are both poignantly contingent. The order of lines and stanzas frequently changes. Prahladji himself had written down the stanzas in one order with me and later sung them in a different order with Shabnam. In some cases performers would consider the order important and would point out what is correct and what is a mistake. In others they wouldn't care. What is actually interesting here is how texts get frozen. I am creating a little canon by publishing my work. Shabnam is creating one by recording a particular version and reinforcing it by printing the texts in a book that goes with the CD. From then on, people who use my book or her CD will have a strong impression of what is the right order. They will quote it, analyze it, and spread it, because it is available from a fixed source, not just an ephemeral performance. The authority of frozen text will ripple out in all directions. In 2003 Shabnam and I met the Gundecha brothers—renowned *dhrūpad* singers of Bhopal. They were going to sing two Kabir bhajans for a CD she was producing. When I asked how they got the particular texts they sang (imagining that they might have learned from the oral tradition), they said they only use words that are authorized by being printed in a book! Similarly a tailor in Damakheda village, who sang Kabir bhajans and was a *mahant* (religious propagator and ritual authority) in the Dharamdasi Kabir Panth, said, "For us to sing it, it must be in a book. Anybody can make up a song and put Kabir's name on it. If it's in a book, it has authenticity [*pramāṇiktā*]."

Nearly every song we heard from multiple sources in Malwa had variations from one singer to another, often from one occasion to another. The text of *Suntā hai guru gyānī* in the rousing folk rendition by Prahladji is about 75 percent the same as the haunting, slow version sung by Kumar Gandharva, the classical singer who lived an hour's drive from Prahladji's village, and who first heard the song from a wandering yogi (Hess 2009a, 30–31). In Devali village, the thick handwritten collection of bhajan texts that Dinesh Sharma's forefathers had been collecting for a century had a version of *Suntā hai guru gyānī* that was full of spelling variations from the versions we knew and had some lines that were different from anything we had heard. The most striking difference was in the last line:

> *kahe kabīr suno bhāī sadho, narak paḍe abhimānī*
> Kabir says, listen seekers, the arrogant fall into hell.

This jarring line seems to come from nowhere. It has nothing to do with the tenor and mysterious yogic imagery of the rest of the song; it has never arisen in any performed version we are acquainted with. But we know that formulaic signatures can be easily thrown in, just grabbed from the abundance of "Kabir says" lines floating in the air. Someone singing or writing in Devali village a few decades ago produced this closing line, demonstrating that a different *ṭek* or *chhāp* can be easily plugged into an opening or closing position.

In an article on early written traditions, I had once suggested that *ṭek* and *chhāp*—the refrain that opens the song and is repeated throughout, and the formulaic signature at the end—are the most portable parts of a song and can easily get changed and substituted (Hess 1987b). About twenty years later Joel Lee, then a PhD student in anthropology at Columbia University, questioned me about this claim. It sounded plausible, but I hadn't backed it up with enough examples to make it stick. Alerted by Joel's question, I began to notice more examples.[9] The following notes, written in August 2009 in Lunyakhedi village, first set the scene by describing Prahladji's collection of handwritten texts, then conclude with a vivid example of *ṭek* "portability." (See Figure 2.1)

> This morning I find PT carefully stacking old notebooks, straightening up loose, torn, and out-of-order pages. They are his oldest handwritten collections, which are falling apart. Rodents have taken bites from the corners. He has decided to revisit them today. There are

FIGURE 2.1. Prahladji's hand on an old handwritten bhajan notebook. Photo by Smriti Chanchani.

many old bhajans that they haven't sung for a long time. He starts to talk to me about them. Such conversations are a treasure-house of knowledge about the culture of singing and interpreting Kabir and others.[10]

Browsing through, PT pauses on one *sākhī*. A key word is *prārabda*, which means fate or results of previous lives. He interprets it, saying that its real meaning is about our karma in this life, emphasizing our power to shape our own fate. But, he says, the Kabir Panthis and other sectarians have wrongly construed it to suggest that some higher power outside ourselves, and unknown actions in earlier lives, determine our fate. One interpretation brings forth our power and agency, the other kills it. That higher power, that energy, is within ourselves, he says.

Next he speaks of the Nath Panth. He says that both sects [Nath Panth and Kabir Panth] are made up of mainly low-caste, uneducated people. Upper-caste people controlled the temples, so low castes put forth a religion insisting that God is an *energy* (he uses the English word), a power that is within ourselves.

He comes upon a set of texts marked *kīrtan*, starting with hymns to Krishna. "In those days," he says, "we used to sing all this—Krishna and Ganapati, *saguṇ* bhakti. We sang for festivals and functions." Along with Krishna I see the names of Shankar and Parvati, and *rāmchandrajī kī āratī*. He starts singing a Krishnaite text in a repetitious melody. His brother Ambaram, standing nearby, joins in, smiling as he remembers those long-ago days. The heading *kīrtan* appears on multiple pages. In contrast is bhajan, a heading that applies to Kabir, Gorakhnath, and other *nirgun* poets. On one page in the *kīrtan* section, he points out to me that a Kabir bhajan has been sung as if it is a Vaishnav *kīrtan*. The entire bhajan, familiar to me, is widely attributed to Kabir. I have heard versions of it often and have seen it in printed collections. But here the refrain begins with a sign of Vaishnav ownership: *om hari kīrtan se dil na churānā re, is jīvan kā nahī ṭhikānā re.*[11] At the end, instead of Kabir's signature, *om hari kīrtan* is repeated. Prahladji provides an interpretation: the Vaishnavs liked the bhajan but didn't like Kabir, so they just removed his name and called it *hari kīrtan*.

We could go on till the end of time cataloguing variations in words, phrases, and sequences in performed or written versions of what is recognizably the "same" song. In most cases there is no point in trying to say which came first, or to designate one as primary, the other as variant. Prahladji's *Zarā halke gāḍī hānko*, an all-time favorite in Malwa, is a song I have not heard or read anywhere else. But certain parts of it show up in a popular song, *Man phūlā phūlā phirat jagat meṇ*, which I found in a printed bhajan collection picked up in a Delhi market and heard on a cassette by Madhup Mudgal. A sobbing woman appears in the Malwa bhajan: *bhilak bhilak kar tiriyā rove*. In the Delhi book it is *lapaṭi jhapaṭi ke tiriyā rove*. Her sobs are evoked with different words, but in both cases it is a rhyming-repeating, onomatopoetic word pair. We also have in both songs the image of the "wooden horse" (*kāṭh ki ghoḍī*) for the litter on which a dead body goes to the burning ground, and the sudden flare-up of the funeral fire compared, incongruously, to the happy bonfire of the Holi festival. The same formula—the woman sobbing that she has lost her partner, while Kabir comments that the one who joined them is the one who broke them apart—appears in yet another song, sung by Kumar Gandharva (Hess 2009a, 80). While noticing these overlaps between otherwise quite different songs, I see that *Man phūlā* contains lines that appear in yet other poems in the *Bījak*—for example, *haḍ jarai jas lakaḍī, kes jarai jas ghāsā*—bones burn like sticks, hair burns like grass.

All the texts compared in the last paragraph share themes of death and the tenuousness of family attachments. On their own, the compositions may seem to have integrity as poems, but these variations and duplications of lines and passages in different contexts tell a different story. While some full poem texts can be passed along nearly intact for centuries (as evidenced by old manuscripts), the common unit in oral transmission is much shorter: half-lines, full lines, couplets, and themes held together by imagery. The pioneering work of Albert Lord on oral-formulaic composition is still illuminating here, even though he studied oral epic, a very different genre, in Yugoslavia, a very distant place.[12]

In some songs it is easier to get the sense of a pastiche of themes and images without much coherence. Shabnam comments on one such song, "*Thārā bhariyā samand māhī hīrā*":

> Traveling through the centuries, from body to body, from singer to singer, some song lines are remembered, but some get lost in transmission, and the song gets completed with images from other songs. And indeed, why not? If you're immersed in the Kabirian pool of poetic imagery, the metaphors start getting familiar, encountered time and again in different songs, till they almost seem like old friends. So why wouldn't they be allowed to enter the body of

> another song, much like a good friend being allowed to gate crash another friend's party? This ... blurring of boundaries and casual breaking of the rules of purity is part of the folk aesthetic. (Virmani 2008c, 41)

Sometimes a structure allows for easy substitution and addition without altering the sense that it is the same song. The song cited above with "*om hari kirtan*" is frequently sung by Prahladji with a different refrain. In his version, all the stanzas begin with *yon saṃsār*, "this world," whose transient nature is evoked in a series of vivid images—a market, a clump of brambles, a paper boat, a glass bangle. The song can be long or short: it doesn't matter if there are four examples or six or seven, each with its own verse. A version of this song is included in Kshitimohan Sen's 1910–11 collection, as well in the Delhi bazaar bhajan book I have referred to. Both lack the lovely repeated refrain of Prahladji's Malwa version:

mat kar mān gumān, mat kar kāyā ko ahaṃkār
kesariyā rang uḍi jāye lo, gulābī rang uḍi jāye lo.

Don't be proud
of your power, don't admire
your body. The golden color
will fly, the rosy color
will fly.[13]

The flexibility and spontaneity of oral tradition occur in the risings and fallings of these "pieces" of poetry.

A charming exchange takes place in Shabnam's film *Chalo hamara des/ Come to My Country* (Virmani 2008a), between middle-aged Prahladji and a very old man he once learned from. Shabnam and Prahladji travel to the old mentor's village, and the two men meet after a long time. When Chenamaruji was middle-aged and Prahladji was young, the older singer shared his own huge repertoire with the younger. Prahladji recognizes the harmonium he used to play, now battered and chipped with age, like the old man's teeth. At Prahladji's urging Chenaji tries to sing, but soon he is breathless. Someone gives him a glass of water. He smiles and says, "Don't trouble me any more. You sing." Prahladji takes the harmonium. "Here is one that you taught me, and I've sung it so many times." He starts to sing, encouraging Chenaji to join in, which the old man does, seeming to gain energy as they continue.

hamen sāhib se milnā hai, arre yār satguru se milnā hai
maiṇ nashe meṇ chūr yār, mere guru se milnā hai,
meṇ nashe meṇ kḥūb yar, mālik se milnā hai

I'm on my way
to meet the guru, on my way
to meet the lord.
I'm smashed, completely drunk, my friend,
about to meet the lord.

As they sing, they seamlessly slide into lines on the same theme, with a tune that is a little different—

sāhib ne bhāng pilāī, aisī bhāng pilāī
akhiyoṃ meṇ lālan chāī ho, satgura ne bhāng pilāī
pī kar pyālā huā divānā, ghūm rahā jaise matvālā

The lord gave me a drink, what a potion he gave me to drink!
My eyes turn red, the guru gave me a drink.
I drank from that cup and went mad,
I staggered around like a drunkard.

Suddenly they pause, look at each other and laugh, Prahladji still strumming the *tambūrā*. "It's the wrong song, isn't it? We started singing another one by mistake!" Thus is enacted in front of us memory's way of retaining and forgetting, arranging and rearranging lines of song by associations of theme, imagery, melody.

Oral folk traditions foster a liberal attitude toward words and meanings, in contrast with situations where there is an obligation to adhere to what is correct. Shabnam once said to me, "It's very hospitable poetry. People can inhabit it." In a written commentary, she discusses oral tradition, highlighting a conversation between two singers in Malwa:

> It was the crack of dawn one winter morning in Malwa. We were on the road, returning from a village concert. A beautiful conversation started between Prahladji and a young and upcoming singer, Arun Goyal. They were discussing the refrain of a song –
>
> Go, go my friend—
> across the seven seas.

Bring back a pearl, oh seeker,
an unpierced one, oh yes!

> When Prahladji sings this song, the seeker is asked to bring up an *anabindiyā motī*—an *unpierced* pearl. But when Arun sings the same song, the seeker is asked to bring up an *anabhinjiyā motī*—an *undrenched* pearl. The two singers debated the merits of that single syllabic shift, and eventually agreed that both poetic options must be sung since both held true to the ideas of Kabir. In one, Kabir invites you to find a pearl of wisdom that has not been strung into a narrow framework of meaning. In another, Kabir invites you to find that pearl which, even while being immersed in the worldly ocean, remains untouched, unattached, unaffected by it.[14]
>
> I marveled afresh at the oral traditions, these open worlds of discourse and dialogue, in which the singers and "receivers" of Kabir's poems were as much its custodians, owners and contributors, participating in the creation and growth of that poetic oeuvre through the lens of their own experiences.
>
> This conversation seemed far removed from the worlds of academic discourse that sought to ferret out the "authentic" Kabir, dismissing millions of poems alive and traveling in the name of Kabir, as "inauthentic." So far removed also from the worlds of holy scripture—of fixed letters on sacrosanct pages....
>
> Many of the songs of "Kabir" sung in this collection bear the signature of poets like Bhavani Nath, Gulabi Das, Bana Nath, Hussain Fakir, Dharam Das and others, about most of whom very little is known except that they were inspired ... to compose their own songs replete with ... Kabirian ideas and images. (Virmani 2008c, 43–45)

The reference to holy scriptures is illustrated by another story that Shabnam told me. She noticed a resistance among some Sikhs to the free-flowing ways of Kabir in folk traditions. This is because Kabir has been incorporated into the Sikh sacred text, the *Ādi Granth*, and thus, in some people's view, rightly removed from circulation. A Sikh singer, after recording Kabir songs, handed her a piece of paper with the texts and declared that he had not deviated a single syllable from the form in the holy book. When Shabnam enthusiastically described a Malwa "bhajan competition" where many groups presented their diverse texts and renditions, a Sikh friend expressed skepticism: "That's not such a good idea. The authentic Kabir is *gurbāṇī*, in the *Granth Sāhib*. We shouldn't fool around with it."[15]

One can get a dramatic sense of the great pool of "Kabirian" themes and formulas in northern and central India by comparing across regions and religious-social formations. Within this oceanic pool are smaller seas that are definable by certain marks but do not have fixed boundaries.[16] They flow, change, overlap, and can only be "seen" when one decides to focus (as in the famous Escher graphics) on foreground and background in certain ways. One can identify *nirguṇ* and *saguṇ* areas; Nath, Sufi, and Kabir Panthi areas; thematic areas featuring the imagery of the yogic body, or of lover and beloved; geographic areas like Rajasthan, U.P., or Bihar. My work with oral Kabir has been mainly in the Malwa region of Madhya Pradesh, where the marks of Nath Yogi, Kabir Panthi, and Rajasthani cultures are strongly identifiable. After immersing herself in Kabir and related poetry/music of Malwa and Rajasthan, Shabnam extended her research to the Kutch region of Gujarat. Her recordings of the Kutchi singer Muralala Marvadi illustrate the extensive reach of thematic and formulaic patterns and—stirring despair in the hearts of those who seek authentic Kabir—the interchangeability of poets and passages. For example, Muralala sings a song attributed to Khīm-*sāhib* whose content is indistinguishable from that of countless songs of Kabir, centered on poetic evocations of the yogic body.[17]

Muralala also sings songs of lover and beloved expressed in a woman's voice. Prahladji in Malwa sings many such songs, often addressed to the *helī* or female friend. So does Mukhtiyar Ali in Rajasthan, which seems to be the epicenter of the *helī* genre. Bhakti poetry of lover and beloved in North India is always inflected by the powerful tradition of devotion to Krishna and Radha, who share a transcendent love. But when it appears in Kabir and other *nirguṇ* poets, it often has a peculiar yogic twist: the beloved is said to reside inside one's own body and to be attainable by yogic practices. The following verses, excerpted from a song sung by Muralala with Kabir's signature, illustrate both the yogic core and the Krishnaite resonance. The name used for the lord is *śhyām*, dark one—rarely found in Kabir and always suggesting Krishna:

Come, let's go meet the five
Let's rein in the twenty-five![18]

Stay with the name
In every corner, the colors fade....

Come, let's go to that sky-dome
where my Dark One stays
I've seen the right and left channels.
The central channel is dancing there!...

A more famous song is *Ghūnghaṭ ke phat khol, tohe pīv milenge*—"Open your veil [*ghūnghaṭ*, the sari end with which village women cover their faces], you will meet the beloved." This refrain sets a tone of Krishnaite romance, but the verses are yogic, saying that the lord/beloved is within your own body and invoking the "empty palace" [*śhūnya mahal*, meaning the body] within which the practitioner should maintain an unmoving meditative posture in order to hear the unstruck sound.[19]

Open your veil
and meet the beloved.

The lord dwells
in every body.
Don't speak harsh words.

Don't be proud of your youth
or your wealth.
That five-colored vest
deludes you.

A lamp glows
in the palace of emptiness.
Stay still,
don't stir.

In the bright palace
a yogic device.
You find the beloved
beyond price.

Kabir says, bliss
is here.
Listen to the boom
of the unstruck drum.

Fluidity in Authorship and Sectarian Affiliation

In the previous section I used the metaphor of an oceanic pool of Kabirian images, formulas, phrases, and themes, adapted from Ramanujan's "pool of signifiers" for the *Rāmāyaṇa*. I also suggested the "ecoregion" metaphor as a way of mapping texts of Kabir and others in North India. Features of these landscapes might include authors' names and religious or sectarian affiliations. What other poets show up in performances as good friends of Kabir? What other poets crisscross with Kabir as claimed authors of the same poems? What sectarian names and terms show up in Kabir's company? In Malwa, songs of Kabir are closely associated with the Kabir Panth and the Nath Panth and with poets belonging to both (Dharamdas, Gorakhnath, Bananath, etc.). In Pakistan, Kabir is found in the company of Sufis. In this section, we will see examples of these crossings and how they affect the substance and attribution of texts.

I am not the first to suggest "mapping" as a metaphor for studying the complex affinities and fluidities of Indian texts that exist in many forms and media. I speak here of mapping Kabir texts amid certain religious associations, names, terms, and poetic phrases and passages. Francesca Orsini, in her work on Hindi and Urdu language and literature, has proposed historico-geographical maps, maps of genres, and more.[20]

Prahladji sings *Shūnya ghar shahar* with Kabir's signature line; Kumar Gandharva's version of the same song gives authorship to Gorakhnath.[21] Kumarji sings another song attributed to Gorakhnath, which Muralala of Kutch, Gujarat, sings under the name of Kabir.[22] And Muralala sings a refrain almost universally associated with Kabir, *Man lāgo mero yār fakīrī meṇ*, with a different set of verses, all attributed to Mirabai. The refrain is the same; the stanzas are different, but with a similar theme—preferring simplicity and poverty over wealth and luxury. A couplet recited as Kabir's by Prahladji is attributed to Bulleh Shah in Rajasthan. Another "Kabir" couplet heard in Malwa is credited to Shah Abdul Latif in Kutch. Carol Salomon quotes from a Baul song: "If circumcision make you a Muslim, what is the woman? If sacred thread makes you Brahmin, what is the woman?" These famous lines of Kabir (so I always thought!) are attributed to the Bengali poet Lalon Shah/Lalan Fakir (Salomon 1996, 192). A Baul song cited by Lisa Knight as *Man siksa* is virtually identical to the Kabir song I know in Malwa as *Jāg musāfir jāg* (Knight 2011, 117).

As I kept uncovering these cross-region, cross-language, and cross-poet attributions of the same lines and passages, I still clung to the notion that a figure called Kabir was separable from the rest. That faith was momentarily shattered when I happened upon a citation in Francoise Delvoye's article, "The Thematic Range of *Dhrupad* Songs Attributed to Tansen, Foremost Court-Musician of the Mughal Emperor Akbar": "Here Tansen, to whom the following composition is attributed, addresses his mind: *Dhireṁ dhireṁ re mana dhireṁ saba kachu hoi* . . . / 'Slowly, slowly, O my mind, everything takes its time!' " (Delvoye 1994, 422).

I was shocked! But why should I be after all these years? I cherish this as a couplet at the very center (if such a metaphor is permitted) of the Kabir corpus. Delvoye doesn't cite the second line, but most likely it would be the one I know: *mālī sīnche sau ghaḍa, ritu āve phal hoi.* It's one of the few *sākhīs* that I can always produce from memory. I used it to make an important statement at the opening of one of my books. Delvoye's attribution of this line to Tansen is a tipping point. Maybe nothing belongs to anybody in this sprawling set of poetic traditions. Kabir would undoubtedly approve of this conclusion. Didn't he famously say *koī nahīṇ apnā* (no one belongs to anyone)? Wait, who knows whether he really said that or not?

In Malwa a Kabir singing session with Prahladji, Kaluramji, Narayanji, or some other Kabir specialist would have a generous sprinkling of songs attributed to other poets—but not just any others. They would be *nirguṇ* poets, and the other names were usually associated with either the Kabir Panth, to which many of the locals belong, or the Nath Panth.[23]

The Kabir Panth has a number of distinct lineages that claim descent from Kabir himself (see chapter 7). In this section I refer only to the Damakheda-based Kabir Panth, which introduces the figure of Dharamdas and poetry attributed to him. Damakheda, a village near Raipur, Chhattisgarh, is the headquarters of one of the largest Kabir Panth formations. Its many followers, spreading from Bihar in the east to Rajasthan and Gujarat in the west, are also called Dharamdasis, because they believe that Kabir's first and greatest disciple was the merchant Dharamdas, who established the sect during Kabir's lifetime on the express orders of the master.[24] In this sectarian environment, the names of Kabir and Dharamdas often come together. Many songs are attributed to Dharamdas, and many others include the names of both Kabir and Dharamdas. Once Prahladji showed me a thick collection of Kabir bhajans edited by Yugalanand, a Damakheda devotee. The great majority of poems concluded with an unvarying half-line, "Kabir says to Dharamdas." Prahladji suggested that many of these songs were traditionally sung with no mention of Dharamdas, but that sectarians had pasted in the *chhāp* that supported their version of history.

The Nath Panth is a sect of yogis, long present in North India in both renunciant and householder streams, tracing their origin to Gorakhnath, whose dates are uncertain. Some scholars suggest that Kabir's forefathers were householder Nath Panthis, that the culture of this tradition pervaded their community even after their conversion to Islam, and that the religious/experiential language of the Naths would still have been common in the family during Kabir's lifetime.[25] "Jogi" singers continue to wander in North India, their repertoire dominated by Kabir.[26]

There is an immediate affinity between Kabir and the Nath yogi tradition. In every collection and location where I have encountered Kabir's poetry, there is always a strong representation of poems about experience in the body, laced with poetic uses of the technical language of yoga. Once I visited the Kabir Panth *samādhi*-temple in Magahar, where Kabir is believed to have died. This shrine is kept by the Kabir Chaura (Varanasi) tradition of Kabir Panthis, who are quite distinct from the Dharamdasis. Hanging out with the white-clad Kabir Panth sadhus was a tall and voluble Nath yogi in bright red robes, with the large round earrings that mark Nath initiates, giving sect members the alternate name of *kānphaṭas*, pierced-ears. The genial yogi joked with me and invited me to visit him in nearby Nepal, where he lived. Magahar itself is next door to the larger city of Gorakhpur, named after the great yogi Gorakhnath, where the headquarters of the organized Nath tradition is located. Though I didn't probe his interest in Kabir, his presence there to me was emblematic of the long-running relationship between Naths and Kabir.

Apart from anecdotes, there is ample textual evidence of this affinity. I have referred to musicologist Edward Henry's documentation of Nath singers in the area around Varanasi (Henry 1988, 160ff.). Nearly all their songs carry Kabir's signature line. In addition, I have studied an anthology of over five hundred song texts collected by a famous Nath yogi master in Malwa in the early twentieth century. Shilnath lived in Dewas for about twenty years before moving to the Himalayan foothills in the last phase of his life. His *dhūnī* (the fire associated with wandering sadhus) has been preserved ever since, and an institution has grown up around it, the Shilnath Dhuni Sansthan. A large temple has recently been completed, dwarfing the *dhūnī* itself. For many years the *dhūnī* was a gathering place for singers of *nirguṇ* bhajans. Kumar Gandharva, the great classical singer who lived in Dewas, used to sit there at night, listening to and singing with the wanderers.[27] Shilnath was so fond of bhajans that he put together a large collection, printed in 1915 and reissued at various points since then. The vast majority of poems in his book are attributed to Kabir, with only a few carrying the names of Gorakhnath and other Nath poets. There is a haunting story of how he decided (as great yogis are able to do) on the moment of his death. Asking a disciple to sing Kabir's beautiful song *Ham pardesī panchhī bābā* ("I'm a bird from another country"), he expired as the song drew to a close.[28] Combing through the first one hundred poems of Shilnath's collection, I found that *all* of them had Kabir's signature.

The investigation of sectarian associations and crisscrossing authorships could be similarly carried on with studies of Kabir in Sikh, Sufi, Dadu Panthi, and other environments.

Fluidity Driven by Ideology

So far we have discussed ways in which natural variations in hearing, memory, and other associative processes will alter oral Kabir texts; and we have glimpsed a larger picture in which the contents of songs often consist of modules—themes, metaphors, lines, passages—that are quite portable. We have also seen that the practice of singing "Kabir" embraces other poets with whom singers associate him. Thus different singers may attribute the same poem to different poets. This book does not undertake a full investigation of the historical and ideological networks that link Kabir with one set of poets, traditions, and vocabularies here, another set there. But we have hypothesized physical and cultural ecoregions in which oral texts, mingling with written, recorded, and performed ones, produce a Kabir with somewhat distinct colors and tendencies. As in a Venn diagram, these regions overlap and can never be absolutely distinguished; nevertheless, the differences are palpable. Another way in which the differences can be traced is through sectarian ideologies.

Long ago I did a comparative study of three major textual traditions of Kabir, located in three geographical regions and sectarian milieus (Hess 1987b). I found that the western collections based in Rajasthan were rich in language and symbols associated with devotion to Krishna (including Vaishnav names of God and expressions in a female voice of intimate relationship, in union and separation, with the divine lover), while the eastern *Bījak*, associated with the Varanasi-based Kabir Panth, had very little language of that sort. The other distinct western tradition—the *Ādi Granth* compiled in the late sixteenth century by Sikhs in Punjab—along with relatively high Krishnaite language, had more content supporting the guru-centered and "plain-speaking," nonrenunciant religious ideology of the Sikhs.

A wonderful example of sectarian influence on texts turns up in Gurinder Singh Mann's important work on the manuscript history of Sikh scripture. The Goindval Pothis, assembled in the early 1570s, are very close to the *Ādi Granth* as canonized in 1604, but also have intriguing differences. Mann has told me that there are three Kabir poems in the Goindval Pothis of approximately 1572 that do not appear in the 1604 *Ādi Granth* or in any other old collection as far as he knows. These three poems, as yet unstudied by scholars, now constitute the very earliest manuscript appearance of Kabir. Mann has also revealed a fascinating bit of information from his study of the earliest manuscripts. Two Kabir poems were written into the 1604 Kartarpur Pothis but then crossed out and excluded from the *Granth* forever after. Both were *ulaṭbāṃsī*, "upside-down language" poems with outrageous, nonsensical, sometimes shocking imagery. *Ulaṭbāṃsī*s appear everywhere that one finds oral and written Kabir, east and west. They belong to an older tradition of mystical poetry using such enigmatic language in meaningful ways.[29] One of the deleted poems from the Kartarpur manuscript seems to have been particularly offensive to Sikh sensibility, depicting crazy mixed-up family relations, with the opening line, "People, look at God's betrothal. The mother married her son and lived with her daughter." Whoever crossed it out wrote "useless" in the margin. The Sikh gurus apparently had a strong preference for plain language and domestic propriety. They also emphatically avoided anything that had even a whiff of tantric influence (Mann 2001, 114–15).

Examining the first hundred poems of the Nath anthology collected by the renowned yogi Shilnath in Dewas,[30] I found not a single Krishnaite name of the divine—no Krishna, Hari, Madhav, or Govind, all of which appear abundantly in the western manuscripts and occasionally, if rarely, in the *Bījak*. In fact even *rām*—a common divine name in Kabir poetry everywhere—is much rarer in the Nath anthology than elsewhere. The metrically equivalent and religiously neutral *nām* (name) is preferred. There is not a single poem in this set emphasizing *viraha* (a woman's anguished separation from the beloved). The word "beloved" appears once, but the context is a statement that the beloved is in your own body. There is throughout the Nath anthology, predictably, an emphasis on experience in the body.

If in various regions of India Kabir swims in a sea of Hindu or Nath Yogi or Sikh or Kabir Panthi poets, in Pakistan he swims in a sea of Sufi poets. I observed from recordings that Muslim singers tend to use a series of *dohās*, rather than a bhajan preceded by one or more *dohās*, as the structure of a song. On her Kabir album, Abida Parveen has a long track called *Man lāgo yār fakīrī meṇ*. But rather than singing a version of the well-known bhajan of this name, with its series of thematically linked stanzas all ending with the same rhyme, Abida just uses the phrase *Man lāgo yār fakīrī meṇ* as a refrain and goes on for sixteen minutes apparently singing whatever *dohās* happen to arise for her. When the spirit moves her, she sings the tag line, *Man lāgo*. At the end she sings the well-known concluding stanza of the bhajan, *kahe kabīr suno bhāī sādho, sāhib mile sabūrī meṇ, man lago*. Farid Ayaz also follows this kind of structure with the track *Maulā maulā*, on the Kabir Project's CD *Kabir in Pakistan*.

Documenting Sufi singers in Rajasthan and Pakistan, Shabnam Virmani has noted various ways in which Kabir interpenetrates with Sufi saint-poets. Thus in language, symbol, affect, text arrangements, and narrative references, Kabir has affinities with Bulleh Shah, Shah Abdul Latif, Sachal Sarmast, and the richly mixed Muslim-Hindu culture of the Sindhi and Punjabi mystical love legends. All these observations invite new research and discovery.

Religious traditions and sects have their ideologies and preferences. So do individuals. Some singers have told me they prefer *nām* to *rām* and consciously substitute the former for the latter. This indicates a more marked disengagement from Vaishnav and *saguṇ* associations and may be linked to a caste-related preference for the *nirguṇ* position (as discussed in chapter 1). A direct announcement of such a change is heard on one of Prahladji's audio CDs. In a spoken introduction to a verse where the *tambūrā*, a musical instrument, stands for the human body, Prahladji mentions that the first stanza as he learned it said, "First I meditate on Lord Ganapati (Ganesh) and mother Sharada (Saraswati). Ram, please give your *darśhan*." But, he continues, "We prefer to sing *satguru*." Throughout the song, he sings the refrain with *satguru* in place of Ganapati and *guru* in place of Ram.[31]

Over a period of years, Kaluram Bamaniya (profiled in chapter 6) had undergone a strong change of attitude toward the Kabir Panth in particular and Vaishnav Hinduism in general. He made a point of changing *rām* to *nām*, even in well-known songs where everyone else sang *rām*. When I met him in August 2012, he was also inclined to excise the name of Dharamdas. So for instance, in a song that usually concludes *kahe kabīr dharamdās se* (Kabir says to Dharamdas), he sang *kahe kabīr samujhāī ke* (Kabir says, explaining). The rhyme and syllable count fit perfectly.

I too find myself tinkering with texts and translations if the versions available to me give scope for choice. A very popular song begins with the refrain, *Moko kahāṇ dhūṇḍhte re bande, maiṇ to tere pās meṇ*, "Where are you searching for me, friend? I'm right here." All the lines have the same rhyme, echoing "*pās meṇ*" (very close/right here). They make a series of negative statements—I'm not in the temple, not in the mosque, not in holy mountains and rivers, not in ritual, and so on. This structure is a setup for the last line, which will make a positive statement. Our friends in Malwa concluded the song with *maiṇ to hūṇ vishvās meṇ*, which means, "I am in belief/faith." That didn't sit well with me. I was happy to discover that the K. M. Sen text, reprinted in Dvivedi's *Kabīr*, had a version that ended, *Maiṇ shvāsoṇ ke shvās meṇ*—I am in the breath of the breath (Dvivedi 1971, 234). As a Zen student who practiced meditation through awareness of breath, I loved this, and it avoided what I considered the dangerous clichés of "belief." So even though the performers I worked with sang it the other way, I decided it was all right to publish the text and translation in my preferred form. Of course there was a footnote explaining what I had done.

Similarly, there was a song that I transcribed from Prahladji in 2002: *Jo tu āyā gagan manḍal se*, "If you come from the dome of the sky." One of the stanzas came out quite felicitously, I thought, in my translation:

> If in your house
> is a lovely spouse,
> why do you knock
> on a prostitute's door?
> Why walk away
> from the cool shade
> of a tree, to make your bed
> on stones?

There is a four-way wordplay in *nārī sukamnā*, indicating both a lovely wife and the body's central energy-channel in yogic physiology.[32] The Hindi word for house is *ghar*. Sometime in the next year or so, Prahladji started singing *ghaṭ* (body) instead of *ghar*. He declared that he liked this meaning better, but to me it knocked out some of the levels of wordplay. It also skewered my translation, which I was fond of. So I decided I would just stick to his first version (with a footnote).

Shabnam had similar issues touching on poetry and meaning, once she started singing herself. She tells how she changed a word because it didn't make sense within the parallel structure of the verses. She even asked a young poet friend steeped in *sant* poetry and folk music to come up with a new signature line for the same song, since she didn't like the one Prahladji used! According to her, Prahladji seemed to have thrown in a *chhāp* from another song, but it didn't fit and broke the mood and meaning of the song.[33]

Shabnam and I both had ideological bones to pick with some of the texts and contexts we encountered. There was a beautiful song whose melody I came to love before I understood all the verses. It opened with a simple refrain:

> *Lagan kaṭhin hai mere bhāī, guruji se lagan kathin hai mere bhāī.*
>
> Devotion is difficult, my brother. Devotion to the guru is difficult, my brother.

Actually *lagan* is more than "devotion," as explained below. The following commentary, from a 2002 field notebook, shows how my discovery of the troubling meaning of one stanza gave rise to a struggle between attraction and repulsion that affected how I dealt with text:

> I fell in love with the song, understanding only the refrain and hearing the haunting melody with its long sustained notes at the ends of lines. The refrain says, "*lagan* is difficult, my brother." Translating *lagan* is also difficult. It means devotion, dedication, concentration, commitment, perseverance, determination, ability to stick to it to the end. None of these by itself is an adequate translation. *Lagan* has a literal sense of sticking, not letting go. It combines devotion (soft) and dogged refusal to give up (tough). And the pronoun before "brother"—*my* brother—in this particular tender and melancholy melody with an undertone of fierceness—gives the song an extra quality of sad sweetness. In other songs, the poet might admonish the listener, the brother, to get his act together and stop being a fool. But in this one, the singer feels the difficulty. He expresses to himself and to his brother—the close one, the friend, the alter ego—how very difficult it is to stick to the path of truth. (I prefer to call it "truth," but the song says "the guru.") This path is before us.

We don't know if we can do it. Yet, as we sometimes understand, we don't have any choice.

To follow this difficult path requires fearlessness. That is what the successive verses illustrate. They present four conventional figures that all stand for fearless, unwavering devotion to one's truth.

As I figure out the Hindi, my problems begin. These tropes representing heroic ideals don't fit with my culturally informed views. Especially the one about the *satī*, the true and pure woman who is so devoted to her deceased husband-lord that she leaps into his funeral pyre without hesitation. This image of the *satī*, with its horrifying social implications, has become abhorrent to many feminists. Do I stop loving the song? Do I continue to love the song, with reservations? With a large footnote detailing my ideological objections? I opt for the footnote. Here is a translation of the song.

> *Holding fast is difficult, my brother.*
> *Holding fast to the guru is difficult.*
> *Without holding on, you can't do*
> *what must be done.*
> *Your precious life moves on*
> *toward death.*
>
> Desiring raindrops of *svātī*,
> the cuckoo repeats,
> *My love! my love!* She repeats,
> Let me die of thirst right now!
> I don't want any other water.[34]
>
> Casting off wealth and possessions,
> the pure woman goes forth
> to enact her purity.
> Gazing at fire without fear
> she leaps into the flames.
>
> When two armies face off,
> the warrior goes to battle.
> Cut to pieces, he falls to earth,
> but never runs from the field.
>
> The deer who knows
> the secret sound of the Word

sets out to hear.
Hearing the Word, he gives up his life
without the slightest fear.

Give up hope
in your body.
Fearlessly sing!
Kabir says, holding fast like that
you'll naturally meet
the guru.

Holding fast to the guru is difficult,
my brother.

Flash-forward a few years. Shabnam has become a singer. Her love of music was one of the factors that led her into this project in the first place. It's no surprise that she started learning the beautiful Malwi folk tunes and singing the poetry along with our mentors in the field, above all Prahladji. (See Figure 2.2) I did this too, immediately on starting my fieldwork. I remember lying in a Dewas hotel room in early 2002, my little cassette player plugged into my ears, singing *Panchhīḍā bhāī* over and over again as I followed Prahladji's voice, trying to get the enchanting melody right.

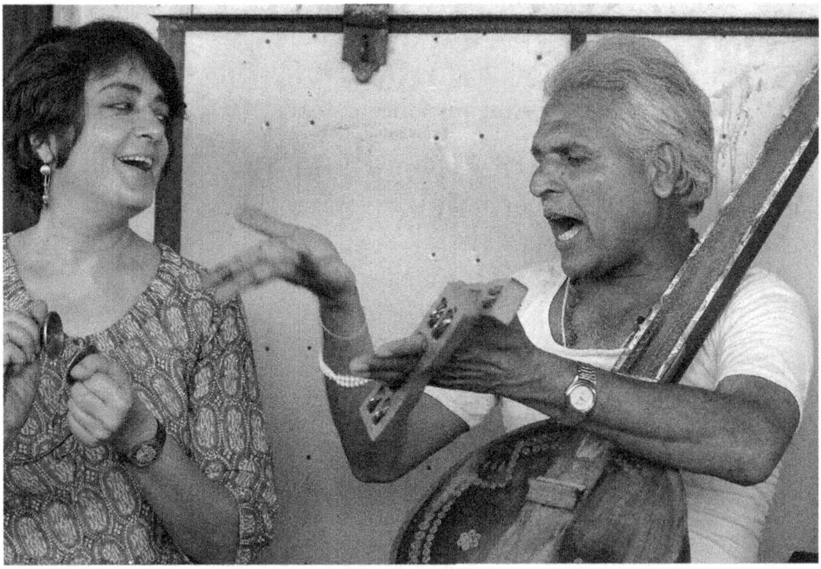

FIGURE 2.2. Shabnam and Prahladji singing together. Photo by Smriti Chanchani.

But with Shabnam things took a different turn. She had a strong, rich voice, a musical gift, and some training. She took up the *tambūrā* and learned to play it well. The first time Prahladji surprised her in a concert by announcing that she would sing a bhajan, she was deeply embarrassed. But there was no escape from him. He didn't let go, and the rural audience applauded insistently, wanting to hear what this camera-wielding woman from Bangalore could do. They weren't disappointed. After some quavering moments, she got into the spirit and belted it out as she had learned to do from her folk gurus. The applause was uproarious. This habit of calling for one bhajan, or two, continued. It took a while, but she got used to it. Shabnam practiced at home. To sing the songs was inextricable from her process of research and creation as a filmmaker. Her repertoire grew—faster and faster as the songs became part of her. Friends started sitting in on her singing sessions at home. They wanted to sing too, and to hear her explanations of the poetry. They held up recording devices. The gatherings, which they called *satsangs*, expanded. There was singing, listening, discussion. Eventually someone who was organizing a Kabir festival in another city asked her to give a concert. Yes, they wanted the films, yes, they wanted performances by folk artists Prahlad Tipanya, Mukhtiyar Ali, and others they had met through the Kabir Project. But they wanted her too—as filmmaker *and* singer.

Shabnam and I participate in the openness and flexibility of oral tradition—which means we make choices that express our own ideological and aesthetic preferences. We try to be responsible in our interventions, but within certain limits we change and shape things. We do this in the process of selecting, organizing, translating, and interpreting songs. Shabnam now also does it as a performer. She ran into the *satī* problem with another lovely song, *Yūṇ hī man samajhāve*—"Teach your mind like this." Again, there was a series of stanzas, this time about concentration, each with a ruling metaphor. The metaphors were vivid and appealing: an acrobat climbing a wire, singing while her husband beats the drum; a village girl carrying a full water pot on her head; a snake that licks up dewdrops in the forest; a pearl diver who plunges into the sea. But in the middle came that troublesome *satī*—the woman who single-mindedly enters the flames out of devotion to her deceased husband.[35] Shabnam decided she wouldn't sing that stanza. Dropping a stanza is common in oral tradition.

We told Prahladji about our problems with the *satī* metaphor and ideal. He and others we spoke to didn't buy into our critique. I once discussed it with a group of educated women in a Kabir Panth gathering, explaining why I thought this image should not be perpetuated. They disagreed. "We are not fools," they said, "we don't plan to jump on our husbands' funeral pyres. We don't believe widows should do that. To us, this image is about courage and devotion. That's what we take from it." One of the women, the wife of a highly placed official, went further in affirming gendered values that were clearly different from mine: "To us Indian women, our husband is everything." While she and others present agreed that nobody believed in widow immolation anymore, the inner principle of fearlessly entering fire for one's beloved inspired them. They wouldn't accept my point that the gendered nature of this trope still oppresses women.

In 2006 Shabnam organized a recording session in Lunyakhedi. Prahladji sang *Yūṇ hī man samajhāve*, including the stanza about the *satī*. Shabnam, who was creating a set of audio CDs for the Kabir Project, decided to edit it out. A few years later I observed her responding differently to the same lines, under different circumstances. In the 2011 Malwa Kabir Yatra (eight days of traveling and performing, mostly in villages), at a moment of utter exhaustion when he was unexpectedly asked to sing in the morning after a night with no sleep, Prahladji asked Shabnam to sing along with him. He sang *Yūṇ hī man samajhāve*, including the *satī* verse. When he got to that verse I saw a flicker of doubt in her eyes, but then she sang right along, supporting him.

Surfing, Globalizing

Shabnam's four feature-length documentary films have been seen by many thousands of people, and their reach continues to expand.[36] The Kabir Project's ten audio CDs and one DVD of bhajan performance, with accompanying books that provide texts and translations, have reached many listeners. The next (and perhaps final) big task that the Kabir Project team in Bangalore have taken up is an internet resource for which they find the word "archive" a bit stuffy and antiquated. They sometimes call it a web-*duniyā*, web-world, and they have named the site (using an image from a bhajan) *Ajab shahar*—"Wondrous City." It is cutting-edge, interactive, artistically beautiful and intriguing. One can follow its branching paths in multiple directions, clicking between singer, explicator, text, translation, article. One can enter deeply into a keyword or theme. One can toggle between urban and rural pandits. One can shuffle and be surprised. One can browse for free, download songs for a fee, add comments and new material. The team also imagines the site as an online directory and web presence for many folk artists, helping to expand their performance opportunities.

Was Kabir already globalizing when his poetry moved from the eastern part of the Hindi region to Punjab and Rajasthan in the sixteenth century? It has always been traveling; but we reserve the word "globalization" for a much more recent sort of phenomenon, defined by exponential leaps in speed, technological sophistication, and the arcane economic connections of transnational systems. In the globalizing conditions characterized above all by the internet, texts move and change in startlingly new ways, while continuing to move and change in old ways.

When did Prahladji's transition into the global system begin? He was a village man of a poor Dalit family, living at subsistence level, his parents and wife unlettered. He managed to become more educated than others in his family, got a job as a schoolteacher, and became fascinated with a musical instrument, the *tambūrā*, which led to his learning to sing bhajans with other village men. So far, no globalization or noteworthy intervention of technology. The Eklavya Kabir *manch* project of the 1990s (see chapter 6) threw him into more prominence, giving him a chance to show his leadership qualities and to get more recognition as a singer. But the recognition had started in the 1980s and was already well advanced in 1990 when Dinesh Sharma began organizing the Kabir *manch*.

A watershed moment occurred in 1993 with the Eklavya forum's production of two cassettes of Malwi Kabir bhajans. One had a mix of different singers. The other featured Prahladji and his group. The latter became very popular. Soon more Tipanya cassettes came out, produced first by a small company in Jabalpur, then by an outfit in Bhopal. They were hits. His local fame spread far faster than it could have without the "new media." Many people in nearby districts started to hum his versions of Kabir. As his concerts multiplied, they had the added buzz of offering familiar songs, old favorites that people knew from the cassettes. Prahladji's economic status changed dramatically. Typically the cassette company would give him a lump sum at the outset, avoiding the complexity of royalties. These sums were of an order beyond what could have been injected into the family economy at any time in the past. But expenses were also mounting. For example, he needed a large car to get to all his engagements, along with his group and their instruments.

When I first met Prahladji in January 2000, I got half a dozen cassettes as gifts. In 2002 I made a list of twelve cassettes with their contents. Prahladji's home and the adjacent Kabir institute were steadily expanding.

> March 16, 2002, Lunyakhedi
> A phone call came—someone asking for a performance. P. explained to the caller what the cost would be, including fuel for the car and something for the *mandalī*. Then we walked to the *smārak* (Kabir memorial) ground, where he showed me holes that had been dug for pillars for a hall that he plans to build. "Visiting *sants* will give talks. Lots of people will come." He said he'd finance it with a cassette, which could make. . . . He cited a range of figures. "That much?" I asked. "My cassettes do very well," he said with a smile.
>
> March 18, 2002, Dewas
> As I sit on the Srishti Club terrace at 8 a.m., Vijay Kumar, the cleaner, approaches with his broom to see what I'm reading. I tell him about Kumar Gandharva. He's heard the name but doesn't know anything about him. He starts talking about Tipanyaji, who was here yesterday—I introduced them. He knows Tipanyaji's songs from the cassettes. He can sing them.[37]

Prahladji became a role model for younger men. Singing Kabir had not been prestigious before, in fact was a mark of low status. Seeing his growing success and prestige, they were attracted to doing the same.[38]

> March 19, 2002, Lunyakhedi
> I woke up from a nap to find a jam session going on in the next room. A singer from a nearby village was jamming with Devnarayan, our violinist, and a *dholak* player. The singer, Dayaram Sarolia, was showing them on the harmonium how he wanted to do the tune and repetitions—up on the middle rep, then down. He sang well. A *panchāyat* secretary, he started by listening to Prahladji, then came in person to learn from him, now sings on radio and TV. Immediately he told me he'd like to go to America.
>
> December 2010, Berkeley
> Dayaram called me from India. "I've got my passport made," he said. "Oh, very good," I replied. "All I need now is a call from you." I explained that I can't just call people to America, and that Prahladji's visits were made possible by support from the Indian Council for Cultural Relations.

When I organized Prahladji's first American tour in 2003, it was a great success. Indians in the United States were extremely enthusiastic, as were a lot of non-Indian Americans in the general public and the academic world. The Indian Council for Cultural Relations, described as an independent but government-funded agency, sponsored the tour, covering the group's international airfare. We created a CD to offer for sale, since that technology was fast replacing cassettes. Proud of myself for being the mover and shaker behind Prahladji's first performances abroad, I was in for a surprise when I arrived in Malwa in July to prepare for the tour. "We're going to England," he announced as I stepped off the bus into the monsoon mud in Maksi. "What? When?" "August." Someone had invited him to an Indian music festival in London. The whole trip would last just a week. And *that* would be his first performance abroad. So I wasn't the creator of his new international persona. I was just part of a wave that was carrying him forward. Shabnam, in the first year of intensive work on her documentary film project, joined us for three weeks in 2003, shooting scenes from this historic arrival of Malwi folk Kabir in America. In 2009 Prahladji and group had another two-month tour in the United States and Canada. This time Shabnam was an integral part of the tour, as her four major films had just been completed. Screenings and discussions of the films took place along with concerts. Cassettes were dead. We sold many CDs and DVDs. (See Figure 2.3)

FIGURE 2.3. Audio and video CD covers. Photo by Linda Hess.

The interpenetration of urban and rural singing cultures, and the explosion of interregional as well as international communication, have quickly created complex new situations in terms of text, context, transmission, and interpretation. My examples come from the ongoing and transforming Kabir Project; similar examples can no doubt be found in other realms of Indian performance. After six years of research, shooting, recording, editing, and production, Shabnam and her coworkers completed the Kabir Project's first phase: four feature-length documentaries; ten audio CDs and one DVD with performances by eleven featured singers and their accompanists; and six beautifully designed books providing texts, translations, photos, art, and commentary, to go with the recorded songs. Well before these products were finished, the singers and songs she was discovering were capturing attention in Bangalore, Delhi, Mumbai, and other metros. Shabnam herself was singing and explicating on public stages. In 2010, responding to numerous requests, she recorded her own two-CD set.

Kabir festivals have been organized in many cities, bringing together films, live performances, speakers, seminars. Committed to making the project available to non-English-speakers, Shabnam has produced versions of all the films with English portions dubbed in Hindi. In February 2010 there was a nine-day Malwa Kabir Yatra (Malwa Kabir Journey), jointly planned with local singers, Kabir Panthis, and NGO workers, moving through villages and towns with concerts, film screenings, and discussions, in Malwa, where the earliest and deepest connections to date had been made with local Kabir oral traditions. It aroused great interest and enthusiasm. Many urban fans joined the journey. A second Malwa Kabir Yatra, which I attended, took place over eight days in April 2011. Again a contingent of urban Indian and international enthusiasts joined the eight-day trek through six villages and two cities, traveling by bus in sometimes grueling conditions along with artists and organizers. A Rajasthan Kabir Yatra in 2012 was beautifully described in Vipul Rikhi's article "Travels Through Song" (http://www.openthemagazine.com/article/photographic/travels-through-song). These *yātrās*, the big-city festivals, the proliferating new audio, video, and internet resources, have contributed to the growth of urban Kabir fans, including some who learn to sing and play the *tambūrā*. Prahladji, Mukhtiyar Ali, and others have frequently been called to Mumbai, Bangalore, and other cities to coach such groups. Hitesh Shah, one of the Mumbai enthusiasts, wrote to me: "We had a workshop with Prahladji at Priti's place. He is far more riveting in his commentary on the songs, than when merely singing them. Astounding understanding in three hours." Later I met Hitesh again at a four-day workshop in Prahladji's village, using the facilities of the Kabir institute there.

Beyond Malwa, Shabnam has worked with singers in Rajasthan, Pakistan, and Kutch in Gujarat. Some of those singers were featured in her films. Others came forth after the films were finished. She learned songs from all the areas and sang some of her favorites to friends in other areas. Mukhtiyar Ali and Mahesha Ram from Rasjasthan, Prahladji and Kaluram from Malwa, Muralala from Kutch, and Fariduddin Ayaz from Karachi met each other and performed together at urban Kabir festivals. They started occasionally singing each other's songs, bringing melodies from other regions into their own home areas. One night in Lunyakhedi, I saw Vijay, Prahladji's second son, lead a *mandalī* of younger-generation singers in a powerful rendition of *Allah Hu*, which he had learned from Mukhtiyar Ali in person and through the Kabir Project films and recordings.

Perhaps my capacity to be shocked by wild new mixes of genres, styles, artists, and media will end soon, but I was still astonished by this one. Bhanwari Devi is a Rajasthani woman singer with a supremely powerful voice and mesmerizing energy whom I met in 2011 on a tour of Rajasthani villages with Gopal Singh. To me, her vocal power and extroversion were in dramatic contrast with her observance of the rural Rajasthani custom that women keep their faces covered in public: she sang through a layer of sari-cloth pulled entirely over her face. Bhanwari Devi became one of the most popular performers in the ensuing Kabir Yatras in Malwa and Rajasthan. In 2013 someone sent me a link to a performance on *Coke Studio*, a very popular music TV show in Pakistan and India that mingles traditional folk music with rock and post-rock styles, singers, and instruments. There Bhanwari Devi (her face covered with red sari cloth, over which headphones were placed) belted out a Kabir song to rocking amplified instrumentation (along with her son on harmonium). More far out: she was in a *jugalbandī* or duet with Hard Kaur (say the Punjabi-appearing name out loud and note the pun), a tattooed woman rap artist in tank top and skinny pants, who belted out her hiphop lyrics in English. The two women took turns doing passages from their songs (https://www.youtube.com/watch?v=npKCgowu-Bk). The composer-arranger of this combo, Ram Sampath, explained in a "behind the music" video clip that he saw it as a song about two "outlaws": "Both of these women ... [have] big voices, they're not going to step back, they're not going to tone down their voices for anyone. I just had to get these two energies together and watch it blaze down the highway." In the short "behind the music" video, Bhanwari Devi appears with her face uncovered, smiling broadly.

In 2011 the extraordinary Baul singer from Bengal, Parvathy Baul, joined the last three days of the Malwa Kabir Yatra, then came to Lunyakhedi for two days to begin learning Malwa Kabir songs from Prahladji (see http://parvathybaul.srijan.asia). During the *yātrā* she performed in what would have been, for the locals, a strange Bengali language and style, but audiences in village and city responded very positively. I was in Lunyakhedi with her on those two quiet days after the tumultuous *yātrā*. She sat with Prahladji and other family members, who were impressed with how swiftly she learned their songs and sang them in her rich voice. On the second night the families of the three brothers, including all the women and children, gathered in front of the main house. Parvathy put on her ankle bells, tied the drum around her waist, raised her *ektārā*, and danced and sang, her bare feet on the packed earth, her long dreadlocked hair flying along with her voice, mingling with drumbeats and the twang of the *ektārā* string. In the darkness and quiet of the village, ripples of delight went through the group. She also stood and sang out one of the new Kabir songs she had learned. The next morning at 5 a.m., she and I got into a hired car and set off for the Indore airport, two hours away, to fly to our next engagements.

Thus texts and tunes are traveling across far-flung regions suddenly—by air as much as on the ground. There has always been movement of songs from region to region, but it has never been this fast—texts and styles coming whole cloth, not piecemeal and gradual as in the past, when they might be altered bit by bit on the road till they lost the signs of their origin in another place. The bullock-cart of oral transmission has turned into a supersonic plane.[39]

Actually metaphors of physical vehicles can't carry the weight—and the weightlessness—of transmission in the twenty-first century. Many clips from documentary films and live performances are on YouTube. People all over the world pick up songs that ten years ago existed nowhere except in local oral tradition. They transcribe in their own ways, translate, post on websites, add information according to their own lights. The galloping fluency of younger people with cell phone technology in rural India is now a huge factor in the spread of texts and performances. Prahladji's village did not even have landline phone service in 2002. A decade later, the little boys I knew in the family have grown up to be strapping fellows in their twenties who are ripping performances from Shabnam's films and sending them by MMS to others in the neighborhood, or across state lines. MMS? I hadn't heard of it till I found out in 2011 that Dharmendra, the shy son of Kamla and Ambaram, who was having trouble passing school exams as a twelve-year-old, was now an expert at MMS transmission. He sang onstage with his uncle Prahladji, played harmonium, and moved with confidence in larger worlds, his sunglasses flashing, his mobile at the ready. He shot with the video camera during tours. After the 2010 Malwa Yatra, Prahladji's older son and *dholak* player Ajay reported that the hottest new thing in local ringtones was Shabnam singing Kabir! By 2012, Dharmendra and many other young village friends had established Facebook pages.[40]

Listeners are also participating in this new freedom and immediacy of transmission. Countless people use cell phones as a way of engaging with music. They record, play, download and share performances. Scholars have noted the democratizing effects of mass media. In *Cassette Culture: Popular Music and Technology in North India* (1993), Peter Manuel observed how audiocassettes, easily producible by small local companies and copied by consumers, gave considerable control in the circulation and enjoyment of music to people of all classes. He also noted that economic and political interests were mobilizing to reduce freedom of access and exchange.[41]

The internet and mobile phones have raised the play of these factors exponentially. As this book goes to press, we can glimpse the vanguard of a new kind of research in a paper called "Folk Music in India Goes Digital" (Kumar, Singh, and Parikh 2011). Neha Kumar and colleagues studied four sites in the Hindi region that are rich in folk music, including Malwa, Madhya Pradesh, where most of my research is based. They spoke to musicians, listeners, retailers, and radio producers, focusing on these questions:

(i) What are various motivations underlying the sharing and listening of folk music within these communities?
(ii) How are new media technologies influencing these practices and supporting these motivations?
(iii) How do considerations of piracy interact with these changes?

Their ten-page article suggests that in a period of just three to five years, great changes have occurred in producing, consuming, selling, sharing, and performing folk music.

> In the furthest reaches of India's rural heartland, the cellphone is bringing something that television, radio and even newspapers couldn't deliver: Instant access to music, information, entertainment, news and even worship. (Bellman quoted in Kumar, Singh, and Parikh 2011, 2)

They learned that mobile phone shops in small rural towns now keep media libraries on a desktop computer, offering music collections as a perk for other purchases. Shop owners often upload their customers' music libraries before downloading new music. CDs and cassettes have been pushed out of the market. "We stopped keeping tapes … four years ago," said one owner. "No one wants CDs anymore. Only mobile." Another owner who had been in the business a long time said, "The market of CDs and audio cassettes has gone down by 85% in the last 3–5 years." Meanwhile the demand for video is shooting up. "Five years back," said a retailer, "people were only interested in listening to music on cassettes, radio, and CDs, but now people are demanding music with video. They don't buy if you don't give them songs recorded with video." Some shop owners work with local musicians to produce video CDs (quotations in this paragraph from Kumar, Singh, and Parikh 2011, 6).

The researchers learned that mobile phones also act as communal listening devices with friends and families listening together. They observed pilgrims who walked 200 kilometers to Rajasthan's annual Ramdevra festival (which draws 1 to 1.5 million, about half of whom choose to walk). A huge proportion of those pilgrims were listening through earphones to devotional songs on their mobile phones as they walked.

They found that the musicians were ambivalent about piracy:

> Piracy leads to illegal but wider distribution of music and therefore also serves to extend the popularity and fame of many musicians. … [O]ne Bikaner artist said: "Singers are still on the safe side because when people record our music on their mobile devices at any live performance, it spreads like fire. People get to know about our good performance only through these devices and we get publicity as well as more shows to perform at. On the one hand, the CD and cassette business has gone down, but on the other, the demand for our live performances is rising" (Kumar, Singh, and Parikh 2011, 7).

Finally, they reported comments suggesting both a decrease in quality of music and an increase in empowerment of musicians:

> With the availability of low-cost and easy-to-use recording devices, the technological skills and capacity required for producing and distributing music need not be limited only to local businesses. Musicians and/or their troupes and families can be empowered to create, share, and market their own recordings. This would allow more musicians (and not just the more famous ones) to get their music into the market. ... Due to the increase in piracy and low-cost distribution, the quality of music the community is listening to has ... suffered. Access to a much wider variety of musicians, recordings and recording qualities may also lead to a less cultivated sense of taste and thoughtful listening. As an artist from Bikaner stated: "Those who have 500 songs in their mobiles are constantly changing songs without paying attention to any particular song. They don't know what to listen to" (Kumar, Singh, and Parikh 2011, 8).

From YouTube to WikiLeaks to policy debates on net neutrality, we see the internet as a source of tremendous power and as a ground of new contestations. Democratic, egalitarian, and class-transcending forces partake of this power, as do totalizing, repressive, and exploitative ones. Focusing down to Kabir music and texts in early twenty-first-century India (as in a Google map, when we zoom from a huge satellite view to a neighborhood), we can say that the democratizing effects of digital technology, with all their turbulent and unpredictable turns, are in the foreground.[42] How will these instantaneous, local, and global media change the ways in which Kabir texts are transmitted and altered, the people who have power over the texts, and the economic factors that play into the process? Will the arrival and dominance of electronic media be comparable to older transitions in the history of media and transmission? Will there be fundamental differences? These are questions to be taken up by a new generation of scholars.

3

True Words of Kabir

ADVENTURES IN AUTHENTICITY

sāncha śhabda kabīr kā, hriday dekhu bichārā
chit de ke samujhe nahi, mohi kahata juga chārā

Kabir's true word—
look in your heart and think.
They strain their brains but can't understand.
I've been saying this for ages.[1]

AFTER SO MUCH discussion of the fluidity, immensity, and creative complexity of oral traditions, can we pass on without mentioning the question of authenticity? No, we can't, even though the very word "authenticity" is a booby trap for scholars of Kabir. Determination to establish a critical edition and stake out an authentic corpus is associated with Orientalist scholarship, best left behind in the twentieth (if not the nineteenth) century. Yet we can't escape the discussion. While deconstruction, postcoloniality, and reception theory have undermined old notions of authorship and authenticity, more subtle and multilayered notions are still interesting.[2] Either "Kabir" is a vast undifferentiated mishmash of everything ever associated with his name in the last 600 years, or some further process of clarification is possible. This chapter reflects on ways of imagining such a process. On the razor-edge path between claiming to have an authoritative edition and refusing to discuss the matter, we will observe various discourses of authenticity and see where they lead.[3]

The urge toward authenticity is powerful. When discussing texts sung by folk singers, or citing lines of poetry in a talk, I am frequently asked, "Is this authentic? How can we know what Kabir really composed?" Most people assume that there should be a way to discriminate among the centuries of accumulating "Kabir" texts, but criteria for doing so remain stubbornly elusive. Text editors anchor historical claims to early manuscripts. Common sense suggests modern language and anachronism as tip-offs to the inauthentic. Ideology inclines some readers to accept and others to reject the same material, depending on what they happen to believe about Kabir. This chapter will demonstrate methods, findings, and conclusions characteristic of several approaches: (a) studying manuscripts with a view to establishing the earliest verifiable textual records and the subsequent history of texts; (b) attempting to trace intertextualities between written and oral sources; (c) immersing oneself in oral traditions; (d) tracing the metamorphoses of Kabir through historical documents and ethnographic inquiries, with no attempt to find the "real" Kabir; and (e) imagining a large field in which these approaches exist together and sometimes communicate with each other. As a prologue to these explorations, I offer three stories.

A Scholar Changes His Mind

In 1995 Bahadur Singh, an Indian scholar based at the University of Hamburg, Germany, went to Rajasthan to collect oral Kabir. He found Kabir singers in almost every village in the widespread areas he visited. Having recorded 300 songs, he was in the process of transcribing them when he gave a report at a conference in 1997. In his conference paper, amid observations about songs and singers, he says: "For those of us who are interested in Sant literature the most important question is of course that of authenticity." Then he compares the text of a song recorded by classical singer Kumar Gandharva with the versions of two rural Rajasthani singers. Noting that the Rajasthani singers included four lines that were absent in Kumarji's version, he wonders how to prove whether or not these four lines are "genuine." His concluding sentence: "A fundamental aim of future research has to be to develop criteria of authenticity" (Offredi 2000, 419–23).

In a later conference paper on the same research (presented in 1999, published in 2002), Singh is still concerned about authenticity but emphasizes the near-impossibility of establishing it: "In the huge majority of texts, at any rate those orally transmitted, there can be no proof of authenticity or inauthenticity" (Horstmann 2002, 196). He suggests that in the world of oral Kabir, we should renounce our historical cravings and inquire instead into meanings and criteria as understood by singers and devotees:

> The historical point of view ... has no meaning for the Kabir devotees; to them Kabir was a seer and therefore ... he could, quite naturally, have spoken with Mira or with Gorakhnath. ... He could also have foreseen the arrival of rail technology and composed a song where the body is the engine, and the soul-passenger is advised not to lose her ticket. (Horstmann 2002, 195–96)[4]

When Singh asked a blind sadhu singer how he knew that a *vāṇī* (utterance) was really Kabir's own, the singer replied: "If a *vāṇī* has a profound meaning, then of course it is Kabir's; if not, it is only an imitation" (Horstmann 2002, 197).

If Bahadur Singh had stuck to research based on written texts, his assumptions about the importance of authenticity in the narrow sense might have remained intact. But he went into the field, where he awakened to new worlds of text, context, performance, and interpretation. He concluded that our methods of study should be different for these different domains. In the world of oral performance we should be ethnographers, inquiring into the understandings of singers and devotees and dropping the quest for original utterances of Kabir. He leaves open the possibility that in the world of dated manuscripts and critical editions, we can still pursue what is genuine.

The Super-Bijak

The *Mahābījak* is a huge tome assembled by Gangasharan Shastri, a high-ranking *mahant* (religious authority and ritual officiant) of the Kabir Chaura (Varanasi-based) division of the Kabir Panth. This tradition has long accepted the *Bījak* as Kabir's *mūl granth* (root, i.e., original text), the only indisputably authentic collection. The *Bījak* is a small book. So what inspired Shastri to make this very large book, which was published in 1998?

First, Kabir Panthis felt the same tension that Bahadur Singh and I and others who have looked at oral and written traditions have felt. Kabir's popularity throughout North and Central India has little to do with the poems of the *Bījak* or the *Granthāvalī* or any other early written collection.[5] The vast body of bhajans has almost no overlap with the *Bījak*. How can the Panth acknowledge and tap into Kabir's popularity and power in the living culture? They also felt something that might be called sectarian book-envy. Other sects and religions have big books, Shastri observed, and we should also have a big book. In this passage from his introduction (translated from Hindi), he tacitly abandons the position that the *Bījak* is the only authentic text:

> Shri Sadguru Kabir Sahab ... has composed countless verses, filled with countless kinds of wisdom. Never having been collected in one volume, these verses are published only in many small books. Since his compositions have never been fully collected in one place, we haven't had access to the fullness of Kabir Sahab's wisdom. In the Kabir Panth we felt the need for one complete volume containing all the verses. The problem was: among the thousands of verses attributed to Kabir, how to select the genuine ones? We have been working on the *Mahābījak* continuously for the past fifteen years. . . . Especially the Kabir Panthis from Punjab and Jammu-Kashmir urged us, saying that the other sects that came up after us have served their people by collecting all their sacred verses into one volume. But we haven't managed to collect the works of Kabir Sahab, the founder of the entire *sant* tradition. What a shameful matter this is! So many little sects that don't even have any philosophy have still managed to pull all their compositions into one volume. (Shastri 1998, iii–iv)

On June 26, 2002, I discussed the *Mahābījak* with Shastri.

LINDA HESS (LH): Do you consider everything in the *Mahābījak* authentic [*pramāṇik*]?

GANGASHARAN SHASTRI (GSS): Yes, everything is authentic.

LH: Where did you get all that material?

GSS: I spent 25–30 years searching and collecting. I used manuscripts, printed and oral sources, and collections from other sects like the Dadu, Niranjani, and Sikh Panths.

LH: How did you decide what to accept and what to reject?

GSS: I accepted [a text] if it was in accord with the principles [*siddhānt*] of Kabir. There were also linguistic considerations [*bhāṣā vigyān*]—whether

> the language was old or not. But even if the language was modern, if the ideas [*vichārdhārā*] were correct I might still accept it.[6]

The *Mahābījak* made its way to Kalapini Komkali, a classical singer, the daughter and disciple of the late Kumar Gandharva (see Hess 2009a). Since childhood Kalapini has been steeped in the Kabir bhajans her father was famous for singing. While doing fieldwork for the present book, I was also writing a book about Kabir and Kumar Gandharva, a project in which she and other family members were giving invaluable help. Once she asked me to look for a collection of songs by Dharamdas. I found one at Damakheda, Chhattisgarh, the headquarters of the Kabir Panth lineage that reveres Dharamdas as Kabir's original disciple and founder of the Panth. I then got a copy of the *Mahābījak* from Kabir Chaura, Varanasi, a rival lineage, and presented the two books to Kalapini and her nephew Bhuvan, also a classical singer in Kumar Gandharva's tradition. The next time we met, they announced that both books were largely useless, because they were full of inauthentic texts. The Dharamdas book, Kalapini said, was rife with modern language and influence of film songs. Bhuvan scanned the *Mahābījak* and came up with the same judgment: inauthentic. He offered a dramatic example. The *Mahābījak* includes a poem that begins with this couplet:

> *vo jo garbha mẽ dukh thā jabar / tujhe yād ho ke na yād ho*
> *āyā thā tū tab kaval kar / tujhe yād ho ke na yād ho.* (Shastri 1998, 785)
> In the womb, when you felt that strong pain—do you remember or not?
> You made a promise, then you came out—do you remember or not?

The poem continues with eight more couplets, each of which ends with the half-line *tujhe yād ho ke na yād ho*—"Do you remember or not?" This, Kalapini and Bhuvan informed me, was a blatant copy of a *ghazal, Tumhe yād ho ke na yād ho,* that the singer Begum Akhtar (1914–74) had recorded and made famous.[7] The alleged Kabir bhajan and the *ghazal* both begin with the relative pronouns *vo jo* and have the same metrical pattern, repeating the same phrase in the refrain. But the rest of the bhajan text is filled with typical Kabir themes and images, while the *ghazal* follows typical motifs of that genre.[8] To Kalapini and Bhuvan this showed that the book was not worth taking seriously. To an archaeologist of the Kabir tradition, however, it is quite interesting. Through such shards of evidence, we can begin to say something historically credible about the ways in which oral traditions develop and change.

Bhuvan offered another hypothesis: that the prevalence of certain Urdu words like *divānā* and *mastānā* (both meaning "mad" or "ecstatic") in Kabir songs was due to the influence of Urdu poetry in the nineteenth and twentieth centuries. I did a quick check on this by consulting the *Millennium Kabir* (Callewaert 2000), where texts are sorted according to their appearance in early dated manuscripts. In manuscripts of the late sixteenth and early seventeenth centuries, I found that *divānā* occurs with some regularity. So at least that word cannot be linked to the influence of recent Urdu poetry, though there might still be merit in Bhuvan's theory that *ghazals* and other Urdu musical-poetic forms influenced oral Kabir from the nineteenth century onward.

One could dig up many examples of how things get added to the growing corpus of Kabir *vāṇī*. But even after throwing out all the film songs and other flagrantly looted items, we will still be casting about, looking for some sieve through which we can pass the myriad things that supposedly "Kabir says."

Trapped by Authenticity

I gave a talk at the Sahitya Akademi in 2002 in which I took up the debates about authenticity. My intention was to discuss discourses of authenticity, not to determine what is really authentic. But I did not do a good job of this. Journalists reported that I was pressing the search for the authentic Kabir, and some scholars who were present reacted as if I were the ghost of nineteenth-century Indology. One person suggested that I should try thinking about social history. Flustered, I replied that my whole project was about the social life of Kabir. This fact, I realized later, was rendered invisible by my decision to talk on that occasion about the problem of authenticity.

The Hindi scholars of Kabir I have known in the last fifteen years have been extremely dubious if not downright hostile toward critical editing projects, which are redolent of colonial histories and attitudes. At the Sahitya Akademi meeting, the idea of searching for a "core" met with skepticism. Jokes were made about Winand Callewaert's star system, in which he rates poems from early manuscripts with one, two, or three stars, to indicate their proximity to an early core of Kabir texts (to be discussed in detail in the next section). Those in attendance were willing to vote in a lighthearted way when I offered a set of verses and asked them to say which ones could or could not be by Kabir. They did have opinions about the nature of Kabir's voice. But if we had tried to establish criteria, the discussion would have been very contentious.

Reading, Writing, Dating: The World of Text Editors

> "I can understand that a translator of Kabir may look for a nice song without bothering about its authenticity. But let us not start writing commentaries on Kabir and 15th-century Banaras quoting those songs."
>
> (Callewaert 2000, vii)

> "If there is a way to find order in the chaos, it is by looking at the earliest mss." (ibid., 104)

Not only do scholars strongly prefer to work with written texts (as discussed in chapter 2), but a major industry in the economy of textual study has been to *establish* correct texts where multiple forms exist. The practice of producing critical editions has a robust history among European and North American scholars in the nineteenth and twentieth centuries. South Asians have also been serious text editors, a famous example being the nineteen-volume critical edition of the *Mahābhārata*, produced over a period of five decades by a team of scholars headed by V. S. Sukhtankar at the Bhandarkar Oriental Research Institute, Pune, India.[9]

In recent decades there has been a transition in the premises underlying text-editing projects. Basically, the idea of an urtext is going away. From a determination to establish a singular authoritative text—as much as possible, the text actually composed by the author—the enterprise of critical editing has become a historical one that aims to show how a body of texts has developed, with ever-weakening claims to "authenticity." J. S. Hawley, ahead of the curve in this trend, demonstrated a historical approach to Surdas manuscripts in an article originally published in 1979 (later included in Hawley 2005). Kenneth Bryant provides a brilliant and mature statement of the position in his introduction to the monumental edition and translation of poetry attributed to Surdas (Bryant and Hawley 2015). After showing how editors discover multiple versions of the same poem, he asks and answers these crucial questions:

> Which version is "right," "original," or "better"? Which one was sung by a man named Surdas, or might he indeed have sung all eleven, or none? And how might we decide? And why might we care?
>
> The traditional approach to answering such questions rests on the assumption of an authorial original surviving in imperfect copies, which the scholar corrects so as to restore the text the author intended. This does not apply in the case of Sur. While many manuscripts available in India today bear the famous title, no two are remotely the same. There is in fact no "original" *Sūrsāgar* to be reconstructed.
>
> The picture that emerges instead from the early manuscript evidence is of a steadily evolving and proliferating oral tradition. Poems were taught by singer to singer, and the corpus of poems known to the tradition grew rapidly from generation to generation. This growth occurred through two processes: the composition of new poems, and the accretion to the "Surdas" corpus of poems previously ascribed to other, less famous poets. Along with the constant addition of "new" poems, the manuscripts also reflect a ceaseless transformation of the old: each poem appears in almost as many different versions as there are manuscripts that contain it. For the most part these versions differ in ways that suggest, not the careless errors of scribes, but the exuberant and imaginative improvisations of singers. (Bryant and Hawley 2015, xxvi–xxvii)

A similar trend in Kabir text study is reflected in the title of a recent paper by Jaroslav Strnad: "Searching for the Source or Mapping the Stream?: Some Text-critical Issues in the Study of Medieval Bhakti." Strnad foregrounds the metaphor of "mapping" in contrast with "source":

> It can be argued that this kind of variation is closely related to the predominantly performative character of many poems—either authored by the sants themselves or inspired by them and composed by others. It may be futile to search for the "authentic" or original version of a particular poem that has come down to us embedded in the broad current of a living tradition borne for centuries by predominantly oral and performative presentations that involve a significant degree of improvisation. Rather than looking for Ur-texts, philological and comparativist methods might be used to map the dynamic flows—the cross- and undercurrents—that constitute, in the long term, a particular tradition (Strnad forthcoming).[10]

Strnad cites Finnish scholar Lauri Honko (2000), applying his theory of "organic variation" between oral and written traditions to the study of Kabir manuscripts:

> In an oral tradition there may be more than one authorial version and, of course, more than one variant of each of these several authorial versions in consequence of their having been presented by still other performers before their different audiences. The extant Kabirian texts incorporated into different collections ... reflect this orality-based diversity. Yet the texts that have come down to us in the manuscripts appear to be products not only of oral traditions but of written ones as well—two traditions, sometimes parallel and sometimes intersecting.
>
> Under such circumstances, any attempt by authors of "critical editions" to arrive at the original version of a poem (an Ur-text) amounts to little more than the addition of another variant to the already existing ones. Actually, the structure of the pad, with its relatively free ordering of more or less self-contained distichs, is an ideal form for variation through interpolations and/or elisions, as the need may be, of lines, distichs, and even larger blocks of text. These can emphasize, dilute or subtly modify the basic idea of the pad without destroying its internal coherence. (Strnad forthcoming)

Callewaert's premise, cited above, still holds. If we want to treat Kabir as a historical figure—if we want to make any statement about his life, times, thought, and compositions—we have to grapple with the written records and begin to sort out the old from the recent (which, for manuscript scholars, is virtually equivalent to separating the core from the marginal). On this assumption a series of scholars in India and abroad have taken on the task of collecting, analyzing, and editing manuscripts, often providing introductions, notes, and charts that present their understanding of manuscript histories. Some of them seem to be aiming at uncovering an original and authentic Kabir. Others are aware that they are undertaking a historical project that can never reach back to the "original Kabir," though none has stated that position as unequivocally and radically as Bryant has done for Surdas.

Significant names in the history of Kabir textual scholarship include Shyamsundar Das (1928), P. N. Tiwari (1961), Shukdev Singh (1972), Charlotte Vaudeville (1974, 1982, 1993), Winand Callewaert with collaborators Swapna

Sharma and Dieter Taillieu (2000), and Jaroslav Strnad (2013).[11] All of them assembled collections, with varying amounts of scholarly apparatus, that were supposed to be more reliable than the vast and uncontrolled popular Kabir traditions. Scholars who used multiple sources divided their collections into groups by various criteria, such as date, region, or context (sectarian or courtly). They created concordances; compared poems, lines, and words; and devised formulas to determine a credible body of texts. Vaudeville worked with Tiwari's edition, but she granted that its value is limited because it does not discriminate between old and recent collections. Shyamsundar Das, one of the towering twentieth-century historians of Hindi literature, edited the 1928 *Kabīr Granthāvalī* based on a single Rajasthani manuscript, which he thought was written in 1504. The colophon later proved to be false, but everyone agrees that it is an old and important manuscript. Callewaert, Sharma, and Taillieu (2000) have edited in a truly critical way despite problems in the production of their final publication.[12] Strnad, working on one of the most important texts provided by Callewaert, has carried the process to a new level of careful detail.

All of the scholars mentioned above except Shukdev Singh focused their attention on manuscripts from western India. In discussions of Kabir's written traditions, it has been common to speak of western and eastern sources, meaning chiefly the Dadu Panthi and Sikh collections in Rajasthan and Punjab, and the *Bījak* in the Uttar Pradesh(U.P.)-Bihar region (Hess 1987b; Hawley 2005, 279–304). Shukdev Singh, my collaborator in translating the *Bījak* in the late 1970s, published a critical edition of the *Bījak* in 1972, based on manuscripts representing different Kabir Panth lineages. The great obstacle to including the *Bījak* in the search for an early "core" is that the earliest dated manuscript of the *Bījak* that he was able to find was written in 1805. I am not aware of any earlier *Bījak* manuscript that has turned up in the four decades since Singh's edition. This does not absolutely prove that the *Bījak* is a very late arrival in the Kabir tradition, but it is a huge problem for those (including myself) who would like to take it seriously. Of the editors listed above, Vaudeville and Tiwari include the *Bījak* in one of the textual clusters that they reckon with. It is omitted from the set of manuscripts on which Callewaert bases his "early core," because there is no dated copy within his cutoff date of 1681. He does, however, indicate which *pad*s in that early core also occur in the *Bījak*.

There is more to this problem than my personal attachment to the *Bījak* (which was the basis of my doctoral work and first book), or the strong claims of the Kabir Panth that their revered text must be taken seriously. The big problem I see today is that the whole of eastern India is left out when we deal only with early dated manuscripts. Kabir lived in the eastern part of the Hindi region.[13] From present U.P. through Bihar, is there really no verifiable written trace of Kabir earlier than 1800? Why do we have so much material between the 1570s and 1680s from Rajasthan and Punjab, far to the West, and nothing at all from the East, Kabir's own area? We know that the appropriate sectarian organizations, the *nirguṇ panth*s, were present in the West, primed and ready to collect poetry favored by their gurus. The Dadu Panth and Sikh Panth did this work in the late sixteenth and early seventeenth centuries. Were there no comparable *nirguṇ panth*s in the East? Are there historical reasons why eastern sects did not compile vernacular collections, or why libraries or other institutions might have been unstable or destroyed in the East? Callewaert and Lath (1989, 82) mention the wealth of manuscripts in Rajasthan: "Rajasthan is a treasure-house for manuscript hunters. There have not been too many floods, rulers were patrons of art and literature and several *panth*s protected their manuscripts jealously. Was that an imitation of the Jain *bhaṇḍār*s or the result of a sect's *nirguṇ* devotion to the book?" Further historical research is needed.[14]

None of the critical editors claims to be presenting the original utterances that came out of Kabir's mouth. They propose to take us closer to the "core," to show which poems are attested in multiple sources, to eliminate works that belong to manifestly later layers.[15] Callewaert limits his final sources to manuscripts dated 1582–1681, puts them into four groups that he considers relevant for revealing the early provenance of Kabir, and works out a system of one, two, or three stars for a core body of poems, based on how many of these groups of manuscripts a poem appears in. The more stars a poem has, the closer to the center of the corpus he proposes to place it. His edition emanates from a hot core of 48 three-star poems to cooler circles of two-star, one-star, and no-star members of the overall selection of 593 poems.[16]

In 1961, Tiwari devised eleven groups of diversely sourced materials and created systems for prioritizing texts based on how many groups they appeared in. Vaudeville's *Kabīr-Vāṇī* (1982) reproduces and comments on Tiwari's edition. As Callewaert points out, Tiwari mixes dated manuscripts with uncritically edited late print collections, which seriously undermines the value of his edition. Callewaert maintains an early cut-off date for his manuscript sources, has fewer groups, uses computerized methods to analyze their contents, and publishes all the versions, with variants, of the 593 poems that make the cut. He limits his claims about authenticity:

> I argue that with certainty we can only say that the version of Kabir's songs found in the 17th century manuscripts is the version commonly used by singers then. And secondly, the songs which occur in most repertoires, in different regions, have a better chance of having been composed by Kabir. (Callewaert 2000, 2)

He also suggests that the very earliest manuscripts (ca. 1580) give us a glimpse of the songs "that may have been popular in the repertoires around 1550" (ibid.).

Callewaert's method of "catching" early compositions is excellent; yet there are gaps in the net. We must keep in mind the long interval between Kabir's death and the major early manuscripts. Even the earliest large written collection of Kabir—found in the *Goindval pothis* that were compiled in the 1570s in Punjab, close drafts for the 1604 *Ādi Granth*, sacred book of the Sikhs—was assembled more than fifty years after Kabir's death, if we accept the conventional 1518 as his latest possible death date. The gap increases to 170 years if we go with the 1448 death date proposed by some scholars. In chapter 2, we got a ground-level view of how singers and other transmitters change the texts they get, even from day to day. If, with Callewaert, we extend the category of "early manuscripts" to 1681, the temporal effects of orality multiply tremendously.

But the variables are not just temporal; they are also spatial, social, and ideological. When poems show up thousands of kilometers away from Kabir's home, in different cultural, linguistic, religious, and political environments, the kinds of changes they go through are affected by much more than the passage of time. In "Kabir in His Oldest Dated Manuscript," J. S. Hawley describes the Fatehpur manuscript. Preserved in royal Rajasthani libraries and clearly dated 1582, this text contains 345 poems, the vast majority devoted to Krishna. Scattered among these are fifteen poems attributed to Kabir. Hawley comments: "Who is this Kabir, as reflected in the Fatehpur manuscript? Given the work's general orientation, it will come as little surprise that he feels a good bit more Vaishnava than some other Kabirs we know and love" (Hawley 2005, 283). Hawley then lists the Vaishnav names for God that abound in the poems bearing Kabir's name. Along with this presence, he observes absences:

> [T]here is an almost complete absence of Islamic or otherwise Urdu or Persian vocabulary in the language of the Fatehpuri Kabir. … [Kabir] is not … the common enemy of Hindus and Muslims (or rather Turks), as we might expect on the basis of some of the best known utterances attributed to him, since he makes no reference to either group in the Fatehpur poems. We simply do not meet any *qāzis* here, even as the butt of criticism, and when he does on one occasion summon a pundit to the bar (12.3), calling him "brother" (12.2), the man's identity as a Hindu seems not to be at issue. Not once in these poems do we find the celebrated face-off that animates a number of famous Kabir compositions, with Hindus and Muslims arrayed on opposite sides of the caesura only to join common cause as Rām-Rahīm or Allah-Rām before the poem ends—or to be dismissed equally with a stroke of Kabir's sharp tongue. This Hindu/Muslim program is one of the aspects of Kabir that Nabhadas most celebrates in his description of Kabir, probably written sometime between 1600 and 1625, so its absence in the Fatehpur collection is striking. Here we simply do not find the Kabir who talked of yogis, *mahants*, and *śāktas*; of *miyāṅs*, *sultāns*, and *mullāhs*. The whole fabulous street-scene panoply of Banaras is absent, and if Kabir was a weaver, a *julāhā*, you would never know it from the Fatehpur collection. (Hawley 2005, 285–86)

The religious and courtly environments in which these written texts appear significantly shape their content, weighing against the mere power of the early date to persuade us that they "have a better chance of having been composed by Kabir."[17]

Purushottam Agrawal's books and articles (most in Hindi, some in English) since 2000 have made him the leading scholar of Kabir in any language. I admire Agrawal's work and have found him an invaluable conversation partner, provocateur, and friend. In this chapter, I differ with some of his conclusions while always appreciating his sharp arguments and original insights. My discussion of Agrawal's views on texts and discourses of authenticity is based on chapter 4 of his landmark book *Akath kahānī prem kī: kabīr kī kavitā aur unkā samay/The Untellable Story of Love: Kabir's Poetry and Times* (2009a). His commentary on Winand Callewaert's work is on 204–13 of that chapter.

Agrawal is very critical of Callewaert, focusing more on what he perceives as a misguided and haughty attitude than on the ultimate results of Callewaert's careful winnowing of the texts. He perceives a certain neocolonial arrogance, even hints of racism, in Callewaert's assertions of scholarly "rigor." Agrawal's critique raises issues to which all of us should pay attention. But on the question of Callewaert's editing methods (not to mention the implication of racism), the critique is far too harsh. Why aren't previous textual scholars who tried to sift through manuscript collections subjected to similar criticism? Why not also dismiss Hawley's work on the growth of the *Sūrsāgar* (Hawley 2005), Byrant and Hawley's momumental work *Sur's Ocean: Poems from the Early Tradition*, and other critical editing projects with which Agrawal is familiar?[18]

The particular critique of Callewaert seems to have been touched off by his brief suggestion of Brahminical bias on the part of the great progenitor of Kabir studies in Hindi, H. P. Dvivedi: "Kabir very soon was 'appropriated' by interested parties (from the Gorakhnathis and the Ramanandis in the 17th century to the Brahmins like Hazariprasad Dvivedi or other social groups in the 20th century) for their own ideological purpose or benefit" (Callewaert 2000, 2). Later Callewaert says of Dvivedi's introduction, "I cannot help calling [it] a Brahminical appropriation of Kabir" (ibid., 15). These statements lead Agrawal into an intriguing tangent on colonial Indology, the history of Christianity, institutionalized religion, and the politics of scholarship in Indian "vernacular modernity" (a key term in his theory of modern cultural history in India). The critique of Callewaert's editing is intertwined with these larger arguments, as Agrawal detects the scent of colonial presumption and misinformation in the work. He associates Callewaert's "star system" with the European and Christian histories of imperiously controlling texts and narratives—whether through narrow text-editing projects; ruthless elimination of competing narratives (as in the editing of the Bible); or constructions by colonial rulers of the colony's history and culture. Elsewhere Agrawal has written forcefully about intellectual identity politics, presenting searing critiques of Dharamvir and others who make caste identity the key to who can speak of Kabir and how readers should judge what is said (Agrawal 2001). Callewaert's suggestion that Dvivedi is biased because he is a Brahmin calls forth the same critique from Agrawal. While "identity politics" in scholarship is an important topic, I do not intend to take up that discussion here, apart from saying that the accusations against Callewaert are, in my view, excessive. My interest here is in narrower questions about the validity of Callewaert's method of editing the texts.

Unfriendly to the "star system," Agrawal has a very different way of evaluating the manuscript sources. Agreeing in principle that it is important to differentiate some early source(s) from the huge accretions of "Kabir" that have built up over centuries, he makes a strong case for accepting the *Granthāvalī* of Shyamsundar Das—published in 1928 and based on a single Rajasthani manuscript written by followers of the *nirguṇ* guru Dadu in about 1620—as the best representative of the oldest manuscript layers. He points out that of the 403 poems in Das's *Granthāvalī*, 396 are present among Callewaert's collection of 593. Along with this overlap, he explains that the *Granthāvalī* offers a rich range of themes associated with Kabir, with no overemphasis on certain themes at the expense of others, and no censorship of verses even if they run counter to Dadu Panthi views.[19] Convinced that the *Granthāvalī* is relatively free of sectarian bias, Agrawal goes so far as to describe Dadu Panthi compilers as objective and scientific. He discusses a range of attitudes that might have influenced manuscript editors as they chose texts from oral sources to commit to writing:

> Some manuscript-makers drew ideological boundaries around their collections, while others, not concerned with such boundaries, based their collections on scientific, objective models. Because of its objectivity and scientific approach, the *Granthāvalī* is the most credible source of Kabir compositions. ... Unlike the compilers of the [Dadu Panthi] *Panchvāṇī* and *Sārvangī*, those of the *Ādi Granth* and *Bījak* had their own ideological purposes and editorial methods. ... The *Ādi Granth* does not include all the poets and compositions that were available at that time, but only those that would promote Sikh ideas. The same applies to the compositions in the *Bījak*. (Agrawal 2009a, 217–18)

He elaborates on why the *Granthāvalī* seems objective:

> The *Granthāvalī* grasps the personality of Kabir in a persuasive fashion. It gives a balanced view of the Kabir who flashes forth in the oral tradition's poems and legends. Most importantly, we find absolutely no attempt in the *Granthāvalī*'s Kabir to raise up a singular image of Kabir. This is not a robotic or computer-produced Kabir, but rather a human being with rich, multi-leveled sensibilities. Rather than finding mechanical consistency, we recognize a Kabir with internal struggles and debates. There are poems that criticize hypocrisy and oppose the ideology of *varṇāshram* [Brahminical

> doctrines on caste and life-stages]. There are poems soaked in the juice of love, poems in the voice and form of a woman, and poems insulting women. There are poems of yogic symbolism, poems in *ulaṭbāṃsī* ["upside-down language," a riddling and paradoxical style], and poems tinged by Vaishnav symbols, stories and beliefs. It is certainly not the case that the *Granthāvalī* lacks social criticism, but it is also not the case that it is filled only with such "harsh words."[20] (ibid., 215)
>
> The unique importance of the Dadupanthi sources, i.e. the *Granthāvalī* tradition, is that they have preserved Kabir's *vāṇī* without any ideological censorship. The Panth was Dadu's, but Dadu himself had boundless respect and gratitude toward Kabir, and thus it was necessary to collect his *vāṇī* with the utmost care. At the time of compilation, Kabir's *vāṇī* was not passed through the sieve of Dadu Panthi beliefs, and thus the particularity of his voice was preserved. The *Granthāvalī*'s Kabir is not some cut-and-pared-down Kabir; it is the complete Kabir. (ibid., 219)

I question Agrawal's assumptions about Dadu and his manuscript compilers. How is it possible to know the quality of Dadu's respect and gratitude to Kabir, and therefore his care in collecting Kabir *vāṇī*? Why not make the same claim about the Sikh gurus?[21] For comparison, I cite statements in the bibliographical notes of P. D. Barthwal's 1936 work, *The Nirguna School of Hindi Poetry*. At one point he affirms that the *Kabir Granthāvalī* edited by Shyamsundar Das "is singularly free from all sectarian affectation which is usually found in the works officially authorized by sects" (Barthwal 1936, 274). But soon afterward he makes a similar statement about the *Ādi Granth*: "Though Sikhism is at present as much a sect as any, yet the *Granth* is absolutely free from sectarianism" (ibid., 282). In between, he seems to backtrack on his claim of nonsectarianism in the Dadu Panth, suggesting that the compilers of the Dadu Panth's "Panch bani ... have shown no love for Nanak's banis though the latter was earlier in time than Dadu" (ibid., 278).

Agrawal's main argument for the *Granthāvalī*'s freedom from sectarian bias is that it embraces all possible themes and styles, even those that contrast dramatically with each other. I question whether this is automatically evidence of the true Kabir. One might argue the opposite: if Kabir did have a distinct personality and particular views, he might not be best represented by works that include a tremendous diversity of viewpoints. The claim that Das's *Granthāvalī* lacks sectarian bias is further undermined by the presence of verses like these: "Kabir, blessed is that woman who has given birth to a Vaiṣṇava son"; and "Keep away from the Śākta, though he be a Brāhmaṇ,/ associate with Vaiṣṇava, though he be a Caṇḍāl./ Meet him with open arms,/ As if you had found Gopal" (Vaudeville 1974, 186, and S.Das 1970, 41).

I can agree, finally, that the *Granthāvalī* is a very good crystallization of the earliest sources, maybe even the best single collection, as Purushottam Agrawal argues. But I can't accept the argument that it stands apart from all other sectarian collections in its objectivity. To appreciate and evaluate the early written collections of Kabir, we should look equally at all of them, assessing their different sectarian or courtly origins, their geographical locations, constituencies, content, and language—along with their dates. In this effort, the work that Callewaert has done is very valuable. It comes up with a "core" that is quite close to the *Granthāvalī*—thus supporting the latter's particular value. But it also offers much more information that we can work with in various ways.[22] It offers persuasive grounds for the value of the *Granthāvalī*, not simply the assertion that it is more objective or more comprehensive in its styles and subject matters.

To conclude this section on the manuscript mindset, I reiterate that Callewaert does not claim to have found the authentic Kabir or to have produced the definitive critical edition. He simply argues two points: first, "the version of Kabir's songs found in the 17th century manuscripts is the version commonly used by singers then." This is uncontroversial, but we should say "there" as well as "then." These versions were commonly sung by singers at that time and *in those places* where the collections were made. His second claim cuts closer to the bone of the authenticity discourse: "the songs which occur in most repertoires, in different regions, have a better chance of having been composed by Kabir" (Callewaert 2000, 2). This conclusion is intuitively attractive, yet the gaps in the net—particularly the absence of manuscripts from the East, the lapse of time between Kabir's death and the earliest written records, and the long distance between Kabir's home and those early manuscripts from Rajasthan and Punjab—must make it very tentative.[23]

Reading and Listening: The World of Oral-Written Intertextuality

Unlike previous scholars of Kabir, Purushottam Agrawal pays attention to the difference between oral and written traditions and thinks seriously about the former. From the beginning to the present, he points out, oral and written sources have been "face to face" in the development of Kabir. While respectful of manuscript researchers, he states emphatically that the presence of texts in manuscripts cannot be our only model. In this connection he quotes a story told by the Pakistani *qawwālī* singer Farid Ayaz, published by Shabnam Virmani's Kabir Project:

> Shamsher used to ply a donkey cart to earn a living. He knew so much poetry of Kabir. Once I heard him down the lane—playing a small *dholak* [drum] ... singing Kabir. 10–15 people gathered around him and the singing went on through the night. I was just 10–11 years old then. When I heard him sing, tears began to flow from my eyes. That was when a love of Kabir arose in my heart. And I began to listen, understand, fill Kabir inside myself... from such a man, whom the world considers a donkey-cart man! Kabir's knowledge you will not get from universities, scholars and professors. For that you will have to go near Kabir himself. You'll have to break free of all your shackles and go![24]

Just as the written traditions have preserved Kabir over centuries, so have the oral. One of Agrawal's major contributions in *Akath kahānī prem kī* is a theory of modernity that differentiates between Europe-derived "colonial modernity" and Indian "vernacular modernity," tracing their developments and interactions from the early modern period to the present. In the matter of textual histories, he asserts that colonial modernity has bequeathed its obsession with "authentic and consistent" written sources and its ignorant disregard of orality, while vernacular modernity understands and appreciates both. An extensive quotation from Agrawal is worthwhile here:

> In any nation or society, especially in one where so much importance is given to *shruti* ["what is heard," referring generally to oral-aural sacred lore and specifically to the Vedas], where people have hesitated to put the words of their gurus into writing, it is not a sign of intelligence to worship written sources and hold oral sources in contempt. (Agrawal 2009a, 213)
>
> In vernacular modernity and the public sphere of bhakti, and among those of our contemporaries who remain connected with the public sphere of bhakti, the poetry of Kabir is like a living, breathing body. In public insight, memory and imagination, it is a vibrant presence. (ibid., 223)

> Seized by its obsession with written works, shaped by the methods that the church developed to "fix" authorship, European modernity—which spread across the world through imperialism—has desired to turn Kabir's compositions into "the book." The book in that very sense in which Kabir questioned, "What book are you talking about? What Veda and Purana are you listening to?"
>
> Assessing Kabir texts is undoubtedly an important task, but we can only speak of authenticity when we consider other contexts along with that of text assessment. The colonial modernity imported from Europe, its mixture with vernacular modernity, and the difference between their methods—we must be aware of all this. We should resist the temptation to turn poetry into "the book." Along with "*kāgaj*" we need to make space for "*magaj*" [colloquial terms, lit. "paper" and "brain," referring roughly to written and oral]. Only then will we be able to give good answers to good questions. Which compositions are respected as Kabir's by vernacular modernity, and on what grounds? We must also pay attention to the methods of the Dadu Panthis, Kabir Panthis, and the compilers of the *Ādi Granth*. What are the similarities and differences in their priorities?
>
> When we do this, it will not be necessary for "modern" Kabir scholars to cut out the songs that are not found in manuscripts, but that are universally admired by Kabir's community—profound songs like *Moko kahāṇ ḍhūṇḍhe re bande, Jhīnī chadariyā, Santo sahaj samādhi bhalī,* and *Jag se nātā chhūtal ho*. Those that we can't find in manuscripts but that have passed the "rigorous" test of popular acceptance as Kabir *vāṇī*—rather than rejecting them, it would be better to regard them as Kabir's *uparachnā* [extended corpus].[25] And who knows? Perhaps tomorrow, some of these compositions may be found in a written source, an old manuscript. In some textual scholar's star system, they might end up getting three stars, or two, or at least one. (ibid., 224–25)

In one pithy statement, Agrawal cautions us about the folly of ignoring oral traditions:

> Along with rigor, it would be wise to apply some nuance and sensitivity. Along with the panditry of manuscripts, it would be wise to

> weigh in the balance Kabir's saying: "As many as leaves in the forest or sand grains in the Ganga / are the words from Kabir's mouth. / Poor pandit! What can he do?" (ibid., 216)

The mention of "rigor," like the earlier reference to a "robotic, computer-produced Kabir," seems to be another poke at Callewaert. But Kabir's *Poor pandit!* inevitably means *Poor Linda!* and *Poor Purushottam!* too. We agree on the value of oral traditions. But how are we going to combine rigor, nuance, and sensitivity, bringing old attested manuscripts into sustained conversation with free-flowing song? This task does not fall within the scope of Agrawal's book, but my project compels me to pursue it further.

Singers, Folklorists, and Other Listeners

Singers, song-lovers, Kabir devotees, and (some) folklorists—do these constitute a category? They do insofar as we are free to construct any categories we like, based on our observation of common properties.[26] What these terms have in common for me is that they sketch a set of participants whose engagement begins with practice and experience, people and performance, emotion and imagination, poetry and music, rather than with history, documentation, and fact. This reminds me of a famous statement by Keats that has lodged deep within me since high school:

> [A]t once it struck me what quality went to form a Man of Achievement, especially in Literature, and which Shakespeare possessed so enormously—I mean *Negative Capability*, that is, when a man is capable of being in uncertainties, mysteries, doubts, without any irritable reaching after fact and reason.[27]

The people cited in this section appeal to feeling, intuition, and experience. They propose ideas that may seem imprecise but that may also open doors for us.

One day Shabnam was talking with Narayanji, a Kabir singer, and Dinesh Sharma of the NGO Eklavya (see chapter 6). Dinesh said someone should do a study on authenticity. "Between praise of the guru and political statements and everything else, we need a way to distinguish authentic (*prāmāṇik*) from false verses." Narayanji interrupted:

> You won't get anywhere that way. The proof [*pramāṇ*] will come when you yourself live it out in your life. Try to find out for yourself, and you'll see what's authentic. The scale is in your own hands. You yourself have to weigh things and decide. Others can't do it for you.[28]

The appeal to experience arises again and again, once we leave the world of critical editors and historians. When Shabnam was interviewed by oral historian Indira Choudhary, she recalled a meeting with the legendary folklorist of Rajasthan, Komal Kothari:

> We spent two or three days chatting with him. I remember at one point he got a little impatient, a little irritated with me asking questions like, "What is the meaning of this song?" He said, "There is no one meaning of this song. Please understand that. This song is lying in wait." ... The spirit of what he said was that this couplet, song or folktale lies in wait for that moment in your life when some very personal experience of yours will come to inhabit that poem, and the meaning of that song will open up to you. You don't then need to ask anybody what the meaning of the song is—it means what it means to you. ... That's so beautiful. To me, they keep opening up. A song I thought I understood three years ago—today suddenly I'll be singing it, and I'll say, "Oh my god." This is what Kapil Tiwari says in his interview: if you've really experienced something, not just read it as information in a book, then, "*Bahut baatein hongi kabir ke saath.*—Kabir will constantly be in dialogue with you." This poetry will be in dialogue with you, because every day new gems will reveal themselves in it.[29]

Later in a conversation with me, Shabnam enlarged on this point:

> You reach a moment in your life when something opens up to you. I'll hear something over and over and it leaves me cold. Then suddenly at a particular moment, it will open up. That just happened with the *sākhī* "*guru govind* ..." [Guru and God are before me. / Whose feet should I touch? / I offer myself to the guru / who showed me God]. I have always thought it was so tiresome. But just now, I actually experienced Kapil Tiwari as a guru, opening the truth to me, within me. And I am indebted. My debt is beyond measure.

> The *sākhī* opened to me as I opened to it. There is no single objective meaning. You have to inhabit it with your life experience. Then it becomes yours. Everyone has his or her own *prāmāṇik* [authentic] Kabir. This is what Narayanji was saying.[30]

Kapil Tiwari, director of Madhya Pradesh's Adivasi Lok Kala Parishad (Institute for Folk and Tribal Arts, abbreviated henceforth as ALKP) in Bhopal for many years,[31] is devoted to folk cultures: studying, appreciating, supporting, and bringing to public attention this immeasurable and often neglected cultural wealth. He has presided over many projects, ranging across literature, music, visual arts, and theater, producing works that include publications, exhibitions, and performances. It happens that he also has a deep personal connection to Kabir, having spent a formative period in childhood living with an uncle in a Kabir Panth ashram. One of his long-term projects has been on the living oral traditions of the *sant* poets, among whom Kabir is preeminent. For more than a decade he directed a team of researchers who were collecting song texts from ten regional dialects (*bolīs*) that span much of northern and central India. In 2007 ALKP published a set of essays by scholars in each region, highlighting the contents and characteristics of Kabir in their area. They have also planned a collection of about 1,750 song-poems in their original dialects, with Hindi gloss and commentary. In a series of video interviews with Shabnam Virmani in 2004, Tiwari eloquently expounds on oral traditions. The citations that follow are based on those interviews (translated from Hindi by Shabnam Virmani and me).[32]

Tiwari emphasizes the fundamental connection of oral traditions with knowledge grounded in experience.

> In the traditions of bhakti, yoga, tantra, for anyone who is doing practical *sādhanā* [spiritual discipline], knowledge is experience, not hearsay. The latter is mere information. You can't understand Kabir through information. You must go into experiential knowledge. One who has this experience will have a relationship with Kabir. Kabir will talk endlessly with such a person. When you have an experience that transforms your vision, in your soul, your heart—the emotional world of the heart, which is an immense ocean—you will easily understand the essence of Kabir. And then even your dead scriptures will get some credibility and substance.

When asked why he was pouring so much effort into putting the contents of oral traditions into books, he replied:

> I've had to, because the whole oral tradition is in danger. We have shifted everything from *śhabda* [spoken word] to *akṣhar* [written word]. There are huge campaigns to make people literate. These people believe that there is an inseparable link between civilization and literacy. Only when something is brought into writing does it become civilized. How am I supposed to believe that Tijan-*bāī*, who can't even write her own name, let alone read Sanskrit, is not civilized?[33] An entire cultural tradition is alive inside her. It has nothing to do with whether she can sign her name. I know so many educated people. Culturally most of them are totally illiterate! Cultural illiteracy, this is a huge problem today. The government should do something about that. But it's doing the opposite. Those who already have deep knowledge of *śhabda*, they must learn to read, as though that is the only yardstick of civilization and development. Meanwhile those urban illiterates whose ignorance of culture, art, life, and experience keeps increasing—they don't do anything about that. They don't even consider it worth worrying about....
>
> Take an example from my life—I got a doctorate in literature, but we never read the *Mahābhārata*. One of the greatest epics of the world, and I read it only after finishing my doctoral studies. I don't have faith in written traditions. I am forced to do this work [of collecting and printing oral repertoires]. Our entire country has sworn an oath of loyalty to development and progress. They must have literacy campaigns. I am afraid for the oral tradition. I want to save it.

Tiwari shares his personal commitment to experiential knowledge:

> Many years ago I decided to let go of what I had learnt or read from others. I was determined to know life directly, and to know myself. I realized that experience is knowledge. All the rest is information. For instance, a "hot coal"—these are words we can read, but we won't know the burning. When we feel the hot coal on our palm, we know what fire is.[34]

In the domain where we reach (often irritably, to use Keats's word) after fact and reason, older Hindi forms and word choices strengthen a text's claim to authenticity, even as modern diction and usage do the opposite. An obvious criterion for declaring a poem inauthentic is anachronism: it may contain modern objects that didn't exist in Kabir's time, or it may show Kabir interacting with someone who lived long before or after him. The example of the train was given earlier. Here is another:

The seeker aims
at the target, shoots. Hit
by the sky! Hit
by the guru's wisdom! Hit
by the true name!

Up-breath, down-breath. A rifle-shot
to the three-stream confluence.
Light the fuse of love, let the bullet
of wisdom strike.

Take the sword of the elements,
the knife of mind,
the shield of the Word. Let the bullet
of wisdom strike.

In the fort of the body, armies gather.
Two soldiers clash.
The brave warrior stands his ground,
the coward runs away.[35]

The language of rifle and bullet is modern. But the trope of being struck and wounded (*chot lagnā, śhabda kī choṭ*) by a weapon that is the guru's wisdom, the word, the name, or the bhajan, has been well established in the mainstream of Kabir poetry for centuries. Many poems speak of a bow and arrow or a spear; here the weapon has been modernized to rifle and bullet. The yogic terminology of breath, energy channels, and the confluence between the eyebrows, central to all the old Kabir traditions, is still here, as is the traditional figure of the body as a city or a fort. Should the whole song be rejected because of the rifle and bullet?

Kapil Tiwari's views on authenticity in Kabir are bound up with his understanding of oral tradition and experience-based knowledge. Here is what he says about anachronism:

KAPIL TIWARI (KT): The question that interests me is not so much the authenticity of the texts as the truth of that Kabir who is spread far and wide among the people. What dwells in people's hearts and souls? For me, if any authenticity is possible, it is here—in people's memory and behavior, in their songs and music, where the tradition has continued unbroken. As for written traditions—the earliest anthology is the *Guru Granth Sāhib* in Punjab, the Nagari Pracharini Sabha in Varanasi has brought out a critical edition, research on the *Bījak* has gone on. But for me there is a greater authenticity in the Kabir of people's living memory than in the critically edited literature. . . .

SHABNAM VIRMANI (SV): In collecting these song texts you must have come across many things that obviously didn't belong to the fifteenth century. Will you include those too?

KT: Yes, I will include those. When I say that this is a living folk tradition, it means that it is not a thing that's frozen in the past. So it will contain many objects and words that arise from today's reality. For example, when Tijan-*bāī* sings *pandvāṇī*, airplanes appear. There were no airplanes in the *Mahābhārata*, but she has put its characters into airplanes. The power of improvisation makes the *Mahābhārata* meaningful in the twenty-first century. So when folk singers sing Kabir's *nirguṇ* songs, many things can enter that didn't exist in Kabir's time. The singer is a person of our time expressing Kabir's truth, not his literal words. For the singer who seizes Kabir's truth, it makes no difference if the text has a train, a photo, an airplane, a rifle. What's the difference? The truth in which the singer has faith should be present there.

Tiwari asserts that "Kabir's truth" is something deeper than period-appropriate diction, deeper than book-based knowledge, deeper than musical proficiency. He claims that sincere, faith-filled rural singers are likely to know and express it more than educated readers of poetry and philosophy, or sophisticated classical musicians. Is he willing to say what Kabir's essential truth is? Yes. He suggests that the heart of Kabir's truth is *shūnya*—emptiness or boundlessness—an experience in which identity, anxiety, and grasping are gone, past and future are gone, and the innermost spirit (*ātmā*) knows a stillness that fills and erases time. This experience is the outcome of *sādhanā* (practice/spiritual discipline) and faith. It will not come when we are involved in complicated thinking. It is associated with a person who is simple, *sahaj*—a key term in Kabir, and a quality that is unambiguously good in North Indian parlance. The core meaning of *shūnya* may be present not only in those poems that directly use the term, but also in others that deal with various aspects of life and death.

KT: The words that Kabir sang have been preserved for us, the tradition has saved them—a tradition that didn't know how to write but knew how to remember. Kabir's truth was so big that for six centuries, people in this country have remembered it, they can't forget it. They eat, drink and sleep with it. ... The person who knows this life can sing Kabir. I'm telling you, singing Kabir is not a matter of musical skill. Very great music masters, great singers—I'm not disrespecting them, but if their singing is not based on knowing and having faith in Kabir's life, if they don't know the urgency of that search, then they just have a kind of musical grammar. With only that kind of power, you can't sing Kabir. Kabir's truth will not come forth. But a folk singer might really live Kabir on some level.

SV: Don't you think you are romanticizing the folk singers to some extent?

KT: I don't think so.

SV: I could argue that many bhajan *mandalīs* sing these songs in a habitual way without understanding them, without attending to the inner meaning of the words.

KT: The people we think of as illiterate, India's rural people who are not in the tradition of written words—you will be surprised to discover how they understand the principles of Indian truths without the help of written texts. I am not ready to grant that those who sing Kabir do not know Kabir's truth. To know is an experience! How is it possible that a sincere and simple Malwi villager like Prahladji, without having studied grammar or classical philosophy, can know Kabir's truth? How is this possible? I would also say that those who are initiated in a popular tradition of spiritual practice and have a deep faith in that truth, they get strength, a power in their singing, not just skill. As long as that truth is not active, skill in singing can't do much. I'm telling you that someone who knows the philosophy of our classical music tradition cannot sing Kabir's truth, the truth of *shūnya*. They can sing, but you won't see the fire, the heat, the energy of that truth.

Tiwari then discusses the great classical singer Kumar Gandharva (1924–92), who lived in Malwa and was known for his uncannily powerful singing of Kabir and other *nirguṇ* poets. He says that Kumarji's ability to sing Kabir in such a profound way was based on his going out among folk singers and learning from them. Kumarji's actions and statements support this view. He regularly went to sit with the Nath Panthis at the *dhūnī* (fire) associated with one of the great yogis who used to live in Dewas. He listened and learned from them, as from wandering singers who passed by his house. In Kumarji's words:

> The way of singing *nirguṇī bhajans*—it is something unique. Especially those people who belong to the Nath sect, who have very little to do with settled habitations—their world is completely different. Their life is different, their ways are different. ... The ones who really have faith in this kind of life—the voice that comes out of them—that's what I try to practice. One day I was sitting on the veranda of the bungalow where I used to live. A man came to beg. He was singing *Suntā hai guru gyānī*. ... It's not that he was singing very well. But I thought: this is the *nirguṇī* voice; I should definitely practice this. The next day I composed *Suntā hai guru gyānī*. The quality of creating emptiness [*shūnya*] in *nirguṇ* is amazing. It comes from that carefree, nonattached state. ... In *nirguṇ*, this way of expressing, of throwing the voice, is a natural part of their lives. Without having that kind of nature, you can't put forth that kind of voice. Their voice matches their mind. *Maiṅ jagūṅ mhārā satguru jāge, ālam sārā sovai* ... "I am awake, my true guru is awake, the whole universe is sleeping"—that is their world. When they sing, at that moment, who is there? No one is there. The *svaras* that come out there are not the *svaras* that come out in the drawing room, are they? *Nirguṇ* should convey a sense of solitude. (Hess 2009a, 30–31)[36]

Madhup Mudgal, a disciple of Kumar Gandharva, corroborates Tiwari's understanding that rural singers and devotees, unsophisticated in urban terms but possessing faith and a certain kind of life experience, sing Kabir with a power that classical musicians like himself can envy. In Shabnam Virmani's film *Koi Sunta Hai/Someone Is Listening*, he describes the Nath Panthis singing a beautiful, haunting Kabir bhajan as they dance in a procession to the place of Kumarji's cremation:

> When Kumarji passed away, those folk groups came. They sang that song, "I'm a bird from another country." It's very difficult to express—I've never heard singing like that. ... The *mandalīs* came

to the cremation and sang "I'm a bird from another country," playing their small hand-cymbals. I don't know what it was. The atmosphere. It was dusk. There was a certain light. I can't explain it. It was too much. My hair stood on end. It was wonderful, even while we were filled with sorrow. [Now Madhupji sings a stanza of "I'm a bird from another country" with a look of deep concentration.] Then they would sing like this. [He hums a wordless bridge.] With cymbals. That made a deep impact on me. We can't sing like that. We won't get that feeling. For them it's pure devotion (bhakti). I wish our bhakti could be like that. But we have to watch out for the singing too. They are 100% immersed (*līn*). That's the way it should be. (Virmani 2008c)

Kapil Tiwari continues his discussion of Kumar Gandharva:

Kumarji reinvented Kabir for himself by going into the oral traditions. He searched for Kabir in places that were far beyond reading. To know Kabir through reading and to know the Kabir created by and dwelling in the lives of people—these are two very different things. In Malwa, Kabir is created by and dwells within life. That is why the soil can give birth to a singer like Tipanyaji. Folk artists like that are not just born out of the blue. You need that ground, those values, the fragrance of that spiritual practice. Then you can sing! Kumarji left classical behind and searched for this Kabir of the soil, rediscovered him in his own spirit. Finding that experience is a very difficult thing to do. Kabir touches your innermost spirit. Then the music that comes out is something else. Then you flow with Kabir's truth, not the technicalities of music. Music comes after. The words (*bāṇī*) lead the music rather than the music leading the words. That *bāṇī* is so great, it contains such a big truth, it has such fire, that when it starts to walk, music just follows it. It's not that the music is in front and Kabir's *bāṇī* is following it.[37]

This view of authenticity claims a profound central truth that radiates through and illuminates the poetry of the Kabir tradition, allowing us to recognize the poems that appropriately go under Kabir's name. For Tiwari, this central truth is indicated by the word *shūnya*. It can be known by practice, sincerity, simplicity, faith, and life experience, and it can be expressed in song by people who have these qualities. If a poem or song attached to Kabir's name expresses Kabir's truth, it may be taken as authentic.[38]

Those who look for Kabir's core texts in written collections and those who listen for Kabir's truth in oral milieus agree on this point: it is worth searching for the "true words" of Kabir. There is a voice, recognizable by content, language, and style, that belongs to Kabir. He is not interchangeable with Dadu, Nanak, or Raidas (despite marked similarities). He is distinct from Surdas, Mira, and Tulsidas (despite Vaishnav names and metaphors, and the ambiguous overlaps between *nirguṇ* and *saguṇ*). Textual scholars, restricting the field to selected groups of manuscripts, seek objective evidence of what is at the "core" of the Kabir tradition. Those who seek the "heart" of Kabir in oral tradition angle off in the direction of negative capability. They move intuitively. They listen. They point out that Kabir is constantly telling us to *listen*, to turn inward, to look in our own hearts for the truth he is trying to convey. They can cite countless songs and *sākhīs* that affirm this, including the one given at the beginning of this chapter.

Kapil Tiwari points to the term *sākhī* in the Kabir tradition. The general public, including schools that put Kabir in the syllabus, use the term *dohā* for those pithy couplets associated with the poet. *Dohā* is a technical term for a meter with a two-line (or four half-line) format. But in Kabir circles, *sākhī* (Sanskrit *sākṣhī*, eyewitness) is preferred.

> People feel that when Kabir's name comes in the signature line, he speaks as a direct witness, he is testifying to his truth, it can't be false. *Kabir* is saying this. I didn't get it from the scriptures, I didn't hear it from someone else, it doesn't come from my studies of texts. This was born inside of me. . . . Kabir cannot tell anybody else's truth. This is his secret. He isn't saying it just to produce a poem. Kabir was not literate. He didn't read the Shastras, Vedas, Upanishads, Agam, Nigam. He was not in the tradition of classical texts. He found the truth through his own practice and through the grace of his guru Ramanand. And he expressed this experience through poetry. . . . Kabir says, listen brothers and seekers! . . . This is the seal (*mauhar*) on his truth. . . . *Sākhī* means witness, one who sees.

How many times I have been teased as the pandit whose pretensions Kabir was so adept at exposing! I will be introduced as the great scholar from Stanford University, and then someone will quote lines that reduce scholars to ash.

maiṇ kahatā ānkhoṇ kī dekhī, tū kahatī kāgaz kī lekhī
terā merā manavā ek kaise hoe re.

I say what I've seen with my own eyes,
you say what's written on paper.
How can your mind and mine ever get together?

pothī paḍh paḍh jag muā, panḍit bhayā na koī
do ākhar prem kā, paḍhe so pandit hoī.

Reading books upon books, everyone died
and none became wise.
Four letters: love.
Read those and be wise.

My own most famous story, in the tiny circle of those who read books in English about Kabir, is "*Kuchh bajegā!*" (Hess and Singh 2002, 35–37). In that story a Kabir Panthi with a strange name nails me accurately as a Kabir researcher who has no real comprehension of what she is doing. Then he gives a riveting performance that conveys the difference between book-knowledge and experience. Many years later, Shabnam reminds me of another *sākhī* that touches on this matter:

Reading, reading, she turned to stone.
Writing, writing, she became a brick.
Kabir says, did she get any love?
Not a single drop!

No Authenticity, No Author

One can argue that it is futile to try to prove anything by early manuscripts: the variables are out of control. One can also argue against the idea that Kabir has a particular, identifiable voice that can be recognized in oral sources. As demonstrated in chapter 2, "Kabir" poems can be interchangeable with Naths or Sufis, with Mira or Nanak or Tansen. Passages of verse can freely migrate from one bhakti location to another. In casual reading, I've found songs and couplets that for me belonged to Kabir popping up among the Bauls of Bengal and the *bhats* of Rajasthan and claimed by those traditions.[39] Perhaps what we have is just a nebulous mass of lines, phrases, formulas, metaphors, and messages, freely floating in some bhakti-*adhyātmik*-poetic firmament and dropping to earth when certain atmospheric conditions prevail.[40]

A third lens for viewing the phenomena associated with "Kabir" is that of social and historical contingency. Here, one avoids the discourse of authenticity. One examines the present and past through historical documentation and ethnography, studies the history of reception, and traces patterns of language and theme across many sources and contexts.

Sources that show threads of reception include Mughal court documents; Sufi histories; bhakti anthologies, commentaries, and hagiographies; Kabir legends recorded in many places; and works produced by *panths* and *sampradāys*. If we layer the written Kabir texts by date—manuscript and print up to the present—we can do specific inquiries like the one suggested by Bhuvan Komkali in the previous chapter: When is Urdu language, or particular Persianate vocabulary, notable by its presence or absence? We can also do such inquiries geographically, or with other criteria, such as courtly or sectarian location. Work on this kind of history has been done by many scholars cited here—Vaudeville, Hawley, Lorenzen, Agrawal, Mukta, Martin, Pinch.

Younger scholars continue to do fine-grained historical work on interpretations and reimaginings of Kabir. For instance, James Hare has recently written on the *Bhaktamāl* of Nabhadas, a foundational text of North Indian bhakti poets and traditions about which little has previously been available in English. Nabhadas's short verse portrait of Kabir, composed in the early 1600s, is very important as the earliest recorded description of Kabir. It strongly emphasizes Kabir's character as a protester against Brahminical norms (*varṇāśhram dharma*, six schools of philosophy), Hindu and Muslim sectarianism, shallow and showy religious practices; and also as a fearless humanitarian who didn't try to please others but stood for sincerity and depth of experience:

> Kabir didn't care about caste or the rules
> on what you should do
> when you're young, middle-aged, and old,
> or the six philosophical schools.
> Religion without devotion
> was for him no religion at all.
> Yoga, ritual, fasting and charity
> were beneath contempt
> without a heartfelt song.

To Hindu and Muslim he told his truth
through poems, songs, and couplets.
He never took sides but shared his words
for the good of all. He was firm, never tried
to please the world.
Kabir didn't care about caste or the rules
on what you should do
when you're young, middle-aged, and old,
or the six philosophical schools.[41]

Hare (2011a) shows how much this picture changed in one century by examining Priyadas's famous commentary on the *Bhaktamāl*, the *Bhaktirasabodhinī*. Priyadas makes Kabir much more of a conventional Vaishnav, devoted to a personal God usually called Hari, accepting caste, valorizing sect (*sampradāy*), and benefiting from many miraculous divine interventions.

Nearly all scholars will take an interest in the Kabir of historical, social, political, and literary contingency. For some, this is the *only* Kabir who is interesting and credible. Authenticity is not a compelling topic of inquiry.

The Truth about Kabir/Kabir's Truth

Scanning the writings of prominent Hindi literary scholars in the early 2000s, I found many quotations from Kabir but few citations of sources. The writer might introduce a verse with, "As Kabir himself says," or, "We can address this question through Kabir's own words"—without indicating the source. The obvious question was: What do we mean by "Kabir's own words"? Where do we locate "Kabir himself"? In his 2009 book, Purushottam Agrawal advances the discussion significantly by evaluating manuscript sources and seriously engaging with oral sources. However, there still seems to be a problem with circular reasoning. Agrawal emphasizes that we must consider the *totality* of Kabir, not just certain themes. He supports the reliability of the *Granthāvalī* by saying that it contains the full diversity of Kabir's themes. But those very themes are at issue. What is the *totality*? If there should ever be convincing evidence of a "core" body of Kabir works, would all the themes Agrawal admires in the *Granthāvalī* be present, or would some emerge as more or less true to his profile?

If manuscripts are unreliable, what to say about the obscure notion of Kabir's truth? Here too we face the problem of circularity, since ideology may determine what gets defined as Kabir's truth. For example, in the Damakheda *panth,* Kabir's relationship with Dharamdas and their establishment of the sect with its lineage of avataric gurus are taken as sacred truths. Thus mention of Dharamdas in the signature line, or emphasis on guru-bhakti, may weigh on the side of "authenticity" for them, while it may weigh on the other side for people outside the sect. Agrawal places a high value on the poems of love and *viraha* expressed in a woman's voice, so he may consider their presence, along with other types, as evidence for authenticity (Agrawal 2009a, chaps. 8–9). In my earlier work I was inclined to find precisely those poems less authentic, since they were farther from the center of "Kabir's truth" as I preferred to see it (Hess 1987b).

Are rural folk singers concerned about authenticity? Sometimes yes, sometimes no. Occasionally Shabnam or I would raise doubts with Prahladji about a particular song, and he would engage in conversation about it. But these were more our questions than his. In 2002 he frequently sang a song, *Tujhe hai shauk milne kā.* While it had a Kabir signature line, the musical style was clearly not of Malwa. Shekhar Sen, a Mumbai classical singer who had created a very successful one-man show about Kabir, once visited the village and told me that this song came from a movie. I asked Prahladji where he got it. His reply: "I'm not sure, I heard it somewhere and liked it."

In 2001 Prahladji recorded a cassette called *Dhanya kabīr.* The title song sets forth the Kabir Panth mythology about how the baby Kabir manifested himself miraculously on a lotus on Lahartara Pond—not a mortal human being but the divine avatar of the age. Since Prahladji claimed not to believe in that mythology, Shabnam asked why he was propagating it by putting it in a cassette that was sure to be popular. Shabnam also pointed out disturbing marks of recently stoked anti-Muslim sentiment in the lyrics.[42] Prahladji appeared not to have thought about these matters. He liked the peppy tune, and in the heyday of his positive association with the Panth, he might have been showing deference to the sectarian story. After that—perhaps influenced partly by Shabnam's questions and even more by his falling-out with the Panth—this song disappeared from his performances.[43]

Despite the apparent lack of concern over authenticity of particular songs, Prahladji clearly believes that there is a meaning in the name Kabir, a heart to the Kabir tradition, a profile to the great poet and *satguru.* His spontaneous commentaries in performances emphasize certain things again and again: the folly of narrow identities of religion, sect, caste, class, nation, race, gender, as well as other limiting frameworks of thought; the immediate availability of truth and liberation within our own body, *ghaṭ ghaṭ meṇ*, in every body, or *nij ghar*, our very own home; the worthlessness of words (*kathanī*) if not matched by deeds (*karanī*); the path of waking up to the nature of our bodies, minds, habits, behaviors, social situations, lit with flashing moments of humor, satire, warning, challenge, paradox; and the importance of the guru, who sometimes seems to be a person outside ourselves but is often declared to be none other than *śhabda*, the essential Word that must be heard within.

In his book *The Weaver's Songs*, after reviewing the histories of written texts and mentioning the continuous background of oral transmission, Vinay Dharwadker concludes that the Kabir tradition comprises a "community of authors" (Dharwadker 2003, 60). It is thus unnecessary to try to tease out the voice of the individual Kabir who lived in the fifteenth century. This may seem to dispense with the question of authenticity altogether. But it also begs the question of what defines that community. Is it just the tag line "Kabir says," attached to any content whatever? Or is the community of Kabir poets characterized by certain "Kabirian" ideas and approaches? (See Hawley 2009, 24–48.)

Gangasharan Shastri, while mentioning respect for linguistic criteria in editing the *Mahābījak*, obviously considered Kabir's central ideas (*vichārdhārā*) more important. *Vichardhārā* literally means "thought-stream." Once in a speech to an audience of thousands at his own annual event in Lunyakedhi, Prahladji expressed the idea that the river of Kabir's truth had a mighty integrity, a set of great currents that flowed on through history, beyond quibbles over what could or could not be proved about the historical figure Kabir:

> People say that Kabir was a Chamar, a Balai, some low caste. Never mind. Kabir is the source of all. Kabir is not the name of any individual. If that's the way we see Kabir, we don't understand. Kabir is our guru. Kabir is a stream, a flowing river. Kabir is a sign and a message. And he never spoke of a Kabir Panth. "Kabir panth" means Kabir's path. A person who walks on that path is a Kabir Panthi. If we talk of the Kabir Panth along with all the other sects, factions, and religions, we're very far from experiencing the truth. (Virmani 2008b at 57 min.)

Toward a Conclusion

Textual and oral approaches suggest two sorts of tactics. Bahadur Singh hints briefly at these two methods in 1999. One is studying manuscripts. The other is listening to the voices of singers and lovers of Kabir-*vāṇī*. A third approach eschews the search for the "true Kabir," assuming the historical and sociological contingency of all texts and interpretations. All three approaches are good. Sometimes they can talk to each other, sometimes not. It is a good idea for a student to immerse herself in all three, to experience the different worlds that each constructs and the rewards that each can offer. This chapter concludes with observations on the state of the field and suggestions for future study.

However skeptical we may be about the reliability of early manuscripts, no one would say they are irrelevant or uninteresting. Though many textual changes undoubtedly took place between Kabir's death in the eastern Hindi region and the inscription of the poetry 50 to 160 years later in Rajasthan and Punjab, these manuscripts comprise an important set of milestones in the history of Kabir texts. My 1980 dissertation included a study of three Kabir collections that aimed at a comparative assessment of themes and styles in these different sectarian compilations. Published as an article in 1987, this study was very rough by today's standards. I counted the occurrence of key words with my hand and eye—pathetic instruments when compared to today's implacably accurate computers. Such a study should be done again, using computerized searches, with carefully chosen key words and a limited number of manuscript sources.

Along with the change from primitive tabulation to computerized precision, our knowledge of manuscripts has changed since 1987. In addition to Callewaert's *Millennium Kabir*, we have a meticulously edited selection from one of the best early Rajasthani collections, a manuscript dated 1614–1619 (Strnad 2013). We have information on earlier sources, including the 1582 Fatehpur manuscript (Hawley 2005) and the manuscript precursors of the *Ādi Granth*, copied and studied thoroughly for the first time by Gurinder Singh Mann (1996, 2001). The *Goindval Pothis*, assembled in the early 1570s, are very close to the *Ādi Granth* as canonized in 1604, but also have intriguing differences. They push the body of poetry stabilized by the Sikhs back thirty years. Mann has told me that there are three Kabir poems in the Goindval Pothis of approximately 1572 that do not appear in the 1604 *Ādi Granth* or in any other old collection as far as he knows. These three poems, as yet unstudied by scholars, now constitute the very earliest manuscript appearance of Kabir. Mann has also revealed a fascinating bit of information from his study of the earliest Sikh manuscripts. Two Kabir poems were written into the 1604 Kartarpur Pothis but then were crossed out and excluded from the Granth forever after. Both were *ulaṭbāṃsī*, "upside-down language" poems with outrageous, nonsensical, sometimes shocking imagery. *Ulaṭbāṃsīs* appear everywhere that one finds oral and written Kabir traditions, east and west. They belong to a much older tradition of mystical poetry using such language in meaningful ways (Hess and Singh 2002, 135–61). One of the deleted poems from the Kartarpur manuscript seems to have been particularly offensive, drawing a picture of crazy mixed-up family relations, with the opening line, "People, look at God's betrothal. The mother married her son and lived with her daughter." Someone crossed it out and wrote "useless" in the margin. The Sikh gurus apparently had a strong preference for plain language and domestic propriety. They also emphatically avoided anything that had even a whiff of tantric influence (Mann 2001, 114–15).

The biggest problem in my 1987 study is my acceptance of the *Bījak* on an equal plane with the manuscripts from the West. As discussed above, so far we have no reliable manuscript of the *Bījak* earlier than 1805. I have never been a manuscript hunter or a textual editor, so I haven't tried to extend the search. But someone should. I am not ready to believe that the *Bījak* can be entirely discarded as a significant early collection, or that in all of the eastern Hindi region there is no hope of finding evidence of early Kabir texts. David Lorenzen has examined the manuscripts in the Kabir Chaura headquarters in Varanasi without finding an early copy of the *Bījak*. Writing *The Bījak of Kabir* in 1983, and citing P. N. Tiwari's 1961 suggestion to the same effect, I said that "hidden treasures" might be waiting to be discovered in the Kabir Panth ashrams scattered through U.P. and Bihar (Hess and Singh 2002, 166). I also noted that the Bhagatahi lineage of the Kabir Panth, which is smaller and has received less attention than the Kabir Chaura and Damakheda *panths*, uses a recension of the *Bījak* that is shorter than and organized differently from the better known Kabir Chaura version. Shorter is often better in manuscript sifting. The hypothetical manuscript hunter I am conjuring should be sure to pay attention to Bhagatahi centers, as well as looking for other sects in the eastern regions that might have kept collections, as the Sikhs and Dadu Panthis did in the West.

Oral and written traditions can obviously be studied separately. Can they communicate with each other? Perhaps so. I am imagining the possibilities of work yet to be done. A well thought-out computerized study of key words with carefully selected written sources could yield an enlightening picture of themes and salient language in these sources. Computers can now bring forth many types of subtle and interesting information.[44] A researcher might consult with other scholars in the process of choosing manuscripts and key words. It might be possible to include the *Bījak* in such a study, with a different kind of valuation based on the lack of early manuscripts (a negative) and representation of the eastern region (a positive).

Would this sophisticated and sensitive search of written sources reveal a deeper substrate, a more omnipresent thematic-stylistic stream, along with distinguishable regional and sectarian variations? Would it help to establish a distinct voice of Kabir? If so, could we compare our discoveries based on written sources with the voices of Kabir preserved in the living oral traditions that Kapil Tiwari describes with such passionate admiration, and that I have begun to document in this book? There may be imaginative ways to do so. One approach might be an ethnographic inquiry into "Kabir's truth" or the "essence of Kabir" (*kabīr sār*). Tiwari located the essence in the key word *shūnya*. What would others say? In living traditions of the early twenty-first century, I asked a few singers and lovers of Kabir to tell me what they considered Kabir's most important teaching or essential point. The interviews did not go very well. Would more extensive and skillful inquiry of this kind lead to new insights, or just to a series of dead ends in a maze of words?

Both the oral and written approaches should be juxtaposed with social and historical studies of "contingent" Kabir. Some will concentrate on just one of these approaches. Others will find it interesting to try to discover deeper truths (in any sense) about Kabir by crisscrossing among them. Either way can yield good results. I remember something Charlotte Vaudeville said when I first met her in Pune around 1976. Recognizing the vastness of our field of study and the limited nature of what any one person can do, she commented, "J'apporte ma pierre à l'edifice." To this building project, I carry my stone.

4

In the Jeweler's Bazaar

MALWA'S KABIR

THE SONGS OF Malwa tell many stories, opening knowledge in surprising ways. Over time I came to appreciate how rich and precious they are—how they are made from people's lives.

Once in the rainy season, looking from Prahladji's rooftop verandah over the green expanse of the countryside—studded with trees and bushes, shining with silver and slate-colored ponds—I imagined the land littered with piles of jewels. The jewels were songs, multicolored and abundant. Their facets, rough and smooth, reflected the green shoots of peanuts and wheat, the bullock carts and birds, the village walls and wells, the roads, rocks, water, and weather. They reflected families, relationships and emotions, marriages, and cremations.

Through the songs I saw markets and workers—cloth and weavers, pottery and potters, jewelry and goldsmiths, and vegetable sellers with their balance-scales. I smiled at local humor and satire, nodded at plainspoken morality. I also saw inside the body, wondrous landscapes, skyscapes, radiance and resonance, flowers and bees, shimmering in the experiences of poets, singers, listeners.

> The market of jewels is arrayed in your body.
> Take what your heart desires, my dear.
> The jeweler strings diamonds,
> the fool strings stones.[1]

One day Prahladji's wife Shantiji spoke of how the village people had an intimate familiarity with the images in Kabir songs. Over the years, most outsiders who came to Lunyakhedi to meet the famous folksinger paid little attention to his wife or the other women of the household. The women were used to remaining unobtrusive. But Shabnam had featured beautiful interactions with Shantiji in two of her films, and Shantiji had received a lot of enthusiastic feedback from city people for the depth, sensitivity, and clarity of her remarks.

In August 2012, fourteen people from Mumbai, Delhi, Bangalore, and Auroville (plus one American, me) attended a four-day workshop at the Tipanya home in Lunyakhedi. Prahladji, along with his family and *mandalī* members, led sessions where we sang, listened, and discussed. Phalguni, a Mumbai lawyer who knew the songs better than most, requested *Thārā bharyā samand māhi hīrā*—a song whose refrain says, "In that huge ocean there is a jewel. The deep-sea diver plunges and brings it back. In your body the chain of wisdom is twisted. The satguru untangles it."

Each stanza is rich in imagery. Two stanzas evoke the sounds and sights of a village in the rainy season:

> In the garden a nightingale [*koyal*] sings,
> in the forest a peacock cries.
> The waves of [the rainy month of] Savan swell.
>
> Dry grass and straw have been burnt,
> the Tij festival of Savan is coming.
> One day, everything turns around.

There was a discussion of what all this meant. While we city people worked on basic vocabulary, Shantiji came up with a spiritual explication. The dry grass and straw left over from the seasons of planting and harvesting, she said, are the unwholesome tendencies (anger, lust, greed, etc.) within us, which at this point can be burnt up. When that happens everything turns around. We are transformed. A little later she and I talked further.

LINDA (L): People like it when you sing and speak up.

SHANTIJI (S): (smiling) I know they do!

L: You usually keep quiet while your husband does the talking. But you know all the bhajans and understand them well.

S: When you live here and experience all the things mentioned in the bhajans, understanding comes naturally. We hear the *koyal* bird singing, we hear the peacock. We know the rain, the swelling waves of water.

We burn the dry grass. Automatically we understand how things turn around. It's like that when you sit and practice *sumiran* [meditation, concentration on the divine name]. From experience you know what the bhajans are saying.

In this chapter, I try to take readers inside the Kabir repertoires of Malwa, presenting a body of songs that I encountered in the early twenty-first century. Our understanding will always be limited and will sometimes be wrong, as most of us don't hear the *koyal* bird or burn the dry grass. But by listening, singing, and getting to know people, we can learn. If we also happen to know something about the history of written texts, religious and social formations, and bodies of song in other regions, that knowledge will interact in interesting ways with what we learn on the ground in Malwa.

Right away, we have to think about how to organize the material. Do the songs fit into categories, indigenous or otherwise? Can we list themes? Do patterns of composition, association, and meaning emerge in a particular way from oral-musical modes of transmission?

Five He-Snakes, Twenty-Five She-Snakes: Making Categories

Classification is a fundamental way of "making culture." In Kabir lore, we frequently hear the numbers five and twenty-five, signifying the functions and characteristics of physical existence. "Five" is explained either as the five elements of material nature (earth, air, fire, water, space) or as the five senses (sight, hearing, touch, taste, smell). Each of these five is linked to five *prakṛitiyāṇ* (natural substances or processes), their combinations giving rise to twenty-five categories of body-mind experience.[2] Most of us are not the drivers of, but are driven by, these natural processes. So "5-25" in Kabir stands for forces linked to our body-mind systems that keep us bound and unconscious. Sometimes they are imaged as animals, like the snakes of the heading above, or the five *mṛigalā* (male deer) and twenty-five *mṛigalī* (female deer) of other bhajans.[3] Sometimes just the numbers five and twenty-five signify the problematic conditions of material existence.[4]

Traditional categories like 5-25 occur within Kabir songs and couplets. Then there is the question of grouping the songs and couplets themselves. The practice of categorizing texts goes back to the earliest manuscripts. The

Sikh *Ādi Granth* of Punjab classifies the songs by musical ragas and does not classify the couplets. Dadu Panthi manuscripts from Rajasthan do not classify the songs but often organize the couplets into thematic sections called *anga*—meaning limb, organ, part, or (in a literary context) genre. The *anga* convention gradually became influential and today is likely to be seen in printed collections that are not based on particular manuscripts. I have even seen *anga* categories used on an audio CD of *sākhīs* sung by Purushottam Jalota. The *Granthāvalī* manuscript, which probably dates to the early seventeenth century in Rajasthan, has the *sākhīs* organized under fifty-two *angas* that are interesting to peruse.[5] The *anga* sections are very uneven in length, the shortest having two *sākhīs* and the longest having dozens. I will give the first five here and the full list in the notes:

1. *gurudev*—the revered guru
2. *sumiraṇ*—remembering/chanting/meditating on [the divine name]
3. *viraha*—separation [from the beloved]
4. *gyān viraha*—separation in the mode of [yogic] knowledge
5. *parchā*—acquaintance/knowledge/experience[6]

To represent the Kabir repertoires of Malwa, I will also create some headings. There are certain themes I am interested in, such as guru, body, beloved, death, delusion, and joy. There are certain images and keywords I would like to trace—cloth; mirror; jewels; drunkenness; the cord (*ḍor*) that is a vital connector; the country (*deś́h*) where the singer belongs, or does not belong; and the quality of otherness (*nyārā*) or emptiness (*shūnya*) in *nirguṇ* expression. There should also be a category for social criticism—poems that comment on caste, sectarianism, hypocrisy, superstition, arrogance, ostentation, violence. As I continue listing themes and keywords, my proposed categories begin to look like Borges's surreal Chinese encyclopedia.[7] I will not be able to follow all these threads in the presentation that follows. My intention here is to draw attention to the process of category making.

Classifying Kabir compositions is an inevitable exercise, but the way is full of pitfalls. Any given bhajan contains multiple themes. The themes are interdependent. If we hang a certain song on the "guru" theme, it usually just means that the song begins with the guru. Later it may talk about in-breath and out-breath, the mind, the body, or drunkenness. A poem about the beloved soon becomes a poem about the *deś́h*, that "other" country; or a reminder of the imminent withering of the body; or an evocation of the glowing inner world of the yogic practitioner. Even a poem of blatant social satire may have a refrain that directs us back to self-knowledge, urging us to open the window to our own interior.

Kabir poetry itself likes to articulate a space between the presence and absence of categories, both using them and denying them. One poem says: "In this body sun and moon, right here a million stars." Another says: "In my country there's no moon, no sun, no million stars."[8] The latter song exemplifies what I sometimes call "deep *nirguṇ*": it tries to take away everything, leaving us with no ground beneath our feet, no pairs of opposites, no concepts. But in the middle of the same song come two stanzas (mentioning Brahma, Vishnu, Shiva, Veda, and Gita) that could be placed in a category of poems that are critical of religion.

aivī aivī seṇ—Such Signs

Such signs my true teacher showed me—
it can't be spoken with the mouth, oh sadhu

in my country there's no ground, no sky
no wind, no water, oh sadhu

in my country there's no moon, no sun
no million stars, oh sadhu

in my country there's no Brahma or Vishnu
no Lord Shiva, oh sadhu

in my country there's no Veda, no Gita
no song, no couplet, oh sadhu

in my country there's no rising or setting,
no birth, no death, oh sadhu

Step by step a truth-seeker arrives.
Kabir, a seeker, climbed to nirvana, oh sadhu.

I stop writing for twenty minutes and sing the song, joining with Shabnam's voice on a recording. Singing it a few times, getting more of it by heart, I realize that naming themes is only a problem if I try to categorize whole bhajans. Sometimes that works, but more often it doesn't. The way to locate themes in oral texts is in lines, half-lines, passages, and extended metaphors. Lord's oral-formulaic theory blooms in my experience.[9]

Getting our heads out of books and tuning in to oral-performative life reveals a good deal about the dynamics of categories. An interesting organizing factor in a performance is the relationship of *sākhīs* to bhajans—a relationship of which we would have no clue if we knew only written texts. In books, the couplets (called *sākhī, saloku,* or *dohā*) and the songs (called *pad, śhabda/śhabad,* or bhajan) are always in two separate compartments. They are literary genres. In folk performance in the Hindi region, they are nearly always mixed. A bhajan is preceded by one or more *sākhīs*, which should be thematically related to the bhajan. An expert singer can string together a wonderful series of *sākhīs*, each touched off by the last, and each expressing some aspect of what is to come in the bhajan. The *sākhīs* are sung in a musically different way from the bhajans, producing melodic and rhythmic variations that experienced audiences find pleasing. Malwi singers sometimes use a form called *rekhtā*, in place of or along with *sākhīs*, to introduce a bhajan. *Rekhtā* as they perform it is a dense and intense metrical form whose melody has a more dramatic quality than the *sākhī*.[10]

In a performance, songs are connected to each other in intricate and ever-changing ways. Song A may lead directly to song B on one occasion, to song C on another, or to song X on another, and in each case the transition will appear seamless. Sometimes performers refer to traditional classifications found in written collections. For example, they commonly refer to songs about the guru (which are called *guru vandanā*, homage to the guru, or *guru mahimā*, the guru's greatness). Singers also speak of a type called *chetāvanī*, "warning." *Chet* means consciousness, awareness, attention. *Chetnā* as a verb means to wake up or become conscious. *Chetāvanī* songs are those that warn of the imminence of death, the shortness of time, the rare opportunity of human birth, or the massive presence of delusion. They exhort us to wake up.

chet re nar chet re, thāro chiḍiyā chug gaī khet re, nar nugar re
ab to man meṇ chet re, ab to dil meṇ chet re

Wake up, man, wake up! The birds have eaten your fields,
and you still don't know the guru.
Wake up now in your mind, wake up now in your heart.

Ulaṭbamsī, upside-down language, is a type that has a strong presence in written collections through the centuries, and singers also know it as a category. It signifies a class of poems that use paradoxes, riddles, and seemingly nonsensical images to evoke a state of mind beyond the habitual (Hess and Singh 2002, 135–61).

Prahladji told me that there is a general order in which he prefers to present bhajans in a performance. In nearly all cases he starts with one or two bhajans acknowledging the guru. After that, he likes to go from what is relatively easy to understand to what is deeper and more difficult. The early-stage bhajans tend to be more didactic: we are wasting our life; we are ignoring the wisdom that comes from the guru; we are lost in pride, attached to pleasures and possessions, worshiping rocks, rushing off on pilgrimages while ignoring our inner condition. Some of us are even eating nonvegetarian food! These bhajans are often entertaining, with funny examples and down-to-earth imagery. At the other end are those that speak of what can't be spoken. They may string together negations, deny that there is any ground to stand on, and use mysterious language, suggesting a consciousness that does not belong to the conceptual mind.

Actually Prahladji sings the most "difficult" bhajans very rarely in public performances, as he doubts that people can understand them. Because I liked them so much, he produced a great many examples for me. I tried to convince him to sing them onstage more, asserting that people would be able to appreciate them. Sometimes they came forth spontaneously in settings where the mood was right, but mostly he ignored my preference and left them out of public concerts. Some exceptions to this rule can be explained by performative considerations. For example, the *ulaṭbamsī* song *Shodhū śhabad meṇ kanihārī* is funny, and he plays it for its capacity to amuse. "*Koī suntā hai guru gyānī*," full of strange and hard-to-comprehend imagery, has such a vigorous, attractive melody and rhythm that the energy carries it along. It also has comprehensible bits, including the refrain. The audience enjoys it whether they understand the hard parts or not.

While the extreme ends of Prahladji's easy-to-hard progression can be associated with particular songs, the large space in between is ambiguous. A song can dart with lightning speed from the simple to the profound, from the comprehensible to the mysterious. We can be chuckling one moment, thunderstruck the next. Is a song easy or hard? Is it satirical or mystical? Even at the more obvious points—the beginning and ending of a program—I don't think Prahladji adheres reliably to the theoretical order he outlined for me.

More than any logical sequence, Prahladji seems to follow streams of association that are intuitive and feeling-driven. A song is much more than its lyrics. A song is sound. A song is a mood, an environment of emotion—*bhāv* in Hindi. Classification depends on cognitive content. *Bhāv* arises with melody, imagery, rhythm, strings of noncognitive associations, factors that can't necessarily be named—the twang of a *tambūrā* string; the lighting up of a listener's face; strange confluences inside the singer's brain, stomach, nervous system. A song is also performance, and the singer is usually keenly aware of what is "working" with the audience.

So I will follow my own set of associations in the exposition below, and you will understand that this series of headings is a device to make a chapter, inspired by my experiences with singers and texts, conditioned by my own affinities.

Guru

There is no doubt about where to start. We start with the guru. Almost without exception, Prahladji begins a concert with a song in praise of the guru. In *nirguṇ* bhakti—devotion to an ultimate reality beyond form—devotees still have the inescapable human need for form. Icons of God, like the images found in Hindu temples, with their narratives, paraphernalia, and external rituals, are rejected. Where can the devotee direct her attention, her emotional energy, her yearning for awakening, and her gratitude for grace? In the *nirguṇ* world, the guru tends to fill this space. Who is the guru? The guru is both outer and inner. The reference may be to a human being who gives priceless guidance or to an innate source of knowledge that is always with us. This ambiguity makes the guru's presence in the poetry rich and resonant. The guru may be praised in extravagant terms, worshiped as a stand-in for God. But at any moment the song may turn us in upon ourselves, where the guru's knowledge actually exists. Awakening is an experience that breaks boundaries, not a clinging to any form. A guru is one who inexplicably opens the ungraspable door to this experience. A very popular couplet of Kabir says:

> Guru and God are before me.
> Whose feet should I touch?
> I offer myself to the guru
> who showed me God.

Prahladji often opens his concerts with a spirited bhajan that has this refrain:

> The guru gives ease to my mind, always eases the mind.
> The guru cuts through nets of karma,
> and people find joy.
> The guru cuts through nets of delusion,
> and people find joy.

While the song praises the guru from beginning to end, in the middle it touches on an intimate experience deep within the body, where liberation happens in the breath:

> The breaths of right and left streams
> flow into the center.
> Between down and up
> the mind becomes still.

Again and again we seem to hear praise of the outer guru; then the song subtly directs us to what is within ourselves. One song has the refrain, *Guru sam dātā koī nahīṇ*—"There is no giver to compare with the guru." Throughout the song, the natural inference is that the outer human guru is being saluted. But at the end we hear:

> Kabir says, what have you lost? What are you searching for?
> A blind person doesn't see. Brilliance gleams in your body.

Moving through many examples, we will see how the categories, the major motifs indicated in my headings, interpenetrate each other. Later I will introduce a section called "Body." But before we can get there, the "Guru" category has taken us straight into the body. And after we get there, the body will take us back to the guru.

Along with *guru*, Kabir uses the term *satguru*, true guru. Sometimes *sat* seems to intensify the meaning; sometimes the choice seems to be a matter of metrical convenience. I have heard that *satguru* implies God. Kabir himself is called *satguru* by his followers, many of whom regard him as God. I have also heard that Kabir uses the term *satguru* when he wants to differentiate the true guru from all the false gurus, whom he never hesitates to criticize.

In March 2002 I went with the *mandalī* for a performance in Omkareshwar on the Narmada River, during the annual pilgrimage there. We went with huge crowds for *darśhan* at the great Shiva temple. The next morning in predawn darkness, Prahladji and I had this conversation:

LINDA HESS (LH): What do you think about all these pilgrims coming to bathe and take *darśhan*? Do Hindu festivals have any meaning for you?

PRAHLADJI (PT): Nothing special. If you're not clean inside, what good does it do to take a bath? Still, when people come with faith and devotion, some change may take place in them.

LH: What about the Kabir Panth? Do you believe Kabir is the eternal *satya-purush* taking different avatars in the four *yugas*, and do you believe that the Kabir Panth *achāryas* and their lineage are avatars of Kabir himself?

PT: No, I don't believe that. *Satyapurush* means a *purush* (man/person) in whom *satya* (truth) exists. God is truth.

LH: You sing *ho jā hoshiyār sadā guru āge*—be alert, the guru is always in front of you. So who is this guru? Some particular person?

PT: No, this has nothing to do with the gross body (*sthūl sharīr*).

For a long time I felt removed from the guru theme, as I associated it with culturally prescribed forms of obeisance to people who might or might not deserve the reverence they got. But gradually a change took place in my viewpoint. New insights about this and other motifs came in unlikely places, taking me by surprise. In 2003 I organized a U.S. tour for Prahladji and his group, in which they did about thirty-five performances in two months.[11] One day we arrived at Syracuse, having driven across New York state from Rochester. Though we were performing at the university, I had arranged an overnight stay at the Zen Center of Syracuse, whose head teacher was a friend. Our Zen hosts asked if the group could do some informal singing for them that evening. We were tired and rumpled but couldn't say no. Only about eight people showed up to listen, which I thought reduced the likelihood of a spirited engagement. Prahladji asked them about Zen Buddhism. He also knew that I practiced Zen. Someone briefly described their practice. When he declared that he would sing *Mhārā satguru baniyā bhediyā*—a song I barely knew—I tried to explain the refrain in English, consulting with him in Hindi. As the vivid, concrete meanings of the words came through to me, I got more and more excited. I thought that the song described the true vitality of the teacher-student relationship in a way that Zen practitioners, familiar with stories of intimate and subtle encounters between teachers and practitioners long ago in China and Japan, would get.

> *mhārā satguru baniyā bhediyā, mhārī nāḍī re pakaḍī hāṇ*
> *un nāḍī meṇ laharī upje, hiyo hiloro khāy*
> *guru mhāne gyān daī gyā*
> *mhārā tan bīch diyo lakhāy, sumiran chetan kar gyā*

My true guru is a *bhediyā*, declares this refrain. *Bhediyā* has a double meaning: one who can reveal mysterious knowledge (*bhed*); and one who pierces (*bhednā*, to pierce). I explained that this means the teacher has opened my understanding and at the same time has opened me, pierced through me. The process is then described in potent physical images: s/he touched my pulse and waves surged in my veins, my heart rocked (in the waves). This is how the guru gave me knowledge: s/he gave me vision in the middle of my body. The mantras I recited turned to shimmering consciousness.

As he sang, Prahladji was transported. Or was I the one who was transported, understanding these words for the first time? Prahladji closed his eyes and seemed to plunge into himself; then he opened his eyes and gestured toward the people in the room. I never expected the atmosphere to ignite in this little living room where a few tired men from village India were singing to a few Americans who had adopted a Japanese style of meditation. Each stanza got more intense, more exuberant. The repeated refrain was a return to incredulous joy: He touched my pulse and waves surged, my heart rocked, he gave me vision in the middle of my body! How could such a thing happen? Hearing this song performed with such passion by a rural Indian singer in a Zen household in upstate New York, I suddenly felt the meaning of a true teacher, one who knows you, touches you, and seems to give you your own life.

After that, I didn't feel detached from songs that conveyed the wonder of the guru's gift.

Social Criticism

Kabir has a special reputation for his social critique—attacks on hypocrisy, pretension, superstition, sectarianism, greed, and abuse of power. Other bhakti poets may touch on these themes, but no one goes as far as Kabir. He especially delights in showing up the delusion and malevolence of religious people. Belonging to a low-status community (he was an unlettered Muslim artisan, whose recently converted community would have been marked as Shudras in the Hindu hierarchy), he is keenly aware of and quick to denounce caste.[12] So in modern North India, he is a favorite of activists who fight for social equality and who resist communal hatred and violence. A song from the Malwa repertoire that represents this genre well is called "Where did you come from? Where are you going?"

Where did you come from?
Where are you going?
Get the news from your own body!
If you find a true guru,
you'll get the secret.
The window within
will open.

Hindus, Muslims,
both deluded, always fighting.
Yogis, sheikhs, wandering Jains,
all of them lost in greed.

The qazi reads the Quran,
then grabs someone's land.
Not knowing the lord in every breath,
he grabs a chicken, smashes its head.

Someone meditates, stock-still,
but inside his thoughts are jumping.
Outside saintly, inside filthy,
mind tainted, he swallows a fish.[13]

Turning their beads, fasting, painting their arms
and foreheads, making mystical gestures,
taking trips to holy places,
they sing, strum, and please the world,
but miss the news
from their own bodies.

By rote they read the Gita,
without a spark of consciousness.

Kabir says, listen seekers—
coming and going,
they wander on.

This poem consists almost exclusively of social commentary, but with a shot of inwardness. The refrain reminds us of what is in contrast to all this violence, greed, dishonesty, and foolishness in the world: something we can learn by opening a window to our own interior, looking deep into our own body.

Other poems are more inwardly oriented but give us a shot of social commentary.

A carved statue stands in the temple.
Its mouth can't speak.
The priest stands at the door.
Who can go in without his permission?

This stanza occurs in a song in the *helī* genre. Addressed in an intimate voice to a female friend (*helī*), these songs may highlight imagery of lover and beloved, of the mysterious country that is hard to enter, or of the yogic body. The song quoted here, long a favorite in Malwa, never occupied a "social critique" niche in my mind. The main theme is a constant in Kabir: Why are you searching? Why are you running, exhausting yourself, looking for truth or happiness in faraway places and external objects? The musk deer who runs from forest to forest trying to find the source of the enchanting fragrance hovering in the air fails to realize that the musk is in its own body. A subset of the "why are you searching?" theme would include sharp comments on temples, mosques, pilgrimage places, and statues of gods—all emphasizing the delusion of searching outside yourself.

But this stanza about the carved statue goes further. It alludes to untouchability and to the widespread practice of denying temple entry to people of the lowest castes. This is still an issue in India, even though discrimination against "untouchables" is declared illegal in the constitution. For millennia priesthood has been the preserve of Brahmin males, who have literally and figuratively guarded the doors so that their holy images would not be polluted by bodies regarded as intrinsically filthy. So the stanza above is a double-barreled critique. First, the statue is not alive; it has a mouth but can't speak. Second, the statue and its priest symbolize the oppression and exclusion of Dalits by upper castes through the ages. Kabir rejects both in one flourish. In Malwa a large majority of Kabir singers and devotees are Dalits. The meaning of this verse does not escape them.

After dwelling on this stanza, I went back and read the whole song again with different eyes. Suddenly the protest against untouchability appeared everywhere, not just in these lines. The statue is mute, but the real Ram speaks. Where? In every body. *Every* body. The Ganges springs from the sky, from the mountain (the forehead chakra, where three streams meet). Everyone has the same clothes to wash (the five elements, our physical constituents), and it isn't soap that gets them clean. Everyone who finds the true guru, who hears the voice of Ramji within, is stainless. In contrast to the priest who shuts the temple door, Kabir in the last stanza opens the heart's lock.

We conclude with a bhajan that makes specific reference to caste. *Rām rame soī gyānī* asserts that the real *gyānī*—possessor of knowledge—is the one in whom the real Ram roams freely (*ramnā*: to wander happily, to roam, to take delight in). After several stanzas that break down labels, social roles, and expectations of enlightenment in future lifetimes, the song ends like this:

The Brahmin is clay,
the Baniya is clay,
the whole creation is clay.
In this clay, everyone meets.
This is Kabir's message.

Mind

In February 2002 I was on the road with Prahladji for the first time. We went to Magahar, Uttar Pradesh, the place where Kabir is believed to have died; to nearby Gorakhpur, headquarters of the Nath Panth, a sect of yogis associated with the legendary founder Gorakhnath; and to Kushinagar, where the Buddha entered *parinirvāṇa*, as Buddhists like to say—in common language, where he died. Prahladji and I barely knew each other. "Teach me something by Kabir," I said in the car. "On what subject?" he asked. "On the mind," I immediately replied. He shot back:

dauḍat dauḍat dauḍiyā, jahāṇ lag man kī dauḍ
dauḍ thake man thir bhayā, vastu ṭhaur ki ṭhaur

Hearing the *sākhī* for the first time, I didn't understand it. Prahladji started explaining in Hindi. When I finally understood, I said, "Ah!" Kabir understands the mind. He nails it. Here is a translation, not nearly as good as the original.

> Running, running, more running,
> how far can the mind run?
> Tired of running, the mind is still.
> Right here!
> Here it is!

The "it" of the last line is not the mind but the "thing," *vastu*. What thing is this? It is the very thing, the essential thing, the thing one has been searching for.

Five years later, at home in Bangalore, Shabnam sang a string of *sākhīs* on the mind. She was an enthusiastic pupil of Prahladji, singing Malwi Kabir in her robust, melodious voice, skillfully strumming the *tambūrā* with her right hand and jingling the *kartāl* in a lively rhythm with her left. Along with the *sākhī* just quoted, she sang three more:

> Greedy mind, grasping mind,
> thieving mind, jumpy mind.
> Don't chase after the mind's thoughts.
> There's a new thought
> every second.
>
> Don't chase after the mind's thoughts,
> the mind has thousands of thoughts.
> If you can ride on the mind's back
> I'll call you a holy one.
>
> As many as waves in the sea,
> the rushing streams of the mind.
> Pearls comes forth spontaneously
> when the mind rests.

The slow reflective style of the *sākhīs* gave way to up-tempo strumming and jingling as she started a bhajan on the theme of the mind. We sang together—our custom on monsoon mornings in Bangalore, before breakfast.

Teach your mind like this,
teach your useless mind like this.
Without seeking, how will you find?
Without looking, how will you see the secret?
Listen you staggering vagabond,
listen you wise sage.

After this refrain, the song gives a series of parallel examples that show a mind properly attuned.

Like a woman acrobat climbing a rope
while her man beats the drum.
She sings as she climbs, but her awareness
is always on the rope.

Teach your mind like this ...

Like a water-bearer who sets a brimming pot
on her head and walks home.
Swinging, swaying, she chatters away, but her awareness
is always on the pot.

Like a snake that slides through the forest
licking dew.
As it licks, it stays aware
of the gem on its head.
It would give up its life
for that gem.

Like a diver who plunges into the sea,
fully absorbed.
Kabir says, listen, seekers, friends,
he instantly reaches the jewels,
plucks them up
from the sea's floor.

The vivid similes are all about concentration; we could also say devotion. We see here how the fervor of bhakti can unite with the *dhyān* (meditation) of the yogi. There is something that is most precious of all. Not only precious, *essential.* Do you understand? If so, remember it every moment (the practice called *sumiran*, remembrance, also merges here with bhakti and *dhyān*). A key word that occurs in three stanzas is *surat*, rendered here as "awareness." The acrobat, water-bearer, snake, and pearl diver keep their awareness steady no matter what else is happening. This sustained awareness is in stark contrast to the mind's greedy, grabby, hyperactive rush in all directions. The song is also conspicuously set in the middle of everyday life, not in a space of ascetic withdrawal. The traveling circus performers and the women gossiping as they go to and from the well are images straight from rural life. I have seen tightrope walkers arrive at the door of Prahladji's village house, beating their drum and singing their songs. The snake licking dew is a fabulous image, both mythic and mundane, of a creature of earth eating its way through the day.

The latter part of the song emphasizes courage. The snake would give its life for the gem on its head. The *satī* and pearl diver plunge into the fire or the ocean.[14] In other songs we hear of the warrior who enters the battle *sanmukh*, face to face, while the coward turns tail and runs. This readiness to die is not just literal (though in some moments it might be literal). It also refers to letting go of the familiar self, the possessive self, the elaborately structured identity that the mind is devoted to preserving.

Once we are alert to the nature of the mind and the possibility of a different kind of awareness, we recognize references to it in less obvious forms.

> Do one thing fully, all is done.
> Try to do all, you lose the one.
> For plentiful flowers and fruit,
> the gardener waters the root.

Our understanding of "mind" becomes cumulative, associated with ever more motifs and images, in no way confined to a set of poems on the mind. The mind is busy, tricky, complex, on the go. The one thing it doesn't know how to do is stop. In contrast is something still (*sthir/thir*), deep (where the pearl diver plunges), absorbed (*magan, līn*), empty (*shūnya*). The mind can be brilliant and attractive—residing in a many-colored palace (*rang mahal*), reveling in a multicolored bed (*rang bhar sej*). Somewhere, a white banner flutters in emptiness. This other state comes across sometimes as calm and empty, sometimes as drunken and mad. But it is always intense and devoid of distraction.

magan bhaī he lāḍlī magan bhaī
piyā kī suratiyā dekh magan bhaī

Totally gone, my dear, totally gone
seeing the beloved's face, I was lost and gone.

Or in a popular *sākhī*:

kaṭuk vachan kabīr ke sun ke āg lag jāī
gyānī to va magan bhayā, agyānī jal jāī

Kabir's words are searing, just hearing
them sets off a fire.
The wise are completely immersed.
The ignorant burn.

How could one possibly get free from the rule of the mind? This is a problem the mind can't solve. Imagery gives hints. A thread or cord (*ḍor, tār*) is said to stretch. ... Where? How?

My mind is a thief. Make a cord of awareness.

***

The thread of awareness climbs to the sky.

Elsewhere we hear about a peak of emptiness, a white flag, in contrast to a colorful palace, a bright bed. Sometimes jewels are explained as breaths. Sometimes the string of breaths, or the string of jewels, is explained as the thread of awareness.[15]

Body

The body is a pot (*ghaṭ*) made of clay, earth, dust (*māṭī*). The fact of our universal, humble composition is a great equalizer, as in the verse cited above about the brahmin, the merchant, and the whole creation. Remembering this fact tends to cut through any arrogance or sense of superiority.

Clay says to the potter:
why do you press me down?
The day is coming
when I will press you down.

To say we are clay is to say we all die. But the theme of death is coming in another section. Here we take a different angle on the body.

In every body, Ramji speaks.
In every body, the beloved speaks.

The *ghaṭ*, the clay vessel, is the most common image of the body in Kabir. While "clay" may suggest death, a vessel is also a container. Kabir is as interested in what the living body contains as in its eventual disintegration.

Oh bird, my friend,
why do you wander
from forest to forest?
In the city of your body
is the sacred sound,
in your own green garden
is the true name.

Oh bird, my friend,
why do you sit
in the dark?
In the temple of your body
the light shines,
the guru's teaching gleams.

Besides a pot, the body appears as a city, a country, a temple, a field, a fort, a palace, a musical instrument. Occasionally the language is anachronistic, as when a distinctly modern term for a big house shows up:

In the city of the body is a bungalow;
at its center is a secret place.

In what is probably the most famous of all Kabir songs, *Jhīnī chadariyā*, the body is a cloth woven with wondrous subtlety:

Subtle, subtle, subtle
is the weave
of that cloth.

What is the warp
what is the weft
with what thread
did he weave
that cloth?

Right and left
are warp and weft
with the thread at the center
he wove
that cloth.[16]

The spinning wheel whirled
eight lotuses, five elements,
three qualities, he wove
that cloth.

It took ten months
to finish the stitching
thok! thok! he wove
that cloth.
Gods, sages, humans wrapped
the cloth around them
they wrapped it
and got it dirty
that cloth.

Kabir wrapped it with such care
that it stayed just the same
as it was at the start
that cloth.

Subtle, subtle, subtle
is the weave
of that cloth.

The more we turn our attention to songs of the body, the more we recognize it as the very place where the elusive *nirguṇ* experience comes forth. The metaphors that clothe this experience are primarily light and sound, but also include flowing streams and other images.

ek bhāṇ vahāṇ kyā paḍī mhārī helī, kaḍoḍ bhāṇ parakāśh

Why speak of one sun, my friend? There a million suns blaze.

sunn mahal meṇ bājā bāje, kingarī ben sitārā

In the palace of emptiness an instrument plays—flute, lute, sitar.

suntā hai guru gyānī gagan meṇ āvāz ho rahī jhīnī jhīnī

The guru, the wise one, listens.
A voice vibrates in the sky, subtle,
very subtle.

pī le amīras dhārā gagan meṇ jhaḍī lagī

Drink the streams of nectar
that cascade from the sky.

The appearance of "sky" in the last two examples signals the yogic body. In Malwa's Kabir, we are never far from this anatomy of energy centers, channels, streams, breath, root, cave, lotus, sky-dome. The yogic language remains simple, evoking right, left, and center channels (*inglā, pinglā, suṣhumnā*); a spot where three streams meet (*triveṇī* or *trikuṭī*, usually explained as the *ājñā* chakra, between the eyebrows); a vast sky revealed when the unified breath reaches the highest chakra, the thousand-petaled lotus at the top of the head. Along with visual metaphors are sonic ones: thunder, music, roaring; in traditional language, *anahad nād*, the unstruck/boundless sound, or *śhabda*, the Word beyond words, the primal vibration, which the fortunate or deeply devoted can hear in the name that the guru transmits, or in the bhajans that they sing and listen to, or in their body, or in the air.

But it's not all light and sublime sound in the town of the body. There are brigands. There are hunters with weapons. There are hungry animals.

Who owns the city of your body? On the road, five guys robbed you.
Five guys, twenty-five guys. On the road, five guys robbed you.

The poet sings about how even the most famous sages from Sanskrit scriptures, even divine avatars, got robbed by the five and twenty-five. He uses the Hindi-English cognate verb, "looted."

The same message comes through a farming metaphor in another song:

You didn't listen to good advice,
so they've eaten your field.
Five stags, twenty-five does
live on this land.
As long as you stay awake,
they won't eat.
As soon as you fall asleep,
they eat.[17]

And in a *sākhī*:

The good days have gone, you didn't benefit from the guru.
What's the point of crying now, when the birds have eaten your field?

Early on in my travels with Prahladji and his group, I became enamored of "songs of the body"—a category I made up. In April 2002, on a train coming back from a huge Kabir Panth convocation in Bandhavgarh, Madhya Pradesh (M.P.), I asked Prahladji and his brother Ashok to help me compile a list of songs that speak of the body—of how everything we are searching for is immediately available within it, and of the *nirguṇ* reality discovered in the body.

That evening, back in the village after long travels, there was no electricity and everyone was tired. Nevertheless, Prahladji called for all the instruments to be brought out. They sat and sang—songs of the body. Everyone looked beautiful in the dark with the light of one candle, white clothes shining, faces faintly glowing, full moon and stars in the sky. I said: "I don't hear these songs in your programs." Prahladji replied: "We don't sing them in programs because people don't understand them. They are too difficult. In our programs we have to sing what is suitable for our audiences. We have to think of what would help them improve their lives, change their habits, increase their love and goodwill." Many of these songs had slow, haunting tunes; they weren't rousing and fun like most of those I heard on stage and in the commercial cassettes.

The singers started dropping verses and confusing words. Prahladji told me to rewind my tape recorder and made everyone start again. After a while, Ashok got fed up. "How can you sing bhajans when you're so sleepy?" He got up and walked away, as did Ambaram and Ajay. I said, "Everyone's tired after so much traveling. Give it up and go to sleep." But Prahladji insisted on doing two more, just him and his *tambūrā* and *kartāl*, with his wife Shantiji joining in.

I expected no more, but in the morning Shantiji said, "Time for bhajans."

"You have other work to do, don't trouble yourself for me," I replied.

"We have nothing to do," said Shantiji.

Ashok, Ambaram, and Ajay came back. They'd looked up the trouble-some words in the little notebooks where thousands of songs had been written down over the years. Then they sang, full and magnificent, for about forty-five minutes. One song, *Yā ghaṭ bhītar* ("In this body"), really made me cry. When I cry my mind gets clearer, and some of the knots and blocks that tie me up get washed away. I imagined how one day I would write about the Malwa repertoires, and how I would describe this scene. The two-year-old boy, whom they dote on from morning to night, banging little cymbals while the others sing. The men in morning *lungīs* and t-shirts, in the privacy of their own home, singing and looking beautiful beyond words. Prahladji, two brothers, two sons, Shantiji, and the baby grandson all together.

Who can know this? The one who knows!
Without a teacher, the world is blind.

In this body forests and hamlets, right here mountains and trees.
In this body gardens and groves, right here the one who waters them.

In this body gold and silver, right here the market spread out.
In this body diamonds and pearls, right here the one who tests them.

In this body seven oceans, right here rivers and streams.
In this body moon and sun, right here a million stars.

In this body lightning flashing, right here brilliance bursting.
In this body the unstruck sound roaring, streams of nectar pouring.

In this body the three worlds, right here the one who made them.
Kabir says, listen seekers: right here my own teacher.

Who can know this? The one who knows!
Without a teacher, the world is blind.

Family Life

I don't normally think of Kabir as shedding light on family life. He tends to be severe when it comes to human attachments. The phrase *koī nahīṇ apnā* rings through several songs: no one belongs to you. *Apnā*, one's own, is a poignant word in Indian family life. It signals who you are related to, the network of connections that saves you from isolation, a familiar world where you belong. When people wanted to let me know that they were accepting me, not treating me as an outsider, they would call me *apnā*. The noun *apnāpan*—one's-ownness—suggests intimacy.

Familiar and familial are almost the same. Kabir seems to be more interested in what is strange, solitary, other, unexpected, foreign. Sometimes he is downright harsh about the family:

> It's all illusion—mom, dad, the whole family,
> beating your chest in mourning—illusion.[18]

Yet glimpses of family predicaments and bonds of affection in the songs sometimes strike me as tender and compassionate—the relationships all the more poignant as they are fragile and fleeting.

Here are two Malwi songs centered on a persona who has evoked deep emotion in India from the fourth-century classical Sanskrit drama *Śhakuntalā* to the latest Hindi films: a daughter leaving her natal family to stay with her new husband and in-laws, usually far from home in painfully unfamiliar surroundings. In the first song, she begs a brother to help her escape from grief and abuse in her marital home (a situation frequently in the news in India). The brother she addresses might be her own brother on a visit, or someone she trusts in this alien landscape.

> *Go and tell them, good brother,*
> *how it is with these in-laws,*
> *go and tell my father and mother.*
>
> In my in-laws' house, so much pain.
> My sister-in-law torments me.
> Birth, death, pregnancy, the pain
> is too much to bear.
>
> My young brother-in-law is obstinate,
> he torments me so much, oh lord,

he speaks cruel and deceiving words,
I can't bear it, oh lord.[19]

The song goes on to equate the in-laws' house (*sāsariyā*) with the worldly world (*saṃsār*) and the father's house with a divine realm that may be beyond this world. Even though the fourth and final stanza implies world renunciation as a solution to worldly woes, the first three stanzas still convey a sense of empathy with human love and suffering, a touching awareness of the tension between love and nonattachment.

Oh save me, mother, now save me!
That son-in-law has come
to take me away.

This is the refrain to a song I heard several times from Narayan Singh Delmia (of whom we'll hear more in chapter 6) and his young friend Arun Goyal, before I really understood it. It was one of those fast and spirited bhajans that seemed to have a happy feeling. I soon learned that somber themes are often performed in bouncing rhythms and catchy melodies.

The double meaning in this song is sustained from beginning to end; there is no easy resolution in renunciation as in the previous example. Here the pathos of a young girl being forcefully taken from her natal to her marital home by a stranger-husband becomes emblematic of all unreliable connections, all separations, especially the ultimate one. The premature departure of the child-bride clinging to her mother is exactly mapped onto the moment when death comes to wrench everyone away—from family, friends, one's own body. The word for son-in-law (the girl's husband) is *jamāī*, which sounds like Jama/Yama, the lord of death.

Oh save me, mother, now save me!
That son-in-law has come
to take me away.

The son-in-law said, listen, mother,
listen to what I say.
This time I'm really going to take her,
so get her ready fast.
Oh save me, mother. ...

The mother said, listen son-in-law,
listen to what I say.
My little child, my innocent girl—
how can I give her to you?
Oh save me, mother. . . .

Oh this body's made of five elements
and three qualities. It's a thing
that doesn't belong to you.
She can't stay in your house.
Oh save me, mother. . . .

Oh eight rooms and nine doors
are in this body. No matter how much
I run and dodge, he grabs my arm
to pull me away.
Oh save me, mother. . . .

It's the month of Sāvan,
the Tīj festival's almost here.
My girlfriends are calling, my heart is feeling
the wish to play.
Oh save me, mother. . . .

The seven brothers of that darling girl
patted her head.
Kabir says, listen truth-seekers:
she went off
down that road.

Oh save me, mother. . . .[20]

In a crucial episode of his life, Prahladji had a powerful urge to leave his family, to give up all attachments and stay at the peaceful Kabir ashram at Kudarmal. His account of that incident appears in chapter 1. His wife Shanti offers her own description in a filmed interview with Shabnam:

> When my daughter Sona was five months old, he went to an ashram. I don't know what got into his mind, but in the ashram he decided—I'm going to stay here. I'm not going home. Four or five members of his *maṇḍalī* were there too. For four days they argued

with him. Come home! You have three small children, your mother and father, your younger brothers, your sister. What will they think of us? That we went with you and returned without you, leaving you here? But he wouldn't listen. Then the guruji of that ashram in Kudarmal asked him—Son, have you accepted a guru?—Yes, sir.—Will you listen to what a guru says?—Yes.—Then go. Go home and take care of your responsibilities. Stay with your family, and sing bhajans. My husband said—I won't go. The guruji said—Then you have turned against the guru, you're clinging to your own mind. You are not a person who turns toward the guru [*manmukhī ho, gurumukhī nahiṇ*]. Son, I'm telling you to stay with your family. When the guruji told him that, he cried a lot. For fifty kilometers on the road, he went on crying. (Virmani 2008a, translated from Hindi in subtitles)

When all this happened, Shantiji was living in Lunyakhedi with her parents-in-law and the children, while Prahladji stayed separately in villages where he was posted as a teacher. After the Kudarmal incident, they were worried.

SHANTIJI: My mother-in-law and father-in-law were afraid. Who knows? He might abandon his wife and children and take off somewhere. In those days we traveled by bullock cart. We didn't have a motorcycle or a bicycle. So the three children and I, we all went in a bullock cart along with our bedding, clothes, pots and utensils, to Kathbaroda where he was teaching. He came home from school and said—Why have you come here? I said—Wherever you are is my home. He said—No, you should have stayed and taken care of Mom and Dad. I said—They're the ones who sent me here. He said—OK, bolt the door and go to sleep. I'm off to Gorkhedi to sing bhajans. (She laughs.) So we made our dinner and went to sleep.

SHABNAM: How did that make you feel?

SHANTIJI: I felt pain inside, but then I tried to reason with myself. After a while I got used to it. It's all right. It's not a bad thing to sing bhajans. Even while he was so absorbed in bhajans, he also took care of our needs—clothes, food, house, he provided well and looked after the family.

[Shantiji explains how in those days he did rigorous spiritual practice. He went off alone in the middle of the night to meditate, bathed in the

river no matter what the weather, and ate only one meal a day. This routine continued for some years.]
He would sit six hours meditating. ... He liked quiet solitary places, no crowds. I thought, fine. I'm getting this much of a shared life. Is there any lack? God has given me children and this much companionship. It's a lot. My life is happy.

Efficiently shaping, rolling, and cooking chapatis throughout the conversation, Shantiji speaks of Prahladji's detachment, his lack of emotional involvement. (See Figure 4.1)

He doesn't have attachment [*moha*] to anything. We may think that we are his family, related to him as wife, son, daughter, brother, sister. But he doesn't have that kind of affection [*lagāv*]. Like yesterday, you were crying when you thought of your son. He doesn't have that.[21] If we're separated, he doesn't have the kind of affection that will make him remember us. If he's far away, he doesn't miss us.

FIGURE 4.1. Shantiji, Prahladji's wife, makes chapatis during conversation in kitchen. Photo by Shabnam Virmani.

SHABNAM: Is that good or bad?

SHANTIJI: Look, we're ordinary people. For us it's bad. For him it's good, all good. Let's say someone dies. Everyone's eyes will be wet, but not his. He'll say—why weep for the dead? They've gone to their home. One day, everyone has to go. If we talk to him of love, he'll say—love should be only for that one. If you're joined in love to that one, everything else is trivial.[22]

Once I asked Prahladji about the seeming contradiction between detachment and love. Putting so much emphasis on the temporary nature of the body, pointing out again and again that we can die the next day, the next minute, and that our family members will be eager to get rid of the corpse, dismissing bonds of mother, father, sister, brother, spouse as false, was Kabir debunking human relationships? Why was he singing about *prem*, love? "Come to the guru's country, let me tell you about the city of deep feeling, the city of love." If not the ordinary thing that people like to call love, then what is love? Prahladji smiled and said, "Love is the thing that doesn't decrease. Love is the thing that only increases [*ghaṭata nahin, baḍhā rahtā hai*]."

Some *sākhīs* I learned in Malwa comment on the dilemma between staying in the world and leaving it. They come down on the side of cultivating inner freedom—non-clinging and non-harming—right in the midst of worldly life.

sādhū aisā chāhiye, dukhe dukhāve nāhiṇ
pān phūl cheḍe nahīṇ, par rahe bāgh ke māhiṇ

Here's the kind of holy person we need:
one who doesn't get hurt, doesn't hurt others,
doesn't meddle with leaves or flowers,
but stays in the garden.

jāgan hī meṇ sovnā, sovan hī meṇ jāg,
ek to ban meṇ ghar kare, ek ghar meṇ rahe berāg.

To sleep while waking,
to wake while sleeping.
One makes a home in the forest.
One stays home, free of attachment.

Once we were in Bhopal, where Shabnam had organized a recording session for Prahladji and some other artists. We all disliked the atmosphere of recording studios, so she had arranged a beautiful setting in the Manav Sangralaya (Museum of Humanity), bringing field-recording equipment and a sound recordist to one of the spacious thatched-roof clay houses that had been built there to represent the region's varied cultures. Prahladji was in an excellent mood, singing song after song. His individual expression came through much more clearly than usual, since this time Shabnam had requested that he play and sing in the old-fashioned way, with only his own *tambūrā* and *kartāl* for accompaniment. There were no supporting voices, no drums, violin, or harmonium.

After four or five songs, he started one about the *pardesī*, the foreigner, a theme I knew well. One of my favorite songs was *Ham pardesī panchchhī, inī des rā nāhīṇ*—"I'm a bird from another country, I don't belong in this country." Kabir reminds us that we are all foreigners by virtue of the extreme brevity of our stay here, though most of us don't recognize it. The song Prahladji sang that day, addressed to the *pardesī*, had a quiet, melancholy feeling. Shabnam gently played the small cymbals.

Now how can I rely on you,
you foreigner
you traveler
from far away?

The walls have crumbled, the roof has collapsed,
the roof has mingled with dust, ah yes,
you foreigner,
you traveler
from far away. Ah yes.

As long as there was oil in the lamp, ah yes,
your temple glowed brightly,
you foreigner. Ah yes.
Now the oil has run dry, the wick has sputtered out, ah yes,
your temple has gone dark
you foreigner. Ah yes.

The shopkeeper's departed,
the market's deserted, ah yes.
The lock remains
but he's taken away the key
you foreigner. Ah yes.

Kabir says, listen seekers, friends, ah yes.
Your swan has flown
to a town
beyond death
you foreigner. Ah yes.

There was an intimate mood in the room. We could feel the soft contours of darkness and light, the clear sounds of voice and instruments filtering into palpable silence. When he reached the lines about lock and key in the second-to-last stanza, Prahladji's voice disappeared. He tried but couldn't sing. Our French friend Aurelie, who had been quietly taking pictures of the session, caught a close-up—profiled face in deep shadow, eyes closed, bits of glowing light on the nose and around the right eye, two small shining streams of tears.

On the third try, Prahladji managed to sing the stanza in a quavering voice. By the time he got to the end, the familiar "Kabir says," he had recovered. He didn't say anything about it. But after that song, he seemed to have more energy and lightness than ever.

Death

Do I really need to write more about death? I was building up to this section, but now it seems anticlimactic. We have already gotten a strong taste.

Death is a familiar presence in the songs of Kabir, as in those of the Nath yogis, who often rub shoulders with Kabir in Malwa. *Jāo nugurī* (Go, you who lived without a guru), one of the Malwi songs of death that stays persistently with me, was presented in full in chapter 1.[23] Here is another one that we have heard from both Malwi and Rajasthani singers.

Stay alert. A thief is entering the city.
Stay awake. Death is entering your body.

He aims no arrow or pistol,
fires no rifle.
He ignores the rest of the city,
but wants to grab you.

He doesn't break down the fort's gate
or attack the castle.

He's invisible. No one sees him coming or going.
He's strolling around inside you.

The darling kids you clothed and fed
will tie you to a bamboo bed
and toss you out.
They're scared of ghosts.

Kabir says, this is an alien country,
no one belongs to you. Fool,
you came to this world with fists clenched,
you leave with hands open.

We meet death in many "categories" of song. It becomes a dreadful son-in-law and an insidious thief. It is in the house whose walls are made of sand; the lamp with no oil; the unbaked pot that can revert to clay any second; the instrument whose strings have snapped; the leaf that flies from the tree never to return; the silent market where the merchant has gone away.

Don't get attached to illusion,
don't be proud of your body.
The body's an unbaked pot,
a drop of dew.
Let a little breeze hit,
a little gust,
the body turns to dust.[24]

Misguided pride in the body is set against its extreme fragility. In the following song, the body's vigor and attractiveness are summed up in two colors, *kesariyā rang, gulābī rang*—the colors of the fine spice, saffron, and of the delicate rose.

Don't be proud
of your power, don't admire
your body. The golden color
will fly, the rosy color
will fly.

This world
is a bundle of paper.

A few drops fall, it melts away.
The golden color
will fly, the rosy color
will fly.

This world
is shrubs and sticks.
A touch of fire, it burns up.
The golden color
will fly, the rosy color
will fly.

This world
is a patch of brambles
where you get tangled and die.
The golden color
will fly, the rosy color
will fly.

This world
is a market fair
where a fool wastes his savings.
The golden color
will fly, the rosy color
will fly.

This world
is a glass bangle.
A little blow, it shatters.
The golden color
will fly, the rosy color
will fly.

Kabir says, listen seekers—
No one else shares
your karma.
The golden color
will fly, the rosy color
will fly.

The most popular song sung by Prahladji in Malwa is a charming little piece featuring a bullock cart. I don't know why it is so popular, but wherever he goes in Malwa, it has to be sung. If he doesn't get to it, someone will request it, shouting it out or throwing a note on the stage. Maybe it's the nostalgic tug of the bullock cart, with its big painted wheels, its impossibly ancient, oddly comforting, slow, creaky way of moving along. These carts are still common in the countryside but are inevitably being replaced by tractors and other modern vehicles. Maybe the lilting tune of this song helps to make it such a winner—starting at a moderate pace and gradually speeding up, as if the bullock were getting inspired to trot.

The song starts with a description of the cart, painted in bright colors and driven by a woman, with Ram as a passenger. The second stanza is plainly didactic, talking about the danger of getting stuck before reaching your goal, and how the virtuous ones will finish the journey while the bad ones will crack up. Then we hear of healers being called, bringing herbs and roots, but to no avail. The fourth stanza is talking about a dead body, but in strikingly light-hearted terms.

> Four fellows met and soon agreed
> to build a horse of wood.
> They hauled it to the burning ground.
> It blazed up, just like Holi!

The wooden horse is a euphemism for the bamboo litter made to carry a corpse. The comparison of the funeral flames with the raucous bonfires of the Holi festival is decidedly irreverent.

This delightful and well-loved ditty concludes with a grief-stricken woman facing widowhood, and the dour response of Kabir:

> The woman sobbed and cried:
> We were joined, now we're broken!
> Kabir says, listen seekers:
> the one who joins
> is the one who breaks.

Attention Now

Why all this dwelling on death? Does Kabir just have a morbid streak—an attraction to death? Some would say yes. In a well-known song, a woman rejoices at her upcoming marriage to Ram.[25] This has been interpreted as meaning that death is a desirable consummation in which the devotee-bride is finally united with her true husband, God.

I don't think Kabir is promoting death, and I wouldn't tag him as "pessimistic." This idea reminds me of the many times I've heard Buddhism described as a pessimistic religion, because the first of the Buddha's four noble truths states that life is permeated with suffering. The people who call him a pessimist fail to read down to the third noble truth, which states that there is a way out of suffering. The fourth truth presents the path.

The dark presence of death illuminates the preciousness of life. Is that too obvious? In a basic sense, Kabir's solution to the human problem is very obvious. It is *sahaj*—simple, natural, immediate. *Sahaj* is the nature of the awakened state. This is impossible for the complicated mind to grasp. On countless occasions, with many little variations, Kabir says:

> *ab kā dhyān karo mere bhāī, yoṇ avsar nahīṇ āī*
>
> Pay attention now, brother.
> This chance won't come again.

The word *ab*, "now," means the present moment, and *dhyān* means both "attention" and "meditation"; so the first half-line could also be translated as "meditate on/in the present moment." This line comes at the end of a song whose refrain repeats, "You didn't follow the guru's teaching, so the deer have eaten your field." Deer (or birds) eating one's field: again death.

Kumar Gandharva sings a Gorakhnath bhajan whose refrain expresses fear of death:

> Guruji, I'm afraid of that day,
> the day, the hour, the very moment. (Hess 2009a, 112)

Then there are four stanzas, all of which begin with "In this body." The first two show familiar images of death: a garden where a deer grazes, a clay pot that easily breaks. The third compares the body to a busy market, then says, "Do your business in this very moment," leading into the final verse:

> In this body, Gorakh the ascetic says,
> today is the day of bliss.

Could our spiritual problem simply be a matter of procrastination?

> *kāl kare so āj kar, āj kare so ab*
> *pal meṇ pralaya hoegī, bahurīueregā kab*

Tomorrow's job? Do it today. Today's job? Do it now.
In a second the world will end. When will you do the job?

Before leaving the theme of "now," we will look at the texts of two full bhajans.

Seeker, there's something
you're supposed to do.
So do it!
This life is a jewel, hard to find.
You've wandered through eight million
four hundred thousand births. There's someone
you're supposed to meet.
So meet!

You tried mantras, prayers, fasts, deprivation,
you ran through the six philosophical schools,
but never found wisdom beyond wisdom.
You just distracted yourself.

A voice says Vishnu's in Vaikunth,
another says he's in Cow Heaven,
someone else says Sahib's in Shiva's city.
For ages, they've marketed these products.

An ignorant person says God's far away.
Someone who knows says God is close.
A true guru gives this precious hint:
The path to God's in every breath.

The guru's whole mind is revealed.
Someone recites a wordless word.
Bananath says, listen friend:
my true guru's voice
is shouting at you.

(Bhajan: *karnā re hoy*)

It's very close, so why are you searching? Where are you running? Bird, why fly from forest to forest? We have met this motif before. It belongs to the section on the body, because "now" equals "here," and "here" is in our own bodies. It belongs to the section on social criticism, because the absolute equality of bodies guts the ideology of purity and pollution, while the vision of the living body as containing the light, the sound, the breath of truth declares the independence and dignity of all who have been oppressed and excluded. Insistence on the body is crucial; merely declaring equality of souls (separate from bodies) permits social and economic hierarchies to roll merrily along.

Now I'm starting to run with political thoughts and forgetting the main point of this section. There will be much more to discuss about political Kabir, but not here. Here we're trying to stick with something simple, *sahaj*. For instance, Kabir's formula *jaisā kā taisā*, or *jyūṇ kā tyūṇ*. It's one of those rhyming, doubling Hindi phrases that are hard to translate; we could say it means "just like this, just like that." Not different. Not elsewhere. It usually comes at the end of a song. The first chapter gives a translation of the song *Tū kā tū*, "You, only you," which celebrates the presence of the ultimate reality in everything. The last lines say:

jal thal jiv meṇ tū hī virāje, jahāṇ dekhu vahāṇ tū kā tū
kahe kabīr suno bhāī sādho guru milyā hai jyoṇ kā tyoṇ

In earth, ocean, every creature, you shine forth, only you.
Wherever I look, it's only you.
Kabir says, listen seekers,
you've found the guru, exactly here!

The famous *Jhīnī chadariyā*, "Subtle cloth," translated in this chapter, concludes:

dās kabīr jatan se oḍhe jyoṇ kī tyoṇ dhar dīnī chadariyā
Kabir wrapped the cloth with care and kept it just exactly as it was.

A song that will be discussed in the next chapter ends this way:

jo tere ghaṭ meṇ jo mere ghaṭ men, sab ke ghaṭ me ek hai bhāī
kahe kabīr suno bhāī sādho, har jaisā kā taisā
In your body, my body, every body, friend, it's one.
Kabir says, listen seekers: in each, just exactly that.

Prahladji once explained *jyūṇ kā tyūṇ* as evoking an untouched simple (*sahaj*) state. He said it may be used in a situation where a storm or earthquake strikes, but when it's over you find a tree or building standing *jyūṇ kā tyūṇ*, as it was, where it was. Then he said that a true guru is one who makes you return to a condition of *jyūṇ kā tyūṇ* or *jaisā kā taisā*—before all the conditioning of human existence intervened.

The return to the present moment that we've seen in earthy, everyday images also comes in the last stanza of a song in strange, ungraspable *nirguṇ* language:

Nowhere, go there,
swan, go there,
nowhere.
Return, stay there,
nowhere.
You'll have no fear
of birth and death.

That one has no sect, no twelve branches,[26]
no ground to stand on.
You can't say its name out loud
or silently, so whose name
are you trying to remember,
swan?

Without ground, the waterwheel turns,
without cloud, without water,
without a vessel nectar pours,
so drink that nectar,
swan.

Brahma, Vishnu, Shiva, those gods
come and go. That syllable
isn't long or short,
that's the word
you should repeat,
swan.

What's gone will not come back,
so live this moment now.

Kabir says listen, seeker,
build your house
in that country,
swan.

Nowhere, go there,
swan, go there,
nowhere.
Return, stay there,
nowhere.
You'll have no fear
of birth and death.[27]

That Country

There is a country, a *deśh*, that constantly shows up in the Kabir songs of Malwa, though I didn't encounter it when I was farther north and east, in Varanasi, studying the *Bījak*.[28] The *deśh* may be a theme that belongs to Rajasthan and its border areas, as it appears often in Rajasthani songs as well. Or it may be related to the mythology of *nirguṇ* sects like Radhasoami and the Dharamdasi Kabir Panth, which have elaborate descriptions of realms beyond this world where the spiritual traveler goes.

The *deśh* is a marvelous place, a place where we really belong and that belongs to us, though it is strange by normal standards. One song devoted mainly to satirical commentary repeatedly invokes the *deśh* in the refrain:

Why have you forgotten your country, you crazy?
Why have you forgotten your own country?

The deluded gardener tears off a leaf.
In every leaf is life!
She tears a leaf, gives it to a [stone] god.
That god has no life, you crazy!

Why have you forgotten your country?

We have met the theme of the *pardesī*, the foreigner. The song that brought forth Prahladji's tears in Bhopal comments ruefully on the unreliability of everyone with whom we might think of forging a solid bond: they're all foreigners, bound to leave this place as suddenly as they came. In another angle on the *pardesī*, the speaker declares himself a foreigner who belongs somewhere else. I first heard "I'm a bird from another country" on an old, privately recorded cassette of the great classical singer Kumar Gandharva. It haunted me even before I understood the words. Later I found out that Kumarji lived in Malwa and learned many Kabir bhajans from wandering yogis and ordinary rural people. When I heard Prahladji's version of the song, the words and melody were similar though not identical.

I'm a bird from another country, baba,
I don't belong to this country.
The people in this country are unconscious,
every moment sunk in regret,
brothers, seekers, I don't belong
to this country.

I sing without a mouth
walk without feet
fly without wings.
Awareness free
of illusion, I play
in the limitless.

Sitting in the shade, I burn.
In the sun, I'm cool.
My true guru is beyond
sun or shade.
I dwell in the guru.

I'm a bird from another country, baba,
I don't belong to this country.

As reported in chapter 1, while organizing the first U.S. tour of the Malwa singers in 2003, I took inspiration from the repeated refrain of one of their bhajans:

chalo hamārā des / Come to my country.

Songs that talk about the *deś h* often address the *helī*—a dear, intimate, female friend. *Helī* songs constitute another genre that could have had its own section. The epicenter of this genre is Rajasthan, where such songs are numerous; I encountered no *helī* texts during my early work on Kabir in Uttar Pradesh.[29] *Helī* songs are characterized by the frequent cry of address, *mhārī helī!*—my dear friend! The cry is energetic, often high-pitched, with the last syllable sustained on a long note. It punctuates the song, making the communication more immediate, emotional, and dramatic.

The following song stays with the theme of that *deśh* all the way, sustaining a subtle tension between the concrete quality of "country" and the no-quality of *nirguṇ*, *shūnya* (empty), *nyārā* (beyond/ other). It is about an experience that happens in the body; we know this because of the yogic language. While in the body, it also dissolves the body's boundaries.

My country is like this.
Touch the innermost secret and see.

Veda and Quran can't reach the border,
it's utterly beyond speaking and listening.
Above the eight lotuses and ten doors
that one lives.

My country is like this.

Without clouds, thunder crashes.
Without sun, brilliance flashes.
Without eyes, string your beads.
Pronounce the word.

My country is like this.

In the palace of emptiness an instrument plays—
vina, flute, sitar.
One who climbs to the cave in the sky
sees the boundless, the pathless.

My country is like this.

A water-drop falls into water,
not salty, not sweet.
Kabir says, listen friends, seekers,
Someone dear to the guru will get there.

My country is like this.
Touch the innermost secret and see.[30]

Not only "empty" and "other," that country is mad—*divānā*. "Madness" here has the ambiguity it also has in other languages. One can be mad with love; one can be mad because one's experiences and views of the world are so wildly different from the norm.

It's with you but you can't find it.
Someone who knows the guru, someone wise, understands.

Oh seekers, friends,
that country is mad.

I don't go to holy places, don't recite the name,
don't practice asceticism or meditation.
Just as I am, I play in the world. No special image or place.

that country is mad
I walk the path without feet, see without eyes,
without ears hear a flute, without nose smell fragrance,
without tongue taste the essence.

that country is mad
On the lake of simplicity, the swan remembers.
It flies without wings. It pecks up pearls on the bank
of Mansarovar, a well of pure water.

that country is mad.[31]

The City of Love

One of Kabir's most universally cited couplets proclaims love as a kind of ultimate mantra:

pothī paḍh paḍh jag muā, paṇḍit bhayā nā koī
ḍhāī akśhar prem kā, paḍhe so paṇḍit hoī

They all read piles of books, then died.
None became wise.
Read four letters: love.
Wisdom is yours.

It's surprising. That austere Kabir, the one who keeps drawing pictures of death, who takes us to obscure verbal realms where the subject is beyond words, and who is more than a little skeptical of family ties, also likes to sing with full, rich feeling about love. What is the nature of this love?

In one of our musical sessions in Bangalore before breakfast, Shabnam sang a string of *sākhīs* about love.

Love doesn't grow in gardens,
love isn't sold in shops.
One who lacks love is bound up
and heading for hell.

***

Everyone talks about love, love.
No one can recognize love.
This cage holds something that won't diminish.
That's called love.

***

A body not infused with love
might as well be a cremation ground.
Like a blacksmith's bellows,
it breathes without life.

***

Try but you can't hide love
when your body feels it rise.
If you don't speak with the mouth
it makes you weep with the eyes.

***

Come into my eyes!
I'll take you behind my lids,
won't look at anyone else,
and won't let you look away.

***

Make your eyes a room
Spread the bed of your pupil

Drop the curtain of your lids
Please your lord there.

***

You want to taste the juice of love
and keep your pride?
Two swords in one sheath.
Never heard of it!

***

Saying "you, you," I became you.
No "I" is left in me.
Completely surrendered.
Wherever I look—you.

These led into one of our favorite songs:

Come along to the guru's country,
the city of feeling,
the city of love.
The city of feeling, dear helī,
the city of love.

Like the young bud of a *kachanār* tree,
the craftsman has made this body wondrous,
made it wondrous, but with defects.
Come along to the guru's country,
the city of feeling,
the city of love.

The moth's color, golden like turmeric,
flies away at the hour of death,
the hour of death, dear *helī,* the hour of death.
Come along to the guru's country,
the city of feeling,
the city of love.

Don't be proud of your body,
the body's a bag of skin,
a bag of skin, dear *helī,* with many defects.
Come along to the guru's country,

the city of feeling,
the city of love.

Gulabi Das says, from singing these songs
my body has become good.
The body is good, dear *helī*, defects have melted away.
Come along to the guru's country,
the city of feeling,
the city of love.

Love isn't easy to understand within any culture or across the distance between two individuals, let alone across cultures. Who knows if what I'm saying about love in Kabir as represented in Malwi folk songs makes any sense?[32]

Kabir directs our attention and intention toward giving up possessiveness and facing death. The body is dust right now. Why cling to anything? Kabir also shows the body right now as wondrous, revealing the wonder of everything. Pay attention to this moment! It won't come back. Once the leaf is blown off the tree, how will they meet again? Sometimes in Kabir and related *nirguṇ* poets, love is found in the unspeakable fragility of these tender, fleeting relationships. *Jājo jājo re, bhāī mhārā jājo* is a song that conveys this feeling.

Go, go, my brother, go,
cross the ocean, bring back an unpierced pearl, oh seeker.

I found them, found jewels, thousands of them,
but the pearl of the heart I couldn't find.

It has flown, flown away, the bird of the forest.
Where is the temple's dweller now?

Embrace, embrace, my brother, embrace
with outstretched arms. Any moment, separated—when
will we meet?

It's split, split, my brother, the milk of the heavenly cow
has split.
Once the milk splits, the curd will never come together.

It's tied, tied up, my brother, tied in knots.
The string's end has broken off, it can't come loose.

He speaks, speaks, my brother, Dharu Prahlad speaks
to the seeker: meet, meet, forever keep on meeting.

Go, go, my brother, go,
cross the ocean, bring back an unpierced pearl, oh seeker.

In all the categories of this impromptu anthology, I could go on with many examples. Like Prahladji in a performance, I am limited by time/space. I conclude the "love" section, based on my knowledge and mood at this moment, with *Aisī mhārī prīt nibhāvajo*—a song using imagery that has been popular in Indian love poetry, both religious and secular, for thousands of years, but concluding with the typical *nirguṇ* shift, locating the beloved intimately within oneself.

Stay true to my love, oh Ram
Don't leave me in this world-ocean

You are a tree, I am a vine
I'll stay entwined around you
If you fall, I wither
What will become of me?
Don't forget me in this world-ocean
Stay true to my love, oh Ram

You are an ocean, I am a fish
I'll stay inside you
If you go dry, I die
What will become of me?
Stay true to my love, oh Ram

You are a cloud, I am a peacock
I'll stay entranced by you
If you thunder, I call out
(Alternate line: If you burst with rain, I sing to you)
What will become of me?
Stay true to my love, oh Ram

Says Kabir to Dharamdas—
Your beloved dwells in your body
Your beloved makes your heart beat
Don't forget me in this world-ocean
Stay true to my love, oh Ram

Drunken Joy

Out on a field one day, we met Kaluram Bamaniya and his group.[33] It was Shabnam's first ride through the Malwa countryside. The men brought special outfits, matching black vests to wear over their white kurtas, bright red turbans that they put on as we watched, stretching the cloth out twenty feet and helping each other to wrap it. They spread a sheet on the ground and sat down with their instruments. Next to the sheet was a pile of dry cornstalks. Our late arrival put a sinking sun behind them, which subtly colored and softened the light. The soil was rosy brown. After a couple of songs in medium tempo, Kaluram started a new refrain.

> *man lāgo mero yār fakīrī meṇ*
>
> This mind, my friend, has learned to love
> owning nothing.

I had heard the words before but not the tune. It was fast and happy. Trying to translate it, I run into problems. The refrain is short and completely comprehensible to the Hindi audience. But what to do in English with *fakīrī*? It is the state of being a *fakīr*—a renunciant who possesses nothing and wanders carefree. Kabir commonly uses Hindu words to signify a world-renouncer, but this word comes from Arabic and is associated with Islam. *Fakīr* (which in Arabic originally means "poor") has a different feeling, conjures up a somewhat different visual image and set of associations, from the Hindu-connected *sādhu, yogī, avadhūt*. My translation can't really convey the message that there is something "Muslim" and "Sufi" about this word. Then the verb *lāgo*—so common, short and simple, but with a range of meanings. *Lagnā* means to become attached, involved, deeply engaged—usually in a positive way. It's omnipresent in Hindi, taking on various shades of meaning. There's no simple equivalent in English. Taking some poetic license, I have used four words ("has learned to love"). Further, *yār* (from Persian) is more intimate and informal than other common words for "friend." In fact all the key words—the rhyming *fakīrī, amīrī, garībī, jāgīrī, sabūrī, magarūrī, sarūrī*—are from Perso-Arabic roots, which is unusual in the Kabir texts I'm familiar with. Remember as you read that the refrain is repeated after every stanza.

man lāgo mero yār fakīrī meṇ

jo sukh pāvogā rām bhajan meṇ, vo sukh nāhīṇ amīrī meṇ
hāth meṇ tumbā bagal meṇ soṭā, chāroṇ diśhā jāgīrī meṇ
bhalā bura sab kā sun līje, kar gujarān garībī meṇ
ākhir yeh tan khākh milegā, kyon phire magarūrī meṇ
kahe kabīr suno bhāī sādho, sāhib milegā sarurī [sabūrī] meṇ

This mind, my friend, has learned to love
owning nothing.

The happiness you get singing God's name,
you won't get that happiness from money.

A water-gourd in my hand, a stick to lean on,
my kingdom stretches in four directions.[34]

Listen to everyone, good and bad,
live at ease in poverty.

At last this body will meet with dust.
Why strut with pride?

Kabir says, listen seekers:
you meet God
in joy.[35]

Man lāgo mero yār was rocking, lilting, upbeat. But Kaluram's next offering took us even higher: *Man mast huā phir kyā bole. Mast* is an adjective referring to a state of abandonment, a joy that fills you to the brim and beyond, ecstatic, with no trace of agitation. It is defined in dictionaries as supreme happiness, drunkenness, freedom from anxiety, unwavering absorption. *Man,* translated as "mind" in the previous poem, also means "heart."

man mast huā phir kyā bole

halkī thī jab chaḍhī tarāju, pūrī bharī tab kyā tole
hīrā pāyo bāndh gaṭhariyā, bār bār vāko kyoṇ khole
haṃsa pāve mānsarovar, tāl talaīyā meṇ kyoṇ dole
surat kalālin bhayī matavālī madavā pī gayī anatole
kahe kabīr suno bhāī sādho, sāhib mil gayā til ole

The heart is overjoyed. What to say?

Something light can go on the scale.
When it overflows the tray, what to weigh?
You found a diamond, tied it in your scarf.
Why keep opening it to count your riches?
The swan has found Lake Mansarovar.
Why paddle around in ponds and ditches?
The wineseller, awareness, is drunk herself.
She goes on drinking wine, no end.
Kabir says, listen seekers:
here's God—in the pupil of your eye![36]

The heart is overjoyed. What to say?

Kaluram is booming, grooving. Why speak? What to say? The two long, open vowels in *bole* flow like rivers, quicksilver, up and down, swift and free in their channels of melody, exuberant. Everyone in the *maṇḍalī* has got the spirit. They're smiling and their bodies thrum as they bring forth music from instruments and voices. Our companion and guide Narayanji, in a long yellow *kurtā*, jumps up and dances, twirling around and extending his arms in liquid movements. Shabnam kneels, one hand holding the camera, the other spinning above her head, forefinger pointed in a Punjabi-style dance move. The earth and sky are right with us.

Sometimes instead of drunkenness, we hear of madness—using *divānā*, a special poetic word for "mad" that signifies the blessed madness of love and joy:

Don't mess with me!
I'm mad with the name, mad
with the song.
Stand away from me, friend,
get back, the knife
of truth is in my hand,
I'll strike you!
Don't anyone mess with me,
I'm mad with the name, mad
with the song.[37]

The theme of great joy occurs in Kabir performances and collections everywhere. Joy flows, joy floods; so it brings forth imagery of liquids.[38]

Drink! A cascade of nectar pours from the sky.

One drop fills a thirsty person's pot. You can't even dream
of the taste! How to explain this, and to whom?
One drop takes you home.

You have to be thirsty to drink that water. That water
is only for the thirsty. No unfit person can know
this cascade of nectar, this great flow.

Drink the nectar, be deathless, forever free
from the cycles of birth, the rounds of pain.
The vessel of your body is filling. It's full!

That drop of nectar is the guru's word.
That water is the road of life.
Kabir has found the right companions.
Green leaves burst forth
on the branch of love.

Drink! A cascade of nectar pours from the sky.

Sometimes the drink is *amṛit* (nectar), sometimes *ras* (juice, liquid, essence) or *premras* (the liquid of love). One popular song names a cannabis drink—*bhāng*—as the source of drunkenness.[39]

The great flow can be evoked as monsoon rain:

My true guru tells the secret, seekers, friends,
the complete guru reveals it, oh yes,
a boundless rain is pouring.

From the east rushes the eastern wind,
merging with waves in the west.
Whoosh-whoosh, the fountains are bursting,
the torrents of rain unceasing, friends.[40]

Or a marvelous root can yield its liquid essence:

A root of wisdom, the true guru gave me, he gave me
a root of wisdom. That root
was very dear to me, filled
with nectar.[41]

It is worth reprising briefly here the story, told in chapter 2, of Prahladji's visit with Chenamaru a very old man who was the first to teach him bhajans. Shabnam captures the scene poignantly in film. The old bhajan-guru looks thin and frail. His cheeks sprout grey stubble, and his eyes don't seem to focus well. But he is smiling and pleased at the visit. After some reminiscing, Prahladji tries to get him to sing. He protests: "Oh no, I can't do that anymore, don't trouble me." All smiles, Prahladji says, "Aren't I here with you? We'll sing together." Prahladji starts a song that he learned from Chenamaru some thirty years before. It tells of an imminent meeting with the guru, the sahib, the lord. In that meeting all petty possessiveness will melt away, replaced by freedom. All boundaries will disappear. The images of this journey get more mysterious toward the end. But the refrain simply announces drunkenness, *nashā*:

> I'm on my way
> to meet the true guru, on my way
> to meet the lord.
> I'm smashed, completely drunk, my friend,
> about to meet the lord.[42]

Though he had protested that he didn't have the energy to sing any more, during this song and one that followed—also about drunkenness—Chenaji's eyes lit up and he sang along with gusto. One month later he passed away.

No Ending, Just Stopping

Oral traditions, unlike critical editions, don't end. The listener just steps away, knowing that the singing and weaving of texts will go on whether she is there or not. We conclude with a few passages from my field notes in 2011 and 2012.

> At this point there are probably 100 Kabir songs from Malwa that I "know"—meaning that they call forth a smile of recognition from me when they are sung. These are, perhaps, a fair representation of popular Malwa Kabir in the first decade of the twenty-first century. It is startling to run down the contents of a scholarly collection of

Kabir poems and to find none of them. A new singer in a new village is sure to come up with many songs that I don't recognize. Why should I be surprised? Prahladji has at least ten notebooks in which he's been writing since 1977. Almost every page is filled on both sides with handwritten texts. When Eklavya documented the Kabir traditions of the region in the 1990s, they collected such notebooks from many singers, photocopying the contents. They counted about 1500 distinct song texts. (Eklavya 1999)

***

PT has been singing out of the ancient-looking copybooks. One morning I find him copying from a tattered discolored sheet of paper from which the words are disappearing. Other mornings he just takes something, seemingly at random, and the song opens an unbelievable little world that becomes at moments a very big world, through specific, concrete, local images. He explains to me the operation of an old-style still with which Adivasi (tribal) people made liquor. He gives a technical description including two clay pots and pipes and heat in the first pot and eventual rising and condensing of the distilled liquor in the second pot. People who like to say Kabir simply reproduced Advaita Vedanta philosophy in charming vernacular language so that common people could receive it according to their capacities need to understand this. Shankara never gave us an Adivasi distillery. They need to understand the power and beauty of the poetry that arises from people's everyday lives, that totally pervades Kabir and Bhavani Nath and other locally known poets whose names keep cropping up as I sit with someone who knows so much. The distillery is only a token of the incalculable richness of this world of language and experience.[43] PT tells me that the people who dictated these songs to him long ago were completely illiterate, but they had tremendous knowledge. They are gone now.

***

Narayanji, Kaluram, and Ajay have been doing research for the Kabir Project. One task is to find *maṇḍalīs* led by old men and to record what they sing. We went to visit one such group in the village of Chaubaradhira. The leader was the only really old one—the others appeared to be in their 40s, 50s, or 60s. Asked his age, the leader said 70–75. Ajay said: "The last time we were here you said 80–85." The man said something equivalent to "whatever," and added, "How am I supposed to know my exact age?" He looked closer to 80 than 70 to me. He spoke with clarity and sang with energy. Though Narayanji is 67, steeped in Kabir singing for forty years, and incredibly knowledgeable, he reported that they sang songs he had never heard before, and some songs were in musical styles unfamiliar to him.

***

In June 2011, Shabnam asked Prahladji and team to come to Bangalore for a three-day retreat. They went to a quiet place, with two co-workers, Smriti and Aarthi, operating video cameras. Prahladji's assignment was to sing bhajans that Shabnam had never heard before. Seventy-five songs were recorded. They compromised on the ground rule, since Shabnam decided to record some songs she already knew. But about fifty were new to her. And he could have produced many more. Not long after, when I'm with him in the village, I sense the influence of that three-day retreat. Our little informal singing sessions include many songs that are totally new to me (meaning that they are really old for him). Even the young girls at Siya village, whom Narayanji and Kaluram have been teaching, produced surprising things, like one bhajan that mingled the names of Kabir, Mira, and Tulsi, and another that concluded, "Kabir says to black Keshav . . . ." There is simply no end to the number and variety of songs in Kabir oral tradition.

"You Won't Get That Happiness from Money . . ."

We began the last section of songs, "Drunken Joy," with two bhajans that speak of supreme happiness. They reject attachment to wealth and possessions. One line even exhorts the listener to relax and enjoy poverty. It so happens that most of the people who join Kabir *maṇḍalīs* in rural Malwa are fairly poor. They have little land; most don't have steady jobs; and their caste status has made them subject to oppression and exploitation. In the session described above, Kaluram and his group first sang a song about patience, contentment, comfort in poverty, and freedom in nonpossession; they followed with a song about inner joy, fullness beyond words or measure. An observer might wonder: Are they escaping from their economic and social limitations by singing such songs? Are they flying to a fantasy land where poverty is a happy thing instead of a miserable thing? These are questions that we will explore in chapters 6 and 8.

5

Oral Tradition in the Twenty-First Century

EXPLORING THEORY

Sound is not what one should desire to understand.
One should know the hearer.
KAUṢĪTAKI UPANIṢAD 3.8

STUDYING ORAL TRADITION at this historical moment has taken me where I didn't expect to go: into media and communication, technology and neuroscience. Though I did not initially intend to write a chapter on theories of orality, I thought it would be wise to take a look at the scholarship on oral traditions. Starting innocently by reviewing the history of orality theory in the last fifty years, I soon understood that there is no such thing as orality plain and simple. This was the end of innocence. Now what? Should I abandon my project, which had "oral traditions" in the title? Should I abandon the very idea of orality, as recommended by Jonathan Sterne, a brilliant scholar in the growing field of "sound studies"? (More on him below.) Could I develop a smarter concept of orality that would not have to negate everything the twentieth-century orality scholars wrote and that would still escape the bruising critique of Sterne?

This chapter is a nod to a field that is too big for me to embrace but too important for me to ignore. It is strikingly different from the rest of the book, which is grounded in ethnographic and textual study of Kabir in specific places and times. Here, Kabir will rarely be mentioned. I have persisted in writing the chapter because of a central question that textual and ethnographic study can hint at but cannot address directly. That question is: What is the difference in our experience when we receive or perform Kabir orally, as compared to when we read Kabir or receive the poetry through other media? How are we alive in different ways?

Chapter 2 examined what happens to *texts* in an oral-performative world, and what happens to our understanding of texts when we perceive them as existing in that world. The present chapter considers what happens to *people* in oral-performative milieus. What goes on in our bodies and minds, our ways of thinking, feeling, and remembering? Can we make a distinction between the experience of a written text and the experience of a musical text that is sung in live performance? Can we also distinguish the oral-performative from other ways of receiving information that have recently rushed into common experience—audio, video, internet, hypertext, virtual reality? Clearly these questions tax my competence. This chapter is a layperson's exploration. At times I may sound like a cheerleader for the oral, or a grumpy complainer about the digital. Such is not my intention, but it is a built-in hazard as I try to trace out what makes the oral-performative a particular and valuable mode of experience.

To explore these matters, we will wend our way through the following:

(1) Theories of orality, literacy, and media that flourished in the latter half of the twentieth century.
(2) Challenges in the last twenty years to those ideas about orality and literacy.
(3) The concept of "secondary orality," which proposes that electronic media in general and the internet in particular are similar to oral tradition, and that oral tradition and the internet differ in similar ways from print media.
(4) The recent efflorescence of neuroscientific research in the study of media, perception, and cognition.

I will argue that, although there is no pure orality or literacy anywhere, it is still possible to think about oral-performative modes and to study them as distinct from literary and other media. A parallel argument (related to "orality" discourses of the twentieth century) is that, although there is no pure and independent function of the senses, there are still differences among hearing, seeing, and other modes of sense perception, and we can discuss those differences. To test this immediately, look at a tree when the wind is blowing. You perceive the tree through colors, shapes, visible motions, and so on. Close your eyes and listen. You perceive the sounds of wind, the sounds made by leaves and branches as they move, birds in the tree, and so on. Your perception of the tree is primarily visual the first time, aural the second. You could do the same with tactile sensation. What the tree becomes in each case is quite different. How your body and mind are functioning in each case is different. To grant that they are different is easy. To state the nature and significance of the difference is hard.

I will argue further that music has a transformative effect on how we receive and understand text. That is an obvious fact, observed in this humanities-based book through evocative descriptions of and conversations about Kabir music. The scientific ways of substantiating this fact are not obvious. I simply hint at scientific explorations here. The point is to include music as an essential aspect of the oral-performative difference in the Kabir cultures we have been studying.

Finally I will argue that live, embodied presence is key to the oral-performative difference. This argument points both to the individual body-mind experience when people are in direct physical proximity to each other and to the larger dynamics of social interaction.[1]

My conclusion: It is the combination of sound, music, physical presence, and social interaction that produces a distinct oral-performative experience in the Kabir culture of North India.

Orality Studies from the Mid-Twentieth Century

When I started graduate school in comparative literature in 1970, I was immediately made to read Albert Lord's 1960 work *The Singer of Tales* and given those linked names, Parry and Lord, a pair of brave new stars to fix in the firmament of literary methodology.[2] In the 1930s, Harvard professor Milman Parry had discovered relatively "pure" living traditions of oral epic in Yugoslavia. His student Albert Lord had used and expanded Parry's data collection to theorize oral composition and draw lines of demarcation between written and oral poetic narratives, emphasizing the significance of the work to Homeric studies. This produced a great shaking at its comp lit and classics epicenter. Comp lit students in those days had an origin myth: "In the beginning was Homer." Soon the seismic waves spread outward. It was fascinating to think about orality—an utterly different frame of mind, one might even say a different brain—in singers, listeners, poets, cultures. It made us suddenly reflect on what had previously been unconscious: our own inescapable, all-encompassing literacy; our unquestioned assumption that books and writing were the natural and indispensable ways of producing and transmitting knowledge; and our obliviousness as to how that affected the way our minds operated.

Many scholars took up orality, literacy, and media from 1960 on. Among the best known are Marshall McLuhan, Eric Havelock, Walter Ong, Jack Goody, Ruth Finnegan, and John Miles Foley; many more could be named.[3] Writing a book in the 2000s with "oral traditions" in the title, naturally I needed to review this half-century of theory and fieldwork. Because of the moment in media history in which I found myself, the journey took on strange dimensions. Sometimes it felt like going through the looking glass.

There is no world of purely oral text production and reception as there seemed to be, briefly, when Milman Parry came into contact with epic singers in Yugoslavia in 1933. Here we confront a slippage in orality studies that is crucial to our present consideration of them. After Parry and Lord, it became common to imagine an absolute distinction between oral and literary milieus. In *The Singer of Tales*, Lord contends that "the two techniques are ... contradictory and mutually exclusive. Once the oral technique is lost, it is never regained.... It is conceivable that a man might be an oral poet in his younger years and a written poet later in life, but it is not possible that he be both an oral and a written poet at any given time in his career. The two by their very nature are mutually exclusive" (Lord 1960, 129). Twenty-six years later, he remains firm on the separation: "Let there be no doubt on this question ... oral traditional literature without a clear distinction between it and 'written literature' ceases to exist" (Lord 1986, 468).

As long as he is talking about singers who compose orally, Lord's argument makes some sense. The process of *composition* does change when singers begin to read and write the material that they perform. But here is the slippage that caused so much trouble later: from talking about a process of composition, scholars began to generalize about "cultures." Some cultures, they proposed, are oral, and others are literate. We can describe the essential characteristics of these two types of culture, no matter where they are in space and time, no matter what other factors are in play. This essentializing through much of the twentieth century dovetailed with a colonial mentality that infected the thinking of most Euro-Americans. The colonially inflected way of framing cultures tended to align oral with primitive, literate with civilized.

Ruth Finnegan and John Miles Foley, whose many works on orality extend from the 1970s to the present, reject the sharp distinction between oral and literate worlds. Finnegan criticizes what she calls the romantic theory of orality that insists on "'pure' oral tradition, uncontaminated by influence or interference from written or printed forms." She traces this theory back to the early nineteenth century but finds it to be still popular among scholars in the late twentieth century. Finnegan herself takes a lively interest in the interactions of oral and written forms and the interplay of aesthetic, commercial, recreational, and political forces in answering the question, "How do oral poems reach their audiences?" (Finnegan 1977, 140–41). She unequivocally rejects the notion of essentially oral and literary cultures:

> They shade into each other both in the present and over many centuries of historical development, and there are innumerable cases of poetry which has both "oral" and "written" elements. The idea of pure and uncontaminated "oral culture" as the primary reference point for the discussion of oral poetry is a myth. (Finnegan 1977, 24)

Foley similarly dismisses the airtight categories some of the founding gurus proposed: "If research over the past quarter-century has shown anything, it's that the so-called Great Divide of orality versus literacy amounts to an illusion that has outlived its usefulness."[4]

If the Great Divide is an illusion, then what is oral about "oral Kabir"? If oral, written, and diversely recorded texts are not separate but interacting, in what ways is it meaningful to talk about a category called "oral-performative"? Along with writing and print, how do we factor in other ways of freezing text—records, cassettes, CDs, video? While we are thinking about this (and emailing, youtubing, and smartphoning about it), something more vast and confounding opens up. Mediascapes are changing with stunning rapidity around us and within us. Whatever we were saying about the normativity of printed texts is interrupted by the flood of e-books inundating the market and shocking the publishing industry, promising to end the long era of paper-based reading.[5] Internet habits disrupt whatever we used to do when we read. Hypertext blows away practices of attention and coherence. We reach portals where signs say, in their own ways, "Eat me," "Drink me." But instead of a cup or a plate, we get a microprocessor. The rabbit-holes of media are electronically produced. We are tumbling down, over, and up even as we write about media. We can hardly keep track of what is "physical" in the old-fashioned sense and what is produced by electronic stimulation of our neural networks.

Where did I read Foley's statement, quoted above, on the "Great Divide"? Not in any book or journal, but on his website, www.pathwaysproject.org.

Who knows if that sentence, accessed in July 2009, is still "there" as I complete this book, or as you read it? ("There" means an infinite virtual space currently known as "the cloud.") For decades a prominent scholar of oral traditions, Foley has taken what he sees as the next step in building a website to argue and demonstrate that oral tradition and the internet are similar, while both are in striking contrast with written texts:

> The major purpose of the Pathways Project is to illustrate and explain the fundamental similarities and correspondences between humankind's oldest and newest thought-technologies: oral tradition and the Internet.
>
> Despite superficial differences, both technologies are radically alike in depending not on static products but rather on continuous processes, not on "What?" but on "How do I get there?" In contrast to the fixed spatial organization of the page and book, the technologies of oral tradition and the Internet *mime the way we think* by processing along pathways within a network. In both media it's pathways—not things—that matter.[6]

Foley's thesis was anticipated by Walter Ong some thirty years prior to the Pathways website, and by Marshall McLuhan before that. *The Gutenberg Galaxy* was prescient in many of its observations about media. On his first page, McLuhan says: "Any technology tends to create a new human environment. . . . Technological environments are not merely passive containers of people but are active processes that reshape people and other technologies alike" (1962, unnumbered page). He points to script and papyrus, stirrup and wheel, and "the sudden shift from the mechanical technology of the wheel to the technologies of electric circuitry." One of the effects of printing with movable type, he suggests, was that "it created the PUBLIC." Print, unlike manuscripts, had the power to create a national public and was thus indispensable to the rise of nation-states. Electric circuitry, he suggests, signals the demise of nations: "What we have called 'nations' in recent centuries did not, and could not, precede the advent of Gutenberg technology any more than they can survive the advent of electric circuitry with its power of totally involving all people in all other people" (ibid.).[7]

McLuhan referenced radio, television, and primitive computers as "electric circuitry." Digital technology and the internet have propelled us much farther beyond print than he was able to witness, though he foresaw the direction: "Today, after more than a century of electric technology, we have extended our central nervous system itself in a global embrace, abolishing both space and time as far as our planet is concerned."[8] As a website on the history of the internet puts it, McLuhan "made the concept of a global village, interconnected by an electronic nervous system, part of our popular culture well before it actually happened."[9]

Parry and Lord did minute and illuminating work on the characteristics of oral composition and performance, based on fieldwork in particular cultures. They observed how oral poets weave texts together by using formulas, themes, meters, rhythms, and repetitive structures. These conventions make possible great feats of memory and formal mastery while still allowing for individual creativity and unpredictability. Many of the same conventions operate in oral transmission of Kabir poetry, as seen in chapter 2 and elsewhere in this book. Along with these similarities, there are significant differences between oral epics and Kabir songs. Epics are long narratives. Songs are based on short poems. Aesthetically and emotionally, they function quite differently. They command attention in different ways. But formally they have much in common, and students of bhakti song performance in South Asia can benefit from the fine-grained observations of Lord and subsequent fieldworkers on oral poetic narrative.

I will return to Foley's "pathways" website later in the chapter, in a section on the internet and the notion of secondary orality.

Media Transitions

Historians since the mid-twentieth century have tracked transitional moments in media and their wider contexts: the rise of manuscript culture in medieval Europe; the emergence of the printing press; the interactions of manuscripts and books with traditional oral modes of discourse; the effects of print and print capitalism; audio and video recording; and the leap into the age of the internet and virtual reality (to name a few highlights). During periods of transition from one technological era to another, we begin to notice something big going on. McLuhan and Ong talk about a long historical process of interiorizing a new technology. At first, when it is novel, it may be seen as either appealing or appalling. In its full sway, we don't even notice it. Print and the all-consuming power of the written word were taken for granted as natural and inevitable in the twentieth century. Even in the early twenty-first, those of us who lived most of our adult lives in the previous century can't quite see through our models of literacy, though everything is changing.

> [W]hen some previously opaque area becomes translucent, it is because we have moved into another phase from which we can contemplate the contours of the preceding situation with ease and clarity. It is this fact that makes it feasible to write *The Gutenberg Galaxy* at all. As we experience the new electronic and organic age with ever stronger indications of its main outlines, the preceding mechanical age becomes quite intelligible. (McLuhan 1962, 275)

The mind conditioned to print, or to any other primary medium of communication, comes to take that medium, its conventions and assumptions, for granted. McLuhan cites H. L. Chaytor's 1945 book *From Script to Print*, which he credits with inspiring *The Gutenberg Galaxy*.

> [T]he result of the fusion [of sound and sight, speech and print] is that once it is achieved in our early years, we … cannot think of sounds without thinking of letters; we believe letters have sounds. We think that the printed page is a picture of what we say, and that the mysterious thing called 'spelling' is sacred. … The invention of printing broadcast the printed language and gave to print a degree of authority that it has never lost. … So also when we speak or write, ideas evoke acoustic combined with kinesthetic images, which are at once transformed into visual word images. The speaker or writer can now hardly conceive of language, except in printed or written form; the reflex actions by which the process of reading or writing is performed have become so 'instinctive' and are performed with such facile rapidity, that the change from the auditory to the visual is concealed from the reader or writer.[10]

This hegemony of print has held sway among the world's formally educated classes over a period that roughly coincides with that of the great Euro-American empires and the rise of nation-states—the sixteenth through twentieth centuries. Along with most of my readers, I am permeated through and through with its effects. Our brains are shaped by it. We automatically filter language and knowledge through this taken-for-granted technology.

In the early twenty-first century we are experiencing another epochal transformation in communication media, and therefore in our brains. The demise of the book is widely trumpeted, and the brain-shapes of those who live in perpetual connectivity—the branching, spinning, virtual dimensions of the web—are under scrutiny. Is the book really dead? Is the hegemony of print over? I don't know. Even as I reflect on orality and print, the explosions of the new mediascape dazzle my real and virtual eyes.

Media affect what we perceive, how we think, and how we organize our knowledge. I have defined "oral-performative Kabir" as referring to live, body-to-body transmission, where sounds produced by voices and instruments reach ears located in the same physical vicinity. A potential objection to this definition is voiced by Philip Auslander, who, in his book *Liveness,* warns against artificially separating live from mediatized performance—a move often correlated with a higher valuation of what is live. In his introduction, after discussing how television originally modeled itself on a live form (theater) and more recently how live events have modeled themselves on mediatized representations, Auslander says:

> I . . . turn to the way in which the issue of live performance is treated in contemporary performance theory and challenge its grounding of the distinction . . . in ostensible ontological differences between live and mediatized forms. Against that formulation, I argue that the relationship between live and mediatized forms and the meaning of liveness be understood as historical and contingent rather than determined by immutable differences. To conclude . . . I examine several of the conventional explanations for why people value live performance and offer a suggestion of how liveness is being redefined for the digital age. (Auslander 2008 [1999], 7–8)

There is always some arbitrariness in imposing categories on real life. I define oral performance as live body-to-body communication in order to examine the consequences of experiencing Kabir in that distinct way. That doesn't mean I am claiming an *ontological* difference between live and mediatized, or denying that the relationship between them is also historical and contingent. Historicity and contingency must enter the picture when we study, for example, the fate of texts (as in chapters 2 and 4, which focus on texts). When we study the experience of people in transmitting and receiving texts, it is acceptable to limit the range of situations we wish to examine. Even when I specify the situation narrowly in terms of live communication, where the bodies are physically close enough for the listener to hear the performer's voice directly, there is a technological gray area. What if they are using microphones? I include amplified performance in my category of live oral performance, though this is admittedly a slightly "mediatized" event and shows that the boundary is not absolute.

Reflecting on our own experience, we notice certain characteristics of oral and written modes of communication.[11] Oral performances are unrepeatable events in time and involve physical proximity of performers and audiences. They entail a certain fluidity of text, a certain unpredictability of content and interaction. Printed texts are fixed, can be individually owned and returned to, and are normally consumed privately. Memory—particularly ability to remember text—tends to be stronger in oral than in print-based situations. Orality implies sociality, which can be dispensed with in consumption of print and other fixed portable media. Audio and video recordings, which became common in the twentieth century, are similar to print in that they offer fixed texts that can be bought, sold, and consumed privately, though they are dissimilar in other ways. These are the salient characteristics that come to mind most readily when we try to distinguish oral-performative modes of transmission and reception from other modes.

But orality theorists in the twentieth century went further in describing the differences between "oral" and "literate," positing a fundamental difference between "eye and ear," visual and aural experience. They generalized broadly, going from observations about eye and ear to theories of perception, cognition, consciousness, social and cultural formations, sometimes economic and political implications. McLuhan, for example, dwells on changes wrought by the transition from ear to eye through printing. The phonetic alphabet, he claims, thrusts the burden of learning and communicating onto the eye more than any other sense organ. Hearing exists in flowing time, reading in transfixed space. The fixed point of view that becomes possible with print "depends on the isolation of the visual factor in experience." Linear perspective, which developed in the Renaissance simultaneously with printing, begins by establishing a fixed point of view. The person who is speaking and listening, according to McLuhan, lives in a more multisensory, kinesthetic field than one who is reading.

While they had many valuable insights, McLuhan, Ong, and other orality-literacy theorists of their generation went to some very problematic places that are easier to see now than they were in the mid-twentieth century. Exaggerating the dichotomy between orality and literacy they characterized "cultures" as being either oral or literate. Unaware of their location in the lineage of colonial anthropology, they felt they could describe the consciousness and social formations of an "oral culture" wherever and whenever it might exist; this, not surprisingly, led to very awkward ways of talking about "others." McLuhan's racist, exoticizing, evolutionary views about nonliterate people and cultures are based on his eager acceptance of an article by British psychiatrist J. C. Carothers, who was in charge of a mental hospital near Nairobi from 1938 to 1950. In the 1950s, Carothers wrote about "the African mind" in full-throated concurrence with nineteenth-century colonial and evolutionary views on the primitive and the civilized.

The history of twentieth-century theorizing about orality is beautifully summarized in the opening chapter of *Power and the Praise Poem: Southern African Voices in History* by Leroy Vail and Landeg White.[12] Entitled "The Invention of 'Oral Man': Anthropology, Literary Theory, and a Western Intellectual Tradition," the chapter traces two streams of theory about oral traditions, both issuing from the work of Milman Parry and Albert Lord. One stream, including McLuhan, Havelock, Goody, and Ong, posited an undifferentiated "oral man," who coincided roughly with the "primitive" of nineteenth-century colonial thought and the "native" or "tribal" person conjured by anthropologists in the first half of the twentieth. This person was magical, childlike, prelogical, in touch with nature, emotionally active but socially suppressed, incapable of developing as a unique individual. The part of the Parry-Lord theory that they emphasized was the dominance of the formulaic, leading to rigid convention and repetition:

> [T]he often unconscious patterns of narrative and imagery are the methods by which *knowledge* is preserved and transmitted in pre-literate societies . . . . Citing Goody, [Ong] asserts that oral societies are "characterized as homeostatic," living "very much in a present which keeps itself in equilibrium or homeostasis by sloughing off memories which no longer have present relevance." Ong's oral men worldwide are trapped in an endless cycle of repetition until, one day, their history takes off with the invention or importation of signs. . . . [H]is vision of oral communities locked into traditionalism by a determining orality is hopelessly at odds with the actual history of southern Africa over the past two hundred years. (Vail and White 1992, 24–25)

This view of oral literature also contrasts strikingly with Parry's and Lord's emphasis on the *creativity* of the oral composer-performer: "As the romantic title of Lord's book, *The Singer of Tales,* indicates and as Parry always insisted, the whole point of studying oral poetry is to understand and appreciate the individual oral artist's enviable genius" (Vail and White 1992, 25).

The second major stream of Parry-Lord-inspired research and theory includes Ruth Finnegan and a succession of other scholars who have worked in Africa.

> [Their] emphasis upon the creativity of the oral performer . . . has revolutionized the study of praise poetry and narratives, shifting attention away from the stultifying realms of the "collective consciousness" and the timeless "text" and toward the individual artist and the act of creation. The oral poet or narrator is seen no longer as a mere "memorizer," but as an artist, improvising brilliantly within the formulas of his or her own tradition. These are attractive arguments. Not only are they consistent with the obvious fact of the historicity of oral literary traditions, but they also insist forcibly on the nature of literature as literature, putting the creativity of the performer at the center of our attention. (Vail and White 1992, 27)

But there is still a problem, traceable to Parry and Lord's original ideas. Though Parry focused very specifically on the southeastern European oral epic poem, "there was always a tendency . . . to push beyond this narrow focus . . . toward a universal theory of oral literature."

> . . . Lord, too, began with a narrow focus, but he has been similarly imperial in his writing . . . What began as a hypothesis about the making of Homeric verse has come, since the 1960s, to be applied, first, to all oral poetry . . . and second, to all oral literature—praise poems, songs, narratives, moralities, proverbs, tables, and riddles. Oral literature as a worldwide phenomenon has come to be *defined* as literature composed in performance through the manipulation of formulas and formulaic expressions. . . . The link between the separate "literatures" of the world came to lie in their common techniques of composition, while criticism, in Ruth Finnegan's words, confined itself to the study of "detailed stylistic points and formulaic systems leading to statistical conclusions." (Vail and White 1992, 26)

In the last few decades studies of oral literature and performance in Africa have become more sophisticated, turning away from Lord's narrow view of the functions of formulaic repetition and his rigid separation of oral and literary, and embracing far more nuanced and grounded analysis of the circumstances of performance and the dynamics of history.

Having received these indispensable lessons in nineteenth and twentieth-century colonial/racist mindsets and their influence on orality theory, I return to my original question. I would like to say something about the difference in the *experience* of oral and written communication. Nearly all Euro-Americans in the mid-twentieth century harbored far-reaching colonial/racist viewpoints. I submit that it is not necessary to have such views to imagine that human beings, in their various circumstances, have a different relationship to the sense-field and activate different neurophysiological and cognitive processes when they are speaking and listening than when they are reading.

From Orality Theory to Sound Studies

A chance meeting with Jonathan Sterne in 2011 introduced me to "sound studies," which has risen to prominence simultaneously with the explosion of digital technology, virtual reality, new vistas in neuroscience, and the convergence of neuroscience and media studies.

Sterne and others to whom his work has led me—on sound, media, technology, the senses, and the brain—reject much of what twentieth-century orality theorists said. He emphasizes these major problems:

(1) They posit an oral-literate dyad, treating the two as mutually exclusive. This oversimplification leads them to essentialize absurdly, slapping oral ("preliterate") and literate onto a temporal template, implying evolutionary progress, and privileging white European civilization. Sterne demolishes "oral man": "Anyone familiar with the distinctions between, for example, Inuit and Zulu society would find the generalization of both as examples of 'oral man' as 'laughably oversimplified' (Sterne 2011, 220, citing Finnegan 1977, 259).

(2) They separate the senses, assuming that the senses operate in distinct ways that can be characterized, much as oral and literate cultures can

be characterized. This "sensorium" thinking, says Sterne, is "thin and dated" (2011, 220).

> The audiovisual litany [see below] renders the history of the senses as a zero-sum game, where the dominance of one sense by necessity leads to the decline of another sense. But there is no scientific basis for asserting that the use of one sense atrophies another. In addition to its specious reasoning, the audiovisual litany carries with it a good deal of ideological baggage. (Sterne 2003,16)
>
> As a concept of how the human brain works, the "sensorium" was discredited in the late nineteenth century, as physiologists learned there is no single centre of the brain that processes sensory information (not even for individual senses, as it turns out). The evidence for differences between oral and literate culture is based on 50- to 100-year-old interpretations of textual sources. (Sterne 2011, 220)

Taking on the entire history of orality theory, Sterne recommends that we discard the "aging fable" that casts its shadow on the received history of communication.

> The story of communication is staged as a play in three acts: orality, literacy, and electronic consciousness. To offer a gross summary: oral culture is a kind of auditory culture, structured by the impossibility of writing anything down. It is ruled by tradition and collectivity, and it dwells in an enduring present where the past is maintained by feats of memory and memorization alone. Literate culture is visual culture, structured by the dominance of visual epistemologies such as the split between subject and object and the ability to externalize memory and institutional form through the power of writing and eventually print. It allows for greater bureaucratic control and consolidation and for highly orchestrated enterprises, such as science, that transcend time and space. Electronic culture depends on the powers of externalization first developed in literature culture, but it returns to a kind of oral mindset of an expansive present and universal interconnectedness. (Sterne 2011, 208)

In his book *The Audible Past: Cultural Origins of Sound Reproduction* and in a later article, "The Theology of Sound: A Critique of Orality," which thoroughly criticizes the theories of Walter Ong, Sterne proposes that a set of long-accepted postulates are discredited by new knowledge and should be finally retired. These principles he calls the "audiovisual litany":

- hearing is spherical; vision is directional
- hearing immerses its subject; vision offers a perspective
- sounds come to us, but vision travels to its object
- hearing is concerned with interiors; vision is concerned with surfaces
- hearing involves physical contact with the outside world; vision requires distance from it
- hearing places you inside an event; seeing gives you a perspective on the event
- hearing tends toward subjectivity; vision tends toward objectivity
- hearing brings us into the living world; sight moves us toward atrophy and death
- hearing is about affect; vision is about intellect
- hearing is a primarily temporal sense; vision is a primarily spatial sense
- hearing is a sense that immerses us in the world, while vision removes us from it.

> The audiovisual litany's account of the differences between hearing and seeing is rhetorically powerful, but not very accurate. As Don Ihde (1974) has shown in his classic phenomenological study of hearing, many of the aspects of auditory perception writers attribute to the litany do not actually hold up when we closely examine auditory experience. Especially in recent years, anthropologists, historians, and countless others have chronicled organizations of sonic culture that call into question the assumptions about sound, culture, and consciousness implied by the audiovisual litany. ... And yet, in the cultural theory and history that it subtends, the oral-literate-electronic triad continues to exert a surprising degree of influence over the ways in which many scholars characterize the long history of communication in the West and how they differentiate dominant Western constructs of communication from its many Others. (Sterne 2011, 212–13)

Instead of the three-part narrative of orality, literacy, and electronic consciousness, Sterne suggests more nuanced and wide-ranging observation of communication technologies throughout human history:

> What if the invention of writing and its stabilization in print were not the single most important turning points in communication history, but only one of many technological turning points? What if scholars—whose lives' work is dedicated to the written word—have overestimated its world-historical importance? We want to believe Plato that everything changed with writing. We are inclined to imagine writing as the moment that consciousness first allowed itself to be externalized in physical form. But what would happen if we instead submitted the history of communication technology to the rigours of the broader history of technology?
>
> Sidney Finkelstein noted that McLuhan's overemphasis on the historical significance of the phonetic alphabet causes him to underestimate the importance of other forms of exteriorization besides writing:
>
> "Tribal society ... was not 'oral' and 'auditory.' It had its speech 'magic,' incantations, poetic rituals, music and also its 'magic' paintings, sculpture, masks and dances as well as its tools and shapely utensils. There are extraordinary cave paintings dating back 20,000 years. The tribesmen had keen, observant eyes and skillful hands as well as sensitive ears." ...
>
> [The] implications are tremendous. There were technologies prior to writing that served some of its functions. Painting and sculpture externalized memory and solidified institutional forms over time. Musical instruments and musical technique were disciplines of the body that subordinated collective communication to abstract codes, even if they were not semantico-referential codes like those of writing. There are at least four major communication technologies that predate writing and that could conceivably have performed some combination of the functions Toronto School authors attribute to writing: painting, sculpture, architecture (especially its monumental and ornamental forms), and musical instruments. If, with Edmund Carpenter (1960), we believe that language and writing are media, then all of these pre-writing technologies are also "early media." As with modern media, these technologies engage,

> orient, and organize the senses even as they are conditioned by them. (Sterne 2011, 221)

"The Theology of Sound" concludes:

> It is time we left aside antiquated notions of sensation and cultural difference and built a global history and anthropology of communication without a psychosocial, developmental concept such as orality. We must construct new studies of early media and new ethnographies that do not posit the ascendancy of the White, Christian West as the meaning of history. In the process, we must re-read our own historical and anthropological archives, but it is also time that we reach beyond them. (Sterne 2011, 222)

Sterne emphasizes "Christian" along with "White" and "West," as he has argued in this essay that Walter Ong—a Jesuit priest—was committed to a Christian theology of "spirit and letter" that mapped onto his theories of orality and literacy and his ways of valorizing the former. Theorizing a "secondary orality" associated with electronic media, says Sterne, for Ong was tantamount to heralding the second coming of Christ.

Jonathan Sterne, and the doorway to "sound studies" that he has cracked open for me, offer tremendous new possibilities for understanding orality—or (since he proposes to toss out this old concept with its troublesome baggage) for understanding media and cognition. At this point I will mention just a few questions about the reach of his critique.

Sterne may have reduced early media thinkers to their mistakes, ignoring their contributions. McLuhan's essentialist and evolutionary views have been well exposed by Sterne and others such as Vail and White. But McLuhan has another side that seems to contradict these very views. He repeatedly asserts that orality and literacy are *not* linear stages. *The Gutenberg Galaxy* is organized by a "mosaic or field approach" rather than "a series of views of fixed relationships." Instead of chapters he presents 107 short sections with bold headings set between black lines. The headings are thematic, suggestive, associative. "Thus the galaxy or constellation of events upon which the present study concentrates is itself a mosaic of perpetually interacting forms that have undergone kaleidoscopic transformations—particularly in our own time" (unnumbered opening page). He mischievously suggests at the beginning that the last section of the book may be the best introduction.[13] Perhaps too disorganized a thinker to be an effective proponent of linear evolutionary progress, McLuhan often startles me with insightful and intriguing pronouncements.

Sterne's audiovisual litany has a stripped-down form that highlights its oversimplification. (The list could use some editing: at least points 2 and 6 appear to be redundant.) But the ideas Sterne criticizes are not all nonsense. There is something to the temporal-spatial associations that have been attributed to hearing and seeing. What is that something? While the modes of sense perception cannot be understood as separate, there is something distinct about them that should not be erased. How do the senses work, both separately and together? There is something to the idea that reading feeds into more abstract intellectual activity relying on certain kinds of brain function, while oral poetry and song affect the body and nervous system differently. How to describe and explain such differences?

We can agree with Sterne that it is wrong to say the senses are separate, function in distinct parts of the brain, and have a zero-sum relationship where dominance of one sense suppresses the others. We can add that the classic list of five senses is outdated. After that, what can we say about differences between a written and an oral text? Between the experiences of reading and listening? Between live and mediatized transmission? Between the locally embodied and the virtual?

In an email exchange, Jonathan Sterne gave a brief answer:

> I would say those differences are a mix of biology, psychology, culture and context. . . . From a standpoint of ignorance, I would make no generalizations that I would assume are automatically applicable to Kabir's work. I also wouldn't posit a single receiver or experiencer. I would think in terms of audiences and the different kinds [of people] that might come into contact with the text. (email, April 12, 2015)

Sterne's edited *Sound Studies Reader* (2012) gives a wealth of examples of how to investigate sound and audition. He emphasizes audition's "status as embedded in real social relations and its power as a figurative and imaginative metaphor for other registers of human action" (Sterne 2012, 20). Introducing authors in the first section of the book, Sterne repeatedly suggests the dangers of over-generalization:

> Don Ihde's classic phenomenology of sound offers a philosophically informed account of what it means to hear and how auditory experience might have a certain specificity. Jody Berland's essay

> adds the crucial dimension of positionality to our understanding of what it means to hear, considering both the social position of the listener, and her place in a sonic and mediatic culture. Michel Chion further stratifies listening by thinking through it in terms of modes—not all listening is the same, and any aesthetic theory of listening will have to account for the plurality of the process . . . Charles Hirschkind expands this modal approach to listening by thinking in terms of Islamic cultures, rather than the West, and in so doing offers a powerful alternative description of what it means to listen in modernity. (Sterne 2012, 20)

My investigations in the remainder of this chapter perhaps incline to the dangerously general, concerned with understanding the physical nature of perception, the particularity of hearing, and the distinctness of situations in which Kabir texts are transmitted orally by live performers. Throughout this book, describing and demonstrating such differences in various ways, I have argued that that in ignoring oral tradition, we confine ourselves to an impoverished understanding of Kabir poetry and of its reception by audiences. In embracing the study of oral tradition, we enrich our understanding of text and transmission, history and society. We also enrich our own ways of learning and knowing ourselves.

Are Different Senses Different?

Dogen, the great thirteenth-century Japanese Zen teacher and writer, went to China to study Zen/Chan Buddhism, as he was not satisfied with the state of Buddhist teaching at home. When he returned to Japan after five years of practice in Chinese monasteries, someone asked what he had learned in China. He replied: "I learned that the eyes are horizontal and the nose is vertical."

We know from many sources that the senses are not separate. They interact in complex ways that neuroscientists are only beginning to understand.[14] We also know that there are not just five senses; five is a conventional number that Euro-Americans are used to.[15] Amid this complexity and uncertainty, it is worth remembering that the eyes are horizontal and the nose is vertical. The commonsense differentiation between sensory modes is constantly acknowledged by neuroscientists who (unlike me) know how to study the brain.

In *The Universal Sense: How Hearing Shapes the Mind,* Seth Horowitz says:

> About the time I started working on this book, I was contacted by Brad Lisle of Foxfire Interactive to see if I would be willing to be a science consultant for a 3-D IMAX film about sound, titled *Just Listen.* The very idea of this blew me away—how do you take such an immersively visual medium as a 3-D IMAX film and make it focus on something as nonvisual as sound? (Horowitz 2012, 132)

Horowitz learned that a brilliant filmmaking team could in fact use a visual medium to make a sonic point. But this did not obliterate the difference between vision and sound. The difference made the point more dramatic and powerful.

John Henshaw begins his book, *A Tour of the Senses,* with this statement: "If you are lucky, this is what you were born with: two eyes, two ears, a nose, a tongue, a balance mechanism in your inner ear, and a layer of skin brimming over with all kinds of sensors" (Henshaw 2012, 1). He then provides a short paragraph on cach of these sense organs. For example, on eyes and ears:

> The eyes are about halfway from the bottom of the chin to the top of the skull. Lidded and lashed for protection, these superb optical instruments distinguish millions of colors, instantly recognize faces, function in conditions varying from near darkness to intense brightness, and sort out, unaided, tiny differences between particles much smaller than a grain of sand.
>
> On the other side of the head, at about the same level as the eyes, are the ears. The exterior parts, somewhat comical-looking and formed of cartilage, aid and protect the marvelous auditory instruments inside. The ears allow the brain to distinguish and interpret sound waves whose pressures and frequencies vary over astonishing ranges. (ibid.)

Sensory experience becomes complex after sound or light gets past the perceiver-portals: the data gathered by "all this superb instrumentation ... must be filtered, reconstructed, and interpreted, and that is the job of the brain" (Henshaw 2012, 2). Sensory modes do not remain separate once the brain begins to process what is coming in. But the sense organs are separate. The eyes, ears, and other sense organs each process different kinds of physical phenomena. A distinct part of the brain is called the auditory cortex. Parts of the midbrain and brainstem are also specialized for processing auditory stimuli. Having disposed of the oversimplifications of the audiovisual litany as presented by Sterne, we still know that reading a poem produces a markedly different experience from hearing it.

Some Things We Know about Sound

Seth Horowitz's book introduces us to what is particular about sound and hearing. For example, hearing is faster than any other sense:

> Vision is a relatively fast-acting sense that works slightly faster than our conscious recognition of what we see. Smell and taste are slowpokes, working over the course of seconds or more. Touch, a mechanosensory sense, can work quickly (as in light touch) or slowly (as in pain), but only over a restricted range. By contrast, animals and humans can detect and respond to changes in sound that occur in less than a millionth of a second and to the content of complex sounds over the course of hours. . . . Whether it's a humpback whale listening to hours-long song cycles during its migrations or a bat using a submicrosecond difference in echoes to determine if something is an edible treat or a branch to be avoided, sound helps animals find food, mate, play, and sleep; ignoring it can get them eaten pretty fast. Which is probably why vibration detection, including what we humans . . . call hearing, is one of the most basic and universal sensory systems that any earthly organism can have. (Horowitz 2012, 3)[16]

Of all the senses, why does Horowitz call hearing "universal"? He notes that there are "plenty of blind animals," and there are animals that lack sensitivity to touch, smell, and taste. But "we never find . . . deaf animals"—at least not among vertebrates. Since "all animals with backbones hear," he calls hearing "the most universal of the senses" (ibid., 3), and he ties this universality to the fact that sound is everywhere:

> There is no such thing as silence. We are constantly immersed in and affected by sound and vibration. This is true no matter where you go, from the deepest underwater trenches to the highest, almost airless peaks of the Himalayas. In truly quiet areas you can even hear the sound of air molecules vibrating inside your ear canals or the noise of the fluid in your ears themselves. (ibid., 2)

> Sound is everywhere there is life (and other places). Anywhere there is matter and energy, there is vibration, and any vibration can transfer energy and information to a receiver who is listening. And the wide range of vibration perceivable by living things, from the single thud of a footstep ... to the incredibly high-frequency sounds that form a dolphin's natural ultrasound, requires a sensory system thousands of times faster than its slower cousins, vision, smell, and taste. It is this faster-than-thought auditory speed, with a wide range of tones and timbres that visual color cannot hope to match, and greater flexibility than the chemical sensitivities of taste and smell, that lets sound underlie and drive a fantastic range of subconscious elements in the living organism (ibid., 5)

"Universality" is a spatial image, "speed" a temporal one. Encompassing both, Horowitz's language suggests to me that sound and hearing may take us to deeper, less conscious levels of perception, physiological processing, and body-mind integration than other sensory avenues:

> Combined with wildly divergent ways of listening by different species and the increasingly complex ways of using information by living things, the presence of sound drives the evolution, development, and day-to-day function of the mind. (ibid.)

"Fundamental" and "deep" are also spatial images that depend on an up-down metaphor (Lakoff and Johnson 2003). To incorporate the temporal aspect suggested by the inconceivable speed of vibration, I would add the adjective "immediate." Sound may be uniquely suited to provide an experience that is revelatory of present time, verging on an experience that is beyond media.

A Word about Music

We don't need a neuroscientist to prove to us that music is powerful, attractive, and important to human beings. But a few citations from scientists can put us in mind of how this is so, and why, therefore, listening to Kabir songs is likely to be a profoundly different experience from reading Kabir poems.

Everyone knows that music has enormous power to stir emotion—more because of than in spite of its independence from language. Oliver Sacks, the well-known physician, neurologist, and author, reflects on the innate "musicophilia" of human nature in his book of that name.

> This propensity to music shows itself in infancy, is manifest and central in every culture, and probably goes back to the very beginnings of our species. ... We humans are a musical species no less than a linguistic one. ... All of us (with very few exceptions) can perceive music, perceive tones, timbre, pitch intervals, melodic contours, harmony, and (perhaps most elementally) rhythm. We integrate all of these and "construct" music in our minds using many different parts of the brain. And to this largely unconscious structural appreciation of music is added an often intense and profound emotional reaction to music. ... Listening to music is not just auditory and emotional, it is motoric as well. "We listen to music with our muscles," as Nietzsche said. (Sacks 2007, x–xi)

A scientist in a documentary film on the sense of hearing says:

> One of the things that we found is that music activates every region of the brain. Twenty years ago we thought that music was predominantly lateralized, that is, exclusive to the right hemisphere. That turns out to be overly simplistic. What we know now is that music activates both sides of the brain, and the back, the top and the bottom, the outside and the inside. In fact music activates every region of the brain that we've so far mapped, perhaps more so than any other human activity."[17]

Among the types of sensory inputs, Seth Horowitz points to sounds as particularly "powerful stimuli for emotions." Among sounds, "those that evoke the strongest emotional response tend to be those from living things, especially other humans" (Horowitz 2012, 128). After observations on the emotional power of human-produced sounds, he moves to a chapter amusingly titled "Ten Dollars to the First Person Who Can Define 'Music' (and Get a Musician, a Psychologist, a Composer, a Neuroscientist, and Someone Listening to an iPod to Agree)." The chapter on music begins with a description of an amazing percussionist, Dame Evelyn Glennie:

> Glennie owns and plays almost two thousand instruments, from classics such as marimbas and xylophones to custom-made and

> haunting oddities such as the waterphone. What I was fascinated by as I watched her play a short piece she had written was the fact that she wasn't playing the instrument so much as she was playing the room itself. Walking barefoot up to the six-foot-long concert marimba, she positioned herself and the instrument carefully, then rose up on her toes, tilted her head back, and with four mallets struck the first notes and made the whole room *ring*.
>
> ... I felt the stage tremble and walls of sound fill the space and bounce back like a tidal wave toward the source. ... It was as if she had created a sonic sculpture that changed over the course of the first few seconds. ... As Dame Glennie launched into the remainder of the piece, using her whole body to play the instrument, but always with her bare feet in solid contact with the floor, her head thrown back, exposing her neck and body to the vibrations from the marimba, I realized that I was in the presence of someone who personified the complexities that science has ... dealing with music. Evelyn Glennie was filling a space with music.
>
> Oh, and by the way: Glennie is mostly deaf....
>
> When I asked her ... —"What is music?"—her reply was that music was something that you create and listen to with your whole body, not just through your ears. (Horowitz 2012, 134–35)

By using the dramatic example of a musician who can't hear, Horowitz emphasizes the nature of musical sound in live performance as a whole-body and whole-space experience. Vibrations fill body and space. They move in astonishing living patterns, creating sonic sculptures that keep transforming, simultaneously drawing and erasing boundaries, revealing the fluidity of forms. The body, the room, and the objects in it are vibrationally, dynamically sculpted together; barriers between inside and outside, in the moments of this experience, are down.[18]

"Secondary Orality": Is the Internet Like Oral Tradition?

Marshall McLuhan predicted that electric circuitry would operate like a global neural network and that the coming era would overturn the long reign of print, the dominance of the eye and fixed-point linear perspective. Electronic media would be more multisensory, even kinesthetic—in some sense recalling the kinesthetic properties of oral culture. The instantaneous and multidirectional nature of new media would make communication more performative.

Half a century later, twenty years or so into the age of the internet, engineers, biologists, psychologists, neuroscientists, social scientists, and literary scholars (among others) are rushing to advance, explain, and theorize the rapidly evolving electronic communication technologies. Meanwhile all of us are using them, bending our lives around them, our fingers constantly playing across keyboards, stroking silky glass screens, sliding on the smoothest metal mousepads. Writers on literature and culture have been fascinated by the affinities between oral-performative and internet-mediated communication. These affinities could pose a challenge to my argument for the distinct character of oral performance. In this section, I will lay out and refute the case for fundamental oral/electronic similarity

Walter Ong coined the term "secondary orality" in 1971, referring to the electronically mediated culture of radio, television, telephone, film, and early computers. Here he summarizes the concept in a later book:

> I style the orality of a culture totally untouched by any knowledge of writing or print, "primary orality." It is "primary" by contrast with the "secondary orality" of present-day high technology culture, in which a new orality is sustained by telephone, radio, television and other electronic devices that depend for their existence and functioning on writing and print. Today primary oral culture in the strict sense hardly exists, since every culture knows of writing and has some experience of its effects. Still, to varying degrees many cultures and sub-cultures, even in a high-technology ambiance, preserve much of the mind-set of primary orality. (Ong 1982, 11)

The notion of secondary orality gained currency as electronic media moved to the center of our lives. Scholars have applied it to texts as diverse as the Bible and Bollywood movies. The abstract of a web-published essay by Robert M. Fowler is typical:

> As different as ancient, primary oral cultures and postmodern, secondary oral cultures are, there are also some remarkable similarities that are only now emerging into view. In this paper I shall take hypertext/hypermedia as paradigmatic of the new electronic

> information technologies, and explore how coming to grips with hypertext/hypermedia might, paradoxically, help us to understand better ancient oral and manuscript cultures, generally, and the Bible, in particular.[19]

John Miles Foley offers elaborate ways of exploring and experimenting with orality, literacy, and the internet in his website <www.pathwaysproject.org>. On discovering this site, I decided to incorporate some of its ideas into my book. Navigating the links, I prepared to quote relevant passages. Then I paused to reflect on the activity of copying and pasting pages of hypertext into a book, from a website designed to demonstrate, among other things, freedom from the ideology and experience of the book. But this was a passing irony. We know, and Foley recognizes, that the various technologies of communication never stay in their own places but tangle with each other like the proliferating cables behind our computer desks. So I proceeded to cut and paste.

Foley adopts the term "agora" from Plato to refer to a place of public discussion. He uses tAgora, oAgora, and eAgora for, respectively, the textual (written), oral, and electronic platforms of such discussion in our time. He also uses OT and IT for oral tradition and internet. The passages that I collected in the summer of 2009 and on a revisit in 2013 may well be altered or gone by the time my book comes out. But here they are, removed from the fluidity of the internet and stuck in a print object. I retain the underlining of hyperlinks, though you can't put your finger on them and make this page disappear.

In a passage captured in 2009, Where Living Sounds Go to Die, Foley characterizes the act of transferring an oral performance to the tAgora—reducing it to a written text—as "a kind of ritual killing." In 2013 the bloody image is gone (replaced by taxidermy!), and the content is developed more fully. Under Ideology of the text, he enumerates some of the losses incurred by such a transference:

> We lose vocal features such as intonation, loudness and softness, and silence. We lose visual signals like gesture and facial expression, not to mention meanings attached to costume, setting, and props. We lose the musical and rhythmical dimensions of performance. Critically, we lose the background of variability, the network of potentials out of which any single performance emerges. Just as importantly, we lose the contribution of the

> audience, real or implied, and any interaction that influences how the performer proceeds. And, not by any means least, we lose the historical and cultural context, as well as the general idiomatic content of the performance (dimensions that are segregated to other parts of the ruthlessly linear book even in the best-case scenario).

Under Don't trust everything you read in books, Foley recounts "the dire implications" of reducing OT to written text:

> Pity the poor non-textual aspects of the OT phenomena we're trying to understand and represent. Clearly their acoustic and visual dimensions can't be housed between two covers; more basically yet, performer(s) become at best vicarious and any audiences are conspicuous by their absence. On these grounds alone we might as well forget anything but severely flawed representations of oral traditions. Add a DVD or CD? Only if you have a generous publisher, and then the add-ons are irremediably static: uncorrectable, un-updatable, unsupplementable, ever-inert. Thankfully, eCompanions and eEditions can help us move beyond this media impasse, but as yet they're not widely in play.
>
> But most fundamentally it's the quality of immutability, the very characteristic that we textual devotees so highly prize, that blocks our way. Whatever its (supposed) advantages, a commitment to (imagined) immutability deprives OT of its core identity. It guarantees distortion, precludes verisimilitude and emergence. Freeze the performance, reduce it to print and/or static files, and what happens? The life, the ongoingness, the right-now, event-centered nature that defined the performance's most essential reality all perish without a trace. And in their place stands an artifact complete in itself and yet empty—a cenotaph, a triumph of taxidermy.
>
> The moral? Oral tradition can't be captured in texts, no matter how strong our ideological motivation. You just can't trust an em-booked oral tradition—not least because it's an oxymoron and a bald-faced lie.

Foley's <www.pathwaysproject.org> is very interesting site, and I recommend perusing it. But I'm going to argue with one of its basic claims here. My argument has mutated from what it was in an earlier draft of this chapter, because the site itself has mutated. In 2009, Foley declared on the home page:

> The goal of the Project is to explain and illustrate a central thesis—namely, that humankind's oldest and newest thought-technologies, oral tradition and the internet (abbreviated here as OT and IT), are fundamentally alike. Hardly identical, of course, but surprisingly similar in their structure and dynamics.

In 2013, he says:

> The major purpose of the Pathways Project is to illustrate and explain the fundamental similarities and correspondences between humankind's oldest and newest thought-technologies: oral tradition and the Internet. Despite superficial differences, both technologies are radically alike in depending not on static products but rather on continuous processes, not on "What?" but on "How do I get there?" In contrast to the fixed spatial organization of the page and book, the technologies of oral tradition and the Internet *mime the way we think* by processing along pathways within a network. In both media it's pathways—not things—that matter.

A link called "Disclaimer" is more prominent in 2013 than it was in 2009. It has become one of the few bold headings on the left side of the home page. The statements on the home page and the Disclaimer are now more nuanced. The words "fundamentally alike" are replaced by "radically alike." The Disclaimer emphasizes the more subtle idea of "homology":

> The Pathways Project is devoted to exploring the homology between oral tradition (OT) and Internet technology (IT). But let me be careful to stipulate a basic and very important disclaimer: *"homology" does not mean "absolute equivalence."* On the web, and I would add on the web we call OT, it means "the quality of being similar or corresponding in position or value or structure or function."
>
> Nowhere in either the morphing book or the online wiki do I make the reductive claim that these two media-technologies are simply identical. Nowhere is it argued—nor should it be—that the oAgora and eAgora are "the same place."

What the Project seeks to explain and represent is the striking reality that, despite the many obvious contrasts between OT and IT, the two media share a fundamental functionality: navigating through linked networks of potentials. They offer comparable vehicles or sets of strategies for the creation and transmission of knowledge, art, and ideas, strategies that are categorically different from those used in the tAgora. The oAgora and eAgora present similar—even cognate—opportunities for virtual surfing rather than for tAgora trekking.

In other words, the Pathways Project explores a comparison/contrast of remarkably similar but non-identical ways of construing and shaping reality. How do OT and IT affect and even determine the ways in which we communicate? How do the cognitive prostheses they provide differ from our trusty, ideologically ingrained medium of texts? In broadest perspective, then, the central thesis of the Project maintains that OT and IT are homologous in *miming the way we think*—notwithstanding the many obvious contrasts in design and usage between the oAgora and the eAgora.

Next comes a section headed "The 'fine print.'" I quote only topic sentences; under each topic, Foley provides a paragraph elaborating on the point.

To make certain that the scale stays balanced and to avoid simplistic equation of technologies, here are a few ways in which the OT-IT homology resists reductionism and makes room for the innate complexity of media-worlds:

1. *Texts can exist online.*
2. *OT can morph into texts and enter the tAgora.*
3. *Communication can move into and out of multiple agoras.*
4. *Communication in the contemporary world requires multiple citizenship.*
5. *The conversation continues ... (linking to comments on and critiques of the project and Foley's responses).*

The Disclaimer concludes with a new statement, "Coda: Homology and Diversity":

Once again, then, homology describes a relationship of *similarity, but not of identity*. Any idea or concept worth entertaining must account for complexity, counter-examples, and general untidiness,

> and the OT-IT homology at the basis of the Pathways Project is no exception. As the Project seeks to illustrate in many different areas, OT and IT do their media-work not by adhering to verbatim singularity but by navigating pathways through networks of potentials. Variation within limits is the ultimate source of their strength and their staying power. Both of these verbal marketplaces thrive, in other words, by remaining forever "under construction."
>
> The oAgora and eAgora are hardly identical or superimposable, but they are importantly alike in fostering activities that—in their own particular, highly diverse ways—mime the way we think.

All of these changes speak to my argument, which was originally directed against the term "fundamentally alike" and against the marginalizing implications of terms like "Disclaimer" and "The Fine Print." But the objection I am raising remains salient. Please recall the losses so eloquently enumerated under Ideology of the text and Don't trust everything you read in books. Those things are still lost in IT. The affinities that Foley shows between OT and IT are not about *orality*—that is, they have nothing to do with sound, voice, hearing, speaking, listening, presence, context, contact of performers and audiences. They are only about text and thought processes: ephemerality of text, interactivity between consumer and content, the possibility of multiple outcomes, the contrast between dynamic pathways as against static products. The orality I speak of requires the presence together of physical bodies, and the production and communication of sound. Physical presence and social interaction entail a quality of embodiment very different from what occurs with internet communication. This is not just a marginal point. It is crucial.

Is it possible to speak of fullness of embodiment, or of body-mind integration? There are pathways, instantaneity, and unpredictability on the internet as in oral performance. But these electronic pathways are relatively disembodied or dis-integrated, as I will now try to explain. On the internet there is no physical vibration among interacting bodies, no people responding (with combinations of spontaneity and cultural conditioning) to the moment of performance in each other's presence. We are looking at screens. The visual is still hyperdominant. Sounds come out of our computers, true, but they are sounds of simulated objects, not real objects and forces colliding in our vicinity. There's no smell or taste. There's no touch, apart from fingers tapping plastic keyboards or sliding along screen surfaces that are weirdly sensuous in a nonhuman way.

We cannot touch each other on the internet. McLuhan claimed that print was the technology of individualism. Strangely, electronic media often function (despite social media and communication free of spatial barriers) as a technology of hyperindividualism. Think of the icon of the iPod that appeared in countless ads in the early 2000s: the black silhouette of an individual with earbuds, isolated in her music, oblivious to ambient sound, leaping in an attitude of exhilaration on backgroundless billboards, dancing with no partner. There is already a small library of work arguing that our constant connectivity may be destroying our capacity for real connection.[20]

The body tends to be activated and energized in oral performance, immobilized and deadened on the internet. Have your felt yourself go rigid as you disappear down the vortex of your browser or smartphone? Have you stumbled out of your chair with difficulty after hours on the computer, disoriented and stiff, like someone emerging from trance? In electronic worlds, separation of mental and physical, of self and environment, tends to become extreme. This difference touches every comparison we might make.

We can speak, for instance, of memory. In the conditions of oral performance, the powers of memory are enhanced. In the conditions of electronic communication, the powers of memory are reduced. If you were an adult before the advent of cell phones, you know that it was normal to remember significant phone numbers. Now we click our contact list. No one remembers phone numbers. As computer memory grows by fantastic factors, the instantaneity of internet information teaches us that we don't need to remember anything. Experiments show that distractions during any event seriously detract from our ability to remember that event. Distractions are the very stuff of web surfing.

In suggesting an enhanced quality of embodiment for the listener as compared to the web-surfer, I am not, of course, saying that written and electronic communications are disembodied. Every kind of communication is embodied. The key to the distinction lies in the degree to which body/mind/environment are separated. The psychological term "dissociation" may be applicable here. Dissociation refers to a separation between mental activity and physical experience, or to a painful fragmentation of various parts of ourselves.[21] Mild forms are common to everyone's life; extreme forms are identified as disorders. Psychiatrist Daniel Siegel, developing a field he calls "interpersonal neurobiology," uses the terms integration and disintegration to indicate relatively wholesome and dissociative states.[22] The evidence we have been building in this chapter—based on observation of personal experience, checked through forays into the neuroscience of perception and cognition—points to less fragmentation, thus more full, dynamic, integrated embodiment, in oral performance than in functioning on the internet.

Sociality

On December 21, 2012, Charlotte Brown and I had a conversation. At that time Charlotte was a senior at Stanford, doing a thesis on the neuroscience of contemplative practice. She had taken a class with me a year earlier, and we had gotten to know each other pretty well. We started discussing the cognitive and physiological differences between reading and hearing, and soon we were having a conversation about conversation. I recorded it and will present it here as the dialogue that it was. You can see how we moved from topic to topic, sometimes breaking into each other's sentences. What you can't get is the tones of our voices, how we sometimes got excited, sometimes talked slower or faster, sometimes laughed, and sometimes paused, searching for words.

CHARLOTTE (C): Some people learn better by listening to a lecture, others by reading the same material. There's a difference. We develop differently—the way we use our senses, the way senses interact with memory, and so on. ... So why does Horowitz call hearing the universal sense?

LINDA (L): [After a couple of unfinished sentences.] This is stupid. I can't remember, though I read it in the preface. I was scanning the book, trying to discover quickly what chapters were most relevant so I wouldn't have to read the whole book. I read sections of chapters, always focusing on getting the pieces that were useful to me as quickly as possible.

C: Would it be different if you'd been having a conversation with Horowitz? Would you be more likely to remember?

L: Yes.

C: Why?

L: Different responses come into play when two people are physically together and interacting. The trajectory of the conversation is different when they are reaching together toward something of common interest. Each person's responses affect the other, and they go to unpredictable places.

C: The book is a fixed object that you can control to a large extent. You're the only active one.

L: I use certain cognitive functions to search the book. In conversation I use more functions, or use my abilities more flexibly. We're being spontaneous, talking in multiple registers.

C: I have a visual image. The dots of where our conversation goes wouldn't have the linearity of the progression of discourse in a book. It would have a different logic, the logic of two people doing something together. [Charlotte called this "second-person space" and recalled hearing scientists speak of second- and third-person space as factors that changed the nature of communication.]

L: Reading a book is a communication process too. But the presence of more than one person fundamentally alters the process.

C: Yes, there are so many things going on. You're getting cues on many more levels. Even if you're just reciting something, you're getting feedback from the audience, you know the environment you're in, and you tailor your performance to fit that environment.

L: Actually the feedback goes back and forth. You send stuff out to the audience, they laugh—

C: Exactly. It's very dynamic and it takes both parties to tell the story in a way that's memorable. With reading there's still a dynamic process, but it's within you. Maybe I'm going out on a limb, but it seems that with a book there's nothing to isolate the process from all the thoughts that are always going on in your head. It's in the same voice. We're reading in our voice. We're constantly thinking and elaborating on things. But as soon as we're in this more dynamic environment, there's a lot more stimulation, and the likelihood of remembering it goes up.

L: All of these things are not yet about orality, not about hearing and listening. They're about aliveness of communication in person, in the flesh. This is also an important part of what I'm dealing with.

C: Yes, but we were talking about the development of the—

L: Yeah, let's get back to that. I'm just remembering that. You said first of all . . . what did you say about the womb?

C: You start hearing before you start seeing. I don't know if you start seeing in the womb. But you definitely start hearing pretty early on, and it's one of the first neural pathways to be laid out as far as your senses go.

L: Then would it be a reasonable inference that when we are listening, when we are using our hearing, we're tuning into something that's more . . . what language to use? More basic, more old brain—

C: There's an argument that that's where you learn your mother's voice, in the womb. . . . I don't know, it's hard to say. An evolutionary psychologist might make some claim about the early development of the sound system. There's something fundamental about this system—

L: —that brings in a more multilevel experience, whatever we mean by levels. Vision develops later, so hearing is more on some . . . what level? Can we say?

C: It's difficult. Hearing probably develops around the same time as your heartbeat starts.

L: Horowitz has a chapter on music. That's the one I read first. And I've been reading Oliver Sacks's *Musicophilia*. Horowitz says it's very difficult to define music, though we can observe that whatever we call music is very important in every culture. The way that scientists have tried to study music is to focus on some mathematical relationships between consonance and dissonance, and time beats, rhythm. So when you said "heartbeat," I thought "music."

C: Yeah, it's fascinating. It's been found that what people like to listen to is something called the edge of chaos. There's enough order, but enough variability that it's interesting. It's like plain order is boring, and chaos is unappealing.

L: This is so interesting. Now I want you to go back to something you said earlier, which is that everybody learns language orally. Only later do we learn to read, and only even later can we read silently. [We pause the recording to put on water to heat for tea.]

Some of the things we've discussed about the difference between reading and oral-performative communication have more to do with the performative—or as you say, with second-person space—than with the oral. But some of them do have to do with the oral. So the final question I guess . . . this conversation has been very useful to me, but maybe I have to ask some of these guys [like Horowitz, Sacks, Lakoff] who really know about this. Is there anything to be said about the simple fact that something comes in here and vibrates the hairs on your little hearing area here instead of being photons or whatever those things are that hit your retina? I don't even have the language. Even though it gets very complicated as soon as it gets into your nervous system, is there anything to be said about just the fact that it starts in your ear?

C: I wouldn't think so, to be honest. I don't know if you can isolate it to the ear.

L: Could we say something about the fact that it's hearing, that it's sound instead of light?

C: Vibrations instead of photons? They're each as arbitrary as the other. We've synergistically developed that these are the two most useful ways to interact with the environment. We've honed both our eyes and our ears to work within these physical realms. I don't think you can parse them apart. There might be something in our visual system that does a ton of re-creating. Your visual system is very active in that you're always making the visual picture of the world you live in, doing way more than what you're receiving. I'm not sure you're doing that much making up with the auditory system.

L: So the auditory system is less conceptual?

C: Maybe. It was drilled into me that we are always thinking and constructing with the visual system, not so much with the auditory. But something else came to mind as far as embodiment is concerned. In an oral tradition there's more dynamic embodiment.

L: Yes, or more fully integrated embodiment. We can go inductively from common everyday experience. You sit and read a book, your body is locked in, you tend to dissociate mental from physical—

C: Totally.

L: —and even more so when you're sucked into the internet. There's a theory called secondary orality that compares the way the internet works and the way things happen in an oral tradition, claiming that the internet is similar to oral tradition in certain ways. But when you're on the internet or sucked into your smartphone, you get more and more dissociated from the physical world. After two hours your body is stiff, you feel unhealthy, you get up and you're literally stiff, out of touch, and you realize that you've been withdrawn. I've been searching for language to say in what way receiving things in a live oral form is embodied differently. When you're on the internet or reading a book, you're not out of your body, you're still in your body. So I've come up with this idea of dissociation. In psychology it becomes a disorder. Being severely dissociated is one of the things that goes with trauma or with anxiety disorders. It comes up in addiction too. We all know what it's like in milder forms. I don't even know the meaning of the word "mental" anymore as separated from "physical," but somehow we experience that we are mentally cut off, dissociated from our bodies and things in the world. . . . It's really awkward to figure out what language to use about embodiment, about the experience of fuller and less full embodiment. Fuller embodiment is when you don't feel violently chopped up. You know how students feel when they're forced to be intellectual all the time—

C: Yeah!

L: What do we mean when we say "in your head"? We all know what it feels like, and we don't like it. Well, some people may like it because they make money off of it. Or some people don't exhibit the unhealthy aspects of it, so they can be intellectuals without suffering from it. But what do we mean when we say "in your head" in that painful sort of way, where you feel like you're excluding all these other aspects of your life, of yourself?

C: It would be interesting to see what it feels like at that moment when you realize "I need to get out of my head." Your body feels anxious. It might be abandonment. You abandon your body and it's getting anxious. You can forget to eat and sleep. In any kind of flow state—

L: What do we mean by flow state? We know it feels good. We have anecdotal descriptions that people give. I'm sure that the guy with the unpronounceable name has some scientific description.

C: Yes and no. Csikszentmihalyi, the flow guy, his book doesn't go into anything scientific because we're not there. Science is not yet able to wrestle with consciousness.

L: So he's just taking people's impressionistic descriptions of how they feel whole, at peace, out of time—?

C: There are surveys, statistics about how many times the same language comes up, because if it does, that suggests that there's something real. Psychology comes down to statistics.

L: Would it be easy to pull out the kind of language they were testing for, for the flow experience?

C: I can pull up the powerpoints on embodied consciousness that I got this summer [at the Mind and Life conference].

L: So what is disembodied or less embodied consciousness?

C: The reason there is a science of embodied consciousness is that in the 1950s they honest to god believed that by 2000 we'd be able to create a brain in a vat that would have consciousness. In backlash there was the embodied cognition movement—

L: George Lakoff etc.?

C: Yeah.

L: I'm into those guys too. So they were reacting to a theory that cognition can be disembodied—

C: Earlier theorists thought consciousness was in the mind.

L: And the mind was in the skull?

C: The mind's the brain, yeah. The mind is what the brain produces.

L: The Lakoff lineage is saying that all of our cognition is embodied, not that something is more or less embodied. But I'm trying to say that there is such a thing as greater or lesser embodiment, or greater or lesser integration of body-mind. I need to clarify the language. Here's where the problem of simulation and virtual reality comes in. [Giving Charlotte's arm a sudden push.] When I imagine hitting someone's arm, they say the same things happen in my brain as when I really do it. I'm making a case that no matter how indistinguishable to us virtual reality becomes from reality, or no matter how fascinatingly we reproduce physical experience in the simulations of our brain, we never eliminate the category of the physical, of the real. We don't end up saying it's the same thing. I'm clinging to that! Someone would probably challenge my assertion that there is a physical reality that's distinct from any simulation of it.

C: It may be the depth of the processing. If you get a brain scan of someone actually getting hit, or just thinking about getting hit, it happens in the same regions, but the strength of the signal is not the same. The memory associated with it is not the same.

At this point we turned off the recorder. Our conversation shifted into less intense modes until we smilingly said goodbye.

Sadness about Dying Media

Gary Shteyngart's 2010 novel *Super Sad True Love Story* portrays a world not far in the future in which the most disturbing potentialities of today's communication media, in concert with economic and political trends, have ripened to create a darkly comic dystopia. In a radio interview with Terry Gross he describes the character Eunice, "a very smart girl" who lives in a world "where the only things that matter are the things that happen instantly. They pop out at you, and then they're forgotten and we move on to the next thing."

GARY SHTEYNGART (GS): She went to Elderburg College, it's a small women's school ... where she was taught to scan books ... you can just get all the information very quickly and then throw the book away. This is not science fiction, this is actually happening on college campuses now. She majored in Images and had a minor in Assertiveness.

TERRY GROSS (TG): Do you feel like Lenny [the novel's hero]—somebody who is an artifact of the past—because you read books, and even more ... you write books?

GS: It's so depressing. I feel like I'm insane to write novels. I feel like one of those last Japanese soldiers on one of those islands, he's hiding in a cave and still shooting at the Americans ... and he hasn't heard that the emperor has surrendered. That's what I feel like all the time.

TG: What about your texting life and your smartphone life? ... Do you find that your concentration span as a writer or a reader is being changed?

GS: It's over. My concentration, my reading life, it's been shot. ... I'm not against technology. I love my iPhone passionately, I think it's a beautiful piece of technology. But sometimes technology outpaces humanity's ability to process it. ... my mind has been sliced and diced in so many ways, there are so many packets of information coming at me, especially in a city like New York ... even our cabs have television screens and info centers built into the back seat ... it's just shocking.

TG: You say you've lost your concentration. So where are you now as a writer and a reader?

GS: As a reader I go to upstate New York. My i-telephone can't connect well up there. ... my mind begins to readjust and I fall into this idyllic state, and all of the sudden books make sense to me again. I'm so used to my iPhone that sometimes I'm pressing on the cover of the book to make some piece of information light up. ... [Keeping up with technology] takes you away from whatever got you interested in doing this to begin with, which is to sit in a quiet place and try to understand what you are, who you are, and what the world is around you. ... When I was writing this book ... I had to obviously keep track of everything that was happening. Thank God I had a great research assistant. But it was an endless information overload. It made me very very unhappy. ... It began to affect my ... relationships ... I got run over by three cabs because I was so busy getting information out of my i-telephone, pressing it and pressing it and hoping something good would come out of it. Here's the thing about this new technology. I think it's incredibly effective. I just don't think it's made anyone much happier.

We are now always connected, but we don't know what we're connected to. It's just an endless scream of information.[23]

Is Shteyngart romanticizing the book? Am I romanticizing orality? Are Plato and Socrates (at the end of this paragraph) romanticizing conversation? No, the point I am making is not about nostalgia or romance. We see our media in different ways in periods of transition. Along with enthusiasm for and embrace of new media, there is resistance and a sense of loss. Like Shteyngart, I am attached to my iPhone and weirdly in love with my MacBook Air. But I note here the contradictions and highlight some of the consequences of our current media life. Walter Ong captures an ancient moment of contradiction when he points out that Plato (via his character Socrates) criticizes writing as dead, inhuman, tending to externalize and objectify what should remain internal and humanly produced, destructive of memory, and overall an enemy of intelligence. But to have an impact, Plato has to criticize writing in writing:

> [T]o make his objections effective, he put them into writing, just as one weakness in anti-print positions is that their proponents, to make their objections more effective, put the objections into print. The same weakness [exists] in anti-computer positions. ... Writing and print and the computer are all ways of technologizing the word. Once the word is technologized, there is no effective way to criticize what technology has done with it without the aid of the highest technology available. (Ong 1982, 80–81)[24]

As electronic media overwhelm books, we notice what we are losing as well as what we are gaining. Gary Shteyngart lovingly describes a public ritual for reading books.

> In Seattle, my friend ... runs this reading series. People just sit there reading in this beautiful hotel by a fireplace. They show up, hundreds of them, sometimes it's standing room only, and they take out books. Instead of reading out loud, they just read to themselves while this fire crackles and they drink wonderful bourbons. ... That was so touching ... to see a whole community of readers just sitting there, not broadcasting what they're reading. It wasn't about them. It was about the act of reading, which is trying to commune with the mind of another human being without constantly needing to

express yourself, to upload your opinions about something: look at me, look at me, look at me. That's what I've been missing.

When I, as a scholar of Indian poetry who has largely worked with written texts, discover the vitality of the oral-performative traditions in which that poetry still lives, I ask how oral tradition is different and how the difference enriches our knowledge and experience. This does not imply an argument that oral is better than written or that either is better than electronic. It does not imply that written and electronic texts are not moving, enriching, interesting and inevitable. It does not imply that we should "go back" to an earlier, fantasized era. It is just an exploration of the particularity and value of experiencing that poetry in oral-performative modes.

Virtual and Simulated Reality

Neuroscientific research and developments in virtual reality have made it ever more difficult to distinguish between "real" and "virtual" or "simulated" experiences. A recent book by Benjamin Bergen, building on theories of embodied language and thought pioneered by George Lakoff and others, demonstrates how the brain's constant simulation of physical experience is the key to our ability to learn and make meaning. In contrast to a theory of abstract or disembodied meaning that Bergen calls "Mentalese," embodied simulation "makes use of the same parts of the brain that are dedicated to directly interacting with the world. When we simulate seeing, we use the parts of the brain that allow us to see the world; when we simulate performing actions, the parts of the brain that direct physical actions light up" (Bergen 2012, 14). Here "simulation" refers to what happens when we imagine or think about something. Bergen opens his book with a vivid description of a polar bear:

> When hunting on land, the polar bear will often stalk its prey almost like a cat would, scooting along its belly to get right up close, and then pounce, claws first, jaws agape. ... To understand what this means, according to the embodied simulation hypothesis, you actually activate the vision system in your brain to create a virtual visual experience of what a hunting polar bear would look like. You could use your auditory system to virtually hear what it would be like for a polar bear to slide along ice and snow. And you might even use your brain's motor system, which controls action, to simulate what

> it would feel like to scoot, pounce, extend your arms, and drop your jaw. . . . Meaning . . . isn't just abstract mental symbols. It's a creative process, in which people construct virtual experiences—embodied simulations—in their mind's eye. (Bergen 2012, 15–16) [Of course he should also have said mind's ear, skin, tongue, muscles, organs, etc.]

While it is fascinating to realize that we see, hear, feel, taste, touch, speak, and act *in our minds,* activating physical/neurological processes associated with the senses even while our bodies are sitting still and in the absence of actual sense stimulation, I suspect that Lakoff (who introduces the book) and Bergen would grant the primacy and difference of direct sense perception and physical experience, on which these more internal cognitive processes depend.

In *Infinite Reality: Avatars, Eternal Life, New Worlds, and the Dawn of the Virtual Revolution,* neuropsychologists Jim Blascovich and Jeremy Bailenson take us chapter by chapter into ever-deeper virtual waters. We learn that the body-mind responds to virtual reality as if it were simply reality. A helmeted virtual adventurer at the edge of an electronically simulated chasm experiences real fear and excitement, with all their attendant neurological, psychological, and physical reactions. Blascovich and Bailenson assure us that unimaginable, seemingly impossible interactions between the real and the virtual will soon become commonplace. The gap between real and virtual will become increasingly elusive. Yet throughout the book, the notion of a physical reality distinct from virtual reality is a given. They can't seem to talk about the marvels of the virtual without reference to the nonvirtual. They call it sometimes "physical" and sometimes "grounded" reality. The contrast, spoken or unspoken, is everywhere.

Embodiment is at the center of many discourses of human communication and meaning in the early twenty-first century, precisely because of the explosive acceleration in information accessible through computers, the ever more intricate articulations of humans and machines, the attraction of a theory in which the body is just another kind of technology and nothing matters except information. In his foreword to Bergen's book, George Lakoff speaks of the Embodiment Revolution—a post-1970 transformation in thinking about the human and the world, the mind and language. He was brought up with a different paradigm:

> For centuries, we in the West have thought of ourselves as rational animals whose mental capacities transcend our bodily nature. In this traditional view, our minds are abstract, logical, unemotionally rational, consciously accessible, and above all able to directly fit and represent the world. Language ... is a privileged, logical symbol system internal to our minds that transparently expresses abstract concepts that are defined in terms of the external world itself. (Bergen 2012, ix)

Lakoff gives a long list of important thinkers and methodologies in the Embodiment Revolution (not mentioning his own central role, which will be obvious to anyone acquainted with the field), concluding: "Now, at the beginning of the twenty-first century, the evidence is in. The ballgame is over. The mind is embodied" (Bergen 2012, x).

Katherine Hayles's brilliant book *How We Became Posthuman* also grapples with the strong pull in our period to see the body as indistinguishable from the machines with which it ever more inextricably interfaces, to see information as independent of human bodies, to minimize the meaning and value of consciousness and biological particularity. Though she sees the dystopic potential of all this, she is not interested in railing against technology. Technological revolutions are inevitable parts of human evolution. Our new technologies are interesting and enriching as well as disturbing and dangerous. But she is clear about what she regards as the nightmare side of the picture: the erasure of the body. The title of her first chapter suggests the direction in which she hopes we'll move: "Toward Embodied Virtuality."

> This book began with a roboticist's dream that struck me as a nightmare. I was reading Hans Moravec's *Mind Children: The Future of Robot and Human Intelligence*, enjoying the ingenious variety of his robots, when I happened upon the passage where he argues it will soon be possible to download human consciousness into a computer. (Hayles 1999, 1)

She summarizes Moravec's description of an imagined robot surgeon pureeing a human brain and pouring its contents into a computer, so that "the patient, now inhabiting the metallic body of the computer, wakens to find his consciousness exactly the same as it was before" (ibid.). And she observes a trend of thought in recent decades, defined by "the belief that information can circulate unchanged among different material substrates" (ibid.).

Hayles elucidates the "posthuman" by offering a nonexhaustive set of assumptions that characterize it:

> First, the posthuman view privileges informational pattern over material instantiation, so that embodiment in a biological substrate is seen as an accident of history rather than an inevitability of life. Second, the posthuman view considers consciousness, regarded as the seat of human identity in the Western tradition since long before Decartes thought he was a mind thinking, as an epiphenomenon, as an evolutionary upstart trying to claim that it is the whole show when in actuality it is only a minor sideshow. Third, the posthuman view thinks of the body as the original prosthesis we all learn to manipulate, so that extending or replacing the body with other prostheses becomes a continuation of a process that began before we were born. Fourth, and most important, by these and other means, the posthuman view configures human being so that it can be seamlessly articulated with intelligent machines. In the posthuman, there are no essential differences or absolute demarcations between bodily existence and computer simulation, cybernetic mechanism and biological organism, robot teleology and human goals....
>
> If my nightmare is a culture inhabited by posthumans who regard their bodies as fashion accessories rather than the ground of being, my dream is a version of the posthuman that embraces the possibilities of information technologies without being seduced by fantasies of unlimited power and disembodied immortality, that recognizes and celebrates finitude as a condition of human being, and that understands human life is embedded in a material world of great complexity, one on which we depend for our continued survival. (Hayles 1999, 3–5)

So at this moment in media history, feeling an affinity with scientists who emphasize the fundamental importance and value of embodiment, I make a case for the particularity and preciousness of a tradition that is oral, physical, and social. We can't extricate it from its written and printed histories, its digital and virtual futures. But we can take a walk with people who sing and listen, where sound moves through air and flesh, where meanings are made by people together. We may discover in ourselves a longing to encounter this, a joy in entering it. It may be partly an antidote to our technological disembodiment, our carpal-tunnel wrists and screen-addicted brains, our dreadful isolation in connectivity. It may fleetingly dissolve our alienation from ourselves.

Conclusion

On first looking into orality theory, I focused on sensory perception: the difference between hearing and seeing, which mapped on to the difference between listening to songs and reading texts. In the process of research I discovered that defining the distinctness of Kabir oral tradition, while it does involve hearing and seeing, also calls into play several other key processes.

There are differences between ear and eye as portals of sense perception. Though I am not able to explain this precisely, thc differences may have to do with factors like speed of perception, order of prenatal development of sense organs, location in the brain of particular sensory functions, difference between photons and vibrations, perhaps difference in the physical structure of eyes and ears, and no doubt other matters that I am not aware of.

There are differences between receiving a Kabir text through live oral performance and encountering it in the pages of a book, or through other media, including audio recordings, film, and digital devices.

Equally important to the "oral" distinction are three other components: music; enhanced body-mind-world integration in live performance; and the social nature of the experience.

Ultimately the distinction of receiving Kabir through oral tradition must be understood as a combination of all these factors: the particularity of hearing; the quality of embodiment; the power of music; and sociality.

Coda: In the Body

From a Kabir Bhajan

My true guru pierced through me

He put his finger
on my pulse and waves
surged in my veins,
my heart rocked.
He gave me knowledge,
gave me vision
in the middle
of my body.
Syllables burst
into light.

From Field Notes

He strums the *tambūrā*, his eyes light up, and he says, "The sound of the *tambūrā* is so great. Just listen!" The *tambūrā* has a strong and sharp beauty, very different from the classical *tānpūrā*, which is more subtle and self-effacing. There is more variety in ways of playing the *tambūrā*: you can pluck, strum, change the rhythm and sequence of notes. While it is like the *tānpūrā* in playing a few notes repeatedly as background and anchor to keep the pitch, the *tambūrā* has a brighter, more extroverted sound. It jumps out at you. A *jāgnevālī āvāz*, Prahladji says—a voice that wakes you up.

***

Full moon in the village is beautiful. The sky is big. Electric light and pollution are small. The glow spreads magnificently through sky and trees, over humans, houses, and animals. Now in the absolute peak of summer, when the daytime sun is relentless, there is a miraculous cool wind in the night and early morning. They say this wind is special to Malwa. It is blowing now: a strong wind that grabs the hair and skin and pulls thinner trees over on their sides. It's so cool and strong! Makes you want to cry, as if compassion had touched you. Sleeping outside, you feel it building up after midnight till you have to pull a quilt over your body. Like the wind of awakening in a Kabir poem—*gyān kī āndhī*. Like the *shītaltā* of the songs, the coolness that stands for calm and peace, after the scorching heat of the sun.

***

When I sink into music, closing my eyes, I leave the flat, bright realm of clear-cut categories and logical consistency, which has a kind of aggression to it (the aggression of argument, being right, winning the point). I am in a sea of rising and falling images, and a voice pulls me like a current, its quality vibrating in my vital organs. I relax; the mind is not in control. I have taken a ride down to a deeper level of my nervous system. Verbal images, rhythm, and melody float, touch each other, open passageways inside me. New connections are made, new ideas arise. If I try to grasp them too roughly, they evaporate. But immediately after the experience I can gently remember them, and they lead me to new places.

6

A Scorching Fire, a Cool Pool

My poems are soft green,
my poems are flaming crimson.

JOSE MARTI[1]

"THERE ARE TWO main kinds of Kabir songs," said Dinesh Sharma in our first meeting at the Dewas office of Eklavya, an educational NGO, in March 2002. "There are the religious [*dhārmik*] songs about devotion to God, homage to the guru, recitation of the divine name, things like that. And there are the social [*samājik*] songs that criticize caste divisions, intolerance, superstition, pomp, rituals, and so on. We wanted to emphasize the social side."

Two months later I met Dr. Bhagirathi Prasad, an officer of the elite Indian Administrative Service (IAS), who held a high post in the Madhya Pradesh state government. He was the chief guest and inaugural speaker for the annual all-night Kabir celebration hosted by Prahladji in Lunyakhedi village. Sitting next to me on stage, behind the singers, Prasad whispered, "I think singing bhajans is a way to get relief from exploitation and suffering. What do you think?" I whispered that we should discuss this later. He proceeded to give an excellent speech, both serious and humorous. He said it's good that Kabir bhajans bring *shītaltā*, literally "coolness"—a word used in this hot climate to signal relief, calm, inner peace. But, he continued, Kabir did not come only to give coolness. He also lit a fire. He held a torch, he was a burning coal. Prasad quoted a famous couplet:

> Kabir stands in the market, a flaming torch in hand.
> First burn your own house down, then come along with me.[2]

What did Kabir want to burn up? Prasad enumerated various examples, starting with dishonesty and false pretensions. Later he said to me, "I wish

Kabir's followers would not just settle into the pleasure of their bhajans to escape their suffering. I want them to go out and change society, to burn up hypocrisy, exploitation, and injustice."

Both Dinesh, the NGO worker, and Prasad, the IAS officer, pointed to two distinct voices of Kabir. One would turn us inward, the other outward. One would speak to our psychospiritual needs, the other to our social consciousness. This polarity became a recurring motif, once I moved from studying Kabir as poetry on a page to meeting Kabir in his living cultural contexts. Some people talked primarily of the religious Kabir who teaches devotion to the guru and recitation of the divine name; the interior Kabir who evokes yogic concentration, inner light and sound, flowing nectar, the boundless *nirguṇ* reality; the austere Kabir who warns of imminent death and the urgent need to seek spiritual insight, to wake up before you die. Others were interested in Kabir as part of the social and economic order, a low-caste weaver who worked with his hands, a protester who blasted the institutions of caste, debunked religious authority, arrogance, injustice, violence, and greed, radically declared human equality, and reminded us that there's no escape from the imperative to think for ourselves and take responsibility for our own actions. This Kabir also spoke of Hindus and Muslims—their identities and motives, their craziness and violence, and the potential for living together in peace.

The present chapter and the final chapter of the book focus on this question of "social-political" and "religious-spiritual." Studying oral traditions includes learning about the social construction of the figure called Kabir and the interpretation of words attributed to him. People do that kind of interpreting in everyday contexts, and they don't publish their interpretations with Oxford University Press. Just as texts take shape and change shape in the process of singing and listening, so do the meanings of texts and the ways of imagining the poet. The political-spiritual question often comes up among people who are interested in Kabir in the late twentieth and early twenty-first centuries.

How do these two aspects of Kabir get delineated, separated, and reunited? Who embraces one side while neglecting or rejecting the other? Who sees them as connected? When people set aside or suppress one aspect of the Kabir tradition, what are they affirming and protecting? Are they claiming to represent what Kabir himself said and meant? Merely emphasizing what they feel needs more attention? Or protecting their own belief system against a perceived threat?

In this chapter the discussion is embedded in a story—that of the NGO Eklavya and its far-reaching experiment with Kabir in rural and small-town Madhya Pradesh. From 1991 to 1998, Eklavya hosted a *manch*—literally a stage or platform—for singing Kabir and investigating his social-political as well as his religious-spiritual significance. By studying the records of this remarkable experiment, talking with people who were involved, and participating in ongoing oral traditions, I was able to get a glimpse of how Kabir folksingers and others in these settings dynamically create Kabir.

Kabir is uniquely situated among North Indian bhakti poets as a "platform" for such dialogue. We would not be having quite this discussion about Surdas, Mirabai, or Tulsidas. Among the major Hindi bhakti poets, it is only Kabir who speaks out loudly against social inequality, abuse of power, and dishonesty. He does share with Ravidas an iconic status among Dalits and others with minimal economic power and "low" rank in India's caste hierarchy.[3] And he shares with Mirabai great popularity among these same groups, especially in Rajasthan.[4] But only Kabir is famous as a social critic. Only with Kabir do we find trenchant observation of social issues coupled with evocation of profound inner transformation—an experience that we can label inadequately as mystical or spiritual, that turns the habits of mind and the structures of self "upside-down," liberating the individual from egocentric delusions and fears.

Through this story, we will encounter the rich discourses of Kabir singers, listeners, devotees, and fans, the people who continue to create the oral tradition. It is a revelation to learn about the content and process of their thought and debate. Along with a sampling of the discussions that occurred in Eklavya's Kabir *manch*, three singer-participants are profiled at length, adding their vivid personalities and views to those of Prahlad Singh Tipanya, who is featured in other chapters.

Eklavya and Its Foray into the Worlds of Kabir

Eklavya's history goes back to the 1970s when a group of academics and scientists from Delhi set out to create vital new ways of teaching science to children in government schools beyond the metros. Existing science education, they felt, was worse than dead, not only failing to teach but actually creating antipathy toward the learning process. One of the founders, Vinod Raina, gave up a prestigious job in Delhi University. Others, like my friends Anu Gupta and Arvind Sardana who have been with Eklavya in Dewas since 1986, and C. N. Subramanium, the director of the organization when I arrived in 2002, could have confidently looked forward to comfortable urban positions. Instead they moved to Madhya Pradesh where they developed what would become a renowned science curriculum.

Historian Harbans Mukhia wrote about Eklavya in a 2002 newspaper article, after the Madhya Pradesh state government terminated a long-standing arrangement by which Eklavya had brought its science program into government schools. Mukhia and others saw this termination as a regrettable political move.

> The group started working in 1972 under the rather prosaic name of Hoshangabad Science Teaching Programme (HSTP), until ten years later when it acquired the present very evocative name [Eklavya]. The idea attracted a large number of scientists, some of them as eminent as M. S. Swaminathan, M. G. K. Menon, Yash Pal, and many others teaching in the University of Delhi, who involved themselves in the development of the programme. . . . The HSTP and later Eklavya sought to develop the programme well within the framework of the system of school education in Madhya Pradesh and with the approval, cooperation and assistance of successive Governments of the State at costs that were almost ridiculously low. As they went along, they developed expertise in writing new kinds of textbooks, training teachers through short term refresher courses, publishing magazines for children and for teachers, and devising tool kits at a fraction of prevailing costs. In course of time, a social science component was also developed based upon the same principle of proceeding from the familiar to the abstract rather than the other way around. By 2001, the HSTP was operative in 1000 schools in 15 districts and 100,000 children were its beneficiaries. The best testimony to its success has been the excitement and joy the process of learning has brought to the children over the past three decades.[5]

In 1982 the organization adopted the provocative name Eklavya, after the jungle-dwelling tribal character in the *Mahābhārata* epic who, spurned by the high-caste royal guru of archery, dedicates himself to a statue of the guru. He teaches himself, practices independently, and becomes a greater archer than the princes of the land. Perceived as an uppity Untouchable and a threat to the social order, he is rewarded for his achievement by a cruel command from the guru to whom he is unconditionally devoted:

"If you are my true disciple, cut off your right thumb." With this command, the Brahmin military guru Dronacharya and his royal protégé Arjuna intend to disable the brilliantly gifted forest-dweller, ensuring that the status and power of the upper castes will not be threatened. Eklavya complies, demonstrating his courage and devotion as well as the ruthless self-preservation of caste and political power. In choosing this name for their NGO, the founders wanted to highlight the potency of individual initiative and self-education, and the tragic denial of opportunity and waste of talent under an oppressive hierarchical system. In a recent brochure, they say that they intend to rewrite the ending of the story. In the new narrative of democracy, Eklavya refuses to sacrifice his thumb: he now understands and is willing to fight for his right to education.

Harbans Mukhia observes:

> The group of scholars, like the *Mahabharata* lad Eklavya ... opted to pursue their search in near wilderness, away from the glare and distractions of a metropolis and settled down in the small town of Hoshangabad on the banks of the Narmada in Madhya Pradesh. There they set out to get the children to generate knowledge for themselves by putting the textbook aside for the moment and going out in the neighbourhood, looking for special kinds of tree leaves, stones, what not and then asking questions and seeking answers. The questions led them to concepts, and the search for answers to the scientific methods of observation, experimentation, analysis and generalisation. They were to be trained in the critical method of acquiring knowledge rather than in the passive acceptance of knowledge generated by teachers. ... In life too they would learn the application of reason.
>
> There was also another valuable principle implied in it. In the great energy and resources expended in the pursuit of education for the next generation, the poor should not have to satisfy their quest with second rate, leftover education: what their children get too should be good and worthwhile. (Mukhiya 2002)

In the 1980s Eklavya expanded its scope. Besides adding social sciences, developing new textbooks, magazines, toolkits, and teacher training, they experimented beyond the bounds of formal education. The Kabir work was one such experiment, based in communities and not tied to schooling.

In Shabnam Virmani's film *In the Market Stands Kabir*, Dinesh Sharma describes Eklavya's approach to Kabir as he understood it:

DINESH SHARMA (DS): We felt that those ideas of Kabir that are most needed today haven't been coming through—the ideas that are really relevant today, and that attract people like us. The spiritual part isn't so interesting to us. We don't oppose it either. We don't say that it is not present in Kabir-*sāhab*'s tradition or that Kabir-*sāhab* didn't do that. . . . We're saying that there's a need at this time to look at these [social and political] things first. That's the kind of work we are doing. We can consider the other things later.

SHABNAM VIRMANI (SV): What other things?

DS: Other things like yogic practice, spiritual things. They're fine, and for some people they may be first in importance. At that time the Ayodhya Babri mosque conflict was in the air. Temple and mosque. The BJP [political party] was highlighting this. These people, the *mandalī* members, were being mobilized and incited. They were using them to join mobs. We felt it was necessary to point out: You and the great tradition you belong to are being used as pawns by the government and political parties.

While the Kabir *manch* was connected to the longer history of Eklavya's commitments (as explained by R. N. Syag below), the political crisis that Dinesh refers to added new urgency. Communal politics, hatred, and violence were on the rise. Hindu nationalist organizations were drumming up anger against a sixteenth-century mosque in Ayodhya, which they fervently declared stood on the actual birthplace of Lord Ram, an incarnation of God and the hero of the vastly popular *Rāmāyaṇa* epic. They claimed that a great temple to Ram had been destroyed in the sixteenth century by a Muslim king, who had then ordered that a mosque be built over the rubble. Appealing to deep-seated religious sentiments, they demanded that the mosque be demolished and the temple rebuilt on that very spot. At the same time their political party, the BJP, was making impressive electoral gains at the state and national levels.

Throughout this campaign one heard the verses of the beloved sixteenth-century Hindi *Rāmāyaṇa* poet Tulsidas being shouted in rallies. Cries of "victory to Ram" and to Hanuman, his mighty devotee in the form of a divine monkey, rang out. Bhajans and pseudo-bhajans with new texts like *Rāmjī kī senā chalī* (Ramji's army is on the march) and *Mandir wahīṇ banāyenge* (We'll build the temple on that very spot) were blasted over loudspeakers, disseminated on cassettes and discs, and eventually posted on the internet. People's bhakti—their religious devotion, their love of Ram, the *Rāmāyaṇa* story, and Tulsidas's beautiful Hindi poetry—were effectively channeled into the campaign. Ram's warrior nature was emphasized rather than his tender and compassionate side: he was a hero who fought and destroyed the demon race (Kapur 1993). In the speeches, audios, and videos produced by the movement, demons were equated again and again with Muslims and Muslim sympathizers (Hess 1994a).

Many secularist and anticommunal groups were considering how to counter this successful appropriation of religious imagery, poetry, and emotion. Kabir, the mystical poet who criticized the follies of both Hindus and Muslims and whose identity partook of both traditions, was an obvious ally. Besides providing a counterforce to communalism, Kabir was an apt spokesman for other Eklavya values: the critique of caste and superstition, the importance of testing things with your own experience, questioning authority, and affirming human equality and dignity.

Most important, Kabir already had a vibrant presence in the countryside in the form of bhajan *mandalīs*, groups that met regularly to sing his verses. These groups would sing in a lively folk style with a few instruments. They were often initiates of the Kabir Panth (sect), which regarded Kabir as the supreme guru, or even as God. Most of Kabir's followers were of the lower classes and oppressed castes.

Dr. R. N. Syag was the director of Eklavya's Dewas office in the 1990s. Syag-*bhāī* (brother), as everyone calls him, has an open, friendly face, a shock of white hair, and a habit of ending many sentences with a form of Hindi *hai-nā*? meaning, "isn't it so?" or "right?" He says *hai-nā* while connecting with his conversation partner's eyes—a habit of inviting dialogue. Syag-*bhāī* explained the importance of working with community groups that had a life of their own:[6]

R. N. SYAG (RNS): Highly educated people like us can talk about democracy and civil society. But in the traditional society of the village, people are identified by caste. In that society you have to think: Where can I sit down? Or if you're a woman: How should I behave? Given that identities are formed around caste and gender, how do you begin to do something in a village? You can't do it in an academic way, can you? If you want to talk to people, there are boundaries. There are distances. There

FIGURE 6.1. R. N. Syag, during our car conversation presented in chapters 6 and 8. Photo by Shabnam Virmani.

is untouchability. When we realized that these Kabir bhajan *mandalīs* existed, we thought that they provided a very good community-based institution. We could work with them. We could also strengthen them.

The *mandalīs* arose spontaneously. No NGO created them, no government created them. They were filling people's real needs and aspirations. Only then would they survive—right? We saw that men would labor all day, and then at night they would sit and sing so beautifully, and they would get so refreshed. Sometimes they would sing all night and go straight to work in the morning. What was going on here? We began to meet and make friends with them.

Another thing was that we came out of a background of science education. Children learned about science and rational thinking in school. But at home in the village, everything was traditional. The literacy rate was low all through the country. We were creating written materials, but science education can only spread when literacy rates are higher. We had started an All-India People's Science Network. In

1987 there were five *jātas* [traveling educational groups that used music, theater, exhibits, and so on] moving from five corners of the country, raising scientific awareness. There were different emphases in different places. Here in M.P., we were educating people about the [1982] Bhopal gas tragedy, about Union Carbide, multinationals, and so on.

LINDA HESS (LH): What's the connection between scientific awareness and Kabir?

RNS: Why are there so many differences between human beings? Why is there untouchability? Didn't Kabir teach us to ask questions? Kabir said, "One who searches will find." That search is what scientists do. Kabir had cultural roots in the community. Where people's lives were difficult, where there was a need for knowledge and education, we thought Kabir could be a medium. Our first contact was Narayanji. We met him in a bus, carrying his *tambūrā*. We went to his village, attended a performance, got to know people. This was sometime in 1990.

LH: The conflict over the Babri mosque was intense then. Was the problem of communalism also in your minds?

RNS: It was. But if we went into the villages talking about nonlocal things—communalism, political parties—it wouldn't have much meaning. Kabir talked about hypocrisy in all religions, and he made our common humanity a central value. So he provided a good medium to discuss these things.[7] We were a little concerned about whether his attacking religion, criticizing Islam and Hinduism, would prevent people from joining us. But we felt that his appeal to common humanity was the main point, and we emphasized that his criticism was directed against anything that destroyed that human feeling.

The Kabir Manch*: An Overview*

Having decided to delve into local Kabir culture, Eklavya workers collected books and educated themselves about Kabir's poetry and place in history. Dinesh Sharma did much of the groundwork, moving among villages, collecting lists of bhajan *mandalīs,* and holding preliminary sessions. They named the project the *Kabīr bhajan evam vichār manch.* A *manch* is a stage—literally a place of performance and figuratively a platform or space for expressing ideas. *Vichār* means idea or thought. Doing *vichār* means thinking, discussing. So it was a platform for singing and discussing Kabir. On July 2, 1991, the *manch* was officially inaugurated. Its central activity was a gathering on the second of every month at the Eklavya office in Dewas. Many groups came. They sang, talked, and drank tea all night.

Such bhajan sessions are not unusual in the countryside. What was special about Eklavya's program was the *vichār* component. Along with singing, participants were encouraged to discuss the meanings of Kabir's bhajans: to raise questions, seek answers, debate points of disagreement, and relate the content of the songs to their daily lives—the conditions of work, society, family, and so on. This was not something they were used to doing. They usually sang for pleasure and release, the pure joy of singing. You need only to sit with a village *mandalī*, seeing how their enthusiasm and enjoyment build over hours of singing, to appreciate why they like to sing. This enjoyment did not require discussion of meanings; in fact such discussion was likely to hinder the flow of feeling.[8]

Another reason why discussing the meaning of Kabir was awkward at first was that the authority to interpret and preach was usually ceded to the Kabir Panth gurus or *mahants*. Before them, ordinary people kept quiet. Most of the singers had limited formal education. Some were illiterate. Many had dropped out in primary or middle school. Only a few had been to high school or college. Often, when asked to talk about the meaning of a bhajan he had just sung, a singer would just repeat the words. What more was there to explain? But even this presentation of the words without music had an impact, focusing attention on the content and preparing the way for more probing conversations.

Organizers constantly conveyed the message that the singers of Kabir had every right to think and talk about the meanings of Kabir. Their ideas were elicited and respected. Soon they warmed to the format, discussing and debating more freely. Of course singing was always more fun, more physically and emotionally satisfying, than talking. But discussion gradually flourished.

Dinesh Sharma kept extensive documentation of the program: notes and reflections on what happened, audiotapes, press clippings, and correspondence. Sometimes he described his own experience in the logbooks, as in this 1992 note on how it all began:[9] "In 1990, while working on a literacy campaign, I came into contact with many Kabir bhajan *mandalīs* in villages. At the same time I started reading books by and about Kabir, and I discovered that his ideas were quite revolutionary." Dinesh found Kabir proclaiming social equality and calling for justice. He went to his first bhajan program in Tonk Khurd village at the home of Fakirchand—a

FIGURE 6.2. Dinesh Sharma, who organized and documented the Kabir *manch* with the NGO Eklavya, holds a picture of the great Dalit anticaste leader B. R. Ambedkar. Photo by Shabnam Virmani.

member of the sweeper caste. For the first time in his life Dinesh, a Brahmin, entered an "untouchable" home. On another occasion, in the same home, he witnessed his first *chaukā āratī*—the core ritual of the Kabir Panth (about which we will hear a great deal in the next chapter). He collected information on Kabir bhajan *mandalīs* in the area. "I got many names and addresses, but one name was on every tongue: Prahlad Singh Tipanya." So we know that even in 1990, Prahladji was recognized as the most outstanding local singer.

After the first meeting in July 1991, Dinesh sent a letter to the leaders of many *mandalīs*:

> Namaste to all the *mandalī* members.
>
> We met on 2 July in Dewas. Some friends suggested that, along with singing Kabir bhajans, we should try to spread the bhajans and Kabir's thought very widely, and that we should arrange various educational and social activities for the public. The *Kabīr bhajan evam vichār manch* was formed with these aims:

* To bring together Kabir bhajan *mandalīs* so that all could sing and listen.
* To understand and propagate Kabir's ideas.
* To organize Kabir festivals and seminars.
* To encourage activities related to religious tolerance, brotherhood, social and educational change.

Please let all your members know about this *manch.*

In the first two years there was a flurry of activity including performances, discussions, seminars, new youth *mandalīs*, and children's activities. They collected books on Kabir and Ambedkar and set up libraries in villages. They created a play using Kabir bhajans and *sākhīs*—some performers sang while others acted out a play highlighting issues like casteism, superstition, double standards, excessive drinking, and literacy. A small book of socially conscious bhajan texts with an introduction about Kabir's life and thought was published and sold for two rupees. Two audio-cassettes featuring *manch* singers went on sale for twenty-five rupees each. They did a brisk business, and the reputation of the Malwa Kabir *mandalīs* began to spread.

Syag-*bhāī* further describes participants and processes in the *manch*:

The Kabir *mandalīs* already existed. They normally got together to sing in their own neighborhoods every week or two. As to caste—mostly they were Balais, an SC community. But there were others too, some OBCs, some of general castes.[10] There were a few women, not many.

At first they felt there should be a religious atmosphere. There should be a sacred image of Kabir, a disciplined program, no arguments. I said—if Kabir came and saw this program, what would he think? He was the sort of person who liked to get into discussions—right? So if we're doing this in his name, how about trying an experiment? Let's encourage people to have a discussion. We'll have it in one of the rooms of our office, and everyone will sit on the floor, with no sacred image of Kabir, no worship or ritual.

So that's what we did. Tipanyaji and Narayanji were the first ones who got into singing and then discussing the *bhajans*. People liked it and more joined in. Word spread and the numbers kept increasing.

People had notebooks with bhajans written in them, and we selected some to publish in inexpensive booklets. We chose *bhajans* that would help to advance this kind of discussion. We didn't pick out the ones about devotion to the guru and that sort of thing. We took bhajans about caste, superstition, hypocrisy. For instance, there's a song that says you do rituals for your parents when they're dead but don't care for them while they're alive. That type of thing. A lot more people started coming, and Tipanyaji's first cassette was produced.

One booklet had an introduction written by Prakash Kant, a very insightful and educated person. A lot of people objected to it because it described Kabir as a human being, no miracles. How could Kabir-*sāhib* be born from anybody's womb? How could Kabir-*sāhib* die? They saw Kabir in a different way. They had religious faith that wouldn't change in one meeting, or ten meetings. We would just calmly talk about it. We put up some exhibitions, distributed information, showed how people came to believe things that weren't necessarily true. We asked: Where do these misconceptions come from? How are they created?

The *manch* wasn't homogeneous. Some people were educated. Some singers were schoolteachers who had studied science, history, social science. Tipanyaji was one of those. There were some college students. ... But the majority of participants had little education and had a lot of faith in their traditions. I emphasized that this was a dialogue. If somebody says something that you don't like, let him speak. Right? This is the meaning of dialogue, isn't it? If someone says something you disagree with, that's what he's been taught, in his family, in his village. It isn't a matter of blame. We used to say this again and again. If someone thinks in a different way from you, still respect him as a human being. Right? What was his learning process? How did he arrive at this understanding?

We didn't do exhaustive research or try to relate to everything about Kabir. We promoted those aspects which inspired us, and we left other aspects alone. If someone liked to touch people's feet as a sign of respect, that was OK. It wasn't an issue. But nobody was told, "You have to touch so-and-so's feet." The main thing was to have dialogue.

The Hindi daily newspaper *Naī Duniyā* carried a story on the meeting that took place on February 2, 1992:

> Twenty-five men and fifteen women were present. They discussed caste, untouchability, various kinds of social conflict in their villages. Two points emerged most clearly:
>
> 1. If we really want people in society to follow Kabir's ideas, we'll have to do more than sing bhajans. To make these ideas concrete, we must develop solid projects in the villages.
> 2. Along with Kabir, we should study the ideas of Ambedkar. At the end of the meeting, Syag-*bhāī* spoke about Ambedkar's life and thought.

B. R. Ambedkar (1891–1956) was the great leader of the struggle against untouchability and caste oppression in the first half of the twentieth century. A member of the despised *mahār* caste, by a series of near-miraculous circumstances he got educational opportunities that led to his earning a Ph.D. in economics from Columbia University in New York and a law degree in London. Returning to India, he fought unrelentingly for the human rights of untouchables and against the institutions of caste, ultimately becoming free India's first law minister and the chief architect of the Indian constitution. In October 1956, just two months before his death, he converted to Buddhism in a great public ceremony, leading a movement in which millions of Dalits (as many members of the downtrodden castes came to call themselves) have become Buddhists, guided by Ambedkar's writings on the political, social, spiritual, and intellectual suitability of that religion to their aspirations. Ambedkar's parents were members of the Kabir Panth. He sometimes said that he had three gurus: Kabir, Jyotirao Phule (a Maharashtrian who fought against caste in the nineteenth century), and the Buddhist monk who presided at his conversion ceremony. In 1992, Eklavya started an Ambedkar *manch* in Dewas, a smaller forum that ran parallel to the Kabir *manch* for two years. Some of the singers attended both; many attended only the Kabir *manch*.

Here is an example of a dialogue that took place at the Kabir forum, transcribed from an audiotape of the meeting on February 2, 1992. Ramprasad, Narayanji, and Girdharji are members of singing groups; Syag-*bhāī* and Dinesh work with Eklavya.

Ramprasad Golavatiya sang *Pandit vād vade so jhūṭha.*[11]

SYAG-BHĀĪ: For the last 600 years *mandalīs* have been singing Kabir bhajans. And during the same period, Kabir has come to be surrounded by rituals and pomp. This is because Kabir's spiritual bhajans are always sung while his social bhajans remain hidden.

NARAYANJI: Since coming to the Kabir *manch*, we've begun to sing the social bhajans more, because people here like them. In the programs where Panth gurus preside, the spiritual ones are given more prominence. Traditionally you start with homage to the guru. Then *chaukā āratī* (ritual) bhajans, then more about the guru's power, *rekhtā*[12] about the nature of the guru and the individual soul, then bhajans that have to be sung at dawn. Like that the entire night passes. After coming here, I've been freed from many delusions.

GIRDHARIJI: Here we have open discussion. In those programs we have to observe a protocol around the guru. We can't ask questions or discuss anything.

DINESH: In his own time, when Kabir saw social problems and felt the need for social change, he expressed those ideas in his bhajans. If we feel moved by Kabir's philosophy, we should look around and consider the needs of our society today. We should discuss and spread Kabir's social ideas.

SYAG-BHĀĪ: Along with Kabir we should discuss and spread the ideas of Dr. Ambedkar, because Dr. Ambedkar did tremendous work for the awakening of the Dalit community. In our society, even after fifty years of independence, we still have illiteracy, poverty, hunger, unemployment.

RAMPRASAD GOLAVATIYA: To raise consciousness, we can sing and do street theater.

NARAYANJI: Syag-*bhāī*, we who are in the Kabir *manch* need to do some work out in the real world. If we just sit here and have discussions, nothing will happen.

SYAG-BHĀĪ: All movements and projects start with ideas. Discussing ideas brings people together. Then they can raise their voices in the world.

As a title for the book of bhajan texts that they were publishing, participants chose a line from one of Kabir's couplets: *kabīrā soī pīr hai jo jāne par pīr*. The line plays on two meanings of *pīr*. The first *pīr* refers to the Sufi (Muslim mystical) equivalent of *guru*, a wise teacher or spiritual master.

The second meaning of *pīr* is pain or suffering. So the line means, "Kabir says, the true teacher is one who feels others' pain." The newspaper *Naī Duniyā* carried a review written by a friend of the *manch*:

> India's medieval bhakti movement was a social and cultural phenomenon that raised a resounding voice against the social ignorance of the times. ... The actions that saint-poets of the bhakti period adopted to change society, and the poetry they composed, are still relevant today. Kabir had a unique place in the bhakti movement. The bhajans and *dohās* he composed are still on people's tongues in villages, and the tradition of singing his songs in groups has continued for many generations. ... In the first fifteen pages of this booklet, Prakash Kant has written an essay on the social, political, and religious conditions in Kabir's time. He demonstrates that the bhakti movement was born from contemporary social and religious circumstances. In every society, people arise to speak against prevailing falsehood and injustice. Their efforts come together to begin the process of social change. ... If we look at Kabir's bhajans and *dohās*, we will see that on one hand he spoke about social transformation, while on the other hand he presented the spiritual aspect of life. In this booklet, most of the twenty bhajans speak out against the orthodoxies that constrict society.[13]

Some faithful devotees of the Kabir Panth objected to Prakash Kant's introduction, which described Kabir as a human being who was born and died in the usual human ways. They believed Kabir was a divine avatar, who manifested himself as a baby on a lotus in a pond, and whose life on earth was replete with miracles. Because of their objections, the introduction was omitted in later editions.

After the demolition of the Babri mosque and subsequent communal mayhem and murder across northern and western India, many groups organized to resist the waves of hatred and violence. The Uttar Pradesh state government sponsored a *Sadbhāv Yātrā* (Goodwill Journey) "to mobilize the public against communalism, spread the message of tolerance, peace, and compassion, and revive the spirit of communal harmony and devotion preached long ago by the *sant* poet Kabir."[14] They asked Eklavya to send *mandalīs* to join the *yātrā*, whose highlight was a weeklong traveling cultural program led by the Indian People's Theatre Association (IPTA).

A caravan of actors, writers, speakers, and singers moved along the roads from Varanasi to Magahar, the sites of Kabir's birth and death. Journalist Akhilesh Dikshit "Dipu" almost ecstatically describes the impact of these artists—their exuberance, simplicity and sincerity; their continuous singing through eight days of travel; the beauty of the tunes combined with the power of the words. Malwa's ever-popular song *Zarā halke gāḍī hānko*—"Move your cart along lightly"—became an anthem, with everyone joining in again and again as they walked. Dikshit observes: "The performance of the Dewas *manch* artists released a flow of Kabir poetry in this eastern region that will remain fresh for years to come" (Dikshit 1993).

About midway through the eight-year duration of the *manch*, Eklavya devised a questionnaire to get information on the ages, castes, and education of participants, as well as the history of each *mandalī*. Some of the questionnaires were lost, but in 2002 we were able to find fifty-eight of them, each representing one *mandalī*. The great majority of participants list their caste as Balai (also called Balahi)—in Malwa a Dalit caste with relatively high status among the Dalits (who have their own hierarchies).[15] A scattering of other castes are listed, including Chamar, Raidas, Goswamy, Rajput, Jat, Darzi, Chaudari, and Khati. When asked their occupation, most say *mazdurī* (labor) or *khetī* (farming). A few say they are shopkeepers, handymen, or teachers (*dukān, mistrī, paḍhāī*). Their ages range from the twenties to the fifties, with the occasional teenager. Under "education," we see notations like "3rd," "5th," or "7th" (indicating the highest grade completed), and sometimes *nahīṇ* (none). Many *mandalīs* say that they have been functioning for a long time, ten to thirty years, and that such singing is traditional in their families. Some newer ones cite Eklavya's Kabir *manch* as their inspiration for starting. A few mention the support of Prahlad Singh Tipanya and Narayan Singh Delmiya. One new group says it was inspired by Tipanyaji's cassettes. The groups covered by the questionnaires are 100 percent male. I was told that a female *mandalī* occasionally appeared at the Kabir *manch*, and I have met some women who sing Kabir. But it is clear that Kabir singing in Malwa is almost exclusively a male culture.

Meetings on the second of the month continued until 1998. A 1995 brochure stated that over 500 *mandalīs* had been involved and that monthly programs were being held in three villages as well as in Dewas. In 1993 Eklavya received a modest grant from the Indian Council of Historical Research to support documentation and text collection. Thousands of bhajans were typed up from the handwritten notebooks of *mandalī* members.

In cases where singers were unlettered, or old and frail, special efforts were made to transcribe songs from their oral presentation. Eklavya produced a lengthy report in 1999, with a historical introduction in English and an account of the Kabir *manch*'s activities in Hindi, followed by a collection of bhajan texts transcribed from the Malwa oral tradition, including notes and appendices. As a title for this report, they used the first line of a Kabir couplet:

> Kabir's words are searing, just hearing
> them sets off a fire.

It was interesting for me to discover, when I searched for the rest of the *sākhī*, that the second line changes the point of view to an interior one:

> *kaṭuk shabda kabīr ke, sun to āg lag jāī*
> *gyānī to vāṇ magan bhayā, agyānī jal jāī*
>
> Kabir's words are searing, just hearing
> them sets off a fire.
> The wise are completely immersed.
> The ignorant burn.

Magan, translated here as "immersed," usually refers to total absorption in meditation or devotional love. It could be associated with the coolness of inner peace which, in the opening of this chapter, was described as opposed to the fiery struggle against injustice. In two short lines this *sākhī* welds fiery intensity with calm concentration. Only the ignorant, those who miss the point, burn up.

Other Urban Activists Who Became Involved in the Manch

Kabir bhajan *mandalīs*, mostly but not entirely rural, comprised the core of Eklavya's Kabir *manch*. In addition, city people from Indore, Dewas, and Ujjain, who were not singers or religious devotees of Kabir and who tended to be highly educated, were also drawn to the monthly meetings. These were people who had affinities with Eklavya and with Kabir. Whether artists, intellectuals, NGO workers, or activists in other arenas, they were interested in strengthening secularism, reducing inequality, and addressing injustices that affected the least powerful and privileged elements of society—seen through the lenses of caste, class, gender, religion, ethnicity, access to education, and so on. For example, there was Prakash Kant, an educator of Dewas who wrote the introduction to the first edition of the published bhajan collection, *Soī pīr hai jo jāne par pīr*.[16] There was Kiran Sahni, an Indore theater director who later put up a production of a famous Hindi play on Kabir.[17]

Suresh Patel of Indore was an officer of the Cotton Corporation of India, a government agency under the Ministry of Textiles. Inspired by Eklavya's *manch*, Suresh embarked on a sustained effort to enlist the power of Kabir's words and music in projects that would support and strengthen people at the lower ends of the economic and social scale. He founded an NGO called *Kabīr jan vikās samuh*—Kabir's Community for People's Development. When I met him in 2002, he took me to see two current projects. The first was a sort of preschool for children of varying ages who had never gone to school:

> [From my notebook, August 3, 2002]
>
> We visit a very poor settlement of Maharashtrian *ādivāsīs* ["tribal" people who had come to the city in search of work]. The children used to be sent out all day to collect plastic bags from the street to be sold by the kilo. Three years ago they started this program to prepare kids to enter government schools. They had to persuade the parents, who wanted the kids to earn money. Now they have a shabby little room with water puddled at one end, but it's clean, and the kids look sparkling. Volunteers from inside and outside the community started teaching the kids, both content and discipline. In three years, 150 kids who were not in school have entered government schools. They're about to start a new batch. A spirited woman leader talked to us, gesturing vigorously. The kids smiled broadly and talked readily.

The other project was an after-school gathering place for children in a lower-middle-class neighborhood, where Kabir's poetry and songs were used to inspire educational activities. It was a small but clean and bright space, with art projects on the walls featuring lines from Kabir. They held a bhajan program the day I came. Narayanji joined Tarasingh Dodve, an excellent singer from Indore, and Arun Goyal, a vivacious young man with a fine voice who had come from his village for this program. Along with Suresh's coworkers, about twenty children and a few guests were present.

They sang songs that emphasized social issues, touching on religious delusions, hypocrisy, and social inequality. The program did not have a drearily didactic or politically doctrinaire feeling. Everyone plunged into the joy of music, generating experiences that were both personal and social. After three hours, I wrote in my notebook:

> Amazing explosion of selfless, joyful, mutually supportive singing, especially between Arun and Narayanji, younger and older, cascades of love and joy between them. A 13-year-old boy played *dholak*. [He turned out to be Tarasingh's son.] They threw the song verses like a ball between them, each smiling affectionately as the other picked it up, joining forces to build the energy ever higher. Narayanji got up and danced—the first time I ever saw that. The children looked happy and talked easily. When asked to sing, several stood up and sang Kabir *dohās* without hesitation.

Suresh Patel had a doctorate in Hindi literature. Like many of the highly educated artists, intellectuals, and activists I met in Malwa, and unlike many of my friends in Bangalore, Delhi and Mumbai, he spoke with me in Hindi, not English. The following translated excerpts are from a filmed interview conducted by Shabnam Virmani.[18] They are abridged and presented here in a continuous form.

> I grew up in a village near Jabalpur [eastern Madhya Pradesh], where I saw poverty, discrimination, untouchability, hypocrisy. And I saw how human dignity arises even in the worst circumstances. It was a majority *ādivāsī* (indigenous) area. The women had barely enough clothing to cover their bodies. When I saw all this in childhood, I began to think about it. In Tagar village, where my maternal grandfather lived, there were traditions of both folk and classical music. There were always Kabir bhajans and *satsangs* going on. I saw how people worked together and helped each other as they participated in Kabir *satsangs*. Some Kabir Panth sadhus came there. I found them different from other sadhus—not so much hypocrisy.
>
> Later when I finished my education, I took a job with the Cotton Corporation of India and came over to this side, Malwa [western

Madhya Pradesh]. Again I noticed that the cotton farmers hardly had any clothes to wear, though they were providing clothes for the whole world. I was moved to try to understand this. At that time I felt very close to Kabir, who 600 years earlier was facing these same things—hypocrisy, superstition, untouchability, poverty, exploitation, cruelty.

Then I heard that Eklavya had started a *manch* in Dewas, with bhajans and discussions. I wanted to organize something like that in Tagar too. I met Syag-*bhāī*, Dinesh Sharma, Prakash Kant, and they said they could send a group. Prahlad Singh Tipanyaji came with his *mandalī*. These were very interior villages. We had a three-day program, everyone was excited. The girls were drawing pictures, writing *sākhī*s on the walls. They collected money among themselves. Prakash Kantji came. Intellectuals, journalists came. People from other villages heard it was going on and they came.

We felt that Kabir-*sāhib*'s devotional bhajans were very well known, whereas his bhajans about social change and hypocrisy, and his own ways of attacking these things, were little known and rarely sung. Even the bhajans that focused on social issues were somehow changed, turned into something else. Kabir himself was becoming a kind of god, and the full force of his words was being lost. It suited some people to promote that kind of thing, it was convenient for them, so they made sure those bhajans were sung and emphasized. Like this one—

> In seven continents and nine world-divisions
> no one is as great as the guru.
> The creator can fail,
> but the guru always succeeds.

The people who came regularly on the second of each month—mostly they just wanted to sing their bhajans. The majority were poor and from Dalit groups. In Eklavya there was an atmosphere of equality. Everyone ate together, sang and discussed together, raised questions. Everyone had the right to speak. They didn't find these values in their villages or in the larger society. Some *mandalī*s were invited to various places to support communal harmony and social awakening. They went on All India Radio and Doordarshan and became more widely known. But the biggest break was with

Tipanyaji's first cassette, *Soī pīr hai jo jāne par pīr*. We stayed in contact after he visited Jabalpur and we encouraged him to get his bhajans into the market. He was inexperienced, and so were we. The company Sonotek in Jabalpur—they said it's nice, but who will listen to it? We said we were sure about the power of Kabir's songs, though we were also a little worried, since the message is so deep.

> *kabīr kī bānī aṭpaṭi, jhaṭpaṭ lakhi na jāy*
> *Jo jan jhatpat lakhi le, vākī khaṭpaṭ hī mit jāy.*
>
> Kabir's words are tricky, quite hard to get quickly,
> but if you see quickly, duplicity's gone!

[The humor of the verse depends on the rhyming sounds of three words translated as tricky, quickly, duplicity—*aṭpaṭi, jhaṭpaṭ, khaṭpaṭ*.]

But I had confidence people would listen to it. After the cassette came out, the Sonotek guys told me their studio's fortunes were made from it. The demand just kept growing. Who could have guessed? A whole series of results came out of this cassette. Dr. Kapil Tiwari organized programs all over M.P.[19] And things kept developing. Until then nobody was paying any attention to Kabir, aside from the Kabir Panth.

[The camera goes to a picture of Kabir on the wall.] A special feature of this picture is that he is working. He dedicated his life to the culture of work. Here his whole attention (*dhyān*) is on his work. He's wearing little clothing and concentrating fully on his work. I find this very suitable to Kabir-*sāhib*. He was living and working among the people, talking with them, eating and drinking with them, sharing all their sorrows and struggles, and composing his poetry. [This description is in implicit contrast with the usual Kabir Panthi representation of Kabir, seated as a great guru, with a lot of clothing, a tall pointed hat, and a hand raised in formal teaching gesture associated with sages and saints.]

Suresh, his close coworker Chhotu Bharti, and others have continued to link the voice of Kabir with their efforts to support people in the quest for equality, dignity, and equal opportunity. Over the years we have met a number of times—in Indore, in Suresh's ancestral village Tagar, and in Khandwa, a college town where we joined faculty members in a public forum on Kabir. I had a habit of questioning Suresh and Chhotu about "inside" and "outside." I would say: Kabir taught us to speak out about the pain and injustice in society, but he also taught us to investigate ourselves, to follow some *sādhanā* (spiritual practice), to find a place of profound awakening within. Was it acceptable—was it true to Kabir—to emphasize the first part and ignore the second? Taking my question seriously, for a while Suresh and one of his colleagues tried practicing yoga and meditation. But eventually Suresh commented that I overemphasized the "inner" part.

I often remember the reply of Chhotu when asked what he felt was the most important teaching of Kabir. Without hesitation, he replied, "There is a great power hidden inside of everyone. We should find that power!" Then he and Suresh added, almost in chorus, "But we won't achieve this just by singing. We must do concrete work."

The hidden power Chhotu refers to is usually understood as the presence in everyone of the supreme reality, which reveals itself poetically in images of boundless sound and light, and which makes all bodies and all persons absolutely equal. Countless Kabir poems express this:

> As oil is in a sesame seed,
> as fire is in flint,
> your lord is in you.
> Wake up if you can.

***

> What are you searching for, dear friend?
> What are you running after, dear friend?
> In every body, Ramji speaks.
> In every body, the beloved speaks.[20]

***

> Kabir says, what have you lost? What are you seeking?
> The blind don't see. Light is blazing in your body.[21]

***

> Wherever I look, nothing is empty, nothing is lacking.
> This body is filled with light.[22]

***

Oh bird, my friend,
why do you wander
from forest to forest?
In the city of your body
is the sacred sound,
in your own green garden
is the holy name.

Oh bird, my friend,
you're sitting in the dark.
In the temple of your body
the light shines,
the guru's teaching gleams.
Why do you wander
from forest to forest?[23]

For many listeners these lines point to an inner spiritual awakening, often implying the necessity of a guru to show the way. For Chhotu, "Your lord is in you, wake up if you can," resonates as a political inspiration. The light that blazes within the body signifies not only enlightenment in the spiritual sense, but *power.*

From our first conversation, in July 2002, Suresh and Chhotu showed how an orientation toward social struggle and service produced a certain consistent way of reading Kabir. With my interest in inner transformation, I would consistently point to the other side.

LH: Was Kabir mainly concerned with reforming society, or was he more interested in the spiritual side?

SURESH PATEL (SP): Kabir was interested in the common people. He showed a way that was simple and open to all, not just the elite.

When Suresh asked why I was interested in Kabir, I touched on various points, emphasizing my attraction to Kabir's fearlessness.

SP: How does a person get free of fears? Why are people fearful? Because they have no security, no money, no education, no legal rights. They have poor health, both physical and mental. We can bring them to fearlessness by changing these things.

LH: But even when we have education, rights, money, and all the rest, we are still not free from fear. Right? (to Chhotu) How can we transform our condition from fearfulness to fearlessness?

CHHOTU: We need to recognize ourselves. When we recognize the strength (*tākat*) within ourselves, we become less and less afraid.

Scenes from the Manch

Though I wasn't present at these events in the 1990s, I could imagine them on the basis of Eklavya's logs and audio recordings, my later conversations with participants, and my many experiences with Kabir singers. Listening to ten-year-old tapes, I reflected on the sheer numbers of songs that the singers knew. Song after song, poetic verse after verse, all through the night, with the vigorous beats of the *dholak*, the ring of cymbals, the clear plucking and strumming of *tambūrā* strings, the single and combined male voices, some melodious, some rough—the room and the people in it were enveloped in Kabir. Together, in mind and body, they possessed immeasurable knowledge of Kabir.

Each meeting began with a bhajan by a group that had been chosen to lead off, after which all present would introduce themselves. Then each group would get a chance to sing, a leader from the *mandalī* would be asked to comment, and general discussion could follow. Though the program continued from 9 p.m. to dawn, often there was time for only one bhajan from each of the many groups that showed up.

In a yellowing register one can read Dinesh's records of the first year, with notes on each monthly meeting, written swiftly as the meeting was going on. The second gathering, on August 2, 1991, was summarized like this:

> Eighteen *mandalīs* sang one bhajan each and were asked to say something about the meaning. We found that most of the *mandalīs* could not explain the full meaning of a bhajan. They all benefited from the discussion in which they heard other people's ideas about the meaning.
>
> As a goal for future programs, they said that people of all castes should sit together and discuss social problems such as casteism, untouchability, etc. Other topics that they wanted to take up were:

- History of Kabir Panth.
- *Chaukā āratī* ritual. Difference between two traditions of Kabir panth—one gives great importance to *chaukā* while the other doesn't. Why? Some say Kabir opposed *chaukā āratī* but later it became a means of involving people in Kabir programs.
- Plan to produce cassettes and booklets.
- Why are there no women participants here?

On September 9, 1991, they took up meanings of words and concepts as well as questions about Kabir's life:

> What are the five *tattvas* (elements) and three *guṇas* (qualities) that Kabir often mentions? What is an *avadhūt* (the wanderer whom Kabir addresses in many songs)? What is the difference between *guru* and *satguru* (teacher and true teacher)? Between *ātmā* and *paramātmā* (the individual divine spirit and the supreme divine spirit)? What is the importance of *satsang* (good company/spiritual companionship)? What are the deeper meanings of *alakh* (unseen) and *adbhūt* (wondrous)? What happened in Kabir's own life? What kind of person was Ramanand (believed to be Kabir's guru)? Why did Kabir speak disrespectfully of Ramanand in one song? [parentheses added by LH]

In one entry, Dinesh made a list of verses that challenged and taunted Brahmins, a second list showing how Muslim clerics were similarly challenged, and a third giving examples of songs devoted to the guru's greatness. The last type, *guru mahimā,* was always cited by Eklavya workers as the sort of thing they were trying to get away from, preferring to emphasize Kabir's radical social thought and anti-authoritarian spirit. For them the constant litanies of homage to the guru represented the hold of traditional religion with its hierarchical structures, which tended to keep people passive and subordinated.

In an early meeting of the *manch,* Hiralal Sisodiya sang the well-known *Santo dekhat jag baurānā* (translation in Hess and Singh 2002, 3–4), then commented on it:

> In this bhajan Kabir says, look, brother, these beliefs we hold on to are false. They have us all tangled up. If we get together, we can break through them—beliefs about temples, monasteries, heavy books, Puranas, Shastras. We keep these conservative traditions,

we say that this is our tradition, but it's not true. All these things have been made by human beings. Nobody has these traditions in them when they're born. If you're born in a Hindu house, you become a Hindu. If you're born in a low-caste house, they call you low caste. And we go around with these orthodoxies loaded on our backs. The religions [he alternates between *dharma* and *mazahab*, Hindu and Muslim terms for religion] go on telling us we have to do rituals, idol-worship, pilgrimage, fasts, we have to put marks on our arms and foreheads, follow rules. Like this, they deceive people. We should be free from these rules. Human beings naturally want to be free.

Kabir also says that if we are really human, we won't harm other creatures. The *sant*s made a strong point about violence. As the divine spirit is in you, so it is also in other creatures. Just as you are conscious, they are conscious. Just as a light is burning within you, it is burning within them. If they are going to die, let them die by themselves, don't kill them. Many commit violence to fill their stomachs or to please their tongues. There are lots of other foods in the world, fruits and vegetables. Why do we have to kill in order to eat? Humans didn't give them [animals] life and don't have the right to take their lives. We shouldn't even kill insects. Kabir said:

Don't torment a living being, we all share one breath.
Though you hear a thousand scriptures, you won't get free of that death.

After the first six months, Dinesh wrote enthusiastically of a change in the gatherings:

Now it seems the people themselves have taken up leadership of the activities, without any formalities. Forgetting differences between high and low, rich and poor, laborer and employer, and other social constructions, they pose questions to each other, going beyond their own limited ideas and beliefs. Sometimes they discuss a single word for thirty minutes, examining it in fine detail. They look at bhajans, mythologies, characters in the traditional literature, philosophy, and discuss everything fully.

Then Dinesh imagined that this could continue and spread independent of Eklavya. He hoped that they would carry this spirit to other social and religious settings, that they would no longer sit silent, not daring to ask questions or express ideas.

In 2004, I discussed these records with Arvind Sardana, a longtime worker in Eklavya's Dewas office who was present throughout the period of the Kabir *manch* and became director of the whole Eklavya organization in 2011. Arvind suggested that it was a bit too optimistic to imagine that such changes would continue and spread without structural support like that provided by the Kabir *manch*: regular organized meetings; bus fare and tea; someone keeping records in a register; collection and publication of bhajans; outreach to larger worlds as in the Sadbhav Yatra; above all the remarkable mixing of people of different social, educational, and economic backgrounds in an atmosphere of mutual respect, equality, congeniality, and enjoyment. Such support was necessary to create something new, sustained, and far-reaching. When Eklavya discontinued the official Kabir *manch* in 1998, these structures dissolved. But there is evidence that individuals experienced lasting changes, and that the Kabir culture of the region was affected in a number of subtle ways. Some of the individuals are profiled below in their own words. Examples of social and cultural impacts also arise in the story of the *chaukā āratī* ritual and Prahladji's relationship to the Kabir Panth, told in chapter 7.[24]

The organizers succeeded in their goal of raising social issues through the medium of Kabir, but they did not try to control the scope of the conversation. Singers sang whatever they wanted to, including plenty of songs praising the guru or describing esoteric inner experiences. They delved into the meanings of spiritual terminology, history, psychology, and social, moral, and political questions, without any sense of limitation, often making connections that might be missed by someone who is inclined to separate the "political" and the "spiritual."

Social meanings sometimes came out in contexts that were surprising to me. On one occasion in 1992, Prahladji and his group sang the rollicking "*Sāhib (satguru) ne bhāng pilāī, akhiyoṇ meṇ lālan chhāī*"—"the lord (or alternately, the true guru) gave me a marijuana drink, my eyes turned red." Far from being a political song, it evokes the joyful "drunkenness" of getting suddenly enlightened through the guru's grace and seeing the divine in every creature and every particle of nature. The signature lines at the end have the names of both Ramanand and Kabir.

guru rāmānand tumarī balihārī, sir par ṭhokar aisī dīnī
sāheb kabīr bakshīsh kar do, yah agam bānī gāī

Ramanand was a famed Brahmin teacher, a devotee of Ram, who came to Varanasi from the South and is widely believed to have been the guru of Kabir as well as other bhakti poets of diverse castes. For someone familiar with conventional history, an obvious way to translate the verse would be this:

> Guru Ramanand, I surrender to you. You gave me such a bang on the head!
> Lord, give Kabir your blessing as he sings this ungraspable song.[25]

On the 1992 tape, I heard Prahladji briefly explicate the whole song. When he got to this verse, he gave the conventional meaning, then offered another interpretation. Ramanand followed the *saguṇ* devotional path, worshiping the Ram avatar who had form and attributes—the son of King Dasharatha in the *Rāmāyaṇa* story. He must have taught his disciples to worship images. It could be that after meeting Kabir, he came to understand the truth of *nirguṇ* devotion. "When Kabir-*dās* wrote, 'In every bush and tree, everything living, moving and unmoving, my lord is blooming,' " Prahladji suggested, "he [Ramanand] must have realized this in his own experience—the lord is everywhere, in everything. Then Ramanand must have said, 'Lord Kabir, give me your blessing.' "

If we take this interpretation, the "ungraspable song" (*agam bāṇī*) refers to *nirguṇ* expression, and a very different translation emerges:

> Guru Ramanand says, I surrender to you. You gave me such a bang on the head!
> Lord Kabir, give me your blessing as I sing this ungraspable song.

I first heard the story of Ramanand's being Kabir's disciple from one of the leaders of the Dharamdasi Kabir Panth in Damakheda. There was a text, he said, a *goṣhṭhī* or dialogue between Kabir and Ramanand, which concluded with Ramanand having a great awakening to the truth of *nirguṇ* bhakti and taking Kabir as his guru. My initial response to this was urbane amusement. I knew the genre of these *goṣhṭhī*s. Every sect had them: their founder encountered other great gurus and sectarian leaders, debated with them, and vanquished everyone. The idea that Ramanand had become Kabir's disciple ran so wildly counter to received tradition that I just smiled.

But when I heard Prahladji coming up with this interpretation in a 1992 tape from the Kabir *manch*, I got a bang on the head myself. At that point I could not dismiss it as a generic "my guru is greater than your guru" narrative. Prahladji was citing the lines of a Kabir bhajan that he and many others in the room sang. His interpretation was clearly and reasonably based on the text. Was it a Dalit protest against the superiority of the Brahmin guru?

The Brahminical shadow over Kabir had become a matter of intense debate among the urban cognoscenti following the publication in 1997 of Dr. Dharamvir's *Kabīr ke ālochak* (*Kabir's Literary Critics*). Dharamvir is a scholar who undertook to expose Brahminical prejudice in the way Kabir was treated by the giants of mid-twentieth-century Hindi literary criticism—Hazariprasad Dvivedi, Ramchandra Shukla, and Parashuram Chaturvedi.

Dvivedi's 1942 book *Kabīr*, a classic in Kabir studies, does not attempt to demonstrate historically that Ramanand was Kabir's contemporary and guru. Taking that for granted, Dvivedi waxes eloquent on how the arrival of such a guru must have transformed Kabir. As Dvivedi puts it, Kabir was a rough jewel before that moment, a harsh critic of others' delusions, perhaps excessively influenced by the Nath tradition where cocky, independent yogis valued their own efforts and achievements and belittled others. But when Kabir found his guru in Ramanand, he realized the depth of bhakti—devotion, love, self-surrender. He experienced previously unknown ecstasy and was transformed into something far greater than he could otherwise have been. This, according to Dvivedi, was Ramanand's grace.[26]

Dharamvir asserts that Dvivedi's account has a subtext: For Dvivedi, it is unthinkable that the unlettered Muslim/Shudra weaver Kabir could achieve greatness on his own. This was possible only after he was perfected by and subordinated to a Brahmin guru. Listening to the Eklavya tape, I realized that five years before Dharamvir's book provoked controversies among urban intellectuals, Prahladji had argued that Ramanand had ultimately surrendered to Kabir. The reversal of the commonly accepted identities of guru and disciple shows that objections to Ramanand's authority had a longstanding presence in grassroots Kabir culture. The arguments of Prahladji and Dharamvir are different. The urban writer, based on his reading of Dvivedi, asserts caste bias on the part of Dvivedi and other twentieth-century Brahmin critics. The singer, based on his reading of a Kabir-attributed song text, links the superiority of Kabir to Ramanand with the superiority of *nirguṇ* to *saguṇ* bhakti. But there is a connection between the two arguments. *Nirguṇ* traditions are deeply entwined with the struggle against caste oppression—a relationship that David Lorenzen explores fully in *Praises to a Formless God*, and that I have discussed in chapter 1.

An interesting sidelight on Ramanand's place in Kabir's life came unexpectedly in a conversation with Narayan Singh Delmia, who is profiled at length later in this chapter. Near the end of our interview in 2002, Narayanji asked me a few questions about my research, including this exchange:

NARAYAN SINGH DELMIA (ND): Did you learn about Kabir? Who were his mother and father? Did you learn that?

LH: About Kabir's life? I read in books various stories that have been told about Kabir. This isn't really historical. From a historical point of view we can't prove much about what happened in Kabir's life. Is this what you're asking me?

ND: Did you learn the names of his mother and father?

LH: I heard that Niru and Nima [Muslim weavers] were his parents. I also found the story that a Brahmin widow had abandoned him and he was adopted by Niru and Nima.

ND: You heard that he was a Brahmin widow's son. And did you hear who his father was?

LH: No, I didn't hear that. Why are you asking? What have you heard?

ND: I haven't read it, but I've heard that he was Ramanand's son.

LH: That's an interesting story! I have never heard that. . . . I don't believe he was the son of a Brahmin widow. I have always assumed that he was a Muslim, born in a Muslim family. Later when he was recognized as someone very great, the Brahmins wanted to claim him. They didn't like the idea that he was a Muslim. But nowadays many people believe that story about the Brahmin widow. What do you think about the story that Ramanand was his father?

ND: I feel it is likely to be true. I will try to learn more about this. I will buy some books and try to find out.

LH: I would be surprised if that story is written anywhere.

ND: I think it is written in Rajneesh's book.

In this conversation, one of Kabir's Dalit followers simultaneously affirms Kabir's intimate tie with the famous Brahmin guru and radically demotes the guru by suggesting that he broke his vow of celibacy to father an even greater guru, the Julaha saint of Varanasi.

While educated urban participants were interested in Hindu-Muslim communal issues on the national level, the village singers were more likely to apply Kabir's critiques of religion and hypocrisy locally to the religious formation they knew best: the Kabir Panth. The Panth became a focus of debate and criticism. The next chapter provides an introduction to the Kabir Panth and its distinct lineages. Here just a few points will be mentioned. The Panth's relationship to Hinduism is not simple. While it was created partly as an alternative to caste-ridden, Brahmin-dominated, ritual-filled Hinduism, it also came to reproduce many Hindu forms. The Panth tradition to which most Kabir devotees in Malwa belong, based in Chhattisgarh and known as the Dharamdasi or forty-two-generation lineage, is the most elaborately Hinduized of all the organized Kabir Panths. In the Dharamdasi "branch," the head guru's lofty status verges on divinity, and authority is vested in a wide network of *mahants* who function as ritualists, initiators of disciples, local gurus, and preachers. A particular ritual called *chaukā āratī* is considered indispensable to the Panth's various functions.

The open, egalitarian, and demystifying thrust of the *manch* contrasted with the ritualizing and authoritarian tendencies of the Panth. Dinesh told me that the chief Kabir Panth *mahant* of Dewas had once come to the *manch* and remarked, "Why do you ask such people to interpret Kabir? What do they know? This is something that only the Panth gurus should do." The day he came people were quiet, hardly daring to speak. "Fortunately," Dinesh said with a smile, "he never came back."

Dinesh made a chart in the logbook, comparing the *manch* to Kabir Panth activities. Table 6.1 below provides an abridged version.

A discussion on October 2, 1991, began with a comparison of Kabir *sākhīs* that seemed to have contradictory messages. The singers came up with their own theory of interpolation, considering who might have inserted what false verses for their own self-interest, and what this implied for their understanding of Kabir and themselves. Here is Dinesh's account, written in the logbook:

Narayanji sang a bhajan that included these lines:

> Don't sit with bad companions—
> they never mention Ram.
> A wedding procession without a groom—
> what's the point?

Table 6.1 Comparison of Kabir Manch and Kabir Panth Activities

Activity	Manch	Panth
Opening	No invoking of authority. General welcome, everyone introduces self.	Dedication to guru. *Mahant* gives sermon.
Arrangements	Nothing special.	Tents, lights, loudspeakers, etc.
Status	Everyone has equal status, respect, chance to talk.	Guru sits on a high seat. He talks, others listen.
Expense	No charge, only bus fare.	Must offer coconut, money. Coming "empty-handed" not acceptable.
Discussion	Yes	No
Relating To Organizers	Open, respectful, friendly, approachable.	Ordinary Kabir Panthi doesn't have the nerve to question the guru.
Goals	Focused on well-being in this life, nothing about after-life or final salvation.	Always talking about *moksha* (salvation) and *satlok* (heavenly world beyond this one).

Prahlad Singh Tipanya raised a question: Did Kabir hate bad people? [As everyone knew, there were many songs and couplets that warned against bad company.] If so, then what about this *sākhī*:

> Kabir stands in the bazaar, wishing everyone well.
> He's not anyone's friend, not anyone's foe.

Narayanji replied with another *sākhī*:

> From good company goodness,
> from bad company grief.
> Kabir says, wherever you go,
> keep your own true company.[27]

Hiralal Sisodiya continued the discussion: If we search through the bhajans and *sākhīs*, we can easily find two that have Kabir's signature, and even though Kabir was one person, the lines say very different things. The two seem to contradict each other. It may be that in certain places, or in response to certain events, Kabir had particular thoughts. It's all right if there are differences in the ideas he expressed. But if the ideas are totally opposite, then, according to me, somebody has passed some fake coins in the market, calling them Kabir's coins. Here's another example. In Kabir's bhajans we see [criticism of] hypocrisy, pomp, ritual marks on the body, temples and mosques. But we also find some bhajans under Kabir's name that promote guru-worship, ritual, sacred books, homage to Ganesh, and so on. Should we fall into these delusions? What should we do?

Prahlad Tipanya said: There are always people in society looking out for their own self-interest and power. They might have inserted this kind of thing in the bhajans. The gurus themselves are hypocritical and pompous in the way they do the *chaukā āratī* [ritual], making ordinary people throw away their money.

GIRDHARIJI: Why do we do *chaukā āratī*?

NARAYANJI: We sit here and oppose *chaukā āratī*, but we ourselves sponsor *āratī*s when the time comes.

GOVARDHANLALJI: The gurus fill us with false promises and beliefs. They say, if you don't do this, then after you die, you won't go to heaven.

NARAYANJI: Why do we fall into their traps?

MANGILALJI: We lack confidence and courage. We feel weak, so we get caught in their snares.

SISODIYAJI: We need to become courageous. The first step is knowledge. First look at yourself, then you can think about the infinite universe. If we come to know ourselves, it's a big thing.

A note in the register for July 2, 1992, the first anniversary of the *manch*, describes a conversation with several participants in the predawn hours. "After a year," Dinesh asks, "do you see any change in yourselves?" He summarizes their response:

We used to have religious fear [*dhārmik ḍar*]. If you don't do this you'll suffer, you won't get salvation. Now we're not afraid. There's no point. Our self-esteem was weak. Now we feel more power and self-confidence. We used to think of Kabir as a Hindu god, an avatar. Now we think of him as a great human being. Narayanji commented on a *sākhī*: "Gold, virtuous folk, and holy ones can break

> and become whole again and again. / A false person's like a clay pot: one blow, it shatters." Before we just said it, but now we understand it and apply it in our lives.

That same night, Narayanji had sung *Santo jīvat hī karo āshā. ... man hī se bandhan, man hī se mukti ...*—"Seekers, fulfill your hopes while you're alive.... It's your own mind that binds you, your own mind that frees you." Explicating the song, he emphasized that there's no point in dreaming about happiness or wisdom after death. Our suffering and our freedom, our problems and their solutions, are all right here.

Three Singer-Participants and Their Experience of the Manch

Narayan Singh Delmia, Hiralal Sisodiya, and Prahlad Singh Tipanya were often mentioned as having taken leadership roles in the *manch*. Prahladji receives extensive attention throughout this book, especially in chapters 1 and 7. Here I will profile Narayanji, Hiralalji, and a younger singer whom I came to know in the 2000s, Kaluram Bamaniya.

Hiralalji

Hiralal Sisodiya, in his sixties when I met him in Ujjain in 2002, had long been a politically conscious person. A staunch follower of B. R. Ambedkar, he had converted to Buddhism along with millions of other former "untouchables." He was a member of the Bahujan Samaj Party (BSP), which seeks to unite poor and disenfranchised sectors of Indian society, particularly the lower castes, electing representatives who would serve their interests. Hiralalji had studied up to the seventh grade and had worked for many years in a cloth mill in Ujjain.

Dinesh Sharma, Hiralal's brother Lalchand, and I drove from Dewas to Ujjain to meet Hiralalji. He spoke with fluency, simplicity, clarity, and color. His words here are presented largely as a continuous statement, with brief bracketed indications of questions posed by Dinesh and me.

> The main purpose of the Kabir manch was to help people understand themselves, what they truly are inside ... Kabir's philosophy first of all is against hypocrisy. People in our country, especially poor people,

FIGURE 6.3. Hiralal Sisodiya. Photo by Shabnam Virmani.

are deeply entangled in hypocrisy and superstition, and in the caste system. The wall of casteism rises up between human beings. Often there is no love, no sense of brotherhood, between people of different castes. A kind of poison is created, which Kabir wanted to eliminate. Kabir wanted equality. … The Kabir *manch* as I see it tried to shed light on hypocrisy, superstition, orthodoxy, casteism. … In this country there are many delusions about God. Kabir said, brother, God is within each person. It is called *chetan svarūp* (consciousness-form). Some people call it *ātmā*, or *buddhi*, or *chetnā*. Kabir said:

> Where are you searching for me, friend? I'm right here.
> Not in Gokul or Mathura, not in Kashi or Kailash.[28]

So the temple, the mosque, all these religious places we've created—it's a kind of commercial business (*dukandārī*), a way of perverting our intelligence, when in fact the supreme being (*paramātmā*) is within every person. This is what Kabir taught. And this is what we were doing with the Kabir manch, spreading Kabir's ideas, awakening people, freeing them from all kinds of problems, delusions, superstitions.

[On being asked what they did at the monthly meetings.]

There were bhajans and interpretations. For the listeners who didn't have much knowledge, there were explanations. Those who had some understanding in their own hearts about Kabir's words, ideas, and ideals—they clarified these things. This was helpful to people. Some decided to lead their lives according to those ideals, and even now they are living that way. In that atmosphere, along with Kabir, the words of other sants also were discussed. Philosophy was discussed. That's what happened at the Kabir manch.

[About his own history with Kabir.]

I had been drawn to Kabir's ideas since I was twelve or thirteen years old. Gradually I changed. Gradually I got some joy, peace, and happiness. Through my brother Lalchand I learned about the Kabir *manch*. I started going and even took some responsibility there. When I heard it was ending, I still went [on the 2nd of the month], because I didn't want to believe it was true. I kept thinking about it. There were still many people from Ujjain who I wanted to take to the *manch*. I had already brought several people there, to learn about Kabir's ideas, to get that happiness and peace.

[About Kabir Panthi gurus who occasionally came to the meetings.]

They wore their beads, caps, brow marks, arm marks. But their system, their way of thinking, was tied to ritualism. [The next comment refers to the fact that the Kabir Panth strictly prohibits alcohol, cigarettes, and nonvegetarian food.] It's good if people give up drinking, if they stop being drunkards. But so what, if there's not a revolution of ideas? This is the most important revolution. When it takes place within a person, his whole life is turned around. He is transformed. After a revolutionary change, you can imagine a person becoming Kabir or Buddha or Nanak or Ravidas or Dadu. Kabir's philosophy puts the greatest emphasis on a revolution of ideas. And it's for everyone—not for certain persons or castes. It's universal. In India there are many sects and schools of thought that have spread all kinds of delusion. They won't let some people enter the path. Even today, they don't let people in. Kabir wanted people to understand their own nature (*nij svarūp ka bodh*). Recognize yourself! The supreme being is not far away.

Hiralalji was very critical of the Kabir Panth, and he didn't hesitate to challenge Panth authorities on their own turf. He relished telling us stories of how he provoked the *mahants*.

> One time I ran into Rajaramji Dangi from Jhonkar village—nowadays he's a teacher here in Ujjain, living in Bhanjushri colony. He was with his guruji, Keshavdasji from Jhonkar. They came to the Eklavya *manch*, and the guruji sang a bhajan with his *mandalī*. Before the bhajan he sang a *sākhī*:
>
> > Step over the bounded—human. Step over the boundless—holy.
> > Step over both bounded and boundless—unfathomable thought.
>
> I asked him to explain the *sākhī*. I said, you are a sant, so *sāhabjī*, please explain it. Instead of explaining, he got angry with me. So I told a story. Two men who lived in the desert went to Australia. In the desert there's a shortage of water. In Australia they found a good hotel with running water. The water came out of the faucets, and they were bathing. They were having a good time. But their passport was only valid for one week. They were from the desert, where there was always a shortage of water. After a week, it was time to go back to India. Their guruji was ready to go, but those two men were unscrewing the faucet from the pipe. He said, "Hey, our plane is leaving soon, we need to go. Where are those two guys?" He went looking for them in their room, and they were unscrewing the faucet. They wanted to take the faucet home. Why? Because water came out of it. They said, "We'll attach it there and water will come out. We're very short of water there." Keshavdasji is like that.
>
> Dangiji was angry with me. He said, "Is this the way you talk to my guruji?" I said, "Brother, you are turning on the faucet, but the water source is far away. You want to get water just by having a faucet. In our society, we have sants and mahants like that: empty faucets. There's no water in them." That's what I said.
>
> Another Kabir Panth guru, Mangaldas Sahib, used to come to our meetings, and so did other sants and mahants. When we would ask them very politely to explain the bhajans, they refused, saying we should have only bhajans here, no explanations. We wanted understanding, but if any of the listeners raised a question, it seemed those gurus had a problem. That's why I had to tell that story.

[He speaks of the *chaukā āratī* rituals that are central to the Dharamdasi tradition of the Kabir Panth. One form of the ritual is *chalāvā āratī*, done on the occasion of someone's death.]

There's not even a religious discourse in a *chalāvā āratī*. I see it as a new orthodoxy, a phony ritual propagated by the gurus. I have spoken against it in a number of places. I have challenged Kabir Panthi gurus and *sants*. There was one *divānjī* [ritual assistant], his name was Kashinathji. He lived here in Ujjain, in Ashok Nagar. He has passed on. In *chalāvā chaukā āratī* they say that they want to bring peace to the soul of the deceased. So I said to him: "You say you're bringing peace to the soul of this dead man. Do you have any proof of this? Kabirji says,

> Everyone went from here, with loads and loads piled on.
> No one came from there. Run and try to ask.[29]

"The soul of the person to whom you're bringing peace has gone away. Did he send you a letter saying I'm peaceful or not peaceful, hungry or thirsty, happy or unhappy? Have you got any proof?" That guru also got angry with me! He said, you only want to criticize Kabir's teachings, nothing more. I said, I'm not criticizing, I'm talking about Kabir's philosophy. Kabir's philosophy is very pure, and you're ruining it, turning it into a commercial business. That's not acceptable to me. That's why you have these *chaukā āratī*s and *satsangs* so often in the villages. *Chaukā āratī, ānandi āratī*, with Kabir Panthi *mahants* sitting in the center, wearing their special shirts.

Once I went to Pavasa village. Shyamdasji from Tonk Kala had gone there for a program. He was wearing his pointed cap and marks on his forehead. In full costume, he was sitting under the canopy. I asked him: Are you Dharamdasji? Are you Kabirji? The person who had organized that *chaukā*, who belonged to the Malviya [Balai] community, said to me, "Sisodiyaji, don't say anything, he'll get upset." I said, "I'll definitely say something. When you put on an outfit like that, should I call you Dharamdasji, or should I call you Kabirji? What should I call you? Tell me!"

I am opposed to all this. Kabir never wanted this kind of ritualism. Not a bit! Kabir's wisdom was pure nectar. Anyone who drinks of that wisdom, who grasps it and knows that truth, will experience stillness and joy upon joy. In the villages they often do this ritual without even mentioning Kabir's teaching. It's terrible.

As our conversation drew to a close, Hiralalji pulled together the various threads of what he had told us.

> Eklavya's Kabir manch was a medium for all human communities, a medium for the birth of a revolution in ideas. The goal was to give all people some peace in their hearts and minds and to encourage the broadening of their imaginations. To eradicate confusion and darkness and to create light. That's why I was so very happy to discover the *Kabīr bhajan aur vichār manch,* and that's why I went there so regularly. Whenever I got an announcement, I went there. Whatever I have received from the satguru—four annas, eight annas, whatever I have been able to understand, I want to share it. If someone becomes a Kabir Panthi and puts a rosary or a bead on a string around his neck, does this mean that he has learned how to think? That a revolution of ideas has taken place in him and his superstition and orthodoxy have been erased? These are difficult matters. Kabirji says:
>
> You're a *sant*? So what? Don't play till you're ripe.
> Crush half-grown mustard seeds—no oil, no pulp.[30]
>
> So what if someone puts on the dress of a *sant* or a Kabir Panth *mahant*? The mustard seeds have to be ripe before you can extract oil from them. Oil doesn't come out of unripe seeds. *Sant*s and *mahant*s should be ripe, mature. Only if they are ripe can they make others ripe. Most of those *sant*s and *mahant*s wandering around, whether they belong to the Kabir Panth or some other Panth, they're putting on a pious show, they're out to get money. Whether the lives of others improve or don't improve—they don't care.
>
> Finally he turned to Dinesh.
>
> Now I want to make this request to you: please start the Kabir *manch* again. Let the *mandalī*s come, let them sing bhajans. I have a little time left in my life. Whatever little morsels I have, I want to share, so that others can also have a revolution in ideas. I want to share, so that the human community can move on the path of truth. You deserve our gratitude for creating the Kabir *manch*. Please start it again!

Narayanji

Narayan Singh Delmia, a well-known Kabir singer of the area, was employed by Eklavya to help with communications and arrangements—strenuous tasks in that pre–cell phone era when many villages didn't even have land line connections. Getting to know Narayanji over the last few years, I have seen that he is a wonderful organizer, a person of keen intelligence and clear ideas who has a way of bringing people together, including and encouraging everyone. When others are singing, if the mood is right, he is likely to get up and dance, gracefully whirling and moving his arms, the pleasure of the moment apparent on his face. His social and religious ideas are quite radical; without compromising them, he seems to know how to express them with humor and sensitivity, in ways that won't polarize a group. When the *manch* decided to create youth *mandalīs*, Narayanji was the one who organized and trained them. A few years later, when the Bangalore Kabir Project and Eklavya supported programs to develop women's *mandalīs* and to bring Kabir creatively into schools, Narayanji was the leader they called on. Though his formal education went only up to the third grade, his quest for knowledge has been lifelong.[31] Narayanji has deeply internalized Kabir's poetry. When I met him in 2002, he was fifty-eight, a slender man with white hair and a quick smile. He lived in a small house in Barendwa village, Ujjain district.

On August 1, 2002, I went to Barendwa for a singing session with some of Narayanji's friends and neighbors. He had arranged a room, its walls

FIGURE 6.4. Narayanji breaks into dance at a village performance. Photo by Hari Adivarekar.

made of smooth whitewashed clay. It had just one tiny window. Outside everything was dripping with rain, the sky densely overcast. And the electricity was down. We couldn't sit outside under a tree, as we would have done in clear weather. Inside it was very dark. Someone lit a "chimney," a small kerosene-fueled lamp that looked like a candle. Then a rope was swung over a ceiling-beam to hang a lantern. They lit the lantern, and the space suddenly became warm, intimate, and lively, with big shadows playing against the white walls. Narayanji led off.

> "Sometimes, Lindaji, I don't know what to think about Kabir—whether he was a human being or God."
> "Which way are you leaning right now?"
> "I think he was human."

He spoke now, as he often did, with a smile that conveyed a combination of amusement and irony.

Then we went around the circle, about sixteen men, young, old, and in-between, and each introduced himself. One tall man with a black beard said he was Raju Das, a *mahant* of the Kabir Panth. "For me, Kabir is God." Most of the others didn't express an opinion. But when the singing started, they were all ready. One man played a *dholak* for everyone. The *tambūrā* was passed around. The *mahant* turned out to be an enthusiastic and tuneful singer, and a virtuoso on the harmonium. His right arm stretched out to emphasize an emotional point while his left hand kept playing on the keys. This gathering had been called for me, but they all knew each other and blended easily. Singing, they were relaxed and in their element. Narayanji had a way of bringing forth many voices, giving everybody a chance.

Later that month we sat in a garden behind the Jain temple in Maksi, the nearby market town. Dinesh was with us. I asked Narayanji to tell me how he got started singing Kabir.

> I liked singing and playing music from the time I was ten or twelve. I was a good dancer too. I danced a lot—in my village, in Maksi, and other places. I also acted in some very good plays, up to the time when I was about fifteen. After that I played instruments and worked in bands. Once I went to a Kabir program in Bhind [near Gwalior]. I was a little scared because some big senior people were there. So I hid myself and sat far off. I didn't even know if they'd

let me come in. But they asked me to sing and play, and the senior people liked it a lot. From about the time I was thirty, I was singing with my *mandalī*. We used to go to Kabir Panth *chaukās* and other functions. I tried to do every bhajan with care and concentration. I was quite in demand.

I really liked singing, right from the beginning. I sang *kīrtan* and bhajans and played instruments. This went on for years. People started telling me I needed to get a guru, because without a guru I wouldn't get [spiritual] knowledge. So I looked for a guru. I went to Shipra and got initiated by a guru there. I didn't pay attention to what *panth* he belonged to, but he took a lot of *gānjā* and *bhāng* [hashish and marijuana], so he couldn't have been in the Kabir Panth. He was a good guru. Later I went to Radhasoami and made Maharaj Charan Singh my guru.

Tipanyaji and I used to sing together in those days. We sang at All India Radio, and in various functions. We just picked up the *tambūrā* and went off to sing.

One day on a bus, when he was carrying his *tambūrā*, Narayanji got into a conversation with Syag-*bhāī* and Dinesh. That's how his association with Eklavya and the Kabir *manch* began. He helped with the initial organization and attended regularly for all eight years.

At first the other people didn't join the discussions. But I sang bhajans and talked about them. After a while, they started talking too. Syag-*bhāī* asked everyone—why are you singing bhajans? They said because we enjoy it, and because we want to get *mukti* [liberation]. Syag-*bhāī* said you only get *mukti* when you give something up. So you're not going to get *mukti* from this.

Other questions came up. Why do you worship idols? Why do you touch people's feet? Gradually we began to understand more, our knowledge increased. We went to different villages, created new *mandalīs*, had discussions with them. When we saw some confusion, we would talk about it. For example, we would say, "You do ceremonies for snakes, you worship Bhairū Mahārāj or other gods and goddesses. Nothing will come of this." They sang Kabir bhajans but still worshiped idols, believed in gods and goddesses. I would say, brother, many of Kabir's bhajans talk about this. [Narayanji sang some verses from a harshly critical bhajan, which is translated in full at the end of chapter 8.]

Serve the true guru, you idiot.
Why have you forgotten your country?

The confused gardener tears off leaves. Every leaf is alive!
He offers torn leaves to a god's image that has no life.

You make the goddess's form of mud and worship her,
then grab her leg and toss her in the water. What happened to her
power?[32]

You call priests from all over. They march around your house,
break a coconut, offer the shell to god, and eat the meat themselves.

In this way we sang bhajans and moved to higher levels of understanding.

When asked if they had discussed these things before the Kabir *manch* started, he said they had, but not in such depth.

"You always liked singing," I said, "but there are many poets and many types of bhajans. Why did you especially choose Kabir?"

He said he liked other bhajans too, but there was one type that he was especially drawn to, and that Kabir excelled in:

When Kabir saw Hindus and Muslims clashing, he tried to bring them together. This kind of *sākhī*—

Hindu? I don't think so. Muslim? Afraid not.
The hidden essence is in both faiths. I play in both.

A doll of five elements, a trick makes it hang together.
I ask you, pandit, which is bigger? Word or creature?

The hidden came from the unseen—defects stuck to it here.
Reverse, merge with the unseen—defects disappear.

Seeing Hindus and Muslims in that situation, Kabir created this type of bhajan. I loved it. And the ones about gods, goddesses, image-worship—I sang many of those. I also liked singing bhajans about caste and untouchability.

Narayanji spoke of how his experiences in the *manch* had changed him.

I used to believe in gods and goddesses and worship them. When my wife gave birth to sons and daughters, I used to take them to the Brahmin to be named. But when my daughter and son had their children, I didn't take them to any Brahmin. I named them myself, or my wife named them. I was less deluded than before. Now I don't worship gods or goddesses.

There was a young woman in the village, a relative of ours, who didn't have children. People said, go see this god or that goddess, take her to Gujarat. Then she will get children. A lot of people have gone to Gujarat. Maybe children were born afterwards and maybe they weren't, but I don't believe in any of that. I took them both, the husband and wife, to be tested by a doctor in Indore. We found out that he didn't have what you need to make a baby. Seed. If he doesn't have that, where are children going to come from? I didn't go for help to any god or goddess. I gave up all superstitions. I began to think in a scientific way.

And you can be sure of this: I absolutely don't accept any caste distinctions. I take food and water from anyone's house, and I'll bring food and feed it to anyone, in any house. I wasn't like that before. I myself practiced untouchability.[33] I hated people who I thought were below me. But after getting involved in the Kabir bhajan *manch*, it was as if my body had been totally turned around [*palaṭ gayī*]. That's how it was. Turned around. Yes, yes, my ideas completely changed. What was I doing? Where was I going? I realized how wrong I had been. … After that I started reading books. I read Kabir. I read about Islam. I also read Rajneesh. I began to realize something frightening. I was completely on the wrong track. Now I understood clearly, without a doubt, how I needed to change.

Picking up on Narayanji's mention of *mukti*, which usually means liberation of the spiritual self from *saṃsārā*, the worlds of birth and death, I asked if there was really such a thing as *mukti*, and if so, what was it? He explained it in an unconventional way:

If you let go of something, then you are free [*mukt*]. For instance, I smoked *bīḍīs*. Now I'm free from *bīḍīs*. I have no desire. I'm free. I ate meat. Now I have no desire for it. I'm free. I drank liquor. Now I'm liberated. Whatever my religious life used to be—I believed in Bhairū Maharaj or Bajarangbalī or some other god—I am liberated from that too. I don't want these gods. The only gods I want are human beings. Living, conscious, you and me, here, having a conversation. Those are the gods I want. They are the ones who can turn me around. If I'm on the wrong path, you can tell me, or you can take my hand and walk with me. If I go to those pictures and statues of gods, nothing will change in me. That's what I think.

I asked Narayanji to say more specifically what happened at the *manch* that changed him so much.

One thing that I liked very much was that there wasn't any trace of caste consciousness. [Looking at Dinesh, he continues.] Another thing I liked was that, from the very start, you helped me. Months after turning the work over to me, you still helped. When we were together, you washed the cups and plates and mugs. No matter what castes came to the Kabir *manch*, and all kinds of castes came, even though you were a Brahmin, you washed the mugs. So I thought about it. If a Brahmin can do this work, why shouldn't I?

In Anu and Arvind's house, they would always serve me food.[34] They showed me so much love. Even today they love me. Anu and Arvind are 100% pure gold. Sometimes Anu was sitting and talking with me, so Arvind would make the tea. Yes, and sometimes he would make a meal and serve it. He has such a good nature. I liked it so much that in my heart I thought, why shouldn't I help my wife like this, in my own house? And I have helped her, quite a few times. Many times. Syag-*bhāī* also did this kind of work. I went to his house, and there was never any consciousness of caste. I asked him, "Syag-*bhāī*, there are no pictures [of gods] in your house. So who do you believe in?" He said, "Narayanji, I believe in you. What do I have to do with pictures?" Being exposed to these kinds of ideas was refreshing. My mind became more and more open.

Then I went to a lot of different places in organizing the *manch*. I formed new *mandalīs*. I went to the houses of *chamārs* [a caste that traditionally deals with leather and dead bodies of animals]. Where I wouldn't have eaten before, I ate. Where I wouldn't have slept before, I slept. And in my heart I didn't feel—how could I come into this house? I felt—these people are very poor. Where did they get such a good quilt to cover me with? Sometimes I slept on the ground. Once I went to the house of someone in a very low caste. I slept with only a cotton *dhotī* to cover me, on a thin straw mat. I didn't think, how can I associate with him? I thought, this brother is very poor. Seeing such people and such circumstances, my way of thinking changed. The old feelings weren't there any more.

In late December 2002, Narayanji organized another bhajan-singing gathering for me in his village. A lot of men, women, and children got together in the verandah in front of his house, spreading out into the open space beyond. I was introduced to a man who, the locals assured me, was 110 years old. As the night went on, I was freezing even while wrapped in a blanket, but the 110-year-old man seemed to be comfortable in minimal cotton clothing, his bare legs stretched out.

The old Kabir singing tradition, Narayanji said, was with the *ektār*—literally "one string," a simple instrument with one or two strings. He showed me an old broken-down *ektār* he had. The practice of using the five-stringed *tambūrā* came later, and the use of other instruments, like harmonium and violin, was much more recent. Now no one uses *ektār* except a few who wander around begging.

The singing started to roll. I noted that while Narayanji didn't have the powerfully penetrating voice or the electrifying presence of Prahladji, he had the gift of building group spirit. He did a call and response with other singers, steadily raising the energy level. Around him were many people smiling, singing, playing instruments, moving their bodies.

Over the next few years, I found myself in a variety of settings with Narayanji. When called upon to sing, he often chose a song that aimed barbs at delusions that he noticed in the vicinity. Once we were in Dinesh's village house. Dinesh's father, a Brahmin priest, was hosting a bhajan session that included but wasn't limited to songs of Kabir. There was a big shrine in the house, replete with Hindu gods, and clearly the site of regular worship. When he got a turn to sing, Narayanij sang the bhajan that begins with the deluded gardener who breaks off leaves and flowers to offer to a lifeless statue. Later I asked him, "Why did you choose that bhajan on that occasion?" He replied, "They had a big temple, didn't they? Wouldn't they be offering all these things to the statues of their gods?"

On another occasion we went to a place that was called a Kabir ashram but was full of images of Hindu gods, along with images of Kabir depicted as a god. They did an elaborate Hindu *āratī* ceremony followed by bhajans. Narayanji sang a satirical bhajan that criticized ritual and spoke irreverently of the *Bhagavad Gita*. The guru of the ashram got angry.

Narayanji also likes to sing rousing songs that touch on current politics. One of his favorites is *Āzādī*, the Urdu word for "freedom." In this simple call and response, he sings out a line, and others participate by shouting the last word, *āzādī*. The chorus is, "Freedom, freedom, everyone wants freedom!" Each stanza mentions a different category of people who want freedom.

This of course is not a song of Kabir. Neither is the *Mandir-masjid* song that responds to the conflicts in Ayodhya and associated communal tension and violence.

Temple, mosque, church—you've divided up God.
You've divided earth, divided the sea. Don't divide humanity.

Hindu says, "My temple! Temple's my true space."
Muslim says, "My Mecca! Mecca alone is true."

They fight, fight and die, fight and get destroyed.
Who knows what cruel, cruel things they do?

Who does this? Look! Who walks here? Learn!
You've divided earth, divided the sea. Don't divide humanity.

For the sake of power, politicians claim to serve the nation.
They join upholders of religion, while we face desperation.

Your brother's cut to pieces, but the politician's honored.
Once he gets the votes and wins, it's time for exploitation.

Temple, mosque, church—you've divided up God.
You've divided earth, divided the sea. Don't divide humanity.

When asked why he was singing non-Kabir songs in Kabir bhajan programs, he said that he had reflected on what Kabir might have done if he were living now, and that reflection inspired him to sing these songs.

LH: Why do you think the Eklavya people started the *manch*?

ND: They were thinking, OK, these people sing bhajans, but do they understand what they're singing? Do they have knowledge about it? Do they realize its importance? They thought of providing some education that would bring about change. They never said, don't do this or that. Slowly, gently, lovingly they provided a space. If they had talked in another way, the whole thing would have broken up. They worked at a very slow pace, so that it wouldn't break, but people would come together, and their understanding would increase. I would set up dates to go various places—here the 8th, there the 10th. Whatever I was learning, I would go and tell it to the *mandalīs*.

LH: They came regularly? They liked it?

ND: Yes, if they didn't like it, why would they come?

LH: Why did they like it so much?

ND: They saw that there was absolutely no discrimination [*bhedbhāv*] here. There was no untouchability here. Their superstitions were diminishing from the bhajans and the discussions.

LH: They enjoyed meeting with the other *mandalīs*?

ND: They enjoyed it a lot. And even now, though the *Kabīr bhajan aur vichār manch* is over, they still have a lot of affection for each other. Those few people who were there from the beginning, they still feel a great fondness for each other. When it ended, people felt very sad. Why did it end? What happened?

LH: Do you remember any particular debates or discussions that left a strong impression on you?

ND: People used to talk about Dinesh—he's a Brahmin, he can't really be interested in these things. What does he have to do with Kabir? Why is a Brahmin sitting with us? He's just doing it for money, because it's his job. He's not really sincere. But I didn't agree. I had seen Sharmaji's nature. He put in so much time, drank tea with us, came to our houses and ate food with us. Once he came to my house with Arvind-*bhāī*. I didn't have any good bedding. And it was raining. You know in rainy season, the quilts get a bad smell. But Sharmaji said, I'll use that quilt. I didn't have a fan. It was a place where you might think sleep is impossible. I realized that these two, Arvind-*bhāī* and Sharmaji, they can go anywhere, sit anywhere, sleep anywhere.

LH: Were there were any problems in the way the *manch* was done, anything you'd change if it were to be done again?

ND: I didn't see any problem. There was food, there was tea and water, everyone enjoyed it. If anyone didn't enjoy it, they just didn't come. There was a little trouble about money at first, they were giving everyone bus fare, but it was too much to give bus fare to everyone who came. So we decided to give bus fare to two featured *mandalīs* each time. There was some uproar about Kabir Panth *mahants* who expected to be placed on a high seat and treated with reverence. They were told that everybody would be treated equally. We wouldn't set up a high seat for them. They didn't like it. They said no one should go to such a place, where we are insulted, where we aren't respected. Some people would only come for Tipanyaji. They'd come and ask: is he here or not? If not, they left.

LH: Why?

ND: He had a wonderful style of singing. In Malwa there's nobody like that. His cassettes are very good, he has done a great job of spreading Kabir. This is the gift of Eklavya. They introduced him to Suresh Patel, who invited him and recommended him. Then he had cassettes, he was invited to Lucknow, to Doordarshan. This is Eklavya's gift.

DINESH: But he also had a great talent. That's why it happened with him and not other *mandalīs*.

Kaluramji

Kaluram Bamaniya, a well-known Kabir singer in Malwa when I started my work in 2002, was a generation younger than the three singers we have met so far. Recognizing his rich, powerful voice and beautiful repertoire, Shabnam Virmani included him along with Prahladji when she produced the double CD set *Kabir in Malwa* (Virmani 2008e). In the 1990s,

FIGURE 6.5. Kaluram Bamaniya singing. Photo by Smriti Chanchani.

during the Eklavya *manch*, he was a beginner. I knew him and enjoyed his music throughout my decade in Malwa.

The following profile is based mainly on a conversation he and I had in August 2011. In addition, excerpts from Shabnam's filmed interviews (2004–05) are italicized and set off by asterisks. It is interesting to note that Kaluram's name, like those of Prahladji and Narayanji, reflects the common practice among Dalits of adopting names associated with upper castes. "Prahlad Singh Tipanya" and "Narayan Singh Delmia" include Singh, the marker of a Rajput or *kśhatriyā* identity. In talking about his life, Prahladji mentions how upper castes in his village objected to Dalits' using the name "Singh" (chapter 1). "Bamaniya" means "Brahmin"—making for a startling juxtaposition with "Kaluram," which combines the popular name Ram with *kālū*, meaning "black." Such a name would only be found in a Dalit family.

KALURAM BAMANIYA (KB): I was born in Tonk Khurd village in 1970. I went to school till 3rd standard, but our situation was precarious, so I had to quit school and start working for others. I would take the cattle out to graze. Later I did farm work and labor. My grandfather, father, and father's brother used to sing bhajans. I sat with them, played *manjīrā*, and started singing. By the time I was about ten, I could sing bhajans and play the *tambūrā*. While working as a laborer or plowing fields, I kept singing, enjoying it more and more. Then I went to Rajasthan.

LH: Rajasthan?

KB: I ran away without telling anyone. I was a restless kid. I never paid attention to my studies. Instead of going to school I'd go for a swim in the lake.

LH: How old were you?

KB: I think fourteen or fifteen. In Savai Madhupur Bajaria I met Ram Nivas Rao, a wonderful singer. He had such a sweet voice. He was well known there the way Tipanyaji is here. I was working at a restaurant near the bus station. One day Ram Nivas Rao was going off with his *tambūrā* to sing bhajans. I spoke to him, and he told me I should come to the function at a nearby college. That day I sang two bhajans for him. He liked my singing. I stayed in that place twelve or fourteen months. I used to go to his performances and sing bhajans with him. I learned about classical *tāl* (rhythm) and how to play a few instruments. If I'd stayed longer I would have learned a lot more. I was still singing in Malwa style. When I went back to my village, I kept singing. I was the only one in my family who was performing. They kept trying to stop me, but I continued. Eventually I got a B rating on All Indian Radio, then a B High.

***

[Shabnam talks with Kaluram, Dinesh Sharma, and Dayaram Sarolia as they drive along in a car.]

KB: *I'm not very educated—only 3rd standard pass. But I cleared 8th through the informal system. I got through the 5th because Indira Gandhi died. They promoted everybody without exams.*

SV: *Why?*

DINESH: *Things were irregular, too many holidays. Schools were closed because of riots.*

KB: *I cleared 6th the same way. … (Shabnam looks puzzled.) Rajiv Gandhi died. (General laughter.)*

***

LH: Did your family belong to any Panth?

KB: No, they worshiped Hindu gods and goddesses like Bhairu and Durga, and they ate meat and drank liquor. They would sing bhajans while drinking country liquor. I also took meat and alcohol, but when I joined the Kabir Panth I gave them up. That was fifteen years ago.

LH: How did it happen that you took initiation from [Kabir Panth *mahant*] Mangaldasji?

KB: I had gone to Pitampur near Indore with my wife and children to work in a factory. Back home my brothers got initiated in the Kabir Panth. They were asked to sing bhajans, but they weren't good at singing, so they called me. One day they came over to my place, and I got some liquor and meat. But they refused to eat and told me that they had taken *dikśhā* from the guru. They persuaded me to take it too. I was impressed that they could give up meat and alcohol and thought there must be something really powerful about this *dikśhā*. Then I went back home, found a *mandalī*, and started singing. Guruji praised me.

***

SV: *When the Eklavya forum started, were you part of it from the beginning?*

KB: *We joined very early on. I had the position of* divān, *assistant, to the most important mahant in Dewas. I was with him for at least ten years. I would prepare the space for the rituals, make the* kanthīs *[wooden bead on a string, given at initiation, worn around the neck] and distribute them. I did all kinds of work. I walked around carrying a stick, with my sleeves rolled up like a goon. If anyone said anything against the guru, I would hit them. So no one said anything (laughs.) But the ideas we got from the Eklavya forum gave us a new kind of strength. We realized that Kabirji was saying that these things are false. Then I lost interest in all that.*

SV: *So you're not a* divān *anymore?*

K: *Only in name. I don't do the work anymore....*

SV: *When the Eklavya* manch *started, were you and Tipanyaji and Narayanji all together?*

KB: *No, we were opposed to each other. Sometimes we were close to fighting.*

DINESH: *Kaluram was very traditional, and Tipanyaji was very progressive at that time. We asked Tipanyaji to be a leader of the Kabir manch. People respected him a lot. He was a teacher, like a guru, and received a lot of respect. We felt he was a capable person to facilitate the meetings. ... Narayanji and Tipanyaji were both leaders. Kaluram belonged to the more traditional faction. They opposed our discussions. But still, Kaluramji used to come regularly to Eklavya and stay through the night.*

KB: *I wasn't opposed to the discussions. I just thought, "They are deluded, and I will set them straight." They thought I was deluded. It was a kind of competition. But they won, I lost! (laughing)*

***

KB: At the ashram I was Guruji's assistant, and I wouldn't let anyone speak against him. But after going to Eklavya for a while, I started feeling distaste for the superstitious and showy ways of the Kabir Panth. Initially I didn't like Eklavya because they sang less and talked more. But gradually I realized how important it was to know the meaning of those words and the power behind them. ... I started disliking going to the ashram. I developed an allergy [uses English word] toward Guruji. I actually started having arguments with him. Guruji told me that he had no connection [*lenā-denā*] with the outer world. I said to him, "You are living in this world, so how could you not be connected to it? Why not just leave this world and go live somewhere up in the sky?" ... Now I haven't seen him for six or seven years. I never go there.

LH: Was your guru angry with you?

KB: Very angry. So angry that he wanted to bring me down. He tried to keep me poor, to prevent me from singing. He wanted me to come back and beg forgiveness. But I stuck to my position. ... The Kabir Panth mostly consists of lower classes of people. But they offer up coconuts, flowers, money. They are exploited. Eklavya didn't say you should do this or that or follow any particular belief. The Eklavya people would ask questions. Is it a good thing that you go out to meet your guruji while your children are at home doing nothing? And they encouraged discussion about the bhajans.

LH: Now after all these stages of your life, you have a lot of opportunities to perform as a singer. What is your experience?

KB: Because of Kabir's *vāṇī* [words], because of singing, I get opportunities to meet many people and exchange ideas. All this has happened because of the *vāṇī*. *Sant vāṇī* is very powerful. I am fortunate that my father and grandfather taught me these bhajans. Because of media, cassettes and modern technology, *sant vāṇī* has spread very far. I am grateful to you and Shabnam for helping me to get access to stages in such good places. But there are many other good singers. Tipanyaji and Kaluram aren't the only ones. Bhairu Singh Chauhan, Dayaram Sarolia, and others are also very good singers who deserve to be on the stage and aren't getting such good opportunities. It's unfortunate that they haven't been able to share the stage with us.[34]

Eklavya Organizers and How They Were Changed

Syag-*bhāī*

One day in 2003, Shabnam and I unexpectedly ran into Syag-*bhāī* in Bhopal. As we were all heading back to Dewas, a four-hour journey away, we shared a hired car. Shabnam had her camera and shot a long conversation on the road (more of it will be offered in chapter 8). Here we include the portion where Syag-*bhāī* speaks of how the *manch* affected him. The main change he describes was in an enhanced appreciation of the capacities of ordinary people, independent of institutional connections, schooling, and economic status. While he still wanted everyone to have access to established structures of power, including formal education, his orientation had changed. The starting point now was what ordinary people had, rather than what they lacked. This vision played a role in his leaving

Eklavya a few years later, to join with others in forming another NGO, Samavesh, that worked more directly with people wherever they were and not just through formal education.

SV: You have talked a lot about dialogue. It was two-way. Did you feel there were changes in the Eklavya people?

RNS: The Eklavya people also learned through dialogue and experiments.

LH: Did you personally learn anything from the people in the *mandalīs*?

RNS: I learned a lot. I learned how much strength is in common people, much more than I had realized. My faith in common people increased a lot. I became less attached to formal education and realized how much could be done with people [who had little or no schooling]. My conviction about this became firm. Now the work I'm doing is all community-based. Previously I worked to improve school education, train teachers, create curricula and materials. Gradually I changed emphasis. We started to work with literacy, with the *panchāyatī rāj* policy in M.P. through which women become officers in the *panchyat*—women who were illiterate, who belonged to scheduled castes. ... Some of us decided to create Samavesh, whose entire focus is this [community-based] work. ... The Kabir bhajan *mandalīs*—they had a spiritual, or you might say nonmaterial inspiration. We wanted community groups that were focused on people's basic life needs—for women, small farmers, etc. Autonomous groups that wouldn't be dependent on government or NGOs. ...

We saw a struggle between two types of systems. One, as I said before, was our traditional system, in which people believe in different castes, different status for men and women, different treatment of girls and boys, everywhere difference. On the other hand we have modern democracy where you are a citizen. As a citizen you are equal. If you go to vote, they aren't going to say you're a woman so you can't vote. Equal citizenship. How can we convey these things to people: these are your rights, you can work in the schools, you can work in the *panchāyat*. As Kabir said—there is a power inside of you, and you should connect with that power. Some are searching for that power outside (he gestures outwardly), some inside (he gestures toward his chest). We are saying there are social powers through which the schools run, the *panchāyats* run. Recognize those powers. What are they? In our elections, some people aren't allowed to advance, although they can really do this work. The power to become *sarpanch*, to direct others, to sign orders. Who would really be the best *sarpanch*? We are encouraging this kind of debate. What is our agency? Where is our money going? Why are we poor? Are we poor because of our past lives, or because of the systems that are operating in this life?

As Kabir in his time tried to understand a whole spiritual world, we are preparing people to understand the social and economic realities of today's world. ... Can people read the constitution and understand it? Can they understand the law? Can women understand what their rights are? From the Kabir *manch* I got a stronger conviction that this is possible. If people can devote this much time and energy to a spiritual world, they can also devote time to changing this world. And these very people are the ones who will change our world!

Dinesh Sharma

While Syag-*bhāī* oversaw the whole project and was the principal guiding hand from Eklavya's side, Dinesh did most of the groundwork, attending to countless details, traveling, organizing, keeping records. He underwent a personal change on a very different level. As the son of a Brahmin priest living in a large village with his parents, wife, daughter, and son, he confronted his own deeply embedded caste identity and changed his life in concrete ways, encountering resistance in himself and in his family along the way. The following is from a filmed interview conducted by Shabnam (Virmani 2008b). Dinesh is driving a car, she is in the front seat with him, and in the back seat are Kaluram Bamaniya and Dayaram Sarolia, two Dalit Kabir singers who have a relaxed and friendly relationship with Dinesh.

My family has been connected to the Singaji Panth for generations—my father, his father, his father, I don't know how far back it goes.[35] So I've been hearing this since childhood, it's in my blood. Our house was a Singaji ashram. My father was the head of a *mandalī* that sang bhajans of the *sants*. They always sang Kabir, along with many other *sants*. The Singaji Panth is all upper caste. My father is a respected *yagyachārī*, a conductor of rituals. For the busy season, two or three months a year, he's hardly in the house. Rituals were always going on at home, and the bhajan *mandalī* met three times a month ... singing for four or five hours....

Before joining Eklavya I completely believed in caste distinctions. Even after joining Eklavya, I had those ideas. I was brought up in that kind of family. When we started the *manch*, I was going to people's houses ... talking about these things. It was very challenging for me. The first time I had to eat [in a lower-caste home] ... really, Dayaram (he turns toward the back seat), I was in a state. I'm telling you the truth. Daya, when I had to eat a meal, I mean I had to stay there and night came, there was no way out. In my mind this question was going round and round—to eat or not to eat. It was a big thing. Half of my mind was saying, hey man, get out of here, eat somewhere outside. Then after eating, I felt—what have I done? What have I eaten? This conversation kept going on inside of me.

But I came to realize I was not wrong to do this. If I want to do this work with all my heart, then I must first break these patterns in myself. Gradually all these worries decreased. A little example, a very small thing but still .... In our family we always put the vegetable on one plate and the *roṭī* [bread] on a separate plate. But you (turning to the guys in back) put the vegetable and *roṭī* all on the same plate. When this happened it seemed very weird to me. Very very strange. I took my pen and moved the *roṭī* away from the vegetable on the plate. That's what I had learned. Then the water was in the big pot, and there was a dipper on the pot, and they served everyone from that dipper. I felt anxious. They were putting the dipper on the floor. What if something dirty got into the water pot? Then the children drank directly from the dipper, they put it to their mouths, and then they gave me water from the same dipper. I worried about that.

Kaluram tells how surprised he was the first time Dinesh ate with them, not separately. Dinesh comments: "Because I was a Brahmin, some people had doubts about me. They thought this is his job, that's the only reason he's doing it. But those who got to know me understood that it was sincere." Dayaram fondly remembers a night when they reached someone's house at 2 a.m. and all ate sweet *roṭīs* out of the same plate. Dinesh continues:

Everything worried me, eating, drinking water, taking tea. But gradually I learned to do everything, I accepted it, and my courage [*himmat*] increased. Eventually my old ideas went away. When I went home to my family, they weren't happy about it. Even today my wife won't eat the leftover food from my plate.[37] She says—who knows where you've been going, whose food you've been eating? So she won't take what's on my plate. (Kaluram and Dayaram are laughing in the back seat.) …

Changes have taken place in my family. We've become much more open—my brothers and sisters-in-law, the children, even my parents. The Singaji bhajan *mandalī* members were all upper caste, but gradually we invited Kabir *mandalī* people to sing with us. Narayanji came several times and led bhajans. Everyone ate and drank. I said if we're talking about the *sant* tradition, singing these bhajans, and in our own house we don't act accordingly, what does that mean? They granted that this was right.

I have learned many things from spending time with the bhajan *mandalīs*. I have learned humanity [*insāniyat*].

Toward a Conclusion

Participants in Eklavya's Kabir *manch*—NGO workers, city activists, village singers—carried a range of beliefs and aspirations that could be channeled through Kabir bhajans. Cross-cultural conversations occurred as people who were primarily motivated by political concerns met with people whose lived experience with Kabir was primarily religious, musical, emotional. Sometimes these varying aspects were present within the same person—an internal dialogue. Some people changed a lot, some a little, some not at all.

At one end of the spectrum Prakash Kant, a Dewas teacher, left-leaning social activist, and friend of Eklavya, responded to my usual questions about "political" and "spiritual":[38]

PRAKASH KANT (PK): We have one clear goal—working for social justice. Social struggle. To the extent that Kabir supports this struggle, we embrace Kabir. If Tulsi is useful, we'll use Tulsi, just as we'll use Mira, Ambedkar or Karl Marx. I don't deny Kabir's spiritual side. That is of course present in his works. It's because of that that he still lives today, after 600 years. If that weren't there, we would never have heard of him.

LH: You are interested in social change and find Kabir useful for that. Do you personally find any importance in the spiritual side?

PK: Personally I don't believe anything of that kind. For me it's useless. I see problems in society that I want to solve. Other people may sing and be happy. They don't feel the need to change society. That's fine, let them be happy. But I can't be happy with that. I need to work for something else. So I'll use Kabir as much as possible. Kabir was human, he had his limits. So for some things, he won't be helpful in my work. I'll have to look elsewhere.

On another occasion Anu and Arvind introduced me to an Urdu poet named Naim, who lived in Dewas and had been a student of Namvar Singh at Jawaharlal Nehru University in Delhi.[39]

LH: For you, what represents Kabir's core message, his actual personality? What's most important for you in Kabir?

NAIM (N): The courage [*himmat*] with which he was able to criticize contemporary society. There's no one to compare with him in this. Maybe Nirala has something of that quality, 500 years later. Kabir was of the "fourth class" [*chauthā varg*, i.e., a *shudra*—those born to serve the upper three classes in the classical Hindu caste system]. He had nothing to do with temples, mosques, or sects. He was completely against these things. But now they make temples and sects in his name. Even his wife and children disagreed with him according to the stories we have heard. He was an all-around *vidrohī*, a resister.

LH: You have talked about the songs that look outward, the social criticism. What about the songs that look inward, the spiritual ones?

N: (with a broad smile and a dismissive gesture) I'm an atheist, I don't have anything to do with God. But probably in India, without the spiritual part, nobody would listen to him or remember him. In this country you need God to get your message out.

This reminded me of a similar remark by a journalist in Raipur, Chhattisgarh. Sunil Kumar loved Kabir and hosted a Kabir bhajan program in his house when I was visiting. Like Naim, he told me he was an atheist and had no interest in Kabir's religious message. "But," he joked, "without the religious content, Kabir would have lasted about as long as a communist slogan."

It was interesting to me that the first example Naim cited to illustrate Kabir's courage was the great bhajan sung by Dewas's own brilliant classical vocalist, Kumar Gandharva—*Nirbhay nirguṇ guṇ re gāūngā*. I have written elsewhere about this song (Hess 2009a, 38–40, 88). The first word, repeated many times, is *nirbhay*—fearless.

NAIM: When Kumar Gandharva sang Kabir, he sang with such power, from deep within. One could understand even difficult things just from the way he sang. *Nirbhay nirguṇ guṇ re gāūngā*! "Fearless, formless, that's the form I'll sing!" He sang that with tremendous energy and courage.

LH: What is meaningful for you in that song?

N: Whatever you know to be true and right—you should speak it out and be afraid of nothing.

LH: You keep mentioning the short refrain—*nirbhay nirguṇ guṇ re gāūngā*. "Fearless, formless, that's the form I'll sing." What about the rest of the song, all the stanzas? (pause) Do you know what the other stanzas are? Do you remember them?

N: (laughing) I don't remember them!

LH: It's all about yoga practice. The first stanza is about sitting in a firm posture and getting control of the *muladhār* chakra, the lowest center. Later it's about breath, the right, left, and central energy channels, and so on. He arrives at the pinnacle of emptiness where the limitless, unstruck sound resounds—*shūnya shikhar par anahad bāje*. From that peak he makes his music—*chhattīs rāga sunāūngā*, "I'll sing thirty-six ragas." Do you think that even symbolically, that peak of emptiness where you hear such music might be relevant for your social and political meanings? [At this point the conversation was interrupted and did not resume.]

With these and earlier examples, we sketch out a category of educated people with urban backgrounds who are interested in Kabir as a social critic and as an ally in political struggle. They may ignore, block out, or criticize the religious-spiritual aspects of Kabir. They may find that side of their admired ally annoying, embarrassing, or irrelevant (a position that Nehru often found himself in vis-à-vis Gandhi). When pressed to explore the matter further, they may say that Kabir was interested in religion/spirituality, as are his present-day devotees, but that they are not. They feel perfectly justified in enlisting Kabir in their struggles in this selective way—using what is useful, disregarding what is not useful or what might be counterproductive. Some activists who have engaged deeply with Kabir and with the community of Kabir lovers and devotees in rural Malwa discuss the question with sensitivity and nuance, still clearly coming down on the side of social engagement, outward-turning vision.

In a very different camp, there are hard-line Kabir devotees who attempt to suppress secular and social-activist readings of Kabir. In one program Syag-*bhāī* gave a welcoming speech that linked the teachings of Kabir with the importance of spreading the benefits of education to all. A local Kabir Panth *mahant* stood up and objected: "What does Kabir-*sāhib* have to do with the issues of schools, government policies, textbooks? Kabir-*sāhib* is telling us only to repeat the divine name and revere the guru. Don't misguide us!" Just as political activists foreground Kabir's politically relevant messages, Kabir Panthi *mahants* and devout disciples shine a light on what suits their ideology, emphasizing guru worship, ritual, and recitation of the divine name.

When Kabir devotees defend their "religious" views, they are not necessarily being apolitical. In some cases they are enforcing their own views and suppressing others, by means that range from argument to violence. When some Kabir Panthis objected strenuously to the way Prakash Kant represented Kabir in his introduction to the Eklavya bhajan booklet, a decision was made to remove the essay from later editions (see references to Prakash Kant, p. 261 above). This was a direct clash of "truths." Prakash Kant said, "Kabir was human, so he had his limits." The protesting devotees said that Kabir was not human but an incarnation of the supreme being, who manifested himself as an infant on a lotus in a pond. They were in no way willing to countenance Prakash Kant's talk of Kabir's being born to a woman in a Muslim family, and so on.

Elsewhere I have shown how this kind of censorship has taken a much more serious turn. Television director Anil Choudhury was attacked and harassed for years because of an episode of his *Kabir* serial where Kabir appeared to be simply human. He was ultimately forced to shut down the serial. Singer and actor Shekhar Sen was threatened with violence if he didn't cut certain parts of his performance at Magahar (stories told in chapter 7). The most serious incident involving our Malwa friends was when a squad of Gujarati Kabir Panthis attacked Prahladji and Shabnam after a 2010 music performance and screening of *Kabīrā khaḍā bazār meṇ* in Vadodara. The film (Virmani 2008b) focuses on Prahladji's relationship with the Dharamdasi Kabir Panth and the nature of its central ritual (treated at length in chapter 7). Displeased with the content of the film and the murmur that Prahladji was an opponent of their guru, they beat up Prahladji and threw rocks at the window of a car in which the two of them were trying to escape. The glass shattered over their bodies.

The censorship of Prakash Kant's introduction gives a hint of what was at stake for both social-political activists and orthodox Kabir Panthis. Sectarians were protecting the ideology and authority structure of their Panth, which was threatened by the historical, human-centered, rational and egalitarian approach of Prakash Kant's essay. Eklavya members and their urban allies, insofar as they "demoted" the popular devotional, spiritual, and guru-centered poetry, were protecting their more materialist worldview, their belief in scientific rationality and social equality.

Through the *manch*, some of Malwa's Kabir singers were awakened in a new way to Kabir's social teaching and its relevance to their lives. They also came to realize how they had been conditioned by their religious sects to think narrowly about what it meant to be Kabir's devotee. The three profiled in this chapter—Narayanji, Hiralalji, Kaluramji—took a sharp turn away from institutional guru-worship, faith in ritual, and acceptance of inequality in the social order. Hiralalji had moved in this direction long before the *manch* began and was thrilled to discover a forum where his convictions about Kabir could be expressed in a nourishing environment. Influenced by the *manch*, Narayanji and Kaluramji moved away from sectarianism and toward social commitment, assertion of their rights, an agenda of equality and liberation—all linked to Kabir. But none of them was moved to debunk or deny the deeper meaning of the "guru," the appropriateness of singing songs venerating the guru, or the value of spiritual practice and experience. They could see a link between Kabir's poetic evocations of sublime sound and light within the clay vessel of the body, the dignity of their own bodies, and the absolute equality of all bodies. They held these spiritual views together with a healthy skepticism about institutions and the corruptibility of individuals.

The political activists seemed more wedded to the idea of a split between spiritual and political than the singers. They tended to be put off by the language of worshiping and abjectly surrendering to the guru. Though they really respected and liked the singers and said they had no objection to religious faith, views, and songs, many of them had an alert system about religion in their minds. Religion was trouble. The Kabir singers described here were less likely to imagine a sharp divide between social and spiritual. Inner and outer connected for them. Kabir's emphasis on inner freedom, equality and dignity as consequences of *nirguṇ* devotion, the presence of the highest reality within this body, the nearness and here-and-now immediacy of what they were seeking, the importance of *karma* in this life, not some vague future life, the power of the mind to bind or liberate—all this was empowering to them.

In a filmed conversation, Shabnam asked Narayanji directly about the social-spiritual split. "Some say Kabir *bhajan* singing inspires oppressed and exploited groups to struggle against injustice. Some say it's an escape. People enjoy singing, get lost in the emotion and withdraw from the world of struggle. What do you think?" Narayanji replied with his usual look of amused irony: "It depends on the personality. Both things are possible." His smile suggested to me that the political zealots and the religious zealots could both easily get things wrong. Understanding Kabir called for a more subtle appreciation of his rich multidimensional messages.

A Last Story

[From my notebook] August 28, 2011
I haven't stayed in touch with Dinesh Sharma since he left Eklavya in 2003. About three weeks ago we ran into him in Tonk Khurd village. He was in a car with his wife; we were in another car going to meet one of the "old men's" *mandalīs*. We stopped to talk. He was very thin and told us he had a liver disease. He had been to Mumbai for surgery. Some days later we heard he was feeling sad and forgotten by his old companions. So today we organized a visit to his house in Devali village: Anu, my dear friend from Eklavya; Prahladji; Narayanji; Kaluramji; and me. He was very weak. He sat up with us for a while, but had to keep lying down. He showed Anu all the hospital reports. One of them said, in English, that he had carcinoma of the liver. He indicated to her that most of his family didn't know this. We stayed for three hours. There was tea and conversation. We looked at the wedding album of his daughter, who got married in 2009. She was sitting with us, holding her six-week-old baby. At one point, infused by a warm feeling, he got up and insisted that someone go out and buy samosas to serve us. I convinced the singers to sing, though they had hesitated. There were no instruments. Dinesh made a request: *Ab thāro kai patiyāro pardesī.*[40] Prahladji closed his eyes for at least a minute, then started singing in a soft, sweet voice.

Now how can I rely on you,
you foreigner
you traveler
from far away?

The walls have crumbled, the roof has collapsed,
the roof has mingled with dust, ah yes,
you foreigner,
you traveler
from far away. Ah yes.

As long as there was oil in the lamp, ah yes,
your temple glowed brightly,
you foreigner. Ah yes.

Now the oil has run dry, the wick has sputtered out, ah yes,
your temple has gone dark
you foreigner. Ah yes.

The shopkeeper's departed,
the market's deserted, ah yes.
The lock remains
but he's taken away the key
you foreigner. Ah yes.

Kabir says, listen seekers, friends, ah yes.
Your swan has flown
to a town
beyond death
you foreigner. Ah yes.

Dinesh had tears in his eyes. When we left, he got up and walked outside with us to the car, twenty yards away. We made plans for old friends to keep visiting him.

August 31, 2011
Prahladji called early in the morning. "Dinesh has expired." Today we all went to his cremation—Anu, Arvind, Dinesh Patel and Shobha of Eklavya, and me. We reached the village cremation ground from Dewas just before they covered his body with fuel and lit the fire. In fact they waited for us. Prahladji kept calling on the phone, saying where are you now, how soon will you be here? There was a platform on the edge of a big pond. Dinesh's

body was wrapped in white, but his face was showing. It looked warm, not dead. We each knelt at his feet, then moved toward his head to say a last goodbye. His son was crying hard, and a few young men kept their arms wrapped around him. Anu, Shobha, and I were the only women present. They lifted the bamboo litter (which Kabir calls a "wooden horse") and placed it on stacks of large round cowdung cakes, then piled many more cowdung cakes on top. They put straw bundles around the edges. The son and some other relatives went around lighting the straw. It flared up; a blast of heat hit us. Then everyone sat down across the road to wait. About a hundred men. They wait till the body is pretty much burnt. It was really hot, someone guessed 42°C. After a while Prahladji stood up and suggested we have a *shraddhānjalī*, "reverent offering," in which people could say a few words about Dinesh. He started, then Anu, Arvind, me. Dinesh's older brother spoke briefly. Dinesh was only forty-four, the youngest of all the siblings. The brother asked for a minute of silence before we dispersed. Everyone was given some pieces of cowdung to throw on the pyre. They called it something like *panchānjalī*, "five-offering"—for the five elements.

We went to their house in the village where all the women sat crying, neighbor women along with family members. Such a clear division of labor—men outside burning the body, women at home crying. His poor wife was sitting in a dark corner facing the wall. It was stifling. When Anu approached and touched her, she cried more and more. The corner was so hot and airless. I never saw her face but touched her back with my hands. After some time we left, making eye contact and hand contact with every member of the family.

Move your cart along lightly,
My Ram is riding.
Move your cart slowly, slowly,
My Ram is riding.

My cart is colored brightly
with wheels of rosy red.
A pretty lady holds the reins.
The passenger is Ram.

What if the cart bogs down in mud
with the destination far?
Those who do good will get across,
the criminals will crash.

Healers came from every land,
they brought their herbs and roots.
The herbs and roots were of no use
since Ram had left the house.

Four fellows met and soon agreed
to build a horse of wood.
They hauled it to the burning ground.
It blazed up, just like Holi!

The woman sobbed and cried:
We were joined, now we're broken!
Kabir says, listen seekers:
the one who joins
is the one who breaks.

FIGURE 6.6. Dinesh Sharma with singer Dayaram Sarolia. Photo by Shabnam Virmani.

7

Fighting over Kabir's Dead Body

IT'S A GOOD story, one of the two most often told about Kabir.[1] In fact it's so good that the Sikhs tell a similar story about what happened on the occasion of Guru Nanak's death.[2] The master passes on peacefully, but even before he draws his last breath, his followers (who have been only temporarily united by his charismatic presence) begin fingering the hilts of their swords. As the warmth drains from his skin, their temperatures rise. Soon they are engaging, weapons drawn, in a full-scale confrontation. Over what? Ritual!

The Hindus want to cremate their beloved teacher to the soothing drone of mantras from the Veda. The Muslims want to bury him while chanting verses from the Qur'an. The earliest hagiography of Kabir, Ananta-das's *Kabir Parachai*, says simply, "The Hindus and Turks ... formed ... band[s]. One band said, 'You should burn him.' The other band said, 'You should bury him.'"[3] Then it tells how his physical body disappeared amid piles of flowers brought for the occasion. Later embellishments heighten the drama and give it a political tinge. Nawab Bijli Khan and Maharaja Virsingh Baghel gallop in with troops. A pitched battle is averted when someone discovers that Kabir's body is gone.[4] Tellers of the tale commonly add that, finding only flowers under the shroud, each faction took half of the flowers to bury or burn, as they pleased.

It's no coincidence that this story attaches to Guru Nanak and Kabir, and not to other poet-gurus of the period. Both Nanak and Kabir deliberately occupied an ambiguous space between Hindu and Muslim communities. In his enlightenment story, Nanak enters a river and emerges after three days with these words on his lips: "There is no Hindu, there is no Muslim." From that formula we can understand that there *were* Hindus, there *were* Muslims, they were often entangled in rivalries and conflicts, and Nanak wished to underline the deluded nature of their fighting as he offered a spiritual truth deeper than their precious religious identities.

Kabir is identified with Muslims by (for example) his name, his Julaha weaver caste, his parents, and the common appearance of "Sāhab/Sāhib" as a name for God. He is identified with Hindus by (for example) his guru Ramanand, his frequent use of yogic terminology, his apparent acceptance of reincarnation, and the common appearance of "Ram" as a name for God. The poetry attributed to him features countless satirical jabs at the foolishness and hypocrisy of both Hindus and Muslims. It also condemns the general idiocy and viciousness of clinging to one's own sectarian identity while attacking others on the basis of theirs. In a famous poem that resonates with the story of Bijli Khan and Virsingh Baghel (as well as with murderous communal conflicts today), he says:

> Saints, I've seen
> the world is mad . . .
> The Hindu says Ram
> is the fountain of love,
> the Turk says Rahman.
> Then they kill each other.
> No one understands.[5]

This first story of fighting over Kabir, like many to follow, has a special bite: the fighting devotees have to forget Kabir's central teachings in order to engage in the conflict.

A law of cultural politics everywhere is: collective entities will fight over possession of their heroes, origin stories, and histories; they will also fight over the proper ways to honor and reinforce their icons and narratives. These collectivities may be identified in terms of religion, caste, language, ethnicity, nation, or ideology (to name some obvious examples). When a sense of the sacred enters the discourse, some of the most interesting battles will take place on the fields of ritual and myth.[6]

In this chapter we will learn about contestations in the late twentieth and early twenty-first centuries over narratives, doctrines, and rituals associated with Kabir. The famous story recounted above suggests that such debates may have started the moment he ceased breathing. Why are people still fighting? They are driven by considerations of both power and faith, and it is often difficult to disentangle the two. Institutional turf battles involve the usual types of power: control over followers; accumulation of land and wealth; and wielding of political influence.[7] The faithful are driven by personal feelings of devotion; by loyalty to traditions and gurus; and by fear that they will be in trouble if they don't believe or behave as they have been told. In India, religious feelings are protected by law; people whose feelings are hurt can assert their rights as believers fairly aggressively, with some confidence that the law is behind them, as we will see below.

Two main points will emerge from this inquiry. First, studying how people fight over their heroes, doctrines, histories, and symbols provides valuable insight into the history of religion. Second, these contestations take place both publicly and privately, among leaders and followers. Usually we hear only about the public part: authority figures and published documents tell the stories. In this case, we have the opportunity to see both institutional leaders and ordinary people getting into the fray. Should the followers of Kabir be doing rituals? Sectarian gurus will naturally express and enforce their views. But in this case, on the issue of the *chaukā āratī* ritual, I was also able to observe a dramatic unfolding of the debate among Kabir devotees in the Malwa region of Madhya Pradesh. Thus the story will be both top-down and bottom-up. We will see how the issues play out institutionally as well as on a more intimate level among friends and family members.

Kabir Religion

If Hindus and Muslims were hotly contesting their claims to Kabir at the time of his death,[8] that situation soon changed. The Muslims seem to have lost interest, while Kabir's Hinduization proceeded rapidly (Lorenzen 1981a). Although he harshly criticized certain Hindu beliefs and practices (such as divine avatars, image-worship, and caste), there were also many positive references to Hindu tradition in his poetry.[9] On the whole, Hindus could easily accommodate Kabir in their diverse and flexible religious spaces. In the fluidity of oral tradition and the dynamics of sect formation, texts and practices that were compatible with Hindu forms and ideas flourished.

Soon there was a story to show that Kabir was not *really* the son of Muslims, but had been adopted. His true mother? A Brahmin widow, of course! Why not a Kshatriya, Vaishya, Shudra, or "untouchable"? For the same reason that he could not be a Muslim. A great, holy, enlightened being, according to certain hegemonic views, should be a Brahmin. Today the story that the newborn Brahmin Kabir was set afloat on a pond at the edge of Varanasi, to be found and adopted by the Muslim weavers Niru and Nima, is widely believed by Hindus. Members of the Kabir Panth do not accept the story of the Brahmin widow, but most of them reject the idea that Kabir was the biological child of Muslim parents. He was, according to most Kabir Panthis I have spoken to, an avatar of God who appeared floating on a lotus pad on Lahartara Pond at the outskirts of Varanasi. The Muslim Julahas Niru and Nima became his foster parents after finding and adopting the miraculous baby.[10]

The Hinduizing process gained momentum in a sectarian environment. In its symbols, rituals, and structures of authority, the Kabir Panth has used generally Hindu and particularly Vaishnav models and terminology: gurus and mahants, *āratī* and *sandhyā pāṭh, dīkśhā* and *prasād, tulsī* beads, occasional Sanskrit chants, and a likeness of Kabir in the place normally occupied by a Hindu divine image. But they haven't imported all Hindu forms equally. Notably, they tend to refuse caste; their leaders often speak strongly against caste, and their institutions and functions generally appear free of caste distinctions. This social emphasis corresponds with their membership—the vast majority being from formerly untouchable castes and poor agricultural classes in rural North India.[11]

The Kabir Panth was founded either prior to the master's death in 1518 (or 1448) or in the late sixteenth or seventeenth century, depending on whose story you listen to and what evidence you find persuasive. Whenever it started, it gradually became heavy with authority, as religious institutions founded in the names of anti-authoritarian teachers are wont to do. Naturally, the Panth felt entitled to claim ownership of Kabir. They were the engine that produced his ongoing honor and glory, along with thousands—then hundreds of thousands, then millions—of disciples. They spread his teachings far and wide, kindling the lamp of awakening in the hearts of initiates. Inspiration from Kabir created the Panth. As time went on, the Panth created Kabir. After all, he could no longer create himself. He was dead. As he muses dryly in a poem: "When you die, what do you do with your body? Once the breath stops, you have to put it away" (Hess and Singh 2002, 61).

David Lorenzen has studied the history and practices of the Kabir Panth more extensively than any other scholar. For details, one can refer to his many articles and books, and for earlier research one can consult colonial scholars such as Wilson, Crooke, Westcott, and Keay. Here I will provide a brief introduction.

We don't know when or where the earliest version of the Kabir Panth began. There are today several "seats" (*gaḍḍī*), also called "branches" (*śhākhā*), that claim genealogies of gurus going back to Kabir. In this chapter, I refer only to the two largest and most influential traditions, which I identify as the Kabir Chaura and the Dharamdasi or Damakheda traditions.[12] The word *śhākhā*, literally "branch," might give the impression that the two are related through some central organization, but that is not the case. They have independent histories, separate guru lineages, distinct literatures, and a relationship that is not necessarily friendly.[13]

The Kabir Chaura sect is headquartered at Kabir Chaura Math (monastery) in Varanasi, Uttar Pradesh (U.P.), where Kabir himself lived. Its founding is attributed to Surat Gopal (or Shruti Gopal), a disciple of Kabir. The Dharamdasi sect is based in the village of Damakheda near Raipur in Chhattisgarh, a linguistic and cultural region in central India that in 2000 became a state, carved out of the eastern side of Madhya Pradesh.[14] Dharamdas, revered in this branch as the most intimate and important direct disciple of Kabir, is believed to have started the Panth during Kabir's lifetime at the master's behest. The Dharamdasis also call their sect the "*bayālīs vaṃśha*" or "forty-two generation" tradition. Kabir prophesied, they believe, that this sect would remain the authoritative source of his liberating teachings for forty-two generations of gurus in unbroken succession. Given that today, after more than five hundred years, they are only at the fifteenth guru, the prophecy suggests that their *gaḍḍī* will prevail for a very long time.

Both the Kabir Chaura and Dharamdasi sects have followers in widespread areas across northern, central, and western India. Both believe that their tradition started first, and the other followed. Some Kabir Chaura spokesmen, following scholar Kedarnath Dvivedi, have asserted that Dharamdas was not contemporary to Kabir but lived at least a century later (Lorenzen 1991, 60). Though both Panths accept the *Bījak* as Kabir's authentic composition, for Kabir Chaura the *Bījak* is the only sacred and authentic text. The Dharamdasis are ambivalent about the *Bījak* and place a much higher value on the *Anurāg Sāgar* (Ocean of Love), which they believe Kabir composed and Dharamdas wrote down. The two works are very different. The Dharamdasis also regard a number of other works as authentic—many of them having the word *sāgar* (ocean) in the title.

The Dangers of Drama

Yogis say, "Yoga's the top,
don't talk of seconds."
Tuft of hair, shaven head,
matted locks, vow of silence—
who's gotten anywhere?
Brainy ones, gifted ones,
heroes, poets, benefactors
cry, "I'm the greatest!"
They all go back where they came from
and don't take anything along.
(Hess and Singh 2002, 53–54)

In 1987, the first episode of a serial on Kabir aired on Doordarshan, India's national television network. This was before the genre of religious serials on TV exploded with the unprecedented popularity of the epic *Ramayan,* which went on for over a hundred episodes in 1988–89, and was followed immediately by the ninety-six-episode *Mahabharat. Kabir* was a relatively low-profile enterprise, written and directed by Anil Choudhury a graduate of the National School of Drama who had worked in theater before moving into the world of television and movies in Mumbai. Choudhury was fascinated by Kabir. How did a poor, low-caste, uneducated member of a Muslim artisan family become such a powerful and popular figure in Brahmin-dominated Varanasi? Choudhury read many books, spoke to academic and religious authorities, began writing a script, and shot the first episode in 1985. He loved the project and described himself as being in a state of *naśhā* (drunken joy) while working on it.

But he was soon sobered by a series of lawsuits filed against him by followers of Kabir, most of them associated with a Gujarati branch of the Panth. When I met Choudhury in 2003, he spoke of six initial cases, both civil and criminal, filed in Ahmedabad, Surat, and Delhi. The main issue was that he had depicted Kabir as a human being, while these Kabir Panthis believed he was God. According to them, Kabir was not born but became an avatar when he manifested himself as an infant on Lahartara Pond. They objected strenuously when the serial showed a nonmiraculous birth and a normal family life, including a mother who slapped him when he misbehaved. Choudhury described arriving at court hearings to find hundreds of Kabir Panthi men shouting and brandishing *lāṭhīs* (long sticks) at him.

Choudhury's life became nightmarish. He was threatened and harassed. Describing a period when he was still trying to produce episodes, he spoke of spending two days shooting, two days editing, and two days in court. Ultimately becoming depressed and fearful, he canceled the project after airing about a dozen episodes. He had to pay heavy legal expenses himself and suffered serious financial loss. Even in 2003, he was uneasy talking to me and asked me not to record the conversation. Later I heard that the number of cases had eventually multiplied beyond the initial six. Though he claimed that none of the cases had merit and all would have failed if brought to trial, his attackers were able to make his life a hell by continuing to file new cases.

It is important to mention that not all Kabir Panthis shared the viewpoint of those who sued and intimidated Choudhury. Sant Vivek Das—today the Acharya or top religious authority of the Kabir Chaura tradition, and at that time too an influential voice at Kabir Chaura—helped and supported Choudhury through these struggles. (We will hear more of Vivek Das in the coming section on ritual.)

My conversation with Anil Choudhury took place at the Mumbai residence of Shekhar Sen, a gifted classical singer, music director, and actor who had created a one-man play called *Kabir*. Sen's show has been very successful; at the time of this writing, he has done hundreds of performances in India and abroad. But he too has felt the repressive hand of Kabir's true believers. In 2003, he organized a tour that was also a pilgrimage for him. It went from Varanasi to Magahar (near Gorakhpur in U.P.)—the places where Kabir is believed to have been born and died. Sen had scheduled performances in fourteen places along the way, shouldering most of the expenses himself.

But as he neared Magahar, a threatening headline appeared in a local Hindi newspaper: "Rivers of Blood Will Flow If Shekhar Sen Brings His Show to Magahar." This time it was sadhus (initiated renunciant followers) of the Kabir ashram in Magahar, affiliated with Kabir Chaura in Varanasi, who objected to the way Kabir's life was depicted. The sticking point for them was that Sen showed Kabir as a married man with children. They insisted that Kabir never married and was a celibate sadhu. If the headline was to be believed, some devotees might be willing to kill for this point! Just before going to Magahar, Sen had performed to an appreciative audience in nearby Gorakhpur. A group of young men there suggested that they could accompany him to Magahar and beat up anyone who disturbed his performance, but Sen declined the offer.

Sen met with the *mahant*, or religious head, of the Magahar Kabir Panth ashram, along with other locals including sadhus and schoolteachers. They displayed books that stated that Kabir was celibate, never married, and of course never had children. Sen replied that he had read all these and more; that he had other sources that described Kabir's wife Loi and his son and daughter Kamal and Kamali; and that one of the Kabir Panthi biographies they cited made absurd and even obscene claims.[15] He declared that Kabir belonged to all humanity, not just to the Kabir Panth, and he mentioned that his grandfather was Acharya Kshitimohan Sen—famed as a pioneering researcher of Kabir's oral and written poetry in the early twentieth century, the man who provided Rabindranath Tagore with the texts that were the source of Tagore's *100 Poems of Kabir*. Kabir, Sen asserted, was his heritage as much as the Panth's. Though the *mahant* at Magahar was an educated man and sympathetic to the artist's position, he emphasized the problem of dealing with believers who had little education and a strong faith in Kabir as their God. They couldn't help being extremely upset at seeing Kabir represented in a way that contradicted what they had been taught. Saying that he did not wish to cause grief to anyone, Sen agreed to remove offensive portions of his script in Magahar (but *only* in Magahar).

Was that the end of the story? No. In March 2006, Sen was to perform in Surat, Gujarat. He had been invited by one group of Kabir devotees; but another group sent a telegram stating that his drama was offensive and had to be stopped. He again offered to speak with them, but before that could happen, he heard from an attorney associated with the friendly group. The outraged Kabir Panthis had gone to court to try to restrain him from performing. The friendly group's attorney was prepared to defend him. Sen sent photocopies of literary sources that supported his representation of Kabir.

At that point in the conversation I became exasperated and asked Sen why he bothered to defend himself at all. He was an artist and had a right to write his own script. What law had he broken? What could they do to him? He reminded me that in India, religious *feelings* are protected. Along with obvious offenses such as damaging or defiling places of worship, disturbing religious assemblies, and trespassing with malicious intent, the law criminalizes insults, words, or even sounds that offend religious feelings.[16] Though a conviction would result only if the defendant was found to have injured feelings with deliberate intent, complainants can hound a person almost indefinitely with accusations and lawsuits. Anil Choudhury's woes are testimony to the perils facing an artist who incurs the enmity of religious groups.

Sen cancelled his *Kabir* performance in Surat and performed a show about Tulsidas.[17]

The Importance of Ritual

Why bump that shaven head on the earth?
Why dunk those bones in the water?
Parading as a holy man,
You hide yourself, and slaughter.
Why wash your hands and mouth, why chant
with a heart full of fraud?
Why bow in the mosque, and trudge
to Mecca to see God?. . . .
Does Khuda live in the mosque?
Then who lives everywhere?
Is Ram in idols and holy ground?
Have you looked and found him there?
Hari in the east, Allah in the west,
so you like to dream.
Search in the heart, in the heart alone.
There live Ram and Karim!
Which is false, Qur'an or Veda?
False is the darkened view.
It's one, one, in every body!
How did you make it two?

(Hess and Singh 2002, 73–74)

Rituals in the Kabir Panth could be considered inherently controversial, because Kabir debunked rituals. In the poetry it is clear that his problems with rituals include the delusions and hypocrisies they encourage and the hard lines of status they reify.

But sects (like nations, families, and individuals) require rituals. They need ways to solemnize membership, to conjure up the unseen founder, to renew their vows and symbolize their hopes, all the while invoking their communion with each other, their continuity with past and future members, their difference from nonmembers, and the differences in status and function among members. They need special times to get together and do their rituals. Along with ritual structures, they need structures of authority. Some people have special rights to interpret the master's words and tell his stories, initiate new members, represent the sect, and shape its policy. These special people also run the rituals and become the vessels of ordinary devotees' reverence and faith. They may be in a position to command obedience and receive material benefits.

Chaukā Aratī *and Authority in Two Traditions of the Kabir Panth*

Nearly all branches of the Panth regularly practice a ritual that they call *chaukā āratī*. *Āratī* is a generic term for the most common kind of Hindu worship, involving various offerings to the divine, with some items being returned as blessed gifts to the worshipers. It culminates with the waving of burning lamps before the deity in Hindu settings, or before the guru or image of Kabir in the Kabir Panth. *Chaukā* means square and refers to the specially adorned four-sided space that must be prepared for the rite as it is practiced in the Panth.

David Lorenzen's essay, "The Rituals of the Kabir Panth," describes the ritual life of Kabir Chaura sadhus and includes translations of key texts that participants recite and sing in their daily and occasional rites. Though he is well aware of the ironies of sects and rituals operating in Kabir's name, Lorenzen declines the easy critique and concludes that in some notable ways the form and content of these practices do reflect Kabir's teaching:

> Kabir Panth rituals are not simply the product of an abject capitulation to the social and cultural pressures that foster Sanskritization, Hinduization, and socioreligious homogenization. In the first place, the rituals . . . are quite simple and inexpensive compared to those of more orthodox Hindu monasteries and temples. More important, however, is the fact that the Kabir Panth rituals express, in both actions and words, an implicit opposition to many of the accepted religious and social norms of more orthodox Hinduism at the same time that they incorporate the basic structure and many formal elements of more orthodox rituals. (Lorenzen 1996, 248)

It is this question—whether the rituals give decorous expression to or make a mockery of Kabir's teachings—that became a matter of heated controversy in the Panth leadership and among some devotees a few years after the publication of Lorenzen's article.

During the period of Lorenzen's fieldwork, 1976–94, *chaukā āratī* seems to have been an uncontroversial part of the lives of sadhus and lay followers at Kabir Chaura in Varanasi and its affiliates. Kabir Chaura recognizes two types of *chaukā*: the *ānandī* ("joyful") and *chalāvā* ("custom[ary]"). The former is done on happy occasions such as initiation of new members; the latter is done when someone dies. In addition to these two, the Dharamdasi branch prescribes two more: *solah sut* (sixteen-son) *chaukā āratī* and *ekottarī* (101) *chaukā āratī*—the former to celebrate a birth or to produce progeny, and the latter a very large-scale version of the rite performed only when the supreme guru, the lineage holder, is present.

Gangasharan Das/Shastri,[18] for many years the *adhikārī* or administrative head of Kabir Chaura Math, and for about a decade the Acharya or religious head, wrote in a guidebook on administration and conduct in the Panth:

> The *chaukā* is done in a prescribed way by all Kabir Panth devotees, sadhus and mahants, similar to the way sacrifices [*yagya*] and fasts [*vrat*] are done. If a Kabir Panth disciple or sadhu is ensnared in any difficulty, he should worship the Lord by means of *chaukā aratī*, and the trouble can be removed. *Chaukā āratī* is a pure form of worship [*sāttvik pūjā*], and everyone can do it. By organizing a properly performed *chaukā aratī*, a person can be released from all his sins, and his consciousness can be purified. Ultimately by the grace of the guru and the supreme lord [*parameśhvar*], he can attain the state of *kaivalyā* ["singleness," highest meditative state, enlightenment], and all the bonds of this world will fall away. *Chaukā āratī* should also be done on special occasions like births and weddings. At the time of death, *chalāva āratī* should be done for the peace of the [departed] soul. It is very important to do *chaukā āratī* for the welfare of the world. *Chaukā āratī* is not the worship of gods and goddesses [*devī deva*]. It is worship of the lord through the medium of the guru. This is the source of human well-being. (Shastri 1983, 8)

The last few sentences indicate the centrality of the guru in this ritual. In the western square marked as the consecrated seat, a human guru—usually an authorized *mahant* of the Panth—sits and receives the worship. He becomes the form of the lord.

Dharamdasi literature is more explicit about the origin and meaning of *chaukā āratī*. Kabir himself created the ritual and proclaimed that its practice should continue forever:

> In the Kabir Panth, *ānandī chaukā āratī* is a widespread and universally respected method of worshipping the guru. It is *pūjā* of the manifest *satyapuruṡh*, the primordial *brahmā*. In it, the visible and present guru is the very form [*svarūp*] of Satguru Kabir Saheb. Every devotee is moved to arrange this *pūjā* in his/her home, and they do it with great reverence on every happy occasion. This *pūjā* is the way to attain the manifest supreme being. (Prakashmuni Nam Saheb 2004, 15)

The author—who is the Acharya, the lineage holder, of the Dharamdasi sect—paraphrases a passage from the *Anurāg Sāgar* that describes the first performance of *chaukā* by Dharamdas for Kabir, explaining the spiritual meanings of various physical actions:

> Breaking the straw symbolizes rising above the three *guṇas* [qualities of material existence]. The *kanthī* [*tulsī* bead worn on a string around the neck] is dedication to *satyapuruṡh*. Taking the name is attaining the form of the swan [*haṃsa*], or opening the door of spiritual knowledge. And to receive the certificate is to attain liberation. ... This *pūjā* was held for the first time in the home of Dhani Dharamdas in Bandhavgarh. Satyapurush Sadguru Kabir Saheb himself designed it, and this very form has been preserved by the lineage-gurus and passed on to the faithful. This *pūjā* is a message of immortality in the world of death; it is the creation of Satyalok [the heavenly Realm of Truth] on this earth. The power to do it correctly rests only with lineage-gurus or with those *kaḍihār* ["helmsmen," a term used in the Dharamdasi Kabir Panth for *mahants*] whom they select and authorize. (ibid., unnumbered page).[19]

This *chaukā* origin story is part of a larger narrative of Kabir's becoming an avatar, selecting Dharamdas as the founder of his "forty-two-generation lineage," ordaining that Dharamdas and his wife Amin-mata would produce the first occupant of the *gaḍḍī* in the form of their son Muktamani Nam Sahab, and ensuring that all the other lineage gurus would emerge from the same family. These gurus are also called avatars:

> Muktamani Nam Sahab himself is a portion [*aṃṣa*] of Satyapurush[20] with a special form [*svarūp*], special qualities [*guṇ*], and special divine power [*śhakti*]. From him alone the forty-two lineage holders are created. They all have special form, special qualities, and special power. Thus we see that a portion of Satyapurush takes avatarhood forty-two times in the family of Dharamdasji through the seed-lineage of Muktamani Nam Sahab, and from them alone living beings can get liberation. The duties of the lineage-seat holder and the burden of propagating the Panth are beyond the capacities of ordinary people. Therefore Kabir Saheb agreed to send a portion of himself in the form of the forty-two-generation lineage. (ibid., "o")

From this, we understand that *chaukā āratī* is closely linked to maintaining the powerful authority of the Panth gurus in the Dharamdas tradition. At its center is worship of the guru. During the *chaukā*, the local *mahant*, the lineage holder of the Panth, Kabir, and God (Satyapurush) are conflated. In addition to being a medium for worshiping Guru-as-God and God-as-Guru, the *chaukā* is supposedly able to deliver amazing practical results, from washing away sin and improving mental health to seeing God, reaching heaven (Satyalok), and attaining final liberation. Gṛindhmuni Nam Sahab—father and predecessor of the present lineage holder, Prakashmuni Nam Sahab—wrote of the centrality and incomparable power of the ritual:

> In our lineage, *chaukā āratī* holds the first place among prescribed actions. Nothing else has been given as much importance as this. Whatever auspicious activity or important social work one may do, nothing can be complete without *chaukā*. ... Birth, marriage, death—in all these circumstances, the completion of *chaukā* is essential. *Chaukā āratī* is a kind of scientific knowledge. In *chaukā āratī* the five elements are mingled in a scientific way, and a tremendous power comes forth from this. Both physical and spiritual components are present in this mysterious creation, and one can thus gain success in both realms.

* *Chaukā āratī* produces many authentic fruits.
* From *chaukā āratī*, a person's spirit becomes pure and long-term bad habits are destroyed.
* Mental problems diminish.
* Doing *chaukā āratī* sharpens your true intelligence; you can directly see Satyapurush. The spiritual joy that comes from doing *chaukā āratī* is of a world beyond this one. We call that world Satyalok. All worlds become stainless and beautiful through *chaukā aratī*; they become deathless. Through *chaukā āratī* one is released from countless sins, and one attains the supreme being (*paramātmā*). Without doubt, through *chaukā āratī* a person attains a peaceful and auspicious state. (ibid., 101–3)

A Kabir Panth Convocation in Chhattisgarh

For five days in February 2002 I attended the annual *melā* (fair, gathering) in Damakheda, a village about two hours' drive from Raipur, the capital of Chhattisgarh. Aside from the big buildings in the Panth compound, the village appears ordinary. But once a year, it fills with countless devotees. People camp in tents, or under the huge canvas cover of the main assembly area, or in nearby fields. An immense kitchen operation provides two cooked meals a day to devotees who sit in rows as fast-moving volunteers ladle vegetables, *dāl*, and rice from stainless-steel buckets and drop deep-fried bread on leaf plates. As hundreds finish their meal, hundreds more take their places.

The main organized activity at the *melā* is listening to discourses and songs that start in the morning and continue late into the night. Followers also form long lines to do homage, called *bandagī*, to the Acharya of the sect, Prakashmuni Nam Sahab—often referred to as Huzur-sahab. Carrying coconuts and other offerings, they reach his presence after waiting in a long queue and enact an individual rite of devotion, bowing at his feet, looking into his eyes three times, touching the coconut to their bodies in a prescribed sequence, repeating *sāhab bandagī* ("homage to the lord") and leaving a monetary donation. Whenever Huzur-sahab emerges from his quarters, he is rushed by devotees who wish to touch his feet or make a gesture of homage. Those who can't get near watch from stairways or other vantage points, drinking in the experience that Hindus call *darśhan*—seeing someone or something holy. In the evening they eagerly await his arrival on the stage: the climax of the series of speakers and singers who have performed through the day. A rustle of anticipation and three blasts from a trumpet announce his imminent arrival. He sweeps in with an entourage including two grey-bearded guardians with embossed silver staffs who stand at attention to the right and left of the stage through his long presentation.

On my third night at the Damakheda *melā*, I witnessed *ekottarī* (101) *chaukā āratī*, the grandest form of the ritual, in which the lineage guru officiates. I saw it again at a *melā* in Bandhavgarh two months later.[21] Manuals describe *ekottarī* as requiring the materials of *ānandī chaukā* multiplied by 101, along with some extra items. These materials include coconuts, fruits, flowers, betel leaves and nuts, eight types of dried fruit, mango leaves, cloves, cardamom, saffron, perfume, crystallized sugar, camphor, sandalwood paste, and vessels of silver, gold, and brass. The sung and recited texts are particular to *ekottarī*.

The *chaukā* space for the ritual was very large, the array of objects very elaborate. Scores of *mahants* in their special costumes, each with a set of paraphernalia, sat in rows in a roped-off square. Tens of thousands of devotees were crammed into the area, which became more and more impenetrable in the circles closer to the guru's seat. The excitement was tremendous. When Huzur-sahab entered with his entourage, it was only with great exertion that monitors could keep the narrow passageway clear and control the surge of bodies that wanted to move toward him. Singing continued throughout the ceremonies.

The most dramatic part was the lighting of over 800 ghee-burning lamps, each wick embedded in a base made of fresh wheat-flour dough. It took several men ten or fifteen minutes to light them all, and the job looked dangerous as more and more flames shot upward. I found the heat under the low canvas roof to be stunning, especially when I climbed onto a platform to see better. The temperature rose suddenly with the altitude, and I felt as if my head were on fire. From my vantage point about twenty yards away, the *chaukā* area looked like a sea of fire. Smoke filled the air; only the open sides of the pavilion allowed us to keep breathing. For thousands of devotees, it was essential to approach the Acharya and do *bandagī* directly, one on one, before leaving the *āratī* arena. This process went on for hours.

With Kabir Singers and Friends in Malwa

My first extended road trip with Prahladji was to the *melā* in Damakheda in February 2002. There I discovered that he had a privileged place on the stage. He and his group were allowed to sing much longer than others. The Acharya beamed at him when they were both present. He praised Prahladji's wonderful bhajans and sometimes requested favorites. In April I traveled with the group again to the Bandhavgarh *melā*. It was on the way back to Malwa from Bandhavgarh, in the train with family and friends, that Prahladji revealed to me that he had become a *mahant* in February. That moment is described in chapter 1. A controversy about his decision, about the *chaukā āratī* ritual and the Kabir Panth, ensued in his local community and went on until it reached a resolution in 2005.

To understand this controversy, one needs to know about the Eklavya Kabir *manch* that is the subject of chapter 6. The *manch* made Kabir singers, devotees, and friends of the area a more cohesive and self-conscious group than they would otherwise have been. While the program was originally organized by Eklavya staff, internal leadership soon developed among singers. Prahladji was a highly respected leader in the group. Others who played prominent roles included Narayan Singh Delmia and Hiralal Sisodiya, profiled in the previous chapter. Those who gathered on the second of the month spent countless hours singing and discussing Kabir, with topics ranging from broad social issues to minute inquiry into the meanings of words. From these discussions a critique of the Kabir Panth, its authorities and rituals, developed. I will remind readers briefly of what Hiralalji and Narayanji reported about this.

On being asked whether Kabir Panthi *mahants* came to the *manch*, Hiralalji said:

> Yes, some gurus came. They wore their rosaries, caps, forehead marks, other marks. But their system, their way of thinking, was tied to ritualism. Fine, the Kabir Panthis give up drinking, give up intoxication. But so what, if there's not a revolution of ideas? The most important revolution is in your ideas. When a revolution of ideas takes place within a person, his whole life is turned around. The person is transformed. ... In India there are many sects and schools which have caused all kinds of confusion. Kabir wanted a revolution of ideas. He wanted people to understand their own nature. Recognize yourself! The supreme being is not far away!

> As far as I understand it, Eklavya's Kabir *manch* was a medium for this—the birth of a revolution in ideas in all human communities. The goal was to give all people some peace in their hearts and minds and to encourage the expansion of their imaginations. To eradicate the confusion, the darkness, in their spirits, and to create light. That's why I was so very happy to discover the *Kabir bhajan aur vichār manch*, and that's why I went there so regularly. ... If someone becomes a Kabir Panthi and wears a rosary or a bead around his neck, does this mean he has become a good thinker, that his superstition and obscurantism have been erased?

Narayanji was quite radicalized by his experience with the Kabir *manch*. After many years as a locally popular Kabir singer, he realized that he was still in the grip of superstition and prejudice and was doing the very things that Kabir criticized. He had worshiped gods and goddesses, but he gave that up. Though a member of a formerly "untouchable" caste himself, he had looked down on castes below his in the hierarchy, treating them as untouchable; he had relied on Brahmin priests for ceremonial functions; and he had joined the Kabir Panth. Under the influence of the *manch*, all this changed. Caste status no longer shaped his behavior. He saw all people as equal and bearing intrinsic dignity. He was moved by the respect and love he received from the Eklavya staff, by their freedom from bias and pretension. He gave up superstitious practices and became critical of the Kabir Panth *mahants*, who seemed to be exploiting people, staging rituals to get money and assert their authority.

By all accounts, Prahladji had shared these kinds of ideas. Certainly since I had known him, he had always preached passionately against sectarianism, casteism, and other small-minded identities. He tried to undermine prejudice, and he emphasized the delusion of searching for truth in external forms and practices.

By the time I started my research in Malwa, the Kabir *manch* had been over for four years. Prahladji had become a regional star, his cassettes enjoying vigorous sales, his recognition extending to highly placed people. As reported in chapter 1, I was not pleased when he told me in April 2002, on that train coming home from Bandhavgarh, that he had become a *mahant*. Along with his pointed hat and other paraphernalia, he had received a *panjā*, a lengthy official document granting permission to propagate religion (*dharm prachār karnā*) and declaring his rights and responsibilities as a *mahant*.

A Dharamdasi Kabir Panth *mahant* is empowered mainly to do two things: to preside over the *chaukā āratī* ritual and to initiate disciples. He also pledges allegiance and obedience to the Panth and the Panth's guru. This did not fit the image of Prahladji that I wished to cherish. In that train rolling from Bandhavgarh to Malwa, we began our many discussions and debates on the subject. I was disappointed that he seemed to be buying into the ritualism and authority structure of the sect. I dreaded seeing him become more priestly and preachy. It made me gloomy to contemplate his energy draining from where I thought it belonged, in his unique calling as a singer, into humdrum sectarian functions that anyone could perform. He argued vigorously and cogently for his decision. First, he said, many people wanted him to be their guru, and in effect he *was* a guru. He had told me several dramatic stories about people insisting that he and he alone should initiate them. But he had no authority. He wanted a way to make it official. Then he argued that the Kabir Panth was doing good work in bringing Kabir-*sāhab*'s message to so many people. There was nothing wrong with rituals as long as one didn't perpetuate delusions about their purpose. Rituals were just a way of bringing people together to share understanding of Kabir and to encourage them to lead good lives.

For several years, Prahladji had hosted an annual Kabir festival on land adjacent to his house, which the state government had granted for the creation of an institute devoted to Kabir. In 2002, the function was scheduled for May 25—Buddha Purnima, the full moon night commemorating the Buddha's birth and enlightenment.[22] On that day, in extreme heat, I was slowly moving around observing preparations. Ambaram's son Dharmendra was on a ladder in the simple temple that Prahladji had built, pasting bright paper flowers between painted verses of Kabir. A tall festive gateway had been erected. White triangular flags flapped from poles and rooftops, bearing the motto *satyanām* (true name). Huge tents without walls were set up to shelter the audience. Dozens of people were making food.

I saw Shantiji, Prahladji's wife, cleaning the wide front verandah of the house with a purifying solution made from cowdung. Then Kabir Panthi sadhus started extending cords, hanging strings of flowers, spreading cloth seats. Meanwhile, spectators and singers, sadhus and gurus, were drifting in. Prahladji was rushing from place to place, looking after arrangements and welcoming guests. He had slept very little in the past few days; his voice was hoarse. His family members were in the same condition.

In the late afternoon a crowd suddenly materialized near the house. I got there just in time to see events take a dramatic turn. This was the performance of Prahladji's first *chaukā āratī*. I was taken aback by how weighty and solemn it felt. At one end of the crowd, two attendant sadhus were dressing him in special clothes—a long shirt, beads, yellowish marks on forehead and arms, the hat. Then he walked gravely to the verandah, stepping on a cloth pathway, not at all his usual social self. He sat down on the *gaḍḍī*, the special seat in the center of the *chaukā*. I had heard that this was "Kabir's seat." Many devotees believed that the person who sat there became Kabir himself. I watched Prahladji being worshiped by a series of people starting with his wife, then his son and daughter-in-law (the married women with their faces completely covered, in *ghūnghaṭ*, as is customary in this community), and other family members, waving the tray that contained flaming wicks and ritual materials.

Prahladji and his attendants went through the order of the *chaukā*, chanting, gesturing, moving things around, according to the ritual rules. At the heart of the event, dozens of individuals went before him one at a time to do *bandagī*; they knelt at his feet, offered a coconut and some money, and went through a routine of looking up at his eyes, then down again, three times, while placing their joined hands in right, left, and center positions. I did it too. He appeared to be very concentrated, acknowledging no one in a personal way.[23]

Eventually those who wished to "take the name," or be initiated by him, did so, one at a time. He whispered the mantra in each one's ear and gave them a *kanthī*, a single *tulsī* bead on a string to wear around their neck. His feet were washed and the water distributed as *charaṇāmṛit*, a holy substance. Most people received a few drops in their cupped right hand and swallowed them. Then *prasād* was distributed, as usual in a Hindu rite of worship—cut-up fruits and little sugar balls. Everybody wants *prasād*. It transfers the holy essence of the rite in a concrete form, conferring blessings. By that time I had retreated to one of the rooms off the verandah, as the crowd had become suffocating. Prahladji's wife came in, smiling broadly, offering *prasād*. "Take this," she said, "it's a ticket to Satlok." Was she serious? Her smile was a bit mischievous. Satlok is the Kabir Panth's version of Heaven. It means "World of Truth." Kabir Panthis sometimes talk about it as if it's a place where good devotees can go when they die.

Later that night, as he introduced the singing program, Prahladji gave a speech. Once again he said what I'd heard him say so often: that it doesn't matter whether you wear white clothes or red clothes or no clothes; if

FIGURE 7.1. Prahladji performs *chaukā āratī* ritual during his period as a *mahant* of the Kabir Panth. Photo by Smriti Chanchani.

you're not pure inside, if your way of living, your thoughts and deeds, aren't right, then all your appearances are just a show, a sign of your pride. Then he said: "May it never happen that I think like this—I am a great bhajan singer or a *mahant* or somebody who holds a high position. May that never happen. If you see me with that kind of pride, you should understand that I have fallen." His voice started to crack as it often did, but this was different. I realized he was crying. He was praying and crying, on that day when the pomp of mahantship had begun for him and he'd passed the mantra to his first crowd of initiates, praying that he wouldn't get lost.

The Debate

For the next three years, my Kabir-connected friends in Malwa were debating Prahladji's decision to be a *mahant* and to do *chaukā āratī*. Hiralal Sisodiya said, "For all those years in the Kabir *manch* he was with us, criticizing pomp and pretension, *mahants* and rituals. Now look! He's a *mahant* himself, and he's doing *chaukā āratī*. What's going on?"

A relative of Prahladji told me that the whole family was upset when he became a *mahant*. First they worried it was a step toward leaving the family entirely, as he had tried to do on a previous occasion (chapters 1 and 2 tell that story). The other reason was that he had been an articulate critic of the sect and its rituals, but now he had no ground to stand on. "It's like someone smoking cigarettes but telling other people not to smoke."

Hiralalji told stories about his own habit of publicly challenging *mahants* and their followers (see his profile in chapter 6). Narayanji, who had known Prahladji for many years, had often sung with him, and was related by marriage, was disturbed and critical. In the 1990s he had come to believe that the Kabir Panth *mahants* did more harm than good. He had seen evidence that some of them were corrupt, that their positions of authority in local communities could easily bring out the worst in them. He and Hiralalji both described *chaukā āratī* as a kind of business (*vyāpārī*) or setting up shop (*dukāndārī*) to get money and gifts. They felt it exploited poor people. They also felt it encouraged superstition, whereas Kabir had relentlessly attacked superstition. Panth gurus and official writings promised that people would be delivered from their sins or would attain heaven or final liberation by participating in *chaukā āratī*. What could be farther from Kabir's real teaching? It led people astray and sent the wrong message to the next generation.

Narayanji also said with a smile that had a tinge of disgust, "They are drinking the water that they use to wash his feet."

I was not neutral. I had become close to Prahladji and the whole family. In August 2002 (as described in chapter 1), I had ritually become Prahladji's sister with corresponding ties to everyone else in the family. I felt more free to argue with Prahladji without there being any question about the underlying love and trust between us. Being his *elder* sister, I actually had the right to criticize and make jokes about him—which the rest of the family, conventionally tied to deference and obedience to the male head of household, found quite enjoyable.

In 2003, Shabnam Virmani had joined our circle, working on her series of films and audio CDs in which Prahladji would figure prominently. One of the four feature-length documentaries she eventually produced focused on stories and issues about the Kabir Panth, *chaukā āratī*, and Prahladji's role as *mahant* (Virmani 2008b). From Malwa to Damakheda, from Delhi to New York, Shabnam and I would spend countless hours with Prahladji and his singing group, along with other friends and relatives. Accounts of our discussions about his decision to become a *mahant* and perform *chaukā āratī*, which could fill many pages, are summarized here.

When challenged, Prahladji did not back down but gave arguments for the value of ritual that students of religion will find familiar. Ritual creates community. It is necessary for initiation, giving and receiving the name, an act by which people make a commitment to join Kabir's tradition. Kabir's teachings communicate on many levels, and most people aren't ready right away to understand the highest teachings. Ritual helps them to begin the process. On these occasions, they can listen to Kabir's songs and receive good guidance. If abuses or delusions have developed in the way ritual is practiced, a wise leader can remove them. Prahladji made a point of telling participants that the *chaukā āratī* had no magic powers and that receiving the name in itself would not transform their lives. They had to change their behavior and deepen their knowledge. They should never think that the Kabir Panth was the only true religion. It was just a path like other religious paths. They should never shrink the greatness of Kabir down to narrow sectarian attitudes.[24]

Of course there were many people who did not criticize Prahladji's mahantship. They accepted the forms and structures of the Panth and associated his new activities with a good tradition. Many wanted to be his disciples.

Prahladji felt the pressure from former comrades in Eklavya's Kabir *manch* as well as from me and other urban friends. Occasionally he would laughingly admit defeat in a discussion and resolve not to do *chaukā āratī* anymore. But then he would do it again. He would say that he was helpless, that people insisted that he do it, and he couldn't say no.

In 2004, when Shabnam was shooting her film about Prahladji and the Panth, he was expressing somewhat heretical views even while continuing to practice as a *mahant*. At a Kabir Panth *melā* with Shabnam, standing aside from the main activity, he said:

> I want people to complain about me here, so that there will be some debate. Otherwise there's none. Who has raised any debate up to now? Whatever Sāhab [the head guru] does, everyone follows. That's what I'm supposed to do too, go by the book. But I won't. If I don't agree with something, I won't do it. Whoever agrees, let them do it. If there's any trouble, I'll face it [smiling]. Maybe Kabir-*sāhab* will be angry with me! They may

> call me an enemy of the guru [*gurudrohī*] [laughs]. There's a book of poetry about the greatness of the guru that has such *sākhīs*, it's unbelievable. Anyone who lets his ears hear criticism or insults of the guru will go deaf, or will go to hell. Or if you listen to any insult of the guru, you're a criminal and should be beaten up [laughs]. . . . Or it's a sin to set foot on the shadow of your guru. That kind of thing. But what is a guru? Kabir says, "*ye sab guru hai had ke, behad ke guru nāhīṇ*—these are all gurus of the limited, there's no guru of the limitless." Who is the guru of the limitless (*behad ke guru*)? "*Behad apne aap upaje, anubhav ke ghar mahin*—the limitless comes forth by itself in the house of experience." When you break through these boundaries, there's no need for all this [gesturing toward the forms of the sect].[25]

Eventually Prahladji introduced innovations in the *chaukā*. He stopped sitting in the ritual square dedicated to Satguru Kabir. Leaving it empty, he sat to the side. He forbade distribution of the *charaṇāmṛit*, the water from his own foot-washing. He told people that showing reverence to the guru was fine, but they shouldn't be clamoring to do *bandagī*, bowing and scraping to him excessively. "When do you do *bandagī*? When there are two. But now you and I have become one, so where's the need for bowing?" He refused to take money, or allowed only a symbolic offering of a rupee or two. He stated that *mahants* should not expect to get their income from ritual activities but should earn a living from their own work, as Kabir did. *Satsang* (gatherings with songs and discourses), *nām-dān* (giving the name, initiation), and *chaukā aratī* should be done as service, without pecuniary rewards. On a trip to Maharashtra in 2002, I noted his saying, in a conversation with other *mahants*, that more than 90 percent of *mahants* take on that role only to fill their stomachs and collect cash. He defined the true guru–disciple relationship as one in which there is no *len-den* (giving and taking), a relationship where participants freely give knowledge and respect, not money and goods.[26]

News of these innovations and critiques reached the sect leadership in Damakheda. They were not pleased. They did not like his presumption that he could unilaterally change the established form of the *chaukā*. They did not like the imputation of corruption among *mahants*.

Ire of the Acharyas

Prahladji liked meeting different gurus. He had taken initiation in several *nirguṇ* sects over a period of twenty-five years, including the Nath Panth, Radhasoami, the Damakheda Kabir Panth, and the Parakh Panth of Abhilash Das. Though he was now sure that he wouldn't deviate from the Kabir Panth, he still respected the gurus of different branches and sometimes visited leaders of traditions other than Damakheda. He had a dream that all the sectarian groups might get past their differences and unite in the larger cause of serving Satguru Kabir. When in Delhi, he often went to the Kabir Bhavan, a new center built by Vivek Das, the religious head of the entire Kabir Chaura network.

Vivek Das became the Kabir Chaura Acharya in 2000. In his early youth, by his own account, he had been a Naxalite, or member of a revolutionary Maoist movement that organized violent uprisings in the pursuit of justice for the poor and disenfranchised. Coming to understand the futility of violence, he became a Kabir Panthi (see closing scenes of Virmani 2008b). He was a young sadhu when I first visited Kabir Chaura in 1976. After the death of the elderly Acharya Amrit Das in 1988, I had heard there was some jostling for leadership. For over ten years the more conservative Gangasharan Das—who at a certain point had begun to call himself Gangasharan Shastri, indicating his wish to take on a more Brahminic identity—had held the position of Acharya. But after some wrangling and deal-making, Gangasharan had moved to a temple on the bank of the Ganges, and Vivek Das had assumed leadership at Kabir Chaura.

Gangasharan Shastri supported the long-observed tradition of *chaukā āratī*. He also unhesitatingly called himself a Hindu and a Vaishnav.[27] Soon after taking leadership, Vivek Das came out strongly against *chaukā āratī*. In a conversation in 2002, he told me he was urging his followers not to do it, though he wasn't strictly forbidding it. He also said that he was about to publish an aggressive critique of the Dharamdasis, who in his opinion did not deserve to be called Kabir Panthis. Having just enjoyed the hospitality of the Dharamdasis, I challenged Vivek Das on the usefulness of attacking rival factions of the Panth. I pointed to the title of a book he had edited, *Ḍhāī akśhar* (Two-and-a-Half Letters). In a famous couplet of Kabir, those letters spell *prem*, love, which is said to contain more wisdom than all the holy books of the pandits. If this is so, I asked, then why spend your time attacking other people who are devoted to Kabir? Don't you have better things to do? Vivek Das replied, "I do many other things, but this is important too. Kabir was aggressive. He attacked deluded people. If people are on the wrong road, Kabir would not hesitate to say, 'You're on the wrong road.' "

In two books published in 2003, Vivek Das invokes the radical Kabir who stood against conventional religion, questioned authority, and satirized pretension and superstition. He attacks a tendency in the Panth that he calls *paurāniktā*, meaning doctrines, stories, texts, and practices that mimic the Sanskrit Puranas and the Vaishnav traditions associated with them. The number-one offenders are the followers of Dharamdas:

> In the middle of the seventeenth century, *paurāniktā* swept into the Panth like a storm. Dharamdas was the leader of this. Dharamdasji was a Vaishnav devotee who accepted the Kabir Panth after coming under the influence of a Kabir Panthi *sant*. As soon as he arrived, there was an influx of *paurāniktā* so overpowering that a question mark was placed over all the actual facts about Kabir. In the form of false dialogues between Kabir and Dharamdas, dozens of books were composed (*Anurāg Sagar, Bodh Sāgar*, etc.). Because of these Puranic writings, ordinary people were led far from Kabir's true wisdom. In these "ocean" (*sāgar*) volumes, buckets full of insults and filth were unloaded on Kabir's contemporary disciples. His disciples were addressed as thief, . . . dweller in hell, and other demeaning terms. The *Bījak*, Kabir-*sāhab*'s basic work, is the universally revered religious text in the Kabir Panth. But in these Puranic "ocean" books, the Bījak's wisdom is referred to as the worms in the *guler* fruit, and the composer of the *Bījak* is called the messenger of death. (V. Das 2003a, preface)

Vivek Das criticizes the Dharamdasis' propagation of an avatar theory, not only about Kabir, but also about the progeny of Dharamdas who ascend to the leadership of their "forty-two-generation" lineage. He criticizes the notion that Kabir's closest disciple was an extremely wealthy merchant. He brands the "ocean" literature as 99 percent lies. And he underlines the fact that all these books promote *chaukā āratī*.

In a volume called *Ghaṭ kā chaukā* (The Chaukā in the Body), Vivek Das attacks the *chaukā* ritual and the centrality it has assumed in the lives of Kabir Panthis. The main text is based on a lecture that he gave to Kabir Panthis in Trinidad and Tobago. They had mounted a major *chaukā āratī* for his visit on the full moon of the month of Kartik [according to the

Hindu system of lunar months]. He scolds them heavily for doing so. His language is vivid, his condemnation unequivocal:

> Kabir-sahab opposed these phony forms of worship.
>
> Kabir gave a great message of awakening, and today his followers have joined the Idiot Panth, the Puranic Panth.
>
> Worshiping through the *chaukā āratī* is a powerful assault on Kabir's revolutionary ideas. (V. Das 2003b, 4, 20, 25)

Vivek Das sarcastically dismisses the priestcraft, the expense, the greed for offerings, and above all people's deluded belief that they will avoid death by breaking coconuts or achieve liberation by writing a mantra on a betel leaf and then eating the leaf. He declares that these delusions are destroying the Kabir Panth. After cataloging the sorts of external practices that Kabir rejected, he says, "To know the spiritual self within your own body is the essence of all worship" (V. Das 2003b, 7). His title, *Ghat kā chaukā*, recalls the earliest reference to the *chaukā* in the ritual texts that Lorenzen studied.[28] There seems to be an understanding, rooted in early layers of the Panth, that the outer *chaukā* is only a symbol of an internal process of transformation:

> The *chaukā* that Kabir-sahab wanted to tell us about is the *chaukā* inside every human being. That is what we need to know, that is the light we need to kindle and spread. Only then can we break the head of the lord of death. Without that, even if we break a thousand coconuts, even if we perform not just 101 but thousands of *chaukā aratī*s, we'll get no benefit. (V. Das 2003b, 29)

In this essay too, Vivek Das emphasizes that the worst offenders, the greatest purveyers of ritualized delusion, the leaders in turning the Kabir Panth into a Puranic fools' Panth, are the Damakheda-based Dharamdasis (see V. Das 2003b, 21).[29]

In the Dharamdasi *melā*s that I had attended, Prakashmuni Nam Sahab also criticized rival branches of the Panth. Though he did not single out Kabir Chaura in 2002, he spoke sharply against dissident groups of Dharamdasis that split off from the mainstream, and he strongly underlined the authenticity and sole authority of the forty-two-generation lineage. The crucial importance of the *chaukā āratī* ritual cannot be questioned in the Dharamdasi Panth. Once when

I mentioned to one of the Prakashmuni Nam Sahab's close lieutenants that I hoped to ask the Acharya some questions about *chaukā āratī*, he responded somewhat angrily, suggesting that I didn't understand the *chaukā*'s real meaning or the challenges of transmitting Kabir's teaching to followers with little or no education.

Perhaps failing to appreciate the seriousness of their differences, or hoping despite everything to bring them together, in 2004 Prahladji invited both Acharyas to grace the occasion of the annual Kabir celebration that he hosted in his village. But he went one step further: in published announcements of the event, he indicated that both would actually be there. Later he said that this was a mistake, that he had only meant to mention both as sources of inspiration. But he was severely upbraided in phone calls from Damakheda for publishing such a claim without getting Huzur-sahab's permission. That same year, at the annual *melā* in Damakheda, the climate changed dramatically for Prahladji. Huzur-sahab was not only chilly. He made critical remarks about Prahladji when they were seated on the stage before tens of thousands of people.[30]

Things came to a head in June 2005, when Acharya Vivek Das asked Prahladji to perform on Kabir Jayanti (Kabir's birthday) at his center in Delhi. Prahladji agreed, and the publicity was circulated. When Acharya Prakashmuni Nam Sahab heard of it, he summoned Prahladji to appear before him in Raipur, Chattisgarh, nearly 800 miles away from Delhi, on the same day. Prahladji refused, citing his prior commitment. There was a showdown in which Prahladji defied the command of his Panth guru, stating that his loyalty is only to Kabir, not to any Panth. He stayed away from the required annual meeting of *mahants* in Damakheda. In October 2005, a gathering of *mahants* convened by the Acharya took disciplinary action. Pradladji's *panjā*, or authorization to be a *mahant*, was revoked. The days of wearing the pointed hat and conducting *chaukā āratī* were over.

"Isn't it ironic," I asked Prahladji one day in his village house, "that you had dreams of bringing together all the different Kabir Panths—you thought you'd unite Vivek Das, Prakashmuni Nam Sahab, Abhilash Das, and the rest—and now you seem to have aroused even more enmity and factions?"

"What did I know," he replied, "when I took *dīkśhā* from Abhilash Das in 1994? I thought the Kabir Panth was all one thing, not Varanasi and Damakheda and Allahabad and Kharsiya and on and on." He laughed and walked out of the room.

Conclusion

Popes wear tall hats, observant Jews wear yarmulkes, mullahs wear beards, Sikhs keep their hair uncut, the Dalai Lama shaves his head. Tibetan Buddhists, while teaching nonattachment and emptiness, practice some of the most elaborate rituals on the planet. Taking a break from my research in Malwa one year, I went to Dharamsala where the Tibetan government-in-exile is based. There I witnessed a "long-life ceremony" for the Dalai Lama, who had recently recovered from a serious illness. Monks in rows droned hallowed verses. Bells and long-necked trumpets resounded. A veritable mountain of offerings rose on one side of the sacred space—foodstuffs and other items symbolizing nourishment and life. The Dalai Lama himself received the community's good wishes, so complexly bodied forth in physical form, with his usual smiling grace. Euro-American guests in a special reserved section (myself among them) seemed happy and respectful. I have never heard admirers of Tibetan Buddhism seriously criticize the Tibetan penchant for ritual in light of the Buddha's simple lifestyle and teaching of emptiness.

Why did a controversy over ritual erupt among Kabir devotees in Malwa and elsewhere in the early 2000s? Why did I feel invested in it? How was this controversy related to the fights over whether Kabir was born in a lotus or from a woman's body, and whether he was celibate or had biological children? What was at stake?

Everyone concerned had a stake in the representation of Kabir: the central leaders and local authorities of the Panth; the singers; the devotees; the scriptwriters for stage and screen; the American scholar-translator; the Indian filmmaker. Some of us, while deeply admiring the character and poetry of Kabir and believing in the value of his contributions to humanity, also receive material gain and worldly recognition from our association with Kabir. Devotees who don't make a profit from the master still build their identity around him. No one is disinterested.

Like all organized religions, the Kabir Panth has found ritual indispensable in maintaining itself institutionally. Ritual creates solidarity, distinction, authority. It provides symbols and concepts that are easy to understand, even if there are also claims of deeper meanings. It gives people something to do.

The Dharamdasi Kabir Panth has followed one well-traveled road in the history of religions by claiming that the founder of the religion actually established the ritual and enjoined its performance. They show this founding moment in a sacred text that was, they affirm, dictated by Kabir. Going even further, they claim divinity not only for the master but also for the lineage of gurus he established. The ritual specifically enacts worship of the guru and his duly named representatives, powerfully enforcing authority and obedience. In the normal course of human affairs, the ritual becomes a source of income for some *mahants*.

The Kabir Chaura branch of the Panth has used *chaukā āratī* in the usual ways—to solidify the community, to provide followers with symbols and prescribed acts, to promote guru-devotion, to get donations. But since Kabir Chaura believes in only one authentic book of Kabir's compositions, the *Bījak*, and since the *Bījak* says nothing of the ritual, they don't claim that Kabir commanded its performance. They also don't have father-to-son succession in leadership of the lineage, or any claim to avatarhood of the Acharyas.

Vivek Das has taken another well-precedented course in the history of religions, that of the reformer. Harking back to the "original" teaching and spirit of Kabir, he excoriates the accretion of ritual, superstition, and mythology. He notes that the main rival branch of the Panth has tried to delegitimize his branch by insulting and demoting the *Bījak*. He comes back with harsh arguments that serve to delegitimize the rival, at the same time promoting reform within his own organization.

On the ground, all these things look much more personal.

Coming from a very poor rural family and a low-status caste, Prahlad Singh Tipanya achieves fame, prosperity, and respect as a Kabir singer and teacher. But he still longs for the legitimacy of institutional affiliation, the authority of conventionally sanctioned guru-hood.

His family members support his decisions; they don't have much choice. But some express discontent, saying he should not have become a *mahant* and should not be doing *chaukā aratī*.

Some of Prahladji's old comrades from the Kabir *manch* criticize him based on their understanding of Kabir's message. They are convinced he has taken the wrong path, which they find all the more regrettable as he has become powerful and influential. But there are other layers in this conversation. Some people (not the ones named in this chapter) resent his success and his seeming to turn away from them. Some, while speaking of Kabir, also have issues that are more local and personal.

Linda, the American scholar-translator of Kabir, and Shabnam, the filmmaker from Bangalore, play their roles. Whether actively taking a position or simply witnessing as the camera rolls, they are not taken lightly. They are impressive and well funded; they are enthusiastic and warm; they sing, laugh, and debate; they become friends, sisters, aunties. Both are highly educated, politically secular, and left-leaning; both are inspired by what they see as Kabir's nonsectarian spirituality, remarkable independence, and social radicalism; both have their educated urban constituencies to think about.

Then we have to remember the *Kabir bhajan evam vichār manch*. It is likely that this controversy wouldn't have occurred at all—at least not on the scale that it did—had it not been for Eklavya's sponsorship of the *manch* in the 1990s. We can never know for sure how crucial Eklavya's role was, but it was certainly important.

In these concluding remarks, the top-down observations (about sect leaders, institutional motives, historical patterns in religion) may come across as more cogent than those that reflect bottom-up movements, global crosscurrents, and personal relationships. Fragmentary glimpses of people's lives and interests do not add up to a clear conclusion. But I sometimes think that fragments reflect reality better than perfectly cogent arguments.[31]

The Last Laugh

Kabir says, when I was born,
the world laughed and I cried.
Let's hope that when it's time to go,
the world will cry and I'll laugh.

Everyone knows the main meaning of this popular couplet. Babies are born crying while their families celebrate. Kabir hopes to live a good life—in which case, people may be sad to see him go. And he hopes to be so free of attachment to this life, so fearless, that he'll go out with a smile while others cry in sorrow.

Kabir was quite serious, but he also had a great sense of humor. The matters we have been discussing are both serious and funny. With his sharply penetrating insight, did Kabir know that his followers would fight over his dead body? Was the decision to have a good laugh an alternative to despair? Do we, his followers and admirers, keep reconstructing his body and then arguing over how to dispose of it? Is he still laughing?

8

Political / Spiritual Kabir

jal meṇ kumbh kumbh meṇ jal, bāhar bhītar pānī
phūṭā kumbh jal jal hī samānā, yah sab akath kahānī

pot in water   water in pot
outside   inside
water
pot shatters
water merges
with water
you'll never tell
this tale

TO CONCLUDE THE time we have spent together (300-plus pages here imagined as time), let us reflect on outside and inside. In considering Kabir oral traditions, we have looked at texts, performers, audiences, circumstances, and interpretations. This closing chapter is in the realm of interpretation, but by now we are aware of how all the other elements come together to give rise to interpretation.

I conclude on this particular interpretive question—"political/spiritual," placed parallel to Kabir's "outside/inside"—because it has turned out to be a preoccupation for me and for many Indian friends and colleagues who study, perform, revere, love, and deploy Kabir. A previous chapter was devoted to this topic as it plays out among singers, admirers, and devotees of Kabir in Malwa. Here the conversation is more urban, and it ranges more widely. We start with India and Kabir, then venture into periods long before Kabir in India and into places beyond India, looking at examples of music and spirituality intersecting with, or veering away from, politics and society.[1]

The discussion is broad, but the argument that drives it is particular. Many left-leaning thinkers, activists, and social workers (with whom I often align politically) are repelled by religion. Influenced by Marxian thought, they tend to see religion as false and retrogressive. Materialist in orientation, they label religion as otherworldly and superstitious. "Spirituality" isn't any better, as they associate the term with "spirits," nonmaterial wraiths that people unfortunately believe in. Marxian or not, social justice activists may be put off by antirational, antiscientific, quietist tendencies in religion, and these associations spread beyond religion to other human activities "tainted" by emotion, receptivity, acceptance, surrender. In this chapter I address the sense of alienation between "religious/spiritual" and "social/political." Some of us feel a longing to reconcile them, but we should recognize that there is good reason for the alienation. Both the conflict and the longing to reconcile are fundamental. We could evoke it in a variety of word pairs: "surrender/control," "acceptance/struggle," "one/two," "passion/dispassion." The word "love" might come up. Kabir seems to be interested in how we grapple with seemingly irreconcilable opposites.

> This is the big fight, King Ram.
> Let anyone settle it who can.

***

> You can get free by your own strength
> or the beloved can free you.

***

> If I say yes it isn't so,
> and I can't say no.
> Between yes and no a space
> my true guru's place.

I propose that we can reasonably interpret Kabir texts as supporting the coexistence and mutual nourishment of inner and outer, spiritual and political; that there is also good reason to think of spiritual and political as opposed to each other; and that it is necessary, in historical and social analysis, to discover not only how texts may be interpreted but also how people have actually applied those texts to their lives and struggles. It is not enough to say that in principle Kabir supports the interdependence of inner and outer. We need to observe how people have brought political and spiritual together or kept them apart and in what ways they have argued for their interpretations. Kabir becomes political when people engage with him in the political sphere—a fact that will be illuminated through the history of the American folk songs known as Negro spirituals.

We will, of course, have to define the terms—spiritual, religious, political. As usual, we start with a story.

Fear of Bliss

We are in Delhi's Habitat Centre, that expansive campus of art galleries, theaters, and cafes where scenes of high culture unfold every day. It is December 2002. Memories of communal slaughter in Gujarat, like the aroma of fresh blood, trouble our minds.[2] Many artists and intellectuals have had their say since the carnage of February and March, taking a stand against the politics of violent, hate-fueled religious nationalism. Tonight painting, poetry, and music come together to evoke a different vision of Indian culture. Acclaimed artist Haku Shah has created a series of paintings based on texts of great Sufi and *sant* poets. The marvelous Hindustani classical singer and social justice activist Shubha Mudgal has composed music for the poems. The brilliant literature professor Alok Rai has written an essay for the exhibition catalog, and he will introduce tonight's performance. They all share this message: the India we wish to identify with and strengthen is one of richly intermingling cultures, where Hindus, Muslims, Sikhs, Christians, Jains, Buddhists, and Zoroastrians, along with the unaffiliated and nonbelievers, at least respect and at best appreciate each other, and where secular democratic institutions uphold the equal rights and safety of all. The poetry of Islamic Sufism and Hindu bhakti celebrates this deep-flowing culture and criticizes intolerant, oppressive sectarianism and casteism. Tonight we allow the combined powers of art, poetry, and music to inspire us.

Professor Rai opens the event, speaking of the collaboration of Haku Shah and Shubha Mudgal:

> [It] not only revisits a part of our culture that is deeply rooted in the values of religious pluralism and harmony, but also revitalizes these ancient ideas in these troubled times. We believe that a better knowledge of our deep roots in pluralistic traditions is central to how we define ourselves as a society today. Diverse symbols ... constitute the basis from which we conceive of and articulate our vision of the kind of culture and community that we wish to be. But our

> pluralistic religious roots are often drowned out in the current violence and misunderstanding ... around religion. (Rai 2002, 3–4)[3]

He goes so far as to claim that the voices of popular medieval devotion prefigure the modern values of "human rights ... dignity, equality, and non-discrimination," and that the poets spoke particularly "to peasants, to women, and to members of lower castes" (ibid., 4).

But he also issues a warning, which makes me think of the genre that Kabir singers call *chetāvanī*, a poem that says "Beware!" In the Kabir world the *chetāvanī* poem usually warns of the imminence of death: "Watch out! Wake up!"[4] We could say that Alok Rai is conveying a *chetāvanī* from the viewpoint of the political left. Beware of religion! Beware of mystical music! Don't let yourself go! Although many distinguished thinkers have invoked the voices of *sants* and Sufis in these dark days, there is a palpable discomfort on the left about getting too entangled with their *religiosity*. Going hand in hand with the well-known Marxist aversion to religion is something we could call the fear of bliss. "Bliss" is a strong word; I mean to include in it the semantic range of joy, delight, beauty, aesthetic passion, love.

Rai mentions a story about Lenin—actually a story that Gorky told about Lenin. We will get a full rendition further on, but now we note how it is embedded in Alok Rai's message as he introduces Haku Shah's art and Shubha Mudgal's music, both based on *sant* and Sufi poetry.

Rai warns against the "seduction" of the mystical, articulating carefully around the dangers of attraction to "transcendent experience." Referring to Sahmat's *Anahad Garje* concerts soon after the 1992 destruction of the Babri mosque as well as to tonight's program,[5] he says there was "some embarrassment on the political left about this seeming surrender to the idiom of religion. Perhaps there still is—perhaps with ... good reason....There is [a] danger that such beautiful, teasing, mysterious images and such sudden, insidious music—at once ambush and seduction—is likely to make one vulnerable. Lenin warned against something similar in the context of listening to Beethoven's *Appassionata*: the world continues to be a hard, brutal place, despite the music and its evocations of harmony."

What Rai praises in Kabir and the rest has nothing to do with their devotion to God or their interest in blissful ego dissolution. He identifies—at least from his words on this occasion—only with their secular and rational humanism. Referring to a well-known poem, Rai says that Kabir helps us remember that the world is mad.[6] The bhakti tradition "represents an attempt to induce, to imagine and invent—through metaphysical injection, through the cultivation of feelings—a gentler, humane society" (ibid., 10).

"Metaphysical injection"—what a strange phrase! Is it a sterilized version of bhakti, devotion, the passion for personal transformation, liberation and love?

We begin to sense the depth of the political and intellectual aversion to "transcendence" that Rai refers to. Religious discourse is the obvious target, but that discourse gets allied with any experience that breaks through the boundaries of the self and transports the individual into a space of joyful boundlessness. Music has a particular power to do that, along with other arts. Indian aesthetic theory over millennia has linked religious and aesthetic transcendence, said to merge in a blissful experience of oneness that finds expression in a language of liquidity—*rasa*.[7]

Here is the story of Lenin and Beethoven's *Appassionata*, as reported by Gorky. The context is a tribute on the occasion of Lenin's death, replete with descriptive details that present a vibrant human portrait of the revolutionary leader.

Listening to Beethoven's sonatas played by Isai Dobrowein at the home of Y. P. Peshkova in Moscow one evening, Lenin remarked:

> "I know of nothing better than the *Appassionata* and could listen to it every day. What astonishing, superhuman music! It always makes me proud, perhaps naively so, to think that people can work such miracles!"
>
> Wrinkling up his eyes, he smiled rather sadly, adding: "But I can't listen to music very often, it affects my nerves. I want to say sweet, silly things and pat the heads of people who, living in a filthy hell, can create such beauty. One can't pat anyone on the head nowadays, they might bite your hand off. They ought to be beaten on the head, beaten mercilessly, although ideally we are against doing any violence to people. Hm—what a hellishly difficult job!"[8]

This is one way of entering our central problem. Political and spiritual can be painfully—hellishly—opposed to each other. Even while showing his deep sensitivity to music, Lenin rejects the superhuman ("ethereal" in the alternate translation given in n. 7) beauty of the *Appassionata*. He can't bear its effect on his nerves. It takes away his aggression. While listening, he feels love for his fellow beings. He wants to stroke them on the head and whisper loving words. But his political self says they are not to be trusted and should actually be beaten on the head mercilessly. Theoretically he and his comrades are against violence, but . . . . His anger at the filthy hell of a world where people are crushed by poverty and exploitation explodes not only against the exploiters but also against those who create beauty in the midst of hell. Gorky, a literary master, captures the subtlety of the moment in this anecdote, noting that Lenin wrinkles up his eyes and smiles sadly as he speaks of his own inability to tolerate the music he adores.

At the Habitat Centre, after invoking Lenin to warn against the ambush and seduction of mysticism and music, Alok Rai underlines the need to find "a language in which to talk about cruelty and exploitation, about the persistence of avoidable suffering . . . [to] signal our commitment to the living, to the lives and livelihoods, ever more threatened, of ordinary people" (Rai 2002, 10–11).

As if one's ability to be mindful of cruelty and exploitation were radically incompatible with one's ability to experience joy listening to Beethoven or the music of Kabir! I object. Don't those who engage in social-political struggle also need joy, love—even transcendence, if that word refers to the melting of boundaries, the dissolving of fear and hate? Lacking such vulnerability, do they risk becoming cruel and dry?

An ominous echo of Lenin's worry turns up in a statement by Golwalkar, the ideologue of the quasi-military, Hindu nationalist RSS.[9] Referring to the emotional looseness of bhakti, he warns:

> All our great authorities on mental discipline have ordained us not to succumb to overflow of emotions and weep in the name of God but to apply ourselves to a strict discipline of day-to-day penance. Effusion of emotions will only shatter the nerves and make the person weaker than before leaving a moral wreck. (quoted in Bhatt 2001, 143)

Ultimately Alok Rai admits that "worldly rage against exploitation and injustice" falls short. There are human needs that remain unaddressed by "the mere removal of deprivations—the arid metaphysics of consumption. These emotional needs and transcendent yearnings . . . also need to be addressed by a cultural movement that seeks . . . to involve whole human beings, and not only parts thereof" (Rai 2002, 11).

But the attitude toward these "emotional needs and transcendent yearnings" is profoundly ambivalent, to say the least.

Defining Terms: Political, Religious, Spiritual

The definitions of political and spiritual will begin by echoing the dichotomies of outer and inner. "Political" suggests outer-directed concern with institutions of society and state, conditions of justice and injustice. Political thought and action, then, are directed toward controlling or changing the material conditions of people's lives and the structures of power that govern them. "Spiritual" suggests inner-directed processes of self-knowledge and self-transformation. We will continue to raise the question of whether it is possible to move beyond these polarities, keeping in mind that merely "dissolving the opposites" is a move that has its own dangers.

If we are going to talk about "spirituality," we need to consider in greater detail the relationship and recent divergence of "religion" and "spirituality." I will not take up here the genealogies and meanings of the word "religion" in English and its cognates in European languages, or their differences from Indian terms that cover similar ground.[10] But in Euro-American academia until very recently, locating Kabir in the domain of religion would not have raised an eyebrow. We have long classified devotional and mystical literature as "religious." My specialization in Indian bhakti poetry got me jobs in departments of religious studies.

In the last few decades, starting in Euro-America and gradually spreading among certain classes in other parts of the world, we have seen a drive to separate "spirituality" from "religion." To put the matter crudely, religion is supposed to be bad, while spirituality is good. The "spiritual but not religious" trend took off with the rapidly accelerating economic and cultural globalization of the late twentieth century. "Spiritual" people often take lore and practices from various cultures and time periods, mixing and matching to taste. They tend to appear in the higher strata of class structures, whether in Euro-America or in Anglophone circles in India (as reflected in the "lifestyle" sections of the Indian English press). In many (though not all) cases they need leisure and money to pursue their spiritual dreams. A *New York Times* piece on California's Esalen Institute conveys the flavor:

> At twilight, not far from a cliff overlooking the Pacific Ocean, a Mayan shaman spoke of the return of Kukulkan to dozens of listeners sitting on the floor inside a yurt. ... Mr. Vergara would soon lead his listeners in breathing exercises and chants to Kukulkan, as part of a weeklong workshop mixing yoga and Mayan rituals at the Esalen Institute, the fabled spiritual retreat. ... [A]s the retreat center prepares to observe its 50th anniversary ... people are still making pilgrimages here, drawn by Esalen's focus on healing, melding of traditions, and mantra of "spiritual but not religious." ... The recent appointment of a boutique hotel founder to Esalen's board of trustees, [critics] say, reflects the increasing emphasis on money-making packages, which range from $405 for sleeping bag accommodations for a weekend workshop to $1,595 for a luxury room.[11]

I am skeptical about the attempt to divorce religion from spirituality. Some of the most exquisite artistic testimonies of mystical experience[12] and spiritual aspiration have been created by people who were thoroughly ensconced in institutional religion—people like John of the Cross, Teresa of Avila, Basavanna (a South Indian rebel against established religion who established a new religion), Amir Khusrau and other Sufis, and the Buddhist monk-scholar-poet Shantideva (referenced below). Many icons of the burgeoning new spirituality are committed to established religious traditions (for example, Pema Chodron, cited below, and of course the Dalai Lama). An example recently highlighted by two major Kabir scholars troubles the religious-spiritual separation. David Lorenzen begins his book *Praises to a Formless God* with a song by Blind Willie Johnson, a gospel and blues singer from South Carolina who died in 1945 and who is said to show "an amazing affinity" with Kabir (Lorenzen 1996, 3). Purushottam Agrawal (2011) enthusiastically endorses the comparison, citing a line by Willie that says God is not in the pulpit and should be sought outside the church. Line-by-line, says Agrawal, two songs by Kabir and Willie appear to be almost translations of each other. But in our enthusiasm about Willie's prospiritual/antireligious insight, we should not forget that he was a churchgoing man and a preacher, who at the time of his death was operating a House of Prayer in Texas.

"Religious" and "spiritual" are historically and socially intertwined. Rejecting religion and embracing spirituality is too easy. It oversimplifies the ways in which religions actually function and perpetuates the alienation of secular intellectuals from the majority of their fellow citizens. But

I accept that there can, within limits, be a distinction and that "spiritual" as distinct from "religious" may be useful in a discussion of Kabir.[13]

When the word "spirituality" is preferred to "religion," we can be sure that the speaker wishes to focus on the individual and turn away from the institutional. The traditions of Kabir poetry, whatever their variations and uncertainties, always emphasize individual awakening, delve into the intimate depths of individual consciousness, and criticize the abuses and failures of institutional religion. He is, among other things, a canny psychologist. One could describe Kabir's concerns as psychospiritual or simply psychological. The latter could imply, on one level, personal insight, transformation, relief of suffering; and on another level, a space where the personal meets a domain of awareness and wisdom that is no longer merely personal.

Purushottam Agrawal on Religion, Spirituality, and Kabir

Among recent scholars of Kabir, Purushottam Agrawal is unique in the scope, creativity, and intellectual power of his writings. Most of his publications are in Hindi, though a few articles are available in English, and he is preparing a major book on Kabir in English. Here I will engage with his discussions of religion and spirituality, and the political implications of both terms.

In a remarkable collection of short essays published in 2004, Agrawal explores the intersections of religion, spirituality, politics, secularism, poetry, and imagination from multiple angles. The book is called *Nij Brahm Vichār: Dharm, Samāj, aur Dharmetar Adhyātma* (*A Transcendent Thought of One's Own: Religion, Society, and Secular Spirituality*). Keywords visible in many essay titles are *dharm, dharmsattā, ātma, adhyātma, dharmetar adhyādmiktā*—religion, religious authority, self, spirit, secular spirituality. Some essays focus on Kabir and poetry. Some discuss politics and history. Two take up what the author regards as Marx's positive understanding of spirituality.[14] Nearly all are firmly rooted in Indian contexts. Originally written as a series of columns in the Hindi daily *Jansattā*, these essays are daring and profound and will reward thorough reading. Here I will just give a taste.

At the outset of *Nij Brahm Vichār*, Agrawal speaks of his lifelong curiosity about and preoccupation with religion—its powers, its claims, and the huge chasm between what is said about it and how we actually experience it.

> They say that God is one and all the religions are just different roads to reach the one God. Then why are the roads full of crashes? Why do the travelers keep having such atrocious fights? They say that religion never teaches us to be enemies. Then why, when we look at history or glance at what's going on around us, does it seem that religion teaches us only to be enemies? They say that all religions teach love and compassion. Then how do so many religious followers get initiated into hatred? (Agrawal 2004, 9)

Another set of coexisting but contradictory facts leads Agrawal toward a definition of spirituality.

> When it comes to self-preservation, human beings have an aggressive instinct. At the same time, sympathy for the pain of others and some conception of justice are also human instincts. Humans are wrapped up in themselves yet always ready to expand themselves. When Rousseau imagined a "social contract," his basic premise was that human beings have at once a drive for self-preservation and a natural kindness. Let us recall the remarkable image of Harishankar Parsai-ji: "Humans occupy no fixed location. Who can say when a person will become a hyena or an embodiment of compassion?"
>
> To settle these opposing possibilities, we seek a way to compose a meaningful whole. Between the hyena and the avatar of compassion, could there be some harmony that would give meaning to an ordinary person's life? Even more, that would provide coherence to centuries and millennia of memories, and to our visions of the future? That would provide some ground for seeing our personal struggles as united with those of the world? The search for this ground is the spiritual search. It is a search for the expansion of the self, the possibility of going beyond the self. (ibid., 48)

One especially beautiful essay is inspired by the late Hindi writer Bhisham Sahni to whom Agrawal pays homage in the essay *Jigyāsu manuṣhya kā chhoṭā-sā nijī dharm* ("For the Human Seeker, a Small Personal Religion"). Agrawal comes close to the heart of what spirituality means to him when he speaks in this essay of the "thrilling realization of the connectedness of all existence" (2004, 34). The word I translate as thrilling (*romānchak*), reflecting traditions of both aesthetic and religious thought in India, literally means causing the body's hair to stand on end. Such a realization may come spontaneously. Often a certain discipline is involved. Religious traditions have developed practices that cultivate concentration, self-awareness, devotion, and reduction of the mental and physical conditioning that keeps us locked in our habits, attachments, fear, and grasping. An overall term for such practices in India is *sādhanā*. In his 2009 book on Kabir, *Akath kahānī prem kī*, Agrawal has combined and expanded several of the earlier essays to form a long chapter entitled *Kabīr ki sādhanā*, which I would translate as "Kabir's spiritual practice," but which Agrawal has rendered in an English version as "Kabir's pursuit"—perhaps to keep it as secular and neutral as possible.

In a lecture in 2009, Agrawal expanded on the meaning of *adhyātma*, the Hindi/Sanskrit word that we render as "spirituality":

> Kabir's criticism of Hinduism or Islam, other religious traditions like the Nath Panth, and in an indirect way even the Buddhist and Jain traditions, to my mind actually reflects a search for a fundamental connection with the cosmos ... without the mediation of organized religion ... spirituality without religion. Let me add that spirituality is an extremely inadequate translation of *adhyātma*. *Adhyātma* in Indian tradition does not mean things pertaining to the other world. It certainly does not mean the spirits with whom you could talk with the help of a priest; it does not mean that at all in the Indian tradition. *Adhyātma* etymologically means to go beyond yourself. In the eighth chapter of the *Gītā*, the question is put to Lord Krishna: please tell me, what is *adhyātma*, what is *brahma*? The answer is a quintessential understanding of the entire Indian tradition. The *Gītā* makes Krishna say: *swabhāvo adhyātmo muchayate*—your very nature is known as *adhyātma*. (Agrawal 2009c)

Agrawal is eloquent and brilliant in exploring the meaning of spirituality and differentiating it from religion. He strikes tellingly at the ways in which organized religion becomes invested in power and dogma, offering security, purity, hierarchical authority, and profit motives while draining agency, consciousness, personal responsibility, and equality. In a creative application of Marxism, he argues that religion brings about alienation from one's own spirituality, just as capitalism brings about alienation from one's own labor.[15] But to my mind he goes too far in setting up religion as the nemesis and destroyer of spirituality. In this analysis, spirituality is good—more than that, it is the essence of the human species (*prajāti sār*) (2004, 25); and religion is bad—more than that, it is diabolical. By repeatedly invoking the parable of the Faustian pact, Agrawal suggests that when naturally spiritual human beings cave in to the promises and enticements of religious power, they are making a deal with the devil that they can never take back![16] This view seriously oversimplifies religion and its intricate connections with spirituality.

Agrawal later seems to soften this sharply dichotomizing critique, turning binary opposition into dialectic—but only after elaborating at greater length on the dark side of religion:

> I am not suggesting that religion is nothing more than this [the dark side of the Faustian pact]. On the contrary, I insist that religion should be understood in its dialectical totality. It is essential that religion be seen as a composite of spirituality, a faith-system, a code of behavior, ethics, and social identity. Religious imagination is much more than violence, vengeance, and obsession with purity of blood. It also has something very sacred, sublime, and auspicious. Not only the lives of illustrious figures like Gandhi, Khan Abdul Gaffar Khan, Martin Luther King, and Raman Maharshi, but also the lives of millions of ordinary pious people bear witness to this fact. I am not proposing a religious war against religion; I am insisting that religion and its role be understood dialectically. One needs to distinguish between religious viewpoints that accord importance to religion's spiritual aspect and those that turn it into the image of an unassailable power structure. One needs to choose one's side in the incessant conflict that goes on between these two trends. Comprehending the role of the spiritual impulse in the constitution of religion, one needs to ask the question: Is it possible to conceive of spirituality outside the domain of religion? Kabir's practice provides an unambiguous and thrilling answer. Yes, it is indeed possible. (Agrawal 2009a, 329–30)

A Working Definition of Spirituality

The definition I use in the rest of this chapter has much in common with Purushottam Agrawal's, but it doesn't rely on the broad rejection of religion that occupies most of his writing about Kabir's *sādhanā*. I use the word "spirituality" to refer to (1) an inner-directed process of cultivating self-knowledge and alleviating suffering; and (2) an impulse to break free from the narrow bounds of self-centered individuality, to know one's connection to all living beings, to nature, to matter and energy. Thus it is *both* highly individualistic *and* oriented toward a loosening of the boundaries of the individual self. This nexus has interesting implications for the spiritual/political question.

Experiencing our connection to the whole living and nonliving universe does not mean that we forget our everyday identity or lose the ability to brush our teeth or get to work on time. But a spiritual aspirant is drawn to the possibility that the boundaries of the narrowly conceived self may grow thin and dissolve. This kind of experience has been ardently desired by human beings in many times and places. It may be conceptualized in various ways. Commonly it is understood religiously: that reality which is revealed when the ego-self dissolves is called God, or the impersonal yet vibrant and all-pervading Brahman, or Buddha-nature. Yet it need not be religiously conceived. In artistic creation the ego-self may become "lost" in this way, no longer controlling and fearful and limited, but deeply concentrated, open, and connected to a fantastically larger flow of reality. When a listener/viewer/reader takes in an artistic creation, the same thing may happen. Intense love between human beings is valued as it opens an avenue to this kind of experience. Sex can also be a gateway. This little catalog is far from exhaustive.

The desire to lose ourselves in something larger can also be sinister. It can lead us to identify with aggressive nationalism, militarism, authoritarian organizations, cruelly repressive religions, sick cults. But this caveat does not discredit spiritual aspiration. It just underlines the truth conveyed by the razor-edge metaphor in the *Kathā Upaṇiṣhad*: "Sharp like a razor's edge is the path, the sages say, difficult to traverse." We need to keep examining our fundamental values, our habitual patterns and blind spots, the strong pull of dishonesty, in order to avoid falling off that edge into one or another dark delusion.[17]

Pema Chodron, a teacher in the Tibetan Buddhist tradition, explains *bodhicitta*, the aspiration to awaken:

> [*Bodhicitta*] lifts us out of self-centeredness ... it fulfills our wish to lessen the pain of self-absorption and our wish to benefit others. ... Shantideva explains that our intention to free all beings from suffering can become irreversible, bringing benefit equal to the vastness of the sky. This happens when we no longer question the wisdom of thinking of others; we truly know this to be the source of indestructible happiness. Something shifts at the core of our being. ... This is the happiness of egolessness. It's the joy of realizing there's no prison; there are only very strong habits, and no sane reason for strengthening them further. In essence these habits are insubstantial. Moreover, there is no solid self-identity or separateness. We've invented it all. (Chodron 2005, 7–14)

This is one way to describe what's at the core of what I call the spiritual path: to be lifted out of self-centeredness, to lessen the pain of self-absorption (having recognized that it is painful), and to act for the benefit of others—realizing that dissolving the painful core of self-centeredness, and acting out of an open heart for the benefit of all, are actually one and the same thing. Is it clear how this spiritual process can merge, for some people, with social and political commitment? Aspiring to act for the benefit of all, relatively free from the prison of greed and self-obsessed fear, we may find it natural, even inevitable, to engage with movements to liberate the grievously oppressed, to transform structures that perpetuate deprivation and violence, to stop the destruction of the earth.

The eighth-century Buddhist poet Shantideva is a source of inspiration for those who believe that devotion to individual spiritual liberation and devotion to relieving suffering in the social-political world are united at the root. Take, for example, this stanza:

> All the violence, fear and suffering
> That exists in this world
> Comes from grasping at self.
> What is the use of this great monster for you?
> If you do not let the self go,
> There will be no end to suffering.
> Just as, if you do not release a flame from your hand,
> You can't stop it from burning your hand.[18]

The world is in the throes of tremendous suffering from preventable causes—poverty, inequality, hunger, prejudice, exploitation, disease, violence, war. Individual and collective action to alleviate the suffering of others issues naturally as compassionate and intelligent people respond to these circumstances. But many have perceived that outer-directed activism is only half the story. These problems are created in the first place by people who are driven by greed, fear, hate. Fires burning inside us cause us to ignite fires outside. Revolutionaries who fight to topple murderous, exploitative regimes often build new regimes that are murderous and exploitative. Inner and outer transformation depend on each other. Shantideva states this proposition convincingly. A Kabir *dohā* uses similar imagery:

> *I! I!* A terrible thing.
> Run from it if you can.
> Friend, how long will you keep
> fire wrapped in cotton?

But the relation between transforming the self and helping others isn't just a happy osmosis. There is tension—sometimes irreconcilable—between them. To truly investigate and transform the self has often seemed to imply renunciation of the world. And to understand and transform the world has often seemed to require a rejection of both institutional and introverted forms of religion. In some instances the problem is ontological, arising from a dualistic split between "material" and "spiritual," and the need to affirm one while denying the other. The problem is also practical: someone striving in either of these two fields often finds that she doesn't have time for the other, that the other entangles her and diverts her from her essential work. The other is dangerous. In a dualistic framework, the other may be evil.

Making Lenin Listen to Beethoven

In the historical unfolding of revolutionary politics, the subtlety seen in Gorky's portrayal of Lenin is usually lost. Rigid adherence to ideology may suck dry the springs of compassion and creativity. Materialism, perhaps conceived in the compassionate impulse to attend to the basic needs of all people, may lead to aridity and dehumanization. Artists, writers, and intellectuals, projected as enemies of the state, may be suppressed, imprisoned, tortured, killed. The generic human drive for power, parading in the guise of devotion to ideology and the state, corrupts sincere efforts to create a new order. Such developments have been seen in twentieth-century communist states such as the USSR, China, and Cambodia. This sort of thing happens in totalitarianism of the right as well. It also happens, in less spectacular and more insidious ways, in imperfect democracies throughout the world, prominently including the United States.

For German director Florian Henckel von Donnersmarck, the story about Lenin and the *Appassionata* became the inspiration for a film about East Germany—*The Lives of Others*, released in 2006.[19] Von Donnersmarck saw in the East German state the systematic stifling of artistic creativity, social trust, love, and compassion in the name of a sterile and ever more ruthless ideology, coupled with the usual corruption and lust of men (and occasionally women) in power. The central character is Captain Gerd Wiesler, a successful officer in the Stasi or secret police. He lives alone. We get a glimpse of the barely conscious ache of lovelessness in his life when he begs a prostitute who visits his apartment for a brief transaction to stay a little longer. She refuses. In the course of duty, Wiesler bugs the home of a leading theater director on whom a corrupt official is trying to pin evidence of disloyalty to the state. Wearing huge earphones, Wiesler listens for many hours to the lives of the playwright and his artist friends. He becomes privy to their discussions of literature, their playfulness and sorrow. He listens to the words of love and the sounds of lovemaking between the playwright and his actress girlfriend. He hears beautiful music. He hears Beethoven. And he undergoes a transformation.

Von Donnersmarck explains the genesis of his film in an interview:

> Lenin had few close personal friends and one of his closest friends ... was Maxim Gorky, the Russian writer. ... After Lenin's death Gorky wrote that Lenin had once told him ... something like this. ... The *Appassionata* is my favorite piece of music, Lenin says, but I don't want to listen to it anymore, because ... when I listen to it, it makes me want to stroke people's heads and tell them nice stupid things. But I have to smash those heads, bash them in without mercy in order to finish my revolution. ... I thought, so this is what Lenin feels like. Now let's see if we can find a way to force Lenin to listen to the *Appassionata*. Out of that I constructed this idea of a man just sitting there with earphones on his head, expecting that through these earphones he's going to hear words

> of his ideological enemies. But actually he's hearing music that is so beautiful that it ... makes him rethink that ideology. ... Lenin changed into a Stasi officer who's sitting in a surveillance center monitoring people. ... Who would be playing that kind of beautiful music if not artists? ... That was going to be the basic setting: a Stasi officer monitoring artists and changing through that close proximity with them.[20]

At the beginning of the film the Stasi officer and the state he serves represent the worst possible outcome of "Lenin's choice" between music and political orthodoxy. At the end the officer—catalyzed by listening with those big earphones, by exposure to art and love and to the lies and cruelty of the political system—has made another choice.

No Separation

To represent the view that the political and spiritual cannot and should not be separated in Kabir, I call on two of the most eloquent and passionate scholars of Kabir whom I met in my journeys—both city men with PhD degrees in literature, both preferring to do their public speaking and writing more in Hindi than in English: Purushottam Agrawal and Kapil Tiwari.

Agrawal shares the leftist antipathy to organized religion but refuses to surgically remove Kabir's spiritual expressions while embracing his humanism and social-political commentary. Both as a reader of poetry and as an observer of human experience, Agrawal will not disown Kabir's "transcendent yearnings":

> Again and again Kabir's poetry reminds us: between worldly and transcendent, inner and outer, social and spiritual, there is no opposition. To understand this non-opposition, there is no need to search "outside." If there is any way to get free of the incompleteness that haunts us, to be released from the habit of chopping our fullness into pieces, it will be through realization "within the body" [*ghaṭ bhītar*] of our human essence: "Search and you'll find it instantly, in a split second. / Kabir says, listen seeker: it's the breath of your breath." (Agrawal 2009a, 36)

Agrawal finds inner and outer not only not-opposed to each other in Kabir but also mutually dependent, each impossible without the other. He cites Kabir's phrase *bāhar bhītar sabad nirantar*—"the word [that resonates] endlessly inside and outside."

> To listen to the unbroken continuity of worldly and transcendent, outer and inner, social and spiritual, to listen constantly to the word resounding endlessly inside and outside and to live in accordance with their interdependence—this is what Kabir calls *ghaṭ sādhanā*, spiritual practice in the body. . . . His much-cited and much-praised social consciousness and social criticism develop from his spiritual search. Kabir's *ghaṭ sādhanā* throws his revolutionary enthusiasts into great embarrassment; but without it, his social consciousness and criticism are impossible. When Kabir looks at society, he sees it through the eyes of that dream which is revealed to him by *ghaṭ sādhanā*. (Agrawal 2009a, 37)

Addressing an audience at a Kabir festival in Bangalore in 2009, he speaks more personally:

> If you look at the poetry, it will be very, very difficult—to my mind impossible—to make a distinction between a spiritual and political Kabir. . . . When I say the word "spiritual," please first translate that in your mind to Hindi, Sanskrit, Kannada, whatever, into *adhyātmik*. Don't take it in the sense in which it is used in contemporary English.[21] In my way of approaching Kabir, you cannot really make a distinction between spiritual and political, between universal and specific. You can be conscious of the specific manifestations of the universal. You can be conscious of political moments. But you cannot say, as many of my friends insist—look here, we are interested in Kabir only so far as he is critical of Hindu bigotry or Muslim bigotry or of caste order or of Brahminism or of Brahmin supremacy, and all that. The rest of Kabir we are not concerned with. Of course you can do that. I mean, nobody can stop you from doing that, but I think you would be doing an injustice to the poetic praxis of Kabir. . . . A certain component [of Kabir] is attractive to us because we are beset with some problems in which we find Kabir can be used

> as an associate or as a tool. Let me repeat I have nothing against that. My only point is this: please do not reduce Kabir only to a social reformer or only to a prop in our political activity. Kabir is, and many poets for that matter are, much bigger and much more complex than that. (Agrawal 2009c)

We met Kapil Tiwari at length in chapter 3. For many years the director of the Adivasi Lok Kala Parishad (Institute for Folk and Tribal Arts) in Bhopal, he is a passionate advocate of the arts cultivated by ordinary people, and he has an intense personal connection with Kabir. The following is part of an interview conducted and filmed by Shabnam Virmani in 2004. Tiwari firmly resists the attempt to separate political and spiritual/religious (he does not distinguish between the latter two terms) in Kabir.

SHABNAM VIRMANI (SV): Do people from different positions in society selectively appropriate Kabir based on their own aims?

KAPIL TIWARI (KT): Absolutely, people make use of Kabir to fulfill their own agendas. This has nothing really to do with Kabir himself. Revolutionaries find certain parts of Kabir useful, right? When he's attacking the pandit or criticizing the mullah, right? Their agenda is fulfilled with such poetry, it confirms their ideology. This aspect of Kabir's poetry and its truth serves their agenda very well.

But this is not the point of Kabir's criticism. He insists that if there is such a thing as religion [dharma], it lies within. All the various forms of external religion are not to be trusted, not authentic. They lead people astray. This is why Kabir criticizes temple and mosque, pandit and mullah. When social movements pick and choose among Kabir's words for their own purposes, surprisingly they resist Kabir's spirituality, Kabir's truth, Kabir's transcendent experience. They don't trust those words of Kabir. It's a strange irony. The part of Kabir that seems poetically interesting and important to them is where he sharply criticizes gross religion and its profiteers. That is useful for them. But when Kabir says, "I am listening to the boundless unstruck sound," they get uncomfortable. They don't even want to mention this Kabir. I am speaking to you of an integral Kabir, a Kabir we can know in his wholeness, including both his social criticism and his spirituality.

SV: And these are two aspects of one reality. They are totally connected.

KT: They are joined together! They cannot be separated, because whoever enters into true religion will simply have to criticize those kinds of people who, with no experience of their own, just set up their business in the market of religion. They use the gods, they use holy books, they use mantras, they use worship and ritual. They turn religion into a lie, they cut religion off from the truth.

SV: And it's fundamentally hypocritical—the same religion that declares that the supreme being exists in everyone then propagates the caste system, calls people sweepers and untouchables, and persecutes them.

KT: Shabnam, I would say it in these words—that from time immemorial in various religions, it is only such people who have held sway: the ones for whom religion is a livelihood, a job, not a thirst, not a search. So once every few centuries when a man like Kabir is born, he has to take on these people. Tulsi had to collide with them, Mira had to collide with them, and Kabir had to collide with them. After a genuine spiritual experience, social poetry criticizing such people is not only possible, it is inevitable. But the point of that social poetry, its core, is that it arises from the ground of spirituality in order to safeguard spiritual truth. It's not just a frivolous criticism of somebody. It's an attack on the politics of religion, not religion itself.

SV: On one hand revolutionaries have selectively appropriated Kabir. On the other hand, upper-caste Brahminical Hinduism has incorporated him into its fold. Would you agree with this?

KT: To a great extent it is true. The point is that priest-dominated religious shops cannot run for too long without a true experience or a truly spiritual person. Tulsi was persecuted [by the Brahmins] in Kashi. Today it's a fact that 80% of the religious shops run because of Tulsi.

A person like Kabir is born only rarely, maybe once in many centuries. When he's alive, Brahmins, pandits, and big scholars of scripture attack him brutally. As soon as he's gone, they want to use Kabir to make their shops credible. They know that Kabir's existence was a very rare thing, and it can be used to lend credibility to their religion, their version of truth, their temples and sects. It's quite amazing how, when Kabir was alive, the priest-dominated society couldn't tolerate him. Yet for centuries afterward, they keep peddling their merchandise in the name of his truth. The fact is that both sides have misused Kabir. Social activists used Kabir for their own ends, and the same is true for those on the spiritual side, who quote and cite Kabir not so that the truth of Kabir may spread, but to gain legitimacy for themselves.[22]

Taking Lenin Seriously

We can say that there's no problem between inner and outer, that they are wedded to each other. We can argue this convincingly, based on texts by Kabir and others, and on our own intuition. But there is a problem. "Inner work" can eclipse social reality. It is a high, a way of getting drunk (think of all the songs about *naśhā*, drunken joy). Who wants to attend to the ugly, messy, intransigent world when a crystalline radiance is expanding within us, making us indescribably happy?

The lord gave me a marijuana drink, what a potion he gave me to drink!
Redness rises in my eyes, the guru gave me a drink.

I drank from the cup and went mad, staggered around like a drunkard.
The locks of a thousand lifetimes sprang open,
my body was filled with light. Redness rises in my eyes.. . . .

In every bush and tree, everything living and unmoving, my lord is blooming.
Wherever I look, no space is empty. Wherever I look, no place is void.
Every body is utterly filled. Redness rises in my eyes.[23]

Spiritual seekers often turn away from the world in order to get inner freedom. Their quest calls on them to let go, to give up entanglements. They need a quiet place to practice. As Lenin noticed, a taste of that transcendent beauty and joy can take away your will to fight. Spiritual insight undermines the oppositional sense of self and other. No one appears to be your enemy. A profound acceptance creeps through your cells.

Drink! A cascade of nectar pours from the sky.
One drop fills a thirsty person's vessel. You can't even dream
of that taste! How to explain this, and to whom?
One drop, and you're home.[24]

The "spiritual" call draws us to enter a state of deep concentration, one-pointedness, no longer painfully fragmented. In these states, the distraction and turmoil of the world recede. We may deliberately turn away from the turmoil, shut it out. Nothing must be allowed to interrupt this incalculably valuable experience for which our whole being longs. One of the limbs of classical eight-limb yoga is *pratyāhāra*, closing the doors of the senses.

Monks and yogis go into isolation and radically simplify their needs to attain this. Their withdrawal from society is evidence of the tension between the complications of social engagement and the need to create special circumstances for attaining deep states of consciousness. World renunciation and asceticism have strong histories in Hinduism, Buddhism, and Jainism, India's three ancient and still flourishing religions. In ancient India people argued, sometimes vehemently, about the competing calls of spiritual and social commitment. Patrick Olivelle has assembled a wonderful set of passages from Hindu and Buddhist sources under the title "Ascetic Withdrawal or Social Engagement" (Lopez 1995, 533ff.). Some texts urge total withdrawal from the world in the interests of spiritual attainment while others predict gruesome karmic consequences for those who do not fulfill their social responsibilities. Over the last two millennia, Indian thinkers have sought ways to harmonize renunciation with social engagement despite their apparent incompatibility. The *Gītā*'s *karma yoga*, the Dharma Shastras' four stages of life, the Sikhs' insistence on householder life and refusal to have an ascetic branch, and the location of many bhakti saints among common working people are famous examples. But these examples are as much evidence of the extreme tension as they are resolutions of it.

D. R. Nagaraj comments insightfully on why social criticism by premodern yogis and mystics does not necessarily translate into fuel for twentieth-century social justice activists:

> [A] whole range of indigenous yogis and sadhus, for whom colonialism hardly mattered either as a transitory phase or as a force to be resisted, had tried to deny, quite forcefully, the centrality of caste hierarchy in the scheme of things. In this regard, Shishunala Sheriff and Kaivara Narayanappa, the two yogis of Karnataka, and the Satnamis and the Mahima movement of North India come to mind immediately. Apparently, the chief reason for their inability to influence historical events in any significant way was that they did not either see or present the problem (untouchability, in this instance) as a political one, which was necessary for the

> regeneration of Indian society as a whole. To be precise, they did not see their society as part of a nation-state. For these indigenous radicals, the task of fighting the caste system had been one of the spiritual requirements of their tradition ... They were the conscience of smaller communities. ... their tradition had always treated temporal power as something alien, on which very little or no positive influence could be exerted" (Nagaraj 2011, 24–25).

Once I asked a Dalit activist in India whether those who had followed Ambedkar in converting to Buddhism showed much interest in meditation. He said that some groups were practicing meditation, but others resisted it, saying, "They're trying to take away our anger!" Dalit scholar Harish Wankhede, whom I came to know at Stanford University, put the point more sharply in a Facebook post on Dec. 20, 2014:

> Spirituality is the fodder of self-engrossed individuals. It only closes our eyes not to see the everyday vices and crimes organized by the religious mafia. Similarly, peace is ... rhetoric in democracy that disallows us to take radical moves against the brutal and corrupt political regimes. Sermons for spirituality and peace are the powerful tools of the ruling elites to curtail our revolutionary aspirations and to keep us mere recipients of doles given by never-existent God and corrupt political leadership. Only a critical rejection of such sovereign ideas may bring any good to the worsening society and polity.

Kancha Ilaiah, whose book *Why I Am Not a Hindu* argues for the historical and cultural distinctness of Dalit-Bahujans from Hindus, overturns the spiritual meaning commonly associated with a famous verse from the *Bhagavad-gītā*: "You are entitled to action [or work] but not to the fruits of action [or work]" (*Gītā* 2.47).[25] This verse is fundamental to the teaching of *nişhkāma karma*—performing one's ethical duty, or appropriate action, free of narrow attachment to the desired results. I have always seen *nişhkāma karma* as a profoundly valuable teaching. Ilaiah begs to differ. He points out that Dalit-Bahujans are closely identified with and give positive value to physical labor, unlike advocates of Brahminical orthodoxy, who regard such labor as polluting and beneath them. How useful it is, then, for the upper castes, identified with their own "purity," to instruct their classes of servants and despised outcasts that they have a right and duty to perform work, but no right to enjoy or possess the fruits of their work.

At a Kabir Panth gathering, I heard a guru speak to a group of devotees about how to concentrate on reciting the divine name. He said, "If outside they are shooting guns, let them shoot. Your work is to be totally immersed in the name. Lose yourself in the name." I was horrified, as this was soon after the 2002 communal massacres in Gujarat. I deeply disapproved of the idea that pursuing personal bliss was a good reason to ignore the suffering and violence close at hand—especially when the violence was perpetrated in the name of religion.

Lenin (along with others in Marxian traditions) is deeply wary of any call to a private ecstasy that blurs the analytical intelligence and undermines the will to carry on class struggle amid concrete political-economic realities. He warns us not only against spirituality but against music! Yet his sad smile and expressive wrinkling of the eyes, as described by Gorky, show that he was sensitive to the "hellishly difficult" nature of the task.

Religious Folk Music and Politics: An American Case

In March 2007, Bernice Johnson Reagon came to Stanford University. Musician, activist, and scholar, Reagon was deeply involved in the American civil rights movement; was founder-director of "Sweet Honey in the Rock," a popular women's *a cappella* ensemble specializing in music related to the black heritage, with which she performed from 1973 to 2004; and is author of many books and articles. I attended her Stanford presentation, called "Song Culture of the Civil Rights Movement." It was an amalgam of history, images, audio tracks, and live performance.

Throughout the program I was thinking about Lenin's problem with the *Appassionata* and Indian leftist/secularist reservations about the *sants* and Sufis. They might love the music, yet they found it dangerous and felt they had to shut it down at a certain point. For most African American participants, the civil rights movement was steeped in the life of the black church. Martin Luther King was a Baptist minister whose Christian faith was inseparable from his other commitments. They did not feel that they needed to shut down either the religious or the musical and emotional elements of their culture for the sake of the struggle.

At the end of her presentation, when Reagon invited questions, I raised my hand. "Some people think that passionate, joyful music, especially combined with religious sentiment, is bad for revolutionary movements. Lenin said something about this. There was a fear that it would lead to escapism, excessive indulgence in emotion, forgetting about the world. Do you think there's a danger that this kind of music can wreck your political edge?"

Reagon stood like a tree in the middle of the stage and looked straight at me. "We felt what we were doing was related to something much greater than us. The music was a direct line to that. When we sang together, we were tapping into an infinite source of power that was running through us. It gave us courage, joy, unity, and the strength to carry on." When someone else asked a related question, she stood still for a moment, then started to sing "Kumbaya," quietly at first. Audience members joined in. Many of us had been part of that era. Gradually people began standing up, swaying, linking arms in the familiar chorus. Reagon sang the verses in a crescendo of energy, improvising on the closing syllables, her rich and colorful voice ranging up and down the scales in unexpected melodies, carrying us along till we joined with ever more enthusiasm on the chorus. Thus, instead of discussing the power of song theoretically, she made us experience it.[26]

For those of us who had sung those songs during the civil rights period and in later movements for peace and justice, the singing struck immediately at our hearts, cutting away distraction and fear, reminding us of the best things we ever did, the most selfless moments we ever had, the best access to the kind of love that King called *agape* love and that Gandhi said was another word for *ahimsa*. King had observed, "The freedom songs are playing a strong and vital role in our struggle. They give the people a new courage and a sense of unity. . . . They keep alive a faith, a radiant hope in the future, particularly in our most trying hours" (W. Martin 2005, 48).

Negro spirituals have a lot in common with bhajans. These devotional songs, composed by African Americans who embraced Christianity, go back to slavery times and continue to be popular today. Using stories from the Bible, expressing deep personal feeling, evoking intense relationships with persons on earth or in heaven, praying or dreaming of better times to come, they speak simultaneously of religious faith and human experience. They run the gamut of all possible emotions, expressing sorrow, jubilation, weariness, despair, awe, fear, hope, love, visions of liberation, and determination to fight. They do all this with poetic imagination and musical genius. It is folk music, without the complexity and refinement of classical musics that require years of training. But like the Kabir music of Malwa and Rajasthan, it is brilliant and compelling.

Scholars have discussed the social and psychological implications of Negro spirituals, just as we have been doing with Kabir bhajans. Did songs of faith and dreams of heaven foster passivity and resignation to their abysmal existence as slaves? Did the emotional expression and physical release of their singing sessions serve as a safety valve, providing temporary pleasure and relief but robbing them of their will to resist or to analyze the material roots of their oppression?

Almost unanimously, scholars have affirmed that from the earliest times, the spirituals reflected a double consciousness: on one hand an intense religious faith articulated in the idiom of an Africanized Christianity; on the other hand, a recognition that the stories of Israelites escaping from slavery, of heroic individuals delivered from torture and murder, of heavenly places where everyone would have shoes, were also about *this* world and their aspirations for freedom in it.

When Israel was in Egypt's land
let my people go.
Oppressed so hard they could not stand
let my people go.
Go down Moses, way down in Egypt land,
Tell ol' Pharaoh
let my people go.

***

Didn't my Lord deliver Daniel, deliver Daniel, deliver Daniel,
Didn't my Lord deliver Daniel, then why not every man?
He delivered Daniel from the lion's den,
Jonah from the belly of the whale,
He delivered the children from the fiery furnace,
then why not every man?

***

I got shoes, you got shoes,
all God's children got shoes.
When I get to heaven gonna put on my shoes,
gonna walk all over God's heaven, heaven, heaven.

Everybody talkin' 'bout heaven ain't goin' there, heaven, heaven,
gonna walk all over God's heaven.

***

Steal away, steal away, steal away to Jesus!
Steal away, steal away home,
I ain't got long to stay here.

In the nineteenth century, as slave insurrections and escapes mounted, the conscious use of spirituals as code for resistance increased. Clearly, enslaved Africans employed spirituals and other folksongs as secret coded communications, announcing plans for escape, revolt and clandestine meetings, or cheering on comrades in battle.

An example of a song composed for one purpose, but used secretly for other, masked purposes, is the familiar spiritual "Wade in the Water." This song was created to accompany the rite of baptism, but Harriet Tubman used it to communicate to fugitives escaping to the North that they should be sure to "wade in the water" in order to throw bloodhounds off their track. An improvised version of this song when it was used for this purpose was:

Jordan's water is chilly and cold,
God's gonna trouble the water;
It chills the body but not the soul,
God's gonna trouble the water.

Wade in the water;
Wade in the water children.
Wade in the water;
God's gonna trouble the water.

If you get there before I do,
God's gonna trouble the water,
Tell all my friends I'm comin' too.

Tubman's and others' improvisations on already existing spirituals, employing them clandestinely in the multilayered struggle for freedom, were repeated at many times and places. (Jones 2005, 50, 54)

We must emphasize that, with this rising political consciousness, the meaning of the songs did not change from spiritual to political. It was always, and would always remain, both.

> [Harding] has shown us, convincingly, that the signs of active struggle were present from the onset of African captivity, flowing like a river toward the ultimate, certain goal of complete freedom and justice. . . . At the same time they retained complete faith in the endorsement and guidance of spiritual forces larger than themselves. In their African-derived frame of reference, there was no contradiction between this absolute faith in the divine and the concomitant assumption of responsibility for personal and collective action. (ibid., 44)

At one point in the splendid book that I have been citing, Arthur Jones imagines a gathering of present-day African Americans with their ancestors from both America and Africa.

> We are now aware of the collective voice of the ancestors, singing to each of us in the sound chambers of our individual spirits. As we begin to hear the melodies and words of the songs within us, we find ourselves preparing to join in the singing, gesturing to our children . . . we begin singing. Our sound grows in intensity and we are now one large chorus, chanting in multiple rhythms and harmonies: "Sometimes I feel like a motherless child . . . I'm troubled in mind . . . Were you there when they crucified my Lord?" The sound of our music continues to expand, finally filling the room; we are shouting! We sing one song after another; we feel our individual spirits intermingling. It is a chilling, ecstatic experience. (ibid., 39)

No fear of bliss here!

In the 1950s and 1960s, use of spirituals in the political arena took another step. "During the Civil Rights Movements our freedom songs no longer operated in code," writes Bernice Johnson Reagon (2001, 3). They tinkered with the words of old songs (as is common in folk traditions), continuing to play on the ambiguity of the inner and outer meanings of peace, freedom, liberation, devotion, and struggle. People rallying, marching, going to jail, risking their lives on "freedom rides" that challenged segregation on Greyhound buses, sang songs full of spirit. For many people the songs were still God-centered, associated with church and with the history of enslaved ancestors, but that did not detract from their power in this world. For those who were not religious, the songs were still powerful and stirring.

As an example of conscious alteration, Reagon discusses the song that gives her book its title, "If You Don't Go, Don't You Hinder Me." In the line, "I'm on my way to Canaan land," they changed "Canaan" to "freedom." This made it nonsectarian and clearly applicable to the present struggle. But she also explains sympathetically what Canaan meant in the stories and sermons of the black Baptist churches she attended in her childhood:

> [It] was about a life beyond this experience we were having on earth. . . . an "over yonder," an "up yonder," an afterlife—"across our Jordan River," on "the other side of death." Those stories and sermons held those songs for us until we began to fight against racism in this country and then the same songs, old songs, became new—lining up for use in the struggle, change a word here or there and there you have it—a freedom song, a new instrument for the struggle for freedom. (Reagon 2001, 4–5)

This Canaan, this "over Jordan" about which we hear, for example, in the beautiful spiritual "Deep River," was a land where everyone would be clean, happy, and free: "When I get to heaven, gonna put on my shoes, gonna walk all over God's heaven." It was a land where degradation and deprivation were lifted, and where enslaved people who had been sold away from their family members would be reunited: "Soon I will be done with the troubles of the world, troubles of the world, troubles of the world, Soon I will be done with the troubles of the world, I'm going to live with God. No more weeping and a-wailing . . . I'm going to meet my mother . . . father . . . sister . . . brother."

We may be reminded of Satlok for the Kabir Panthis, Begumpura for the followers of Raidas, the *amar deśh* or *deśh divānā* (country of no-death or of divine madness) in Kabir's songs.[27] We may hear the resonance between a black American song and a Kabir song that both start, "I'm on my way":

> I'm on my way to freedom land. I'm on my way to freedom land.
> I'm on my way to freedom land, I'm on my way, praise God, I'm on my way.

If you don't go, don't hinder me. If you don't go, don't hinder me.
If you don't go, don't hinder me, I'm on my way, praise God, I'm on my way!

I asked my sister, come and go with me, I asked my brother, come and go with me,
I asked my friend, come and go with me, I'm on my way, praise God, I'm on my way!

***

I'm on my way
to meet the guru, on my way
to meet the lord.
I'm smashed, completely drunk, my friend,
about to meet the lord.

About to shed my greed and grasping,
living free.
Shedding crimes, tricks and lies,
living free.
This world-ocean pulled me down;
I've won the victory.
A joyous meeting
waits for me.

The spiritual quest is difficult and calls for extraordinary devotion, inner strength, and courage. Kabir expresses this in songs such as "*Lagan kaṭhin hai mere bhāī*," "Holding on is difficult, my brother" (translated in chapter 2). Civil rights activists, changing "I" to "we" in an old spiritual, invoked the same courage and devotion in their multileveled songs:

We shall not, we shall not be moved.
We shall not, we shall not be moved.
Just like a tree that's planted by the water,
We shall not be moved.[28]

Kabir frequently reminds us of a great light within everyone—usually understood as the presence of ultimate reality or God. People in the civil rights movement, like Chhotu in Indore (chapter 6), saw this light not only as the presence of God but also as a source of tremendous power to stand up against oppression and prejudice.

> This little light of mine, I'm gonna let it shine,
> let it shine, let it shine let it shine.
> Everywhere I go, I'm gonna let it shine. ...
> Way down in Montgomery, I'm gonna let it shine. ...
> Right there in the jailhouse, I'm gonna let it shine. ...

Even while "shining" fiercely in the political arena, many civil rights activists still believed that the light was the presence of God. They had no need to choose. Each side energized the other.

A perfect mix of religious and political references appears in the following song, which ranges from biblical characters in jail to the chains associated with slavery to the twentieth-century civil rights movement. The original chorus, "Keep your hand on the plow," was changed in this twentieth-century adaptation to "Keep your eyes on the prize." Remember that throughout the song, as in a Kabir bhajan, there are many repetitions of the refrain, "Keep your eyes on the prize, hold on." I have shown only two.

> Paul and Silas bound in jail
> Had no money for to go their bail
> Paul and Silas thought they was lost
> Dungeon shook and the chains come off
> Freedom's name is mighty sweet
> And soon we're gonna meet
> I got my hand on the gospel plow
> Won't take nothing for my journey now.
> *Hold on, hold on, keep your eyes on the prize, hold on.*
>
> Only chain that a man can stand
> Is that chain o' hand on hand
> I'm gonna board that big Greyhound
> Carry the love from town to town
> Now only thing I did was wrong
> Stayin' in the wilderness too long
> The only thing we did was right
> Was the day we started to fight.
> *Hold on, hold on, keep your eyes on the prize, hold on.*

Another parallel between the religious songs of the black church and Indian bhakti is the continued vitality of oral tradition even amid writing and copyrighting. Charles A. Tindley, in the early twentieth century, was the first great composer of the genre known as gospel music.

> Most of the time when we sang these songs, we did not acknowledge Tindley as composer, because the songs came to us via the oral tradition without Tindley's name being connected. … The singer of a Tindley composition often sang the song as a church song and sometimes seemed to think it was of her or his own creation. This may seem fraudulent with our Western sense of copyright; however, within the Africa-based tradition it is understandable. Within the Black tradition one is not really considered a singer until one has found one's own way of presenting a work. … "Stand by me" performed by harmonica virtuoso Elder Roma Wilson, the Five Blind Boys of Alabama, the Caravans, and the Violinaires, are all original compositions based on the Tindley composition. They are singing Tindley's song transformed by their own creative interpretations. (Reagon 2001, 19)

Tindley himself drew from the oral tradition in writing the songs he then copyrighted, for example in his 1901 composition "I'll Overcome Someday." The anonymous church song "I'll Be Alright" was probably a source for him. Thus the composer Tindley, "operating within the African American oral tradition, may have drawn from his traditional core as much as he gave to it" (ibid., 20). Tindley's version, further adapted, emerged as the anthem of the entire civil rights movement and eventually spread throughout the world. With an altered tune and a change from "I" to "we," it became "We Shall Overcome." I have often heard this song in India, with the Hindi words *ham honge kāmyāb ek din.*

We conclude this excursion into black American "bhajans" with a sampling of lyrics from six songs that ring with the mingling energies of music, spirituality, and liberation.

Over my head I hear music in the air,
Over my head I hear music in the air,
Over my head I hear music in the air,
There must be a God somewhere.

***

Sometimes I am tossed and driven, Lord,
Sometimes I don't know where to roam.

I've heard of a city called heaven
I've started to make it my home.

***

Sometimes I feel like a motherless child
Sometimes I feel like a motherless child
Sometimes I feel like a motherless child
A long way from home. a long way from home.

***

There is a balm in Gilead to make the wounded whole,
There is a balm in Gilead to heal the sin-sick soul.
Sometimes I feel discouraged and think my work's in vain.
But then the holy spirit revives my soul again.

***

Oh freedom, oh freedom, oh freedom over me!
And before I'll be a slave I'll be buried in my grave
and go home to my Lord and be free.

***

Give me your hand, give me your hand,
all I want is the love of God.
Give me your hand, give me your hand,
we must be lovin' at God's command.[29]

Ways of Being Political with Kabir

Kabir has never been used as deliberately and comprehensively as the Negro spirituals were used in movements for justice and liberation. Nevertheless, we can summarize various political understandings and deployments of Kabir that turned up in the present research. Such understandings play out in different ways with different groups—rural Indians, urban Indians, internationals, intellectuals, artists, upper castes, lower castes, women, men. And of course there are many differences within these groups.

Prahladji is political in that, when expounding on stage, he often highlights Kabir's social-political messages: the sharp criticism of caste, of religious sectarianism and prejudice, of public greed and hypocrisy. But he does this in a general way. He doesn't comment specifically on political events, parties, leaders, movements. I never heard him refer to the Gujarat carnage of 2002. When he mentions the delusions of *mandir-masjid-gurdwārā* (Hindu temple–Muslim mosque–Sikh house of worship), many listeners will think of the physical and political battles over the "disputed site" in Ayodhya. But he doesn't speak of it.

Shabnam decided to make this association explicit in her film *Had-Anhad/Bounded-Boundless*. In fact, it was the horrific communal violence in Gujarat in 2002 that moved her to start the Kabir Project in the first place. *Had-Anhad* opens with a scene in Ayodhya and a conversation with locals who celebrated and had participated in the demolition of the Babri mosque in December 1992. They expressed militant support of the Hindu god Ram, hostility to Muslims, and determination to build a Ram temple on the site of the razed mosque. Shabnam juxtaposed this "Ram" with the "Ram" of Kabir. "Who is Ram?" her narrative voice asked, and the film explored the question among Kabir Panthis, Muslims, and Hindus, mostly featuring Sufi singers of Kabir in India and Pakistan. The opening scene caused some anxiety among friends who watched the rough cut. One close adviser suggested that it should be removed.[30]

Narayanji is political in the life-transforming seriousness with which he took the issues raised by Eklavya's Kabir *manch* in the 1990s, and the consistency with which he maintained the changes in his worldview and behavior that began then (detailed in chapter 6). He stopped observing caste differences in local Dalit hierarchies, he stopped depending on deities, he stopped calling Brahmins for rituals, and he started living out the message of equality by committing to educating girls in his family and encouraging them to work in the world. He also led the way in encouraging and training women Kabir singers—a surprising innovation in the Kabir culture of the region.

Suresh Patel and Chhotu Bharti in Indore are directly oriented to social-political concerns (see chapter 6). For them, Kabir's message of radical equality implies working actively on behalf of those groups and classes that have least power. Through their *Kabīr jan vikās samuh* they set up educational programs for migrants, after-school meeting places for children in poor neighborhoods, and village festivals that combined singing with consciousness-raising.

Higher-profile movements that resist oppression related to caste, religion, ethnicity, gender, and poverty occasionally use songs or organize concerts in the course of their political activities. But they do not adapt songs of Kabir and other *sants* and Sufis in a way comparable to the American civil rights movement's use of Negro spirituals. The reasons must include those to which Alok Rai introduced us. Left political appropriation stops short of embracing Kabir's inwardness, as the left is generally unsympathetic toward religion, suspicious of transcendence, fearful of bliss. A counterexample was the Sadbhav Yatra in Uttar Pradesh in 1993, following the destruction of the Babri mosque and outbreak of violence and bigotry against Muslims (see chapter 6). Organizers from the famous leftist theater group IPTA (Indian People's Theatre Association) invited the Kabir singers of Malwa for the weeklong traveling political show, and those singers marched at the head, churning up joy and inspiration all the way. Here the insight of German film director von Donnersmarck is relevant. The Sadbhav Yatra was organized by theater people. When it comes to sustaining our full humanity amid tough political struggle—permitting reason, emotion, imagination, and faith to exist all together—artists are better than dry ideologues.[31]

Conversations with Friends

At the beginning of this book, introducing the study of oral traditions, I said that to know Kabir we have to know people. We conclude, then, with a series of personal conversations that explore the political/spiritual question.

In Valley School, Bangalore, 2005

Shabnam interviewed Krishna Nath, a writer and traveler who had been engaged in some of the pivotal political struggles of India in the twentieth century. He was at the forefront of those who resisted Indira Gandhi's 1975–77 Emergency, which had been a shocking move toward dictatorial rule.[32]

> I came from a family burning in the fire of revolution. More than half my life I spent in the socialist movement—in jails, villages,

universities, wandering in the Palamu forests in Bihar. We felt that if the economic structure would change, there would be a change in consciousness, in literature and culture. We felt that we must put every ounce of our life energy into this. First independence, then later a struggle to remove a single family's dynastic rule. When that developed we felt a certain hopelessness. But we struggled against it. I was the one who suggested the slogan *Indirā hatāo, deśh bachāo* ["Remove Indira, save the country"]. But even then, the change and reform that we wanted both *bāhar* and *bhītar*, outside and inside—it came neither outside nor within our minds. In those days we used to feel that turning away from the struggles of the real world, sitting in meditative poses and listening to *anahad nād* [the unstruck sound], was escapism. Those who were immersed in *anahad nād* probably felt: these idiots are wasting their time and breaking their heads, trying to bring change in the outer world. We thought that changing the external world would change people's minds. Today looking back, I don't see a *bhītar* and *bāhar* contradiction at all. Outside and inside are just the trickery of language [*shabda kī māyā*].

Between Bhopal and Dewas, Madhya Pradesh, August 2004

One of my most memorable conversations on "political and spiritual" happened in a car, on the day Shabnam and I ran into R. N. Syag by chance in Bhopal. We hired a taxi together to go to Dewas, three hours away. Syag-b*hāī* was introduced in chapter 6 in the context of Eklavya's K*abīr bhajan evam vichār manch* (platform for singing and discussing Kabir). Here is the part of our conversation that belongs in this chapter. Shabnam had her camera, so it was all recorded. The speakers are Shabnam (SV), Syag-*bhāī* (RNS), and me (LH). We spoke in Hindi.

SV: In the process of the Kabir *manch*, did you personally have any change in your religious or spiritual views?

RNS: That's a tough question. What kind of thing is this spirituality? (*Yeh adhyātmik kyā chīz hai?*) I didn't understand "spiritual" then, and I still don't. I relate to people. For me, happiness is based on people forming relationships and having faith in each other. Listening to bhajans is fine, we can enjoy that. But where do you draw a line and say that something is religious or spiritual? I see religion as consisting mainly of externally imposed dogmas. What interests me is how people form relationships, what barriers arise between them, how relationships get broken. This is what I want to understand. For me, there was never any religious or spiritual question about Kabir. If other people are spiritual or religious, I have no objection. People seek meaning in their lives in various ways, and they go wherever they find satisfaction.

SV: So for you religion is basically a negative thing?

RNS: I feel that when people are lacking a support system, when there is a vacuum in their lives, then they get help from religion. . . . Different people will define spirituality in different ways. But I find satisfaction on the human level—from work, family, friends, one's whole circle. If there is any problem, any painful situation, we analyze it. This or that is the reason, and this is the solution. We won't find the solution in some other world. If a poor man doesn't have a strong base, he might turn in that direction. Maybe even rich men don't have so much social strength. I don't know many rich people so I can't really guess.

LH: Many Kabir poems speak of the Lord or the unstruck sound. What do you think of all those bhajans?

RNS: My friend Suresh Patel has gone into that in greater depth. As I keep saying, my main interest is in social work, the physical world, and amid this, people and their struggles. So the world of the unstruck sound where some other kind of happiness is supposed to come—I have no experience of it and no desire to experience it. Some people who came to the *manch* thought these things were important. They would say—you are studying in primary school, you haven't had the pleasure of going to university, so how would you know anything about that joy? I have no answer to this kind of thing.

Previously in the villages people weren't getting vaccinations or immunizations. For smallpox they believed in a mother goddess, they worshiped her as Shakti, right? But when the disease was entirely eliminated the goddess was no longer relevant, and people stopped worshiping her.[33] Gradually people come to understand that the cause of all our problems, our illnesses, our poverty, is a system that people have created. Who are those people, and why did they want to create that system? My interest is in understanding this. I saw limitations in the *manch*. A number of young people were also interested in these [rational, scientific] questions. But there were many people whose interests were in the spiritual line. Some said, don't keep raising these questions. If you do, the pleasure of bhajans will be spoiled, and the discussion of these questions will also be spoiled. So we created another circle—*Dr. Ambedkar vichār manch.* Some people went both for the Kabir bhajans and for the Ambedkar *manch.* Some people went to one and not the other. In the Ambedkar *manch,* there was more analysis. What are our problems, what is their root cause, what role does the system play, why don't our systems work? We invited people to give talks and lead discussions. This made sense to me, because the social world is made by human beings. The structure of the family, the structure of society, of caste—only human beings can change them.

LH: You have asked where we find satisfaction in life, and you answer that we find it through work, friends, family, and through acting with our communities to solve real problems in the world. Very good. We face problems in the real world, like education, political rights, and so on. This is a very rational view. Yet within human beings there are elements that are not rational. Many people have internal problems that seem to be out of their control. They want to understand themselves. Why do we do things that we know are not good to do? Why are we not happy? Why are we so fearful? Why do we feel a lack of love? We would like our actions in to be based on love. We would like our behavior to arise from love. But it's not like that. Why? This becomes a kind of inner search.

RNS: All right. What will be your method of searching? Will it be psychology, or neurology? Whatever your method, it will have its own system. If it's a spiritual search, I have no objection. If someone finds happiness in that way, it's fine with me. But the body is our instrument, it is the basis for our finding happiness. Today in this country and in this world, when millions of people don't have their basic bodily needs met, when they're dying like flies before our eyes, if you say "I'm off on a quest for spiritual happiness," I can only say that this is not the way that I would get happiness. . . . Diverse viewpoints are good. If someone gets happiness and energy from religion, if it's useful to them, I don't say it's a bad thing. Everyone's experience is legitimate.

We can compare research on diseases. As I was saying, fifty years ago people believed that the goddess Shakti controlled disease. Even today in villages people often say something has happened to the soul [*ātmā*]. Someone else can say that the disease is a psychiatric or neurological problem. Whatever the method, it should be less mystified. It should be available to all, not limited to you or me.

LH: Kabir says, *Dukh meṇ sumiran sab kare, sukh meṇ kare na koī*. Everyone takes up spiritual practice when they're suffering, no one does it when they're happy. There was suffering in my life thirty years ago. I was searching. Did I need a doctor? A psychiatrist? Gurus? Lovers? I tried a lot of things, but nothing worked. My life was a mess. Even before things reached such a crisis, I was attracted to this kind of search. Where would I find a world view and a practice that would enable me to recognize and understand myself, especially the ways in which I had tied myself up inside and lost my freedom? How could I get liberated [*mukt*] from something if I didn't understand it? I'm not talking about the big religious liberation [*mukti*], release from the cycle of birth and death. But in this life, how could I get free from these problems? I heard about Buddhism and started doing a Buddhist form of meditation. I learned a lot from that. You may say, and it may be true, that this is an activity for the leisure classes. But I couldn't get away from it. My own behavior was destroying me. Why was I doing this? It seemed I had no control over it.

SV: This is also relevant to our relationship to society. If you're destroying yourself, your mind and heart become very constricted. You can't do anything for others.

LH: Yes, if I have no love for myself, how will I love others?

RNS: There can be various causes for this. Our childhood, socialization, family composition, school structure, local environment. There is no reason why we have to look beyond this world for an answer. I'm saying that whatever we are today is created by *this* world.

LH: I'm not saying that the solution is outside this world. But the problem I'm describing is also internal, and it's very deep.

RNS: It may be deep, that's another matter. A disease may be very deep, but the cure can only come from human beings.

LH: OK, so to solve these problems we must look at society?

RNS: That's what I believe.

LH: I also believe it. Even Kabir believes it. He criticizes society, but never in separation from our inner experience. You yourself said that a great source of Kabir's power is that he constantly asks us to look within ourselves, to learn from our own experience (see chapter 6). That's what I was trying to do. How? By sitting. That's all. Sitting still. Observing the breath. This isn't an easy task, because the mind is always running in different directions. The mind does not want to sit in one place. So I learned about my mind, I learned about my body, my desires, my fears. And inevitably I would reach a place where I was helpless, blocked, couldn't make any progress. What did my meditation teachers say? Sit right there, where there is no solution. Where you find only obstacles. Sit there. Observe mind, body, feelings. Learn. There's no rest or stability in the mind? Fine. What is in the mind? Thus slowly, slowly, slowly, I learned something, but not by rational methods. I learned by experience. What is the breath? What is consciousness? What is responsibility? What is morality? What is in our hands, and what is not in our hands? What should our attitude be toward that? And above all—my real desire, my real pain—it seemed to be something about the heart. Why was the heart so narrow? It was terrible that my heart couldn't seem to open. I wanted to do something for society, wanted to help others, but how? This question was very urgent for me. I had no choice. Slowly things began to change. Something opened. I saw that whatever I did would be incomplete if I didn't understand my own condition, my fear, greed, grasping mentality. I wouldn't be able to do any good work in the world in that condition, with a heart that couldn't open. So this is my spiritual story. If you don't have that kind of deep dissatisfaction within yourself, it's great. I see that you are doing your work wholeheartedly. It's really good. But it seems to me that many people have some kind of problem of the heart.

RNS: What is the root cause of this problem? Were you born with it? Did it come from some spiritual power? Or did it come from the social and economic environment? You say your heart was closed. Was it biologically closed? You say that through spiritual work your heart could open. I can give you ten examples of how a closed heart can be opened through social and cultural work. There are various paths. This is your experience. I have not taken that path so I can't comment on it. My experience tells me that whatever problems we have, we should look for the causes in our families, societies, schools, systems. Some problems are being solved, others are being created. We continue to work with that. We should think about happiness and comfort. How many comforts do we need? How many clothes? Do we need to have a bigger house? What else? What brings satisfaction? I would say that if there is some spiritual process, then it can be demystified. What you have learned in thirty years somebody else might be able to learn in three years.

SV: This is what Goenka-ji has done with his *vipassana* [meditation] courses. Completely demystified, nonsectarian, no religion involved. It is a demystified technique which he feels is valuable in society.

RNS: I'm saying that there are some people who do fine without any spiritual practice.

LH: Completely right. I would add that everyone has some kind of faith which helps them go on. It doesn't have to be faith in God. But it's beyond rationality. Despite all the obstacles, we keep living, we keep making efforts. It's not rational. From some source we get this inspiration. You have your faith, I have mine. Even when we can't solve a problem with our brains, we continue to believe in life. In that sense we are all believers.

RNS: Sure. We have faith in the people we work with, faith in ourselves. That's how our work can go forward. No argument. But there is a process of change in the world. When we see that the forces in the world are very oppressive, we look for a solution. Where did science come from? Great problems can open new paths. In the past, people looked for a supernatural answer to every problem. ... Science was not just plucked out of the air. It arose from needs. It was to understand the world and to do something about the world that all the streams of science emerged, including anthropology, sociology, psychology. Universities have a great role. Academics can come together with activists and we can accomplish a lot. We don't have to stay in our separate compartments.

LH [REACHING OUT AND SHAKING HANDS WITH SYAG]: On that point, we have achieved unity!

The next day I reflected in my notebook on the conversation. I had talked about the connection between inner and outer in my own history, but the personal story might have obscured more general implications. Why is there so much cruelty, exploitation, violence, inequality, refusal to share resources necessary to life? Many people are lost in deluded self-interest, clinging to what they have and driven to amass more, urgently seeking to attain a sense of security, which continuously eludes them. How do we get free of such compulsions? How do we stop lying to ourselves as well as others? How do we penetrate and go beyond the fears that paralyze us and cause us to act in ways that serve our imagined self-interest, our individual "security," while we ignore or harm others? How to wake up from the fractured dreams of violence, greed, and self-clinging? Just as structural change won't come just from singing bhajans, inner transformation won't necessarily occur by setting up schools and health centers. In both social change and spiritual work, we are seeking to be liberated from our narrow, painful, fearful selves.

In Madison, Wisconsin, November 2011

After hearing Alok Rai in 2002, I planned to argue against the position he seemed to represent in referencing the story of Lenin and the *Appassionata.* Later it seemed wiser to inquire more directly into his views. I tried to connect with him in India, but we couldn't work out a meeting there. Finally in 2011, I caught up with him at the South Asia conference in Madison. First I quoted to him his own words about the "seduction" of the mystical, the dangers of attraction to "transcendent experience," and the "embarrassment on the political left about this seeming surrender to the idiom of religion."

ALOK RAI (AR): I suppose it goes back to Nehru's own ambivalence about religion, because at some level he inherits this nineteenth-century rationalist confidence that religion is superstition and that the task of socialism lies in shedding all that. The sort of early twentieth-century H. G Wellsian confidence—

LH: But also Marxian and materialist?

AR: Also Marxian, of course. And the issue has obviously come up on the Indian left with regard to the issue of using a religious idiom or not using it. They've struggled with all kinds of figures—Kabir, Tulsidas, even Vivekanand for that matter.

LH: Well yes, because of the way that Vivekanand and Tulsidas have been appropriated, I would struggle with them too. But Kabir, who is in no way going to support the politics of hate or religious nationalism? Still they will struggle with him because of the religious problem?

AR: Because of using the religious idiom.

LH: Is that all you want to say about it? Do you yourself struggle with Kabir for that reason?

AR: I don't. I don't think so. But a religious idiom comes packaged differently for different groups of people. To shift it from the ground of socialism to something else—for instance the embarrassment that Kumkum Sangari struggles with writing about Mirabai. What is a feminist to do with someone who makes surrender a form of liberation? I suppose there are two aspects to it. It has partly to do with using religion as a sort of mobilization device. But there's also a further purpose—not making merely an instrumentalist use of religion, but using it to organize the emotions that religion gives rise to.

LH: Some of the people I interviewed in Dewas aren't worried about the instrumentalist view. They say openly—we are struggling against injustice and inequality. We'll use Kabir if he helps us. We'll use Marx if he helps us. We'll use Ambedkar, we'll use anybody, and we'll discard anything [in their work] that doesn't help us. There's an assumption that the part of Kabir that stresses going inward, that talks about attaining certain states of concentration and awakening and illumination ... I can see you're already reacting—

AR: Yes, with that the left is distinctly uncomfortable. I'm not personally. I am not.

LH: Tell me why they are and you're not.

AR: Speaking personally—and I am a bit embarrassed, let me say quickly, because many of my friends would find this a surrender to that idiom. But I think of myself as having a kind of transcendental longing without expecting that transcendental longing to be gratified by some available system of faith, which is what religion is. At its best, at its finest, it is that. Of course religion is a lot of other, more inferior things. But at its finest it is an established set of answers—

LH (BREAKING IN): Not established! Constantly contested! And a figure like Kabir also calls on you as an individual. He resolutely refuses to be institutionalized. So if that is the case, in your longing for something transcendental—would the testimony or the poetic voice of Kabir interest you?

AR: Yes, unmistakably. The particular occasion that I referred to, *Anahad Garje*, was very, very moving [see n. 5 below]. This was in the immediate aftermath of Ayodhya [the destruction of the Babri mosque by Hindu mobs and subsequent widespread communal violence].

LH: Regarding the embarrassment at feeling moved by the music, maybe we could get back to the Lenin-Gorky conversation. At first I was really—I'm looking for a more sophisticated word, but I was upset, I was put off. I thought: there's something really wrong with that viewpoint, when Lenin says I love the *Appassionata* but I'm not going to listen because it opens me up, it makes me too vulnerable, makes me want to caress people when I should be smashing their heads, and so on. I found that a dangerous and destructive kind of attitude. And so did the German filmmaker who saw how that attitude helped to create the East German dystopia. He did it brilliantly. He was inspired by the same story. Do you think his construction of Lenin was fair?

AR: There are two moments. One is that he is moved by the *Appassionata*. Somehow one doesn't imagine Stalin listening to the *Appassionata*. Here is someone who confesses to being moved, so moved that it actually interferes with his capacity for action. To experience the dilemma as a dilemma already says something about the person. The fact that he chooses what he chooses points to something else.

LH: My first impulse was to take off polemically against Lenin on the basis of this story, though I didn't know much about Lenin. Then when I looked carefully at two translations, I found it more interesting. As you say, he starts out by saying I am deeply moved by it. It makes me proud, he says, perhaps naively so, that people can work such miracles, produce such marvels. Then Gorky's description shows him wrinkling up his eyes, smiling sadly. So the next thing he says seems to include a sense of irony, an awareness that he's saying a double-edged thing. I want to say sweet things and pat the heads of people who can create such beauty, but I need to be bashing their heads, though theoretically we are against violence. … He may be joking with himself a little. But this crossroads where he stands, and the choice that he seems to make … if he is really making that choice, if he's choosing the path of a steely-eyed ideology of the state where you really have to beware of opening your heart, of being vulnerable, then it does create the danger that the filmmaker expanded upon, of a sterile, heartless, brutal totalitarian state.

AR: The Soviet Union was a large-scale playing out of choosing that road.

LH: Coming back to India and the Sufi-*sant* poets and the embarrassment of the left, you speak of the religious idiom of the poetry. But it isn't just religious. As I said, you could speak of it as an individual movement toward self-knowledge—

AR: A moment of silence, a moment of wonder, a moment of existential bewilderment.

LH: For that you have to be open, you have to be vulnerable, you can't be in control. But there's more than a spiritual or existential moment. There's also the power of the music, which you were talking about when you made that comment. You said we're listening to this powerful music, but we ought to exercise a certain caution. You didn't show your vulnerable side when you said that. You identified yourself with Lenin's warning.

AR: In my public speaking I present myself as being more certain than I really am. In conversations like this I can be tentative, I can be uncertain. But there's something about a podium....

LH: So you sided with what appeared to be Lenin's position on that, in warning us. Watch out, don't get too carried away. Don't bliss out on the music without remembering what Lenin said.

AR: It's also because of the attempt by Sahmat to organize the Sufi and bhakti concerts [in 1993]. There was a controversy at that time. I was marking that, not taking a personal position.

LH: I'm interested in the question of whether you need to choose.

AR: I would think that being vulnerable and sensitive to the pain of others is actually a very important first step in a human politics, a politics that's capable of being human.

LH: And a key to the inhumanity of some communist states [in the twentieth century], when they abandoned that.

AR: I would say that. But I'm also conscious that there's a tradition of the left that speaks of scientific socialism, understood in a nineteenth-century way, almost a technocratic socialism.

LH: Maybe we should be more forthcoming in not aligning ourselves with such a tradition. Instead of bowing to that tradition on the left, maybe we should not bow.

AR: I actually want to signal the opposite. It is this [vulnerability] which is a sign of the capacity for goodness.

In Lunyakhedi, August 2012

[From my notebook]
I'm at a workshop where fourteen people from big cities have come to get the flavor, music, and meaning of Kabir bhajans in Malwa. They have been infected by the Kabir folk music bug in urban festivals and concerts, Shabnam's films and CDs, *satsangs* with Prahladji and other folksingers in Mumbai and Bangalore homes. For five days they are in the village singing, listening, learning, conversing. On the third day, when Prahladji, Kaluramji, and Narayanji are here together leading the singing and discussion, I notice that the songs and conversation are all about the fine points of inner spiritual meaning. Even when Kaluramji sings a bhajan where the central metaphor is a broom, and God is cast as the universal sweeper (*bhangī*,

> the quintessential untouchable), the interpretation offered is purely spiritual. So I raise the question: What happened to all the social consciousness you singers developed in the Eklavya Kabir *manch*? Isn't this bhajan an expression by Dalits about their own dignity and value, and a protest against casteism? You spent so many years discussing how Kabir has both a social and a spiritual side, and in the *manch* you gave special attention to the social side. Now it seems there is nothing to talk about but breath, consciousness, emptiness, chakras, love, wordless joy, and the nature of the guru.

There follows a somewhat surprising discussion. First Prahladji (PT) and Kaluramji say that it's problematic and can even be dangerous to sing the songs that criticize caste and religion in public programs. They give examples of how upper-caste and religious people can react to this kind of thing. I say: Here you are not on a public stage but in your own home with sympathetic people. Still you aren't singing those songs or raising those questions. PT says: What's the need? These people already understand and agree with the social message of Kabir. Then he goes to another argument that is familiar to me from the years I've known him. If you say directly to somebody's face, "Your ideas about caste or religion are wrong, you should change them," it won't do any good. That approach isn't effective. But if they are moved by the bhajans and the *bāṇī*, if they understand deeply the spiritual message, they undergo a true change from within. He gives examples of how this has happened—as with a village *ṭhākur* (member of a ruling caste) who was full of caste prejudice but who changed from within after being moved by the bhajans and PT's way of explaining them. It is only a spiritual change that is enduring (*sthāī*), he says. I have often heard this from him. Falguni, a lawyer from Mumbai, agrees. She says that when you truly realize the equal presence of the same radiance, the same divinity in every body, evoked by Kabir in so many powerful and poetic ways (and by implication, when you see the same sorts of lies, pretensions and delusions in everyone), then automatically your social views and behavior will change.

But I am not satisfied. I suggest that it's also important to talk overtly about these things, and to take action in the social and political sphere. For every dose of Gandhi (who focused on changing hearts and resisted legislation and structural change), we need a dose of Ambedkar (who fought for legal, educational, and other structural safeguards for equality and justice, and who constantly called out the hypocrisy and cruelty of existing institutions). Many of the workshop participants appreciate this discussion.

I think most of them have social and political commitments in the cities. But they are also deeply drawn to the psychospiritual depths that Kabir's words open up. They wish to refresh themselves here, to draw from that well—or perhaps, like the pearl diver who appears in the poetry, to plunge into that ocean.

In Berkeley, California, June 2012

"I'm in despair about the Buddhists," said my friend Joanna Macy, author, activist, and meditator.

"What do you mean?" I asked, though I had a hunch.

"They're becoming more self-centered. They're not paying attention to the problem that engulfs us all. Have you seen the cover of the latest *Shambhala Sun*?"

I had seen it. *Shambhala Sun*, one of the glossy American Buddhist magazines that are showing remarkable staying power amid the general decay and death of paper journalism, had featured in large type across its cover the heading "I want to be...." Beneath that was a vertical column of adjectives: Peaceful, Insightful, Loving, Grounded, Skillful, Wise, Genuine. Each adjective was linked to an article in the magazine that would guide the aspirant in that direction. To Joanna, this seemed to signal a metastasizing narcissism, one of the dangers of an inner-directed spiritual practice. "*I* want to be like this. *I* want to look like that. *I* want to transform *myself*."

Joanna, a Buddhist practitioner and an elder of the American engaged Buddhist community now in her eighties, has devoted many years to writing and to public work aimed at saving the earth. She was partly speaking with humorous hyperbole when she claimed to be in despair about the Buddhists. But she was also pointing to a deeper meaning. "Despair" isn't just a negative word for her: one of her earliest innovations was a workshop model that she called "Despair and Empowerment." The idea was that people had to move out of denial, to allow themselves to feel the despair and grief that would arise if they really faced the massive extinction of species and the death of ecosystems, in order to awaken and join in efforts to reverse the destruction of the natural world. Joanna has been tirelessly engaged in work to connect all of us to the earth's crisis, to related issues of justice, and to each other for many decades. A look at her website (www.joannamacy.net) will demonstrate the commitment, freshness, and imagination of all she does. When we met that day, she had just published a new book and was continuing to lead workshops and mentor younger people all over the country. She describes her work since the 1960s as grounded in Buddhist teachings, systems theory, and deep ecology.

Here is the point of this vignette. Devotion to spiritual practice, insight, and personal transformation *is not* opposed to political commitment, socially engaged compassion, and work for justice. And devotion to the personal spiritual path *is* opposed to such engagement. This contradiction has been felt through the millennia. Why did the Buddha leave his wife, newborn child, and kingdom to wander possessionless through forests, practicing asceticism and meditation for years? Why did he establish a tradition of renouncers? Fast-forwarding 2,500 years, why do many Buddhists in the practice centers of California cultivate such an exquisite awareness of their own psychological states and the nuances of their personal relationships while not managing to find time for the death of the planet? Transforming oneself can be a full-time job. It can fill the horizon. It is very interesting. On the other hand, changing the world can be more than a full-time job. Activists are understandably impatient with "navel-gazers"; yet without self-knowledge and self-connection, activists are likely to burn out, to become violent or bitter or unconsciously shaped by the very things they are fighting against.

To say that inner and outer are not opposed is to solve nothing. It is true and untrue. To say that inner and outer are opposed is equally true and untrue. The contradiction must be lived out and investigated in every circumstance in which it arises. Kabir is a provocateur. Kabir is a deep well of poetry and thought. In the field of reception and interpretation, we confront the welter of circumstances in which the question can be asked. We see how others have dealt with this problem, and we work out solutions for ourselves.

Emailing with Vipul Rikhi, September 2012

In a generous commentary on a draft of this chapter, novelist and poet Vipul Rikhi said:

> Resolving this dichotomy is more important to you than it might have been to Kabir. . . . Why does everyone need to be an activist? Or why does everyone need to be a spiritualist? Or why must there be a "resolution" to this dichotomy that is satisfactory to the mind? Does

one really need to lay down a ground where the political-spiritual debate will be resolved forever? In the end … everyone does what they feel is fit. You may call it dharma. In a symbolic sense, this is the idea of the four estates (the priests, warriors, traders, workers). If a buddha needs to go away, why shouldn't he? If people feel deeply called to protest against various structures and forms of exploitation, without devoting too much time to inner questions, why shouldn't they?

I agree with Vipul that we do not need to resolve the debate forever. But this statement should also not resolve the debate forever, breeding complacency. Taking a position can be very important. "Taking no position" is a position. I hear truth in Kabir's "If I say yes, it isn't so, and I can't say no. . . ." And I hear truth in the cracked voice of Florence Reece, a Kentucky woman who composed a song in 1931 when coal miners were fighting for decent working conditions against brutally cruel bosses:

> Which side are you on boys? Which side are you on?
> They say in Harlan County, there are no neutrals there.
> You'll either be a union man or a thug for J. H. Blair.
> Which side are you on boys? Which side are you on?[34]

Skyping with Shabnam, Bangalore and Berkeley, August 2013

After an unexpectedly intense conversation, we put together in writing the main points that Shabnam made.

> If you define political as outward, material, and structural, and spiritual as inward and personal—if politics only means "movements" run by "activists"—you've already capitulated to a false dichotomy.
>
> Look at Lila-*behn* in Bisalkhedi village. She and her friend, the other Lila, have been so determined to learn bhajan singing from Narayanji and Kaluramji for the last few years. Someone might view their bhajan singing as an insignificant pastime, one that doesn't do anything to change society.
>
> But on meeting them, chatting and spending time with them, I see so clearly how they are negotiating quite oppressive patriarchal

power equations within their families in order to go out and sing. They are resisting social attitudes that disapprove of women singing and playing instruments, and attitudes of discomfort when all of this gives women mobility and agency. It was poignantly pertinent too, that all the bhajans they sang that day when we visited them were about seeking the true Beloved. The songs directly juxtaposed the limited frameworks of family and husband against a more transcendent reality. It seems to me that in aspiring to a transcendent experience they are negotiating real social and familial power relations, very much in this world. Why is this not defined as "political"?

Look at Ram Prasad Aradiya and his *maṇḍalī* in Dhunsi village—men who work as laborers, who are economically and socially marginal, who may live at subsistence levels, who are not accorded a sense of dignity and personhood by the caste-ridden structures of mainstream society. In the *satsang*, we witness them claiming that space as their own, with a sense of joy and ecstasy. Watching them dance and sing, I recognize the sense of power and personhood that the poetry and music are filling their bodies with. Tellingly, the song they are singing is "*Ānand bhayo re āngana mā*" ("Joy has come to our courtyard"). Tell me, if this is not political, what is?

Of course, someone might view this *satsang* as a space of inaction, sitting around and playing *manjīrās*, while the real job of revolution waits outside. But who are we to say that the power and agency and dignity that these poems and songs give does not spill out of the *satsang* space and into the spaces of lived social reality? How would we map subtle inner shifts of consciousness? How can we not call these "political"?

In that packed room in Dhunsi, where we filmed Ram Prasad's *mandalī* singing and playing while others spontaneously jumped up to dance, there was a shelf with pictures of Dr. Ambedkar and Satguru Kabir side by side. We had a conversation about them. One man said Ambedkar was their guru for social and political rights, and Kabir was their guru of spiritual and inner worlds that gave them joy, strength, solace, perspective on the nature of this world and their lives in it. These two went together naturally. Ambedkar didn't need to join a bhajan *mandalī*. Kabir didn't need to create a political party and fight elections. Both did what was true to their nature, and together they created a life-fulfilling wholeness.

Oh Freedom

I complete this chapter in late August 2013, when Americans and others are celebrating the fiftieth anniversary of Martin Luther King's "I Have a Dream" speech, delivered at the historic 1963 March on Washington for Jobs and Freedom. I attended the march. I was twenty-one years old at the time. Today, as I drive across the San Francisco Bay Bridge, my radio is vibrating with the sounds of that era. The boundary-crossing meanings of "liberation" are in the air. The expansive powers of song are evident as I sing out with the radio, loud as if I were still there—

> Oh freedom
> Oh freedom
> Oh freedom over me!
> And before I'll be a slave
> I'll be buried in my grave
> and go home to my Lord and be free!

The broadcast continues with parts of Pete Seeger's Carnegie Hall concert of June 1963, which highlighted music of the civil rights movement. He talks about the awe-inspiring courage and faith of those who faced vicious dogs, fire hoses, phalanxes of riot police, tear gas, and bullets with solemnity, dignity, humor, and joy. Their joy was defiant. They would march in silence, not responding to threats and obscenities, until the moment they were arrested, and then they would burst into a dance and a song:

> I ain't scared of your jail 'cause I want my freedom,
> want my freedom, want my freedom,
> ain't scared of your jail 'cause I want my freedom,
> want my freedom now!

Kabir and his *nirguṇ* poet friends won't solve the political-spiritual problem for us. But they will provoke and challenge us not to forget our humanity under any circumstances, and to figure out what that means and what work we are called to do.

Seeker, there's something
you're supposed to do.
So do it!
This life is a jewel, hard to find.
You've wandered through eight million
four hundred thousand births. There's someone
you're supposed to meet.
So meet!

You tried mantras, prayers, fasts, deprivation,
ran through the six schools of philosophy,
but never found wisdom beyond wisdom,
just stumbled on in delusion.

A voice says Vishnu's in Vaikunth,
another says he's in Cow Heaven,
a third says the Lord's in Shiva's city.
For ages, they've marketed these products.

An ignorant person says God's far away.
Someone who knows says God is close.
A true guru gives a precious hint:
The path to God's in every breath.
The guru's whole mind is revealed.
Someone recites a wordless word.
Bananath says, listen friend:
my true guru's voice
is shouting at you.[35]

Even when they criticize society and religion in the harshest terms, they are calling us back to ourselves, to life, compassion, the aspiration to nonviolence.

Why have you forgotten your country, you crazy?
Why have you forgotten your own country?

The deluded gardener tears off a leaf.
In every leaf is life!
He tears a leaf, gives it to a stone god.
That god has no life, you crazy!

The branch is Brahma, the leaf
is Vishnu, the flower is Shiva.
He tears a flower, gives it to a god
that has no life.

You call priests from all over.
They march around your house,
break a coconut, offer the shell to god,
and eat the meat themselves.

You make fine rice pudding
to offer to god's image.
A dog pees on the god,
a squirrel eats the pudding, you crazy.

When your father's alive, you throw a shoe at him.
When he dies you take him to the Ganges.
Alive, you wouldn't feed him.
Dead, you feed crows in his memory.

You pray to Bhairu and Bhavani for a child,
you pay by cutting off a goat's head.
Kabir says, listen seekers:
don't chop off the head of someone else's child!

Why have you forgotten your country, you crazy?
Why have you forgotten your own country?[36]

They know sorrow and death, but they are not afraid of joy.

This mind, my friend, has learned to love
owning nothing.

The gladness you get singing the name,
you won't get that gladness from wealth.

At last this body will meet with dust.
Why strut with pride?

Kabir says, listen seekers:
you meet God
in joy.[37]

They can think and analyze, but as artists they burst beyond the experiential and expressive limits of logic and analysis. They don't separate body and spirit, and this is a key to their political and spiritual genius.

No moon, no sun.
Without sun, explosions of light.
Ah! Don't go to another world,
dear friend, see the light right here.

Dear friend! A mute person
sings beautiful melodies,
a deaf one hears, a lame one leaps
and dances, friend, a blind one
starts to see.

Dear friend! In the dome of the sky,
a drunken yogi blazes.
There's no fire or holy ash, friend,
and no one to blaze.

Dear friend! On the peak of emptiness,
a fight breaks out.
It's no place for cowards, friend.
Who can rely on a coward?

Dear friend! Gulabi Das sings,
the lock on my heart has opened!
Bhavani Nath says, friend,
my body shines.[38]

Notes

INTRODUCTION

1. I would like to clarify the use of "North India" in the book's title. The region including Madhya Pradesh is often referred to as Central India, distinguished from North India. Indeed "Madhya" means "middle," and the region is located nearly in the center of the subcontinent. However, another way of speaking of major regions is to distinguish simply between North and South India. That classification refers to language families, with the Sanskrit-based Indo-Aryan languages in the North and the Dravidian languages, which had completely different origins, in the South. It is in this latter sense that I use "North India" in the title.
2. Some poets in the Sikh *Ādi Granth* sometimes sign off with *suno*, but it is not constant as in Kabir. Interestingly, while *suno* is present in the vast majority of well-known written and oral compositions of Kabir, it is absent in most Kabir-attributed verses in the *Ādi Granth*.
3. In the introduction to Hess and Singh 2002, a section called "Rough Rhetoric" analyzes this vocative style. Hess 1987a is an earlier version.
4. Chapter 1 discusses *anahad nād* along with other terms used for this profound sound, such as *shabda*, *bāṇī*, etc.
5. As Jack Hawley has pointed out to me, we don't *know* that Kabir was illiterate. Some of his modern devotees believe that he was not only literate but knew Sanskrit and read ancient scriptures. This view seems to be motivated by their feeling that it is insulting to call him illiterate. We will never know for sure whether Kabir could read. But there is no evidence that he ever wrote anything down, and his traditional body of works includes these often-quoted lines: "I don't know ink or paper, / these hands never touch a pen. / The greatness of four ages / Kabir tells with his mouth alone" (Hess and Singh 2002, 111–12). In Varanasi in the 1970s, I met Hazariprasad Dvivedi, the great Hindi critic, creative writer, and author of a

classic book on Kabir. Referring to this couplet, he told me that while the English term "well-read" has been translated into Hindi, the traditional term is *bahuśhrut*, "well-heard." Kabir did not read or write, suggested Prof. Dvivedi, but he learned by oral tradition the contents of the Upaniṣhads and other literature.

6. "I agree with the critic who said that reading was not merely the mental absorption of a text, but a physical act in which the colour, weight and texture of the book, together with the physical context (beach, bed, comfortable chair, train) contributed toward the total experience" (Sacks 2000, 73).
7. This was Imre Bangha, the great Hungarian scholar of early North Indian literature (and expert in manuscript study). We were introduced by Ashok Vajpeyi at the lounge of Delhi's India International Centre Annexe, which friends sometimes referred to as Ashok's office. I don't remember the date—sometime between 2002 and 2005.
8. Many other scholars have studied Indian texts in close connection with their performative and social contexts. For instance, anthropologists Ann Gold (1992) and Susan Wadley (2004) have worked closely with singers of oral epics in Rajasthan. Kirin Narayan (1997) has written beautifully of Himalayan folktales as told among women. Milton Singer, a trailblazing anthropologist of the previous generation, used "cultural performance" as a primary category of analysis (1972, esp. chaps. 3 and 6). Parita Mukta (1997) has studied Mirabai as she is constructed by people of "low" caste and class in rural Rajasthan. Nancy Martin's work on Mirabai and Kabir (2000, 2002) also focuses on how poets, poetry, and meanings are produced in the cultures of ordinary people in Rajasthan. Paula Richman has devoted herself to demonstrating, in several richly elaborated works, the performative heart of the *Rāmāyaṇa* in a multitude of contexts. A number of J. S. Hawley's works are very important to my present study. But none of these scholars focuses on oral texts and their relation to written and otherwise recorded texts the way I do. Christian Novetzke (2008) and Philip Lutgendorf (1991) come closest to my endeavor, each working with a specific North Indian bhakti poet, attending to history and studying their texts in performative as well as written forms. Lutgendorf works with a more or less fixed text, the *Rāmcharitmānas* of Tulsidas. Namdev, like Kabir, does not have a fixed canonized text, so Novetzke pays a great deal of attention to the many forms and processes by which Namdev's poetry gets written down and transmitted orally.
9. Examples of introductions in English by scholars who take a serious interest in texts and their histories: my works of 2002 [1983]; 1994b; 1987b; Vaudeville 1993; Dharwadker 2003; Callewaert 2000; Lorenzen 1991; Hawley 2005, especially chaps. 14–15.
10. Though his exact dates are unknown, 1398–1518 are commonly cited. Some scholars who doubt the accuracy of the conventional (and miraculous) 120-year lifespan have suggested a death date around 1448.

11. Some say he was born in this Muslim family, while others believe he was adopted by Muslim parents after his birth mother, a Brahmin widow, set him afloat on Lahartara Pond. For the histories of various Kabir legends, see Lorenzen 1991 and Lorenzen 2006, chap. 5.
12. The *Adī Granth* was finalized in 1604, but its precursor manuscripts, known as the *Goindval Pothis*, were compiled in the 1570s. See Mann 1996 and 2001.
13. There are several distinct lineages of Kabir Panthis. See chapter 7 below for an introduction.
14. My favorite essay setting this forth has long been A. K. Ramanujan's "Who Needs Folklore?" (1999 [1990]). Wendy Doniger's illuminating article, "Fluid and Fixed Texts in India," appeared first in Flueckiger and Sears 1991, with a version in Doniger 1995, 56–64.
15. Callewaert 2013; Callewaert 2000; Mann 1996 and 2001; Hawley 2005; and Agrawal 2009a. My early work on this: Hess 1987b.
16. See Fish 1972 and 1980. Kenneth Bryant (1979) brought this kind of reader response analysis to Hindi bhakti poetry in his book on Surdas. I was inspired by both authors when I wrote "Rough Rhetoric," first published as Hess 1987a, later included in the introduction to Hess and Singh 2002 [1983].
17. For example, Hess 1993, 1994a, 2006; Hess and Schechner 1977.
18. "Folk" has become a contested term in discussions of music and other forms of culture. In speaking of folksingers and folksongs in this book, I refer to a music that is quite easily accessible to local people and is not characterized by the kinds of complexity and refinement that require years of training. This loose definition, I realize, leaves a lot of gray area.
19. An earlier version of this chapter was published in Banerjee and Dube 2009. This is also the central story of a documentary film, Virmani 2008b.

CHAPTER 1

1. Ashok Vajpeyi, mentioned at various points in this book, is a great poet and writer in Hindi, a cultural leader who has shaped and led important institutions (like the Bharat Bhavan in Bhopal, the Lalit Kala Akademi in Delhi, and the Mahatma Gandhi International Hindi University, now in Wardha, Maharashtra). He is an ever-present, effervescent contributor to Indian cultural and intellectual life. He has been unstintingly generous and encouraging to me and at crucial moments has been the one who made it possible for my work to go forward.
2. Bhajan: *Panchhiḍā bhāī*.
3. Most people refer to our friend respectfully as Tipanyaji, in deference to his status both as a renowned singer and Kabir expounder and as a schoolteacher. Over the years, Shabnam and I and others associated with the Kabir Project began using his first name, Prahladji. We never discussed it, but it just happened. Though this was a bit startling in local culture, I think we tacitly made the

move because we addressed other local singers by their first names, and some democratic impulse in us wanted to grant equal respect to all the singers.

4. For information on the Kabir Panth, see chapter 7.
5. Some of the other names of poets we hear when Malwa *mandalīs* sing "Kabir" are Dharamdas, Gorakhnath, Bhavani Nath, Gulabi Das, Shivguru, Bananath, Bherya, Ishwardas, Ramdas, Ramanand, Brahmanand, and Nanak. Many of them are associated with the Nath Yogi tradition (on which see Henry 1991; A. Gold 1992).
6. Questions about women and gender in Malwa Kabir singing culture don't get much attention in this book. We touch briefly on gender issues in conversations with Prahladji's wife Shantiji and other family members, and in occasional stories and descriptions—for instance, two male singers have since 2011 taken up the unusual project of training some women and girls to sing Kabir. It would be worthwhile to examine gender more fully in relation to Kabir, including who sings, speaks, and worships; and how people understand the representation of women and female voices in Kabir's poetry. That project is not, however, taken up in this book.
7. Chapter 6 is devoted to Eklavya's Kabir *manch*.
8. This is a standard trope in the poetry. Swan (*haṃsa*) and heron (*bagulā*) are both white water birds, but the former represents the pure spiritual essence while the latter is hypocritical and impure. Though it stands still like a yogi in meditation, it is just waiting to spear a fish (nasty non-veg food).
9. Bhajan: *Rām rame soī gyānī.*
10. See Bhattacharya 1996; and chapter 6 below, n. 16.
11. [PT] at the beginning of a quotation means that the speaker is Prahladji. In the rest of this section, till the subheading that begins "Inside and Outside," all the inset quotations are spoken by Prahladji in interviews conducted in February and March 2002.
12. Prahladji refers here to the common Kabirian phrase *choṭ lagnā*, to be struck or wounded. One is struck by the Word or the guru's teaching. It leaves a "wound," a mark that changes a person profoundly.
13. The lines are in a bhajan referred to sometimes as *Aisī khetī kījai*, sometimes as *Nīch sangat mat kījai*. It is on his MP3 recording entitled *Syānī surtā*.
14. See n. 8 above.
15. See n. 21 below and the "Guru" section of chapter 4.
16. Often called *chetāvanī* or warning song, a wake-up call, causing one to become conscious. Discussed as a theme in chapter 4.
17. *Koī suntā hai* is translated and discussed in Hess 2009a. It is also the title of one of the four documentary films by Shabnam Virmani, collectively called *Journeys with Kabir*.
18. Bhajan: *Maharam hove soī lakh pāve, aisā deśh hamaṛā.*
19. Bhajan: *Nirbhay nirguṇ*, translated and discussed in Hess 2009a, 39–40 and 88.
20. Bhajan: *Laharī anahad uṭhe ghaṭ bhītar*, also referenced in the Introduction.

21. The *nād(a)* is discussed in many Sanskrit and vernacular sources related to yoga, philosophy, and music.
22. The guru—very important in Kabir poetry and *nirguṇ* religiosity—will be discussed in chapter 4. Here we can note an ambiguity that tends to get lost amid the literal-mindedness of *guru-bhakti* in Indian tradition generally and in the Kabir Panth particularly. In poetry attributed to Kabir, the guru can be a human being to whom one owes profound reverence for revealing the path to liberation; or it can be the divine presence within oneself. If asked, Prahladji usually emphasizes the guru within. In one of my favorite old stories, a man named Gayabanand said he had three gurus: Satguru Kabir, his initiating guru in the Kabir Panth, and the guru in his own heart (Hess and Singh 2002, 36). Incapable or deceitful gurus also appear as objects of satire in the poetry.
23. A version of this poem was included in Kshitimohan Sen's 1910–11 collection of Kabir poetry, which was the source of Rabindranath Tagore's 1917 English collection *100 Songs of Kabir*. These 100 poems (plus others from the Sen volumes, a total of 256) are given in Hindi in the appendix to Hazariprasad Dvivedi's *Kabīr;* the poem under discussion is no. 8 (p. 241). In that version the Hindi for "in this body" is *is ghaṭ antar* instead of *yā ghaṭ bhītar*, and the repeated refrain sung in Malwa—"Who can know this? The one who knows! / Without a teacher, the world is blind"—is not present.
24. Bhajan: *Guru sam dātā koī nahīṇ.*
25. For example, the Kabir, Dadu, and Raidasi Panths.
26. In his study of "Prahlad the Pious Demon," Lorenzen (1996, 31) argues that the author(s) of the *Bhāgavata Purāṇa*, a major Sanskrit text revered by Vaishnav/Krishnaite *sampradāys*, "strongly support the Brahmanic ideology of *varṇaśhramadharma*. Above all, the text stresses the necessity of offering respect and charity to the Brahmins. The final five discourses ... of book seven ... mainly consist of a lengthy dialogue between Nārada and Yudhiṣthira on the virtues of *varṇāśhramadharma*. Jan Gopal's *Prahilād charitra*, on the other hand, promotes the more egalitarian and generally anti-Brahmin ideology commonly found in *nirguṇī* texts."
27. There have been recent programs to train women priests, and there are certain special circumstances in which non-Brahmin priests serve, but these rare exceptions prove the rule. See, for example, an article in *The Hindu*, a national English newspaper, published on May 23, 2014, titled "Pandharpur Temple Allows Women, Men of All Castes as Priests": http://www.thehindu.com/news/national/other-states/pandharpur-temple-allows-women-men-of-all-castes-as-priests/article6038635.ece?homepage=true.
28. The Hindi word *kāī* means rust, moss, scum, mold, verdigris, indicating some foreign substance that accumulates on the surface of a purer substance because

of its exposure to other materials and circumstances. "Scum" isn't a perfect translation, but I don't have a better one.

29. They lack *mukti* presumably because they (especially Vishṇu with his avatars) keep reappearing in new forms, going round in the cycles of birth and death.
30. A beautiful dialogue in this regard occurs in Virmani 2008a, a scene where Prahladji is in a train traveling to Banaras.
31. On the other hand, Advaita Vedanta is philosophically entirely *nirguṇ*, yet the institutions founded by Shankara are relentlessly casteist, restricted to Brahmins. The conditions under which caste ideology and oppression develop are much more complicated than one's theological orientation. Yet in the specific case of vernacular *nirguṇ* bhakti, we can observe the historical preference of *nirguṇ* traditions by oppressed castes for the reasons we have discussed.
32. Bhajan: *Jāo nugurī kāyā.*
33. Relating to all the family members in the three households has been an important part of my life in Lunyakhedi, so I would like to mention at least in a note who they are (as of 2015). In Ambaram's and Kamla's house live their two sons, two daughters-in-law, and two grandchildren. Ashok and Sumitra have two sons, Mithun and Arjun, and a daughter, Rachna. Mithun married at seventeen; his fifteen-year-old wife didn't come to live there at first, but they fixed up a little room for the young couple. She moved in about two years later and now has two children. Rachna was twelve when I first came in 2002. In 2010 she got married and moved to her husband's village. Prahladji and Shantiji also have two sons and a daughter. The daughter, Sona, lives with her husband, but often comes to her natal home with her daughter and son. The older son Ajay and his wife Sangita have two boys. They lived in Lunyakhedi for most of the time I've known them, but in 2012 shifted to a flat in Indore, with frequent visits to the village. Their main reason for the move was to get better education for their sons. The younger son Vijay got married along with his cousin Mithun, in 2005; Vijay and Seema have a son and daughter. Prahladji's elderly father lived in the main house but frequently trudged in and out of the others, until his passing in 2014. Another boy, Shri, the son of Prahlad's sister Gita, lived in Lunyakhedi with his Uncle Ashok and Aunt Sumitra for most of his life.
34. For a description of these events by Prahladji's wife Shantiji, see chapter 4.
35. Taken from Shabnam's footage, though it does not appear in any of the finished films.
36. Details on what the *panjā* said are in chapter 7.
37. For more on Syag-*bhāī*, see chapters 6 and 8.
38. One of Shabnam's four feature-length documentary films in the *Journeys with Kabir* series features Prahladji and me and focuses on the cross-cultural reach of Kabir's voice. It is entitled *Chalo hamāṛa des/Come to My Country.*

39. This is a formal ritual of the Kabir Panth, in which Prahladji was at that time serving as a *mahant*—guru and ritual authority. Chapter 7 tells the story of his mahantship and all the issues it raised.
40. This DVD as well as all the documentary films and other media produced by the Bangalore-based project can be acquired through the website www.kabirproject.org.

CHAPTER 2

1. Aditya Behl was an astoundingly creative scholar and friend whose death in 2009 at the age of forty-three left many of us grief-stricken.
2. The wonderful work of Christian Novetzke (2008) on orality, literacy, performance, and authorship in the tradition of the Marathi bhakti poet Namdev is highly relevant and recommended—especially chaps. 2 and 3.
3. On the question of Kabir's (il)literacy, see Introduction, n. 5.
4. See Hawley 2005, 194–207, for a detailed study of how the body of poetry attributed to Surdas grew from century to century, in layers traceable through dated manuscripts. In the same volume (24–47), Hawley explains how newer compositions become linked with the names of older poets. All of the processes mentioned here are observable in today's oral performances and will be demonstrated in this chapter.
5. See chapter 3 for a detailed account of important Kabir manuscripts.
6. Hess 1987b; Vaudeville 1993; Callewaert 2000; Dharwadker 2003, Introduction; Agrawal 2009a, chap. 4; Hawley 2005, 279–304.
7. Callewaert and Lath (1989, 55–118) provide a valuable essay called "Musicians and Scribes." They cite evidence in sixteenth- to eighteenth-century texts of the widespread practice and importance of singing bhajan/*kirtan* in bhakti sects and wider cultures, and they closely examine written sources for evidence of oral transmission. Much of their attention goes to signs of music observable in written texts (raga categories and metrical features that would have been expressed as musical rhythms). They also note indications of how texts were altered in singing. Comparing written versions, they show that refrain and signature lines were easily portable, as I have noted in this chapter with examples from performance. The common addition of "fillers" like *re bhāī* and other short phrases are seen in variants, along with changes in stanza order, dropping of stanzas, lines, or half-lines, or substitution of those units. Their observations of such textual dynamism are based on written sources, while mine are based on live performances.
8. Dinesh Sharma appears prominently in chapter 6, which also explains how the NGO Eklavya collected many hundreds of song texts from singing groups in the area.

9. Later in this chapter Prahladji speaks of the wholesale substitution, in a sectarian collection, of "Kabir says to Dharamdas" for more common forms of "Kabir says." I also note the appearance of a famous Kabir refrain, *Man lāgo mero yār fakiri meṇ*, in a song sung by Muralala of Kutch with the signature line of Mirabai. The refrain *Koi jānega jananahār*, in the Malwa Kabir bhajan *Is ghaṭ antar*, turns up in a verse by the Rajasthani Niranjani Panth *sant* Turasīdās (cited in Baid 2012, 2). This footnote could turn into a very long catalog.
10. The oldest notebook gives a nice glimpse of Prahladji's history, recording the moment when his focus switched from studying economics to singing and collecting bhajans. At the beginning, I see the heading ECONOMICS in English capital letters. He studied economics for his BA. "Adam Smith: Economics is the science of wealth" is written in English, then the same thing in Hindi. He lists prominent economists including J. B. Say, J. A. Mill, Carlyle, Ruskin, Prof. Lannen, on and on, with one Indian name, Prof. J. K. Mehta. The next section, "Characteristics of wants: Human wants are unlimited," is in English and Hindi. There follow notes on consumption, land, productivity, consumer's surplus, decentralization of industries, and mobility of labor. English words appear less and less. Then suddenly the bhajans start. There is no return to economics. Near the beginning of the bhajans a date is recorded: 28 Aug. 1977.
11. The Kabir bhajan is well known. Each line begins with *ye/yoṇ sansār*—this world (of birth and death)—and continues with images of impermanence. The verses in Prahladji's notebook were: *ye sansār os kā motī, dhūp paḍe uḍ jānā re / ye sansār hāṭ kā melā, saudā kar ghar jānā re / ye sansār ūṇḍā kuā, rapaṭ rapaṭ mar jānā re / ye sansār bor kā jala, ulajh ulajh mar jānā re.*
12. For more on the work of Lord and other twentieth-century scholars of oral texts, see chapter 5.
13. A full translation of the song appears in chapter 1.
14. Another switch between two words that sound similar but have different meanings is in the song that I translate as "In this body" (see chapter 4). Prahladji sings in the first stanza: *yā ghaṭ bhītar ban aur bastī, yāhī meṇ jhāḍ pahāḍā/ yā ghaṭ bhītar bāg bagīchā, yāhī meṇ sinchanahārā.*" The last word means one who waters, referring to the gardens and groves in the verse. In Shubha Mudgal's sung version, the last word is *sirjanahārā*, meaning the creator, the one who made the gardens and groves. They also have different words in the repeated phrase at the beginning of all the lines: *yā ghaṭ bhītar* in one, *is ghaṭ antar* in the other. But these variants have exactly the same meaning and are metrically equivalent.
15. Callewaert and Lath contrast the "freezing" effect of strict canonization in the *Ādi Granth*'s sphere of influence with the continuing vitality of oral tradition elsewhere: "Unlike the case for the Sikh tradition, the manuscript tradition in Rajasthan does not seem to have stopped the development of the oral tradition. The oral tradition in Rajasthan has remained dynamic and has continued to be

a vital source for Santa songs and sayings, even after a rich manuscript tradition was established. The two traditions have run parallel up to the present day. The oral traditions have remained alive and active, till perhaps two generations ago, adding to and modifying earlier material" (1989, 97). But why would they suggest that the dynamic oral tradition ended two generations ago? I would refute that claim, as evidenced in this chapter.

16. In a famous essay titled "Three Hundred Ramayanas: Five Examples and Three Thoughts on Translation," A. K. Ramanujan says: "One may ... say that the cultural area in which *Ramayanas* are endemic has a pool of signifiers (like a gene pool), signifiers that include plots, characters, names, geography, incidents, and relationships." These signifiers continuously move among oral, written, and performance traditions (Ramanujan 1999, 46).
17. The cup filled with the name— / Seeker, drink it fearlessly. / I found my true guru today. / My awareness has climbed to the sky. // In the bee's cave, my lord sits, / The bee is buzzing there, / The seeker takes an inward posture, It fills to the brim. // With no clouds / Lighting strikes / An unbounded light / Bursts into showers.
18. On these numbers see chapter 4.
19. The popularity of this song is probably related to its performance in a 1950 Hindi film, *Jogan*, with Nargis and Dilip Kumar.
20. In *Before the Divide: Hindi and Urdu Literary Culture* (2010), Orsini takes us beyond the entrenched categories of Hindi and Urdu by showing historically how and why these categories were constructed and also showing the dynamic multilingual and multicultural worlds in which people of the fourteenth through eighteenth centuries actually lived. In an earlier article she presents an idea that resonates with my "ecoregions" but is more elaborated: "[W]e need new maps that will include Hindi, Urdu, Persian and Apabhramsa. We need historico-geographical maps, starting from the Sultanate period, which go beyond Delhi and take into account regional kingdoms and the network of cities and the qasbas of Avadh and Bihar. We also need topologies that will map the spaces of literary production and consumption, in order to note the contiguity or distance between literary actors and to move beyond impressionistic and anecdotal evidence of 'cultural contact' between writers and performers of different traditions. Finally, we need a map of literary genres" (Orsini 2005, 397). Yet another article gives more emphasis to oral-performative modes: "Fifteenth-century Hindavi literature consists mainly of songs, *doha* couplets and *katha*s, narratives. Some were indeed produced at regional or even smaller courts, but others in the open 'Bhakti public sphere' (Agrawal) or towns and villages. Songs (and singer-composers ...) were highly prized and at the centre of courtly performances, as well as of devotional practices and temples. Both *katha*s, songs and *doha*s were genres practiced by a range of different poets—Naths, Sants, Sufis, Jains, *bhakha* and

sometimes also Persian court poets—and the high degree of intertextuality in terms of titles, names, tropes and images shows that they circulated among all these domains, evidence of a general intelligibility of genres and aesthetics" (Orsini 2012, 238). Orsini cites Nalini Delvoye's work on music in the Sultanate period and later: "[Delvoye] has done much to show precisely how these different locations—both courtly and religious—were connected, and how singers, songs and musical aesthetics circulated between Sufi *sama'* sessions, courtly *mehfils* and *sabhas*, temple functions and devotional gatherings" (Orsini 2012, 240).

21. Kumarji also sings *gaṛh* instead of *ghar*, which has an entirely different meaning. Prahladji's son Ajay told me that once his father's *mandalī* was singing this bhajan at the *Shīlnāth dhūnī* (a Nath Panth center in Dewas, described later in this chapter), and the gathered Nath Panthis got quite angry when they heard Kabir's signature line at the end. Besides being obviously wrong in their view, this constituted disrespect to their revered founder.
22. The two texts are unmistakably the "same" song, with the refrain "I'm afraid of that day," but they contain fascinating differences. For Kumar Gandharva's version, see Hess 2009a, 112–13. Muralala's performance of the song was posted on YouTube by the Kabir Project, <http://www.youtube.com/watch?v=LcI_6ToTuhY&feature=plcp>.
23. Poems attributed to the Sikh gurus almost never come up. The one prominent exception is *Sakal haṃs meṇ rām virāje*, a song with Nanak's signature that Prahladji and other Malwa friends sing often.
24. Some scholars assert that Dharamdas actually lived much later. "Raghavdas's *Bhaktamāl* ... was composed in the early years of the eighteenth century, that is, some hundred years after the establishment of Dharamdas's Kabir Panth. ... Raghavdas counts Dharamdas as one of Kabir's nine direct disciples, but Dharamdas's lifetime was actually about a century after Kabir's" (Agrawal 2009a, 164–65).
25. The best-known scholar to advance this view, influencing many later thinkers, is Hazariprasad Dvivedi (1971[1942]).
26. Henry 1991, 160–88; Henry 1995; D. Gold 1999, 2002; D. Gold and A. G. Gold 1984. A lovely short film by Anal Shah shows a singer of this tradition singing in the lanes of Varanasi: <http://www.youtube.com/watch?v=RzB3c-xdOyk> (uploaded 2008, accessed 2012).
27. For a fuller description of Shilnath, his published bhajan collection, and the institution honoring him in Dewas, see Hess 2009a, 19–23. Virmani's film *Koī suntā hai* includes discussion of Kumarji's visits to the Shilnath ashram and brief footage of the place.
28. The story, briefly told in Hess 2009a, 21, is movingly recounted by Madhup Mudgal in the film by Virmani (2008c) and transcribed in chapter 3, p. 138–39.

29. Hess and Singh 2002 contains an essay by Hess on this genre, "Upside-down Language" (135–61).

30. For details on this collection see Hess 2009a, 19–23.

31. Prahladji got this song from Gujarati singer Hemant Chauhan, whom he admires greatly and sometimes calls his "ideal" (*ādarśh*). Hemantji sings *ganapati* in the first verse, which PT changes to *satguru*. PT retains the homage to Sharda (Sarasvati), but he explains the name to me in a way that effaces the icon of the Hindu goddess of learning and the arts, wife of Brahma. According to him, Sarasvati's name indicates that she is the goddess of *svar*—voice or sound in relation to music.

32. In one reading *nārī* is woman and *sukamna* means lovely, delicate, happy, delighted. The translation "lovely spouse" reflects this meaning, as *nārī* often means wife as well as woman. In another combination, *nāḍī* is channel or nerve, a yogic term for the channels in the subtle body through which energy or breath courses. *Sukamnā* then is *suṣhumnā*, the central channel running along the spinal cord. Through spiritual exercises the yogi attempts to direct the breath into the central channel instead of the normal, repetitively cycling right and left channels. The word for this central channel, *suṣhumnā*, is of feminine gender. The energy that rises through the *suṣhumnā* is *kuṇḍalinī*, also understood as female.

33. The song was "*Aisī mhārī prīt*," which Shabnam sang on her own first CD set. The *chāap* she found incongruous was one that was familiar to her from "*Saudāgīr ab kyoṇ bhūlyo jaī*."

34. *Papihā* or cuckoo: a conventional figure in love poetry. She adores the drops of water that fall only during the *nakṣatra* or asterism of *svāti*, a constellation of stars in the moon's path that occurs for a very short time each year. She refuses to drink any other water. No thirst will drive her to touch any water but the drops of *svāti*. Her cry, "*piyā, piyā*," sounds like the word for "beloved."

35. A full translation with discussion is in chapter 5.

36. They have been screened on countless occasions in India, at least a few times in Pakistan, and in a number of other countries. Kabir festivals have blossomed in many cities, featuring live performances and film screenings. Some of the films have been shown on NDTV, a major cable channel, or made available on the internet.

37. My discussion with Vijay went deeper, revealing that he not only knew the songs popularized by Prahladji's cassettes but also was familiar with the *nirguṇ* theology and spirituality that are espoused by sects like the Kabir Panth and Radhasoami, and that seem to have great influence among people of low-caste status. He talked about the power of the Name. I asked if he also worshiped Ram and Krishna. He said yes, but he considered them to be holy persons, not Bhagavan (God). Using three names for the one he regarded as supreme, he said that Niranjan-Satyapurush-Mahakal was far above them. If you practice the name in every breath, through the guru's grace, you may experience that.

I asked if he also worshiped Devi. He said, "Yes, Devi is Yogamaya who created this whole universe. She created Brahma-Vishnu-Mahesh. Originally there was *shūnya* (emptiness). Out of *shūnya* she appeared, just like that, by herself. Satyapurush is *shūnya* (empty), *nirākār* (formless)—the absolute highest."

38. See discussion of the contempt in which upper-caste people had held the *tambūrā*, and how that had changed, in chapter 1. This conversation is transcribed from Shabnam's film *Kabīrā khaḍa bāzār meṇ/In the Market Stands Kabir*. Also see reference to the *tambūrā* in the description of the *mandalī*'s village sendoff for London in chapter 1.
39. Jack Hawley suggests that I shouldn't underestimate the amazing speed with which Kabir traveled via urban networks even in the sixteenth century. Personal communication, February 2012.
40. In 2013, an internet search for a particular song took me to a site called freebhajans.com. The first item in the Google search results was a video of Shabnam singing *Man mast huā phir kyā bole*—and guess where? At my house in Berkeley, California, in 2009, with Prahladji and the *mandalī* accompanying, and a room full of my family and friends (http://www.freebhajans.com/category/kabir-amritvani).
41. A similar process appears to be underway with digital media as discussed, for example, in Tim Wu's 2011 book *The Master Switch: The Rise and Fall of Information Empires*. "Although the Internet has created a world of openness and access unprecedented in human history, Wu is quick to point out that the early phases of telephony, film, and radio offered similar opportunities for the hobbyist, inventor, and creative individual, only to be centralized and controlled by corporate interests, monopolized, broken into smaller entities, and then reconsolidated. Wu calls this the Cycle, and nowhere is it more exemplary than in the telecommunications industry. The question Wu raises is whether the Internet is different, or whether we are merely in the early open phase of a technology that is to be usurped and controlled by profiteering interests" (*Booklist* review, cited on amazon.com web page for Tim Wu's book, accessed July 3, 2014).
42. The ominous and antidemocratic potential of the internet is increasingly under scrutiny, for instance in Robert W. McChesney's *Digital Disconnect: How Capitalism Is Turning the Internet against Democracy* (New Press, 2013). In summer 2013, in the wake of Edward Snowden's revelations about secret government collection of vast amounts of information from our daily internet lives, a spate of articles addressed the end of the open internet. The prospects were definitely not democratic. One of many such commentaries: "Snowden's remarkable decision and the various details that have emerged about the NSA's massive program to capture and store data off the Internet and, reportedly, from servers run by Microsoft, Apple, Facebook, Yahoo, and others mark a watershed moment. I, and many others, have posted about this type of surveillance scenario before, but a young NSA contractor fleeing the United States for Hong

Kong to expose the reality and scale of the U.S. government's eavesdropping is a chilling, worldwide wake-up call about our rights in an increasingly connected world. . . . there seems to be enough evidence to bear out what I and many others have been pointing out for years: that the technology to establish widespread, constant surveillance finally exists, and we are in danger of exactly the type of police-state scenario that many are starting to fear in light of revelations about PRISM." Paul Venezia, June 17, 2013, http://www.infoworld.com/d/data-center/the-end-of-the-open-internet-we-know-it-220707.

CHAPTER 3

1. This is *sākhī* 74 in the *Bījak* (S. Singh 1972, 154), translated in Hess and Singh 2002, 96–97. A slightly different translation is given here.
2. Influential early articles in the unfolding of postcolonial and deconstructionist theory include Barthes 1978 [1967], "The Death of the Author"; and Foucault 1977 [1969], "What Is an Author?"
3. John Stratton Hawley's 1988 article "Author and Authority in the Bhakti Poetry of North India" (reprinted as "Author and Authority" in Hawley 2005, and summarized in Hawley 2009, 24–28) was an early and perspicacious view of the author question in the Indian bhakti context. See also Novetzke 2008, chap. 2.
4. A song about the train and rail ticket is sung by Kabir singers in Malwa, but attributed to a different poet, Ishwardas.
5. In an early article, I told a story about how I discovered that there was no overlap at all between the *Bījak*, the singular holy book of the Kabir Chaura branch of the Kabir Panth, and the *Śhabdāvalī*, a collection of popular bhajans published by the Kabīr Chaurā Math in Varanasi (Hess 1987b, 118). David Lorenzen addresses this gap in "Kabir's Most Popular Songs" (Lorenzen 1996, 205–24).
6. The in-person interview was tape-recorded at the Kabir Chaura Math, Varanasi. This portion is translated from Hindi. The same criteria are given in the preface to Shastri 1998, iv. Further in the preface to that volume, Shastri says they drew from the *Guru Granth Sāhib*, Rajjab's *Sarvāngī*, and a text from the Nagari Pracharini Sabha attributed to Sevadas. In addition he traveled far and wide hearing songs. "Traveling across regions, hearing the songs of Kabir from the mouths of people, I was plunged into a bottomless sea of utterances. Many men could go on all night singing Kabir. I couldn't know what they had composed themselves and what was really by Kabir. . . . I went to the tribal areas of Maharashtra, Gujarat, and Bihar. When I asked them to sing bhajans, they sang in a language I couldn't understand. All I could pick up was '*kahe kabīr suno bhāī sādhu*.' Beyond that I had no idea what they were saying." Noticing that the tribal people did not sing Surdas, Mirabai, or Tulsidas, but they did sing Kabir, he speculated that Dalits, Adivasis, and people of "backward castes" felt that Kabir's words touched their lives more closely than those of other major poets (Shastri 1998, iv).

7. The *ghazal* is an Urdu poetic form, popular in sung as well as recited performance, with particular patterns of rhyme and meter that are not typical of Kabir bhajans. This claimed Kabir poem partakes of the meter and rhyme forms of the *ghazal*.
8. The lyrics and a scratchy recording of Begum Akhtar are available at http://www.hindigeetmala.com/song/vo_jo_ham_men_tum.htm (accessed Aug. 2013).
9. http://www.bori.ac.in/mahabharata_project.html.
10. I have discussed the idea of mapping Kabir in chapter 2, referring to Francesca Orsini's proposals for mapping Hindi-Urdu literature.
11. As this book was in production, in August 2014, I attended a gathering of scholars who work on early Hindi texts. There I realized that a significant new name should be added to my list: the Czech scholar Jaroslav Strnad. He has worked on what may be the earliest verifiable Rajasthani manuscript that has a large number of Kabir compositions. His 2013 book is entitled *Morphology and Syntax of Old Hindi: Edition and Analysis of One Hundred Kabir Vani Poems from Rajasthan*. Though the title and the bulk of the book are concerned with linguistic analysis, Strnad has also done the full work of a textual editor. Part one is "Edition of the *Pads*," with minute attention to the kinds of decisions a textual editor must make.
12. A number of typographical errors and other points of confusion have been reported, and Callewaert is in the process of preparing a corrected edition.
13. If only for poetic resonance, I cite a well-known couplet recorded in both the *Bījak* and the *Kabīr Granthāvalī*. This is *Bījak sakhī* 194:

    bolī hamārī purv kī, hame lakhe nahi koy / hamko to soī lakhe, dhur purab kā hoy.

    "My speech is of the east, no one understands me. / Only that one understands me, who is totally from the east."

14. I have gone no farther than a few casual conversations with other scholars on this topic. At a workshop on early Hindi literature in Bulgaria in July–August 2014, some of the luminaries in the field agreed that the plethora of good early manuscripts in Rajasthan could be attributed to several factors including: the influence of the Jains, who revered books and had a tradition of establishing libraries; the relatively stable Rajput courts with their interest in preserving cultural artifacts; and the dry climate. In the East the climate was much worse, leading to rot and white ants destroying manuscripts. Courts in the East were less stable. The Jain influence was absent. Conversation partners on that occasion included the very knowledgeable Monika Horstmann, Imre Bagha, and Kenneth Bryant. Historian William Pinch, in an earlier correspondence, made similar suggestions. In an email on Oct. 4, 2012, he said:

> "I'm sure a lot of this has to do with the greater stability, size, and longevity of the courts in the western areas, especially Jaipur/Ajmer, Jodhpur, Orchha, etc., and the emergence of a manuscript tradition and interest in sant/bhakta hagiography (Nabhadas etc.) connected to those courts. The eastern side was also subject to greater political vagaries, what with the rise of the Company. Another factor was the patronage that the more 'egalitarian' *sampraday* like the Dadu Panthis and Nanakshahis received from the western courts. One doesn't, I think, see that kind of patronage in the east, though surely there must have been some. The big and medium-sized eastern states, like Darbhanga, Dumraon, Ramnagar, Bettia, Hathwa, Tekari raj, would have had libraries, but many of them were frittered away during the '70s or caught up in litigation. ... And no doubt they preferred more in the way of brahminical, Sanskrit mss. Still, none of this seems satisfying. Perhaps it has to do with the fact that Bhumihar Brahmans and Maithili Brahmans dominated the eastern courts, whereas Rajputs ruled in the west—and the latter were more keen on patronizing the newer *sampraday*."

Another fruitful line of research may be among sects that have been neglected so far by scholars. Tyler Williams has recently completed a Columbia University dissertation on the Niranjani Panth of Rajasthan. Closely examining manuscripts of *sant* poetry, Williams is turning up valuable new knowledge about their contents and histories. This *panth* is still in western India. Will someone bring forth new discoveries from the East?

Francesca Orsini, in an email exchange, suggests looking into the geography "of *maths*, libraries, *gaddis*," as well as the social composition of sects in the eastern Hindi region: "I would be very interested in the early history of the Kabir panth and their attitude towards writing and collecting books, and to the *math* (if there is one) and family of Malukdas. The Dadu panthis and Sikhs were clearly very much into *pothis* and *granths*, and Sufis, also in the east. But in the east, what was the social composition and investment in writing of the Sants and their successors (and followers)?" (email, Sept. 1, 2013).

15. Even that limited claim is subject to doubt. As Purushottam Agrawal says (2009a, 218), the fact that a text doesn't appear in an early dated manuscript doesn't prove that it didn't exist at an early date.
16. See Callewaert 2000, 75 for details of the four groups and star-distribution. See also Dharwadker 2003, 33–41 and Hawley 2005, 194–207 for further light on early "cores" and expanding "complete works."
17. Agrawal (2009a, 204–5) offers a cogent discussion of the Fatehpur manuscript.
18. For instance, Imre Bangha's website on the *Kavātāvalī* critical edition project, http://tulsidas.orient.ox.ac.uk/ (accessed July 2014).

19. No examples are mentioned. It would be helpful to see examples of how Kabir poems in Dadu Panthi manuscripts go against teachings of the *panth*.
20. This is a reference to the *sākhī* that begins *kaṭuk shabda kabīr ke*, "Kabir's harsh words," cited in full in chapter 6.
21. Particularly relevant is Guru Amardas, who served as the third Sikh guru from 1552 to 1574. Gurinder Singh Mann (2001) has shown in chapter 7 of *The Making of Sikh Scripture* that Guru Amardas was most likely responsible for adding the *bhagat bāṇī*, including Kabir, to the developing text that would become the *Ādi Granth*.
22. If we compare the narrower collection of Callewaert's starred poems to the *Granthāvalī*, the overlap may be even closer than the above numbers show. This would support Agrawal's view that the *Granthāvalī* is the best single "core" text (or at least one of the best), and it would also speak well for Callewaert's method.
23. A note from the field of Buddhist manuscript studies sets the right tone for evaluating Kabir manuscripts as well. In an online article about the search for an authentic Buddhist canon, Linda Heumann quotes Oskar von Hinüber, a Pali scholar: "Nobody holds the view of an original canon anymore." Paul Harrison of Stanford University elaborates: "If everything just proceeds in its own vertical line, and there is no crossways influence, that is fine; you know where you are. But once things start flowing horizontally, you get a real mess. Having something old, of course, is valuable because you are more likely to be closer to an earlier form. But notice I'm careful to say now 'an earlier form' and not 'the earliest form.' A first-century B.C.E. [Gandhari] manuscript is going to give you a better guide to an earlier form than an 18th-century Sri Lankan copy will. But that's not an absolute guarantee, just a slightly better one" (http://www.douban.com/group/topic/22375578/, accessed Sept. 2011).
24. This passage follows the translation in Virmani 2008f, 9, cited in Agrawal 2009a, 218.
25. Agrawal coined the term *uparachnā* here, and I made up an English term to translate it.
26. On the matter of category formation I can never forget Borges's great fabrication of the Chinese encyclopedia, to which I and many others have been introduced through the preface to Foucault's *The Order of Things: An Archaeology of the Human Sciences*: "This book first arose out of a passage in Borges, out of the laughter that shattered, as I read the passage, all the familiar landmarks of my thought—our thought, the thought that bears the stamp of our age and our geography—breaking up all the ordered surfaces and all the planes with which we are accustomed to tame the wild profusion of existing things, and continuing long afterwards to disturb and threaten with collapse our age-old distinction between the Same and the Other. This passage quotes a 'certain Chinese encyclopedia' in which it is written that 'animals are divided into: (a) belonging to the Emperor, (b) embalmed, (c) tame, (d) sucking pigs, (e) sirens, (f) fabulous,

(g) stray dogs, (h) included in the present classification, (i) frenzied, (j) innumerable, (k) drawn with a very fine camelhair brush, (1) et cetera, (m) having just broken the water pitcher, (n) that from a long way off look like flies.' In the wonderment of this taxonomy, the thing we apprehend in one great leap, the thing that, by means of the fable, is demonstrated as the exotic charm of another system of thought, is the limitation of our own, the stark impossibility of thinking that. But what is it impossible to think, and what kind of impossibility are we faced with here?" (Foucault 1994, xv).

27. John Keats's letter to George and Tom Keats, 27 December 1817. http://www.poetryfoundation.org/learning/essay/237836?page=2.
28. From film footage in the Kabir Project archive.
29. This is a slightly edited version of a transcript of the interview. I am grateful to Chintan Girish Modi for sending me the transcript and pointing out this passage.
30. Conversation on July 16, 2005.
31. Tiwari retired in 2011; I haven't been able to find out the exact date when his directorship began.
32. This interview is preserved in Shabnam Virmani's collection of footage though it was not used in any of her documentary films.
33. Tijan-bāī is a brilliant performer of *Mahābhārata* stories in a vernacular performance genre called *panḍvāṇī.*
34. Here we must cite a well-known poem of Kabir:

   The pandits' pedantries are lies.
   If saying Ram gave liberation
   saying candy made your mouth sweet
   saying fire burned your feet,
   saying water quenched your thirst,
   saying food banished hunger,
   the whole world would be free.

   (For a translation of the whole poem, see Hess and Singh 2002, 54.)
35. Bhajan: *Har har mārūngā.*
36. I first met Kumarji's family—his wife Vasundhara, daughter Kalapini, and grandson Bhuvan—in Dewas in 2002. They added another instance to the well-known stories of Kumarji's frequent visits to the Shilnath *dhūnī* singing circles and his first encounter with *Suntā hai guru gyānī* through the voice of a wandering yogi. An old unlettered woman lived on the "hill of Devi" in Dewas, where Kumarji and his family also lived. He called her Mirabai and used to invite her home and listen to her sing. The family brought her to meet me one day. I still have a cassette of her singing. She is no longer alive.
37. Kumarji said he didn't make up the melodies he composed but found them present in the poetry (Hess 2009a, 23). However, he also relied a great deal on Shilnath's printed collection for the texts he sang (Hess 2009a, 21–23).

38. After reflecting on these statements by Tiwari, I want to ask him if he would ever mark a poem as inauthentic, not aligned with Kabir's truth. If so, what examples would he give? What does he think of what Shabnam has called "obvious corruptions" in the oral tradition? For example, the song *Dhanya kabīr*, recorded by Prahladji and group, recites as fact the miraculous birth of Kabir on a lotus and includes modern stereotypes of violent enemies against whom true *dharma* must be protected.
39. Salomon 1996; Knight 2011; Snodgrass 2006.
40. I am reminded of V. Raghavan's 1966 *The Great Integrators: The Saint-Singers of India*. Raghavan, a renowned Sanskritist, traced many similes, extended metaphors, and themes in their frequent appearances among bhakti poets all over India, in every major language. He also showed how some of these common tropes can be traced all the way back to the Upaniṣads. Though his book was clearly oriented toward India's postindependence preoccupation with national integration, and though he spoke of a unitary "bhakti movement" no longer granted by scholars, he was right in observing the very widespread sharing of extended metaphors and other patterns of imagery and symbolism.
41. My translation of the stanza on Kabir, *chappay* 60 in Nābhadas's *Bhaktamāl* [Garland of Devotees], ed. S. B. Rupkala, Lucknow, 1962.
42. *bachāyā hindū dharma ko hinsakoṇ se*: He [Kabir] saved the Hindu religion from its violent (opponents).
43. On the story of his relationship with the Panth, see chapter 7; and Virmani 2008b.
44. In 2010, an undergraduate student majoring in computer science, Nicelio Sanchez-Luege, took a class with me. Nicelio did a statistical study using translations of Kabir poems by Rabindranath Tagore, Robert Bly, and me. A chart with colored dots representing statistical findings on the three translators suggested to me the power of such visual patterns to reveal different ways of seeing. He concluded in his unpublished course paper: "The stated goal of the project was to verify whether Kabir's poems were suitable for statistical analysis, and whether translator was a statistically significant variable in PCA. Kabir's poetry is certainly apt for statistical analysis. Despite the project's naïve word-count method (using all words), PCA showed clear stratification according to translator. The statistical significance of the results makes this project a suitable prototype for larger-scale projects. Computational statistics allows for staggering amounts of data, thus a study including every translated Kabir poem is plausible from a computational perspective. In addition to more data, future studies may add more variables to further explore correlations in the data. The emergence of translator as a significant factor using such simple methods warrants further investigation into the relationship between translator and poem. A more sophisticated study would include variables such as the region of the original text, the year it was printed, and who transcribed it. Each translator may have implicit bias in any of these variables. Such a study could add an arbitrary amount of

variables to analyze Kabir's poetry from different cultural, regional, and linguistic perspectives."

An updated indication of the possibilities of computer analysis of Kabir texts comes from my colleague and collaborator Jaroslav Strnad, whose work on manuscripts has been discussed earlier in this chapter. "[A proposed] initiative called ENIAT (Early New Indo-Aryan Texts) ... [aims] to offer electronic versions of texts suitable for quantitative processing by way of word lists, concordances, keywords etc. (sophisticated software for these tasks already exists and is easily available). When I finished the typing of *sākhīs* into my computer it was quite easy to convert... into ASCII Latin alphabet which can be comfortably searched even by the most ordinary tools incorporated into the MS Word, for example. Searching for particular words and phrases is no problem now" (email, Feb. 7, 2015).

CHAPTER 4

1. Bhajan: *Kaī ḍhūnḍhtī phiro mhārī helī.*
2. According to one Kabir Panthi book that Prahladji showed me, *pṛithvī* (earth) is related to *haḍḍī, mās, tvachā, lobh, raktavāhiyā; jal* (water) to *kaph, pitt, rakt, prasved, vīrya; agni* (fire) to *ālasya, janhai, nidra, kshadha, tṛiṣha; vāyu* (wind) to *śhakti prayog, dhāvan, prasāraṇ, sakuchan, sharīrik vṛiddhi; akāśh* (space/ether) to *kām, krodh, lobh, moh, ahaṃkār.*
3. The male and female snakes appear in *Gyān kī jaḍiyāṇ*, the deer in *Thane gam nī rākhī bhāī, to gayā khet sab khāī.*
4. Why are the 5 male, the 25 female? My first guess is that women are generally understood as more troublesome than men in the realm of spiritual endeavor, and more linked to materiality. So the larger class of problems related to material existence would be female. Some say that it's simply a matter of grammatical gender: the words for "element" (*mahābhūt*) and "sense" (*indriyā*) are masculine, the word for "process of nature" (*prakṛiti*) feminine.
5. See chapter 3 for discussion of the *Granthāvalī* edited by Shyamsundar Das, published in 1928, and regarded by Purushottam Agrawal as the most reliable of all Kabir manuscripts.
6. The remaining categories as listed in Das 1970 [1928]: *ras, lāmbi, jarṇā, hairān, lai, nihakarmī pativratā, chitāvaṇī, man, sūṣhim mārag, sūṣhim janam, māyā, chāṇak, karaṇī binā kathnī, kathaṇī binā karaṇī, kāmī nar, sahaj, sānch, bhram vidhauṃṣhaṇ, bheṣh, kusangati, sangati, asādh, sādh, sādh sākhībhūt, sādh mahimā, madhi, sāṛagrāhī, vichār, upadeśh, besās, pīv pichhāṇan, birkatāī, samrathāī, kusabad, sabad, jīvan mritak, chit kapaṭī, gurusiṣh herā, het prīti saneh, sūrā tan, kāl, sajīvani, apāriṣh, pāriṣh, upajaṇi, dayā nirabairatā, sundari, kastūriyaṇ mṛig, nindyā, niguṇā, bīnatī, sākhībhūt, belī, abihaḍ.*
7. See chapter 3, n. 26.

8. These and all otherwise unidentified lines from poetry are unpublished texts that I have learned solely from oral performance—the songs of Malwa.
9. For more on Albert Lord, see chapter 5.
10. I encountered the term *rekhtā* connected to Kabir only because Prahladji has a few *rekhtā* compositions that he often sings in the place where usually *sākhīs* are presented, or in combination with *sākhīs*, before the bhajan. Imre Bangha provides a fine article on *rekhtā*. "The Persian word *rekhta* ('poured, interspersed, mixed') had several technical meanings. Prior to the eighteenth century, it was part of musical terminology. It also referred to a mode of writing, namely to poetry written in a language that mixes lines, phrases and vocabulary from Hindi and Persian (. . . [this] also includes the Arabic vocabulary imbibed by Persian), in which the Hindavi component is normally Khari Boli and sometimes Braj Bhasha or a mixture of the two. As a musical term, Rekhta appears in Alauddin Barnavi's musicological treatise … (1655) … as a kind of text in which one sets the words of both langauges to a *raga* and a *tala* … [which] indicates an early link between Rekhta and Hindustani music. … In the eighteenth century, Rekhta appears also as the name of Khari Boli mixed with Perso-Arabic vocabulary [notably used by the Urdu poet Mir]" (Bangha 2010, 25–26). Of the four *rekhtās* I transcribed from Prahladji, three have Kabir's *chhāp* and one that of Paltu Das. Only one has a conspicuous mix of Hindi *khari boli* and Perso-Arabic language. The other three are characterized by yogic terminology.
11. Described in the conclusion to chapter 1.
12. In the simplest version of traditional Hindu social stratification, there are four *varṇas* (classes). In texts known collectively as Dharma Shastras, the top three *varṇas*—*brāhmaṇ*, *kṣhatriyā*, and *vaiśhya*—are considered "twice-born," as they are permitted to partiake of upper caste rites of passage. The fourth class—*śhūdra*—is separate and defined as a servant class, created to serve the upper three. The groups who came to be known as untouchables are yet another level, outside the *varṇa* hierarchy and much lower in status and ritual purity than the Shudras. The commonly referenced "caste system" is much more complicated than this, and its history is contested.
13. The heron is proverbial for false holiness. Pure white, it stands still like a yogi, but its only purpose is to spear a fish.
14. One stanza sung by Prahladji and generally not included by Shabnam and me is on the *satī*, or woman who burns herself alive on her deceased husband's funeral pyre. See discussion of this poem and this trope in chapter 2.
15. A few examples: *Nirbhay nirguṇ* as sung by Kumar Gandharva (Hess 2009a, 88–89); *Rang mahal; Piyujī binā; Panchhiḍā bhāī*—three songs often sung by Prahladji; Mukhtiyar Ali's explanation of the jewels in a *sākhī* that he sings in the film *Had anhad/Bounded-Boundless* (Virmani 2008d). The bhajans are full of references to the mind (*man*, Sanskrit *manas*) and other faculties and levels of consciousness (*chit, ahaṃkār*, etc.) that are treated more systematically and

abstractly in Sanskrit philosophical traditions. But it would be a big mistake to think of the content of *nirguṇ* poetry as merely a crude vernacular version of yoga/tantra/advaita/*sāṃkya* philosophy.

16. Right, left, and center are *inglā, pinglā,* and *sukhman,* the three major yogic energy channels
17. Bhajan: *Ṭhane gam nī rākhe bhāī, gayā khet sab khāī.*
18. Bhajan: *Mat kar māyā ko ahaṃkār, mat kar kāyā ko abhimān.*
19. Bhajan: *Ketā jājo jī bhalā bhāī.*
20. Bhajan: *Ab ke bachāī le morī mā.*
21. *moha*—attraction, attachment, love, affection, delusion. Note the convergence of these various meanings. *Lagāv,* similarly, means attachment, connection, fellow-feeling, affection.
22. By "that one," he refers to God or ultimate reality. I have no doubt that he would sometimes say the things that Shantiji refers to, but I have seen Prahladji cry on several occasions. The first time was at the airport in 2003, when the group was leaving for India after our two-month tour in the United States, and we were all crying. Another instance was in the Bhopal recording session described below in this section.
23. Once at a mountain retreat where Prahladji had been called for a workshop, he ruminated on how Kabir might have hit upon the subject of this song and others: "Kabir always said *kahat kabīr.* It is a *kahnā-sunnā* (speaking-hearing) thing. Direct. Kabir didn't write or read, but his thinking and understanding were so powerful. He looked at things directly and understood." At that point he looked at the thick ranks of flowers in front of us, on the edge of the Himalayan hill—orange, pink, violet. "Kabir would have seen flowers like this. He noticed that some were buds, some were dried up and dead, some were at the peak of their beauty. A gardener came along and started picking the flowers. Kabir noticed that he didn't take the buds or the dried-up ones: only those that were in full bloom. Right there he understood. So he created that *sākhī—mālī āvat dekhiyā, kaliyāṇ kare pukār / phūl phūl chun liye, kāl hamārī bār*—Seeing the gardener come, the buds cry out: / he's picking the flowers one by one. Tomorrow it's our turn.

    And the bhajan *Jāvo nugarī kāyā.* He must have seen someone who died, the body lying in front of his house, a fine big house, a palace, with so much care taken on the windows, the doors, the stairways. The body is like that. It's beautiful, with its doorways and colors. He must have seen the body lying in front of the house, and he understood. You made a beautiful palace but you couldn't stay in it. The one who stayed there is gone."
24. Bhajan: *Mat kar māyā ko ahaṃkār mat kar kaya ko abhimān.*
25. Bhajan: *Dulahanīṃ gāvahu mangalachār.* This is the first *pad* in the first section (*rāg gauḍī*) of S. Das's *Kabīr granthāvalī.*

26. Barthwal (1936, 281) explains how Dharamdasi literature sets forth the creation of twelve false branches of the Panth. "Anurāga Sāgar suggests a bitter dispute regarding succession to the headship of the Dharamdāsī branch in the sixth generation from Dharamdās. They also contain recriminations against other panthas founded on the teachings of Kabīr. According to the Anurāga Sāgar and other works, in Kali Yuga, Kabīr works for the release of souls untrammelled by any promise to Niranjan. Still the latter has cheated out of him the secrets of the *Name* and has given birth to the twelve Nirguna sects (Dwādaśha Panth) who prevent the righteous from coming to the shelter of the successors of Dharamdās whose family Kabīr is said to have ordained the true leadership continuously for forty-two generations." Barthwal names some of the founders of the twelve *panths*, including derisive nicknames given by the Dharamdasis.

    A Kabir Panthi guru named Rampal (who was re-arrested in 2014, on a list of serious charges, amid violent resistance by his followers) set up a website promoting his own lineage and contesting claims to legitimacy by others. Here he quotes and comments on the passage from *Anurāg Sāgar* that proclaims establishment of the twelve *panths*: <http://www.kabirpanth.jagatgururampalji.org/fourteenth_mahant_native_seat.php>
27. Bhajan: *Begam kī gam kar le re haṃsā.*
28. This is an example of how mapping oral traditions can reveal the influence of regional and sectarian cultures on the living body of Kabir literature.
29. This may be because I was focusing on the fixed text of the *Bījak*, not listening to folksingers in the countryside.
30. Bhajan: *Aisā des hamārā.*
31. Bhajan: *Bheḍā hai par miltā nāhīṇ.*
32. English lacks other words that carry the resonance of "love," but Hindi-Urdu has quite a few including *prem, pyār, iśhk, prīti, sneha,* all of which occur in Kabir and other *nirguṇ* poets.
33. Chapter 6 provides a profile of Kaluram.
34. *jāgīrī* in the Mughal period refers to a land-grant with authority to rule.
35. On this occasion, Kaluram sings *sabūrī* (contentment or patience) in the last line. I have also heard *sarūrī* (joy) in this line and have translated the latter here.
36. *til ole*, the last two words, are interesting. *Til* can mean sesame seed or the pupil of the eye. *Olā* has two separate meanings—a hailstone (not relevant here); and a screen, or figuratively secrecy. Archaic meanings are given as *gupt bāt, bhed, rahasya*—hidden matter, secret, mystery.
37. Bhajan: *Maiṇ divānā nām kā.*
38. Bhajan: *Pī le amīras dhārā gagan meṇ jhaḍī lagī.*
39. Bhajan: *Satguru ne bhang pilāī, akhiyoṇ meṇ lālan chhāī.*
40. Bhajan: *Barkhā agam chalī āī.*
41. Bhajan: *Gyān ki jaḍiyā, daī mere sadguru.*
42. Bhajan: *Hame satguru se milnā hai.*

43. I have heard many times that Kabir in particular and *nirguṇ* in general are just "simple" renditions of Advaita Vedanta philosophy—something like the way stained glass windows made the Bible accessible to illiterate peasants in medieval Europe. Kabir gives us *māyā, ātma, paramātma, karma, mokśha,* and advice to eradicate the five passions, with some extended metaphors from the Upaniṣhads, all in a nice simple Hindi for the common folk. At first this made some sense to me, but over the years I have gone from vague irritation to wholesale rejection of this claim. Kabir's eye sees a world that doesn't exist in Sanskrit philosophy. It is a flesh-and-blood eye, gazing at people in their everyday activities. It is a critical eye with a voice to match, calling out abuses and lies. The voice shows a sense of humor with a satirical slant. A different kind of intelligence is operating. Consider these among countless examples:

When your dad was alive, you wouldn't give him a scrap of bread.
When he's dead, you shave your head and feed his soul through a crow.

***

One voice says Vishnu's in Vaikunth,
another says he's in Cow Heaven,
a third says the Lord's in Shiva's city.
For ages they've marketed these products.

Shankara (my straw man for Advaita) does not give us chickens and widows, shopkeepers and dogs. Shankara has a shaved head and does not make fun of men with shaved heads. Kabir's evocations of the everyday lives of ordinary people are not just colorful add-ons. They create a fundamentally different vision.

CHAPTER 5

1. Linguist Deborah Tannen observes: "[S]trategies associated with oral tradition place emphasis on shared knowledge and the interpersonal relationship between communicator and audience. In this, they 'elaborate' what Bateson (1972) calls the metacommunicative function of language: the use of words to convey something about the relationship between communicator and audience. Literate tradition emphasizes what Bateson calls the communicative function of language: the use of words to convey information or content" (Tannen 1982, 2–3). In his essay in the same volume, Wallace Chafe describes how "speakers interact with their audiences, writers do not" (ibid., 45).
2. In 2012, Lord's famous book was in storage in Stanford's library system and had to be called out of exile to be read, showing the generational rise and fall of stardom in academia.
3. Works that pay particular attention to the interplay of oral and written modes in religious scriptures and in India include Coburn 1984 and Graham 1987.

4. <www.pathwaysproject.org>, accessed in July 2009.
5. As recently as 1987, in *Beyond the Written Word: Oral Aspects of Scripture in the History of Religion*, William Graham wrote: "We live in a world increasingly dominated by the printed word—a world, as the novelist Italo Calvino has put it, 'dense with writing that surrounds us on all sides,' whether in newsprint, magazines, and paperbacks, or on billboards" (ix). In the post-2000 world the adverb "increasingly" is not applicable; it should in fact be replaced by its opposite.
6. In 2013, I found that the website had changed quite a bit since I had gathered quotations from it four years earlier. This is Foley's revised and improved statement of the main thesis.
7. Perhaps McLuhan deserves some credit for making the connection between print and nationalism, a central point in Benedict Anderson's famous 1983 work *Imagined Communities.*
8. McLuhan 1964, cited at <http://www.livinginternet.com/i/ii_mcluhan.htm>.
9. <http://www.livinginternet.com/i/ii_mcluhan.htm>, accessed December 2012.

   Another interesting prophetic statement by Nicola Tesla is quoted on the same page, even more striking as it was much earlier. Tesla said in 1926: "When wireless is perfectly applied the whole earth will be converted into a huge brain, which in fact it is, all things being particles of a real and rhythmic whole. We shall be able to communicate with one another instantly, irrespective of distance. Not only this, but through television and telephony we shall see and hear one another as perfectly as though we were face to face, despite intervening distances of thousands of miles; and the instruments through which we shall be able to do his will be amazingly simple compared with our present telephone. A man will be able to carry one in his vest pocket."
10. Chaytor 1945, cited in McLuhan 1962, 88.
11. By speaking of "our own experience," do I imply a universal "we" that won't hold up to examination? I leave this as a debatable question.
12. I am grateful to Sean Hanretta for introducing me to this work
13. It's not a coincidence that the first global web-browser, launched in 1993, was called Mosaic.
14. We can now learn in detail about what is happening neurologically and cognitively when we read. Stanislas Dehaene's 2009 book *Reading in the Brain* is a scientifically sophisticated, widely accessible and fascinating study. It's clear that visual and auditory functions, written words and speech, are enmeshed with each other in complex ways. But they are also separable; they are not the same.
15. "If this book does nothing else, perhaps it will convince you that there are more than five senses. … The idea that we have exactly five senses dates back at least to Aristotle. … Nine would be a much better much better estimate" (Henshaw 2012, 6–7).

16. Later Horowitz gives further details on how hearing is much faster than seeing: see 96ff.
17. *Hearing: Science of the Senses,* a film described at <http://films.com/ItemDetails.aspx?TitleId=26468> (accessed June 5, 2013). In the preview clip available on the site, this speaker is unidentified.
18. Does this mean that we must fundamentally imagine sound as vibration, produced and experienced through many bodily and environmental factors, not necessarily tied to reception by ears? We could say this, but we must also say that the ears have been specially constructed to receive and further transmit such vibrations. In all but very exceptional circumstances, ears are central and crucial to the reception and negotiation of sound.
19. <http://homepages.bw.edu/~rfowler/pubs/secondoral/index.html>, accessed July 17, 2009.
20. For example, Carr 2011 and Turkle 2012.

    There is a visually and verbally witty four-minute cartoon video called "What the Internet Is Doing to Our Brains," inspired by Nicholas Carr (2011), at <http://www.karmatube.org/videos.php?id=4057> accessed August 2013. Carr is heard calmly narrating at some points, along with a more frenetic voice that simulates our state of mind when careening around from link to link. The video shows how the constant distraction of email and internet practices destroys our ability to pay sustained attention to anything. Attention is the key to intelligence, creativity, and ultimately, the piece proposes, our humanity. The video is persuasive and entertaining. And it comes to us via the internet. When I received an email that directed me to it, I interrupted whatever I was planning to do at that time to follow the links.

    Here is an intriguing statement on technology and love by the novelist Jonathan Franzen:

> "Let me toss out the idea that, as our markets discover and respond to what consumers most want, our technology has become extremely adept at creating products that correspond to our fantasy ideal of an erotic relationship, in which the beloved object asks for nothing and gives everything, instantly, and makes us feel all powerful, and doesn't throw terrible scenes when it's replaced by an even sexier object and is consigned to a drawer.
>
> "To speak more generally, the ultimate goal of technology, the telos of techne, is to replace a natural world that's indifferent to our wishes—a world of hurricanes and hardships and breakable hearts, a world of resistance—with a world so responsive to our wishes as to be, effectively, a mere extension of the self.
>
> "Let me suggest, finally, that the world of techno-consumerism is therefore troubled by real love, and that it has no choice but to trouble love in turn." *New York Times,* May 28, 2011, <http://www.nytimes.com/2011/05/29/

opinion/29franzen.html?_r=1&nl=todaysheadlines&emc=tha212&pagewanted=all>.

21. Wikipedia does a pretty good job with its brief definition of "dissociation": "a term in psychology describing a wide array of experiences from mild detachment from immediate surroundings to more severe detachment from physical and emotional reality. It is commonly displayed on a continuum. The major characteristic of all dissociative phenomena involves a detachment from reality—rather than a loss of reality as in psychosis. In mild cases, dissociation can be regarded as a coping mechanism or defense mechanism in seeking to master, minimize or tolerate stress—including boredom or conflict. At the nonpathological end of the continuum, dissociation describes common events such as daydreaming while driving a vehicle. Further along the continuum are non-pathological altered states of consciousness.

    "More pathological dissociation involves dissociative disorders. . . . These alterations can include: a sense that self or the world is unreal . . . ; a loss of memory . . . ; forgetting identity or assuming a new self . . . ; . . . fragmentation of identity or self into separate streams of consciousness . . . and complex post-traumatic stress disorder. Dissociative disorders are sometimes triggered by trauma, but may be preceded only by stress, psychoactive substances, or no identifiable trigger at all."
22. See Siegel 2012 and <http://drdansiegel.com>.
23. On National Public Radio's *Fresh Air*, Aug. 2, 2010.
24. McLuhan had discussed Plato's critique of writing two decades earlier (1962, 25).

CHAPTER 6

1. Pete Seeger's famous song "Guantanamera" is a setting of the Cuban poet and freedom fighter Jose Marti's poem. Seeger gives a translation on CD 2 of the album *We Shall Overcome: Complete Carnegie Hall Concert* (recorded on June 8, 1963).
2. Eklavya chose another fiery line as a title for the official report on its project with Kabir singers: *kaṭuk vachan kabīr ke, sun ke āg lag jāī*, "Kabir's words are searing, just hearing them sets off a fire" (Eklavya 1999).
3. Official government designations include Scheduled Castes, Scheduled Tribes, Other Backward Castes (abbreviated as SC, ST, OBC). The first two roughly line up with "Dalit" or former "untouchable" groups, the third with groups loosely affiliated with Shudra castes.
4. See, for example, Mukta 1998; N. Martin 1999, 2000, 2002; Hawley and Juergensmeyer 2007, chap. 1.
5. Harbans Mukhia, "Eklavya loses thumb again." *The Hindu*, Aug. 5, 2002, <http://www.thehindu.com/2002/08/05/stories/2002080500251000.htm>, accessed in August 2011.

6. Translated from a conversation in Hindi.
7. Eklavya workers were interested in a wide range of social-political issues, including caste, poverty, religious authority, superstition, exploitation, communalism. Many urban artists, intellectuals, and activists in the 1990s and 2000s were attracted to Kabir and the Sufi-*sant* heritage because of their dismay at the country's communal turn, the resurgence of religious nationalism and resulting social division, hatred, and violence. Shabnam Virmani began the Kabir Project because she had been so disturbed by the extreme communal violence in Gujarat in 2002. But Malwa Kabir singers had different priorities. The two top issues for them were caste and organized religion, particularly the Kabir Panth with which many of them were affiliated. Communalism was a more remote topic that didn't affect their daily lives. The politics of nationalism was even more remote. All the musicians in the Kabir *manch* were born as Hindus in the broadest sense of the term. There were no Muslims. Rather than prejudice or exclusion, this reflects the fact that historically in India, Kabir has been embraced by and folded into the Hindu community far more than the Muslim. (See interviews on Muslim views of Kabir in Virmani 2008d and Lorenzen 1981a.) The disconnect between Malwa Kabir singers' views and national politics was shown by a younger musician who told me in 2004 that he was considering going into politics with the BJP. I was appalled. Did he realize that the BJP was linked to the Sangh Parivar and Hindu nationalism, and that the Sangh Parivar's values were terribly opposed to Kabir's? He didn't.
8. In March 2002 I visited Dinesh Sharma's home in Devali village. His father was the leader of a large *maṇḍalī* that sang in a different style from the Malwa style, associated with the Singaji Panth in the Nimar region of M.P. They obviously got pleasure and a high out of it, singing loudly for several hours in a call and response fashion with drums and cymbals. Many closed their eyes for concentration. There wasn't much melody. The tempo regularly changed from slow to fast and back again. The drummer seemed to dance with his upper body and head as he played. But when, at my request, the leader started giving long explanations in Hindi of each verse, he went to sleep on his drum. I then said the explanations should stop, and he came back to life. I ask how their bodies and minds changed after hours of singing. He answered, "We feel love for *paramātma*." I asked again, emphasizing the body. "We feel lightness" (*halkāpan*). They didn't seem to have any interest in the critical, socially relevant songs of Kabir. From the words I picked up, their songs featured mythologies of Kabir's career as an avatar; moral admonitions ("having received a human body, why don't you keep it pure?"); yogic imagery. Toward midnight they built up to an intense pitch, cymbals swinging and banging, drummer in the middle totally absorbed, his head dancing. They gestured, their bodies went up and down vertically, voices got fuller. A smaller circle of about twelve at that point, they were all very

concentrated. I retired but heard that they started singing a folk genre called *phagun*, and from jumping in their seats started jumping on their feet, dancing and shouting till 3 a.m.

9. All material from Kabir *manch* tapes, registers, and files has been translated by LH from Hindi unless otherwise indicated.
10. See n. 2 above.
11. The poem, from the *Bījak* (Hess and Singh 2002, 54–55), goes like this:

> The pandit's pedantries are lies. / If saying Ram gave liberation, / saying candy sweetened the mouth, / saying fire burned your foot, / saying water quenched your thirst, / saying food banished hunger, / the whole world would be free. / The parrot gabbles *God* like a man / but doesn't know God's glory. / When he flies off to the jungle, / he'll forget God. / If you don't see, if you don't touch, / what's the use of the Name? / If saying money made you rich, / nobody would be poor. / If you love lust and delusion, / you can't get a glimpse of God. / Kabir says, God is one. / Love the one or shuffle off in chains / to the City of Death.

12. See chapter 4, n. 8.
13. Article dated February 6, 1992.
14. Lucknow edition of the *Times of India*, April 22, 1993.
15. Much information on the Balais (or Balahis) in this area, including some of the Kabir singers I knew and worked with, is available in "Caste, Class and Sect: A Study of the Balahis in Malwa circa 1940–1994," a master's thesis submitted to the History Department of Delhi University by Shahana Bhattacharya in 1996. At the time of this writing, Bhattacharya is on the faculty of Kirori Mal College, University of Delhi. She was kind enough to provide me with a copy of her thesis, which I had seen in the Dewas Eklavya office. She notes in her preface that the Malwa lower castes in general, and the Balahis in particular, have a striking familiarity with Kabir's teachings, though only about 15 percent of the Balahis she surveyed were formally members of the Kabir Panth. About their status, she wrote: "balahis, both by their own standards, and those of most other castes in the area, are considered to rank the highest among all the 'untouchable' groups in the caste hierarchy in Malwa. The ritual distance that exists between, say, the balahis, and the bagris, chamars, and other scheduled castes . . . seems to be enhanced by the distinctly higher economic status of the balahis today" (vii).
16. The same title was given to this booklet of socially conscious song texts (discussed and translated above, p. 263–264) and to the first audiocassette by Prahladji's group, produced by the *manch* in 1993 (see reference to the cassette in Suresh Patel's interview).

17. The play was *Kabīr* by the great Hindi writer Bhisham Sahni (1915–2003). Were the director and the playwright related? I don't know. Kiran Sahni and his group are shown rehearsing and discussing the play in the film *Kabira khaḍā bazar meṇ* (Virmani 2008b).
18. Around 2004. Shabnam's tapes aren't marked with dates, but they are classified carefully for easy retrieval. This cassette is marked MP Raj DV1, the interview beginning about 22 minutes into the tape.
19. On Kapil Tiwari, see chapters 3 and 8.
20. This song, *Kaī ḍhūnḍhtī phiro mhārī helī*, is sung by Prahladji in an early section of Shabnam Virmani's film *Chalo hamārā des/Come to My Country*.
21. This song, *Guru sam dātā koī nahīṇ*, is sung by Shabnam and Prahladji during the closing credits of the film *Chalo hamārā des/Come to My Country* (Virmani 2008a).
22. Bhajan: *Sāhib ne bhāng pilāī*.
23. Bhajan: *Panchhīḍā bhāī*.
24. In 2014 Narayan Singh Delmia took the lead in reorganizing the Kabir manch, with monthly meetings and some financial support from private donors. In 2015 I heard that it had taken off and the groups were gathering enthusiastically.
25. The word translated as "blessing" is *bakśhīśh*, which in common parlance is a tip or gratuity. This is an unusual usage. Discussions of how best to translate it led to this imperfect solution. It seems to be a rough and whimsical use of an unexpected marketplace image—like *bhāng*.
26. For a rigorous examination of the historicity of Ramanand, see Agrawal 2009a, chap. 5 (Hindi); and Agrawal 2009b, 135–70 (English). Agrawal (2001) has sharply criticized what he regards as the extreme identity politics and other issues in Dharamvir's later writings. He draws scholars Winand Callewaert and J. S. Hawley into his criticism insofar as they accept Dharamvir's critique of Dvivedi's "brahminical bias" (see chapter 3 above). See also Horstmann 2002,115–42 (her essay, "Hazariprasad Dvivedi's Kabir," in the volume she edited).
27. The implication is: stay in touch with yourself, let your own nature bring forth good company.
28. Holy places associated with Krishna and Shiva.
29. A *sākhī* from the *Bījak*. Hess and Singh 2002, 121.
30. This is a variant of *sākhī* 280 in the *Bījak* (Hess and Singh 2002, 123). Oil was sold for cooking, pulp for animal fodder, so both were useful.
31. He once told me a story about how his wife sent him out with money to buy *rākhīs*, the ornamented string bracelets used for the Raksha Bandhan festival. This important family-oriented holiday celebrates the relation between brothers and sisters. Females tie the bracelets on the arms of males who are in their actual families or with whom they have created a ritual relationship. Narayanji took the money and couldn't resist spending it on a book—in this case one by Osho (Rajneesh), whose commentaries on Kabir and other spiritual matters

have received much praise. He went home without the *rākhīs* and was in big trouble with the women in the family.

32. The verse refers to Gangaur, a festival devoted to Gauri (Parvati), popular in Rajasthan and parts of M.P. and Gujarat, with fervent participation by women devotees.
33. There are hierarchies and degrees of untouchability practiced even among those castes whom upper castes lump together as untouchable.
34. Anu Gupta and Arvind Sardana, who have worked for Eklavya in Dewas for many years. They are always my hosts when I stay in Dewas. In 2011 Arvind became the director of the whole Eklavya organization.
35. Shabnam and I are both outsiders to rural Kabir culture in different ways. The fact that we had power to open doors for local people shaped our relationships in various ways, which we often reflected on and talked about—with each other and with Malwa friends.
36. Singaji was a *nirguṇ sant* of Madhya Pradesh, born in the late sixteenth century, whose followers tend to be of higher castes.
37. In a culture where people generally avoid touching leftover food, a wife's eating her husband's leftovers is a kind of intimate practice, as well as an expression of purity hierarchies.
38. The conversation occurred in August 2003 with Arvind Sardana and Prakash Kant at the Dewas Eklavya office.
39. Namvar Singh is a very eminent Hindi literary scholar and critic who has written important works on Kabir. It was he who first told me about the Eklavya Kabir *manch*, when we met at a conference in Heidelberg in 2000. He urged me to go there and write about what Eklavya and the *mandalīs* had done together.
40. See chapter 1 for a description of another poignant occasion on which this song was sung.

CHAPTER 7

1. Special thanks to David Lorenzen, who responded to my inquiries with a stream of information that helped me to complete the article that was the original form of this chapter (Hess 2009b). David has been a reliable (and forgiving) friend and colleague since we first met in Varanasi in 1976.
2. Here is a version of this well-known story from a Sikh website: "Feeling his end was near, the Hindus said we will cremate you, the Muslims said we will bury you. Guru Nanak said: 'You place flowers on either side, Hindus on my right, Muslims on my left. Those whose flowers remain fresh tomorrow will have their way.' He then asked them to pray and lay down covering himself with a sheet. Thus on September 22, 1539 in the early hours of the morning Guru Nanak merged with the eternal light of the Creator. When the followers lifted the sheet they found nothing except the flowers which were all fresh. The Hindus

took theirs and cremated them, while the Muslims took their flowers and buried them." < http://www.sikhs.org/guru1.htm>

3. Lorenzen 1991, 125. Lorenzen dates this text at around 1600 (ibid., 10–13).
4. Ibid., 41. A song chanted regularly in Kabir Panthi rituals refers specifically to this episode (Lorenzen 1996, 251).
5. *Bījak śhabda* 4, translated in Hess and Singh 2002, 42. (I have slightly changed my own translation here.)
6. By "myth" I mean not falsehood, as in common parlance, but sacred narrative—the stories communities tell to convey the deepest truths about their founders, histories, and understanding of reality (Dundes 1984).
7. According to the official state website in 2007, Chhattisgarh's population includes 44.7 percent Scheduled Castes and Tribes. These communities are indispensable for politicians. The site notes that religious reform movements stressing equality have been important in Chhattisgarh, and it provides a paragraph on the Kabir Panth.<http://chhattisgarh.nic.in/profile/corigin.htm#mainhistory>. At the two Kabir Panth *melās* I attended in Damakheda and Bandhavgarh in 2002, the then Chief Minister of Chhattisgarh, Ajit Jogi, made conspicuous appearances, and the speeches included warm mutual praise from the leaders of the Panth and the state government.
8. Usually given as 1518. See Lorenzen 1991, 9–18.
9. When I say that "Kabir" was critical or positive or emphasized certain points, I refer to themes that are common across all the important collections attributed to him.
10. David Lorenzen notes that not all members of the Kabir Chaura–based division of the Panth believe Kabir was an avatar who manifested himself on Lahartara Pond. In particular, he says that its current leader Vivek Das (about whom more below) does not believe this (email, July 3, 2006). The Damakheda-based Dharamdasi Kabir Panth does teach this miraculous version of Kabir as avatar.
11. Caste distinctions are notoriously entrenched in Indian society, and a particular outpost of the sect will only be as enlightened as its leadership. The Chhattisgarh website cited in n. 7 above states: "The Kabir Panth does not believe in caste hierarchies. However in contemporary times the Panth has been divided along caste lines. The only time that they do not adhere to caste hierarchies is in the presence of the Chief Guru on the birth anniversary of Kabir." Keay observes that Kabīr's attempts to preach against caste "met with little success" and that separate *chaukā āratī* rituals were arranged for different castes (Keay 1931,109). Lorenzen finds the Kabir Chaura ritual practices quite free of caste distinctions (Lorenzen 1996, 249–50). I have heard Acharya Prakashmuni Nam Sahab of Damakheda speak vigorously against the caste system and was told that he had arranged high-profile marriages, including that of his own brother, across castes. On the other hand, in a film interview (Virmani 2008b), Hiralal Sisodiya

laughingly dismisses claims that the Kabir Panth is truly caste-free, reciting a funny couplet about the perpetual resurfacing of caste practices.

12. David Lorenzen has been a mine of information on the various Kabir Panth traditions for many years. During the writing of this chapter, he pointed out to me that one important tradition, the *Pārakhī* sect headed by Abhilash Das, are atheists who seem to have considerable Jain influence: "Abhilash Das's group is an offshoot of the Burhanpur *śhākhā* which, in theory at least, follows the Purandas '*Trijya*' commentary on the *Bījak*. Puran Das (and Abhilash Das) believe in immortal *jivas* [souls] but not in *ishvar* [God]. This doctrine, and the Burhanpur *śhākhā* in general, seem to be much influenced by Jainism, which of course follows a similar doctrine. The Burhanpur sadhus also worry a lot about eating bugs (*jivas*), etc. like the Jains. . . . Abhilash Das is an impressive organizer and a very prolific writer. He has his own printing press. His *Kabīr darśhan* book is important. He spends part of the year in Allahabad, part in Calcutta, and part on tour (especially in the Nagpur region). He has a fair number of sadhus under his control and also a group of women sadhus. He is said to be a Brahmin of a family somehow related to Ram Chandra Shukla" (email, July 6, 2006). Abhilash Das passed away in 2013.
13. For a summary of stories about Kabir's disciples and the Panths they founded, see Lorenzen 1991, 55–65. Recent historical accounts in Hindi of the Kabir Panth with its various branches have been written by Dr. Rajendra Prasad (1999), who is affiliated with Damakheda; and Vivek Das, Acharya of Kabir Chaura (2003a). An important early scholarly work by P. D. Barthwal, *The Nirguna School of Hindi Poetry*, has an extensive annotated bibliography that gives evidence of early rivalry within as well as among Kabir Panth lineages: "These works … show what shape the teachings of Kabir took at the hands of his followers mostly those belonging to the Dharamdasi branch. They also help in constructing the history of that branch. For instance, Anuraga Sagar suggests a bitter dispute regarding succession to the headship of the Dharamdasi branch in the sixth generation from Dharamdas. They also contain recriminations against the other panthas founded on the teachings of Kabir" (Barthwal 1936, 281).
14. A rival faction of Dharamdas-following Kabir Panthis is based at Kharsiya in Chhattisgarh.
15. Some Kabir mythology claims that he had five penises.
16. "CHAPTER XV of the Indian Penal Code: OF OFFENCES RELATING TO RELIGION. 145[295A]. Deliberate and malicious acts, intended to outrage religious feelings of any class by insulting its religion or religious beliefs.

    Whoever, with deliberate and malicious intention of outraging the religious feelings of any class of 146[citizens of India], 147[by words, either spoken or written, or by signs or by visible representations or otherwise], insults or attempts to insult the religion or the religious beliefs of that class, shall be punished with imprisonment of either description for a term which may extend to 148[three years], or with fine, or with both.] ...

298. Uttering, words, etc., with deliberate intent to wound the religious feelings of any person—Whoever, with the deliberate intention of wounding the religious feelings of any person, utters any word or makes any sound in the hearing of that person or makes any gesture in the sight of that person or places, any object in the sight of that person, shall be punished with imprisonment of either description for a term which may extend to one year, or with fine, or with both" (<http://www.helplinelaw.com/bareact/bact.php?no=15&dsp=ind-penal-code&PHPSESSID=cf79e2d637bbaa65e271dd8bd3a3913a> accessed in 2008).

As I learned in excellent papers by Barton Scott and Cassie Adcock at the 2014 annual meeting of the American Academy of Religion, this law was enacted under colonial rule, not in independent India. Thanks to Ajay Skaria for referring me to this illuminating article, which locates the history of Section 295A in the 1920s: Neeti Nair, "Beyond the 'Communal' 1920s: The Problem of Intention, Legislative Pragmatism, and the Making of Section 295A of the Indian Penal Code," *Indian Economic Social History Review* (2013) 50: 317–340.

17. A violent attack on Prahladji and Shabnam by Kabir Panthis occurred in Vadodara (Baroda), Gujarat, in 2010. After his falling-out with the Dharamdasi Kabir Panth in 2005 (recounted later in this chapter), some of the devout followers of that Panth and its Guru became quite hostile. At a Kabir Festival in Vadodara, Prahladji had a concert, and Shabnam's film *Kabirā khaḍā bāzār meṇ* was shown. After the program, as they were walking to their car in the parking lot, a gang of Kabir Panthis confronted them and started beating Prahladji. They managed to get into the car and the driver took off. The attackers threw rocks; a window shattered over Prahladji and Shabnam. Another group of attackers was blocking the main gate. The skillful driver managed to escape without further injury to anyone.
18. Gangasharan Das was the name he used when I met him in the late 1970s. He later changed his name to Gangasharan Shastri.
19. See also Barari 1980. The title refers to the helmsman as one who holds the mysteries of the *chaukā*.
20. This is the name used in the Damakheda Kabir Panth for the supreme being who sends forth avatars in each of the four ages. Satyapurush is like Vishnu for Vaishnavs.
21. Bandhavgarh is a remote spot in the far north of Madhya Pradesh, known today for its tourist-attracting wild animal reserve. It is important in this branch of the Kabir Panth as the home of Dharamdas, the wealthy merchant who gave his money to his guru Kabir and became the founder of the Panth. They believe that Dharamdas spent years with the master in a cave at the top of a high cliff, receiving teachings and preparing to establish the true lineage of Kabir's followers. The teachings would be written down in the form of the *Anurāg Sāgar*, this sect's

most cherished text. Acharya Prakashmuni Nam Sahab had organized the *melā* at Bandhavgarh for the first time in April 2002, saying it was a longtime dream of his to bring the Kabir Panthis to this spot and lead a pilgrimage through the forest and up the cliff to the sacred place of origin.

22. The function was always held on a *purnimā* (full moon) date. The choice of Buddha Purnima that year was partly just how the scheduling happened to work out, but everyone was also aware of the special importance of Buddha and Buddhism to B. R. Ambedkar, the great leader of untouchable liberation.
23. Years later Prahladji told me that the first time he did *chaukā āratī*, he had an experience, an insight, that caused a tremor (*ghabrāhat*) in him. What is really happening with *bandagī*? It is not that the disciple looks to the guru to get something, or that the guru has an idea of doing something to the disciple, but that they look into each other's eyes and see themselves. Suddenly he realized that they are one, there is no difference, and that is the true meaning of guru and disciple.
24. These views are summarized from several video conversations filmed by Shabnam Virmani.
25. It is remarkable to note that Prahladji gave this interview in 2004, while attending the great annual gathering of the Kabir Panth and still a mahant. *Describing outrageous excesses in certain verses that enjoin absolute obedience to and veneration of the guru, he laughed at the absurd claim that "if you listen to any insult of the guru, you're a criminal and should be beaten up." In 2010, this is exactly what happened to him. He was beaten up by Panth zealots who called him a gurudrohī* (see pp. 309-310 and p. 431, n. 17).
26. One weakness in Prahladji's argument was that he was well-off, having a government job as a schoolteacher as well as substantial income from his success as a singer. Other *mahants* were likely to be poorer and to have fewer choices.
27. Lorenzen 1981, 162. Gangasharanji made the same statement in a 2003 conversation with me.
28. "The earliest reference to the *chaukā* seems to be that of the above translated 'Jñān gudarī' ("Quilt of Knowledge"), which states:

> He disperses all his egotism and pride, / as he lights his body's chauka. // Making mind the sandalwood, intellect the flowers, / welfare his bow of respect, he finds the root. // Making faith the flywhisk, love the incense, / he finds the pristine name, the form of the Lord.

... the date of the 'Jñān gudarī' is unknown ... The oldest manuscript ... is dated ... 1838 C.E. ... The presence of the 'Jñān gudarī' in the *Sandhyā pāṭh* booklets of almost all branches of the Kabir Panth, however, suggests that it is an old composition, perhaps older than the split of the Kabīr Panth into its Kabīr Chaurā and Dharmdāsī branches. This split cannot be dated with any assurance either, but it probably took place over 300 years ago" (Lorenzen 1996, 238).

29. In a 2007 update, based on his visit to India in January, David Lorenzen wrote to me about the implementation of *chaukā āratī* reform that Acharya Vivek Das had called for in the Kabir Chaura sect. Vivek Das had compromised with other leaders who wanted to keep the *chaukā*. They had started to describe it as "guru puja," keeping the forms almost identical but eliminating references to Satyapurush—the supreme being who, especially for the Dharamdasis, is seen as the source of Kabir's four avatars in the four ages (email from Lorenzen, January 30, 2007). Meanwhile Vivek Das's attack on the Dharamdasis had grown even sharper. In a 2006 book, *Vaṃsha kabīr kā aṃśa*, he goes so far as to refer to them as "cockroaches."
30. I did not attend this *melā*, but got a report from Shabnam Virmani, who caught some of these comments by Huzur-sahab on video.
31. The power of fragmentary evidence has been forever impressed on me by Gyanendra Pandey's brilliant article "In Defense of the Fragment" (Pandey 1997).

CHAPTER 8

1. Other prominent scholars have written on political interpretations of Kabir. The most prominent and persistent on this theme is David Lorenzen, many of whose works are listed in the References. I have cited Purushottam Agrawal in this chapter. His *Akath kahānī prem kī* (2009a) and earlier works are highly recommended. Dr. Dharamvir's *Kabīr ke ālochak* (1997) presented a Dalit interpretation that vigorously criticized Brahmin scholars of Hindi literature who had previously dominated the discourse. Monika Horstmann gives a glimpse in English of Dharamvir's critique of Hazariprasad Dvivedi (2002, 124–25). Gail Omvedt (2008) writes of Marathi and Hindi bhakti poets as "anticaste intellectuals." Nancy Martin urges us to observe subtle ways in which bhakti figures like Kabir, Mirabai, and Ravidas give strength and inspiration to low-caste and economically poor people in rural North India. Invoking both Christian liberation theology and James Scott's "weapons of the weak," she says that low-caste communities share messages of equality, the dignity of work, the nonseparateness of body and spirit, and faith and joy under hard circumstances, which sustain them in meaningful ways: "The theology … articulated in narrative and song by Meghvāl performers in rural western Rajasthan … is not revolutionary, but rather speaks of loving God in the midst of suffering and pain. It is a theology of dignity and self-respect, which privileges the wisdom and religious authority that are particularly the province of the poor and disenfranchised" (N. Martin 2002, 202).
2. The rise of Hindu nationalist politics in the 1990s, accompanied by growing polarization between Hindus and Muslims (as well as Christians and other minorities), has been noted in chapter 6. The worst flashpoints of communal violence were in 1992–93, triggered by the demolition of the Babri mosque in Ayodhya; and in 2002 in Gujarat, when the burning of a railway car in Godhra caused the deaths of fifty-eight Hindu pilgrims returning from Ayodhya, leading in turn to months of violence mostly victimizing Muslims.

3. Quotations come from the published essay in the catalog, on which his more informal opening remarks were based.
4. *Chetāvanī* is discussed as one of the local ways of categorizing Kabir bhajans in chapter 4.
5. SAHMAT is an organization created in 1989 after the murder of Safdar Hashmi, a theater director, writer, and activist. Hashmi was attacked in broad daylight during a street theater performance. "Writers, painters, scholars, poets, architects, photographers, designers, cultural activists and media persons formed the Safdar Hashmi Memorial Trust," carrying out "a resolve to resist the forces threatening the essentially pluralist and democratic spirit of creative expression" <http://www.sahmat.org/aboutsahmat.html>. SAHMAT is both an acronym for the Safdar Hashmi Memorial Trust and a Hindi word meaning agreement or harmony. The organization has been active continuously since 1989. In 1992, after the demolition of the 1526 mosque in Ayodhya known as the Babri Masjid, SAHMAT produced a series of concerts in Ayodhya featuring bhakti and Sufi music and poetry. The concert series was called *Anahad garje*, a phrase from Kabir that means "The unstruck sound roars."
6. *Santo dekho jag baurānā*. An English version is in Hess and Singh 2002, 42.
7. For a brief and evocative account of how *rasa* theory reaches across aesthetic and religious domains, see Goswamy 1986. Discussions of *rasa* in the arts go back some two thousand years to the classic *Nātya Śhastra*. Major adaptations of *rasa* in the religious realm are seen in the works of Abhinavagupta, the eleventh-century philosopher of Kashmir Shaivism (Masson and Patwardhan 1970) and the *rāgānugā* bhakti of Gauḍiyā Vaishnavism (Haberman 1988). Chapter 4 has a section on themes of "liquid joy" in Malwa's Kabir.
8. <www.marxists.org/archive/gorky-maxim/1924/01/x01.htm>, accessed August 2013. Alternate translation by George Lukacs on the same site: "Gorky recorded Lenin's very characteristic words spoken after he listened to Beethoven's Appassionata sonata: 'I know the Appassionata inside out and yet I am willing to listen to it every day. It is wonderful, ethereal music. On hearing it I proudly, maybe somewhat naively, think: See! people are able to produce such marvels!' He then winked, laughed and added sadly: 'I'm often unable to listen to music, it gets on my nerves, I would like to stroke my fellow beings and whisper sweet nothings in their ears for being able to produce such beautiful things in spite of the abominable hell they are living in. However, today one shouldn't caress anybody-for people will only bite off your hand; strike, without pity, although theoretically we are against any kind of violence. Umph, it is, in fact, an infernally difficult task!' " <http://www.marxists.org/archive/lukacs/works/xxxx/lenin.htm>
9. Rashtriya Swayamsevak Sangh, founded in 1925, widely regarded as the most powerful component of the Sangh Parivar or family of political and cultural organizations that have coalesced around Hindu nationalism since the late 1980s.
10. Among many sources on this are King 1999 and Masuzawa 2005.

11. http://www.nytimes.com/2012/08/20/us/as-esalen-celebrates-its-past-its-future-is-debated.html?hpw, accessed August 2013. Among recent books mapping the spiritual-religious terrain is Jeffrey Kripal's *Esalen: America and the Religion of No Religion* (2008). Others include Goldberg 2013; Bender 2010; Schmidt 2012. Kripal and Goldberg are especially knowledgeable about Indian influences on "the West." Bender traces a peculiarly American spirituality that focuses on "individual meaning, experience, and exploration" but has "historic roots in the nineteenth century and a great deal in common with traditional religious movements." Schmidt looks at both Asian and American sources in his book, which, according to a publisher's blurb "explores America's abiding romance with spirituality as religion's better half."

    Thanks to Kathryn Lofton for references to Schmidt and Bender. In response to my question about the class location of the "spiritual not religious" crowd, Lofton says that their fieldwork does demonstrate a "bourgeois demographic" and a widespread consumer culture of spirituality in contemporary America. But she also says that the subject is more complicated. Bender and Schmidt trace American spirituality back two centuries. Lofton adds: "the language of 'spirit' and 'spirituality' has always circulated in evangelical circles … and evangelicalism has (a) a critical relationship to the question of institutional power, (b) a wide-ranging class demographic" (email, Oct. 18, 2012).
12. Purushottom Agrawal (2000, 133–37) has critically traced the genealogy of "mysticism" and found it to be problematic. His essay title, translated from Hindi, is "The Politics of Calling Kabir a Mystic." I still use the word sparingly, lacking a good alternative.
13. Have the conditions of late capitalism (alienation, individualism, competition, mobility erasing connection with place, weakened family ties, growing isolation) undermined the traditional ways in which religions served human needs, opening a wider split between "religious" and "spiritual"? On July 28, 2013, I listened to *New Dimensions*—a US radio program, on the air since 1973, featuring spiritual speakers of all kinds. The guest was David Bennett, author of a book on near death experiences and the wisdom associated with them. Near the end of his interview, he spoke of hosting circles of people at his home in central New York. Avoiding labels with religious baggage, he called these people simply "experiencers" and said the circles provided a greatly needed sense of community for people who had spiritual experiences. I noted to myself that community was one of the major functions of traditional religious organizations. Then he spoke of the power of ceremony, describing a "gratitude ceremony" he did every morning and mentioning the altars set up in various rooms of his house. The interviewer affirmed the value of ceremonies: through repetition and symbol they have a deep impact on consciousness. We can see where this is going: when the social solidarity and ritual provided by religion are pushed out the institutional door, they come back in the spiritual window.

14. The first is *Dharm, adhyātma aur marksvād* ("Religion, Spirituality, and Marxism)." The second, *'Dharm kī adharmik samīkshā' aur dharmetar adhyātma* ("'Nonreligious Investigation of Religion' and Secular Spirituality") continues the discussion of Marx while responding to another author's critical comments. Other essays including *Dharmsattā banām ātmasattā, adhyātmasattā* ("Religious authority vs. individual authority and spiritual authority") also refer to Marx on spirituality, all citing the *Economic and Philosophic Manuscripts of 1844*.
15. "Marx says in the 1844 *Manuscripts* that just as labor gets alienated—your own physical activity gets alienated and becomes labor, a commodity to be sold and purchased in the market—similarly, your basic nature, the essence of your being human becomes alienated in the form of religion, becomes a commodity, an activity imposed upon you from an outside agency, divine or diabolical" (Agrawal 2009c,).
16. This idea is first laid out clearly in "*Dharmsatta banām ātmasattā, adhyātmasattā*" (2004, 23–26), but references to the Faustian pact are repeated many times throughout the book as well as in Agrawal 2009a.
17. Kabir sometimes uses imagery of the narrow passage:

Kabir's house is at the top / of a narrow, slippery track.
An ant's foot won't fit. / Oh man, you're loading a bullock!

***

Dear friend, the formless courtyard / is very narrow.
You can't get in. / If you get in, you'll meet the beloved....
Let's go / to the guru's country
where you can't get in / or out.

***

The lane of love is very narrow.
Two can't get in.

18. Cited in Tulku Thondup, "The Buddha Said Four Things," *Shambhala Sun* 10, no. 5 (May 2002): 38. Available online, Tulku Thondup Rinpoche "World Peace Begins in Your Mind," <http://www.kosei-shuppan.co.jp/english/text/mag/2007/07_456_8.html.>
19. It won the Academy Award in 2007 for best foreign language film.
20. From an interview with Terry Gross on National Public Radio's *Fresh Air*, Aug. 10, 2007.
21. Agrawal may be misrepresenting contemporary English usage of "spiritual," which is not necessarily different from his understanding of *adhyātmik*.
22. This is part of the footage shot by Shabnam Virmani, but it was not used in any of the four documentary films she produced. It will eventually be uploaded on the website that will go under the name "*Ajab Shahar*," under construction as this book goes to press.
23. Bhajan: *Satguru ne bhāng pilāī*.

24. Bhajan: *Pī le amīras dhārā gagan meṇ jhaḍī lagī.*
25. Dalit-Bahujan refers to a modern political alliance of the castes that orthodox Brahmanism marked as untouchable or defined as Shudra, the fourth *varṇa* category whose members were born only to serve the upper three *varṇas*.
26. See Reagon 2001 and W. Martin 2005. From the former: "In the vortex of the struggle, the personal and the social were indeed political. While the Movement obviously fought over the public and tangible, it also concerned itself with the private and interior landscapes of black people's lives. It concerned itself with the affective, the emotional, and the psychological. As the singing preachers always want to know from their audience: 'How do you feel?' Part of their charge is to help people 'feel' better, if only for a moment. In fact, nurturing the 'soul' is absolutely vital cultural as well as social work" (50).
27. On Begampura, see Omvedt 2008, 106–7, and introduction: "The bhakti radical, Sant Ravidas (c. 1450–1520), was the first to formulate an Indian version of utopia in his song 'Begumpura.' 'Begumpura,' the 'city without sorrow,' is a casteless, classless society; a modern society, one without a mention of temples; an urban society as contrasted with Gandhi's village utopia of Ram Rajya. 'Begumpura' describes a land with no taxes, toil, or harassment, where there is no hierarchy but all are equal. Finally, calling himself a 'tanner now set free,' he proclaims that he wanders freely with his friends: the right to walk anywhere in a settlement, city or village is a unique matter for dalits." See also chapter 4 above, section on "That Country."
28. This song had previously been adapted for use in the labor movement of the 1930s: "The union is behind us, we shall not be moved." "Sweet Chariot: A History of the Spirituals" is a website (accessed August 2013) built largely out of Arthur Jones's work. One page <http://ctl.du.edu/spirituals/freedom/civil.cfm> has a chart showing examples of changes made "From Slave Spiritual to Civil Rights Movement Freedom Song." The site also lists other sources on music in the civil rights movement.
29. These lyrics have been extracted from various recordings that I have listened to.
30. Shabnam comments that many people have expressed anxiety about politically charged scenes. Friendly viewers might say, "The film was great, but why did you have to put in the Ayodhya part and the Wagah part? How are they relevant?" She showed the film in Godhra, where the 2002 Gujarat communal violence began when fifty-eight Hindu pilgrims were killed in a railway car fire. There, she said, viewers hated the film and attacked it in her presence as offensively anti-Hindu. However, the overall response to the film among viewers in India and abroad has been overwhelmingly positive.
31. In this connection I'd like to mention two great artists whom I've come to know in the course of this project—the singer Shubha Mudgal and the painter Ghulam

Mohammed Sheikh—committed to struggles against communalism and caste oppression among other causes, and unafraid of "the religious idiom."

32. Krishna Nath's comments are translated from a Hindi conversation that was captured on video by Shabnam Virmani but not used in any of her four documentary films..
33. This is not accurate. When smallpox disappeared people attributed other diseases to the goddess and found ways to keep her relevant. See Ferrari 2007, 2009.
34. Hear this in Florence Reece's voice at <http://www.youtube.com/watch?v=Nzudto-FA5Y> and in Pete Seeger's recording at <http://www.youtube.com/watch?v=msEYGqlodrc>.
35. Bhajan: *Karnā re hoy.*
36. Bhajan: *Kyoṇ bhūlīgī ṭhāro des.*
37. Bhajan: *Man lāgo mero yār fakīrī meṇ.*
38. Bhajan: *Binā chandā re binā bhāṇ.*

References

Agrawal, Purushottam. 2000. "Kabīr ko 'rahasyavādī' kahane kī rājnīti" (The Politics of Calling Kabir a "Mystic"). In *Vichār kā anant*. New Delhi: Rajkamal Prakashan (Hindi).

——. 2001. "*'Jāt hī pūchho sādhu kī . . .' Asmitāvādī atichār ke sāmne kabīr kī kavitā*" ("'Ask Only about the Holy Man's Caste . . .' Kabir's Poetry Confronts the Excesses of Identity Politics"). *Bahuvachan* 2, no. 6 (January–March 2001): 311–25 (Hindi).

——. 2004. *Nij Brahm Vichār: Dharm, Samāj aur Dharmetar Adhyātma* (*A Transcendent Thought of One's Own: Religion, Society and Secular Spirituality*). New Delhi: Rajkamal Prakashan (Hindi).

——. 2009a. *Akath kahānī prem kī: kabīr kī kavitā aur unkā samay* (*The Untellable Story of Love: Kabir's Poetry and Times*). New Delhi: Rajkamal Prakashan (Hindi).

——. 2009b. "In Search of Ramanand: The Guru of Kabir and Others." In Banerjee and Dube, eds., 135–70.

——. 2009c. "My Personal and Political Kabir." Partial transcript of a lecture given at a Kabir Festival in Bangalore, <http://sunosadho.blogspot.in/2011/03/purushottam-agarwals-kabir.html>. Video of the lecture at https://www.youtube.com/watch?v=bWyTFl6s62s#t=381

Auslander, Philip. 2008. *Liveness: Performance in a Mediatized Culture*. 2nd ed. New York: Routledge.

Baid, Neha. 2012. "*Niranjanī sampradāy kī anya nirguṇ sampradyoṃ se mat-bhinnatā*" ("Philosophical Differences between the Niranjani Sect and other Nirgun Sects"). *Paper delivered at the International Conference on Early Modern Literatures in North India. Aug. 3–6, Indian Institute of Advanced Study, Shimla (Hindi).*

Banerjee, Ishita, and Saurabh Dube, eds. 2009. *From Ancient to Modern: Religion, Power, and Community in North India*. New Delhi: Oxford University Press.

Bangha, Imre. 2010. "Rekhta: Poetry in Mixed Language." In Orsini, ed., 2010, 18–83.

Barari, Mahant Sukritdasji. 1980 [1947]. *Chaukā-chandrikā, arthāt kaṇḍihārī bhed (Moonlight on the Chaukā, or the Helmsman's Mysteries)*. Kharsiya, M.P.: n.p. (Hindi).

Barthes, Roland. 1978. "The Death of the Author." In *Image-Music-Text*, ed. and trans. Stephen Heath. New York: Hill & Wang. Originally published in French in 1967.

Barthwal, P. D. 1936. *The Nirguṇa School of Hindi Poetry*. Benares: India Book Shop.

Bellman, E. 2009. "Cellphone Entertainment Takes Off in Rural India." *Wall Street Journal*, November 22.

Bender, Courtney. 2010. *The New Metaphysicals: Spirituality and the American Religious Imagination*. Chicago: University of Chicago Press.

Bergen, Benjamin K. 2012. *Louder Than Words: The New Science of how the Mind Makes Meaning*. New York: Basic Books.

Bhatt, Chetan. 2001. *Hindu Nationalism: Origins, Ideologies and Modern Myths*. New York: Bloomsbury Academic.

Bhattacharya, Shahana. 1996. "Caste, Class, and Sect: A Study of the Balahis in Malwa, circa 1940–1994." M.Phil. thesis, University of Delhi.

Blascovich, Jim and Jeremy Bailenson. 2011. *Infinite Reality: Avatars, Eternal Life, New Worlds, and the Dawn of the Virtual Revolution*. New York: HarperCollins.

Bryant, Kenneth E. 1979. *Poems to the Child-God: Structures and Strategies in the Poetry of Surdas*. Berkeley: University of California Press.

——, ed., and John Stratton Hawley, trans. 2015. *Sur's Ocean: Poems from the Early Tradition*. Cambridge, MA: Harvard University Press.

Callewaert, Winand M., in collaboration with Swapna Sharma and Dieter Taillieu. 2000. *The Millennium Kabir Vāṇī*. Delhi: Manohar.

——. 2013. *From Chant to Script*. Delhi: DK Printworld.

Callewaert, Winand M., and Mukund Lath. 1989. *The Hindi Songs of Nāmdev*. Louvain, Belgium: Peeters Press.

Carr, Nicholas. 2011. *The Shallows: What the Internet Is Doing to Our Brains*. New York: Norton.

Chafe, Wallace L. 1982. "Integration and Involvement in Speaking, Writing, and Oral Literature." In Tannen, 35–54.

Chodron, Pema. 2005. *No Time to Lose: A Timely Guide to the Way of the Bodhisattva*. Boston: Shambhala.

Coburn, Thomas B. 1984. "'Scripture' in India: Towards a Typology of the Word in Hindu Life." *JAAR* 52: 435–59.

Crooke, William. 1999 [1896]. *The Tribes and Castes of the North-Western Provinces and Oudh*. 4 vols. Calcutta: Asian Education Services.

Das, Shyamsundar, ed. 1970 [1928]. *Kabīr granthāvalī*. Varanasi: Nagaripracharini Sabha (Hindi).

Das, Vivek. 2003a. *Kabīr ka sach*. Varanasi: Kabirvani Prakashan Kendra (Hindi).

——. 2003b. *Ghat kā chaukā*. Varanasi: Kabirvani Prakashan Kendra (Hindi).

——. 2006. *Vaṃśha kabīr kā aṃśha?* Varanasi: Kabirvani Prakashan Kendra (Hindi).

Das, Vivek, and Krishna Kalki, eds. 1998. *Ḍhai akśhar.* New Delhi: Kabir Bhavan (Hindi).

Dehaene, Stanislas. 2009. *Reading in the Brain: The New Science of How We Read.* New York: Penguin.

Dehalavi, Mahant Sudhadas, ed. 1970. *Chaukā āratī paddhatī, arthāt kaṇḍiārī gutakā.* Damakheda, M.P.: Vansh pratap gaddi, Kabir Nagar (Hindi).

Delvoye, Francoise "Nalini." 1994. "The Thematic Range of *Dhrupad* Songs Attributed to Tansen, Foremost Court-Musician of the Mughal Emperor Akbar." In *Studies in South Asian Devotional Literature,* ed. Alan W. Entwistle and Francoise Mallison, 406–29. New Delhi: Manohar.

Dharamvir, Dr. 1997. *Kabīr ke ālochak.* New Delhi: Vani Prakashan (Hindi).

Dharwadker, Vinay. 2003. *Kabir: The Weaver's Songs.* New York: Penguin.

Dikshit, Akhilesh. 1993. Article in Lucknow edition of the *Times of India,* April 22, 1993. Clipping kept in Eklavya files.

Doniger, Wendy. 1991. "Fluid and Fixed Texts in India." In Flueckiger and Sears 31–41.

——. 1995. *Other People's Myths: The Cave of Echoes.* Chicago: University of Chicago Press.

Dundes, Alan. 1984. *Sacred Narrative: Readings in the Theory of Myth.* Berkeley: University of California Press.

Dvivedi, Hazariprasad. 1971 [1942]. *Kabīr.* Delhi: Rajkamal Prakashan (Hindi).

Eklavya. 1999. *Documentation of Kabir's Verse as Sung by Kabir-Panthis of Malwa.* Dewas: unpublished project report (English and Hindi).

Ferrari, Fabrizio M. 2007. "Love Me Two Times: From Smallpox to AIDS, Contagion and Possession in the Cult of Śitala." *Religion of South Asia* 1, no. 1: 81–106.

——. 2009. "Old Rituals for New Threats: The Post-Smallpox Career of Śitala, the Cold Mother of Bengal." In *Ritual Matters,* ed. C. Brosius and U. Hüsken, 144–71. New York: Routledge.

Finnegan, Ruth. 1977. *Oral Poetry: Its Nature, Significance, and Social Context.* Cambridge, UK: Cambridge University Press [2nd rev. ed. 1992, Bloomington and Indianapolis: Indiana University Press].

Fish, Stanley. 1972. *Self-Consuming Artifacts: The Experience of Seventeeth-Century Literature.* Berkeley: University of California Press.

——. 1980. *Is There a Text in This Class? The Authority of Interpretive Communities.* Cambridge, MA: Harvard University Press.

Flueckiger, Joyce Burkhalter, and Laurie J. Sears, eds. 1991. *Boundaries of the Text: Epic Performances in South and Southeast Asia.* Ann Arbor: Center for South and Southeast Asian Studies, University of Michigan.

Foucault, Michel. 1977. "What Is an Author?" Trans. Donald F. Bouchard and Sherry Simon. In *Language, Counter-Memory, Practice,* ed. Donald F. Bouchard, 124–27. Ithaca, NY: Cornell University Press. Originally delivered as a lecture in 1969.

——. 1994 [Pantheon 1971]. *The Order of Things: An Archaeology of the Human Sciences.* New York: Vintage. (Orig. *Les Mots et Les Choses* published in French in 1966. The translator is not named in any English edition.)

Gold, Ann Grodzins. 1992. *A Carnival of Parting: The Tales of King Bharthari and King Gopi Chand as Sung and Told by Madhu Natisar of Ghatiyali, Rajasthan.* Berkeley: University of California Press.

Gold, Daniel. 1999. "Nath Yogis as Established Alternatives: Householders and Ascetics Today." *Journal of Asian and African Studies* 34, no. 1: 68–88.

——. 2002. "Kabīr's Secrets for Householders: Truths and Rumours among Rajasthani Nāths." In Horstmann 2002.

Gold, D., and A. G. Gold. 1984. "The Fate of the Householder Nath." *History of Religions* 24, no. 2: 113–32.

Goldberg, Philip. 2013. *American Veda. From Emerson and the Beatles to Yoga and Meditation: How Indian Spirituality Changed the West.* New York: Harmony.

Goswamy, B. N. 1986. "Rasa: Delight of the Reason." In *The Essence of Indian Art*, ed. B. N. Goswamy, 17–30. San Francisco, CA: Asian Art Museum.

Graham, William A. 1987. *Beyond the Written Word: Oral Aspects of Scripture in the History of Religion.* Cambridge: Cambridge University Press.

Haberman, David. 1988. *Acting as a Way of Salvation: A Study of Rāgānugā Bhakti Sādhanā.* New York: Oxford University Press.

Hare, James. 2011a. "Contested Communities and the Re-imagination of Nabhadas' *Bhaktamāl.*" In *Time, History, and the Religious Imaginary in South Asia*, ed. Anne Murphy, 150–66. New York: Routledge.

——. 2011b. *Garland of Devotees: Nābhādās' Bhaktamāl and Modern Hinduism.* Ph.D. diss., Columbia University.

Hawley, John Stratton. 2005. *Three Bhakti Voices: Mirabai, Surdas, and Kabir in Their Times and Ours.* New York: Oxford University Press.

——. 2009. *The Memory of Love: Sūrdās Sings to Krishna.* New York: Oxford University Press.

Hawley, John Stratton, and Mark Juergensmeyer. *Songs of the Saints of India.* New York: Oxford University Press, 1988.

Hayles, Katherine. 1999. *How We Became Posthuman: Virtual Bodies, Cybernetics, Literature, and Informatics.* Chicago: University of Chicago Press.

Henry, Edward O. 1991. *Chant the Names of God: Musical Culture in Bhojpuri-Speaking India.* San Diego, CA: San Diego State University Press.

——. 1995. "The Vitality of the Nirgun Bhajan: Sampling the Contemporary Tradition." In Lorenzen 1995, 231–50.

Henshaw, John M. 2012. *A Tour of the Senses: How Your Brain Interprets the World.* Baltimore: Johns Hopkins University Press.

Hess, Linda. 1987a. "Kabir's Rough Rhetoric." In *The Sants: Studies in a Devotional Tradition of India*, ed. Karine Schomer and W. H. McLeod, 143–66. Berkeley, CA: Religious Studies Series, and Delhi: Motilal Banarsidass.

——. 1987b. "Three Kabir Collections: A Comparative Study." In *The Sants: Studies in a Devotional Tradition of India*, ed. Karine Schomer and W. H. McLeod, 111–42. Berkeley, CA: Religious Studies Series, and Delhi: Motilal Banarsidass.

——. 1993. "Staring at Frames till They Turn into Loops: An Excursion through Some Worlds of Tulsidas." In *Living Banaras: Hindu Religion in Cultural Context*, ed. C. A. Humes and B. Hertel, 73–101. Albany: State University of New York Press.

——. 1994a. "Marshalling Sacred Texts: Ram's Name and Story in Late Twentieth Century Indian Politics." *Journal of Vaiṣṇava Studies* 2, no. 4 (1994): 175–206.

——. 1994b. *A Touch of Grace: Songs of Kabir*. Translated with Shukdev Singh, introduction by Linda Hess. Boston, MA: Shambhala.

——. 2002 [1983]. *The Bijak of Kabir*. Translations by Linda Hess and Shukdev Singh. Essays and notes by Linda Hess. New York: Oxford University Press.

——. 2006. "Ramlila: The Audience Experience." In *The Life of Hinduism*, ed. John Stratton Hawley and Vasudha Narayanan, 115–39. Berkeley: University of California Press.

——. 2009a. *Singing Emptiness: Kumar Gandharva Performs the Poetry of Kabir*. Calcutta: Seagull. Distributed outside India by University of Chicago Press.

——. 2009b. "Fighting over Kabir's Dead Body." In *From Ancient to Modern: Religion, Power, and Community in North India*, ed. Ishita Banerjee and Saurabh Dube. New Delhi: Oxford University Press.

Hess, Linda, and Richard Schechner. 1977. "The Ramlila of Ramnagar." *Drama Review* 21: 51–82.

Honko, Lauri. 2000. *Textualization of Oral Epics*. Berlin: De Gruyter Mouton.

Horowitz, Seth S. 2012. *The Universal Sense: How Hearing Shapes the Mind*. New York: Bloomsbury.

Horstmann, Monika, ed. 2002. *Images of Kabir*. New Delhi: Manohar.

Jones, Arthur. 1993. *Wade in the Water: The Wisdom of the Spirituals*. Marynoll, NY: Orbis Books.

Juergensmeyer, Mark. 1991. *Radhasoami Reality: The Logic of a Modern Faith*. Princeton, NJ: Princeton University Press.

Kapur, Anuradha. 1993. "Deity to Crusader: The Changing Iconography of Ram." In *Hindus and Others: The Question of Identity in India Today*. New Delhi: Viking.

Keay, F. E. 1931. *Kabīr and His Followers*. Calcutta: Association Press (YMCA).

King, Richard. 1999. *Orientalism and Religion: Post-Colonial Theory, India and "The Mystic East."* New York: Routledge.

Knight, Lisa. 2011. *Contradictory Lives: Baul Women in India and Bangladesh*. New York: Oxford University Press.

Kripal, Jeffrey. 2008. *Esalen: America and the Religion of No Religion*. Chicago: University of Chicago Press.

Kumar, Neha, Gopal Singh, and Tapan Parikh. 2011. "Folk Music in India Goes Digital." ACM Digital Library. Proceedings of the SIGCHI Conference on Human Factors in Computing Systems, 1423–32.

Lakoff, George, and Mark Johnson. 2003. *Metaphors We Live By*. Chicago: University of Chicago Press.

Lopez, Donald, ed. 1995. *Religions of India in Practice.* Princeton, NJ: Princeton University Press.

Lord, Albert B. 1960. *The Singer of Tales.* Cambridge, MA: Harvard University Press. (40th anniversary edition published by Harvard in 2000 includes a CD with photos, audio, video, and an introduction by editors Stephen Mitchell and Gregory Nagy.)

——. 1986. "Perspectives on Recent Work on the Oral Traditional Formula." *Oral Tradition* 1/3: 467–503.

Lorenzen, David N. 1981a. "The Kabir Panth: Heretics to Hindus." In Lorenzen 1981, 151–71.

——. 1981b. "The Kabir Panth and Politics." *Political Science Review* [Jaipur] 20: 263–81.

——, ed. 1981c. *Religious Change and Cultural Domination.* Mexico: El Colegio de Mexico.

——. 1987. "The Kabir Panth and Social Protest." In Schomer and McLeod, eds., 281–303.

——. 1991. *Kabir Legends and Ananta-Das's Kabir Parachai.* Albany: State University of New York Press.

——, ed. 1995. *Bhakti Religion in North India: Community Identity and Political Action.* Albany: State University of New York Press.

——. 1996. *Praises to a Formless God: Nirguni Texts from North India.* Albany: State University of New York Press.

——. 2006. *Who Invented Hinduism? Essays on Religion in History.* New Delhi: Yoda Press.

——. 2006 [1987]. "Traditions of Non-Caste Hinduism: The Kabir Panth." In Lorenzen 2006, 78–101.

Lutgendorf, Philip. 1991. *The Life of a Text: Performing the Ramcaritmanas of Tulsidas.* Berkeley: University of California Press.

Mann, Gurinder Singh. 1996. *The Goindval Pothis: The Earliest Extant Source of the Sikh Canon.* Cambridge, MA: Harvard University Press.

——. 2001. *The Making of Sikh Scripture.* New York: Oxford University Press.

Manuel, Peter. 1993. *Cassette Culture: Popular Music and Technology in North India.* Chicago: University of Chicago Press.

Martin, Nancy M. 1999. "*Mira Janma Patri* and Other Tales of Resistance and Appropriation." In *Religion, Ritual, and Royalty*, ed. Rajendra Joshi and N. K. Singhi. Jaipur: Rawat Press.

——. 2000. "Mirabai and Kabir in Rajasthani Folk Traditions: Meghwal and Manganiyar Repertoires." In *The Banyon Tree: Essays on Early Literature in New Indo-Aryan Languages*, ed. Mariola Offredi, vol. 2, 391–418. Delhi: Manohar Press.

——. 2002. "Homespun Threads of Dignity and Protest: Songs of Kabir in Rural Rajasthan." In *Images of Kabir*, ed. Monika Horstmann, 199–214. Delhi: Manohar Publications.

Martin, Waldo E. 2005. *No Coward Soldiers: Black Cultural Politics and Postwar America*. Cambridge, MA: Harvard University Press.

Masson, J. L., and M. V. Patwardhan. 1970. *Aesthetic Rapture: The Rasādhyāya of the Nātraśāstra*. 2 vols. Poona: Deccan College.

Masuzawa, Tomoko. 2005. *The Invention of World Religions: Or, How European Universalism Was Preserved in the Language of Pluralism*. Chicago: University of Chicago Press.

McLuhan, Marshall. 1962. *The Gutenberg Galaxy: The Making of Typographic Man*. Toronto: University of Toronto Press.

——. 2005 [1964]. *Understanding Media: The Extensions of Man*. New York: Routledge.

Mukhiya, Harbans. 2002. "Eklavya loses thumb again." *The Hindu*. <http://www.thehindu.com/2002/08/05/stories/2002080500251000.htm>

Mukta, Parita. 1997. *Upholding the Common Life: The Community of Mirabai*. Delhi: Oxford University Press.

Nagaraj, D. R. 2011. *The Flaming Feet and Other Essays on the Dalit Movement in India*. Calcutta: Seagull Books.

Narayan, Kirin. 1997. *Mondays on the Dark Night of the Moon: Himalayan Foothill Folktales*. New York: Oxford University Press.

Novetzke, Christian. 2008. *Religion and Public Memory: A Cultural History of Saint Namdev in India*. New York: Columbia University Press.

Offredi, Mariola, ed. 2000. *The Banyan Tree: Essays on Early Literature in New Indo-Aryan Languages*, vol. 2. New Delhi: Manohar.

Omvedt, Gail. 2008. *Seeking Begampura*. New Delhi: Navayana.

Ong, Walter. 1982. *Orality and Literacy: The Technologizing of the Word*. New York: Routledge.

Orsini, Francesca. 2005. "A Review Symposium: Literary Cultures in History." *Indian Economic and Social History Review* 42: 377–408.

——, ed. 2010. *Before the Divide: Hindi and Urdu Literary Culture*. New Delhi: Blackswan.

——. 2012. "How to Do Multilingual Literary History: Lessons from Fifteenth and Sixteenth-Century North India." *Indian Economic and Social History Review* 49, no. 2: 225–46.

Pandey, Gyanendra. 1997. "In Defense of the Fragment: Writing about Hindu-Muslim Riots in India Today." *Representations* 37 (Winter 1992); reprinted in *Subaltern Studies Reader, 1986–1995*, ed. Ranajit Guha, 1–33. Minneapolis: University of Minnesota Press.

Parry, Milman. 1971 (posthumous). *The Making of Homeric Verse: The Collected Papers of Milman Parry*, ed. Adam Perry. New York: Oxford University Press.

Prakashmuni Nam Sahab ed. 2004. *Āśhīrvād: Śhatābdī Granth*. Damakheda, Chhattisgarh: Shri Sadguru Kabir Dharamdas Sahab Vanshavali, Pratinidhi Sabha (most pages unnumbered) (Hindi).

Prasad, Rajendra. 1999 [1981]. 3rd ed. *Kabīr panth kā udbhav evam prasār* (*The Origin and Spread of the Kabir Panth*). Damakheda: Shrī sadguru kabīr dharmdās sāhab vanṣhāvalī pratinidhi sabhā (Hindi).

Raghavan, V. 1966. *The Great Integrators: The Saint Singers of India*. Ministry of Information and Broadcasting: Publications Division.

Rai, Alok. 2002. "Reinventing Tradition." In *Haman hain ishq, That Love Is All There Is*. New Delhi: India Habitat Centre.

Ramanujan, A. K. 1999. *The Collected Essays of A. K. Ramanujan*, ed. Vinay Dharwadker. New Delhi: Oxford University Press.

Reagon, Bernice Johnson. 1966. *Songs of the Civil Rights Movement 1955–1965: A Study in Cultural History*. PhD diss., Howard University.

——. 1987. "Let the Church Sing Freedom." *Black Music Research Journal* 7.

——. 2001. *If You Don't Go Don't Hinder Me: The African American Sacred Song Tradition*. Omaha: University of Nebraska Press.

——. 2004. "The Music Kept Us from Being Paralyzed: A Talk with Bernice Johnson Reagon." In *Black Notes: Essays of a Musician Writing in a Post-Album Age*, ed. William C. Banfield, 193–97. Lanham, MD: Scarecrow Press.

—— 2005. "The Power of Song." A musical production composed and directed by Reagon, performed by children, sponsored by the Public Library of Flint, Michigan. The entire script is available at <http://www.fpl.info/powerofsong/script.shtml>.

Rosenberg, Bruce A. 1987. "The Complexity of Oral Tradition." *Oral Tradition* 2, no. 1: 73–90.

Russell, R. V. 1916. *The Tribes and Castes of the Central Provinces of India*. "Kabirpanthi," vol. 1, 233–45. Available online: <http://www.gutenberg.org/files/20583/20583-h/20583-h.htm#d0e6746>.

Sacks Albie. 2000 [1990]. *The Soft Vengeance of a Freedom Fighter*. Berkeley: University of California Press.

Sacks, Oliver. 2007. *Musicophilia Tales of Music and the Brain*. New York: Knopf.

Salomon, Carol. 1996. "Baul Songs." In *Religions of India in Practice*, ed. Donald Lopez. Princeton, NJ: Princeton University Press.

Schaller, Joseph. 1995. "Sanskritization, Caste Uplift and Social Dissidence in the Sant Ravidas Panth." In *Bhakti Religion in North India: Community Identity and Political Action*, ed. David Lorenzen, 94–119. Albany: State University of New York Press.

Schmidt, Leigh Eric. 2012. *Restless Souls: The Making of American Spirituality*. Berkeley: University of California Press.

Schomer, Karine. 1987. "The Doha as a Vehicle of *Sant* Teachings." In Schomer and McLeod 1987, 61–90.

Schomer, Karine, and W. H. McLeod, eds. 1987. *The Sants: Studies in a Devotional Tradition of South Asia*. Berkeley, CA: Berkeley Religious Studies Series.

Sen, Kshitimohan. 1910–11. *Kabīr ke pad*. 4 vols. Shantiniketan, Bengal: Brahmacharya Ashram (Hindi with Bengali translations).

Shah, Rajula, dir. 2008. *Śhabad nirantar/ Word Within the Word* (film). Distributed by Magic Lantern Films, New Delhi.

Shastri, Gangasharan. 1983. *Achār Samhitā*. Varanasi: Kabirvani Prakashan Kendra (Hindi).

——, ed. 1998. *Mahabījak*. Varanasi: Kabir Vani Prakashan Kendra (Hindi).

Shilnath, ed. 1923. *Ṣhrī Śhīlnāth Śhabāmṛit* (*Shri Shilnath's Nectar of Poetry*). Dewas: Shri Shilnath Sansthan (Hindi).

Siegel, Daniel. 2012. *The Developing Mind: How Relationships and the Brain Interact to Shape Who We Are*. 2nd ed. New York: Guilford Press.

Singer, Milton. 1972. *When a Great Tradition Modernizes: An Anthropological Approach to Indian Civilization*. Chicago: University of Chicago Press.

Singh, Bahadur. 2000. "Kabir: Recited and Sung Today in Rajasthan." In Offredi 2000, 419–24.

——. 2002. "Problems of Authenticity in the Kabir Texts Transmitted Orally in Rajasthan Today." In Horstmann 2002, 191–98.

Singh, Shukdev, ed. 1972. *Kabīr Bījak*. Allahabad: Nilabh Prakashan (Hindi).

Snodgrass, Jeffery G. 2006. *Casting Kings: Bards and Indian Modernity*. New York: Oxford University Press.

Sterne, Jonathan. 2003. *The Audible Past: Cultural Origins of Sound Reproduction*. Durham, NC: Duke University Press.

——. 2011. "The Theology of Sound: A Critique of Orality." *Canadian Journal of Communication* 36: 207–25.

——, ed. 2012. *The Sound Studies Reader*. New York: Routledge.

Strnad, Jaroslav. 2013. *Morphology and Syntax of Old Hindi: Edition and Analysis of One Hundred* Kabīr vānī *Poems from Rājasthān*, vol. 45. Leiden & Boston: Brill's Indological Library.

——. Forthcoming. "Searching for the Source or Mapping the Stream?: Some Text-critical Issues in the Study of Medieval Bhakti." In *Early Modern Literatures of North India*, ed.Tyler Walker Williams, Anshu Malhotra, and John Stratton Hawley.

Tannen, Deborah, ed. 1982. *Spoken and Written Language: Exploring Orality and Literacy*. Norwood, NJ: Ablex.

Tiwari, P. N., ed. 1961. *Kabīr granthāvalī*. Allahabad: Hindi Parishad, Prayag Vishvavidyalaya.

Turkle, Sherry. 2012. *Alone Together: Why We Expect More from Technology and Less from Each Other*. New York: Basic Books.

Vail, Leroy and Landeg White. 1992. *Power and the Praise Poem: Southern African Voices in History*. Suffolk, UK: James Currey.

Vaudeville, Charlotte. 1974. *Kabīr*, vol. 1. Oxford: The Clarendon Press.

——. 1982. *Kabīr-vāṇī: recension occidentale/western recension.* Pondicherry, India: Institut Francais d'Indologie.

——. 1993. *A Weaver Named Kabir.* New York: Oxford University Press.

Virmani, Shabnam. 2008a. *Chalo hamārā des/Come to My Country: Journeys with Kabir and Friends* (film). Bangalore: The Kabir Project.

——. 2008b. *Kabīrā khaḍā bāzār meṇ/In the Market Stands Kabir: Journeys with Sacred and Secular Kabir* (film). Bangalore: The Kabir Project.

——. 2008c. *Koī suntā hai/Someone Is Listening: Journeys with Kumar and Kabir* (film). Bangalore: The Kabir Project.

——. 2008d. *Had anhad/Bounded-Boundless: Journeys with Ram and Kabir* (film). Bangalore: The Kabir Project.

——. 2008e. *Kabir in Malwa* (audio CDs and book). Bangalore: The Kabir Project.

——. 2008f. *Kabir in Pakistan* (audio CDs and book). Bangalore: The Kabir Project.

——. 2008g. *Kabir in Rajasthan* (audio CDs and book). Bangalore: The Kabir Project.

Wadley, Susan Snow. 2004. *Raja Nal and the Goddess: The North Indian Epic* Dhola *in Performance.* Bloomington: Indiana University Press.

Westcott, G. H. 1974 [1907]. *Kabīr and the Kabīr Panth.* Varanasi: Bharatīya Publishing House.

Wilson, H. H. 1958 [1861]. *Religious Sects of the Hindus.* Calcutta: Sushil Gupta.

Index

Poems/songs by Kabir that are translated and discussed in the text are not identified in a consistent way throughout the book. A list is provided under "bhajans—first lines." Page numbers with *t* or *f* indicate entries in tables/figures.

Ādi Granth (also known as Guru Granth Sāhib)
  classification in, 152
  compared to oral traditions in Rajasthan, 406–407n15
  and the *Goindval Pothis*. See *Goindval Pothis*
  Kabir's poetry inscribed in, 5, 75, 88–89, 94–95, 123, 136, 146
  sectarian methods of, 88–89, 127, 130, 406–407n15
  and Sikh views of the authentic Kabir, 88–89, 406–407n15
  as source for Shastri's *Mahābījak*, 411n6
  suno used in the signature by poets in, 399n2
Agrawal, Purushottam, 124, 142, 435n12
  Blind Willie Johnson compared with Kabir by, 352
  Callewaert criticized by, 124–126, 130
  Dharamvir criticized by, 125, 427n26
  Europe-derived "colonial modernity" and Indian "vernacular modernity" differentiated by, 129–131
  on the *Granthāvalī*, 126–127, 128, 143–144
  on Marx, 353, 356, 436n15
  on the mutual dependence of inner and outer, 361–362
  on Ramanand, 427n26
  on religion and spirituality in Kabir, 361–362, 436n21
  on the value of songs not found in manuscripts, 130–131, 414n25
Aisī mhārī prīt nibhāvajo, "Stay true to my love, oh Ram"
  in Shabnam's first CD set, 409n33
  singer's alteration of lines in, 409n33
  translated, 194–195
Ali, Mukhtiyar, 70, 89, 107, 418–419n15
Ambedkar, B.R.
  biographical details, 262
  Buddhist conversion, 262, 367, 432n22
  inspirational example of, 21, 260, 262–263, 283, 306, 382, 387, 390, 394 (*see also* Ambedkar *manch* in Dewas)
  posters of, 21, *259f6.2*

Ambedkar *manch* in Dewas, 262, 382
anahad (boundless), waves of sound suggested by, 2–3
anahad nād (unstruck/boundless sound), 2, 37–38, 90, 169, 308
 Anahad garje concerts (*see* SAHMAT)
 and *Nirbhay nirgun gun re gāūgā*, 37, 308
 political criticism of, 363, 380
Anurag Sāgar (*Ocean of Love*)
 and the *Bījak* ranked by the Dharmadasis, 319, 339
 and Dharamdas, 326, 431–432n21
 and "false" *panths*, 420n26, 430n13
Ayaz, Fariduddin (Farid), 107
 Maulā maulā performed in Malwa and in "*Had-anhad*/ Bounded-Boundless," 70
 Maulā maulā performed on the Kabir Project CD, 96
 on non-scholarly depth of knowledge about Kabir, 129

Babri mosque/masjid, 254, 257, 264, 348, 378–379, 387, 433–434nn2, 5
 Mandir-masjid song, 296
bagulā (heron). *See* herons
bāhar and *bhītar* (outside and inside)
 Agrawal, Purushottam on, 361–362
 "In this body" phrase in bhajans, 40, 171, 183–184
 jal meṇ kumbh kumbh mẹ jal, bāhar bhītar pānī, 345
 Nath, Krishna on, 379–380
 Patel, Suresh on, 271
Bailenson, Jeremy, 243
Bamaniya, Kaluram, 24, 71, 96–97, 107, 195–197, 200–201, 298f6.5, 304–306, 310, 389–390, 393
 interviewed by the author, 299–302
Barthwal, P.D., *The Nirguna School of Hindi Poetry*, 127, 420n26, 430n13
Behl, Aditya, 73, 405n1
Bender, Courtney, 435n11
Bhagavad-gītā
 and *adhyātma*, 355
 Dalit critique of, 367
 irreverently treated in a bhajan sung by Narayanji, 295
 renunciation harmonized with social engagement in, 366
bhajans
 Delhi bazaar bhajan collection of, 85–86
 Gorakhnath bhajans, 56, 183–184
 handwritten and unpublished collections of, 77–78, 92, 261 (*see also* Prahladji's handwritten bhajan notebook)
 historically sung with alterations, 405n7
 kīrtan contrasted with, 84
 published collections (see *Ādi Granth*; *Bījak*; Callewaert, Winand; Dvivedi, Hazariprasad; *Kabīr*; *Kabīr Granthāvalī*; *Mahābījak*; Sen, Kshitimohan; Tagore)
 and *sākhīs* (couplets), 154
 Shilnath's collection of songs in the Nath anthology, 93–94
 spirituals compared with, 369–370, 373–376
bhajans—first lines
 Ab ke bachāī le merī mā, "Save me mother," 173–174
 Aisā deśh hāmarā, "My country is like this," 189
 Aisī khetī kījai, "Plow your fields like this," 31–32, 402n13

Aisī mhārī prīt nibhāvajo, "Stay true to my love," 194–195, 409n33
Aivī aivī sen, "Such signs," 153
Anagaḍhiyā deva, "God without form," 43
Begam kī gam kar le, "Nowhere, go there," 186–187
Bhāv nagarī, "The city of love," 81, 192–193
Bheḍā hai par miltā nāhin, "It's with you but you can't find it," 190
Binā chandā re binā bhāṇ, "No moon, no sun," 398–399
Chalo hamārā des, "Come to my country," 65
Eklā mat chhoḍjo, "Don't leave me alone," 63–64
Ghūnghaṭ ke phat khol, "Open your veil," 90
Guru sam dātā koī nahīṇ, "There's no giver like the guru," 157, 427n21
Gyān kī jaḍiyāṇ, "A root of wisdom," 198, 417n3
Hameṇ sāhib se milnā hai, "I'm on my way to meet the lord," 87, 199, 374
Ham pardesī panchhī, "I'm a bird from another country," 94, 188
Har har mārūngā nishāno sadhu choṭ hai āsmān kī, "I'll shoot and wound the sky," 135
Jāg musāfir jāg, "Wake up, traveler, wake up," 91
Jāgrat rah re, "Stay awake," 179–180
Jā jo jā jo re bhāī, "Go, go, my brother, go," 193–194,
Jāo nugurī, "Go, you who lived without a guru," 48, 178–179
Jhīnī chadariyā, "Subtle cloth," 167–168, 185
Jo tū āyā gagan manḍal se, "If you come from the dome of the sky," 25, 97
Kahāṇ se āyā, kahāṇ jāoge, "Where did you come from? Where are you going?," 39–40, 160–161
Kaī ḍhūnḍhtī phiro mhārī helī, "My dear friend, what are you seeking?" 39, 42–43, 427n20
Karnā re hoy, "There's something you're supposed to do," 184, 396
Ketā jājo jī bhalā bhāī, "Go tell them, good brother," 172–173
Koī mat chheḍo re, meṇ divānā nām kā, "Don't mess with me! I'm mad with the name," 197
Kōi suntā hai, "Someone is listening," 37, 155
Kyoṇ bhūlīgī ṭhāro des, "Why have you forgotten your country," 187, 292, 396–397
Lagan kaṭhin hai, "Holding fast is difficult," 99–100, 374
Laharī anahad uṭhe ghaṭ bhītar, "Boundless waves are rising in my body," 2–3, 37–38
Man lāgo mero yār fakīrī meṇ, "This mind, my friend, has learned to love owning nothing," 96, 195–196, 397–398, 406n9
Man mast huā, "The heart is overjoyed," 196–197, 410n40
Mhārā satguru baniyā bhediyā, "My true guru has pierced through me," 158–159, 246–247
Nirbhay nirguṇ, "Fearless, formless," 37, 308, 402n19, 418–419n15
Panchhiḍā bhāī, "Oh bird, my brother," 1–2, 100, 167, 269, 418–419n15
Pī le amīras dhārā gagan meṇ jhaḍī lagī, "Drink! A cascade of nectar pours from the sky," 57, 169, 198, 365
Rām rame soī gyānī, "When Ram plays inside you, you're wise," 29, 162

bhajans—first line (*cont.*)
Sāhib ne bhāng pilāī, "The lord gave me a marijuana drink," 87, 271, 427n22
Santo dekhahu jag baurānā, "Saints, I see the world is mad," 274–275, 316, 434n6
Santo jīvat hī karo āsha, "Seekers, fulfill your hopes while you're alive," 283
Satguru āngan āya, "When the true guru entered my courtyard," 44
Thārā bhariyā samand māhī hīrā, "In your deep ocean a jewel," 85–86
Tū kā tū, "You, only you," 27, 185
Uḍ jāegā hans akelā, "It will fly away alone, the swan," 61–62
Yā ghaṭ bhītar "In this body," 40, 153, 171, 403n23, 406n14
Yoṇ sansār, "This world," 59–60, 86, 180–181, 406n11
Yuṇ hī man samajhāve, "Teach your mind like this," 101–102, 164–165
Zarā halke gāḍī hānko, "Move your cart along lightly," 67, 265, 313–314
Bhanwari Devi (Rajasthani singer), 107–108
Bharti, Chhotu, 270–273, 374, 378
Bhopal
Adivasi Lok Kala Parishad (ALKP) in, 19, 22, 51, 133, 363
gas tragedy in, 257
Bījak, 75, 78, 85, 94–95, 114–116, 121, 126, 136, 147–148, 187, 319, 339, 343, 412n13, 426n11, 427n29, 427n30
Black Church. *See* gospel music; Negro spirituals
Blascovich, Jim, 243
Brown, Charlotte, 234–239
Bryant, Kenneth, 118–119, 120, 401n16
Buddhism, 183, 347, 355, 391–392
Ambedkar's conversion to, 262, 283, 364, 432n22
ascetic withdrawal and social engagement as competing calls, 366
author's practice of, 97, 158, 383
Dalits and, 262, 283, 367
Dogen, 221
Pema Chodron, 352, 357–358
and PT's U.S. tour, 158–159
Shantideva, 352, 358–359
Tibetan Buddhist rituals, 342

Callewaert, Winand
on the *Ādi Granth*'s influence on oral traditions, 406–407n15
Agrawal's critique of, 124–126, 427n26
Kabir textual scholarship of, 117–118, 120–126, 128, 131, 412n12, 413n16, 414n22
on textual indications of music, 405n7
Carothers, J.C., 213
cassettes
disappearance from the market, 105, 110
featuring artists other than PT, 55, 56, 85, 415n36
featuring PT, 24, 25, 51, 53, 55, 56–57, 103–104, 144, 265, 270, 298, 331
influence on oral tradition, 6, 16, 74, 78, 104, 109, 207, 260, 265, 302
Soī pīr hai jo jāne par pīr (PT's first cassette), 270
caste
Agrawal on identity politics, 125
Dalits, 5, 13, 29–30, 42, 44, 49, 161–162, 251, 259f6.2, 262–263, 265, 269, 278–279, 283, 367, 390, 411n6, 424n3, 433n1, 437n25, 437n27
Dalits' names and, 299

Delmia, Narayan Singh on, 279, 292–295, 331
and Eklavya's Kabir *manch*, 249, 251–265, 267, 273, 275, 294
four *varṇas* (classes), 142–143, 307, 418n12
and the Kabir Panth, 280, 318, 429–430n11
Kabir's social criticism and, 5, 7, 9, 21, 159–162, 249–251
low status and poverty of Kabir singers in Malwa, 201–202
nirguṇ bhakti and oppressed castes, 40–45, 96, 278–279, 403n26
in Prahladji's life and Kabir interpretations, 5, 13, 23, 26, 28–30, 36, 38, 42, 44–47, 84, 145
premodern yogis and sadhus' views of, 366
Ramanand and, 277–279
Shabnam's discussion with Tiwari, 362–363
Sharma, Dinesh on, 304–306
shudra class of Kabir, 307
Sisodiya, Hiralal on, 283–285
stanza about a carved statue on, 42–43, 161–162
Syag, R.N. on, 255, 260, 303
and *tambūrā* playing, 55, 410n38
Chauhan, Bhairu Singh, 55–56, 66, 302
chaukā āratī rituals
criticism and debate over, 274, 282, 287, 335–336
ekottarī chaukā āratī described, 329
Gangasharan Shastri's views of, 338
Kabir Chaura use of, 324–325, 338–340, 343, 432n28
origin story in the *Anurag Sāgar*, 327, 339
PT's innovations, 337
PT's performance of, 333–334, *334f7.1*, 336, 432n23
presided over by Dharamdasi Kabir Panth *mahants*, 280, 325–328, 329, 332
traced to the *Jñān gudari*, 432n27
in two traditions of Kabir Panth, 324–328
Vivek Das's reforms, 338–340, 432n28
Chaytor, H.L., 210
Chenamaru, 86, 199
Chhattisgarh
Kabir Panth in (*see* Dharamdasi Kabir Panth; Prakashmuni Nam Sahab)
melā (fair, gathering) attended by author in, 328–329, 330, 429n7
population demographics, 429n7
Chodron, Pema, 352, 357–358
Choudhury, Anil, 309, 320–321, 322
clay pot as a metaphor for the human body. See *ghaṭ* (clay pot)
communalism, 254–255, 257, 264, 269, 280, 296, 316, 347, 378, 387, 425n7, 430–431n16, 433n2, 437–438nn30, 31
conversations documented by the author, individual conversation partners. *See* Bharti, Chhotu; Brown, Charlotte; Delmia, Narayan Singh; Macy, Joanna; Naim; Patel, Suresh; Rai, Alok; Rikhi,Vipul; Shastri, Gangasharan; Syag, R.N.
couplets. *See sākhīs* (couplets) of Kabir

Dadu Panth manuscript collections, 75, 121–122, 147, 152, 412–413n14
Granthāvalī, 126–127, 130, 152
Panchvāṇī, 75, 126
Sarvāngī, 74, 126
Dalit-Bahujans. *See* caste, Dalits
Das, Gangasharan. *See* Shastri, Gangasharan

Das, Shyamsundar, Kabir textual scholarship of, 120–121, 126
Das, Vivek
biographical details, 338
and *chaukā āratī* rituals, 338–340, 432n28
Dharamdasis criticized by, 338–340, 432n28
Kabir Bhavan built by, 338
PT invited to perform Kabir Jayanti, 341
as a reformer, 338–339, 343, 429n10
support of Choudhury's struggles, 321
Dehaene, Stanislas, 422n14
Delmia, Narayan Singh (Narayanji), 92, 131–133, 197, 200–201, 267–268, *289f6.4*, 310, 378, 427n24
on the *chaukā āratī* controversy, 335
and the *Kabir bhajan evam vichar manch*, 24, 257, 261, 263, 259–260, 280–283, 288–289, 291, 292–295, 331
profile of, 288–298
on Ramanand and Kabir, 279
on social-spiritual split, 311
Delvoye, Nalini, 92, 407–408n20
deśh (country)
as a theme in Kabir's poetry, 152, 187–190
individual bhajans on. *See* bhajans—first lines, *Aisā deśh hāmarā*, "My country is like this"; *Chalo hamārā des*, "Come to my country"; *Ham pardesī panchhī*, "I'm a bird from another country"; *Kyoṇ bhūlīgī ṭhāro des*, "Why have you forgotten your country"
Dewas
education NGO in (*see* Eklavya NGO)
Kumar Gandharva, home of (*see* Kumar Gandharva)
Nath Panth center in (*see* Shīlnāth Dhūnī (Nath Panth center in Dewas)
Dhanya kabīr as a controversial song, 144, 416n38
Dharamdas, 91–93, 96–97, 116, 144, 194, 408n24, 431–432n21
Dharamdasi Kabir Panth, 92, 144, 187, 280, 287, 309–310, 319, 325–326
Anurag Sāgar (*Ocean of Love*) sacred book of, 319, 326, 339, 420n26, 431–432n21
and Bandhavgarh, 59, 170, 326, 329, 429n7, 431–432n21
and the *chaukā āratī* ritual, 326–329
leader of (*see* Prakashmuni Nam Sahab)
rivalry within lineage, 430n13
See also Das, Vivek, Dharamdasis criticized by
Dharamvir, Dr., 125, 278, 427n26, 433n1
Dharma Shastras, 366, 418n12
Dharwadker, Vinay
Kabir identified as a community of authors by, 6, 145
Kabir textual dissemination charted by, 78
divānā
as a term for madness (*see* madness)
and Urdu musical-poetic forms, 117
divine madness. *See* madness
drunken joy, songs about, 195–199, 276, 365, 434n7
Dvivedi, Hazariprasad, 97, 125, 278, 399–400n5, 403n23, 408n25, 427n26, 433n1

Eklavya bhajan booklet. *See Soī pīr hai jo jāne par pīr* (bhajan collection)
Eklavya Kabir *manch*, 11, 15, 24, 251–254, 257–66

Dinesh Sharma as organizer of, 257–260, *259f6.2*, 273–275
Hindu identity of musicians in, 425n7
Hiralal Sisodiya's involvement (*see* Sisodiya, Hiralal)
Kaluram Bamaniya's involvement, 298–302
Narayan Singh Delmia, involvement (*see* Delmia, Narayan Singh, and the *Kabir bhajan evam vichar manch*)
PT's involvement, 24, 55, 103, 265, 276–278, 281–282
scenes from, 273–283
table 6.1, *281t6.1*
urban activists in, 266–273
Eklavya NGO
Ambedkar *manch* organized by (*see* Ambedkar *manch* in Dewas)
and Dinesh Sharma (*see* Sharma, Dinesh)
farewell event for the author, 62–64
history of, 251–254
Kabir *manch* organized by (*see* Eklavya Kabir *manch*)
and science education, 251–252, 256–257
and Syag-bhāi, 255–257, 302–304
transcription of bhajans from oral tradition, 200, 265–266
See also *Soī pīr hai jo jāne par pīr* (bhajan collection)
embodiment
body as theme in poetry, 166–171
disembodiment in electronic communication, 16, 109–111, 232–234, 242–246
and *divānā* (*see* madness)
ghaṭ bhītar "within the body" (see *ghaṭ* (clay pot); *ghaṭ bhītar*)
"In this body" phrase in bhajans, 40, 171, 183–184
Lakoff on the Embodiment Revolution, 243–244
live embodied presence in oral performance, 4, 78, 205, 211–212, 233–234, 237–239, 246–248
naśhā (*see* drunken joy)
Ramanujan on bodily location of texts, 80–81
emptiness (*śhūnya, śhūnyatā*)
in bhajans, 37, 90, 138, 152, 165, 166, 169, 189, 308, 398
as Kabir's core truth according to Tiwari, 136
and ritual, 342

Finnegan, Ruth, 206–208
Foley, John Miles
OT (Oral Tradition) and IT (Internet) homology claimed by, 228–232
Pathways Project website, 207–208, 209, 228–232, 422n6
refutation of the thesis of the Great Divide between oral and written, 207–208
freedom songs. *See* Negro spirituals

Gangasharan Shastri. *See* Shastri, Ganga Sharan
Gandhi, Indira, 1975–77 Emergency, 376
ghaṭ (clay pot)
chaukā āratī ritual related to, 339–340
examples in poetry, 2–3, 37–40, 97, 171, 185, 282–283, 403n23
jal meṇ kumbh kumbh meṇ jal, "pot in water water in pot," 345
as a metaphor for the body in Kabir poems, 39, 145, 166–167, 362
ghaṭ bhītar "within the body"
Agrawal on, 362
and the metaphor of the clay pot (*see ghaṭ* (clay pot))
chaukā ritual within the body, 340, 432n27

ghazal style songs
and globalization, 16
influence on oral Kabir, 117
Tumhe yād ho ke na yād ho, 116
Urdu poetic form, 412n7
Gītā. See *Bhagavad-gītā*
Glennie, Evelyn, 225–226
globalization
antidemocratic potential of the internet, 410–411nn41–42
democratizing effects of digital technology, 109, 111
and media, 78, 106–111, 207–208
oral networks in the sixteenth century, 103, 410n39
of PT, 22, 66–67, 103–105
and "spiritual but not religious," 351–352
substance of the local affected by, 16
Goindval Pothis, 95, 123, 146–147, 401n12
Golwalkar, M.S., 350
Gorakhnath
affinity with Kabir, 91, 93, 114, 402n5
bhajans, 56, 183–184
city of Gorakhpur named after, 92, 162
and Nath Panth, 93, 125
poems in the anthology of Shilnath, 94
Shūnya ghar shahar attributed to, 91
gospel music
Blind Willie Johnson compared with Kabir, 352
composed by Charles A. Tindley, 376
and PT's American tour, 66
Granthāvalī. See *Kabīr Granthāvalī*
Gupta, Anu
and the author, 307, 311, 313, 428n34
and Dinesh Sharma's final days, 311–313
and Eklavya, 251–252
and Narayanji, 294
Guru Granth Sāhib. See *Ādi Granth*
gurus
of Ambedkar, 262
author's connection to theme of, 158–159
in bhajans, 20, 25, 27, 29, 34, 37, 39, 43, 44, 48, 51, 62, 87, 98, 99–100, 132, 135, 138, 150, 154, 156–159, 160, 167, 170, 175, 183, 184, 185, 188, 189, 190, 192–193, 198, 199, 246–247, 272, 276–277, 292, 346, 365, 374, 396, 427n21, 436n17
Eklavya *manch* discussion of, 274, 276–277, *281t6.1*, 282, 285–287, 310
Guru Nanak. *See* Nanak
"guru's greatness" as theme in Kabir poetry and song, 152, 154–155, 156–159, 249–250, 261, 269
Hiralalji and, 285–287, 310, 330
as human beings or the divine presence within oneself, 156, 158, 162, 403n22
of Kabir, 5 (*see also* Ramanand)
Kabir as satguru, 144, 157, 255
in Kabir Panth, 15, 144, 160, 258, 270, 280, 309, 319, 324–327, 329, 332, 336–337, 343, 403n22, 432n28
Kaluramji and, 300–302, 310
in *Mahābārata*, devotion of Eklavya to guru, 252–253
Narayanji and, 291, 295, 310, 335
of PT, 33–34, 36, 54, 175, 199
PT as a, 21, 51, 55–56, 57–59, 301, 332, 337
PT on, 34, 96, 145, 158, 186, 336–338, 341, 409n31, 432n23
Shabnam on Tiwari as guru, 132
Sikh gurus, 95, 127, 147, 408n23, 414n21 (*see also* Nanak)

haṃsa and *bagulā*. *See* heron/crane (*bagulā*); swan (*haṃsa*)
Hawley, J.S., 142, 400n8, 405n4
  on authorship in bhakti poetry, 411n3
  on Dvivedi's "brahminical bias," 427n26
  on the Fatehpur manuscript, 123–124, 146
  historical approach to Surdas manuscripts, 118, 125, 405n4, 413n16
  on Kabir's literacy as unknown, 399–400n5
  on the speed of urban networks in the sixteenth century, 410n39
  on textual histories, 400n9
Hayles, Katherine, 244–245
Henry, Edward O., 93, 402n5
Henshaw, John, 222–223, 422n15
heron/crane (*bagulā*)
  and swan (*haṃsa*) compared, 26, 32, 402n8
  symbolism, 418n13
Hinduism
  Dalit-Bahujans distinguished from, 367
  Das, Vivek's criticism of *paurāniktā*, 339–340
  and Eklavya Kabir *manch*, 282, 425n7
  and Kabir Panth, 280, 316–318, 324, 338
  and Kaluram, 96, 300
  and Narayanji, 291–292, 295, 296
  and PT, 30, 158, 409n31
  and renunciation, 366
  selective appropriation of Kabir, 364
  and temples, 42, 156
Hindu-Muslim connections, 5, 26, 35, 38, 39, 46, 96, 124, 142–143, 160, 195, 250, 254–255, 257, 280, 292, 315–316, 347, 416n42, 428–429n2
Hindu nationalism, 254, 350, 425-n7, 433n2, 434n9
Honko, Lauri, 120
Horowitz, Seth
  discussed by author with Charlotte Brown, 234, 236
  hearing identified as the universal sense, 222–224, 232, 423n16
  on music, 225–226, 236
Horstmann, Monika, 412–413n14, 427n26

Ilaiah, Kancha, 367
inside and outside. See *bāhar* and *bhītar*

Jainism
  and the Burhanpur *śhākhā* of the Kabir Panth, 430n12
  influence on manuscript collection and libraries, 122, 412–413n14
  and Kabir's equal-opportunity critique of religious hypocrites, 39, 160, 355
  Rajasthan influence of, 412–413n14
  and renunciation, 366

Kabir Chaura branch of Kabir Panth
  and *Bījak* (see *Bījak*)
  chaukā āratī used by, 324–325, 338–340, 343, 432n28
  history and locations of, 93, 319, 321
  leaders (*see* Das, Vivek; Shastri, Gangasharan)
  and the *Mahābījak* (see *Mahābījak*; Shastri, Gangasharan)
  rituals of, 324–325
Kabir couplets. See *sākhīs* (couplets) of Kabir
Kabīr Granthāvalī
  Agrawal on, 126–127, 128, 143–144
  Das edition of, 121, 126, 152

Kabīr Granthāvalī (*cont.*)
Rajasthani manuscript base of, 121, 126–127
and sectarian bias, 126–128
Kabir *manch*. *See* Eklavya Kabir *manch*
Kabir *mandalīs*
demographics of, 265
in Eklavya Kabir *manch*, 24, 256–257, 259–260, 264, 273
explanations of bhajans by, 137, 273–274
farewell event for author, 62–64
organized for Kabir *manch* by Narayanji, 291, 294, 297
at Kumar Gandharva's cremation, 138–139
led by Ram Prasad in Dhunsi village, 394–395
of Malwa, 23–24, 255, 258
of older men, 200–201
poverty and low caste status of those in Malwa, 201–202
PT's hosting of, 24, 49–50, 53–55, 104
and the Singaji *mandalī* in Dinesh's village, 304, 306, 425–426n8
Syag-bhāi on, 256, 260, 263, 303
of women, 289, 393–394
and the younger generation, 69–70, 107, 289
Kabir Panth
and Ambedkar's parents, 262
and *Bījak* (*see Bījak*)
and caste distinctions, 280, 318, 429–430n11
censorship of Prakash Kant's introduction, 261, 309
Choudhury attacked by, 320–321, 323
and the Eklavya Kabir *manch*, 280, *281t6.1*, 297–298
and gurus, 15, 144, 160, 258, 270, 280, 309, 319, 324–327, 329, 332, 336–337, 343, 403n22, 432n28
Hinduization of, 280, 316–318, 324, 338
Hiralalji's criticism of, 285–288, 330
and Kabir *mandalīs* in Malwa, 258, 280
and Kabir's manifestation on a lotus on Lahartara Pond, 144, 309, 318, 320, 342, 416n38, 429n10
Kaluramji's relationship to, 96, 300–302
and *Mahābījak*, 114–116
Mangaldas Sahib (*mahant* of Dewas), 26, 49, 280, 300–302
Narayanji's criticism of, 331, 335
PT and Shabnam attacked by, 309–310, 431n17
PT's relationship to, 33–34, 36, 53–54, 58, 84, 145, 158, 332–333, *334f7.1*, 336–338, 341
seats (*gaddī*)/branches (*śhākhā*), 319
Allahabad-based (*Pārakhī*) branch, 33, 430n12
Burhanpur-based branch, 430n12
Chhattisgarh-based branch, 319 (*see also* Dharamdasi Kabir Panth; Prakashmuni Nam Sahab)
Kharsiya-based branch, 430n14
Varanasi-based branch, 93, 319 (*see also* Kabir Chaura; Shastri, Gangasharan)
See also *chaukā āratī* rituals; Kabir Chaura; Dharamdasi Kabir Panth
Kabir poetry
classification of, 151–156
collections of (see *Ādi Granth*; Eklavya NGO, transcription of bhajans from oral tradition; *Goindval Pothis; Kabīr Granthāvalī*; *Mahābījak*; Nath anthology; Prahladji's handwritten bhajan

notebook; Sen, Kshitimohan; Tagore)
computer analysis of, 148, 416–417n44
oceanic pool of images, 85–86, 89, 91
Kabir Project based in Bangalore
author's association with, 12–13
films, audio CDS and bilingual books produced by, 46, 54–55, 66, 68, 71, 101–102, 105, 106, 129, 378, 405n40
initiation of, 425n7
and Shabnam Virmani, 102, 425n7
Kabir says listen. *See* Kabir's signature line
Kabir's life and identity, 5
described as a community of authors by Vinay Dharwadker, 145
myths and legends of, 144, 306, 317, 318, 339, 401n11, 429n10
and Ramanand, 274, 276–279 (*see also* Ramanand)
in play of Shekhar Sen, 321–323
in television serial of Anil Choudhury, 320
Kabīr Smārak Sevā aur Shodh Sansthān (Kabir Memorial Institute for Service and Research), 48–49
Kabir songs. *See* bhajans—first lines
Kabir's signature line ("Kabir says"), 1, 2, 80, 140, 411n6
altering of, 82–84, 86, 91–93, 98, 144, 405n7, 408n21
authority of, 140
and Nath bhajans, 93–94, 408n21
suno used in the signature by poets in the *Ādi Granth*, 399n2
Kabir's social criticism
featured in his poetry, 5, 9, 36, 38–39, 159–162, 251, 282
and social activism today, 306–307, 308–309, 310–311, 347–348, 350, 363–365, 366, 377–380, 386–389, 392–395
Kabir textual scholarship, text-editing approaches, 118–119
Kabir Yatras (Malwa and Rajasthan Kabir Journeys), 102, 106, 107, 108
kahe kabīr suno bhāī sadho, "Kabir says, listen Seekers." *See* Kabir's signature line
Kaluram. *See* Bamaniya, Kaluram
Kant, Prakash
introduction to book of bhajan texts describing Kabir as human, 264, 267, 309–310
on Kabir's birth in a Muslim family, 309
and Patel, Suresh, 268
on usefulness of Kabir for social justice work, 306–307
King, Martin Luther
"I Have a Dream" speech, 395
spirituality and social engagement combined by, 356, 368, 369
kīrtan, 84, 86
Knight, Lisa, 91
Komkali, Bhuvan
on *ghazal* and other Urdu influences on oral Kabir, 117, 142
grandson of Kumar Gandharva, 116, 415n36
Mahābījak viewed as inauthentic by, 116
Komkali, Kalapini 116, 415n36
Kothari, Komal, 132
Kripal, Jeffrey, 435n11
Kumar Gandharva
bhajan embossed on a mirror discovered by, 60
biographical details, 11, 82, 138–139

Kumar Gandharva (*cont.*)
cremation of, 138–139
disciples of, 116, 138
Gorakhnath bhajans sung by, 91, 183–184
Ham pardesī panchhī sung by, 188
Nirbhay nirguṇ guṇ re gāūgā sung by, 308, 418–419n15
and Shīlnāth Dhūnī, 60, 93–94, 138, 408nn21, 27, 415n36, 416n37
Shūnya ghar shahar sung by, 91, 408n21
song text variations, 91, 113, 408nn21, 22
Suntā hai guru gyānī sung by, 82
Tiwari, Kapil on, 137–140
Uḍ jāegā hans akelā sung by, 60–62
Kumarji. *See* Kumar Gandharva
Kumar, Sunil, 307

Lagan kaṭhin hai mere bhāī (bhajan)
author's effort to translate, 98–100
spiritual quest of civil rights activists compared with, 374
Lakoff, George, 224, 238–239, 242–244
Lee, Joel, 83
The Lives of Others, film by Von Donnersmarck, 16, 360–361, 379
Lofton, Kathryn, 435n11
Lord, Albert
colonial framing of cultures based on theories of, 206
oral-formulaic theory of composition, 85, 153, 209
The Singer of Tales, 14, 205, 206, 421n2
Lorenzen, David, 41, 142, 147, 279, 317–319, 324–325, 340, 352, 400n9, 401n11, 403n26, 411n5, 428n1, 429nn3, 10, 430nn12, 13, 432nn26, 27, 432n28, 433n1
Lukacs, George, 434n8
Lunyakhedi village, 11, 19, 28–29, 42, 56–57, 70–71, 104, 108, 150, 249, 389, 404n33

McLuhan, Marshall
critiques of, 212–213, 218–219
cultures essentialized as either oral or literate by, 212–213
The Gutenberg Galaxy, 14, 208–210, 219–220, 422n7, 424n24
on media, 206, 208–210, 226, 233, 422n7
and secondary orality, 227
Macy, Joanna, 391–392
madness
divānā as a term for, 189–190, 197, 373
and emptiness, 165
and Rai's reference to the Kabir poem *santo dekhat jag baurānā*, 348, 434n6
Mahābījak
Urdu poetry added to, 116–117 (*see also* Shastri, Gangasharan)
Malwa
location of this study, 1, 11, 19–20
Malwa Kabir Yātrā, 70, 102, 106–109
repertoires in, 14, 149–151
mandalīs. *See* Kabir *mandalīs*
Marti, Jose, 249, 424n1
Martin, Nancy, 400n8, 433n1
Marvadi, Muralala (Kutchi singer), 70, 89, 89, 91, 107, 406n9, 408n22
Marx, Karl
Agrawal on religious and spiritual views of, 353, 356, 436nn14, 15
aversion to religion, 345–346, 348, 368
Rai, Alok's discussion of, 386–387
Mirabai
and feminists, 386

Kabir refrains attributed to, 91, 406n9
Kumarji's name for an elderly Dewas singer, 415n36
and low caste people, 400n8, 411n6, 433n1
popularity of, 251
PT's singing of songs of, 23
moon and sun motif. *See* bhajans-first lines, *Aivī aivī, Binā chanda, Yā ghaṭ bhītar*
Mudgal, Madhup, 138–139
Mukhia, Harbans, 252–253
Muslims and the Muslim community
and communal conflict, 144, 254–255, 280, 292, 315–317, 362 (*see also* Babri mosque/masjid)
Kabir's association with, 5, 316, 425n7
and Kabir's egalitarianism, 39, 96, 362, 425n7
Kabir's upbringing in a Muslim family, 5, 279, 309, 316–317, 401n11
Muslim singers, 96 (*see also* Ali, Mukhtiyar; Ayaz, Fariduddin (Farid); *qawwali* style songs)
reflected in vocabulary of poems, 26, 91, 124, 195

Nabhadas (author of *Bhaktamāl*), 142–143
Nagaraj, D.R., 366–367
Naim (Urdu poet in Dewas), 307–308
Nanak, Guru, 127, 140, 141, 285, 315–316, 402n5, 408n23, 428–429n2
Narayanji. *See* Delmia, Narayan Singh
naśhā. *See* drunken joy
Nath anthology, Shilnath's collection of songs in, 93–94
Nath, Krishna, 379–380, 438n32
Nath Panth, 89, 93, 355
center in Dewas (*see* Shīlnāth Dhūnī)
headquarters (*see* Gorakhnath)
and PT, 33, 84, 338
songs associated with Kabir of, 91–93, 138, 278, 402n5, 408n21
Negro spirituals
Kabir bhajans compared with, 347, 369, 370, 373–375, 376, 377, 379
King, Martin Luther on, 368–369
meanings in American history of, 368–377
oral tradition and fluidity of texts, 371–373, 376, 437n28
Niranjani Panth of Rajasthan, 412–413n14
nirguṇ
Barthwal's book on the *nirgun* school, 127, 420n26, 430n13
and the body, 168, 170–171
and caste, 40–44, 96, 277–279, 310–311, 403n26, 404n31
and Kabir, 2, 6, 20, 23, 152–153, 186, 189, 193, 250, 277
and Kumar Gandharva, 11, 93–94, 138, 308
and the lover-beloved theme, 89–90, 194
poets, 23, 402n5 (*see also* Gorakhnath)
and *saguṇ* notions of God, 23, 41–42, 44, 89, 96
sects, 33–34, 122, 187, 338 (*see also* Dadu Panth; Kabir Panth; Nath Panth; Niranjani Panth; Radhasoami Satsang)
and Shankara's Advaita Vedanta, 41, 402n31, 421n43
non-scholars' depth of knowledge about Kabir, 250, 273
Vijay Kumar, author's discussion with, 104, 409–410n37
Farid Ayaz on, 129
Tiwari, Kapil on, 136–137

Novetzke, Christian, 400n8, 405n2, 411n3

Olivelle, Patrick, 366
Omvedt, Gail, 433n1, 437n27
Ong, Walter
on media and technology, 209
on orality and literacy, 206, 208, 212–213
on Plato using writing to criticize writing, 241
secondary orality theorized by, 219, 227
Sterne's critique of, 217–219
oral tradition, 8–9, 14, 199–201
and canon creation, 82
continued vitality of, 242, 251, 376, 406–407n15
and critical editions, 118–120 (*see also* Callewaert, Winand)
dichotomizing oral and literate traditions, 14, 76, 206, 212–214
and embodiment, 4, 78, 205, 211–212, 233–234, 237–239, 246–247
historical development of, 116, 119–120
mapping of, 76, 91, 119, 407–408n20, 420n28
and mediatized transmission, 9, 13–14, 74–75, 78, 103, 105–111, 203–204, 206, 212, 220, 227, 242
and the oceanic pool of Kabirian poetic imagery, 85–86, 89, 91
oral-formulaic theory of composition. *See* Lord, Albert
orality theory, introduced, 203–205
Ramanujan, A.K. on, 76–77
secondary orality, 204, 219, 226–228, 237
textual fluidity of Negro spirituals, 371–373, 376, 437n28
and textual spontaneity and dynamism, 80–82, 86–89, 101, 405n7, 406n14
Tiwari, Kapil on, 133–134
twentieth century scholarship on. *See* Finnegan, Ruth; Foley, John Miles; Lord, Albert; McLuhan, Marshall; Ong, Walter; Parry, Milman; Sterne, Jonathan
Orsini, Francesca, 91, 407–408n20, 412n10, 412–413n14

Parry, Milman, 205–206
Parveen, Abida, Kabir Album, 96
Patel, Suresh, 267–272, 298, 378–379, 381, 426n16
Prahladji. *See* Tipanya, Prahlad Singh (Prahladji)
Prahladji's handwritten bhajan notebooks, *83f2.1*, 83–84, 406n10
Prakashmuni Nam Sahab, 49, 326–328, 340–341
on caste, 429–430n11
melā at Bandhavgarh organized by, 431–432n21
Prasad, Bhagirathi, 249–250
PT. *See* Tipanya, Prahlad Singh (Prahladji)

qawwali style songs, 16, 70, 96, 129

Radhasoami Satsang, 33–34, 187, 291, 338, 409–410n37
Raghavan, V., 416n40
Rai, Alok, 347–350, 379
interviewed by the author, 386–389
Rajasthan, 10
Bahadur Singh's research on oral Kabir, 113–114
Bhanwari Devi, 107–108
Dadu Panth in. *See* Dadu Panth
Fatehpur manuscript, 123
Jain influence in, 412–413n14
Kabir Panth in, 92
Kabir and Sufi poetry, 96

and the Malwa region, 11, 19
manuscripts of Kabir compositions, 75, 94, 121–122, 123, 126, 128, 146, 412n11,412–413n14 (*see also* Das, Shyamsundar; *Kabīr Granthāvalī*; Strnad, Jaroslav)
Meghvāl performers in rural western part of, 433n1
Mukhtiyar Ali, 70, 89
Niranjani Path, 406n9, 412–413n14
oral epics of, 400n8
Panchvāṇī poetry collection, 75, 126
Ramdevji devotion in, 30, 110
as region where oral Kabir is popular, 10, 16, 68, 89, 103, 107, 141, 179, 187–188, 248, 406n9, 406–407n15
Sarvāngī poetry collection, 75, 126, 411n6
and *tambūras*, 23, 68
vitality of oral tradition in, 406–407n15
Ramanand
commentary by PT, 277–278
debate over Ramanand and brahminical bias, 125, 276–279, 427n26
historicity of, 427n26
and Kabir's association with Hinduism, 125, 316
as Kabir's disciple, 277–278
as Kabir's father, 279
as Kabir's guru, 140, 274, 277–278
in *Satguru ne bhāng pilāī* "The true guru gave me a marijuana drink," 276–278
Ramanujan, A.K.
author's meeting with, 17
pool of signifiers for the *Rāmāyaṇa*, 89, 91, 407n16
"Who Needs Folklore," 76–77, 80, 401n14
Ramdev, 55–56, 110
Reagon, Bernice Johnson, 368–369, 372–373, 376, 437n26
rekhtā poetic form in Kabir singing, 154, 418n10
Rikhi, Vipul, 392
rural audience, *52f1.1*

Sacks, Oliver, 225, 236, 400n6
Sadbhāv Yātrā (Goodwill Journey), 264, 276, 379
SAHMAT (Safdar Hashmi Memorial Trust), 434n5
Anahad garje concerts produced by, 348, 387, 434n5
Sahni, Bhisham, 354, 427n17
Sahni, Kiran, 267, 427n17
sākhīs (couplets) of Kabir
attributed to both Kabir and other poets, 91–92, 141
bhajans' relationship to, 154
in conversations about Kabir, 32
Dadu Panthi manuscripts organization of, 152, 417n6
examples of, 10, 32, 34, 43, 46, 92, 112, 132–133, 141, 156, 162–163, 249, 263–264, 266, 269, 270, 281, 286, 344, 412n13
examples on love, 190–192
examples on the mind, 162–166
interpretation by singers, 281–282, 419n23
meaning of *sākhī*, 140
in North Indian public schools, 5, 30
painted on temple walls, 49
PT's interpretation of, 84
Sampath, Ram, 107–108
Sanchez-Luege, Nicelio, 416–417n44
Sangh Parivar, 425n7, 434n9
Sardana, Arvind
and the author, 307, 312, 428n34
and Eklavya, 251–252, 276, 428n34
and Narayanji, 294, 297

Sarolia, Dayaram, 104, 302
  and Dinesh Sharma, 304–306, *314f6.6*
  interviewed by Shabnam Virmani, 55, 56–57
  on stigma attached to *tambūrā* playing, 55
satī (widow who self-immolates on husband's funeral pyre)
  controversial verses on, 99, 101–102, 418n14
  as symbol of courage and devotion, 165
Seeger, Pete, 395, 424n1, 438n34
Sen, Kshitimohan, 97, 322, 403n23
Sen, Shekhar (Mumbai classical singer), 144, 309, 321–323
senses
  and body-mind systems (5–25 categories), 151, 417n4
  five senses as a conventional number of, 221–222, 422n15
  hearing as the universal sense, 221–224, 234
  Kauṣītaki Upaniṣad 3.8 on sound, 203
  and orality theory, 14, 78, 204, 215–226, 228–229, 232–233, 235–237, 240, 246–247
  and *pratyāhāra* (closing the doors of the senses), 366
Śhabad nirantar, film by Rajula Shah, 79-80
śhabda (the Word)
  akṣhar [written] word contrasted with by Tiwari, 134
  inner-outer sound associated with ultimate *nirguṇ* reality, 7, 33, 37, 43–44, 58, 112, 145, 169, 399n4
  in the title of Rajula Shah's film, 79
Shabnam. *See* Virmani, Shabnam
Shah, Hitesh, 106–107
Shah, Rajula, film on Kabir singers, 79–80
Shankara and Advaita philosophy, 41–42, 200, 404n31, 421n43
Shantideva, 352, 358–359
Sharma, Dinesh, *259f6.2*
  co-conducting interviews with the author, 283, 290
  and Dayaram Sarolia, 314f6.6
  family's handwritten bhajan collection, 77, 82
  Kabir *manch* organizing and documentation, 55, 255–260, 273–276, 304
  Kabir *manch*'s influence on, 297, 304–306
  last days of, 311–314
Shastri, Gangasharan, 431n18
  on the *chaukā āratī* ritual, 325, 338, 431n18
  on editing the *Mahābījak*, 114–116, 145
Shilnath (Nath yogi master in Malwa)
  anthology of song texts collected by (*see* Nath anthology)
  dhūnī devoted to the memory of (*see* Shīlnāth Dhūnī)
Shīlnāth Dhūnī (Nath Panth center in Dewas)
  and Kumar Gandharva, 60, 91, 93–94, 138, 408nn21, 27, 415nn36, 37
  mirror embossed with an unpublished bhajan at, 60
Shteyngart, Gary, 239–242
Siegel, Daniel, 233
signature lines
  and authenticity, 281–282
  Kabir's (*see* Kabir's signature line ("Kabir says"))
  of poets other than Kabir, 23, 88, 144, 276, 402n5, 406n9, 408n23
Sikh religion

Kabir's poetry inscribed in *Ādi Granth*, 5, 67, 75, 88–89, 95, 121, 123, 147, 151, 397n2, 414n21
legends of founder Guru Nanak, 315–316, 428–429n2
sacred texts (*see Ādi Granth*; *Goindval Pothis*)
sectarian bias, 126–127, 147
Singaji (*nirguṇ sant* of Madhya Pradesh), 23, 304, 428n36
Singaji bhajan *mandalī*, 306, 425–426n8
Singh, Namvar, 11, 307, 428n39
Singh, Shukdev, Kabir textual scholarship of, 120–121
Sisodiya, Hiralal, *284f6.3*
on the *Kabir manch*, 274–275, 281–282, 283–285, 288
on the Kabir Panth, 285–287, 330
Soī pīr hai jo jāne par pīr (bhajan collection)
introduction by Prakash Kant, 264, 267, 309–310
title translated, 263–264
Soī pīr hai jo jāne par pīr (PT's first cassette), 270
songs
Black Church. *See* gospel music; Negro spirituals
of Kabir (*see* bhajans; bhajans—first lines; *ghazal* style songs)
of Mirabai (*see* Mirabai)
Muslim singers (*see* Ali, Mukhtiyar; Ayaz, Fariduddin (Farid); *qawwali* style songs)
spirituality
Agrawal on, 353–356
author's definition of, 357–359
differentiated from religion, 351–353, 435n13, 436n14
and Marxist/materialist/leftist views, 345–346, 348–351, 356, 360–361, 367, 384–385
Sterne, Jonathan, 203, 215–221, 223
Strnad, Jaroslav, 120–121, 412n11, 416–417n44
Sufis
Alok Rai on the culture of, 347
Amir Khusrau, 352
in the film *Had-Anhad/* Bounded-Boundless, 378
invoked against communalism, 347–348, 425n7, 434n5
Kabir related to, 17, 89, 91, 94, 96, 141, 195, 347
language and genres of, 195, 263, 407–408n20
musical styles of, 5, 70, 71
of Pakistan and Kabir, 91, 141
Suntā hai guru gyānī
altered signature of Dinesh Sharma's version of, 82–83
Kumar Gandharva's version of, 82, 415n36
PT's version of, 82
Surdas, textual study of, 118–119, 125, 405n4, 413n16
swan (*haṃsa*)
and heron (*bagulā*) compared, 28, 32, 402n8
symbolism, 60–62
Syag-bhāi. *See* Syag, R.N.
Syag, R.N., *256f6.1*
conversations with author, 255–257, 260–261, 302–304, 380–385
Eklavya *manch* involvement, 255, 260, 262, 263, 302–304
and Narayanji, 291, 294

Tagore, Rabindranath, 322, 403n23, 416–417n44
tambūrā playing
and caste, 55, 410n38
and the *ektār* associated with the old Kabir singing tradition, 295

tambūrā playing (*cont.*)
and PT, 23, 31, 103, 247
by urban fans, 68, 106
Tansen (Mughal court musician), 92, 141
textual scholarship
on Kabir, 118–120 (*see also* Agrawal, Purushottam; Callewaert, Winand; Das, Shyamsundar; Strnad, Jaroslav; Tiwari, P.N.; Vaudeville, Charlotte)
urtext as a focus of, 118–120
Tindley, Charles A., 376
Tipanya, Ajay (PT's son and dholak player), 45, 52, 67, 70, 109, 171, 200–201, 404n33, 408n21
research for the Kabir Project, 200–201
Tipanya, Ambaram (PT's brother), 28, 30, 51–52, 69–70, 84, 171, 404n33
Tipanya, Ashok (PT's brother), 20, *21f1.1*, 28, 30, 45, 51–53, 69–70, 170–171, 404n33
Tipanya, Kamla (Ambaram's wife), 52, 61, 109
Tipanya, Prahlad Singh (Prahladji)
American tours 2003 & 2009, 12, 65–67, 68, 104–105
annual program hosted by, 49, 56, 332–334
audio and video CD's, 105, *105f2.2*
audio cassettes (*see* cassettes, featuring PT)
on authenticity, 144–145
author's first meeting with, 19–21, 104
bhajan notebook (*see* Prahladji's handwritten bhajan notebook)
bhajans learned from Chenamaruji, 86, 199
initiation into several *nirguṇ* sects, 33–35
Kabir Panthi attack on, 309–310, 431n17
Kabīr Smārak Sevā aur Shodh Sansthānka started by, 48–49
life story, 28–36, 47–50, 52–54, 55–59, 64–66, 68–71, 406n10
mahantship in Kabir Panth , 15, 58–59, 330, 331–337, *334f7.1*, 341, 343, 405n39
meditation experience, 34–39, 175–176
performing in Bangalore with *mandalī* and Shabnam Virmani, *12fI.1*
sings with Ashok, *21f1.1*
song composed in honor of his cassette "*Pī le amīras*—Drink This Nectar," 56–57
and the sound of *tambūrā*, 23, 31, 247
urge to leave his family, 53–54, 174–176
Tipanya, Shanti (PT's wife)
and the author, 13, 61
home life of, 30–31, 52, 53, 65, 171, 174–175, *176f4.1*, 332, 402n6, 404n34
interview with Shabnam, 174–176
singing and interpreting bhajans, 149–151, 171
Tipanya, Sumitra (Ashok's wife), household of, 49, 404n33
Tiwari, Kapil
on authenticity, 134–137, 139–140, 416n38
director of Adivasi Lok Kala Parishad (Tribal and Folk Art Institute), 19, 22, 24, 133, 363
interviews with Shabnam Virmani, 132, 133–140, 363–365
on Kabir's truth, 136–137, 148
on Kumar Gandharva, 137–140
on oral tradition, 133–134
on religion and politics, 363–365
Tiwari, P.N., Kabir textual scholarship of, 120–121, 122, 147
transcendence. *See* Rai, Alok; spirituality, and Marxist/materialist/leftist views

unstruck/boundless sound. See *anahad nād*

Urdu
  Fatehpur manuscript's absence of, 124
  Kabir reception reflected in Mughal texts, 92, 142
  mapping of Hindi-Urdu literature by Orsini, 91, 407–408n20, 412–413n14
  Naim (poet in Dewas), 307–308
  Perso-Arabic words in *Man lāgo mero yār fakīrī meṇ*, 195
  poetry added to the *Mahābījak*, 116–117
  rekhtā poetic form in Kabir singing, 154, 418n10

Uttar Pradesh, 10, 75, 121, 162, 188, 319. See also *Sadbhāv Yātrā*

Vajpeyi, Ashok, x, 1, 19, 400n7, 401n1

Vaudeville, Charlotte, Kabir textual scholarship of, 120–121, 122, 148, 400n9

vichārdhārā ("thought-stream"), 115–116, 145

Virmani, Shabnam
  Ajab shahar/Wondrous City DVD on PT's U.S. tour, 66
  Ajab shahar/Wondrous City internet archive, 102–103, 436n22
  attacked by Kabir Panthis, 309–310, 431n17
  author's partnering with, 12–13, 68, 101, 105, 335, 428n35
  Dayaram Sarolia interview, 55, 56–57
  Dinesh Sharma interview, 254, 304–306
  film *Chalo hamārā des*/Come to my country, 46–47, 54–55, 86, 404n38, 427nn20–21
  film *Had-anhad*/Bounded-Boundless, 70, 378, 418n15, 437n30
  film *Kabīra khaḍā bāzār meṇ*/In the Market Stands kabir, 309–310, 410n38, 427n17, 431n17
  film *Kōi suntā hai*/Someone is Listening, 138, 402n17
  films, CDs, and books produced by, 13, 68, 102, 106, 298
  Kaluram interview, 300–301
  Kapil Tiwari interview, 133–138, 139–140, 363–365
  Krishna Nath interview, 379–380, 438n32
  oral traditions researched by, 16, 81–82, 85–86, 87–89, 96, 107, 129, 132–133, 201, 416n38
  on political issues, 378, 393–395, 425n7, 437n30
  and Prahladji singing together, *100f2.1*, 102, 427n21
  PT interviews, 45–46, 58, 336–337, 432n24
  sākhīs on love sung by, 191–192
  sākhīs on the mind sung by, 163–164
  as singer, 100–101, 106, 163
  singing texts altered by, 98, 101–102, 409n33
  Sufi singers in Rajasthan and Pakistan documented by, 70, 96, 107, 378, 418n15
  Suresh Patel interview, 268–270
  See also Kabir Project based in Bangalore

women and gender, 402n6
  Bhanwari Devi (Rajasthani singer), 107–109
  in death rituals, 313
  in Kabir singing culture, 23, 265, 289, 378, 393–394
  in Malwa culture, 4, 52, 61, 303
  and *satī*, 101–102, 165
  women priests, 403n27

Zen. *See* Buddhism

Made in the USA
Middletown, DE
31 December 2020

30502924R00272